I0147936

BIRDS OF KANSAS

BIRDS of KANSAS

Max C. Thompson, Charles A. Ely, Bob Gress, Chuck Otte,
Sebastian T. Patti, David Seibel, and Eugene A. Young

Published by the University Press of Kansas (Lawrence, Kansas 66045), which was organized by the Kansas Board of Regents and is operated and funded by Emporia State University, Fort Hays State University, Kansas State University, Pittsburg State University, the University of Kansas, and Wichita State University

Publication was made possible, in part, by grants from the following: *Chickadee Checkoff,* a voluntary donation program of the Kansas Department of Wildlife and Parks for the purpose of promoting conservation and programs for nongame wildlife; *Kansas Ornithological Society*; Migratory Bird Program of the *U.S. Fish and Wildlife Service,* Region 6; and *Westar Energy Green Team.* The findings and conclusions in *Birds of Kansas* are of course those of the authors and do not necessarily represent the views of these donors.

Library of Congress Cataloging-in-Publication Data

Birds of Kansas / Max C. Thompson . . . [et al].
p. cm.
Includes bibliographical references and index.
ISBN 978-0-7006-1782-1 (cloth : alk. paper)
1. Birds—Kansas—Identification. I. Thompson, Max C.
QL684.K2B57 2011
598.09781—dc22 2010048288

British Library Cataloguing-in-Publication Data is available.

Printed in China

10 9 8 7 6 5 4 3 2 1

The paper used in this publication is acid free and meets the minimum requirements of the American National Standard for Permanence of Paper for Printed Library Materials Z39.48-1992.

Contents

Preface

We have included in the book as much information on the distribution of birds in Kansas as we could. Many members of the Kansas Ornithological Society have contributed records to the production of this book. Databases kept by Max C. Thompson, Charles A. Ely, and Chuck Otte were used extensively. We would like to acknowledge ORNIS, a database portal for specimen collections in the United States, and those curators and collection managers of the following museums who made their data available: Academy of Natural Science, Philadelphia; Burke Museum of Natural History and Culture; Delaware Museum of Natural History; Field Museum of Natural History; Harvard University Museum of Comparative Zoology; Philadelphia Academy of Natural Sciences; Sternberg Museum of Natural History; University of California Museum of Vertebrate Zoology; University of Kansas Museum of Natural History; University of Michigan Museum of Zoology; U.S. National Museum; and Yale Peabody Museum of Natural History. Without the use of this database, we would have missed many unknown specimens. Emporia State University kindly provided us with a list of their specimens. The U.S. Geological Survey, Bird-Banding Laboratory supplied us with Allbirds, a database for banding records.

Many persons stand out as giants in Kansas ornithology. One of those is Marvin Schwilling. His many records supplied information that was unavailable elsewhere. We are sad that he did not live to see the fruits of his labor. The untiring effort of Ed Martinez to band shorebirds at Cheyenne Bottoms has provided us with much data on migratory shorebirds.

Many of us spent untold hours devoting our lives to this book over the past 2 years. Chuck Otte would like to thank Jaye Otte, and David Seibel would like to thank his parents for their support over the years. Charles Ely wishes to thank his wife, Jan, who, sadly, was unable to see the results of her decades of active support.

The following persons were especially helpful with information or production of the book: Henry Armknecht, Danny Bystrak, Jeff Calhoun, Tom Flowers, Matt Gearhart, Pete Janzen, Robert Mangile, Ed Miller, Mike Rader, Nate Rice, Mark Robbins, Stan Roth, John Schukman, Scott Seltman, Thomas and Sara Shane, Abigail Vogels, and Kristof Zyskowski. The color photographs in this book would not have been possible without the monetary support of the Chickadee Checkoff, Kansas Ornithological Society, Westar Energy Green Team, and the U.S. Fish and Wildlife Service, Region 6, Migratory Bird Program. Ken Brunson, Suzanne Fellows, and Brad Loveless were extremely helpful in production of the book. We are grateful to the anonymous reviewers who looked at preliminary copies and especially to Bill Busby, who critiqued the manuscript and provided valuable suggestions.

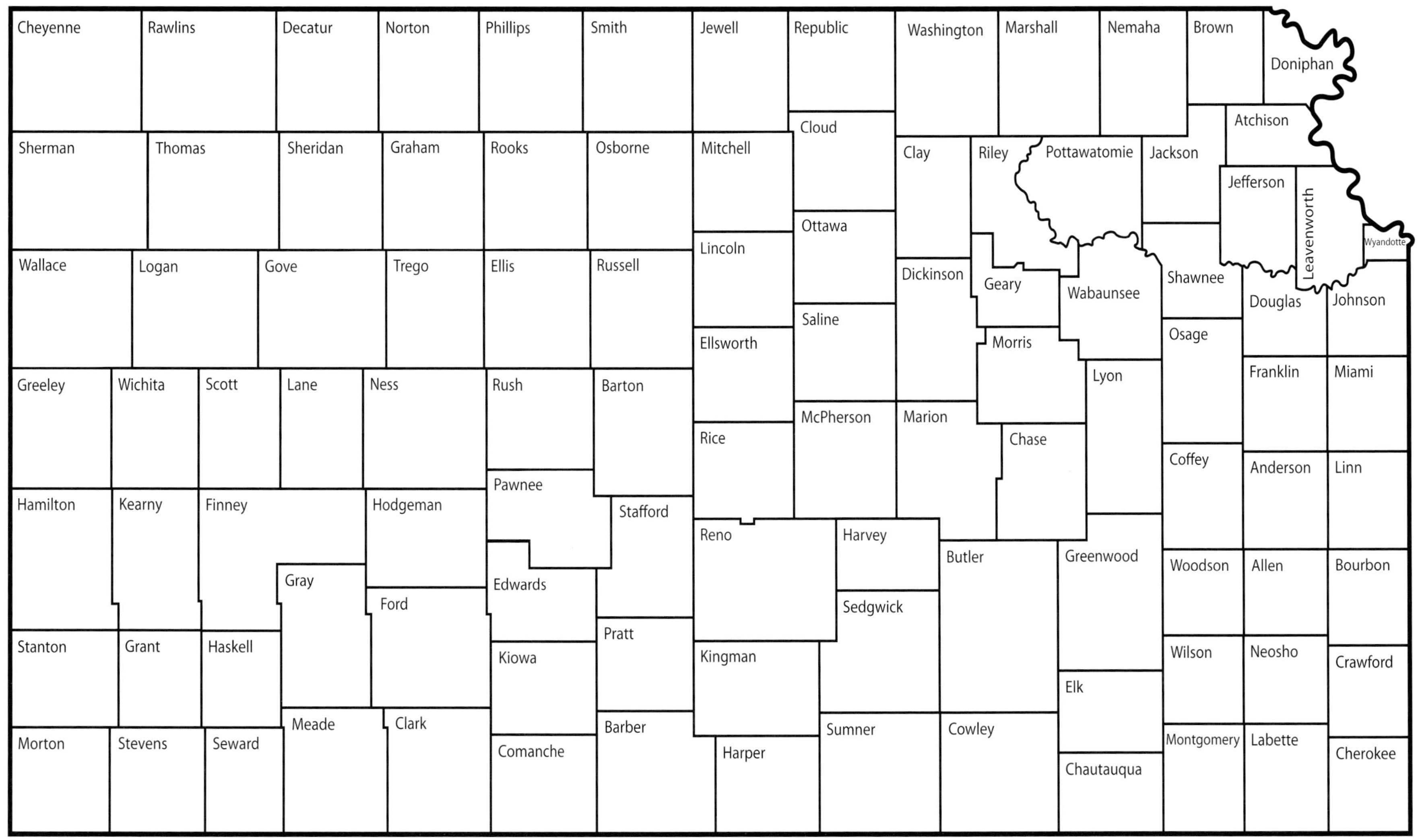
Cheyenne
Rawlins
Decatur
Norton
Phillips
Smith
Jewell
Republic
Washington
Marshall
Nemaha
Brown
Doniphan
Sherman
Thomas
Sheridan
Graham
Rooks
Osborne
Mitchell
Cloud
Clay
Riley
Pottawatomie
Jackson
Atchison
Jefferson
Leavenworth
Wyandotte
Wallace
Logan
Gove
Trego
Ellis
Russell
Lincoln
Ottawa
Dickinson
Geary
Wabaunsee
Shawnee
Douglas
Johnson
Greeley
Wichita
Scott
Lane
Ness
Rush
Barton
Ellsworth
Saline
Morris
Lyon
Osage
Franklin
Miami
Rice
McPherson
Marion
Chase
Coffey
Anderson
Linn
Hamilton
Kearny
Finney
Hodgeman
Pawnee
Stafford
Reno
Harvey
Butler
Greenwood
Woodson
Allen
Bourbon
Gray
Ford
Edwards
Sedgwick
Stanton
Grant
Haskell
Pratt
Kingman
Kiowa
Wilson
Neosho
Crawford
Elk
Morton
Stevens
Seward
Meade
Clark
Comanche
Barber
Harper
Sumner
Cowley
Chautauqua
Montgomery
Labette
Cherokee

Introduction

The number of bird species reliably reported for Kansas is 473, an increase of 47 species since Thompson and Ely (1992) published the second volume of the *Birds in Kansas* nearly two decades ago. A species is included in this book on the basis of a specimen, a photograph, an accepted record by the Kansas Bird Records Committee (KBRC), or an observation that is verified by a competent observer and accepted by the authors. With one exception (Bronzed Cowbird), the species list for this book matches that of the Kansas Ornithological Society's (KOS) *Birds of Kansas Checklist*, 11th edition, as updated through September 2010 by the KBRC (and incorporating the latest taxonomic revisions).

The KBRC was established by the KOS in 1990 as a vehicle to maintain and evaluate records of bird sightings in Kansas. All records submitted to the KBRC are reviewed and evaluated. Minimal data on records receiving a decision by the committee are published by KOS in the *Kansas Ornithological Society Bulletin*, the professional journal for the KOS.

The numerous records used in this book are from databases maintained by each of the authors, especially those of C. Ely and the Kansas Birds Database, which was partially funded by the Kansas Department of Wildlife and Parks (KDWP) and maintained by M. Thompson. Additional records include those published by the KOS in the *Bulletin* and *Horned Lark* (newsletter).

People who observe birds as a hobby are called birders or bird-watchers. An estimated 46 million birders in the United States spend 30 billion dollars per year while observing, photographing, or feeding birds (U.S. Department of the Interior, Fish and Wildlife Service, and U.S. Department of Commerce, U.S. Census Bureau, 2002). About one-fourth of Kansans 16 years of age and older participate in activities involving birds (U.S. Department of the Interior, Fish and Wildlife Service, and U.S. Department of Commerce, U.S. Census Bureau, 2002). Professionals who study birds—ornithologists—are many fewer in number. Many of the larger universities in the United States employ at least one ornithologist among their faculty, including most of those in Kansas.

All birds have state and federal protection except the alien European Starling, Rock Pigeon, and House Sparrow. It is illegal to possess nongame birds, their nests, or their eggs for any reason without a permit from the U.S. Fish and Wildlife Service and the KDWP. Should you find injured or dead birds, it is best to call your local conservation officer for advice.

Several field guides are available for the birder. Check with bookstores or with museum gift shops to find those best suited for your needs. The KOS welcomes those interested in birds. You can obtain information on the KOS and its benefits by writing to the Kansas Ornithological Society, Division of Ornithology, The University of Kansas, 1345 Jayhawk Blvd., Lawrence, Kansas 66045. You can also access publication and membership information via the Internet by going to http://ksbirds.org.

History of Ornithology in Kansas

By Thomas G. Shane[1]

Kansas has a rich and illustrious 200-year ornithological history from the first report of Wild Turkey taken on 26 June 1804 by hunters of the Lewis and Clark Expedition to the present. It started with numerous well-known explorers who began reporting a few species that caught their notice or were important food items, and has grown to an organized and systematic study of all species that venture into the state. The period of exploration increased in sophistication as trained biologists became a part of such

1 Excerpted from a larger unpublished manuscript.

endeavors through the mid-1850s. Following the Civil War, westward immigration increased dramatically and with it the need for more accurate information on the "frontier," with colleges and universities becoming increasingly important.

For Kansas, the period from 1865 to 1879 was especially significant and was marked by a period of heavy immigration, the settling of much of western Kansas, and the development of immigrant trails and railroads through the state. It marked the demise of the vast bison herds and the near extinction of numerous species large and small. The academics of that time became involved in the finding and dissemination of information, including assembling and documenting the first state bird lists, and by the late 19th century they were publishing notes on life-history observations and even county lists. This pattern continued until just after World War II when graduate programs and research became a more serious component of academia. All scientific disciplines underwent a rapid growth in the late 1950s, and research programs, large and small, manned by academics and their students have been the norm for the last 50 years.

In Kansas, as elsewhere, large numbers of nonacademics from early naturalists to modern birders have made major contributions and continue to do so. These dedicated people have helped produce and complete such projects as Christmas Bird Counts (CBCs), the Kansas Breeding Bird Atlas (KBBAT), and bird-feeder counts. Many publish independent studies and are responsible for the majority of additions to the state bird list in modern times. They contributed thousands of observations to works such as this one. Kansas birders as a group contribute to regional and state studies, band thousands of birds, promote conservation, and in other ways contribute to ornithology on a national level.

The Lewis and Clark Expedition followed the Missouri River bordering extreme northeastern Kansas in 1804 (returning in 1806) and mentioned a few bird species. The Pike Expedition traversed the state (October–November 1806) from near present-day Fort Scott to near Red Cloud, Nebraska, then south to the Arkansas River at Great Bend where the expedition divided, exiting the state for Colorado and Louisiana, but with few references to birds. Thomas Say (the first trained ornithologist to visit the state) accompanied the Long Expedition, briefly exploring the northeastern part of the state in 1819 and descending the Arkansas River the next year.

In May 1834 John J. Audubon traveled the Missouri River, collecting, among others, a series of Carolina Parakeets. Additional explorers during the following decades such as Prince Maximilian zu Wied, Josiah Gregg, John C. Fremont, and James W. Abert added about 40 new species. Prior to the Civil War, Spencer F. Baird (Smithsonian Institution) recruited the assistance of U.S. Army surgeons (including William A. Hammond and John X. deVesey, both from Fort Riley) to collect birds during their free time from regular duties. He also organized the ornithological results of numerous government surveys and expeditions, including some to Kansas. Joel A. Allen collected near Leavenworth, Topeka, and Fort Hays in the summer of 1871 and northwestern Kansas that winter. The first longtime resident ornithologist of Kansas was Nathaniel S. Goss, a naturalist devoted to birds. His early collecting was at Neosho Falls and later included most of the state, resulting in many publications including his first catalogue in 1883 and subsequent updates in 1886 and 1891. The Goss Ornithological Collection is now at the University of Kansas Natural History Museum (KUMNH).

Ornithology at the University of Kansas began even before its official opening in 1866 when Francis H. Snow, its first professor of natural science, arrived prematurely and immediately began collecting birds. Although an entomologist, he diligently added bird specimens to the museum collection and published his findings, including three Kansas bird catalogues (1872, 1878, 1903), until near his death in 1909. In the early days of the state, most birds collected were deposited at the University of Kansas. Later, the Museum of Natural History was officially established by the Kansas Legislature to house vertebrate collections of the state at the university. It has since become one of the leading university museums in the nation. The KUMNH bird collection now contains more than 100,000 specimens. The former Southwestern College Museum of Natural History, in Winfield, collection of 9,000 specimens is now part of the KUMNH collection. Other noteworthy bird collections include the former Museum of the High Plains (MHP), now part of the Sternberg Museum of Natural History in Hays (3,500 specimens), and the 1,200 specimens at Emporia State University in Emporia.

David E. Lantz at Kansas State University (KSU) was one of the most active ornithologists at the turn of the century, publishing both a historical list of Kansas birds and a bibliography of Kansas birds in 1899. Arthur L. Goodrich joined the KSU faculty in 1927, taught an ornithology course for decades, and published *Birds in Kansas* in 1946. Harrison B. Tordoff arrived at the University of Kansas in 1950. He began field research and published the first modern Kansas checklist in 1956. The arrival of Richard F. Johnston at the University of Kansas in 1958 was marked by extensive field study of Kansas birds and resulted in the *Directory to the Bird-Life of Kansas* in 1960 and an updated version in 1965.

The publications on Kansas birds were again updated by Max C. Thompson and Charles A. Ely with the publication of their *Birds in Kansas*, volumes one (1989) and two (1992). In 2001, with the completion of the breeding bird atlas project, the *Kansas Breeding Bird Atlas* was published by William H. Busby and John L. Zimmerman. These latter two projects were made possible in large part by the many hours of observation and meticulous data collection by nonprofessional birders. Kansas ornithology is alive and well with both professionals and amateurs contributing to our knowledge of the birds in Kansas.

Bird Distribution and Vegetation

The number of bird species recorded in Kansas is currently 473. This great diversity is partly attributed to the early start of Kansas ornithology, which preceded the extinction of such species as the Passenger Pigeon and Carolina Parakeet, and the extirpation of the Gunnison Sage-Grouse, Ruffed Grouse, and others. Of equal importance is the state's central location in North America. It includes both eastern deciduous forest and the central grasslands and lies within the Central Migratory Flyway. Kansas is a wintering area for far-northern breeding birds such as the Harris's Sparrow and Lapland Longspur, as well as a breeding area for southern species such as Mississippi Kite and Painted Bunting. Other birds such as the Greater Roadrunner and Curve-billed Thrasher enter the state from the arid southwest. The major rivers of Kansas funnel stragglers from the Rocky Mountains when those species experience their occasional irruptions and provide corridors that move eastern species west into the state.

Birds are inextricably connected to ecosystems and their vegetation. In Kansas there are three major ecosystem types—forests, grasslands, and wetlands (including reservoirs). All birders should become familiar with the physiography and vegetation of Kansas in order to appreciate the diverse ecology and wildlife found in the state. Excellent general references include the works of Self (1978) and Collins (1985), and the vegetation map by Kuchler (1974). In addition, birders can become familiar with many of the excellent birding areas in various physiographic provinces by reviewing Zimmerman and Patti (1988).

To the casual visitor traveling on an interstate highway, Kansas seems a treeless expanse of plains and prairie. However, a short distance on either side of these main routes, one can find a great variety of habitats. These areas, usually small and widely scattered, are concentrated habitats that are often as productive, or more so, than larger blocks of the same habitat elsewhere. In much of Kansas, native vegetation communities are now threatened by nonnative invasive species. Tartarian honeysuckle (*Lonicera tatarica*) has escaped from windbreak and ornamental plantings and aggressively established itself in the understory of many eastern and riparian woodland areas. Sericea lespedeza (*Lespedeza cuneata*), once planted as wildlife cover, is now being battled in southeastern and Flint Hills rangeland areas. Landowners and public land managers need to use extreme caution when selecting plant materials and give preference to native species whenever possible.

The topography of Kansas is more gently rolling than flat and slopes upward from the southeast to the northwest. From about 700 feet in elevation in southeastern Kansas near Coffeyville, Montgomery County, there is a rise of about 10 feet per mile to 4,039 feet in the far west at Mount Sunflower, Wallace County. Climatic conditions in Kansas are varied, with annual rainfall increasing from about 18 inches in the west to more than 40 inches in the southeast. The average growing season ranges from less than 150 days in the northwest to more than 200 days in the southeast. Vegetation is determined by temperature and precipitation, as well as the type of parent rock, soil development, and, more directly, human land use over the last two centuries.

Forests

At present, deciduous forest occurs in extreme southeastern Kansas as an extension of the Ozark Plateau, and in the Osage Cuestas (east-central), and the Glaciated Region (northeast) as a westward extension of the eastern deciduous forest. Oaks and hickories dominate, and are multilayered, with an understory of shrubs and herbaceous plants. Among the forested habitats are islands of bluestem prairie in the east-central and southeastern parts of Kansas. Westward to the Flint Hills, the proportion of trees decreases as prairie increases. Originally, this was a mosaic, or intermingling, of forest and prairie, "forest islands in a sea of grass." In the southern portion, chiefly on upland sandstone soils, open groves of blackjack oak (*Quercus marilandica*) and post oak (*Q. stellata*) are interspersed within bluestem prairie in a savanna-style ecosystem of great importance. These are the Chautauqua Hills, or "cross timbers," which extend northward from Oklahoma. Thus, much of eastern Kansas has woodlands, to the delight of birds that like to inhabit thicker stands of trees. Riparian woodlands extend westward along all major rivers and are particularly well developed along the Kansas River from Kansas City to Lawrence. However, in recent decades there has been an increase in forested areas in all riparian regions of central and eastern Kansas. In the east, riparian growth involves a variety of tree species, including cottonwood (*Populus deltoides*), sycamore (*Platanus occidentalis*), willows (*Salix* spp.), elm (*Ulmus* spp.), hackberry (*Celtis* spp.), ash (*Fraxinus* spp.), and various oaks (*Quercus* spp.), typically with a thick understory of saplings and woody shrubs. The number of tree species and the extent and density of vegetation decrease rapidly as one progresses westward. For example, today along the Republican River such eastern birds as the Wood Thrush occur in the understory west to Cloud County. A century ago, with higher water tables, they occurred 150 miles farther west to Decatur County. Oaks are rare west of Cowley, McPherson, and Jewell counties, as are Eastern Wood Pewees, which prefer oaks as breeding habitat. In western Kansas, often the only tree species present is the cottonwood (*P. deltoides*), and the understory is restricted to grasses, indigo bush (*Amorpha* sp.), salt cedar (in floodplains, *Tamarix* sp.), or sagebrush (*Artemisia* spp.).

Much of the original forest in Kansas has been replaced by urban communities and farmland. In these areas, control of natural fire has caused an expansion of secondary forest at the expense of bluestem prairie. Eastern red cedar (*Juniperus virginiana*) is often the first species to take advantage of the absence of fire, but various hardwoods soon also become established.

Grasslands

At least 90 percent of the state was originally grassland. In the west, shortgrass predominated east to about Sheridan, Lane, and Meade counties. Buffalo grass (*Buchloe dactyloides*) and grama grasses (*Bouteloua* spp.) were abundant on upland sites; mixed grasses extended westward nearly to the Colorado border along rivers. Most of this area, known as the High Plains Physiographic Province, is now cultivated, and the remainder is degraded rangeland. As a result, some birds requiring large expanses of shortgrass such as Mountain Plover are today very local or like the Chestnut-collared Longspur have disappeared as regular breeding species. Mixed-grass prairie extended eastward though central Kansas, gradually merging into true tallgrass prairie from about Jewell, Rice, and Harper counties eastward. This prairie was quite variable with different combinations of short-, medium-, and tallgrass species. Shortgrass species were found on the shallow soils of the uplands; tallgrass species, such as big bluestem (*Andropogon gerardii*), Indian grass (*Sorghastrum nutans*), and switchgrass (*Panicum virgatum*), were abundant in moist areas; and midsized grasses, such as little bluestem (*Schizachyrium scoparium*) and side-oats grama (*Bouteloua curtipendula*), occurred elsewhere. A great variety of forbs (nonwoody flowering plants), various shrubs, and trees occurred in ravines and on "breaks." Dominant woody species included hackberry, smooth sumac (*Rhus glabra*), and rough-leaved dogwood (*Cornus drummondii*).

Fully developed tallgrass prairie, dominated by big bluestem, switchgrass, and Indian grass, occurred on thick soils in lowlands and shallow upland soils, especially in the Flint Hills and eastward. Extensive areas of tallgrass prairie, some of them in excellent condition, remain in parts of the Flint Hills. Lower streams are bordered by riparian woods. Characteristic breeding species include Greater Prairie-Chicken and the Upland Sandpiper, both of which occur in much smaller numbers in mixed-grass prairie. Smith's Longspur and Sprague's Pipit are regular transient and/or winter residents, and after the annual burning by ranchers in spring, migrating flocks of American Golden-Plovers and Buff-breasted Sandpipers are a regular sight.

Sand-sage prairie occurred on the sandy soils south of the Arkansas and Cimarron rivers in southwestern Kansas. The largest area, now mostly replaced by irrigated farmland, was in southern Kearny and Finney counties and northern Gray County. Dominant grass species now are sand bluestem (*Andropogon hallii*), little bluestem (*Andropogon scoparius*), and prairie sandreed (*Calamovilfa longifolia*). The dominant woody species now found is sagebrush, followed by wild or sandhill plum (*Prunus americana*) and salt cedar. Characteristic bird species are Lesser Prairie-Chicken, Brewer's Sparrow (locally), and Cassin's Sparrow.

Sand prairie, similar to sand-sage prairie except that it lacks sagebrush, is found on sandy soils south of the Arkansas River in central Kansas, chiefly in Edwards, Stafford, and Reno counties. Grasses are taller, with big bluestem, little bluestem, switchgrass, and prairie sandreed dominant. Woody vegetation consists primarily of thickets of sandhill plum. Bell's Vireo is a characteristic breeder in the thickets; Mississippi Kite is common in planted windbreaks.

The Cedar Hills prairie extends northward from Oklahoma into the Red Hills Physiographic Province of south-central Kansas, from eastern Meade County to western Harper County. It is a heavily dissected, mixed grassland, characterized by red soil and scenic relief. Eastern red cedars are scattered over the slopes, and small patches of woody growth, including hackberry, elm, soapberry (*Sapindus saponaria*), wild plum, and smooth sumac, occur in ravine bottoms and on north-facing slopes. The Black-capped Vireo formerly nested here.

Wetlands

Wetlands occupy only a small area in Kansas, but they are biologically of the utmost importance. During pioneer days, they occurred extensively in floodplains, along major rivers, chiefly in central and eastern Kansas. Most of these marshes were drained or converted to other uses, but new marshes, usually small, have been formed by the impoundment of streams for reservoirs or have been developed for waterfowl hunting. The best known area is Cheyenne Bottoms Wildlife Area (CBWA, Barton Co.), which was originally part of a 41,000-acre natural sink. During the 1950s, KDWP (then the Kansas Fish and Game Commission) acquired about half the area and now manages it for waterbirds and shorebirds. Like all natural marshes, it is at the mercy of a dependable water supply along with the succession toward land as a result of siltation, and thus faces an uncertain future. The most important locality in the central

United States for migrating shorebirds, CBWA is a major staging area for migratory shorebirds, waterfowl, wading birds, and gulls. Quivira National Wildlife Refuge (QNWR, in Reno, Rice, and Stafford cos.) and Slate Creek Wetlands (Sumner Co.) are two naturally occurring salt marshes occurring within Kansas. Both provide habitat for shorebirds, waterfowl, and wading birds. Other important marshes are in Republic, Cloud, and Lincoln counties.

In freshwater marshes, prairie cordgrass (*Spartina pectinata*), sedges, and cattails (*Typha* spp.) dominate, and vegetation may be tall and dense. In salt marshes, inland salt grass (*Distichlis spicata*) and seepweed (*Suaeda depressa*) dominate, but other grasses, sedges, spike-rush (*Eleocharis* spp.), and various forbs may be important; vegetation is usually of low to medium height. Cattails in both freshwater and salt marshes can also become abundant and are especially important to nesting waterfowl, rails, and herons, as well as wintering blackbirds. These marshes are used by a great variety of birds, including waterfowl, wading birds, shorebirds, Marsh Wrens, and blackbirds, as long as open water exists. After the water freezes, these birds are largely replaced by sparrows, often huge roosts of blackbirds, and various raptors, especially when cattails are present.

The only natural lakes in Kansas are oxbows cut off from major channels and ephemeral playas. Though still of importance they have been augmented by a myriad of impoundments from small farm ponds to reservoirs thousands of acres in extent. These continue to have a tremendous effect on the distribution and numbers of many species of birds. No doubt, the reservoirs have created vast amounts of open-water habitat that support great concentrations of waterfowl, gulls, cormorants, and pelicans that migrate through the state. They also attract a host of vagrant species such as Yellow-billed Loon, Magnificent Frigatebird, and Long-billed Murrelet. In western Kansas, sewage lagoons are often the only water sources that attract waterfowl, gulls, and herons.

Disturbed Habitats

The Kansas landscape has been altered dramatically since colonization by Europeans, causing changes in the distribution, numbers, and local composition of the bird life. Although many species have been affected adversely, others have benefited from these anthropogenic changes. Today cropland covers more than half the state, making it the most extensive general habitat type. Most of this acreage is devoted to wheat, sorghum, and corn, hardly prime breeding habitat for most species, but very important for transient and wintering birds, from sparrows and longspurs to raptors and waterfowl. Red-winged Blackbirds, Dickcissels, Horned Larks, Lark Buntings, and others nest in large numbers in fallow fields.

Pasture and rangeland occupy about one-third of the state and are utilized by many of the prairie birds previously mentioned. Remaining habitat is chiefly in the form of plantings in towns, on farmsteads, and as windbreaks. Their importance is most noticeable in western Kansas, where the numbers of many familiar birds, such as robins, orioles, and swifts, have increased greatly since pioneer times. With them come such nonnative immigrants as the House Sparrow and European Starling.

Changes in bird life typically follow changes in vegetation, that is, plant succession. As an example, Sharp-tailed Grouse were reported in Ellis County in the 1870s but were replaced by Greater Prairie-Chickens soon after settlement. As cultivation became more extensive, prairie-chickens were replaced by the introduced Ring-necked Pheasant. Recently, as grasslands have started to become more and more fragmented, prairie-chicken populations have declined precipitously. In the mid-1980s, the U.S. Department of Agriculture's Conservation Reserve Program (CRP) paid farmers to take land out of cultivation and restore it to native grasslands or woodlands. At its peak, more than three million acres of Kansas cropland were put into this program, most of it as grassland and much of it in southwestern Kansas, benefiting grassland-nesting species such as the Lesser Prairie-Chicken. Currently, those contracts have started to expire without an apparent opportunity to be continued and many of those acres are returning to crop production. The impact of this action on the bird life that had been using CRP land is of grave concern.

Explanation of Species Accounts

Unless otherwise stated, our comments refer to birds and their activities in Kansas.

Names: Common and scientific names and the sequence of species follow the American Ornithologists' Union's *Check-list of North American Birds* (7th edition, 1998) and its supplements (through the 50th). Following the name is the species' four-letter alpha code, formulated in the same way as those first used by bird banders but expanded and updated by the Institute for Bird Populations (2010). Use of alpha codes as a shorthand for species names has become a frequent practice on the KSBIRD-L listserv (http://listserv.ksu.edu/archives/ksbird-l.html) and elsewhere. KSBIRD-L is an e-mail discussion group used by both birders and ornithologists for up-to-date bird sighting and for the general discussion of Kansas birds.

Maps: For each species a map shows the counties in which a species has been reported. An accepted sight record (solid black circle) is one that the authors have determined to be valid or at the very least hypothetical in nature. We use a stricter definition for confirmed breeding records (open circle) than used in the KBBAT, usually relying on physical evidence of nesting (see Breeding below for details). If enough data exist for a species we include potential ranges using the following color codes. Purple = year-round resident; in general refers to permanent residents. Yellow = breeding or summer range; based upon verified breeding records, KBBAT data, and whether or not potential habitat exists in counties where the species has not been recorded, or where breeding hasn't been confirmed, but should be looked for in available habitat. Green = migrant or transient range; usually refers to spring and fall migration. Blue = winter range; based upon available habitat and may include counties where the species has not been recorded, but should be looked for. If there are insufficient data to ascertain the type of range, or the occurrence of the species is rare or highly irregular, then the map simply appears white with the respective circles.

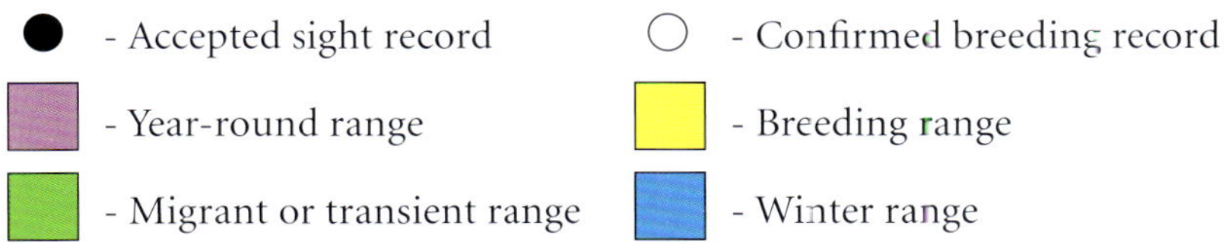

Photographs: A color photograph is provided for each species in this book. The photographs are the work of 27 wildlife photographers. We are grateful to these individuals for allowing us to use their photographs. Many of these photographs were taken in Kansas, but this was not a requirement for choosing. We focused on photographs that were of high quality that also showed unique features, or interesting character, or behavior for the species.

Status: This section is a general statement defining the occurrence of a species. If a species has been recorded only a few times in the state, or if its status is still in question, additional detail is provided. Because this is a general work, our terms are defined broadly rather than quantitatively.

Regular:	Occurs in about the same numbers, in about the same habitats each year.
Irregular:	May vary each year in numbers or distribution.
Local:	Present and/or breeds at only a few localities or is widely scattered over appropriate habitats.
Casual:	Occurs in very small numbers most years.
Vagrant:	Occurs rarely, but can be expected every few years.

Accidental: Far out of its normal range or movement pattern and not likely to appear in the near future.

Indications of abundance refer to presence in proper habitat and are also qualitative.

Rare: Only a few individuals seen in a season.
Uncommon: Small numbers present but found on most bird-watching trips during appropriate season or time of the year.
Common: Easily found, usually in numbers.
Abundant: Found in large numbers.

The status of a resident species is complicated by the fact that the individuals present may represent permanent residents (e.g., House Sparrow), resident and migratory populations (e.g., American Crow), or summering, wintering, and transient populations (e.g., Mourning Dove).

Habitat: Here we provide information on where the species is most likely to occur at various times of the year, ecologically and geographically. We added interesting or unusual behavior and observations both from personal experience and from the literature if germane. Included are data concerning nesting and foraging habitat when available.

Migration: We provide extreme dates of reported occurrence, main migration periods, and, where available, median dates of first arrival and early and late departure dates. Comments on variation from normal patterns and/or variation within the state are sometimes provided.

Breeding: A brief life history is usually given for each regularly breeding species. Included are the basic data concerning nest location and construction and if data are available, clutch size, incubation period, nestling period, courtship, and care of the young. At times we supplement such information from widely available basic sources such as Bent (1929, 1932, 1946, 1953, 1958, 1968), Terres (1980), Thompson and Ely (1989, 1992), and Busby and Zimmerman (2001). Readers are encouraged to refer to these references and the numerous Web sites available for more information. Breeding is reported only when an active nest, eggs, or dependent young have been reported and documented, corresponding to the "confirmed" classification as used in the KBBAT (Busby and Zimmerman, 2001).

Comments: Here we provide aspects of the species we believed would be of interest to the amateur birder or professional ornithologist. In some instances comments relate to more-extensive details associated with one of the aforementioned categories, information on natural history, or unusual behavior for the species.

Banding: For each species we examined the All Bird Data master file supplied by the U.S. Geological Survey, Bird Banding Office, Patuxent Wildlife Research Center (data current through 31 December 2008). For each species we extracted the total number of birds banded in Kansas ("Summarized Banding" file) and all encounters involving Kansas ("Encounters" file). We use the broad term "encounter," which includes any report of a banded bird, alive or dead, subsequent to initial banding and includes color-marked and tagged individuals and provides a more accurate picture of information obtained from banding. For each species we also provide the total number of individuals banded and encountered in-state; the number banded in Kansas and encountered elsewhere with the number from each state, province, or country; and the number of individuals banded or marked elsewhere and subsequently encountered in Kansas.

□ - Banding location ■ - Band encounter location

An open square in Kansas indicates that the species was banded in the state and the subsequent black squares represent recoveries from elsewhere. A black square in Kansas indicates the species was recovered in the state, and the corresponding open squares would be the location where the bird was banded. Postal abbreviations for the states and Canadian provinces and territories are used.

References: While this is a general work, the amount of data and literature relevant to each species necessitated a reference list for each species. Full citations for each reference can be found in the References section. Although not exhaustive, it was an attempt to use the most relevant recent literature and to use older literature for clarification of records.

Abbreviations used in the species accounts include the following:

AB	*American Birds*
AFN	*Audubon Field Notes*
AOU	American Ornithologists' Union
BBO	Bird Banding Office
BBS	Breeding Bird Survey
CBC	Christmas Bird Count
CBWA	Cheyenne Bottoms Wildlife Area
CNG	Cimarron National Grasslands
CRP	Conservation Reserve Program
DMNH	Delaware Museum of Natural History
ESU	Emporia State University
JRR	John Redmond Reservoir
KBBAT	Kansas Breeding Bird Atlas
KBRC	Kansas Bird Records Committee
KDWP	Kansas Department of Wildlife and Parks
KOS	Kansas Ornithological Society
KU	University of Kansas Natural History Museum
KUMNH	University of Kansas Natural History Museum
MBTA	Migratory Bird Treaty Act
MCZ	Harvard University Museum of Comparative Zoology
MDCWA	Marais des Cygnes Wildlife Area
MHP	Museum of the High Plains
MVZ	University of California Museum of Vertebrate Zoology
NWR	National Wildlife Refuge
QNWR	Quivira National Wildlife Refuge
SCW	Slate Creek Wetlands
UMMZ	University of Michigan Museum of Zoology
USFWS	U.S. Fish and Wildlife Service
USNM	U.S. National Museum

Many records in the text are further identified by the county in which they occur. However, the following localities, used very frequently throughout, are identified here only: CBWA (Barton Co.), CNG (Morton Co.), JRR (Coffey Co.), MDCWA (Linn Co.), QNWR (unless noted, Stafford Co.), and SCW (Sumner Co.).

Black-bellied Whistling-Duck

Dendrocygna autumnalis (BBWD)

© David Seibel

Status: Vagrant to casual; primarily in the eastern half of state.

Habitat: Usually in marshes, ponds, even city parks; could potentially occur almost anywhere within the state.

Migration: Observations seem to fall into three time periods: 3 March–21 May, 29 June–26 July, and 10 August–20 September. Most observations have been of single individuals for a few days. One was present in a Salina (Saline Co.) subdivision 3 March–20 May (D. Weibel).

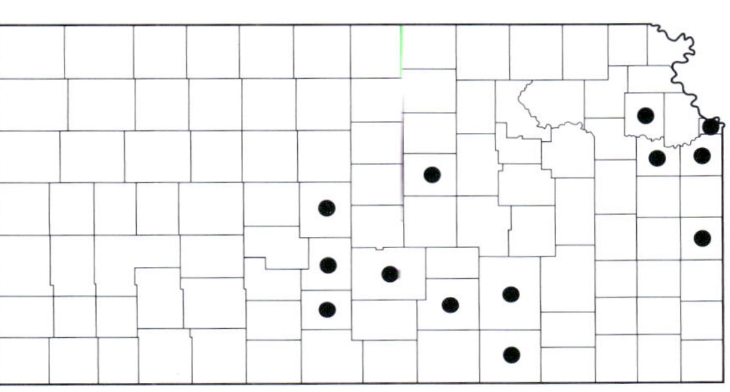

Comments: Its range and numbers have expanded northward in the last 20 years with recent breeding in small numbers in extreme southeastern Oklahoma and in southwestern Arkansas. As such, its continued, if only occasional, occurrence in the state is to be expected. It is, however, a species commonly held in captivity and the possibility of an "escapee" should always be considered. The species has been recorded every year since 2003; some sightings have involved multiple individuals. It is a cavity-nester, will use appropriate duck boxes, and given its rapid range expansion might someday attempt to breed at places like CBWA or QNWR.

References: James and Thompson, 2001; Thompson and Ely, 1989.

Fulvous Whistling-Duck

Dendrocygna bicolor (FUWD)

Status: Casual visitant.

© Brian Small

Habitat: Most often in the vicinity of marshes, or wet areas associated with ponds or reservoirs.

Migration: Sightings are 1 May–26 July and 1–22 September at CBWA; 13–20 April and 26 June–25 September elsewhere. One shot in Pottawatomie County on 28 November (W. Sheets) is now a mount at KDWP headquarters.

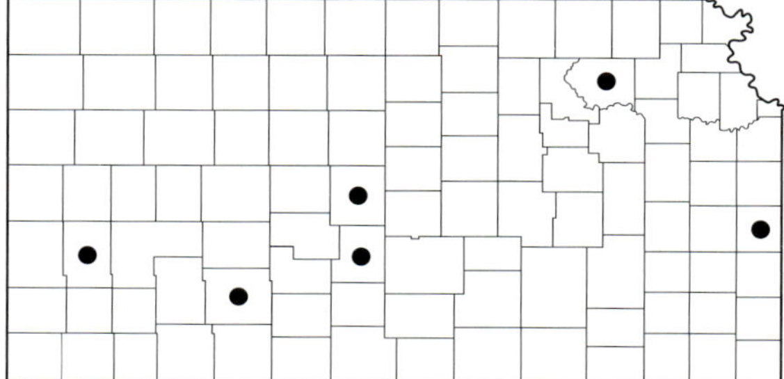

Comments: Formerly known as the Fulvous Tree Duck, it is one of the world's most widely distributed waterfowl species, occurring in tropical and subtropical parts of the Americas and also in more temperate parts of both Asia and Africa. It is frequently kept in captivity, and observers should always consider the possibility, of a sighting being a free-flying escapee. It visits Kansas at rare intervals with reports from 14 different years since 1929. The first report was of three shot at CBWA during 1929 or 1930. It was next reported there during the summers of 1965, 1967, and 1968 with three birds seen at various times, and nesting was suspected in 1965. Most sightings are of one to a few days duration and typically one to three individuals. The most recent account (QNWR) involved sightings from 28 June through 26 July (M. Gearheart and others). There is a specimen of one, shot by a hunter at Lake McKinney (Kearny Co.) and subsequently mounted and displayed (fide T. Shane) but without a date.

References: Hohman and Lee, 2001; Thompson and Ely, 1989.

Greater White-fronted Goose

Anser albifrons (GWFG)

Status: Common to locally abundant migrant statewide; uncommon during winter; casual in summer.

Habitat: Marshlands and wetlands, or on ponds and reservoirs; feeds in agricultural areas such as corn stubble or sorghum fields.

Migration: Flocks arrive by early February, or earlier, depending on the availability of open water. Median earliest arrival in Russell County is 16 February. M. Schwilling reported the arrival of about 10,000 on 21 February 1973. Most migration is during late February to mid-March with few flocks after late March, but with stragglers into late April (28 April, Meade Co.). As with most species of waterfowl, a few individuals remain at scattered localities through the summer. Early fall arrivals include 26 August (Barton and Russell cos.) but arrival is typically later (median first arrival for Barton Co. is 24 September) and with peak migration during the last half of October and early November. During many years most flocks depart by late November, but variable numbers remain into at least January and during winters with open water may actually overwinter.

Comments: Although not as well known as the Canada Goose, it is a common transient throughout the state, at times abundant at CBWA and, especially, at QNWR. During peak passage, the cacophony created by the thousands of white-fronts can be deafening.

Banding: 314 banded; 562 encounters: 3 in-state; 45 from Kansas to: SK (15), AB (8), TX (7), Mexico (6), AK (2), IA (2), NE (2), LA, ND, SD; 514 encountered in Kansas from: AK (184), NU (151), SK (84), NT (67), NE (20), YT (3), ND (2), TX (2), CA. Oldest 19 years, 6 months.

References: Ely and Dzubin, 1994; Thompson and Ely, 1989.

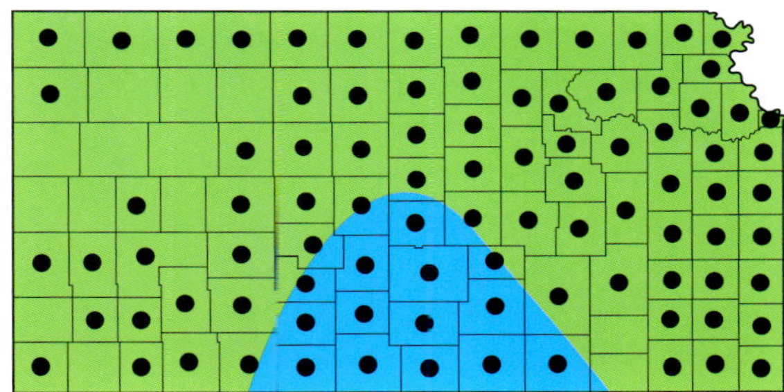

Snow Goose

Chen caerulescens (SNGO)

Status: Common to abundant migrant in eastern and central Kansas; uncommon in the western one-third. Winters on reservoirs until open waters freeze.

Habitat: Usually found in migration at large marshland and wetlands areas such as CBWA and QNWR in association with other migrating geese. Flocks can also be seen resting on larger ponds and reservoirs, and feeding in agricultural fields near refuges and larger bodies of water.

Migration: In spring early-arriving flocks are present by mid-February in the east with spectacular flights between mid-February and mid-March. Migration westward is usually later. Most flocks have departed by late April with scattered individuals, probably ill or crippled, remaining through the summer, usually at the larger marshes. Fall arrival may be as early as early September (median arrival at CBWA is 4 October), but the major flights (up to 400,000 birds, KDWP) are during late October and early November. On the evening of 2 November 1995 a heavy flight overloaded the radar at the Kansas City International Airport, disrupting air traffic. Large numbers remain into early winter or later if open water persists. Large numbers are usually recorded on Kansas CBCs, especially in the northeastern and eastern parts of the state, and more recently at QNWR.

Comments: It is one of the most abundant waterfowl species in the world. Two subspecies are currently recognized: *C. c. atlantica*, or Greater Snow Goose, and *C. c. caerulescens,* or Lesser Snow Goose. The latter is the form seen in Kansas. Additionally, two color morphs of the species exist: white and "blue." Although these forms were formerly treated as separate species, DNA testing has shown that they are color morphs of a single species. The beautiful sight and remarkable sounds of a flock of hundreds of snow-white geese "yelping" as they pass overhead on a cloudless, crisp November morning presents an experience that is not soon forgotten. The species has increased dramatically in numbers and in parts of its breeding range is seriously damaging its breeding habitat.

See page 485 for banding information.

References: Mowbray et al., 2000; Thompson and Ely, 1989.

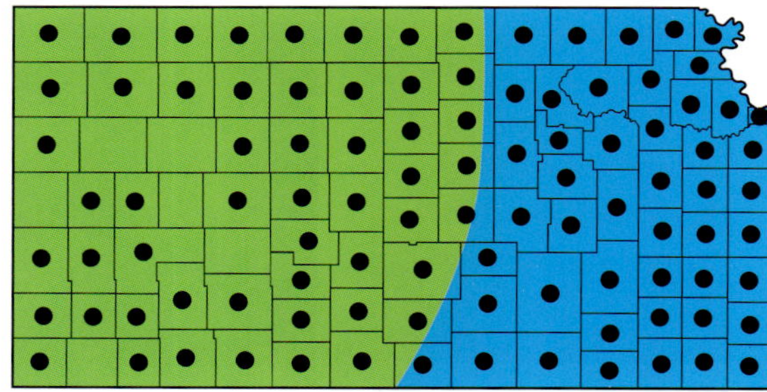

Ross's Goose

Chen rossii (ROGO)

Status: Uncommon migrant and rare winter visitant statewide. Its status has changed dramatically since 1989. Most common in central Kansas, especially at CBWA and QNWR; least common in the west.

Habitat: Generally occurs with other migrating geese, especially Snow Geese (Lesser form), the species to which it is apparently most closely related. During migration, occurs in large marshes and wetlands, agricultural lands containing stubble, and less frequently on reservoirs.

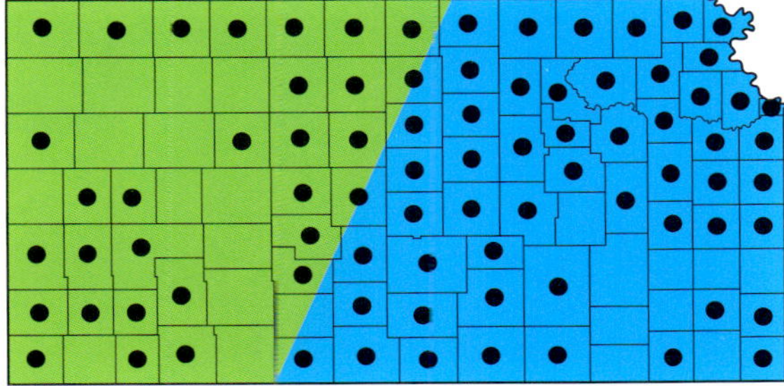

Migration: Extreme dates of occurrence are 2 October and 16 April. Most spring sightings are 12 February–31 March; most fall sightings 4 November–26 December with small numbers remaining during winter when open water persists. One is suspected of having summered near Liberal (Seward Co.) in 1990.

Comments: It was not reported in Kansas until 22 November 1951. During the mid-1960s single individuals spent extended periods at Kirwin NWR (Phillips Co.) and CBWA. By the mid-1990s it was widespread and regularly seen, usually with Snow Geese, throughout most of the state, and it is now a regular transient and winter resident. The species was first described to science in the 1860s, and the nesting range was not discovered until the 1940s. The species was considered rare even in the 1800s and in the early 1900s. By 1931, the total population was estimated at no more than 5,000–6,000 individuals. By 1950, the total species population was estimated to be no more than 2,000–3,000 individuals. By the 1960s and 1970s, several Canadian provinces had taken the initiative and had instituted a restrictive late white goose hunting season with the specific aim of reducing the mortality of this species. Since that time, it has rebounded, and population levels were estimated to be 188,000 in 1988 and 800,000 by 1998. It has also expanded its historically restricted winter range and now routinely winters in parts of Mexico, New Mexico, Texas, Louisiana, and Arkansas. The very rare "blue morph," which occurs in well under 1 percent of all individuals, may represent backcrossing of Ross's Geese with blue-morph Snow Geese.

Banding: Two banded; no encounters.

References: Alisauskas et al., 1998; Ryder and Alisauskas, 1995; Thompson and Ely, 1989.

Brant

Branta bernicla (BRAN)

Status: Casual migrant and rare winter visitant; no records from the west.

Habitat: Usually found near marshes, ponds, or reservoirs or feeding in nearby fields, often with larger flocks of its congener, the Canada Goose.

© Mike Blair

Brant with Canada Goose

Migration: Records of occurrence are from 9 November (Stafford Co.) to 3 May. Most sightings have been in midwinter; spring sightings are 6 March–3 May. One individual lingered in Geary County from 26 November to 4 December 1994, and another was near Hoisington (Barton Co.) from at least 26 April to 3 May 2009. There are records from 12 Kansas counties including a report of 15 individuals from Elk City Reservoir (Montgomery Co.) in December 1973.

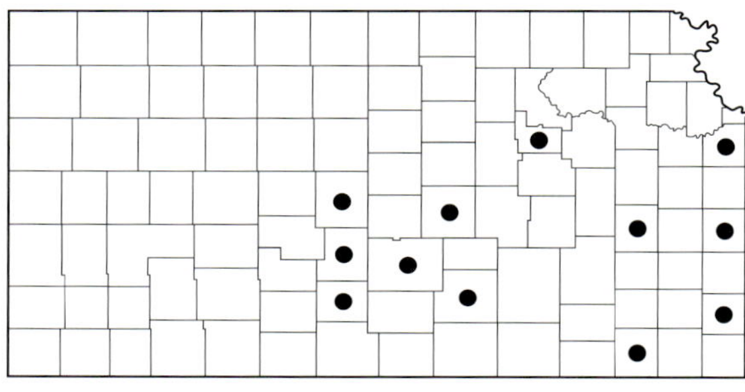

Comments: There are currently two recognized subspecies of this small goose in North America: *B. b. hrota* (the "Eastern Brant" or "Light-bellied Brant") and *B. b. nigricans* (the "Black Brant"). The majority of Kansas birds are *B. b. hrota,* but there are sight records and reports of *B. b. nigricans.* Additionally, some authors recognize that *B. b. hrota* is comprised of two stocks: "Atlantic Brant" and "Eastern High-Arctic Brant," the latter one currently unrecognized. Also, a fourth unrecognized form, "Western High-Arctic Brant" or "Gray-bellied Brant" breeds in the western Arctic of North America. This is a complicated taxon, and unresolved issues of systematics present identification and distribution pitfalls.

References: Reed et al., 1998; Thompson and Ely, 1989.

Cackling Goose

Branta hutchinsii (CACG)

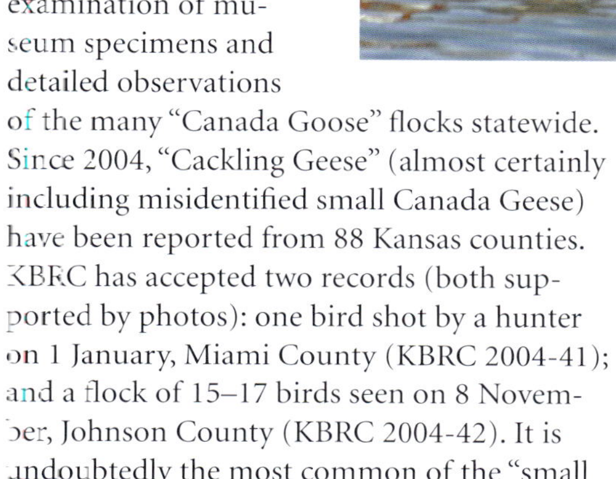

Status: It was considered conspecific with the Canada Goose until 2004, and so few prior records distinguished between the two. Continued confusion with small races of Canada Geese, in particular *B. canadensis parvipes*, keeps its status in Kansas unclear, especially in the west. Resolution will require critical examination of museum specimens and detailed observations of the many "Canada Goose" flocks statewide. Since 2004, "Cackling Geese" (almost certainly including misidentified small Canada Geese) have been reported from 88 Kansas counties. KBRC has accepted two records (both supported by photos): one bird shot by a hunter on 1 January, Miami County (KBRC 2004-41); and a flock of 15–17 birds seen on 8 November, Johnson County (KBRC 2004-42). It is undoubtedly the most common of the "small Canadas" observed during migration; a few may remain during mild winters.

Habitat: Occurs in association with other waterfowl on ponds and reservoirs, and in mixed feeding flocks in agricultural fields.

Migration: Largely unknown. During the 1980s it appeared that movements of small Canadas preceded those of the larger, migrant Canada Geese in the fall and followed those of the larger geese in spring. However, this does not seem to be the situation at present. Also, in recent years small geese are overwintering with larger Canadas and are recorded on CBCs in moderate numbers.

Comments: Differences in size, voice, habitat usage, and migration timing, corroborated by mitochondrial DNA studies, led to the AOU's 2004 split of this species from the generally larger Canada Goose. The Cackling Goose comprises four subspecies, only one of which, *B. h. hutchinsii*, normally occurs in the Midwest. While many Canada Geese are much larger, the smallest may approach or even overlap the size of larger individual Cackling Geese, and small birds should be examined very critically.

Banding: These totals are only those identified as "Cackling Geese" by the BBO. They do not include another 5,183 individuals identified as "small Canada Geese" but undoubtedly including many *B. hutchinsii*. Sixteen banded; two encounters. One banded in Alaska on 1 August 2000 was encountered in Kansas on 29 January 2006; one banded in Kansas on 17 December 1981 was shot in Manitoba on 3 September 1998. Oldest 16 years, 9 months.

References: AOU, 2004; Hertzel et al., 2006; Mowbray et al., 2002; Sibley, 2004; Thompson and Ely, 1989.

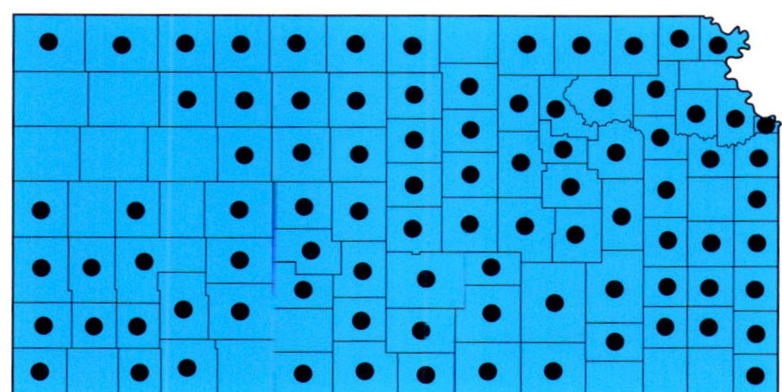

Canada Goose

Branta canadensis (CAGO)

Status: Common statewide migrant; uncommon local breeder in the central and eastern part; moderately common winter resident.

Habitat: Agricultural fields, pastures, wetlands, and marshes, to ponds and reservoirs.

Migration: Peak migration periods occur from mid-October through November, and from January through February. Extreme dates for presumed transients are 3 September (Barton Co.) and 12 April (Cowley Co.). Large numbers remain as long as water remains open, but some will often remain locally despite frozen conditions and with an adequate food supply and freedom from harassment. Flocks migrate by day or night.

Breeding: KBBAT documented the species as a relatively common breeder in eastern and central Kansas with greatest frequencies in the Osage Plains and Flint Hills and the lowest in the High Plains and Smoky Hills. Eggs have been reported 7 April–5 May, and goslings 1 May–26 June.

Comments: Several subspecies representing a wide range of sizes occur in Kansas. The smallest, *B. c. parvipes*, a migrant to be expected mostly in the west, intergrades with the Cackling Goose and can be extremely similar in size and appearance. The large subspecies *B. c. maxima* presumably composed the state's original breeding populations. It was thought extinct until "rediscovered" in Minnesota in the early 1900s. Birds from this (or similar) stock were used to repopulate Kansas. KDWP first established restoration flocks at Kirwin NWR (Phillips Co.) and at CBWA, which successfully bred in 1958 and 1962, respectively. However, lack of sufficient feeding areas and excessive early-season harvest before migrants arrived prevented more than remnant survival. During the 1970s private restorations in Barber and Reno counties were more successful. In 1980 KDWP began the Kansas Resident Canada Goose Management Plan, which resulted in the widespread success seen today, primarily in the eastern half of the state. The species is adaptable in its breeding habitat requirements. Such diverse areas as prairies, wetlands, marshes, farm ponds, golf courses, and urban/suburban office parks with small ponds can be used. In fact, a small pond with a goose tub erected in the middle can suffice. Breeding pairs are monogamous and establish lifelong bonds during their second year.

See page 485 for banding information.

References: Busby and Zimmerman, 2001; Hertzel et al., 2006; Kraft, 1990; Mowbray et al., 2002; Sibley, 2004; Thompson and Ely, 1989.

Trumpeter Swan

Cygnus buccinator (TRUS)

© Judd Patterson

Status: Rare winter resident. Historically, this species was likely a regular migrant through Kansas, but no specimens or documented sightings exist from that era. It has become more common within the last decade as wildlife agencies continue reintroduction and population stabilization efforts in states to the north and west of Kansas. It is occasionally reported on CBCs.

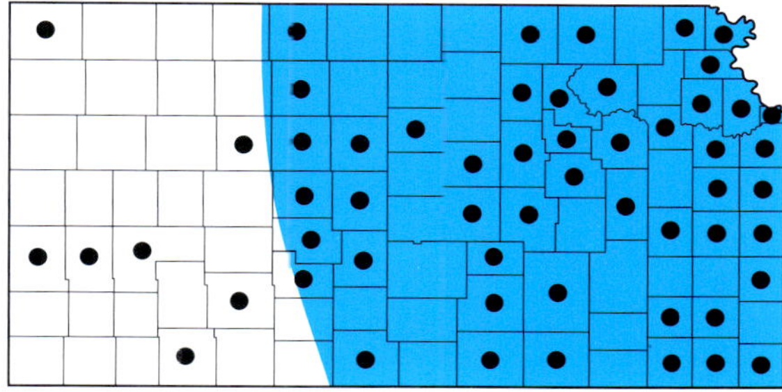

Habitat: Occurs on reservoirs or large marshes and, increasingly, on smaller ponds.

Migration: It is becoming regular at CBWA, QNWR, and eastward. Extreme dates are 14 November (Stafford Co.) and 26 March (Shawnee Co., neck identification collar) with most sightings during midwinter (December–February.) Most sightings are of family groups, and a high percentage includes at least one color-tagged individual. The group wintering in northwestern Kansas during the 1980s was from a "restoration flock" in Nebraska; more recent flocks (where known) were from similar flocks in Minnesota, Iowa, Idaho, and Wisconsin. Fall arrivals are usually mid-November to mid-December. Spring migration begins as early as 6 February (Cowley Co.) and 7 February (Montgomery Co.). Other known departures are 22 February (Anderson Co.), 15 February (Crawford Co.), and 1 March (Rooks Co.) with additional late dates to 26 March (Shawnee Co., wing-tagged).

Comments: It is the largest waterfowl species native to North America. It was common in colonial times, but widespread hunting and loss of habitat reduced its numbers dramatically; by the 1930s, only a handful of individuals remained in the lower 48 states. Conservation efforts have had a dramatic, positive effect upon population levels, but the species remains vulnerable because of its relatively slow reproductive rate. Care should be exercised in distinguishing Trumpeter Swans from Tundra Swans; differences between the species are subtle, and separating the two in the field can often be impossible. Some members of the family groups are often tagged or marked with unique neck bands, making it possible to determine the specific origins of a particular family group. Such markings should be observed closely and reported whenever possible.

Banding: None; 117 encounters, all with auxiliary markers (wing tags, etc.) encountered in Kansas from: IA (80), MN (23), WI (13), ID. At least one other from Nebraska was apparently never reported.

References: Mitchell, 1994; Thompson and Ely, 1989.

Tundra Swan

Cygnus columbianus (TUSW)

Status: Rare migrant and casual early winter resident, chiefly in eastern one-third of the state and at CBWA and QNWR.

Habitat: Occurs both on larger expanses of marshes, wetlands, ponds, reservoirs, and nearby fields; often associates with Trumpeter Swans when they are present.

Migration: Although 9 of 12 extant specimens from the 19th century were taken during spring (7 March–26 April), most modern sightings are from fall and early winter. The earliest arrivals are 15 October (Russell Co.) and 27 October, but arrival is usually early November with peak numbers from mid-November through mid-December. At least partial overwintering occurs if water remains open. Presumed spring transients arrive in mid-February with the peak (much movement) during March. One flock present on 11 February was seen to depart on 11 March. Late spring dates include 26 March (Sedgwick Co.) and 4 April (Cowley Co.) and a very late departure of 26 April (Linn Co.). The largest flock reported was 32 in Osage County on 15 December.

Comments: Identifications should be made carefully, because distinguishing Tundra Swans from Trumpeter Swans can be difficult at best and, in some situations, impossible. Most reports are of family groups, which often spend only a few days in an area before moving. Unfortunately, because of their large size and white plumage, swans are readily visible and until recently often suffered considerable harassment from gunners intent on an easy "target." One group of seven in Sherman County in 1970 was reduced to a single bird in a few days (fide J. Palmquist).

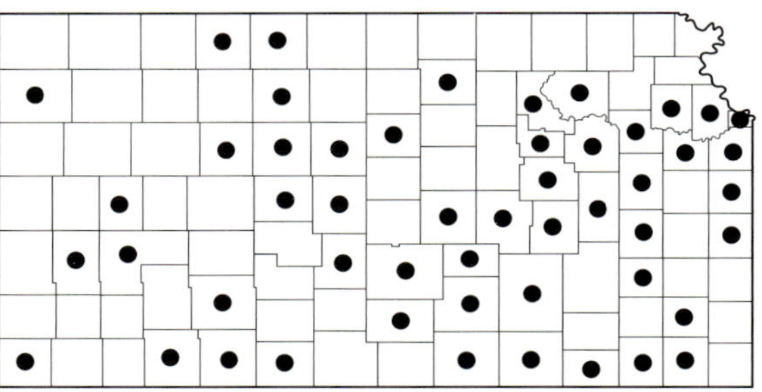

References: Limpert and Earnst, 1994; Thompson and Ely, 1989.

Wood Duck

Aix sponsa (WODU)

Status: Common migrant statewide; locally common breeder in the east, uncommon in the west; rare but regular in winter in the south.

Habitat: Commonly frequents riparian woodlands as well as freshwater marshes; regularly nests in parks and residential areas with mature trees.

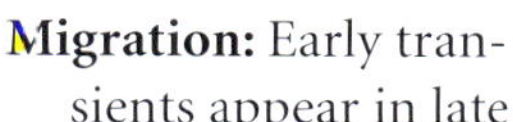

Migration: Early transients appear in late February and increase in numbers through mid-March with most migration from late March through mid-April. The median arrival date in Hays (Ellis Co.) is 3 April. In fall local flocking begins by mid-August or earlier. Most flocks are small with an occasional large flock by late October (1,000, 25 October, Barton Co.). Numbers decline by early November with small numbers remaining into the CBC period. Only a few remain in the eastern one-third of the state after mid-October. Occurrence for the entire winter period is rare.

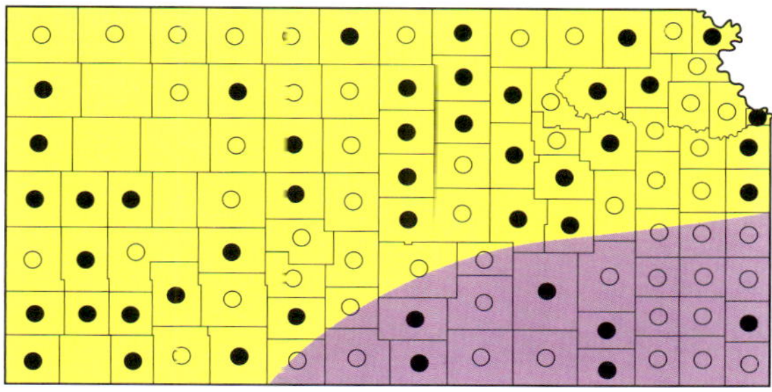

Breeding: It is a cavity nester and has benefited greatly from the erection of nest boxes by conservation agencies and organizations. Eggs have been reported 18 April–24 May, downy chicks 17 May–14 July (once to 22 August), and broods (nonflying young) 17 May–21 June (once to 6 September). The Wood Duck is unique among North American ducks in being regularly double-brooded. The second brood is usually produced by adults, less frequently by yearling females.

Comments: The male Wood Duck is probably the gaudiest duck in North America. The hen, drab and cryptically plumaged, incubates the eggs and broods the young alone. Although the species was feared to be near extinction by the early part of the 20th century, population levels increased steadily through the latter parts of that century and have not only retained their former numbers but are also expanding the former range. The erection of nest boxes, the expansion of beaver populations providing wetland habitat, and limited harvesting have dramatically benefited this species and its recovery.

See page 486 for banding information.

References: Busby and Zimmerman, 2001; Hepp and Bellrose, 1995; Thompson and Ely, 1989.

Gadwall

Anas strepera (GADW)

Status: Common migrant statewide; rare and local breeder; fairly common early winter resident.

Habitat: Usually occurs with other migrating waterfowl, loosely associating with other dabblers on ponds, reservoirs, and wetlands.

Migration: The spring movement closely follows open water and usually peaks during late March and the first half of April. Median first arrivals include 6 March (Ellis Co.). Most birds have departed by early May but with stragglers, especially in the west, are found into June and with nonbreeding but summering birds during most years. Fall migration begins slowly by mid-August and peaks in late October through mid-November. It is usually recorded in good numbers on CBCs if open water remains.

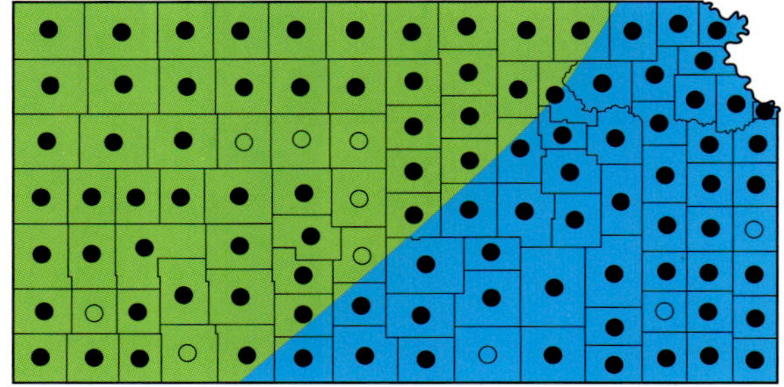

Breeding: KBBAT confirmed breeding only in areas with extensive marshlands: CBWA, QNWR, and SCW. Historically, there are additional confirmed breeding records from Ellis, Grant, Linn, Meade, Russell, Trego, and Wilson counties. It nests in dry areas such as fields or meadows adjacent to, or very near, marshes, wetlands, or ponds. Eggs have been reported 12 June–10 July, and ducklings 30 May and 29 July (Sumner Co.). It is generally single-brooded, but pairs will replace a brood if the first nest is destroyed.

Comments: M. Schwilling noted that it was one of the duck species that was actually increasing in total population size apparently because of its ability to change with changing habitat conditions. It is easy to distinguish from all other North American dabblers in flight, because in both sexes, and at all ages, it is the only one with a white speculum.

See page 486 for banding information.

References: Busby and Zimmerman, 2001; Leschack et al., 1997; Thompson and Ely, 1989; Young, 1993.

Eurasian Wigeon

Anas penelope (EUWI)

© James Arterburn

Status: [Hypothetical]. Accidental visitant; remains on the hypothetical list due to lack of physical evidence (specimen or adequate photograph).

Habitat: Marshes, reservoirs, and ponds, typically with other dabbling ducks (including American Wigeon) during migration.

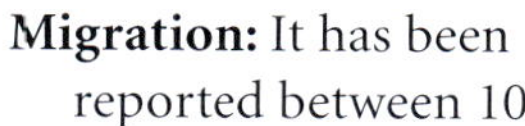

Migration: It has been reported between 10 March and 26 April (five records) and on 1 June. It should be looked for in mixed flocks of dabbling ducks in spring, and perhaps during October–November.

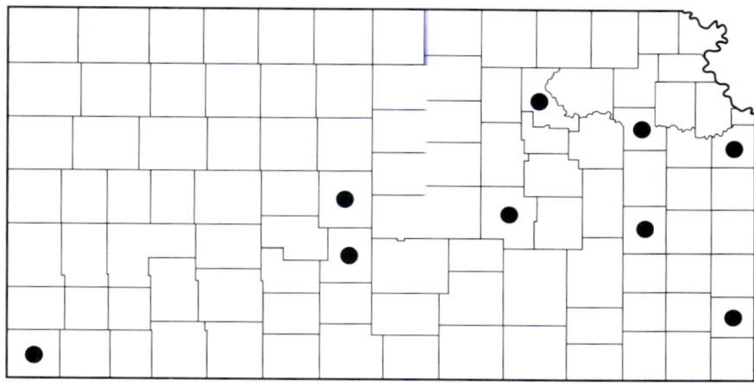

Comments: There are nine accepted records (see map) since 1950; the most recent, a single bird on the Elkhart sewage ponds (Morton Co.) on March 1995 (L. Smith, KBRC 95-16). Exercise care in identifying this species; it is known to hybridize with the closely related American Wigeon. Females and young males of these two species are very similar, and some may not be safely separated under field conditions.

Banding: Five individuals are listed as having been banded, but because all five were banded by a single bander, at the same location and on the same date, these are almost certainly in error.

References: Mowbray, 1999; Thompson and Ely, 1989.

American Wigeon

Anas americana (AMWI)

Status: Common spring and fall migrant statewide; uncommon winter resident; casual breeder.

Habitat: Occurs in marshy wetlands, and on reservoirs and ponds.

Migration: Early arrival is usually related to the presence of open water. Large numbers are usually present by mid-February or early March with numbers declining through mid-April and with stragglers into late May (24 May, Ellis Co.) or early June (24 June, Meade Co.). Scattered individuals are observed during most summers, especially in the west. Fall migration begins by mid-August or (usually) mid- to late September with peak numbers in October or November and with smaller numbers remaining into the CBC period.

Breeding: At least one of three nests reported from CBWA in 1963 was that of a Gadwall. However, a confirmed wigeon nest was found there on 23 June 1973 (three eggs, M. Schwilling), and a brood was observed in Seward County on 12 June 1982 (G. Ernsting). KBBAT did not confirm breeding anywhere in the state.

Comments: It can usually be found in good numbers during migration associating with other dabbling ducks. Large flocks of several hundred birds are not uncommon. A flock of 3,000 was seen at Liberal (Seward Co.) sewage-treatment ponds on 28 December 2009. Wigeon are highly terrestrial and can often be seen in fields adjacent to wetlands or reservoirs, feeding on vegetation. The male makes one of the most easily recognizable duck calls: a three-syllable whistle, often rendered as "whew, whew, whew." The sound is reminiscent of a child's squeaky toy being squeezed.

See page 486 for banding information.

References: Busby and Zimmerman, 2001; Mowbray, 1999; Thompson and Ely, 1989.

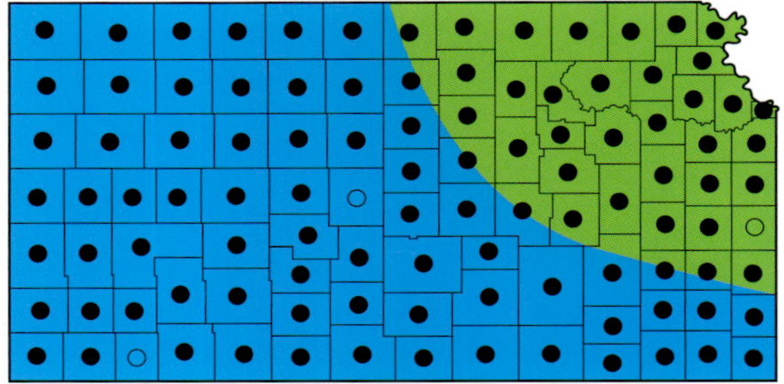

American Black Duck

Anas rubripes (ABDU)

Status: Rare migrant; casual in early winter; few records from the western one-third of the state; casual breeder.

Habitat: Frequents marshes, wetlands, shallow ponds, and reservoirs.

Migration: Migration is early February to mid-March with a late date of 4 April. Fall movement has been as early as 10 August at CBWA but is usually 20 October with the peak from November through freeze-up. Up to 50 individuals were reported from CBWA during the mid-1960s, but, statewide, sightings are typically 1–5 (rarely) individuals. Typical sightings are of a few within huge flocks of other species, for example, three in a huge flock of Mallards in Ellis County on 6 January. In recent years it has been reported most regularly at Melvern Reservoir (Osage Co.) during midwinter. It regularly occurs in small numbers on CBCs.

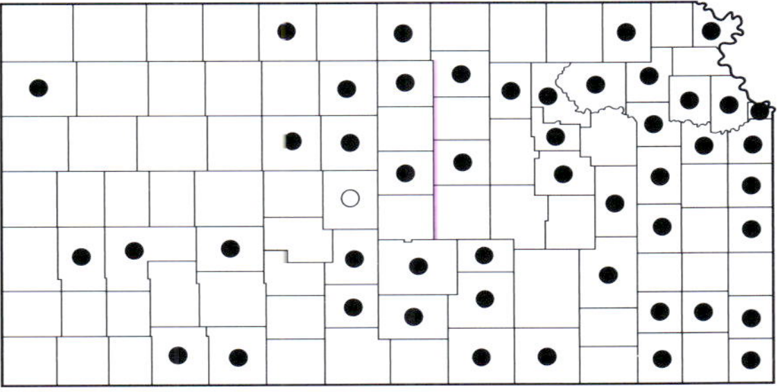

Breeding: It summered at CBWA during the 1960s with as many as 50 individuals during 1963. M. Schwilling found a nest with three eggs on 7 July 1969, and later as many as eight young. It may also have nested following unusually high numbers during fall 1963 and 1965 (M. Schwilling). There are no other breeding records for Kansas, and the 1969 numbers are not likely to be repeated in the near future given the overall population dynamics of the species.

Comments: It is a member of the so-called Mallard "superspecies," which also includes the Mallard and the Mottled Duck and regularly hybridizes with Mallards in the wild. Some authors have suggested that the range expansion of the Mallard, coupled with the release of game farm–raised Mallards and the pressures inherent in the annual harvest of ducks, has led to the genetic compromise of the American Black Duck as a species.

See page 486 for banding information.

References: Loncore et al., 2000; Thompson and Ely, 1989.

Mallard

Anas platyrhynchos (MALL)

Status: Common to abundant migrant; fairly common breeder; abundant winter resident when open water remains.

Habitat: It is plastic and opportunistic in its habitat requirements. Found in marshes, on small ponds and reservoirs, as well as creeks, streams, and rivers; also in grasslands and fields, feeding on grains. Mallards have also adapted well to human interference and can be found in both urban and suburban environments, even breeding in such locales.

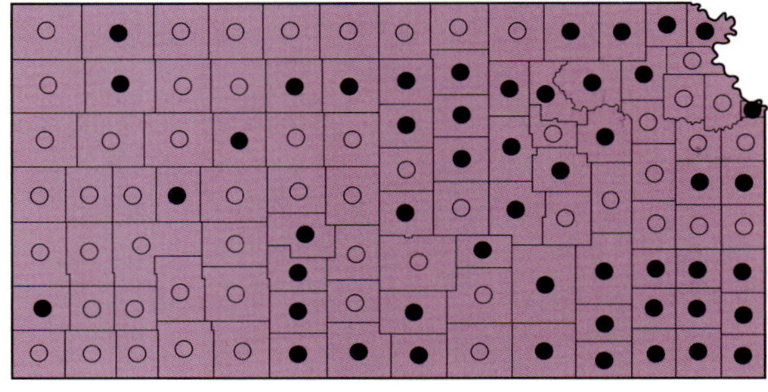

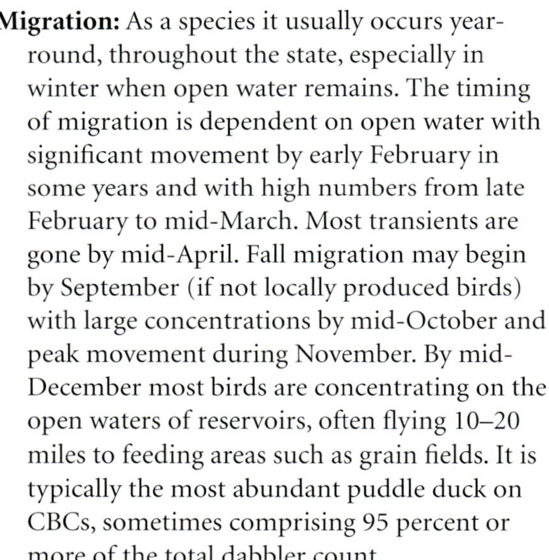

Migration: As a species it usually occurs year-round, throughout the state, especially in winter when open water remains. The timing of migration is dependent on open water with significant movement by early February in some years and with high numbers from late February to mid-March. Most transients are gone by mid-April. Fall migration may begin by September (if not locally produced birds) with large concentrations by mid-October and peak movement during November. By mid-December most birds are concentrating on the open waters of reservoirs, often flying 10–20 miles to feeding areas such as grain fields. It is typically the most abundant puddle duck on CBCs, sometimes comprising 95 percent or more of the total dabbler count.

Breeding: There are confirmed breeding records from nearly all counties. KBBAT project found it to be well distributed as a breeding species in the central and western portions of the state and least common in the Osage Plains, the Flint Hills, and the Glaciated Region. Irrigation ponds and small sewage-retention ponds apparently provide suitable brood-rearing habitat for the Mallard in the central and western parts of the state. Most nesting is usually at CBWA. Eggs have been reported 14 April–17 July (134 clutches), chicks 15 May–30 July and once 6 August, and flying young as early as 1 July. Hens will often attempt a second nesting if the first nest is destroyed, or the brood is lost to predation.

Comments: It is the most common and most familiar duck in Kansas. Peak Mallard wintering numbers occur during the last half of December, with 300,000 birds reported on average.

See page 487 for banding information.

References: Busby and Zimmerman, 2001; Drilling et al., 2002; Thompson and Ely, 1989; Young, 1993.

Mottled Duck

Anas fulvigula (MODU)

Status: Currently a rare visitant to the south-central region; formerly bred at CBWA.

Habitat: Most records are from marshes at CBWA and QNWR. Usually found singly or in pairs at these locales.

Migration: Reports from CBWA are 15 February–30 November. Reports from elsewhere are 11 March (Woodson Co., 1876) and 22 June–29 October. Banding suggests that birds move to Gulf Coast marshes during winter.

Breeding: Breeding was confirmed at CBWA from at least 1963 to 1977. M. Schwilling estimated a population of 12 pairs in 1966 and 25 (individuals?) during the early 1970s. Eggs have been reported 17–27 June and broods 23 June–16 July and 20 August. There are no recent breeding records from Kansas.

Comments: Identification is difficult, and it has been confused with other species since the 19th century. Specimens in museums are often misidentified. The breeding habitat at CBWA has been severely impacted by lack of water on several recent occasions, undoubtedly causing local birds to move elsewhere, at least temporarily. Recent reports from QNWR and SCW during July and August 2009 (up to two birds at one time) may be related to these events. There are currently specimens from Barton and Woodson counties.

Banding: 20 banded; one encounter. An adult male banded at CBWA on 5 March 1968 was shot near Jennings, Louisiana, on 17 December 1969, probably on its wintering grounds. Oldest 1 year, 8 months.

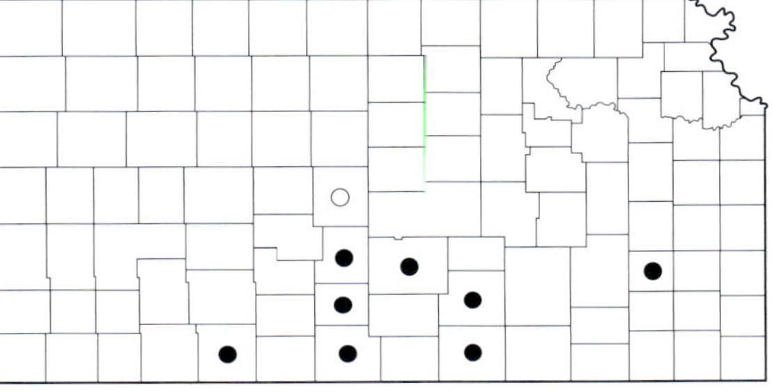

References: Moorman and Gray, 1994; Thompson and Ely, 1989; Tordoff, 1956.

Surf Scoter

Melanitta perspicillata (SUSC)

© Mark Chappell

Status: Uncommon fall migrant through the eastern half of the state; rare migrant in the west; rare in midwinter.

Habitat: Most likely to occur on reservoirs and sewage ponds.

Migration: Fall sightings are between 16 October (Clark Co.) and 29 December with most between mid-October and mid-November. The few spring records are 21 February (Linn Co.) and 19 April (Lyon Co.) to 6 May (Morton Co., had been present several days). A recent report involved two birds found on the Oskaloosa/Perry Reservoir CBC on 14 December 2008.

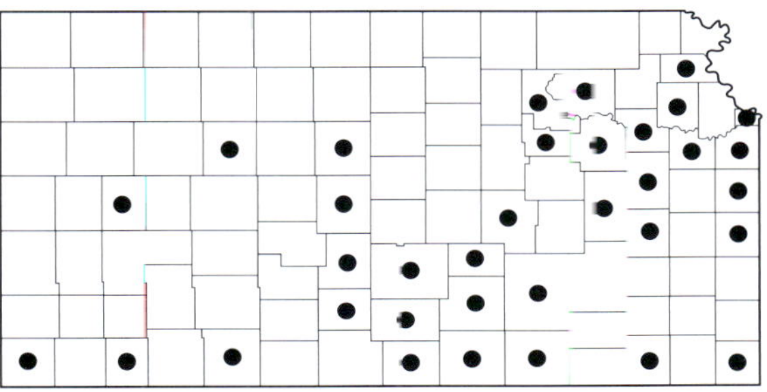

Comments: Prior to 1956, there were eight specimens of this scoter from the state, and two sight records. By 1980, the number had increased with an additional 17 records, involving more than 23 individuals. Only a few have been recorded in the west. The adult male's jet-black plumage, distinctive white head patches, large, multicolored bill, and white iris make it easy to understand the origin of the old colloquial name "skunkhead!" Some care is required in separating female and young male scoters; at some distance, many individuals are simply best identified as "dark-winged" scoters.

References: Savard et al., 1998; Thompson and Ely, 1989.

White-winged Scoter

Melanitta fusca (WWSC)

Status: Uncommon fall migrant; rare winter visitant. Most records are from central and eastern Kansas reservoirs.

© David Seibel

Habitat: Generally on reservoirs, often in association with other waterfowl species.

Migration: Fall sightings are from 15 October (Trego Co.) to 22 December, with most during mid-October through November. The few spring reports are 4 March (Chase Co.) to 6 and 8 May (Jewell Co., R. Lohoefener). Midwinter reports (2 January–27 February) also include one that remained at Lone Star Lake (Douglas Co.) from 30 January through 12 February.

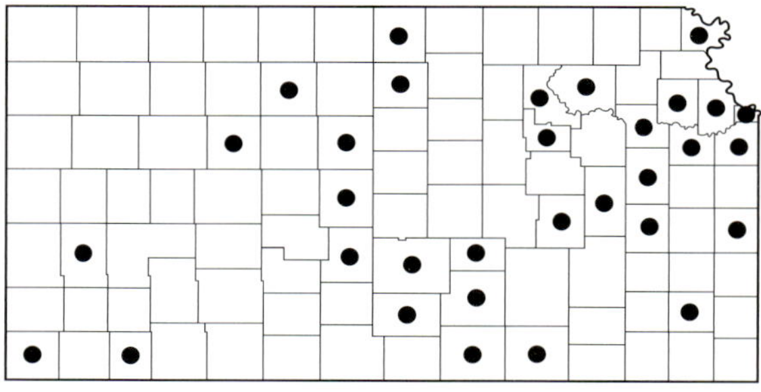

Comments: This is the most common and widespread of the scoters in Kansas. As with the others, the number of sightings increased dramatically with the establishment of reservoirs, better optics, and a deliberate attempt to bird these large bodies of water.

References: Brown and Fredrickson, 1997; Thompson and Ely, 1989.

Black Scoter

Melanitta americana (BLSC)

© David Seibel

Status: Uncommon fall migrant through the eastern and central parts of the state; rare in the west with few records.

Habitat: Most likely to occur on reservoirs and sewage ponds. As with the other scoters the number of sightings increased greatly with the advent of reservoirs and the increased birding that followed.

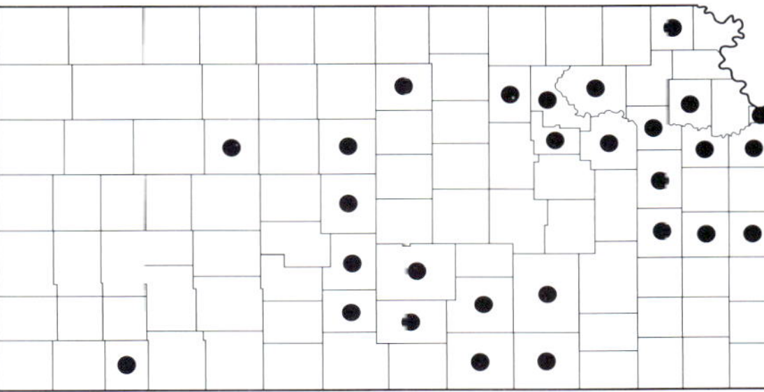

Migration: Nearly all sightings are from fall and early winter during the period 20 October (Pratt Co.) through 19 January (Cowley Co.) with most during November. The few spring sightings are from 18 March (Linn Co.) to 24 April including one present at Milford Reservoir (Geary Co.) 17–26 April 1997. Most sightings were of 1–3, up to 12, birds. Nine were seen in Russell County (4 November), and 3 were shot out of a flock of 12 by a hunter in Cowley County (1 November 1984).

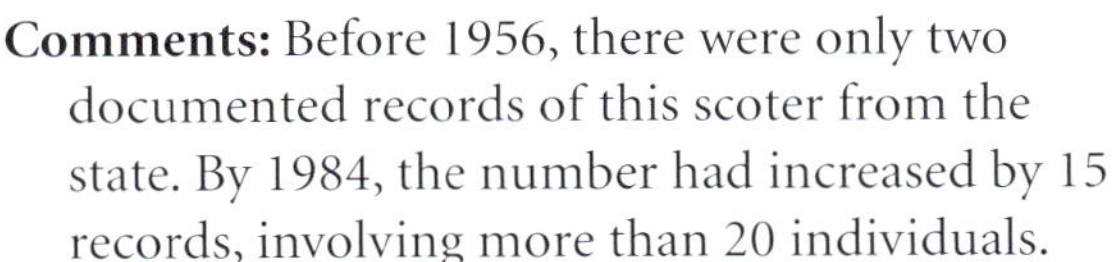

Comments: Before 1956, there were only two documented records of this scoter from the state. By 1984, the number had increased by 15 records, involving more than 20 individuals.

References: Bordage and Savard, 1995; Thompson and Ely, 1989.

Long-tailed Duck

Clangula hyemalis (LTDU)

Status: Low-density transient and winter visitant; most often recorded in central and eastern Kansas.

Habitat: Usually found on reservoirs; also on smaller ponds and basins and even the larger rivers in the eastern part of the state.

Migration: Early fall arrivals have appeared by 21 October (Barton Co.), but most sightings are from early November through the CBC period. Overwintering may occur whenever and wherever open water is present. Numbers are greatest from about 22 February through 5 April with a few present to 20 April (Pottawatomie Co.). Most sightings are of one or two individuals, but five were present at sewage ponds near Lawrence (Douglas Co.) on 1 December.

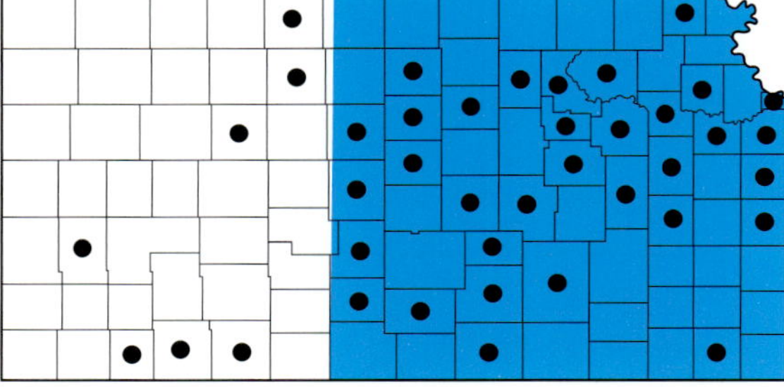

Comments: Although there are few reports from the 19th and early 20th centuries it now occurs regularly most years. It was formerly known as the Oldsquaw, a name derived from the garrulous calling within large flocks, but the few birds observed in Kansas are usually silent. The adult male in breeding plumage is a handsome bird with boldly marked plumage and two greatly elongated central tail feathers, hence its current name, Long-tailed Duck. Most individuals are young birds, or adults in the subdued winter plumage.

References: Robertson and Savard, 2002; Thompson and Ely, 1989.

Bufflehead

Bucephala albeola (BUFF)

Status: Regular, low-density migrant; uncommon winter resident.

Habitat: Occurs on both reservoirs and on smaller ponds and impoundments, usually singly, in pairs, or in small flocks.

Migration: The earliest fall sighting is 9 September (Douglas Co.), but early arrivals are usually in late October (20 October, Morton Co.) with the peak in mid-November. Most have departed by late November, but small numbers remain into December and, if water remains open, may overwinter. Spring arrival is mid-February to March with a peak from late March to early April and with stragglers to 10 May (Sumner Co.). Rarely, a few may spend the summer. A report of breeding (brood of four) from Pratt County in 1989, though highly unlikely, was made by an experienced observer. It is usually recorded on CBCs especially during mild winters, when significant numbers are often reported. In 2007, 281 individuals were reported statewide, and in 2008, 323 were noted. High numbers during winter include 1,000 on 17 November and 2,000 during December 1987 at Winfield City Lake (Cowley Co.).

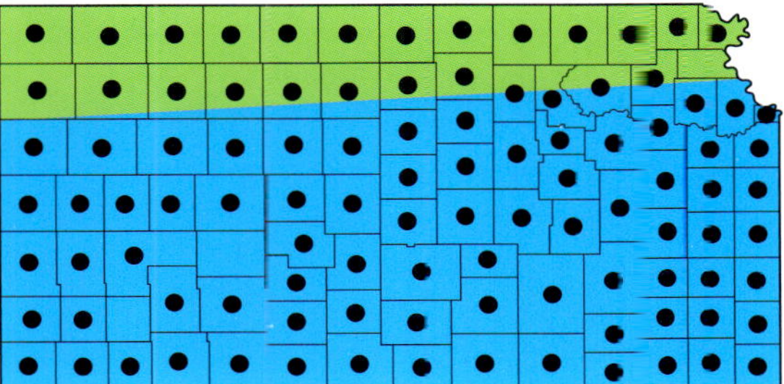

Comments: It is a very distinctive species, and its courtship displays during early March are familiar to most birders.

Banding: 10 banded; six encounters: all encountered in Kansas from: AB (3), NT, SK, TX. Oldest 4 years, 1 month.

References: Gauthier, 1993; Thompson and Ely, 1989; Young, 1993; Young and Thompson, 2008; Young et al., 2009.

Common Goldeneye

Bucephala clangula (COGO)

Status: Common migrant and winter resident on larger reservoirs statewide.

Habitat: Generally limited to large bodies of water and rivers, less often on small ponds.

Migration: In fall early arrival is in late October to early November with the peak in late November. Unless all waters are frozen it can usually be found in moderate to large numbers from mid-December through mid-March. High counts include 2,000 at Marion Reservoir on 20 November, 4,240 on 19 December (Mitchell Co.), and 1,000+ on 28 January (Russell Co.). Spring departure is by mid-March to mid-April with stragglers into early May (4 May, Wabaunsee Co.). An injured individual summered in Pratt County in 1921.

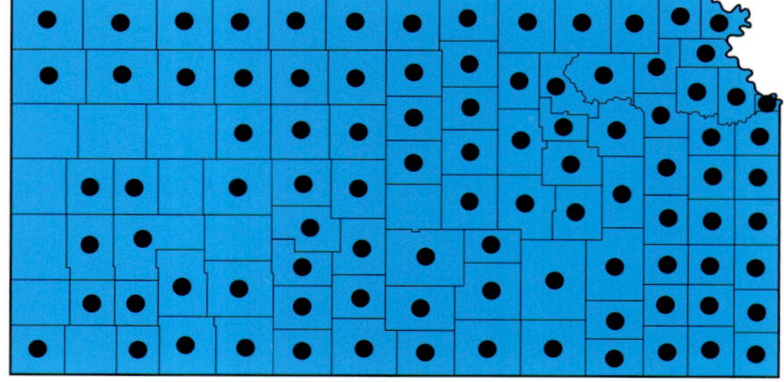

Comments: Expert divers, goldeneyes can effortlessly swim underwater to secure their food. Although seeds, tubers, and leaves are consumed, at least 75 percent of their diet is animal, including crustaceans, mollusks, insects and their larvae, and small fish. It is usually recorded in good numbers on CBCs; 4,814 were recorded in 2008 and 3,559 in 2009. Most reports, and all larger groups, are from central and eastern Kansas. Goldeneyes can often be heard migrating on fall nights because of their distinctive wing whistle, and it is this sound that gave rise to the colloquial name for the bird: "Whistler."

Banding: 10 banded; 10 encounters: all encountered in Kansas from a single locality in Minnesota. Oldest 4 years, 6 months.

References: Eadie et al., 1995; Thompson and Ely, 1989; Young and Thompson, 2008; Young et al., 2009.

Barrow's Goldeneye

Bucephala islandica (BAGO)

Status: Casual winter visitant; the number of sightings (many supported by photos) has increased considerably since 2000.

Habitat: It often associates with flocks of Common Goldeneyes on reservoirs, but also on smaller ponds.

Migration: Current sightings are 12 September (Lyon Co.) and 2 October (Trego Co.) through 17 February (Sedgwick Co.) with most during mid-November through December. The few spring records are 9 February (Osage Co.) through 10 April (Shawnee Co.). A male remained at a small sewage lagoon in Wichita from 19 November through 16 March, leaving when the pond froze solid then returning after it thawed. Many of the records come from KBRC reports.

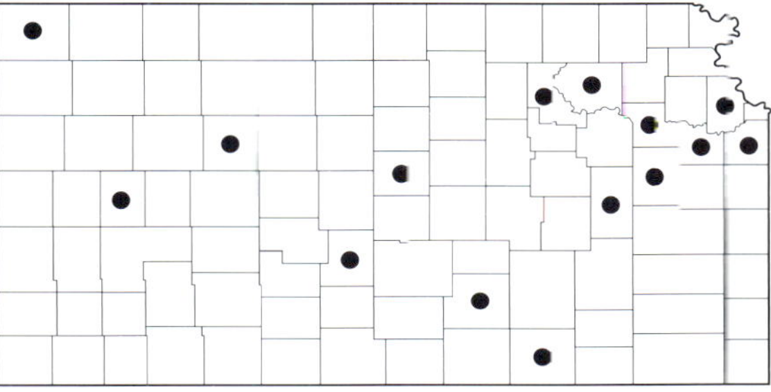

Comments: Specific identification of female and young male goldeneyes can be problematic; care must be exercised in documenting any occurrence of the species for the state.

References: Eadie et al., 2000; Land, 2010; Thompson and Ely, 1989.

Hooded Merganser

Lophodytes cucullatus (HOME)

© Judd Patterson

Status: Common, low-density migrant in the east; uncommon in the west; casual in winter; usually found singly or in small flocks.

Habitat: Favors marshy areas, streams, and small ponds, often among flooded trees.

Migration: Spring transients overlap with wintering individuals, but migrants arrive by at least 24 February (Sumner Co.) with most migration mid-March through mid-April and most departed by early May with stragglers to 25 May (Scott Co.). There are midsummer records for several counties where nesting has not been reported. Fall migration begins in early October (Barton Co.) to late October (Russell Co.) with most records during November. Smaller numbers remain into early winter; overwintering has been reported but is not well documented. It usually occurs in small flocks, but 200+ were reported on 31 January (Miami Co.), 200 on 30 December (Cowley Co.), and 200 on 10 January (Butler Co.).

Breeding: KBBAT confirmed breeding only at MDCWA, but it is a rare but local breeder throughout eastern and central Kansas. Eggs have been reported 3 April–18 May and broods 20 April–11 June ("full size," Jefferson Co.). As a cavity nester, it has benefited from the erection of Wood Duck nest boxes at some of the state's wildlife management areas. Females are parasitic and will deposit eggs in the cavities of conspecifics, as well as other waterfowl species.

Comments: This, the smallest merganser in Kansas, is a handsome, animated bird. The male, sporting a fan-shaped crest, is unmistakable, whereas the drab female is best identified by its small size and its long, narrow serrate bill.

Banded: None banded; 11 encounters: all encountered in Kansas from: MO (6), MN (3), MS, SD. Oldest 4 years, 6 months.

References: Busby and Zimmerman, 2001; Dugger et al., 2009; Thompson and Ely, 1989; Young, 1993.

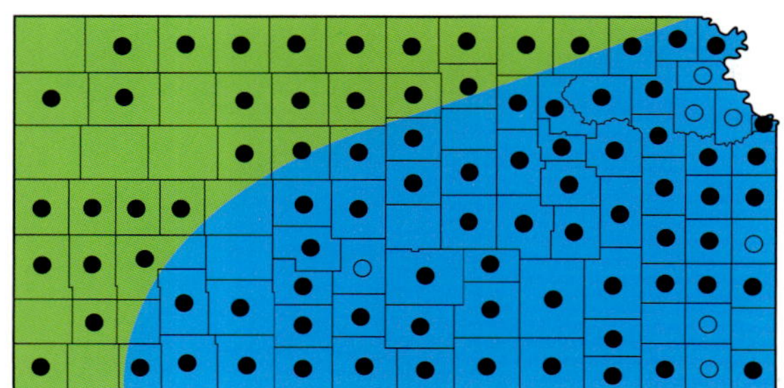

Common Merganser

Mergus merganser (COME)

Status: Common spring and fall migrant; fairly common winter resident (chiefly in the east) when open waters persist.

Habitat: Usually on reservoirs, sometimes in large rafts; individuals and small groups also occur on smaller ponds, impoundments, and rivers.

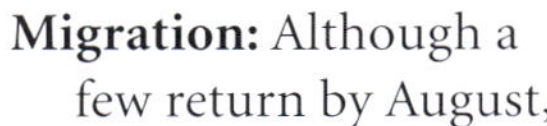

Migration: Although a few return by August, fall migration usually begins in mid-October with significant numbers by mid-November and highest numbers during midwinter, open water permitting. Flocks of 5,000 or more are common on reservoirs from mid-December through February. Higher counts include 12,000 on 20 February and 20,000+ on 5–6 January (Wilson Reservoir, Russell Co.); and 18,040 on 17 December, 15,000 on 24 January, and 25,400 on 19 December (Glen Elder Reservoir, Mitchell Co.). Most have departed by mid-March but with stragglers to 30 May (Morton Co.) and 12 June (Osage Co.). Occasional birds are present during midsummer: 26 June (Phillips Co.) and 24 July (Barton Co.).

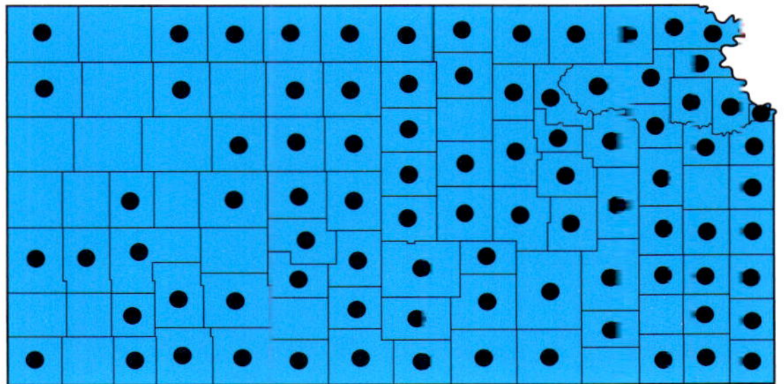

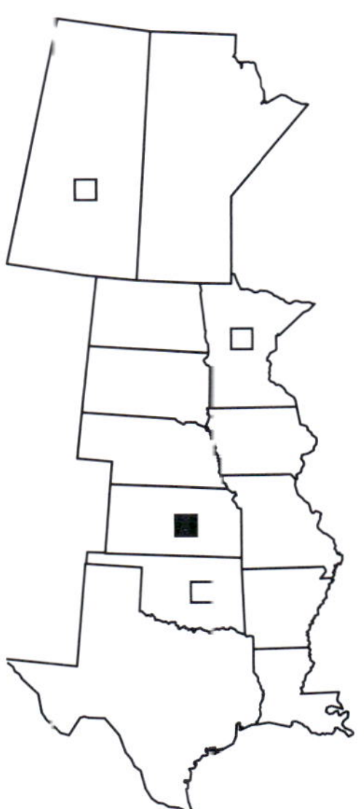

Comments: It is by far the most widespread and abundant of the three mergansers, often appearing in huge rafts on reservoirs during winter. Most typically arrive following major freezing of reservoirs to the north. Kansas reservoirs sometimes host the largest concentrations in the nation on CBCs.

Banding: Five banded; four encounters: all in Kansas from: OK (2), MN, SK. Oldest 1 year, 11 months.

References: Cink and Boyd, 2007; Thompson and Ely, 1989.

Red-breasted Merganser

Mergus serrator (RBME)

Status: Uncommon spring and fall migrant; most records are from central and eastern Kansas.

Habitat: Generally found on larger reservoirs.

Migration: The earliest fall records are 22 August (Seward Co.) and 29 October (Barber and Marion cos.), but most fall records are in November. In recent years, a modest number have been reported on CBCs during mild winters.

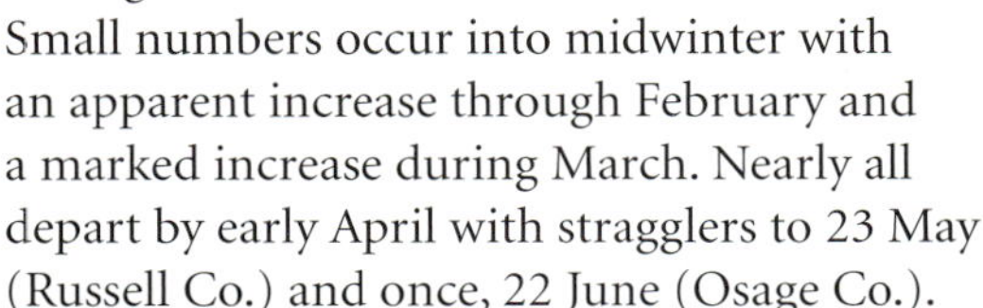

Small numbers occur into midwinter with an apparent increase through February and a marked increase during March. Nearly all depart by early April with stragglers to 23 May (Russell Co.) and once, 22 June (Osage Co.).

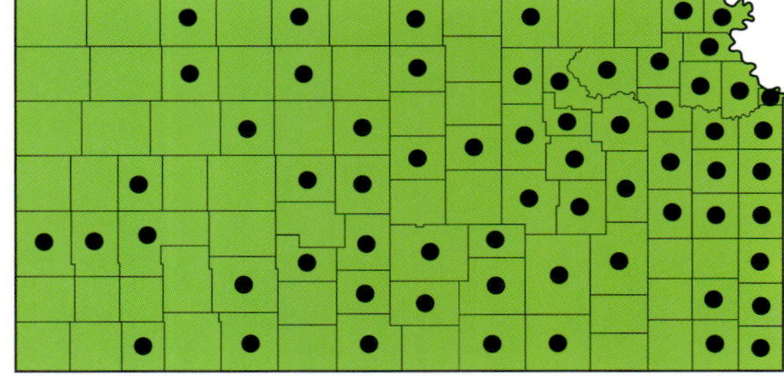

Comments: This is the least common of the three merganser species in Kansas. Some care needs to be exercised in separating females from the similar and much more common female Common Merganser.

References: Thompson and Ely, 1989; Titman, 1999.

Ruddy Duck

Oxyura jamaicensis (RUDU)

Status: Common migrant, statewide; uncommon and local breeder; uncommon in early winter.

Habitat: It frequents both larger reservoirs and smaller ponds during migration. It breeds in marshy areas with significant areas of emergent vegetation.

Migration: Spring arrival usually begins in early March with birds widespread by mid-March and with the peak from late March to mid-April. Although numbers are greatly reduced by early May, small groups typically remain into mid-June (12 June, about 30, Seward Co.; 9–16 June, 4 different years, Ellis Co.). Fall migration probably begins in late August and early September and peaks from late October to mid-November with small numbers remaining into early January. It is usually recorded in moderate numbers on CBCs if open water persists. There are, however, only two reports between 9 January and 18 February.

Breeding: Most confirmed breeding records are from Barton and Stafford counties. There is one report from Ellis County in 1888. Nest-building has been reported 15–18 June, eggs 30 May–30 July (half during 14–27 June), and broods 10 June (Meade Co.) and 15 June (Grant Co.) to 18 August (Sedgwick Co.).

Comments: It is usually found in pairs or in small flocks of 5–20 individuals during migration. It is the only representative in Kansas of the genus *Oxyura*, stiff-tailed ducks, which has representatives worldwide. The name comes from the "stiff" tail, which is often held in an erect position as the bird is swimming.

Banding: 49 banded; three encounters: two from Kansas to: VA, TX; one in Kansas from SK. Oldest 3 years, 8 months.

References: Brua, 2002; Busby and Zimmerman, 2001; Janzen, 2007; Thompson and Ely, 1989.

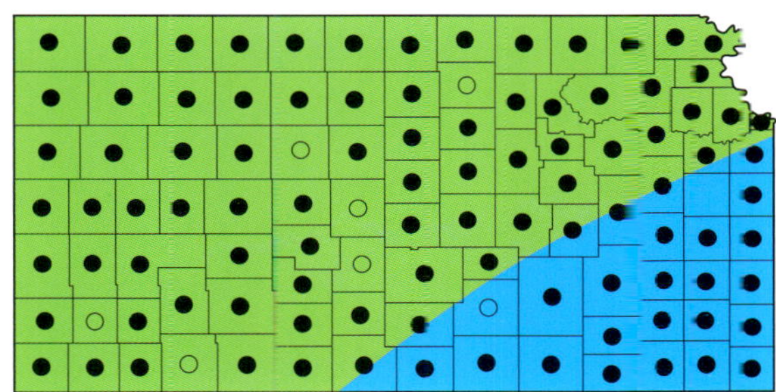

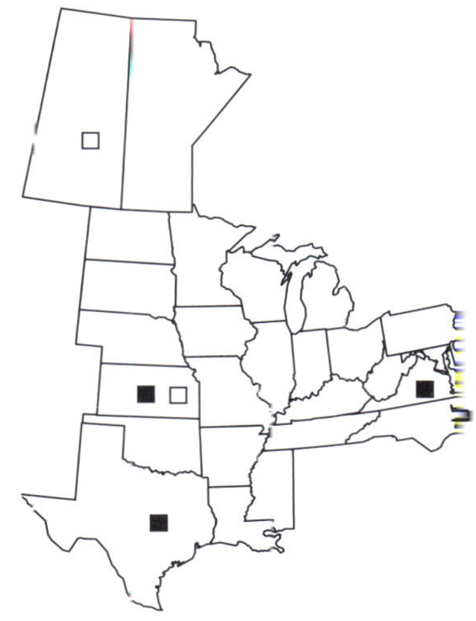

Scaled Quail

Callipepla squamata (SCQU)

Status: Uncommon, permanent resident in the southwest.

Habitat: Generally confined to sand-sage prairie south of the Arkansas River. It seems to have an affinity for abandoned farms and homesteads and is frequently found near farm machinery.

Migration: It is sedentary, and no migration is known to occur. Outside the breeding season, it gathers in coveys like other quail. R. and J. Graber, in 1950, reported coveys of 40 or more individuals in Morton County. Occasional individuals reported outside the normal range are probably escapees from captive flocks.

Breeding: Few data have been reported for actual nesting in Kansas. Specimens that had recently laid were collected on 27 June and 13 July, and a covey of half-grown chicks was seen on 7 July.

Comments: Popularly known as "cottontop," or "blue quail," it reaches its most northeastern distributional limit in southwestern Kansas. It has been known to hybridize with the Northern Bobwhite and one such individual was reported on the CNG CBC in 1978. It is regularly reported in low numbers on this CBC, and irregularly on the Liberal (Seward Co.) count. It is defined by KDWP as an "upland game" bird with a single, statewide "quail" season for the two species.

References: Busby and Zimmerman, 2001; Cable et al., 1996; Dabbert et al., 2009; Graber and Graber, 1950; Kuenning, 1998; Thompson and Ely, 1989; Versaw, 2004; Zimmerman, 1979.

© Mike Blair

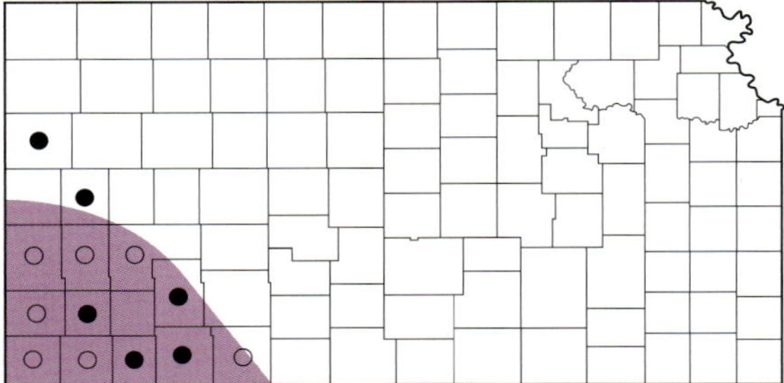

Northern Bobwhite

Colinus virginianus (NOBO)

Status: Common permanent resident.

Habitat: Prefers agricultural fields and grasslands with woody margins; hedgerows and windbreaks with low brushy cover provide essential protection and food, especially during winter months with heavy snow cover.

Breeding: KBBAT found it widespread over most of the state with lowest frequency in the Red Hills and High Plains where it is largely limited to riparian situations. Nest-building has been reported 1–10 June, eggs 3 May–18 August, chicks 15 June–21 August, and flying young 17 July–September. Unsuccessful females may attempt a second brood in late summer or even early fall. An unusually late clutch found on 27 September hatched on 4 October (Franklin Co.). The species is generally sedentary.

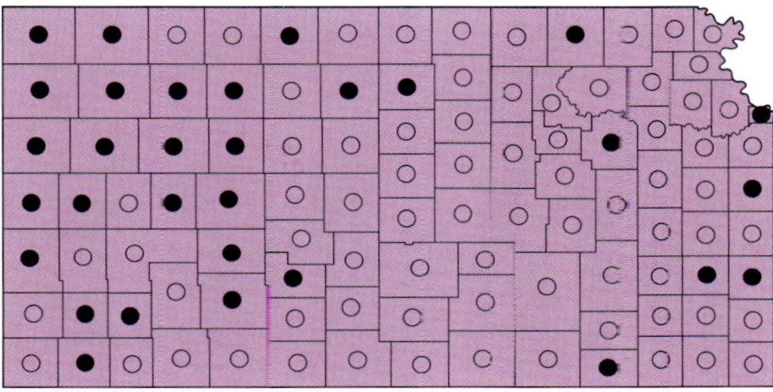

Comments: Fluctuations in populations from year to year are not well understood but are probably due to low survival rates during severe winters and habitat changes from grassland and shrubs to trees, and changing farm practices. It is the second most commonly hunted upland game bird species in the state, and Kansas annually ranks among the top three states where it is hunted.

References: Brennan, 1999; Busby and Zimmerman, 2001; Thompson and Ely, 1989.

Ring-necked Pheasant

Phasianus colchicus (RPHE)

Status: Introduced. Permanent resident statewide; abundant in the western half, uncommon in the eastern half; essentially absent from the southeast.

© Linda Williams

Habitat: Largely associated with agricultural lands, especially cultivated fields interspersed with hedgerows, brushlands, or woody borders.

Migration: A largely sedentary species, pheasants do gather in flocks in the fall and winter, and movements have been observed in response to weather and food availability.

Breeding: KBBAT found it widespread and abundant through the west, in smaller numbers in the Red Hills, Flint Hills, and the northeast, and largely absent from the southeast. Eggs have been reported 17 April–24 June, chicks 12 May–21 July, and flying young as early as 20 June but usually in July.

Comments: Pheasants have been introduced locally by private individuals since early pioneer days. Formal introductions by KDWP began in 1905 and 1906 when 3,000 birds were introduced into 84 counties. Pheasant populations soon increased and expanded in area, and a hunting season was instituted during 1917–1921, and then reopened in 1932. Populations have always fluctuated with short-term climatic change and changing agricultural practices. For example, western Kansas populations were severely impacted by drought and vegetation loss during the 1930s but rebounded in most areas. Declining numbers there are the result of changing agricultural practices. Its near absence from the southeast is still a matter of debate usually attributed to a combination of climate (high spring temperatures and humidity), land use, and soil minerals.

The male is a striking, almost gaudy, bird and, with its long, pointed tail, iridescent multicolored plumage, and naked red face, cannot be confused with any other species. Females are generally brown overall but have the distinctive long, pointed tail. Half-grown young running across roads are sometimes confused with the Greater Roadrunner by the inexperienced observer. It is the most popular upland game bird in the state.

References: Busby and Zimmerman, 2001; Giudice and Ratti, 2001; Thompson and Ely, 1989.

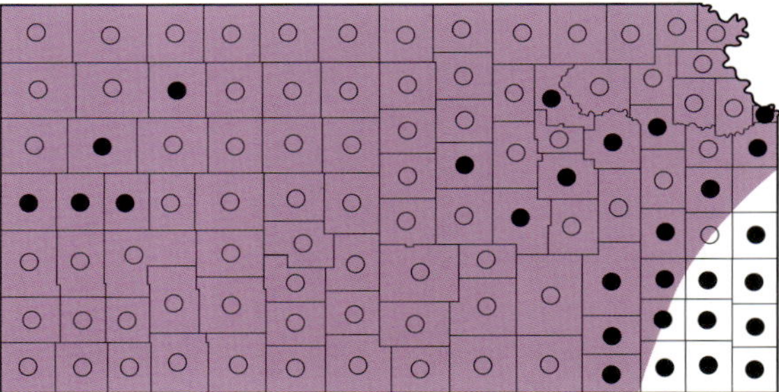

Ruffed Grouse

Bonasa umbellus (RUGR)

Status: Formerly a permanent resident in the eastern part of the state, extirpated by the late 19th or very early 20th century. The only known specimen, taken by A. J. C. Roese in "southeastern Kansas," probably Douglas County, between 1885 and 1910 is mounted and in the collection of KUMNH (KU 31944).

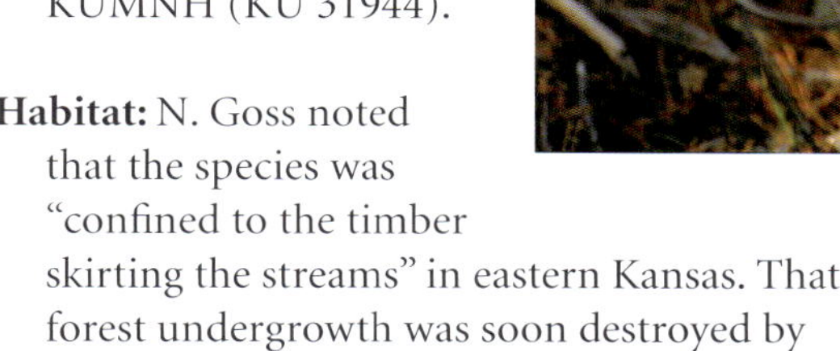

Habitat: N. Goss noted that the species was "confined to the timber skirting the streams" in eastern Kansas. That forest undergrowth was soon destroyed by cattle and various human activities.

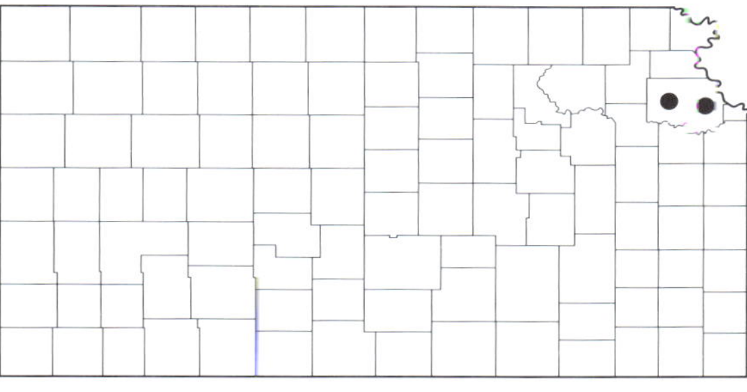

Comments: KDWP began reintroduction of this grouse in 1983. Birds were first released in Jefferson County in 1983 and 1984 with subsequent reports of a brood in 1984 (M. Schwilling) and occasional reports through 1991. Atchison, Bourbon, Doniphan, Douglas, Johnson, Leavenworth, Linn, and Miami counties became additional reintroduction sites during the 1980s with subsequent scattered reports into the 1990s from Atchison, Douglas, and possibly Leavenworth counties. An introduction at Fort Riley by military personnel in 1991 did not become established. Its current status in Kansas is uncertain, but it probably no longer occurs in the state.

References: Goss, 1886; Rusch et al., 2000; Thompson and Ely, 1989.

Gunnison Sage-Grouse

Centrocercus minimus (GUSG)

© The Denver Post

Status: [Hypothetical]. Extirpated. Inclusion of this species on the state list remains an open subject for debate. Its inclusion has been largely because of a published statement by N. Goss: "included as an occasional resident of western Kansas on the authority of Mr. Will. T. Cavanaugh, Assistant Secretary of State, who informs me that while hunting buffalo during 1871, 1872, 1873, and 1874, he occasionally met with and shot the birds in the sage brush near the southwest corner of the State." There are also a few unpublished anecdotal (and unverified) accounts. L. Smith recalls that as a young boy in the early 1930s he retrieved a sage-grouse shot by his brother-in-law while hunting prairie-chickens a few miles west of Wilburton (Morton Co.). This grouse probably occurred in limited numbers in Kansas. It was recorded in nearby Cimarron County, Oklahoma, as recently as July 1920. A specimen from Oklahoma was subsequently destroyed in a fire. J. Young and others stated: "The identity of the sage-grouse known to have occurred in extreme southwestern Kansas and adjacent northwestern Oklahoma is unknown but we postulate that they too were Gunnison Sage-Grouse because of their proximity to the current range of the species." At present, it is unlikely to occur in Kansas because of habitat changes and the disjunction of populations to the west.

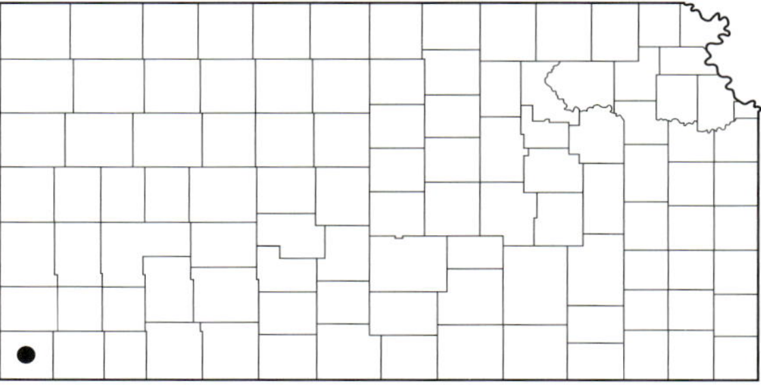

References: Cable et al., 1996; Thompson and Ely, 1989; Young et al., 2000.

Sharp-tailed Grouse

Tympanuchus phasianellus (STGR)

Status: Formerly a resident in the west; extirpated from the state by the end of the 19th or the early 20th century.

Habitat: It inhabited midgrass prairie along streams.

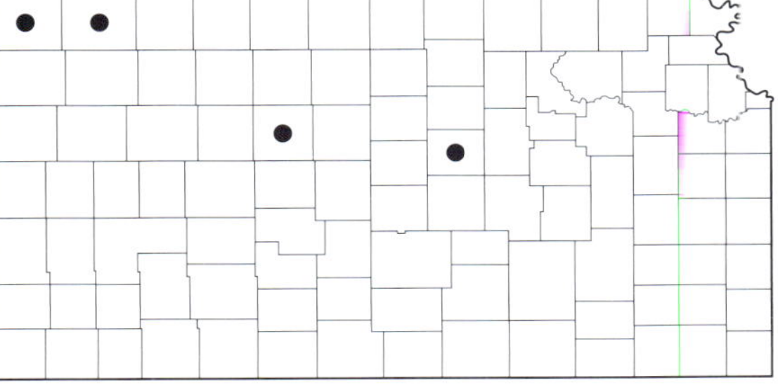

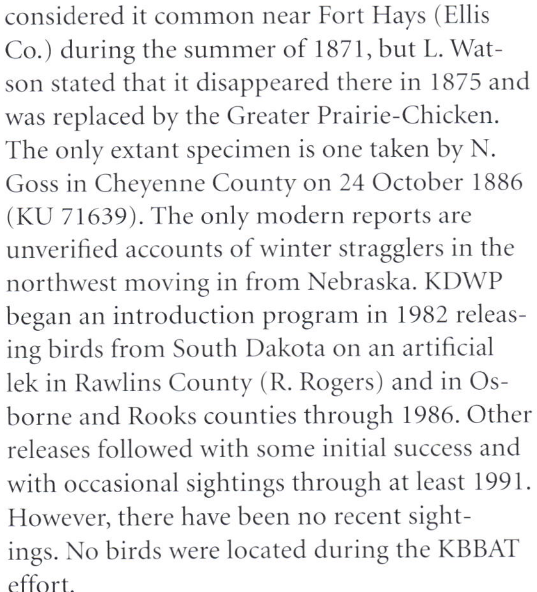

Comments: N. Goss and others considered it "common" in western Kansas and occasional eastward, but there are few firsthand accounts for that period. J. Allen considered it common near Fort Hays (Ellis Co.) during the summer of 1871, but L. Watson stated that it disappeared there in 1875 and was replaced by the Greater Prairie-Chicken. The only extant specimen is one taken by N. Goss in Cheyenne County on 24 October 1886 (KU 71639). The only modern reports are unverified accounts of winter stragglers in the northwest moving in from Nebraska. KDWP began an introduction program in 1982 releasing birds from South Dakota on an artificial lek in Rawlins County (R. Rogers) and in Osborne and Rooks counties through 1986. Other releases followed with some initial success and with occasional sightings through at least 1991. However, there have been no recent sightings. No birds were located during the KBBAT effort.

References: Allen, 1872; Busby and Zimmerman, 2001; Connelly et al., 1998; Cooke, 1888; Thompson and Ely, 1989.

Greater Prairie-Chicken

Tympanuchus cupido (GPCH)

Status: Common but declining permanent resident. Locally common in north-central region of the Smoky Hills and portions of the Flint Hills, becoming less common east of the Flint Hills into the Osage Cuestas and also into northwestern regions where it is known to hybridize with the Lesser Prairie-Chicken (Ellis Co.).

© Thane Rogers

Habitat: Mixed-grass and tallgrass prairie specialist requiring large expanses of native prairie and different kinds of grassland for successful breeding. In the northwest, CRP grasslands appear to provide habitat for expansion of its range. In the Flint Hills, annual burning and early intensive stocking land management practices have severely reduced nesting habitat. Cultivated fields have become an increasingly important component, because the waste grain, or uncut crop fields, provide an abundant food supply during severe winters.

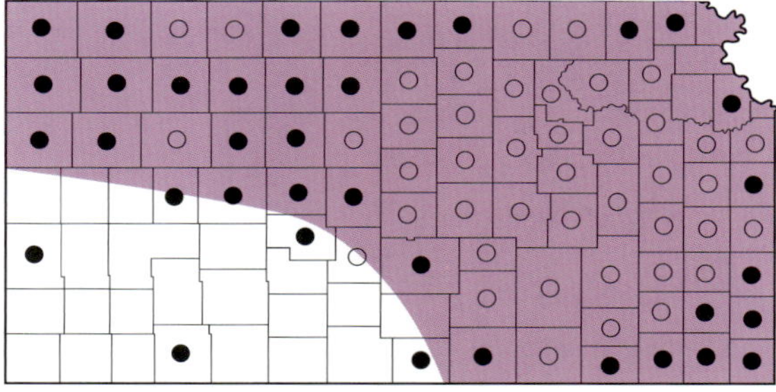

Breeding: Prairie-chickens gather at breeding areas called "booming grounds" or "leks." Leks are usually in elevated uplands with sparse vegetation. A few up to 100 males may gather on the booming grounds beginning in February through April, although limited activity occurs there throughout the year. Females attend the ritual dances, and, if courtship is successful, they will mate. Females normally do not return to the booming grounds after copulation unless their nest is destroyed. Females seek a nesting site in tall, dense cover that is composed of residual vegetation and new growth. Egg-laying occurs from 1 May to 10 June. Young are precocial but remain with the female from 6 to 8 weeks. Nesting and rearing habitats may or may not be the same, although they may occur in the same general grassland type.

Comments: It was abundant on the prairies of eastern Kansas during presettlement days. Near Fort Hays (Ellis Co.), J. Allen considered it rare in 1871 but said it was "advancing westward" every year and "apparently fast becoming common," having first been seen in the vicinity only 2 years earlier. The Kansas population was historically estimated between 400,000 and 880,000 but recent estimates are less than 200,000.

References: Allen, 1872; Applegate and Horak, 1999; Bent, 1932; Clubine, 2002; Cooke, 1888; Horak, 1985; Horak and Applegate, 1998; Janzen, 2007; Johnsgard, 1973; Johnston, 1965; Robb and Schroeder, 2005; Robbins et al., 2002; Robel, 1966; Robel et al., 1970; Seibel, 1978; Svedarsky et al., 2000; Svedarsky et al., 2003; Thompson and Ely, 1989.

Lesser Prairie-Chicken

Tympanuchus pallidicinctus (LPCH)

Status: Locally uncommon permanent resident in the west. Has expanded its range northward as a result of CRP grasslands, although the overall population continues to decline. The only specimen north of the Arkansas River until recently was taken in Logan County, 1 January 1921. This may indicate that the incursion to the north of the Arkansas River is a recent event. It has come into contact with Greater Prairie-Chickens in the northwest where it is known to hybridize.

© Judd Patterson

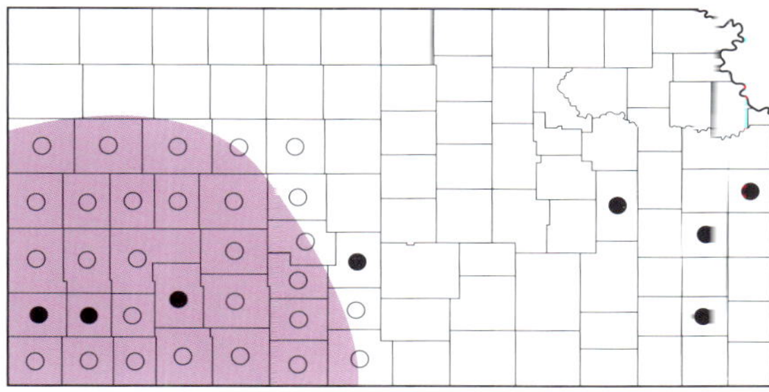

Habitat: A shortgrass and sand-sage prairie specialist in Kansas. CRP grasslands provide habitat for reestablishment in its former range and expansion north of the Arkansas River. Cultivated fields have become an increasingly important component, because the waste grain or uncut crop fields provide an abundant food supply during severe winters.

Breeding: It gathers at traditional breeding areas called "booming grounds" or "leks." After mating, females seek a nesting site in tall, dense vegetation. Eggs have been reported 17 May–1 June with most late May, and chicks 30 May–18 August. Females sit closely while incubating, and some nesting in agricultural fields are killed during mowing or harvesting. Young are precocial and remain with the female for up to 8 weeks. Like the Greater Prairie-Chicken, brood-rearing habitat is a mosaic of habitats that provide cover from potential predators, shade from midsummer heating, an abundance of insects, and seeds or cultivated grains.

Comments: N. Goss reported movements of large numbers eastward in the winter and took two specimens (Neosho Co., KU 71641-42, ID verified). Four additional specimens come from Anderson, Miami, and Lyon counties during January and February from 1881 to 1894 (MCZ 187193, 187194, 25382, 331738, ID verified). Eastward migration in winter has not been recorded in recent times. In 2008, the USFWS reviewed the status and raised its listing priority to a two, indicating that overall threats are of a high magnitude and imminent. Primary threats to the continued existence of the Lesser Prairie-Chicken include loss of habitat to continued agriculture development and loss of CRP grasslands due to reduction in farm bill funding to continue the CRP program.

References: Bent, 1932; Cable et al., 1996; Jarzen, 2002b; Johnsgard, 1973. Thompson and Ely, 1989; USFWS, 2008.

Wild Turkey

Meleagris gallopavo (WITU)

© David Seibel

Status: Common permanent resident east of a line from the Red Hills in the south and Smoky Hills in the north; uncommon to locally common westward.

Habitat: Prefers riparian habitats interspersed with open areas such as clearings, pastures, and farmlands that also offer cover; locally ranges into suburban and urban edges.

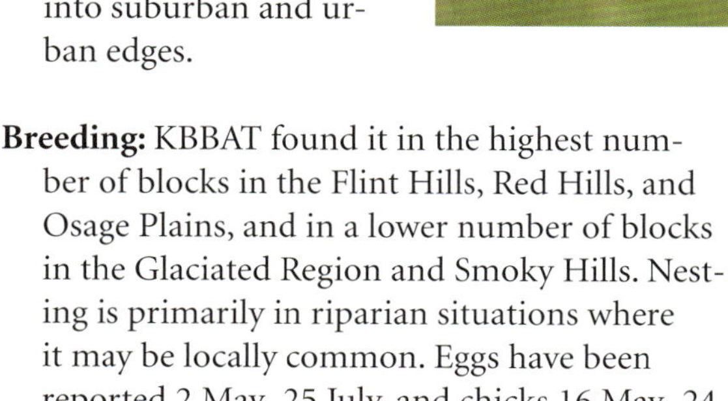

Breeding: KBBAT found it in the highest number of blocks in the Flint Hills, Red Hills, and Osage Plains, and in a lower number of blocks in the Glaciated Region and Smoky Hills. Nesting is primarily in riparian situations where it may be locally common. Eggs have been reported 2 May–25 July, and chicks 16 May–24 September.

Comments: In presettlement days it was abundant along the major river systems. Large numbers were killed by early settlers and travelers, and turkey hunts were occasionally reported in area newspapers. For example, the *Hutchinson News* of 10 April 1873 reported a 1-day hunt by soldiers of Fort Larned in which 200 turkeys were killed. R. I. Dodge presented the tally from a five-man, 20-day hunt southeast of Fort Dodge in October 1872 that listed 154 turkeys among the hundreds of birds and mammals killed. Although the northeastern population was exterminated by around 1900, by 1959 turkeys were reentering the state from Oklahoma, and in 1966–1967 KDWP stocked birds from Oklahoma and Texas at 14 sites in Kansas. These and subsequent introductions were successful, and a season was established in 1974. Numbers continue to increase over much of the state. By the 1980s Kansas was trapping birds for reintroductions in neighboring states. The Wild Turkey is endemic to North America. The domesticated turkey has become well known worldwide as a culinary delicacy.

References: Busby and Zimmerman, 2001; Eaton, 1992; Fleharty, 1995; Johnsgard, 1979; Thompson and Ely, 1989.

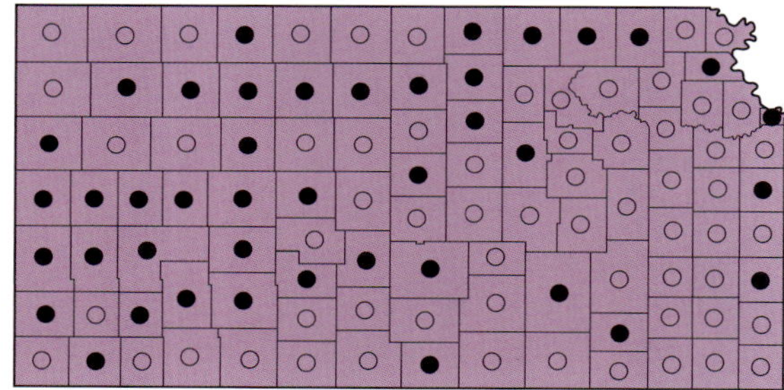

Red-throated Loon

Gavia stellata (RTLO)

© Mark Chappell

Status: Casual fall migrant in the eastern one-third of the state; casual in spring; reported twice on CBCs. The only specimen was taken on the Marais des Cygnes River near Ottawa, Franklin County, on 20 October 1925 (KU 36238).

Habitat: Typically on larger reservoirs; usually as singles.

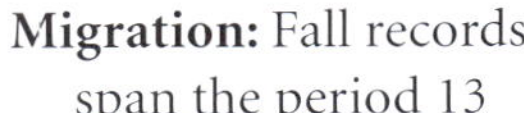

Migration: Fall records span the period 13 October–29 November; spring records, 10 April–18 May. There are three December records: 21 December 1994, Kirwin Reservoir, Phillips County (KBRC 95-07); 16 December 1997, Wilson Reservoir, Russell County (KBRC 97-53); and 21 December 1997, Cowley County.

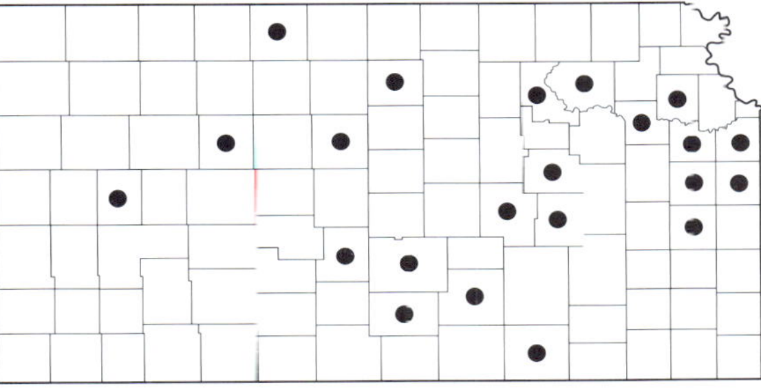

Comments: It is circumpolar in its breeding distribution. In North America normally winters along the Atlantic and Pacific coasts. Population levels in parts of North America seemed to have declined recently for unknown reasons. As with other loons, it was rare in Kansas prior to the building of reservoirs. A marked increase in deliberate birding of these reservoirs during the late 1900s has also been a factor in the increase in sightings. It can be easily confused with other loons and even the Western Grebe under poor conditions, so identifications should be made with care.

References: Barr et al., 2000; Thompson and Ely, 1989; Thompson and Young, 1996, 1999.

Pacific Loon

Gavia pacifica (PALO)

Status: Rare fall migrant; a few birds remain into midwinter (2 February, Kingman Co.). A specimen was taken during November 1970 at Wilson Reservoir (Russell Co.) by a hunter (MHP 2559). One entangled in a fish net at Milford Reservoir (Geary Co.) on 15 November was photographed and released by T. Cable.

Habitat: Usually larger and deeper bodies of water such as reservoirs. Loons need a fairly large surface area of water to become airborne, and these large areas provide loons with such a surface area.

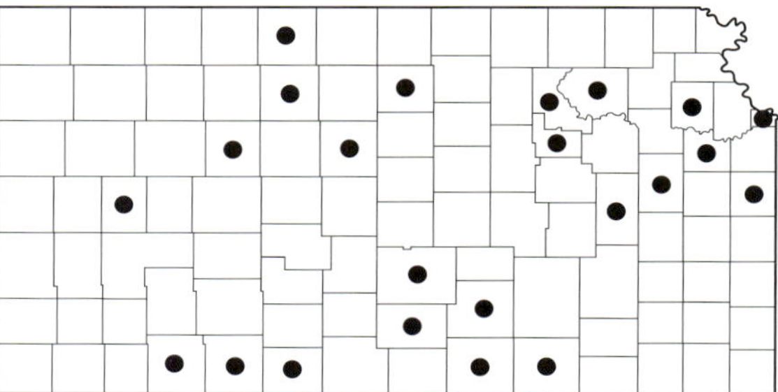

Migration: Extreme dates of observation are 15 August–2 February with most individuals encountered in October and November. The northbound spring migration is unknown and apparently bypasses Kansas. Extraordinarily, a single individual was recorded by multiple observers and photographed on Milford Reservoir (Geary Co.), 28 June–6 July 1998 (KBRC 98-59). A single individual recorded on the Wilson Reservoir CBC on 15 December 2002 had been present for 2 weeks.

Comments: This loon was only "resurrected" as a species distinct from the Arctic Loon (*G. arctica*) within the last decade. There are no records of the Arctic Loon from Kansas, and very few records from the interior of North America.

References: AOU, 1998; Cable, 1987; Russell, 2002; Thompson and Ely, 1989.

Common Loon

Gavia immer (COLO)

Status: Uncommon spring and fall migrant statewide; most common in central and eastern portions of the state; rare winter resident when open water remains in December or January; no unequivocal breeding record.

Habitat: Usually larger ponds and reservoirs statewide. Sometimes in moderately large numbers on the reservoirs in central and eastern Kansas, but single individuals often occur on smaller sewage ponds, especially in the west.

Migration: Most spring migration is from late March through mid-May with extremes of 23 March and 11 June. A few individuals (up to seven at Wolf Creek, Coffey Co., 1983) occasionally remain during summer. It is most numerous in fall (30 August into December) with a peak in mid-October through mid-November. The highest count reported is 54 on 31 October (Perry Reservoir, Jefferson Co.).

Breeding: An intriguing set of photos from the summer of 1988 taken at Milford Lake (Geary Co.) is highly suggestive of breeding. The photos are not of publishable quality and are inconclusive. However, they appear to show an adult Common Loon attending two juvenile birds. Although the juveniles are clearly dependent, they also appear to be capable of flight, possibly even sustained flight. Subsequent attempts to confirm the photos were unsuccessful.

Comments: A well-known inhabitant of the "north woods" and fresh lake waters of northern North America, it is generally restricted to the larger reservoirs in the state. Loons are rarely heard vocalizing in Kansas, and most individuals in the state are in basic, or basic transitioning to alternate, plumage. Although some very large numbers of loons can be found in midwinter just south of the state (e.g., Tenkiller Reservoir in Oklahoma; Table Rock Reservoir in Missouri), no such concentrations occur in Kansas. For example, just 7 were reported on the 2008 CBCs, and 12 were reported in 2007.

References: Evers et al., 2010; Thompson and Ely, 1989; Young and Thompson, 2008; Young et al., 2009.

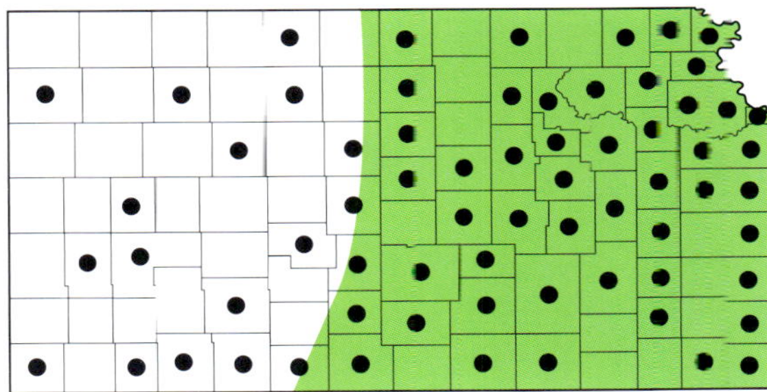

Yellow-billed Loon

Gavia adamsii (YBLO)

© Jim Burns

Status: Accidental; five records. The first report was on 10 December 1995 at Wilson Reservoir (Russell Co.), by M. Rader (KBRC 1996-05). The second record on 23 November 1996, at Cheney Reservoir (Kingman and Sedgwick cos.), was first reported by P. Janzen (KBRC 1996-37). The third record was on 10 November 2002, at Clark County State Lake (Clark Co.; KBRC 2002-32). It was found by C. Hobbs and S. Patti, remained at this locale for several weeks, and was seen by many individuals including B. and N. Beard (KBRC 2002-32A) and K. Groeneweg (KBRC 2002-32B). Video captures were submitted with these last two reports, and the species was removed from the hypothetical list by the KBRC. The most recent sighting, 24 April 2004 at Pottawatomie County State Lake #2, was reported by D. Rintoul and was seen by several others (KBRC 2003-16).

Habitat: Deep-water reservoirs are favored.

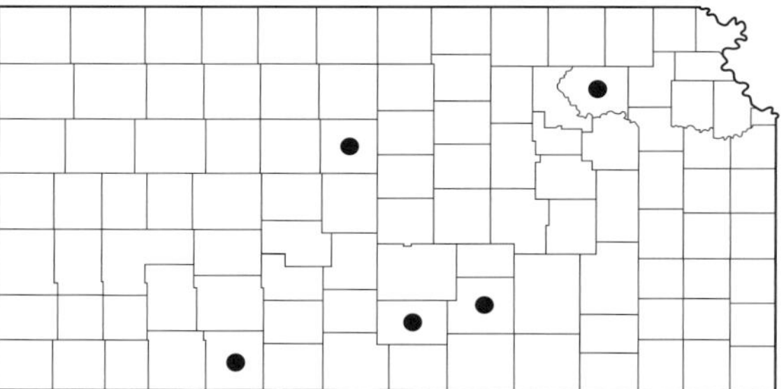

Comments: The largest of the world's loons, it is a relatively rare species in both the New and Old Worlds. Distinguishing Yellow-billed Loons from Common Loons can be difficult, especially at great distances. Since the 1980s it has been found migrating and wintering in the interior of North America, including Kansas and Oklahoma. At least one author has concluded that these interior records likely can be attributed to new identification information contained in modern field guides rather than to any change in loon populations.

References: North, 1994; Otte, 2004; Pittman, 1997; Rintoul, 2003.

Pied-billed Grebe

Podilymbus podiceps (PBGR)

© Judd Patterson

Status: Common migrant statewide; uncommon, somewhat localized breeder statewide; rare winter resident in mild winters, mainly in the south and east.

Habitat: Ponds, reservoirs, and marshes.

Migration: Earliest spring arrivals, usually at CBWA or the larger reservoirs, are dependent on open water and generally begin in February. Median dates of earliest arrival include 4 March (Rooks Co.), 9 March (Barton Co.), and 17 March (Russell Co.). Arrival is later in the west (median arrival, 29 March, Ellis Co.). Late spring dates of presumed transients are 24 April–25 May. Because it usually occurs in small groups, large estimates are rarely made; but peak migration is late March through mid-April. Summering individuals occur during most years and make it difficult to determine the start of fall migration, which probably begins in late August and peaks in late October and early November. High numbers include 1,000 on 25 October on Lake Quivira (Johnson Co.). Arrival and departure dates for spring and fall are clouded by the presence of breeding and wintering birds. It is now reported annually on CBCs, although the numbers vary from year to year. During the period 1949–1971, it was reported on 16 of 23 years that CBCs were conducted. During more recent CBCs, the high count was 705 birds (1998); the low was 20 individuals (2003). It remains unclear whether these birds are late fall migrants or true winter residents. Overwintering occurs if water remains open during the entire winter as in 1998–1999 (Sedgwick, Stafford, and Trego cos.), though data from mid-January and February are few and scattered.

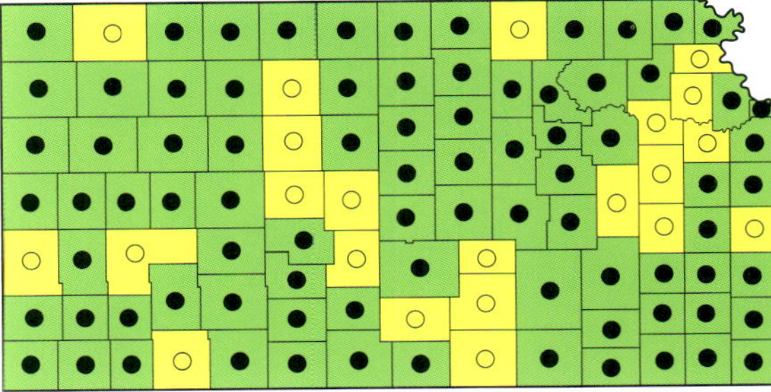

Breeding: It nests singly at the edges of ponds and sloughs where reeds, cattails, or similar emergent vegetation is available for nest construction. Although most nests have been found at CBWA (up to 20 in a single day by M. Schwilling) it may nest wherever local water and vegetation conditions are favorable. Statewide, eggs have been reported 1 May–14 July and flightless young 18 June–2 August (downy chicks) and 7 August. S. Seltman reported 200 juveniles at CBWA on 2 August 1993, and KBBAT reported them in blocks at SCW, Perry Reservoir (Jefferson Co.), the Benedictine Bottoms (Atchison Co.), QNWR, and the MDCWA.

Comments: This is the grebe most familiar to Kansans. In the adult, the brownish plumage and the high arched bill with a black vertical bar distinguish it from all other North American grebes.

Banding: 29 banded; no encounters.

References: Muller and Storer, 1999; Robins and Worthen, 1973; Thompson and Ely, 1989.

Horned Grebe

Podiceps auritus (HOGR)

© Judd Patterson

Status: Uncommon migrant; rare winter resident in relatively mild winters.

Habitat: Marshes, ponds, and reservoirs with sufficient surface area for the birds to become airborne.

Migration: Some early March reports are probably of overwintering individuals. Median first arrivals include 27 March (Russell Co.) and 29 March (Barton Co.). Usual arrival is early April with a peak during mid-April, with most departed by 1 May and stragglers to 19 May (Barber Co.). The highest reported count during spring is 53 on 1 April (Linn Co.). The only midsummer record is 24–25 July (QNWR, E. McHugh and M. Gearheart). Fall migration begins by 22 August with most sightings from mid-October through mid-November and with stragglers into early winter. It is occasionally reported on CBCs, and occasional birds overwinter if reservoirs remain ice-free (Cowley Co., 1980–1981). Late February sightings may be wintering birds or early transients. The largest fall counts are 86 on 16 November and 75 on 9 November (both Russell Co., different years).

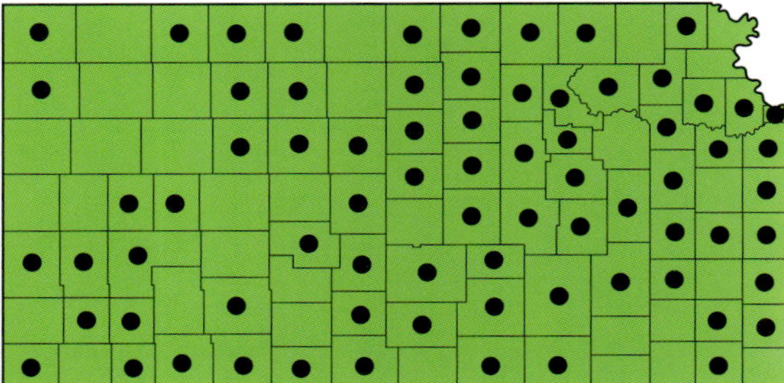

Comments: Care should be exercised in identification, especially when birds are in basic plumage; Eared Grebes are very similar, and the differences are subtle.

References: Stedman, 2000; Thompson and Ely, 1989.

Red-necked Grebe

Podiceps grisegena (RNGR)

Status: Casual. Most records are from eastern and central Kansas. There are currently 18 accepted records for the state and at least 7 others that were not submitted to the KBRC but are considered likely. There are two specimens: one taken on the Kansas River, east of Lawrence (Douglas Co.), on 29 October 1910 (KU 7697); and one found dead on the ice at Marion Reservoir (Marion Co.) on 20 January 2003. This individual had been discovered on 31 December 2002 by A. Powell and was subsequently seen by others. It is presently at ESU.

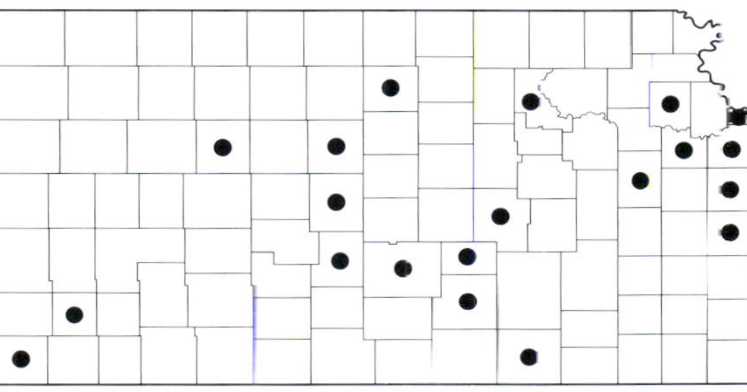

Habitat: Most likely to be found singly on reservoirs or large pools in wetland complexes.

Migration: Fall records span the period 26 August (unverified) through 20 January with most 20 October–23 November. The few spring records are 13 March (Jefferson Co.) through 19 May (Barton Co.), and most were in or near breeding plumage.

Comments: The Red-necked Grebe is nearly circumpolar in distribution and winters primarily on ocean coasts.

References: Stout and Nuechterlein, 1999; Thompson and Ely, 1989.

Eared Grebe

Podiceps nigricollis (EAGR)

© Linda Williams

Status: Common migrant statewide but most common in central and western Kansas; rare, irregular and inconsistent breeder; casual in midwinter.

Habitat: Marshlands and wetlands such as CBWA, SCW, and QNWR, as well as small ponds and larger reservoirs.

Migration: The earliest report is 16 March (Rooks Co.), but arrival is usually late March or early April with the peak from mid-April to early May. Median first arrival is 30 March (Barton Co.). Stragglers remain through 28 May (Ellis Co.) and 8 June (Morton Co.), and there are numerous records of summering birds, usually at the larger marshes, including 50 on 12 June (Seward Co.). High counts include "flocks of 2–40" on 22 April (Barton Co.), 36 on 5 May (Sheridan Co.), and "hundreds" on 22 April (Stafford Co.). Fall migration begins in mid-August and is widespread by late September. It peaks in October with stragglers into November and a few into early January if open water persists. High numbers include 17 at SCW on 9 September, and 15 at Cheney Reservoir on 14 November and 12+ on 10 November (Reno Co.).

Breeding: Breeding has been confirmed in Barton, Kearny, and Stafford counties, and summering birds have been reported in at least five other counties in central and western Kansas. Single nestings were reported from CBWA in 1968 (16 June, clutch seen, E. Martinez), 1972, and 1990. Nesting has been noted in June through August. The first reported colony was noted in June 1982, at QNWR. As many as 107 nests were counted, but all were destroyed by a severe thunderstorm on 13 July of that year. KBBAT reported a colony at Lake McKinney (Kearny Co.). About 25 birds were observed on 17 June, and three nests were under construction (A. Nonhof). On 14 July 1999, the number had increased to 92 nests and 130 attending adults. The total number of nests decreased thereafter with only eight active nests observed on 1 August. On 30 June 2007, CBWA flooded, and 75–100 nesting platforms were seen south of U.S. 156 by T. Mannell. Their success is unknown.

Comments: It is the most common grebe in North America and has a distinct preference for alkaline habitats.

Banding: Three banded; no encounters.

References: Busby and Zimmerman, 2001; Cullen et al., 1999; Thompson and Ely, 1989; Young, 1993.

Western Grebe

Aechmophorus occidentalis (WEGR)

Status: Uncommon transient; casual early winter resident; rare, very local and unpredictable breeder.

Habitat: Usually on larger reservoirs or extensive marshland areas; occurs regularly at CBWA and QNWR.

Migration: Early records include 2 February (Riley Co.) and 12 March (Russell and Linn cos.) with most sightings from late April and early May and stragglers to 15 June (Scott Co.). The high spring count is 14 on 9 May (Barton Co.). Fall reports are more numerous, usually of single birds but with highs of 20 on 30 September (Trego Co.) and 19 on 5 November (Barton Co.). Extreme dates for presumed transients are 31 August (Marion Co.) and 22 December (Rooks Co.). Peak migration is about 20 October–15 November. One remained in Wyandotte County until at least January, and others are believed to have wintered during 1975–1976 (Coffey and Kearny cos.) and in 1998–1999 and 1999–2000 (Linn Co.).

Breeding: A few birds summered at CBWA in 1969, 1970, and 1985, but nesting was not documented there until the summer of 1993 (pair with young) and again in 1994 when at least three pairs and a single were present and five young were produced. KBBAT confirmed breeding at CBWA in 1996, and nesting occurred in at least 1999 and 2000. Two adults carrying chicks and a third adult were present on Lake McKinney (Kearny Co.) on 12 September 1996, and five pairs were reported there 22 August 1997. It was suspected of nesting at QNWR in 1996. Eggs have not been seen, but courtship has been reported 20 April–19 May, small young 6 July–6 August, and nearly grown young on 6 August.

Comments: It requires large areas of water with emergent vegetation for successful nesting. During fall and winter Western Grebes and Clark's Grebes can be a challenge to distinguish, especially at longer distances.

References: Busby and Zimmerman, 2001; Storer and Nuechterlein, 1992b; Thompson and Ely, 1989.

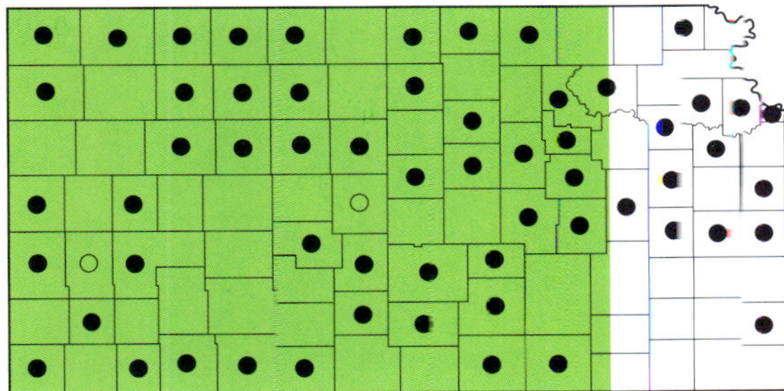

Clark's Grebe

Aechmophorus clarkii (CLGR)

Status: Rare migrant in central and western Kansas; casual elsewhere; during migration, often with Western Grebes, but never in large numbers.

Habitat: Usually on larger reservoirs and large wetlands.

Migration: Fall sightings are 30 August (Barton Co.) through 1 December (Russell Co.) with most during November. The high count is four from Phillips and Russell counties. An individual at Hillsdale Reservoir (Miami Co.) observed from 7 November through at least 29 January 1992 may have overwintered. Spring records are 18 April (Republic Co.) to 24 May (Rawlins Co.) with most in April.

Breeding: Nesting has not been documented, but at least one was displaying with a Western Grebe on 26 April 1997 (CBWA), and several summered there during 1998 (one mixed pair) and in 1999 (two mixed pairs). There are reports of a pair at Lake McKinney (Kearney Co.), 22 August 1997 (unverified) and 5 July 1999 (A. Nonhof).

Comments: It was considered a light morph of the Western Grebe until 1985. The 10th record for Kansas was not reported until 1997, when one or two individuals were documented by many observers between 26 April and 24 May at CBWA (Barton Co.; KBRC 97-23, 97-30), and the species was removed from the hypothetical list. Clark's Grebes and Western Grebes are unique among grebes in having the structural ability in their necks to allow them to use their heads and bills as a "spear" to seize prey. Clark's Grebe can be difficult to separate from the Western Grebe, especially at longer distances. Additionally, "intermediates," or hybrids, have been documented. Apparent mixed pairs have been observed in Kansas.

References: AOU, 1998; Storer and Nuechterlein, 1992a; Thompson and Ely, 1989.

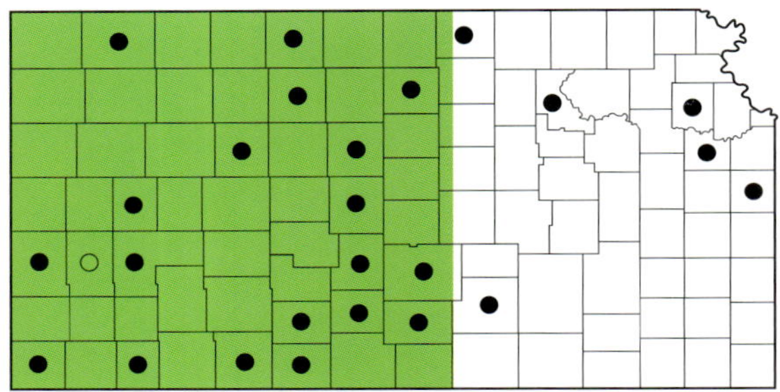

American Flamingo

Phoenicopterus ruber (AMFL)

Status: Accidental. There are two records involving three individuals, but, although well documented, the birds' origins cannot be proven. A mounted specimen now displayed at the QNWR headquarters in Pratt was taken in the fall of 1928 at the Little Salt Marsh (QNWR). From two to six birds were said to have been present, and the specimen is thought to be of wild origin because of its bright pink coloration. In the 1920s, it was not generally known that diet is involved in the development of the pink color, and most captive flamingos were white. On 11 November 1972, a single bird was photographed by an area farmer at Glen Elder Reservoir in Mitchell County and reported by J. Johnson.

Comments: As has been noted by several authors, the origin of these birds remains the subject of some controversy.

Reference: Thompson and Ely, 1989.

© Judd Patterson

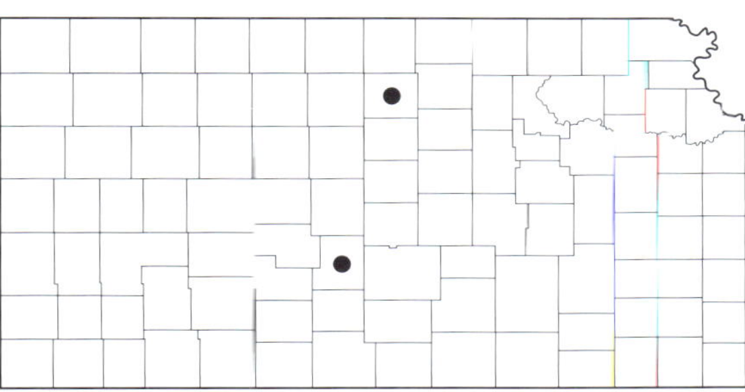

Wood Stork

Mycteria americana (WOST)

© Judd Patterson

Status: Casual visitant. The only specimen was collected on 4 October 1913 by W. Feaster (KU 11798) in Sherman County.

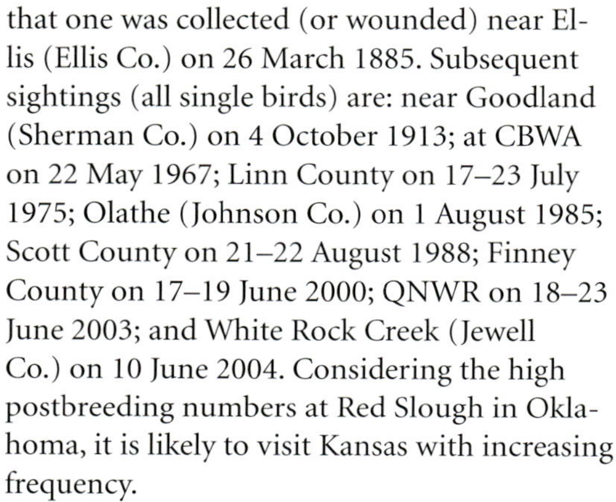

Comments: It visits the state at rare intervals including three during the 19th century. N. Goss noted that it had been seen near Chetopa (Labette Co.) during the spring of 1877, that one had been killed there about 1887, and that one was collected (or wounded) near Ellis (Ellis Co.) on 26 March 1885. Subsequent sightings (all single birds) are: near Goodland (Sherman Co.) on 4 October 1913; at CBWA on 22 May 1967; Linn County on 17–23 July 1975; Olathe (Johnson Co.) on 1 August 1985; Scott County on 21–22 August 1988; Finney County on 17–19 June 2000; QNWR on 18–23 June 2003; and White Rock Creek (Jewell Co.) on 10 June 2004. Considering the high postbreeding numbers at Red Slough in Oklahoma, it is likely to visit Kansas with increasing frequency.

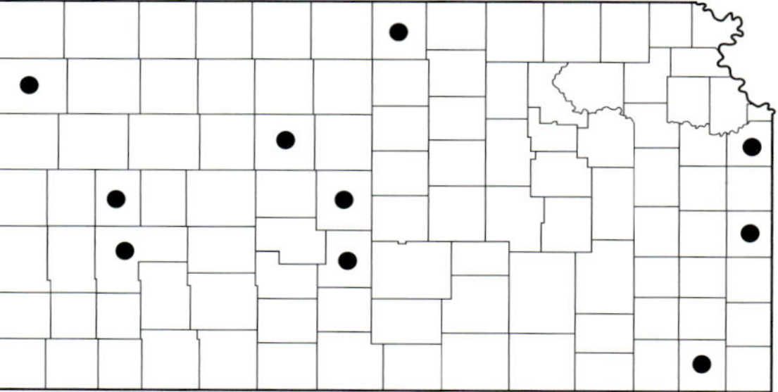

References: Coulter et al., 1999; Thompson and Ely, 1989.

Magnificent Frigatebird

Fregata magnificens (MAFR)

© Judd Patterson

Status: Accidental. There are currently only five accepted records. A specimen collected in Osborne County on 16 August 1880 and identified by N. Goss is now lost. The second, an adult female, observed in Meade County on 16 and 17 June 1982 by M. Goldsberry and T. Flowers (photos) was seen again on 23 July (presumably the same individual) by M. Schwilling. S. Seltman observed one in flight and at close range near Hill City (Osborne Co.) on 8 October 1988. Two recent sightings from Riley County have been accepted by the KBRC. One was seen by T. Cable over Manhattan on 12 October 1995 (KBRC 95-36); the second, an adult male, was fishing over the tubes at Tuttle Creek Reservoir on 9 September 2007 (KBRC 2007-29). In discussing the latter record, the committee noted that two additional species of frigatebirds have been confirmed from nearby states and cautioned observers about the need for more specific information on subsequent reports. A report on 28 July 1997 (Pottawatomie Co.) near Tuttle Creek was not submitted to the KBRC.

Habitat: Truly pelagic; most likely to be found at a large reservoir.

Comments: Any sighting of a frigatebird in Kansas is cause for considerable excitement. Specific identification can be problematic, however; frigatebirds wander widely over the planet, and the several species involved are confusingly similar in plumage. In addition to the Magnificent Frigatebird, there are interior continental records of both the Lesser Frigatebird (*F. ariel*) and the Great Frigatebird (*F. minor*). Care should be exercised in documenting all frigatebirds. Frigatebirds are generally blown inland by Gulf of Mexico hurricanes and should be looked for after storms hit the Texas coast.

References: Diamond and Schreiber, 2002; Frey and Monser, 2009; Parker et al., 1983; Thompson and Ely, 1989.

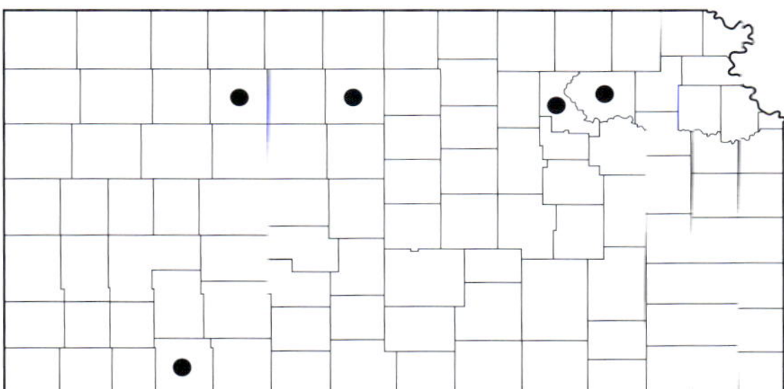

Neotropic Cormorant

Phalacrocorax brasilianus (NECO)

Status: Rare; has been reported with increasing regularity in the state with all sightings from Barton County eastward; a recent breeding record from Barton County; and several winter records.

© David Seibel

Habitat: Generally found in and around marshes, and the edges of ponds and reservoirs; often in association with Double-crested Cormorants.

Migration: Records span the period early March through late October, exceptionally into December. Most of the records have been from JRR and CBWA. They have become increasingly common around Arkansas City (Cowley Co.), possibly a result of nesting in nearby Oklahoma (Kaw Reservoir). Up to 11 were observed from 10 to 12 April 2007, several were observed through October 2008, and one was subsequently reported on the 2008 CBC. Two seen at the outlet tubes at JRR on 28 February 2003 had spent most of the winter there.

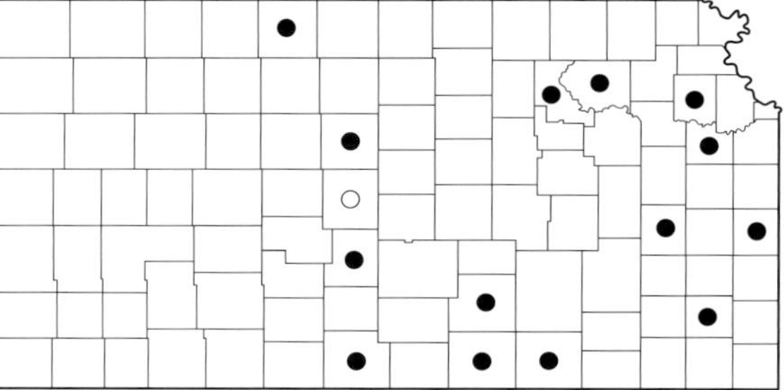

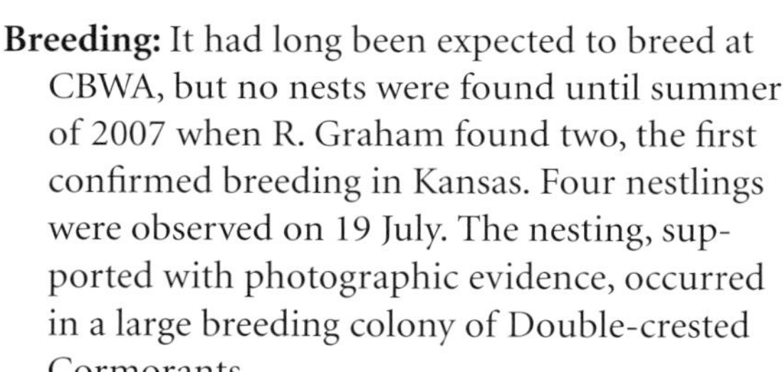

Breeding: It had long been expected to breed at CBWA, but no nests were found until summer of 2007 when R. Graham found two, the first confirmed breeding in Kansas. Four nestlings were observed on 19 July. The nesting, supported with photographic evidence, occurred in a large breeding colony of Double-crested Cormorants.

Comments: It was first reported in Kansas on 2 April 1872 (Douglas Co.) and then went unreported for nearly a century until 18 April 1971 (Barton Co.). It has become increasingly regular since the 1980s.

References: Telfair and Morrison, 2005; Thompson and Ely, 1989; Young et al., 2009.

Double-crested Cormorant

Phalacrocorax auritus (DCCO)

Status: Common spring and fall transient in eastern and central Kansas; uncommon migrant in the west; very local and irregular breeder; casual in early winter when waters remain open.

© Judd Patterson

Habitat: Reservoirs and deeper areas of marshlands and wetlands, especially where dead trees, snags, and roosting areas can be found.

Migration: Significant numbers arrive in late March and early April with the peak in late April and stragglers to mid-May. Earliest median arrivals include 31 March (Russell Co.) and 21 April (Phillips Co.). Nonbreeding birds occur at numerous localities during summer, usually at larger reservoirs. Fall migration begins in early September with significant numbers by late September and early October. The peak migration is in late October, and most have departed by 27 November (Ellis Co.). Numbers decrease through the CBC period and often later during mild winters. Modest numbers are reported on a few CBCs if open water remains.

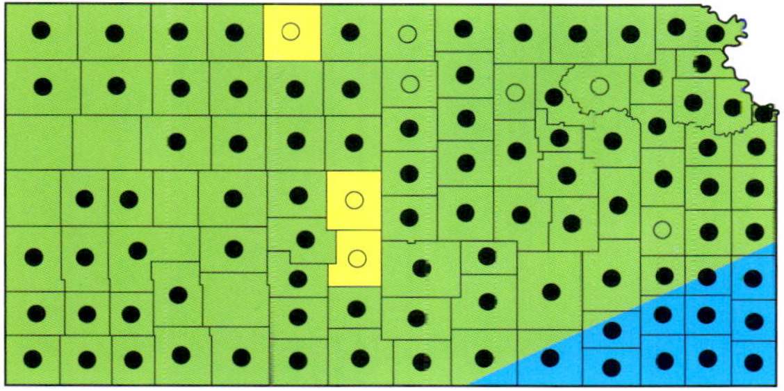

Breeding: The earliest documented breeding in Kansas was at CBWA (O. Tiemeier) in August 1951 followed by the establishment of a colony (with Great Blue Herons) at Kirwin NWR (Phillips Co.) in 1959. Breeding colonies, with year of first breeding and highest total of nests, are: CBWA (1951); Kirwin NWR (1959, 30 nests); Glen Elder Reservoir (Mitchell Co., 1974, 220 nests); Wolf Creek Reservoir (Coffey Co., 1982, 25 nests); Milford Reservoir (Clay Co., 1989, 4 nests); and QNWR (1993, 33 nests). The Kirwin colony fluctuated in numbers with the falling of dead nest trees and fluctuating water levels from 1959 through at least 1987. Populations increased in 1993, and success has continued due in part to a policy of preventing boat traffic near the colony. Statewide, eggs have been present 9 May–20 June, flightless young 8 May–23 July, and recently fledged young 27 July–11 August. The nest is a bulky platform of sticks and twigs.

Comments: After swimming and fishing, birds will often roost in dead trees, wings spread, in order to dry off. Unfortunately, it is often thought to present a problem to human fisheries and aquaculture, and depredation permits are issued by the USFWS to allow reduction of cormorant numbers.

See page 489 for banding information.

References: Busby and Zimmerman, 2001; Hatch and Weseloh, 1999; Parmelee and Stephens, 1963; Thompson and Ely, 1989.

Anhinga

Anhinga anhinga (ANHI)

Status: Vagrant; specimens have been taken in Rooks (1874), Meade (1888), and Barton (1933) counties. Most sightings are during the period 28 April–29 May, with three sightings 23 June–24 July and one in September.

© Judd Patterson

Habitat: Strictly associated with water; migrating birds may be seen flying or soaring at relatively high altitudes.

Comments: Most sightings are of single birds; however, N. Goss reported a flock of five from Meade County in 1888, and A. Richards (pers. comm.) reported six in Phillips County in 1953. At close range, the Anhinga, "snake bird" or "water turkey," is one of the more distinctive North American birds. However, under many conditions identification is more difficult, and some reports have been of cormorants. With its long, snakelike neck, sharp, straight bill, long, fanlike tail, and fully wettable feathering, it is a truly aquatic creature spending most of its life in water or adjacent to it. It seems to strongly favor freshwater, except during periods of extreme drought.

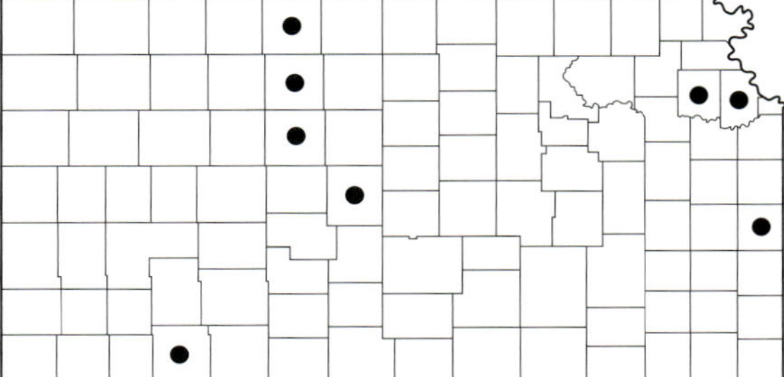

References: Frederick and Siegel-Causey, 2000; Goss, 1891; Thompson and Ely, 1989.

American White Pelican

Pelecanus erythrorhynchos (AWPE)

© David Seibel

Status: Abundant transient statewide though most commonly observed at large wetland complexes and reservoirs.

Habitat: May occur on any pond or reservoir with sufficient surface area for takeoffs or landings and occasionally on larger rivers like the Arkansas and Kansas rivers.

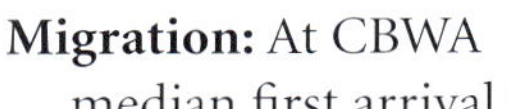

Migration: At CBWA median first arrival is 21 March (earliest 3 March); elsewhere early sightings include 6 February (Osage Co., three) that may be wintering birds. In late February 1996 a large incursion occurred in the east. Peak numbers are in mid-April and include 10,000–12,000 on 22 April (Barton Co.), 5,000 on 24 April (Stafford Co.), and 1,000+ on 22 April (Rush Co.). Most depart in late April. A mass exodus at CBWA on 18 April 1974 reduced the birds present from 12,000 to 300 in 1 day. Up to several hundred individuals (400–500 in 1979) typically summer at CBWA with smaller numbers at Wilson Reservoir (Russell Co.) and Melvern Reservoir (Osage Co.), and even occasionally on small ponds. At CBWA the fall migration is larger than the spring flight but is less well documented and is more variable. Typically arrival is late July or mid-August with most departure by early November. High numbers include 12,000–15,000 on 10 and 18 September (different years) and 10,000–12,000 on 20 October at CBWA. Elsewhere high numbers include 6,500 on 19 September and 6,000 on 30 September (both Stafford Co.) and 2,500 on 10 October (Linn Co.). Numbers decline rapidly after mid-October. Stragglers, and rarely flocks, remain into the CBC period and remain as long as open water is present. Although only 1 white pelican was recorded in 2008, 269 were recorded on the 2007 CBCs. Some of these lingering individuals may be sick or injured.

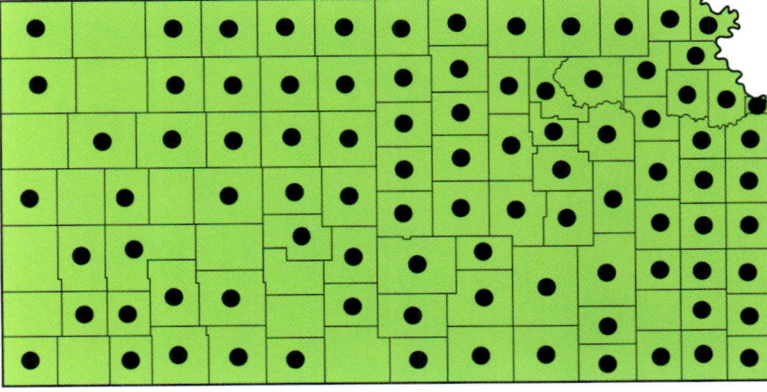

Breeding: There is no known evidence of breeding in Kansas, but birds with breeding knobs on their beaks have summered at CBWA (Barton Co., 1969) and QNWR (1985). Rumors of nesting at Jamestown Wildlife Area (Republic Co.) are without basis. However, recent nesting in the upper Midwest and the continued summering of large numbers in Kansas during some years suggest the possibility of breeding in the near future.

Comments: It is well known for coordinated feeding techniques that include cooperative foraging and synchronized bill-dipping.

See page 489 for banding information.

References: Knopf and Evans, 2004; Thompson and Ely, 1989; Young and Thompson, 2008; Young et al., 2009.

Brown Pelican

Pelecanus occidentalis (BRPE)

Status: Vagrant. There are at least 16 valid records (all single individuals), about half supported by physical evidence. The only specimen is one found dead near Parker (Linn Co.) on 6 June 1916 (KU 10468).

© David Seibel

Habitat: Usually found on marshes, ponds, or reservoirs; does not necessarily associate with the American White Pelican.

Comments: Although any pelican is unmistakable, all dark pelicans should be examined carefully as a number of sightings have proven to be "oiled" white pelicans. Unique among the world pelican species, the Brown Pelican is the only one to have a dark plumage and to engage in "plunge-diving" to catch fish in its distensible pouch. The Brown Pelican is regarded as one of the major success stories of the conservation efforts to combat pesticide use in this country in the 1970s. Although the species was listed as an Endangered Species by the USFWS in 1970, the efforts at regulating the use of such pesticides as DDT and Endrin, as well as efforts directly aimed at this species, were so successful that the Brown Pelican was completely removed from the Endangered Species list in 2009. The population has largely rebounded to its prepesticide levels, and future sightings are expected. What the future holds is unknown after the gigantic Gulf of Mexico oil spill of 2010.

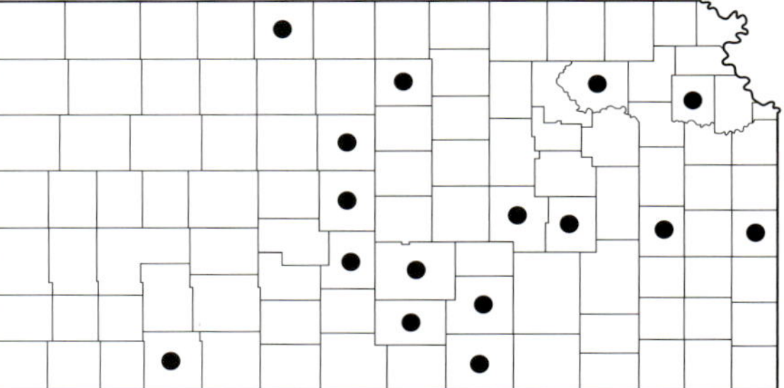

References: Shields, 2002; Thompson and Ely, 1989.

American Bittern

Botaurus lentiginosus (AMBI)

Status: Uncommon transient; fairly common summer resident at larger wetland areas; scattered breeding records elsewhere.

Habitat: Prefers marshland areas with expanses of cattails, reeds, sedges, or other tall emergent vegetation; occasional in damp grasslands that have been unmodified by agricultural practices.

Migration: Median earliest arrival at CBWA is 26 March but elsewhere is more commonly in mid-April. Most migration is late April and early May and is over by 15 May. Early fall arrival is usually late August, with a peak during October, smaller numbers through mid-November, and stragglers to 21 December (Barton Co.).

Breeding: Most nesting has been at CBWA (10 nests in 1963, M. Schwilling) but occurs at scattered localities statewide (Graham Co., 1929). KBBAT reported confirmed breeding at CBWA and "probable" nesting at the Baker Wetlands (Douglas Co.), Benedictine Bottoms (Atchison Co.), and QNWR. Courtship has been reported 29 April, eggs 24 May–27 June, and nestlings 9–17 June. The nest itself is a platform structure usually constructed over water in dense emergent vegetation such as cattails, sedges, or bulrushes, but occasionally in damp fields with tall grasses.

Comments: A medium-sized, stocky heron, it is a solitary, reclusive denizen of cattail marshes. Its cryptic plumage and its ability to blend with vegetation by "freezing" in place when confronted with a possible threat suggest that the species may often be overlooked. During migration, individuals have even been observed in cultivated fields. Its distinctive call, "pump-er-lunk" or "dunk-er-doo," is heard most often during the breeding season; many more birds are heard than seen during the breeding season.

Banding: One banded; one encounter. One banded in Saskatchewan on 1 July 1923 was shot in north-central Kansas in mid-September 1923 probably enroute to its wintering grounds.

References: Busby and Zimmerman, 2001; Lowther et al., 2009; Thompson and Ely, 1989.

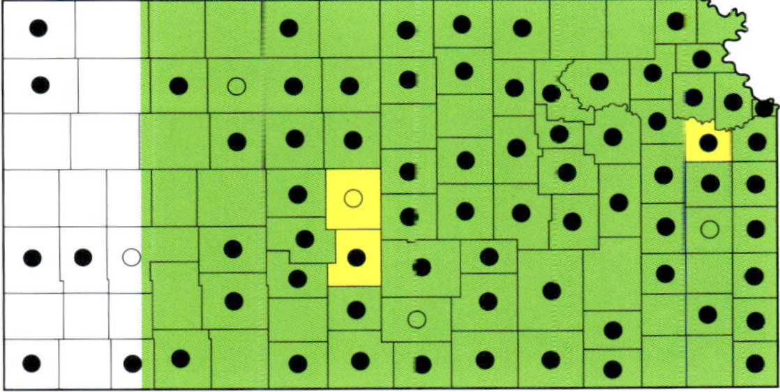

Tricolored Heron

Egretta tricolor (TRHE)

© Judd Patterson

Status: Rare summer visitant; casual breeder.

Habitat: Usually in marshes; singly or in loose association with other herons.

Migration: Early spring dates are 16 April–27 May (Barton Co.) and 23 April–21 May (Stafford Co.). There are a few early June records, but most are midsummer to early August. Late dates are 4–27 September with one on 2 October (Barton Co.).

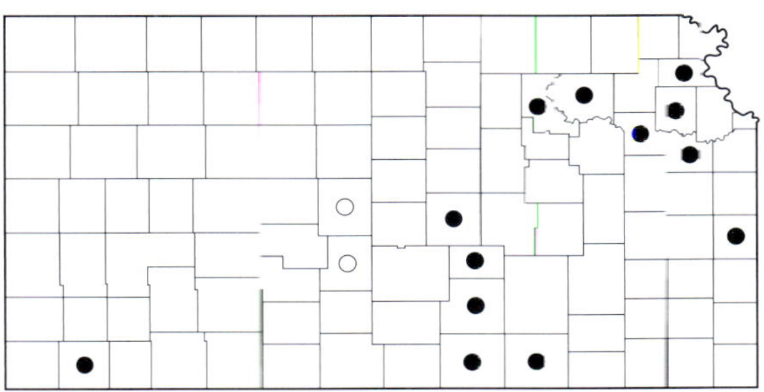

Breeding: Breeding was attempted at CBWA in 1974 but was unsuccessful. It bred successfully there in 1976 and again in 1985. At least two birds were present during summer 1996 at QNWR, but nesting was not confirmed. At least one has been reported sporadically at CBWA and/or QNWR during at least 15 summers since 1965. Eggs were reported 22 June (M. Schwilling), young 23 June, and fledged young 4 July (E. Martinez).

Comments: Nearly all records are from CBWA and QNWR. Most have been of single birds; highest number was 6 on 29 July 1971 (Barton Co.). Three specimens have been taken: about 1923 (Cowley Co., since lost); 9 August 1934 (McPherson Co., at Hesston College); and 23 April 1973 (Barton Co., current location uncertain).

Banding: Three banded; no encounters.

References: Seibel, 1978; Thompson and Ely, 1989.

Reddish Egret

Egretta rufescens (REEG)

Status: Accidental. There are two records. A single bird was found at CBWA on 22 September 1999 by R. Kostecke (KBRC 1999-40). A subadult found at QNWR on 21 June 2003 by G. Friesen (KBRC 2003-35) remained through at least 4 July (KBRC 2003-35A, 35B). It was observed by many birders and documented by numerous photos.

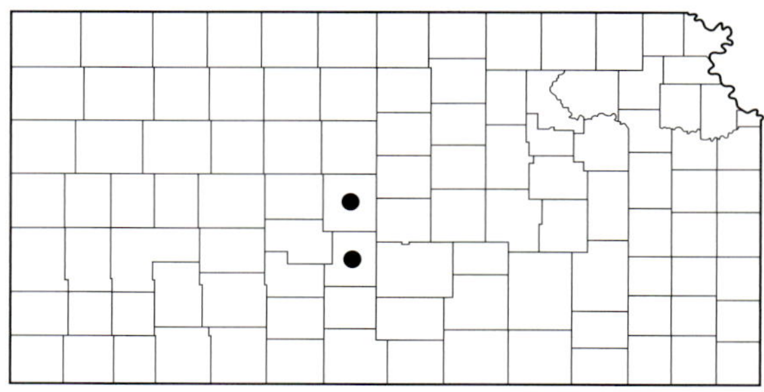

Comments: Two color morphs of this coastal egret exist, dark and white; both Kansas birds were dark-morphed individuals. Reddish Egrets are distinctive for their manner of feeding. Birds run wildly, twist, jump, and wing flap as they chase prey though shallow waters.

References: Lowther and Paul, 2002; Otte, 2004; Rintoul, 2000.

Cattle Egret

Bubulcus ibis (CAEG)

Status: Uncommon transient and summer resident.

Habitat: Marshes, ponds, reservoirs, and pastures; frequently accompany cattle in pastures capturing insects disturbed by the herds.

Migration: Extremely early arrivals are 17 February (Cloud Co.) and 6 March (Anderson Co.), but arrival is usually early to mid-April (2 April, Coffey Co.) in the east and later westward (26 April, Ellis and Meade cos.). Arrival at heronries may be as early as 8 April (Sedgwick Co., 10 birds) but later elsewhere; median first arrival at CBWA is 21 April. Peak numbers of transients are early May to late May (Osage Co.). Birds congregate in favored feeding areas by mid-July with peak numbers in September and decreasing numbers through mid-October. Small flocks and individuals remain to mid-November (13 November, Ottawa Co.; 24 November, Barton Co., three). A flock of five was near Sterling/Alden (Rice Co.) on 10–22 November, and one remained until near freezing temperatures on 2 December. Unusual were 54 at CBWA on 31 October 1973 and 1 in a snowstorm in Pawnee County on 30 October 1979.

Breeding: Up to nine birds were summering at CBWA by 1969, and the first breeding was confirmed there in 1973. By 1982 the colony had grown to about 300, and another colony was developing near Wichita (Sedgwick Co.). Breeding was reported from Reno County in 1983, followed by a colony at QNWR that had grown to 100+ nests in 1999 and involved at least 500 pairs by 1993. More than 150 pairs nested in Lakeview Playa (Meade Co.) in 1997. Within 30 years the breeding population in Kansas had topped 1,000 pairs and is still growing. Nest-building has been reported 16 July (Meade Co.), eggs 5 June–27 July, and young 16 June–7 August.

Comments: Native to Africa, it became established in South America, arriving from Africa in the late 19th century, then expanded its range northward, reaching North America in the 1950s. It was first reported in Kansas during the fall of 1961 (Douglas Co., unverified) and was documented on 26 April 1964 (Pottawatomie Co.).

© Judd Patterson

See page 490 for banding information.

References: Busby and Zimmerman, 2001; Flowers, 1998; Gress, 1984; Telfair, 2006; Thompson and Ely, 1989.

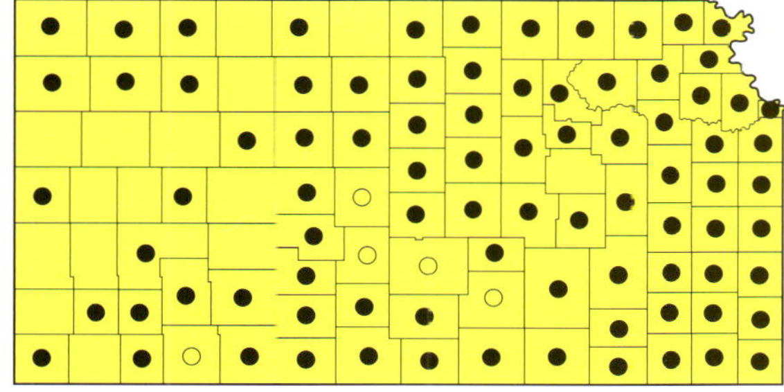

Green Heron

Butorides virescens (GRHE)

Status: Common summer resident in the east, transient and uncommon resident in the west.

Habitat: Usually found singly at the edges of ponds, reservoirs, and streams.

Migration: Peak migration is late April to mid-May with very early dates of 28 and 30 March (Shawnee Co.). Median first arrivals are 25 April (Russell Co.) and 19 April (statewide). Although not a flocking species, individuals do congregate loosely at feeding sites in mid- to late summer. High counts include 50 on 15 August (Jefferson Co.) and 20–30 on 8–12 July (Neosho Co.). Numbers increase by mid-August with most migration during September. A "heavy flight" was reported on 16 September (Shawnee Co.). The median late departure date is 13 September (Russell Co.). Stragglers remain into mid-October (18 October, Harvey Co.; 27 October, Linn Co.) and rarely into midwinter (18 December, Shawnee Co.; 19 December, Russell Co., five birds).

Breeding: KBBAT confirmed breeding in roughly the eastern two-thirds of the state with lowest frequency in the High Plains and, surprisingly, the Arkansas Lowlands. Nesting frequency in the west is obviously low because of the paucity of free-flowing streams. Eggs have been reported from 22 May to 14 July (median 4–5 June), young 30 May–21 July, and recently fledged young 13–27 July. A late hatching date is 21 July. A loose colony of up to 10 nests was observed in Wichita (Sedgwick Co.) for several years (about 1987–1991). It is often double-brooded.

Comments: Often found by disturbing and flushing a single bird, the Green Heron is known colloquially as the "shy-poke" or "shite-poke." It often gives a distinctive "kee-ow" call as it flushes.

Banding: 38 banded; one encounter: in-state.

References: Busby and Zimmerman, 2001; Davis and Kushlan, 1994; Thompson and Ely, 1989.

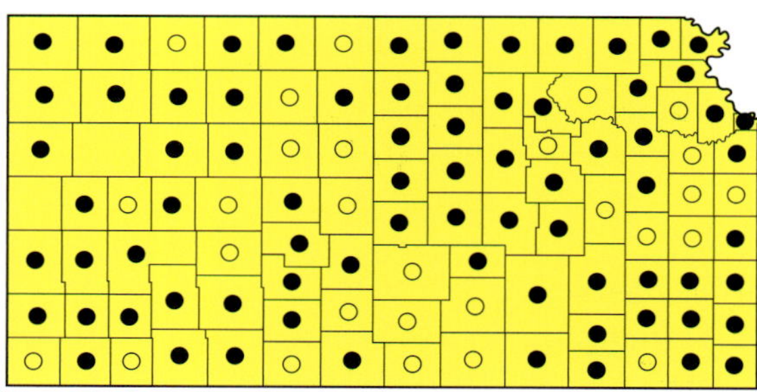

Black-crowned Night-Heron

Nycticorax nycticorax (BCNH)

© Judd Patterson

Status: Common transient statewide; local breeder in central and south-western Kansas; casual early winter resident statewide when waters remain open.

Habitat: Primarily marshes; also edges of ponds, reservoirs, and in riparian growth.

Migration: Very early dates include 24 March (Leavenworth Co.) with usual arrival about mid- to late April. Median first arrival is 7 April at CBWA. Most migration is probably late April to mid-May with most transients gone by late May to 6 June (Mitchell Co.). Scattered singles and small groups are seen statewide most summers. It is common in Meade County by late August, and peak numbers at CBWA are usually in mid-September. Most fall migration appears to be in September and early October. Numbers decrease rapidly during October with stragglers to 11 November (Douglas and Shawnee cos.) and rarely into December. During 1981–1982 an immature was seen at CBWA through December to at least 7 January and was found dead on 23 January.

Breeding: KBBAT documented breeding in two discrete areas: the marshes of central and south-central Kansas, and the agricultural areas of the southwest where most nest in planted shelterbelts. In the latter, ephemeral playa lakes, agricultural irrigation ponds, and small municipal sewage ponds provide the habitat necessary for breeding. The southwest in historic times has been the site of numerous heronries of Black-crowns. The van Winkle Heronry in Finney County held over 1,000 birds in 1952, many times larger than the current one at the Garden City Zoo. Other heronries are (or have been) at Ulysses (Grant Co., 85 nests, 1982), Sublette (Haskell Co., 100 nests, 1982), Lake McKinney (Kearny Co.), playas in Meade County, Elkhart (Morton Co.), and Seward County. In the central part, the largest heronries have been at CBWA (500 nests, 1965 and 1974). Nest-building has been reported 6 May–22 June, eggs 30 May–1 September, and young 30 May–10 August. The species is usually single-brooded, but pairs will renest if the first nest fails or is destroyed.

Comments: For several years birders have observed a nesting colony of 25–35 active nests adjacent to the sewage ponds in Elkhart. The adults are apparently attracted to larval barred salamanders (*Ambystoma mavortium*), which thrive in at least some of the sewage lagoons at this site.

See page 491 for banding information.

References: Busby and Zimmerman, 2001; Cable et al., 1996; Davis, 1993; Taggart et al., 2010; Thompson and Ely, 1989.

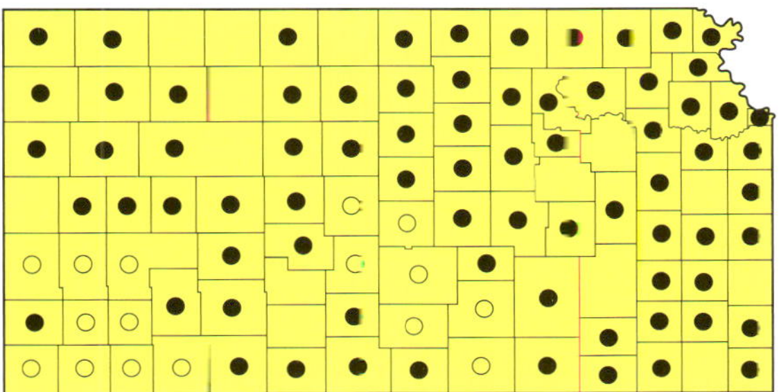

Yellow-crowned Night-Heron

Nyctanassa violacea (YCNH)

Status: Uncommon transient statewide; local summer resident.

Habitat: Usually on wetlands and their borders and edges.

Migration: Spring arrival is 21 March (Cowley Co., previous nest site) through 23 April (Finney Co.) with late spring dates of 22 May (Morton Co.) and 24 May (Ellis Co.). Scattered birds occur throughout most of the state during summer. Most fall migration is probably during September with a few remaining into late October and even November (16 November, Stafford Co.) and once to 18 December (Sedgwick Co.).

Breeding: Unlike the Black-crowned Night-Heron, it nests singly or in small loose colonies, often in upland areas including along residential streets. The largest colony reported was about 50 birds at CBWA in 1969, but only a few nests were found. Several pairs nest each year in city parks or along suburban streets in Lawrence (Douglas Co.); Wichita, Mulvane, and Derby (all Sedgwick Co.); Winfield (Cowley Co.); Topeka (Shawnee Co., since 1979); and probably, unobserved, in other urban areas as well. K. Groeneweg found 11 active nests and 18 adults within a one-half–mile radius in southeastern Wichita on 17 April. Courtship has been observed 17 April, nest-building 25 April–8 July, eggs 16 May–24 June, and young 7 June–22 July. Nest locations range from cattails to large trees and shrubs. Renesting may occur when a first nest is lost early during the breeding cycle.

Comments: A. Sprunt, Jr., describes the Yellow-crowned Night-Heron elegantly: "In full nuptial display, the Yellow-crowned Night-Heron is one of the most exquisite of all North American wading birds."

Banding: 17 banded; one encounter. One banded in Kansas on 1 September 1969 was encountered in southeastern Texas on 19 April 1970, probably on or returning from its wintering grounds.

References: Busby and Zimmerman, 2001; Janzen, 2007; Thompson and Ely, 1989; Watts, 1995.

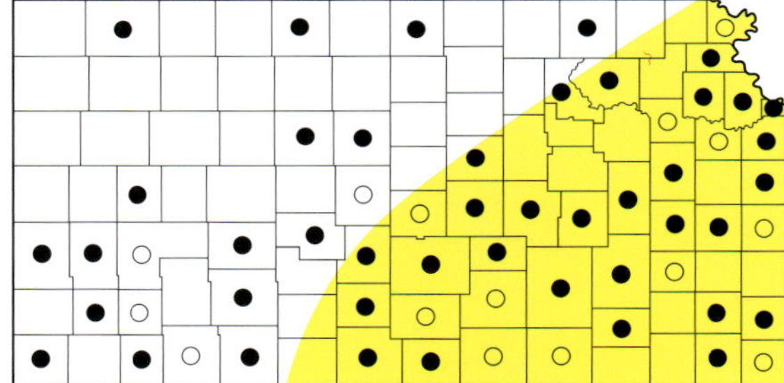

White Ibis

Eudocimus albus (WHIB)

Status: Casual visitant. There are about 14 records during the period 2 May–28 September. The earliest report was 16–17 August 1969 at Lakeview Marsh (Douglas Co.). Most subsequent sightings have been at CBWA or QNWR. There are no specimens, but several sightings are well documented by photographs. The earliest arrival and longest known residence was the immature first seen 2–14 May at QNWR and then at CBWA 19 May–29 July 1971. It was seen repeatedly at both sites and is presumed to have been the same individual. Another May sighting at QNWR was of two present 6–19 May 1998. Most fall sightings have been during the period 9 July–28 September.

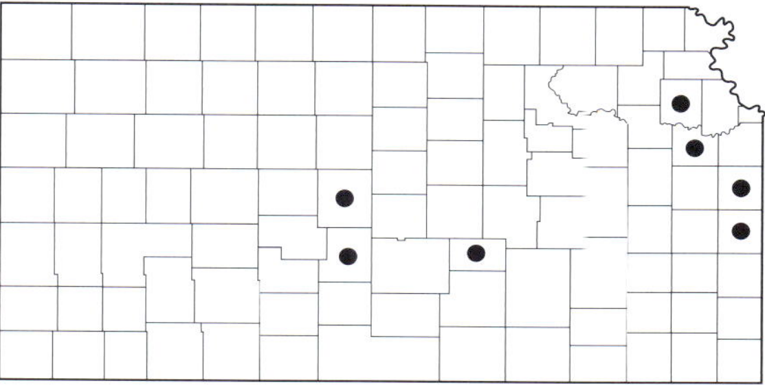

Comments: Both adult and immature birds have been recorded in the state, but most records are of juveniles. Adult White Ibises are strikingly handsome waders. Adults, with their white plumage, black wing tips, and red, decurved bills and red legs, are unmistakable. Juveniles, with their orange-red bills and white bellies, are quite distinctive, as well.

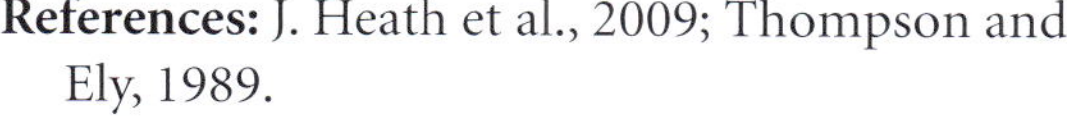

References: J. Heath et al., 2009; Thompson and Ely, 1989.

Glossy Ibis

Plegadis falcinellus (GLIB)

© Judd Patterson

Status: Rare visitant; probably overlooked and underreported. There are 20 records currently accepted by KBRC; additional records were not submitted to KBRC. The first record was an adult found at the West Lassiter Marsh, Perry Reservoir (Jefferson Co.), by J. Brier and N. Liebert on 3–4 May 1992, and subsequently seen and photographed by many others (KBRC 92-32) including L. Moore (AB 46(3):449). An individual with a broken wing found in Morton County 15 August 1991 later died and was preserved (KU 85718). It was sent to Louisiana State University for confirmation where it was concluded that "all signs point to Glossy Ibis," but no positive identification was made.

Habitat: Usually in marshy areas with other ibises and herons.

Migration: Since 1995 numerous individuals have been reported, most from either CBWA or QNWR, and some were in full breeding plumage. These, and other reports accepted by KBRC, are from 7 April to 10 June (most during the last half of May) and 4 July to 13 September (most during August).

Comments: Although nearly impossible to distinguish from the White-faced Ibis except in breeding condition when soft part colors and facial feathering are obvious, many recent sightings appear valid. It is a notorious vagrant whose breeding populations in the Gulf States are increasing rapidly, so its appearance is not unexpected. Improved identification guides and increased scrutiny of ibises by observers are also involved. Nonbreeding individuals are best identified as *Plegadis* sp. Additionally, hybrids between the species have been recorded, making identification more difficult.

References: Davis and Kricher, 2000; Pittman, 1993.

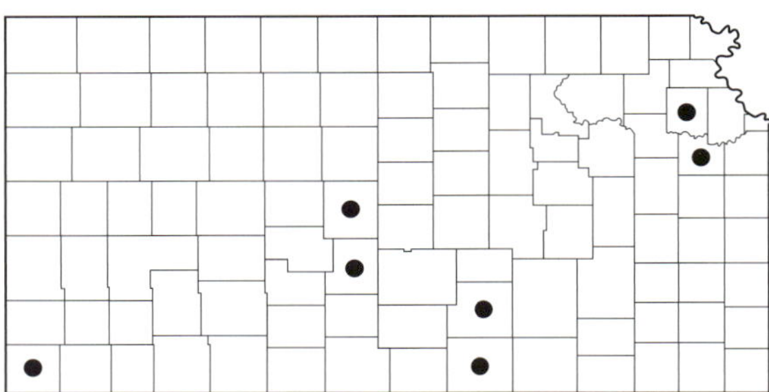

White-faced Ibis

Plegadis chihi (WFIB)

© Judd Patterson

Status: Uncommon spring and fall transient statewide; regular, low-density breeder in Barton and Stafford counties and elsewhere if water conditions permit; casual in early winter during mild seasons.

Habitat: Largely limited to shallow marshes and wetlands; also ephemeral playa lakes, especially in west.

Migration: The earliest reported date is three birds on 31 March (Stafford Co.). Median first arrival dates are 15 April (Barton Co.) and 20 April (Stafford Co.). High numbers for spring include 200 on 26 April (Stafford Co.), 75–80 on 17 April (Morton Co.), and 48 on 21 April (Linn Co.). Flocking begins by 19 July (120, Barton Co.) and 7 August (500, QNWR). An estimated 2,000 birds were present at the latter two localities on 1 September. Most departure is mid-September through October. In recent years reports of late stragglers have increased and now extend to 7 November (Barton Co.) and 18 November (Linn Co.) and into the CBC period (18 December, Stafford Co.; 30 December, Barton Co.).

Breeding: Nesting was confirmed at CBWA (Barton Co., photo by L. O. Nossaman) in 1929 or 1930 and again in 1962 and subsequent years. Breeding was first documented from QNWR in 1981, and it is now a regular breeder at both localities, water conditions permitting. Both colonies are thriving today. Additional nesting has occurred in a Meade County playa and in Finney County. Visiting birds can be expected wherever suitable habitat exists. Nesting at CBWA and QNWR is in marsh vegetation; at the playas in small trees. The actual size of nesting populations has been difficult to determine, because the number of birds present varies from day to day and apparently includes a large nonbreeding element. There is apparently considerable movement between the CBWA and QNWR populations. The highest reported nesting count is 100 pairs at QNWR in 1983. Eggs have been reported 1 June–27 July, chicks 4 July, and fledged young as early as 16 July.

Comments: Its status has changed markedly during the last century, and numbers continue to increase. It was presumably a rare visitant with only five scattered records from 1879 through 1923. A handsome bird with showy glossy bronze and cinnamon plumage, long legs, and a long, sharply decurved bill, it can be confused only with the closely related Glossy Ibis.

Banding: 155 banded; no encounters.

References: Busby and Zimmerman, 2001; Davis and Kricher, 2000; Flowers, 1998; Ryder and Manry, 1994; Thompson and Ely, 1989; Young et al., 2009.

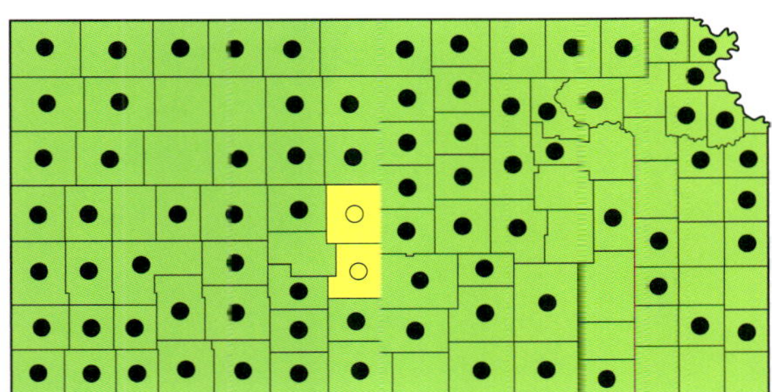

Roseate Spoonbill

Platalea ajaja (ROSP)

© Judd Patterson

Status: Formerly accidental; now vagrant; 9 or 10 records. The first record was a male collected on Four Mile Creek near Douglas (Butler Co.) by R. Matthews on 20 March 1899 (specimen since lost or destroyed). One was reported from Chase County in April 1977 by J. Horak. Subsequently, in 1986, one or two birds were seen at Melvern Reservoir (Osage Co.) 24 August–26 September 1986 and one at CBWA 2–6 September 1986. A report from McPherson County (1996) was unverified. The number of sightings has doubled since 2000 with sightings (some documented by photos) from 30 August 2001 (CBWA, M. Rader), 12 August–26 September 2001 (Finney Co., T. Shane, possibly up to six birds), 9 August 2002 (JRR, one adult and one young), 29 June 2003 (Barber Co., D. Angle), 20 July–6 September 2003 (Barton Co., J. Mayhew), 22 July 2004 (Stafford Co., T. Anderson), and 17 August 2004 (Riley Co., D. Burnett). These dates suggest dispersal from rapidly growing colonies on the Gulf Coast.

Habitat: The species is dependent upon marshy wetlands; its prey consists of aquatic animals, including small fish, crustaceans, and insects and their larvae.

Comments: The spoonbill is one of the most distinctive and most unusual birds in North America. With its pink plumage, reddish wings, long legs, bald head, and spatulate bill, it is not easily confused with other species. It feeds by using its distinctive, tactile bill to the maximum effect; head-sweeping and bill-scything with an open bill ensure capture of prey.

References: Dumas, 2000; Shane et al., 2001; Thompson and Ely, 1989.

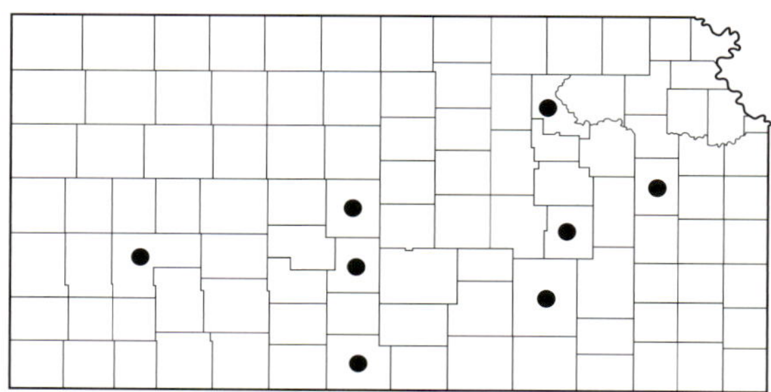

Black Vulture

Coragyps atratus (BLVU)

Status: A rare visitant to the extreme southeastern part of the state; probably a rare resident in Cherokee County. Formerly a resident in southeastern Kansas through at least the 1800s. A specimen secured in Ellis County on 27 March 1885 has since been lost.

Habitat: Most likely to be found in the spring in Cherokee County, especially the wooded outcrops near Schermerhorn Park or near Baxter Springs.

Migration: Most recent records are from Cherokee County during the spring and summer. When Thompson and Ely published their work in 1989, its presence in Kansas was largely historical except for a few recent unverified reports from the southeast. That changed beginning in 1998 when a single bird was found at Schermerhorn Park in Cherokee County (KBRC 98-41) on 25 April 1998. Additional recent reports include a report of two birds from near Baxter Springs on 17 July 2001 (KBRC 2001-32), two birds at Schermerhorn Park on 26 and 28 April 2003 (KBRC 2003-17/17A), and one bird in Cherokee County on 14 June 2003 (KBRC 2003-36). Subsequently, there have been numerous reports from the southeast and reports from Sedgwick County (KBRC 2004-08), Jefferson County (KBRC 2005-25), and Johnson County (KBRC 2006-08). E. Young observed one with Turkey Vultures flying over the Ninnescah River south of Belle Plaine, Sumner County, on 1 April 2007. This is the most recent western record. In 2009, Black Vultures were seen repeatedly in Cherokee County, with as many as five individuals seen at one time in April (M. Gearheart, pers. comm.). Most intriguing was a report from January 2010 in which a pair was observed performing an apparent courtship ritual (L. Herbert, pers. comm.). A single bird was noted at JRR on 14 November 2009 (KBRC 2009-30) by M. Gearheart.

Breeding: The single confirmed nesting is a nest with two eggs taken in Labette County in 1858.

References: Buckley, 1999; Thompson and Ely, 1989.

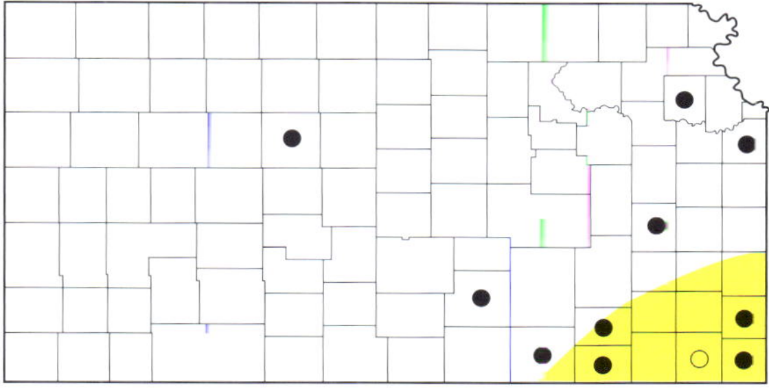

Turkey Vulture

Cathartes aura (TUVU)

© Judd Patterson

Status: Common transient and local breeder; most common in the central and eastern parts; occasionally present during the early part of mild winters.

Habitat: Can occur almost anywhere during spring through fall; often encountered soaring overhead at locales that have significant updrafts.

Migration: A few birds arrive in the south and east during February, including 1 February (Linn Co.), 6 February (Miami Co.), and 13 February (Jefferson Co.), but most early arrivals are mid-March with significant numbers by late March: several hundred on 26 March (Sumner and Cowley cos.) and obvious transients on 24 March (Douglas Co.) and 25 and 30 March (Linn Co.). Arrival in western Kansas is nearly a month later. Median first arrivals there include 2 April (Russell Co.) and 7 April (Barton Co.) with high, migrating flocks on 7 April (Pawnee Co.). Most transients have probably departed by late April. Overall numbers are declining by mid-September but with large flocks developing at roosting sites. Large counts include 75–100 on 20 September (Meade Co.), 300 on 3 October (Butler Co.), and 149 on 7 October (Geary Co.). Most birds depart the state by mid-October. There are a number of records from 8 December through 22 January, perhaps from nearby wintering areas in Oklahoma.

Breeding: It is a low-density breeder statewide due in part to the patchy nature of preferred breeding sites. Nesting may be in a cave, an isolated rocky outcrop, a hollow stump, abandoned buildings, or a barn. Eggs have been reported 3–31 May and young 6 June–14 August.

Comments: The genetic relationship of New World vultures with other bird families remains unsettled and the subject of some controversy. Close relationships have been proposed for both the Falconiformes and the Ciconiiformes (storks). There is also a proposal to place them in a new order, "Cathartiformes." The matter at this writing is unresolved.

See page 491 for banding information.

References: Busby and Zimmerman, 2001; Kirk and Mossman, 1998; Thompson and Ely, 1989.

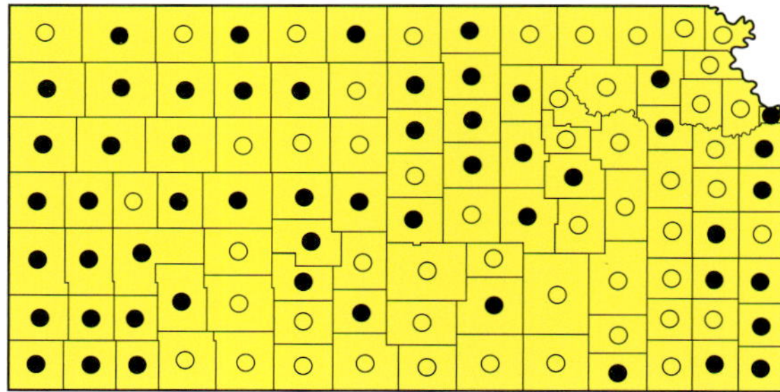

Osprey

Pandion haliaetus (OSPR)

© Judd Patterson

Status: Uncommon to common transient; rare winter visitant around large bodies of water and rivers when open water persists; possibly a summer resident in the southeast and at larger reservoirs.

Habitat: Usually reservoirs and large rivers, often at farm ponds during migration.

Migration: During spring, most common from April through May, with extreme dates of 1 March (Ellis Co., G. Carson) and 7 June (Geary Co., KBRC 99-26). During fall, most migrate in September and October, though occasionally observed in July and August, with extreme dates of 7 July (Labette Co.) and 1 August (Clinton Reservoir, Douglas Co.). Among the few very late dates is 21 November (Pottawatomie Co.). The few winter records include seven observed on CBCs, four in the 1990s and three in the 2000s.

Breeding: Two possible nesting records. At Bone Creek Lake (Crawford Co.), a pair has been observed building a nest on a platform each year since 2005. This activity has taken place during the months of March through June. No eggs or fledglings were observed. Birds have been seen in this vicinity regularly during this decade, but all nesting attempts have failed. A pair was also observed using a nest at Banner Creek Lake (Jackson Co.) in May 2008 (G. Keehn, pers. comm.), but nesting was not confirmed. From 1996 through 2000, KDWP hand-reared and hacked 39 Ospreys at JRR, Wolf Creek Reservoir, and El Dorado Reservoir with the hopes of establishing a breeding population in the state. These attempts were unsuccessful.

Comments: Ospreys feed mostly on fish, and occasionally one will carry a fish in its talons while migrating. Populations have rebounded since the disuse of DDT in the 1950s and 1960s, and confirmed nesting should be looked for in eastern Kansas. Large numbers pass through the south-central region during fall migration. E. Young observed 37 heading south, flying as singles or groups of no more than 3, over 1.5 hours (late afternoon) on 21 September 2006 with an additional 30–40 individuals observed over a 2- to 3-hour period.

See page 491 for banding information.

References: Alderfer, 2006; Janzen, 2007; Moore, 2001; Poole et al., 2002; Rintoul, 2000; Seibel, 1978; Thompson and Ely, 1989; Thompson and Young, 1996.

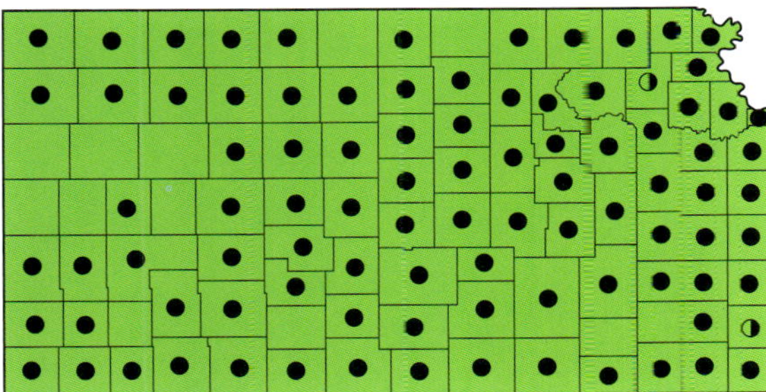

Swallow-tailed Kite

Elanoides forficatus (STKI)

© Judd Patterson

Status: Formerly a regular summer resident in the east, now a rare visitant. Occurred from January to September with nesting confirmed near Neosho Falls (Woodson Co.), 27 April–July 1876; and a nest with eggs collected 27 May 1883 near Abilene (Dickinson Co.) by W. H. Packer and J. Elston. There are four recent records: one observed in Shawnee County, 6 September 1972 ("Woods," unpubl. manuscript, 1976); two individuals in Riley County, 12 July 2001; one documented with a photograph by G. Davis at SCW, 27 August 2005 (KBRC 2005-15), also observed by L. Davis; and one observed by R. Royer in Brown County, 29 May 2008 (KBRC 2008-18).

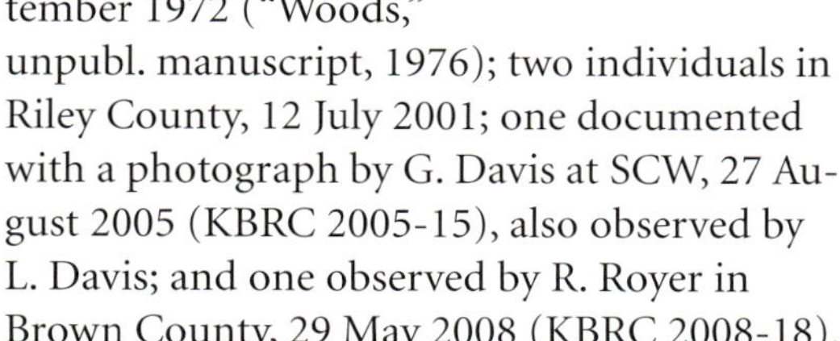

Habitat: Open wetland areas, residential areas, riparian edge, and wet meadows.

Comments: Historically, this species was a summer resident as far north as Minnesota, Illinois, and Ohio, but is now restricted to the southern tier of states from Texas to Florida. Populations appear to be stable and may be increasing. An unsuccessful attempt was made by KDWP to reintroduce the species into the state by cross-fostering young birds in the nests of Mississippi Kites in Meade County (two birds in 1982) and Harvey County (four birds in 1983). One from each site fledged on 25 July and 17 June, respectively.

Banding: Two banded. One cross-fostered in a Mississippi Kite nest southeast of Meade was banded on 2 July 1982. It was killed after fledging but apparently was not salvaged, and the location of the band is unknown. A second bird being cross-fostered near Newton (Harvey Co.) was banded on 2 July 1983.

References: Flowers, 1995a; Meyer, 1995; Moore, 2001; Otte, 2006, 2009; Thompson and Ely, 1989; Tordoff, 1956.

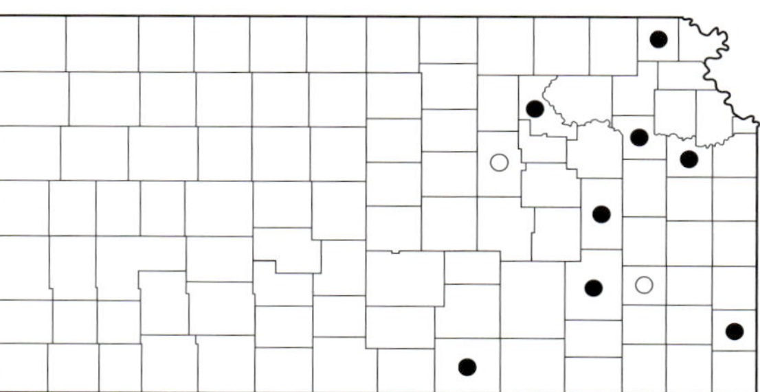

White-tailed Kite

Elanus leucurus (WTKI)

© David Seibel

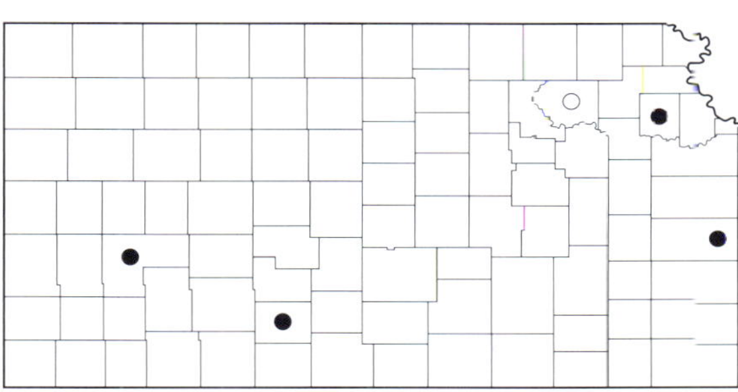

Status: Rare visitant, and bred once. On 6 August 1989 an adult was observed near Olsburg, Pottawatomie County, by G. Radke. On subsequent visits by numerous birders, a pair was observed, and a female was flushed from a nest in the top of a bur oak on 12 August. Two young were observed on 24 August, but the nest was destroyed by a thunderstorm on 8 September. One was observed by G. Salsbury near Greensburg (Kiowa Co.) on 21 April 2000 and one by S. Baugh (Finney Co., KBRC 2001-27) on 29 June 2001. G. Pittman observed a bird that was subsequently photographed and observed by many at the University of Kansas Nelson Environmental Study Area (Jefferson Co.) from 11 to 23 September 2006 (KBRC 2006-21). Other reports are unverified: mid-July 1989 (Linn Co.), 1 April 1989 (Barton Co.), and June 1988 (Barton Co.).

Habitat: Within its normal range prefers open grasslands, savannah, and cultivated fields.

Comments: The White-tailed Kite, formerly known as the Black-shouldered Kite, was on the verge of extinction in the early 20th century, but populations have rebounded, especially in Texas, which is likely the main source for birds found in Kansas.

References: Dunk, 1995; Otte, 2007; Rintoul, 2002; Rintoul and Cable, 1990.

Mississippi Kite

Ictinia mississippiensis (MIKI)

© David Seibel

Status: Common summer resident from central to southwestern Kansas, rare in the east and north. Recent evidence indicates an increase in breeding in the north and southeast.

Habitat: Prefers residential communities, parks, golf courses, and isolated woodlands. In the west it is commonly observed foraging over open fields, especially cropland.

Migration: Usually arrives in late April through May with unlikely early arrival dates of 1 March (Saline Co., unverified) and 7 March 2007 (Pratt Co., unverified). The mean earliest arrival date is 7 May for Barton, Meade, and Rice counties. Late arrival and migration dates are difficult to ascertain due to presence of nesting individuals. Fall migration begins in late August and lasts through early October. Again, the earliest dates are difficult to determine due to nesting. However, large numbers, presumably from local breeding populations, begin to stage in August and early September, and most are gone by mid-September. The median late date for departure is 16 September (Rice Co.). The latest departure date is 29 October (Meade Co., KU 67339). Published winter records of one to four individuals in Cowley County, 19–28 February 1971 and 4 January 1972, are probably erroneous (D. Seibel, pers. comm.).

Breeding: Usually takes place from May to early August, with peak egg-laying from late May through June. Nest-building has been reported 4 May–17 July, eggs 29 May–23 June, nestlings 7 June–14 August, and recently fledged by 1–9 August.

Comments: Populations have been expanding in Kansas since the mid-1900s. After breeding, individuals will disperse northward and return southward during fall migration. Large concentrations have been observed in Garden City (Finney Co.), with 95 birds in two kettles (16 September 2002); up to 120 in Hays (Ellis Co.); 60 at Ulysses (Grant Co., 28 August 2004); 170 in Finney County (20 August 2004); 300+ in Larned (Pawnee Co., 19 August 2003); and 500 in Belle Plaine (Sumner Co., 14 September 2005).

See page 491 for banding information.

References: Parker, 1999; Piper, 1997; Seibel, 1978; Thompson and Ely, 1989.

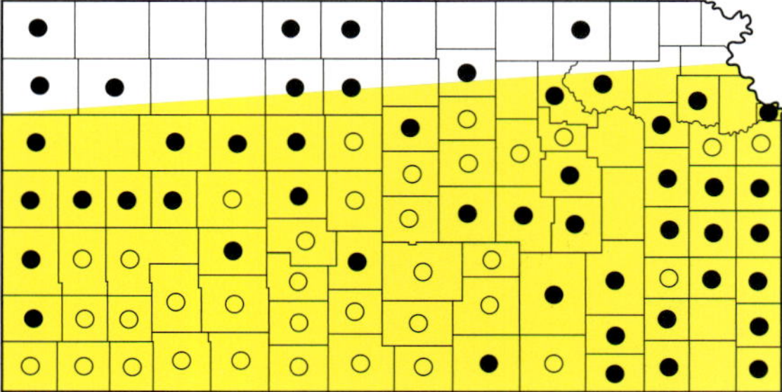

Bald Eagle

Haliaeetus leucocephalus (BAEA)

© David Seibel

Status: Low-density summer resident, primarily in eastern half of Kansas, but west to Hodgeman County; common transient and winter resident statewide; some nesting birds are permanent residents.

Habitat: Prefers open water of larger reservoirs, rivers, and wetlands. Nests in dead trees within coves of reservoirs, or in tall deciduous trees (especially cottonwood), sometimes isolated, along streams and rivers; in winter they roost in large numbers in trees away from human disturbance; often in grasslands, especially the Flint Hills, during the winter, where they feed on carcasses of cattle and deer; in prairie dog towns in the west.

Migration: Difficult to ascertain due to presence of wintering birds, but appears to peak from February through March and continues through April. A few transients linger from May through June. Most nonnesting birds usually appear from September through March. Concentrations of 100+ individuals are common at reservoirs and rivers in the northeast, CBWA and QNWR, and the Arkansas River during the winter.

Breeding: Eggs are laid in late January, normally in February through April; young hatch (average 39 days) in March through May and fledge in about 3 months from May to July. A male fledged from Clinton Reservoir (Douglas Co.) in 1989 mated with a female at Hillsdale Lake (Miami Co.) in 1993. This female was from an egg taken from a nest in Florida in January 1990, hatched and raised in Oklahoma, and fledged from a hack tower at Eufala Lake. The pair bred again in 1994. Several eagles hatched in Kansas have returned to nest in different locations in the state.

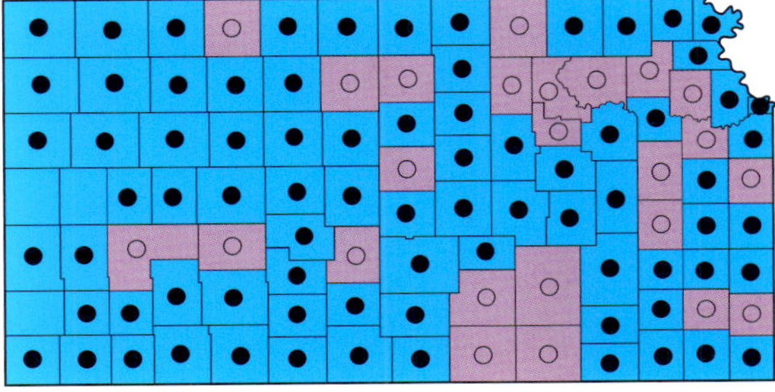

Comments: Removed from the Endangered Species list in 2007 and from the state endangered list in 2009.

See page 492 for banding information.

References: Buehler, 2000; Highfill, 1990; Schwilling et al., 1989; Seibel, 1978; Thompson and Ely, 1989; Tordoff, 1956; Watkins and Mulhern, 1997, 1998, 1999; Watkins et al., 1994; Watkins et al., 1996; Young, 2009.

Northern Harrier

Circus cyaneus (NOHA)

© Jim Burns

Status: Low-density summer resident statewide, except northwestern and southeastern corners; common transient and winter resident statewide.

Habitat: Prefers large tracts of open grassland; during the winter often roosts in large concentrations near wetlands, especially CBWA, QNWR, and SCW.

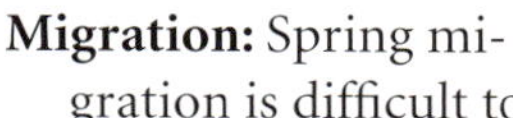

Migration: Spring migration is difficult to ascertain due to presence of wintering birds, but appears to peak from March through April, and lasts through May. In fall, nonnesting birds usually appear from September through November. Most wintering birds are reported from December through February with numbers increasing as snow cover increases in northern latitudes. Large numbers include 100+ on 7 October (Larned area, Pawnee Co., S. Seltman), 59 on 6 February (QNWR), and 40 on 25 February (Russell Co.).

Breeding: Nests on the ground and prefers mid- to tallgrass prairie and CRP grasslands in the west; occasionally uses wheat, alfalfa, or abandoned cropland fields and marshes. Nests located in early crops such as wheat or alfalfa are often destroyed during harvest. Eggs have been reported 6 April–6 July, nestlings 12 June–29 July, and recently fledged young 16 June–19 July. A recent fledgling was observed being fed on 2 September at SCW. The median date for 30 clutches, statewide, is 19 June.

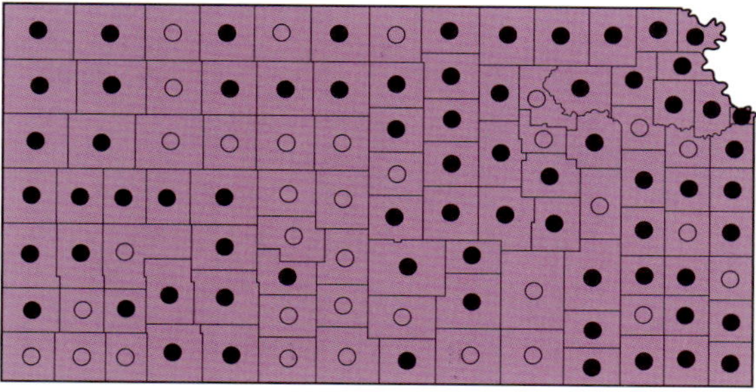

Comments: The Northern Harrier, formerly known as the Marsh Hawk, has decreased in numbers as a breeding species in Kansas due to the loss of native grasslands. The use of CRP grasslands in the west has resulted in increased nesting, but that program is continually under threat by federal budget cuts.

See page 492 for banding information.

References: MacWhirter and Bildstein, 1996; Thompson and Ely, 1989; Tordoff, 1956; Young, 1993.

Sharp-shinned Hawk

Accipiter striatus (SSHA)

Status: Common but low-density transient and uncommon winter resident statewide; rare local breeding resident; recorded all months.

Habitat: Typically woodlands but during migration in open areas, especially along hedgerows, isolated farmyards, parks, and bird-feeding stations. May take up residency in suburbs in the winter.

Migration: Most migration is late March through early May with stragglers into early June. Birds have been observed migrating between 24 April and 10 May. Fall migration usually starts in mid-September with the peak during October. Extreme dates for presumed fall transients are 13 July (Morton Co.) through 28 October (observed movement, Sumner Co.). It overwinters in small numbers nearly statewide.

Breeding: Small numbers nest in the northeastern and south-central regions. KBBAT reported a single confirmed nesting (Cowley Co.). Other confirmed nestings are in Cloud and Pottawatomie counties with scattered reports of possible nesting, chiefly territorial individuals during summer, and one possibly carrying food on 23 July (Linn Co.). The report of an incubating adult in Colby on 5 May 1997 was not confirmed. Most nests are in coniferous trees and seldom seen; nesting takes place from late April through July.

Comments: It is very similar in appearance to the Cooper's Hawk in comparable plumages, and many sightings are fleeting glimpses. Identifications should be made with care and corroborated whenever possible. This is especially true of suspected nesters. It is probably the most common of the accipiters observed at bird-feeding stations and during migration.

Banding: 110 banded; one encounter: one in-state. A bird banded 20 October 1980 was found in the same area 15 February 1984. Oldest 3 years 4 months.

References: Bildstein and Meyer, 2000; Janzen, 2007; Piper, 1997; Seibel, 1978; Thompson and Ely, 1989; Tordoff, 1956; Young, 19[illegible]

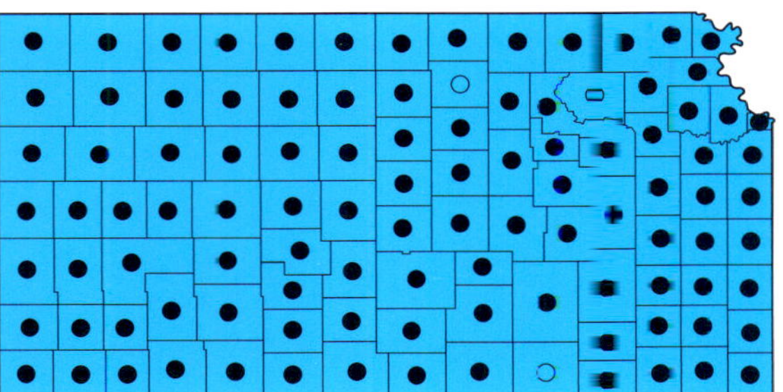

Cooper's Hawk

Accipiter cooperii (COHA)

Status: Common low-density transient; uncommon winter resident statewide; low-density breeder in eastern two-thirds, rare breeder in the northwest.

Habitat: Woodlands; uses open areas during migration, especially along hedgerows and riparian growth; occasional at bird-feeding stations.

Migration: In spring, most migration is mid-March through April, with an extreme late date of 21 May (Morton Co.). Actual migration was observed on 26 April (40, Linn Co.). Scattered individuals, statewide during summer, may be vagrants or perhaps local breeders. Although few data are available, an increase in sightings by mid-August and a rapid increase by mid-September suggest the beginning of fall migration. Most migration is probably during early October.

Breeding: Most nests are in deciduous trees in riparian habitat and in both suburban and urban areas. Nest-building had been reported 6 April (recently completed), eggs 19 April–11 June and 3 July, nestlings 7–13 June, and recently fledged young 17 June. Most reports of nesting are of birds "incubating" but without actually viewing the nest contents. Johnston reported a modal egg-laying date of 25 April.

Comments: It is a widespread but low-density winter resident, often competing with Sharp-shinned Hawks at feeding stations. It closely resembles the latter species, and care should be exercised in making identifications. Breeding populations appear to be increasing and expanding westward with a significant number of these in suburban areas of towns and cities.

See page 492 for banding information.

References: Curtis et al., 2006; Janzen, 2007; Johnston, 1964a; Seibel, 1978; Thompson and Ely, 1989; Tordoff, 1956.

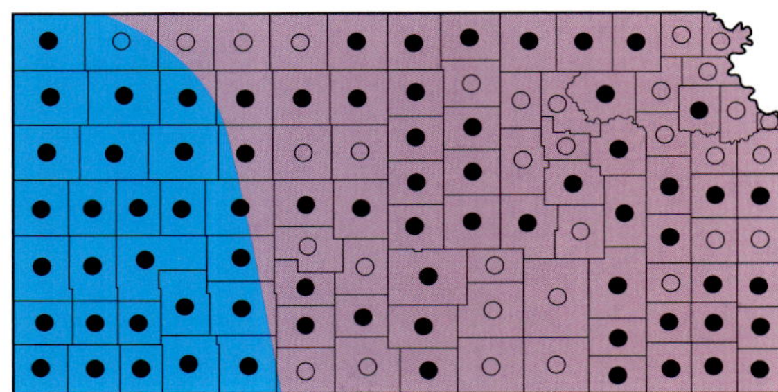

Northern Goshawk

Accipiter gentilis (NOGO)

Status: Rare and irregular winter visitant statewide; rare spring and fall transient.

Habitat: Prefers woodlands and, especially in the west, riparian corridors and shelterbelts.

Comments: It is a boreal species that has periodic irruptions into the Great Plains during winter. Major invasions occurred in Kansas during the winters of 1916–1917, 1973–1974, 1982–1983, 1997–1998, 2002–2003, and 2004–2005. E. Young observed one several times from 7 January to 10 February 2005 in Sumner County. Some sight records have proven to be female Cooper's Hawks or even buteos, so all sightings should be identified with care.

Migration: Normally recorded from October through April with extreme dates of 7 September and 23 April. It appears to arrive earlier in the west (September), and, statewide, most records are from December through January. Spring migration occurs from March through April with late unverified records for 1 May (Pawnee Co.).

Banding: Two banded; five encounters: five encountered in Kansas from: MN (2), WI (2), AB. One banded in Wisconsin, 8 November 1973, was recovered from Labette County, Kansas, in February 1984. Oldest 10 years, 2 months.

References: Cable et al., 1996; Janzen, 2001; Seibel, 1978; Squires and Reynolds, 1997; Thompson and Ely, 1989.

© Mark Chappell

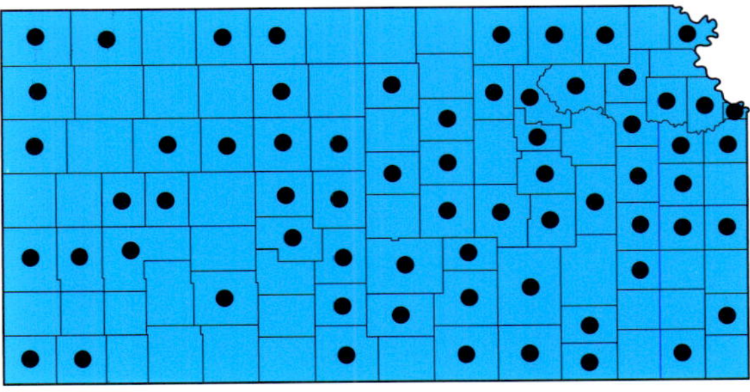

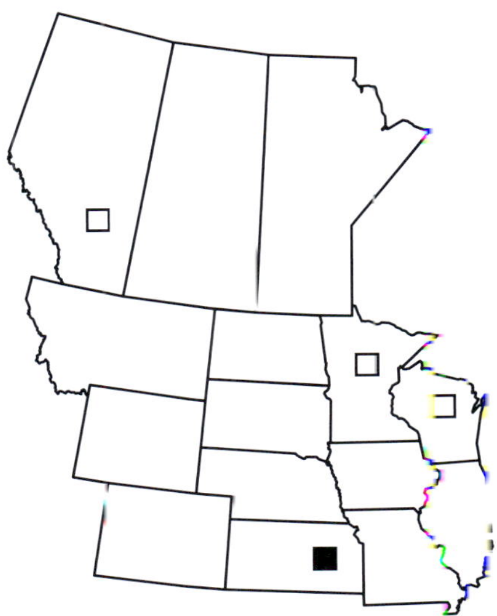

Harris's Hawk

Parabuteo unicinctus (HRSH)

Status: Vagrant. One breeding record. Dates of seven confirmed records range from 31 October to 10 January. A record for 9 September 1998 in Labette County was not fully documented. Two records are from 1918, one collected in Sedgwick County (14 December), the second in Douglas County (25 December). Two records in January are from 1962 (Meade Co.) and 1963 (Mitchell Co.). Interestingly, the Meade County birds remained to nest. Of the remaining records, birds were present for an average of 22 days: 11 December 1972 through 7 January 1973 at CBWA; and 11 November through 5 December 2000 (Cowley Co.).

Habitat: Within its normal range, semiopen grasslands, desert, chaparral, and riparian areas; in Kansas, trees near wetlands and ponds and riparian woodlands.

Breeding: The birds visiting the State Game Farm at Meade Lake (Meade Co.) deserve special attention. An adult female trapped during the first week of January 1962 was crippled and died on 10 January (ESU B964). H. Smith noted at least one additional bird and captured and released a second individual that fall. D. Parmelee and H. Stephens saw three birds on 21 December 1962 and again on 8 February 1963. The pair remained, and H. Smith observed copulation on 29 and 30 March and later saw an individual carrying nesting material and found the nest. D. Parmelee and H. Smith saw an adult on the nest on 13 April, three eggs on 21 April, and one downy chick on 28 May. Unfortunately the nest was destroyed by a storm on 6 June.

Comments: It is usually sedentary, highly social, and possibly nomadic; the latter trait probably explains records for Kansas. Origin of birds in Kansas could be from southwestern populations in Arizona and New Mexico, or from the south via Texas. Some extralimital records are believed to be escapees from falconers and aviarists.

References: Bednarz, 1995; Bunker, 1919; Parmelee and Stephens, 1964; Pittman, 1995; Rintoul, 2002; Snyder, 1919; Thompson and Ely, 1989.

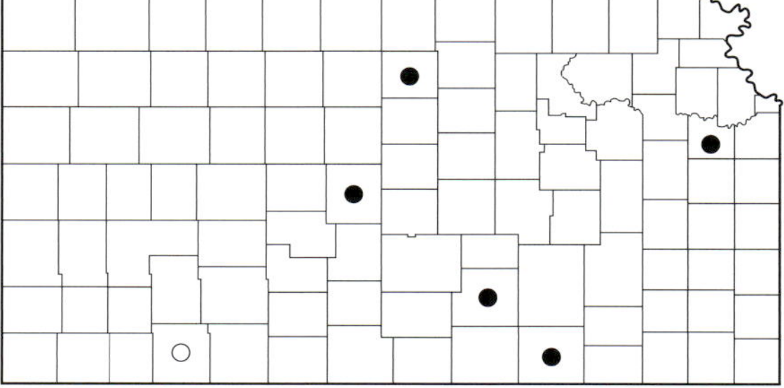

Red-shouldered Hawk

Buteo lineatus (RSHA)

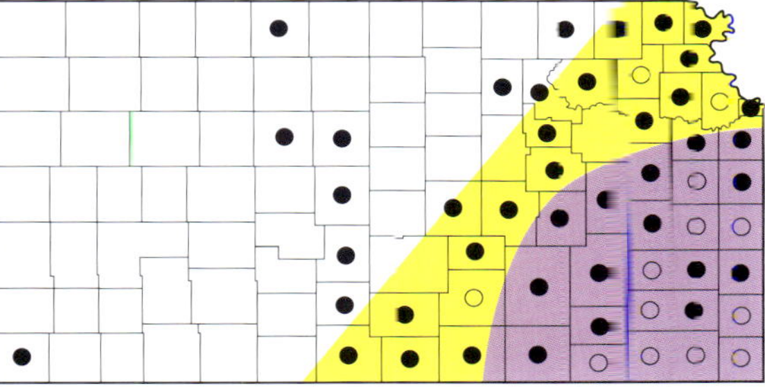

Status: Uncommon breeding resident in the east; probably a rare, local permanent resident in eastern and south-central regions, otherwise rare in winter; casual transient in the west.

Habitat: Riparian and swampy woodlands.

Migration: Difficult to determine due to resident status, but spring migration probably starts in February and lasts through May. During fall, most migrate in September and October, with a few found through at least 16 November (Stafford Co.). Recent winter records from December through January from the eastern and south-central regions are likely overwintering or resident birds.

Breeding: Most nesting occurs in riparian forest. It is typically quite vocal during courtship in March; otherwise nesting activity can go unnoticed. Nest-building has been reported 1 March–2 April, eggs 25 April–5 May, nestlings 25 April–16 June, and recently fledged young 23 June.

Comments: It was considered "common" near Topeka in 1871 through at least 1900 but was rare and local in the extreme east during most of the 20th century. Numbers began increasing dramatically in the late 1990s and early 2000s with a concomitant range expansion. Often secretive, except during courtship; generally observed hunting above tree canopy or perched below. It was removed from the state list of threatened and endangered species in 2004.

Banding: No confirmed bandings.

References: Busby and Zimmerman, 2001; Dykstra et al., 2008; Janzen, 2007; Rintoul, 1999; Seibel, 1978; Thompson and Ely, 1989.

Broad-winged Hawk

Buteo platypterus (BWHA)

Status: Regular transient statewide, rare to uncommon in the east, rarer westward; rare, local breeding resident in the northeast; nesting should be looked for in the southeastern and south-central regions.

Habitat: A variety of woodlands and parks, nesting in deciduous woods; during migration generally observed soaring overhead, sometimes in flocks.

Migration: Reports from 3 to 9 March (Pottawatomie Co.), if correct, are exceptional. Arrival is usually early April (3 April, Cowley Co.; 7 April, Ellis Co.; 8 April, Johnson Co.) with peak migration mid-April through early May. Individuals seen in western half of the state as late as 31 May (Ellis Co.), 10 June (Trego Co.), and 11 June (Morton Co.) are thought to be late migrants, but 21 June (Douglas Co.) and 14 July (Linn Co.) records may be from nearby nesting areas. Records after mid-May in south-central and southeastern counties may represent breeding birds. The fall migration begins by at least 27 August (Cowley Co.) and peaks during September, with records as early as 3 August (Sumner Co.) and 16 August (Lane Co.) and others as late as 31 October (Scott Co.), 3 November (SCW), and 11 November (Shawnee Co.). The earliest fall records could represent locally breeding birds rather than transients.

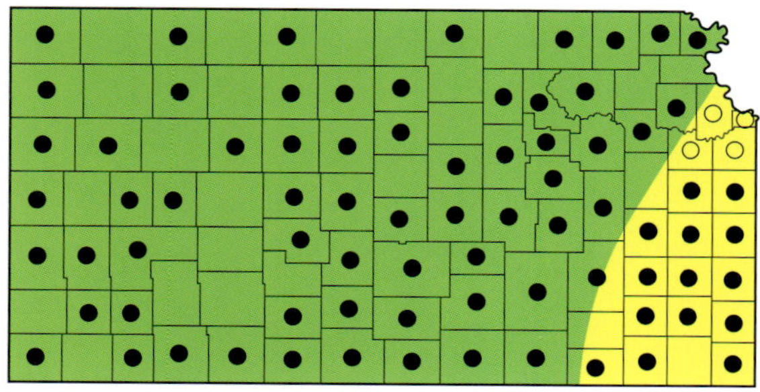

Breeding: KBBAT reported one confirmed nesting (Wyandotte Co.). It has also nested in Douglas, Leavenworth, and Johnson counties and perhaps Shawnee County in the northeast, with several sightings of both adults and young during late spring and summer, but no confirmed nests farther south. The strongest current evidence of breeding in southeastern counties, reported by P. Janzen (pers. comm.), includes one carrying a stick on 5 May 2001 near Caney (Chautauqua Co.) and two adults and one immature seen 26 June 2004 northwest of Fredonia (Wilson Co.). Eggs have been reported from late April to 18 May. Nesting probably continues through June. Young may use the nest for up to 2 weeks after fledging as a feeding and roosting site, with adults remaining on territory for up to 8 weeks.

Comments: An estimated 400 were observed by J. Schulenberg on 30 September 1986 (Lyon Co.). Other large kettles include 150 on 26 April 1991 (Linn Co.) and 50 (mixed-species flock) on 27 September 1996 (Johnson Co.).

Banding: Five banded (three in Ellis Co.); no encounters.

References: Cable et al., 1996; Droege, 2004; Goodrich et al., 1996; Seibel, 1978; Thompson and Ely, 1989; Tordoff, 1956; Young, 1993.

Gray Hawk

Buteo nitidus (GRHA)

© Jim Burns

Status: Accidental, two records. D. LaShelle observed a definitive basic-plumaged Gray Hawk on 15 April 1990 in the Rolling Hills area of Milford Reservoir (Geary Co.). It was seen on 16 April by several other observers, and again on 18 April in the Curtis Creek area, 2 miles north-northwest of the original site. A "small raptor gray under parts and banded tail" observed by M. Anderson at Rolling Hills on 6 April may have been the same individual. The original report (KBRC 91-01) was rejected because the bird was of questionable origin. Upon reevaluation in 1998, the record was accepted, but the location was erroneously reported as Clay County. The second occurrence was a bird photographed by M. Bryant in suburban Wichita (Sedgwick Co.), where it was present from 19 to 30 October 2005 (KBRC 2005-26).

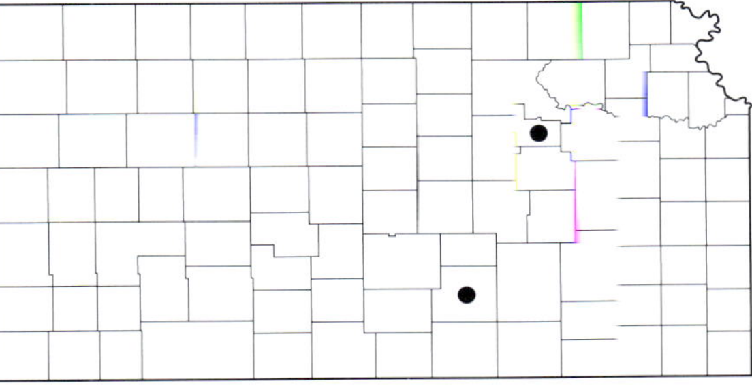

Habitat: Within its normal range, near riparian woodlands and forest edge.

Comments: It is thought to be relatively sedentary in nature, with only three records outside of its normal U.S. range of southern Texas and Arizona (two for Kansas, and one for Illinois in 1871). However, populations may be increasing in these regions, accounting for current Kansas sightings. Birds in Arizona are known to migrate in March and October; interestingly, both of the Kansas dates fall within or near these periods. It should be noted that it is also kept by falconers and aviculturists. The possibility of an escapee was part of the reason the first sighting was originally rejected. The photograph of the Sedgwick County bird showed no sign of previous captivity, and the species was moved from the state hypothetical list to confirmed.

References: Bibles et al., 2002; Davis and Russell, 1990; LaShelle, 1990; Otte, 2006; Pittman, 1992; Rintoul, 1999.

Swainson's Hawk

Buteo swainsoni (SWHA)

Status: Common to abundant spring and fall transient; uncommon summer resident in the west, rare in the east. Formerly, more common; numbers have declined over the last century.

Habitat: Prefers large tracts of open grasslands with scattered trees. During spring, burning or recently burned uplands and recently worked agricultural fields are favored hunting grounds.

Migration: Normally late March and early April through May with an extreme arrival date of 11 March (Sumner Co.). Earlier reports are suspect. Median first arrivals include 2 April (Pawnee Co.) with 160 present on 25 April; 4 April (33 years, 26 March–19 April, S. Seltman); 10 April (Meade Co.) with hundreds present by 17 April; 12 April (Russell Co.); 24 April (Lyon Co.); and "large flocks" on 14 April (western Kansas). Fall migration begins by at least mid-September (40+ on 14 September, Rush Co.), but the large flights are during early October (see Comments) with occasional individuals to 12 and 19 November. None of the few winter sightings (most on CBCs) have been verified.

Breeding: KBBAT reported that 74 percent of all confirmed nestings during the study were from the High Plains; nesting occurs locally east of the Flint Hills. Nest-building has been reported 9 April–15 June, eggs 29 April–15 June (most during the last half of May), chicks 25 May–20 July, and recently fledged young by 20 July.

Comments: Large numbers are observed during spring and fall migration: 172 in burned pasture, Butler County (11 April 2009); 192 at SCW (April 1998) and 250 at Belle Plaine (4 October 2006), both Sumner County; 300 in Sedgwick County (3 October 2002); more than 400 in Geary County on 28 September 2007; up to 500 in late September to early October (Sedgwick Co.); 4,000+ at SCW (5 October 2003); "thousands" in Wabaunsee County (October 1957); "thousands" (3 October) in Meade County; and "large flocks" (27 September) in Wallace County. On 5 October 2003 an

estimated 4,000–6,000 along with hundreds of Turkey Vultures and about 10 accipiters were observed in a 45-minute period flying over SCW. About 1 hour later another large group of Swainson's Hawks were observed over the Arkansas River, northwest of Arkansas City (Cowley Co.), to bring the total to an estimated 8,000 raptors and vultures (P. Janzen, pers. comm.).

See page 493 for banding information.

References: Busby and Zimmerman, 2001; Cable et al., 1996; England et al., 1997; Goldstein et al., 1996; Janzen, 2007; Seibel, 1978; Thompson and Ely, 1989; Young, 1993.

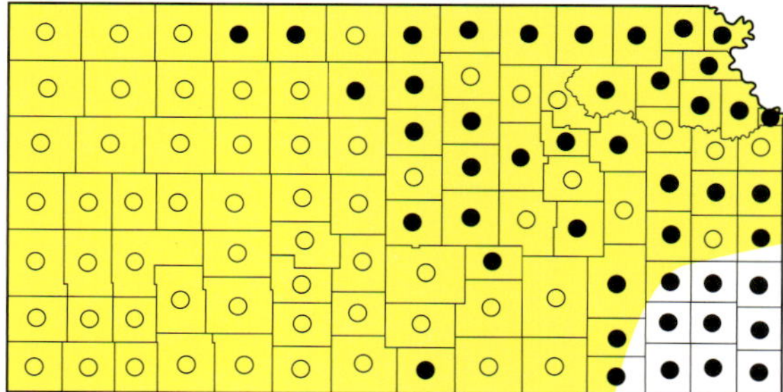

Red-tailed Hawk

Buteo jamaicensis (RTHA)

Status: Permanent resident statewide; abundant winter resident and transient; most abundant and widespread in the east, less common in the west.

Habitat: A variety of habitats, including fragmented areas, grasslands, wetlands, riparian edge, and open woodlands; along roadsides and streams during winter.

Migration: In spring, melanistic birds, characteristic of northern and western populations that do not breed in Kansas, depart the state in March and are usually gone by April, exceptionally to June. During fall migration melanistic birds usually begin to appear the first 2 weeks in October. Winter populations are augmented by transients and winter residents from farther north and west. Numbers during the winter are large with several CBCs routinely reporting more than 100 individuals per year, with the largest counts coming from the Flint Hills region. Manhattan, with 914 individuals (83rd count), had the second highest total ever recorded in North America.

Breeding: Nesting in the west is usually in riparian situations. Pair formation seems to be initiated in October, and by November pairs are commonly seen perched next to, or near, each other along highways and riparian habitats. Courtship occurs from January through March. Copulation has been noted on 24 February, nest-building 24 February–13 April, eggs 3 March–20 May, chicks 23 March–20 June, and recently fledged young 29 May–26 June. E. Young observed downy chicks in a nest at SCW on 11 March, one of the earliest known records.

Comments: The extent to which breeding birds migrate south is not well understood. At least three subspecies are known from Kansas, *B. j. borealis* (nests in east; subsumes "*B. j. krideri*," the pale form often called "Krider's Hawk," and "*B. j. abieticola*," a heavily marked form, both present in winter), *B. j. calurus* (winters and probably nests in the west), and *B. j. harlani* ("Harlan's Hawk," a winter resident). Evidence indicates that Harlan's Hawk may be a separate species.

See page 493 for banding information.

References: Applegate et al., 2004; Busby and Zimmerman, 2001; Dickerman, 1993; Hubbard et al., 2001; Preston and Beane, 2009; Thompson and Ely, 1989; Wolfe, 1961; Young, 1993.

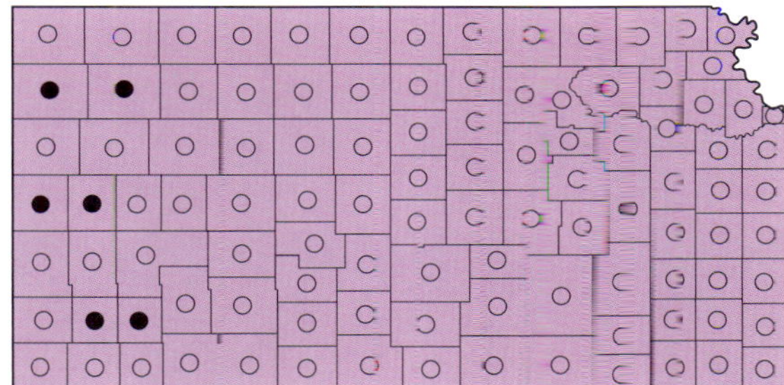

Ferruginous Hawk

Buteo regalis (FEHA)

Status: Low-density permanent resident in the west, common transient in the west, uncommon transient and winter resident in the central region, rare east of the Flint Hills.

© Kyle Gerstner

Habitat: Prefers large tracts of open grasslands, especially shortgrass prairies of the High Plains; often at prairie dog towns.

Migration: Spring migration is poorly known due to presence of wintering birds but appears to peak from February through April. Early departure dates include 16 February (Sumner Co.) and 27 March (Harvey Co.). Late dates include 14 April (Sumner Co.), 18 April (Bourbon Co.), 26 April (Barton Co.), and 18 May (Stafford Co.), with an extreme date of 14 June (Riley Co.). In fall, the main migration appears to be from late September through November. Outside of the breeding range, early arrival dates include 31 August and 5 September (both Barton Co.). Numbers in the west increase as populations are augmented by more northerly birds from late November through March. In the central region most winter records are from December. One individual remained at SCW from 12 to 25 February 1989.

Breeding: It nests on the ground in eroded canyons in the west, occasionally in isolated trees. Nests are a large, bulky mass of sticks and weed stalks lined with finer materials. Prior to the elimination of bison, this fine material consisted of bison bones and wool. A pair often has several nests within its breeding territory and may alternate among them in successive years. Eggs have been reported 14 April–9 June, chicks 6 May–24 July, and recently fledged young 25 June–8 July. The estimated 40–50 breeding pairs has remained stable for many years.

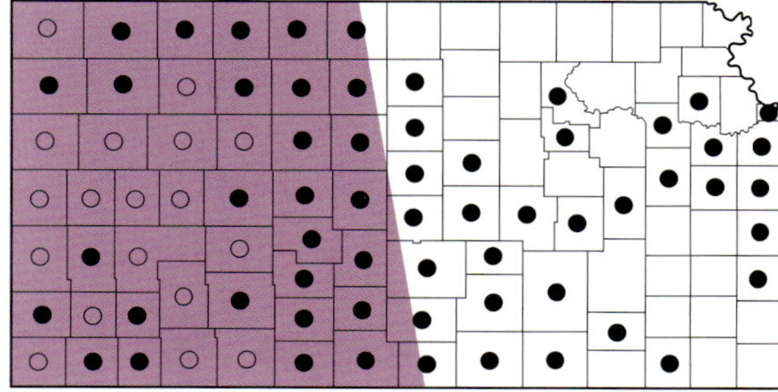

Comments: The primary prey includes rabbits, ground squirrels, pocket gophers, and prairie dogs; hawk populations fluctuate with prey abundance and availability.

See page 493 for banding information.

References: Bechard and Schmutz, 1995; Busby and Zimmerman, 2001; Collins and Reynolds, 2005; Gillihan et al., 2004; Janzen, 2007; Otte, 2005; Roth and Marzluff, 1989; Seibel, 1978; Thompson and Ely, 1989; Young, 1993.

Rough-legged Hawk

Buteo lagopus (RLHA)

Status: Common transient and winter resident in the west and the Flint Hills, uncommon eastward.

Habitat: Prefers large tracts of open grasslands where it feeds primarily on small mammals, especially voles.

Migration: The northern movement is under way by early March, and most have departed by mid-April. Late dates include 20 April (Pawnee Co.) with unusually late stragglers on 17 May (Graham Co.) and 19 May (Rush Co.). In fall, scattered sightings (most unconfirmed) have been reported during August, but even one appearing with a strong cold front in Ness County on 4 September is unusual. Earliest arrivals are usually late September to mid-October with large numbers present and widespread by the first week of November. Dates for late fall arrival are undetermined. Winter birds are observed from November through February with peak concentrations from December through February.

Comments: It appears to be more crepuscular than other hawks. Winter populations are influenced by southern limits of snow cover, and locally by fluctuation of small mammal populations.

Banding: 12 banded; 13 encounters: 8 in-state; 4 from Kansas to: NE (2), ND, TX; 1 banded in Wyoming, 15 June 1942, was recovered in Kansas, 23 December 1943. Oldest 12 years, 11 months.

References: Bechard and Swem, 2002; Johnsgard, 1990; Sullivan, 1995; Thompson and Ely, 1989; White, 1994.

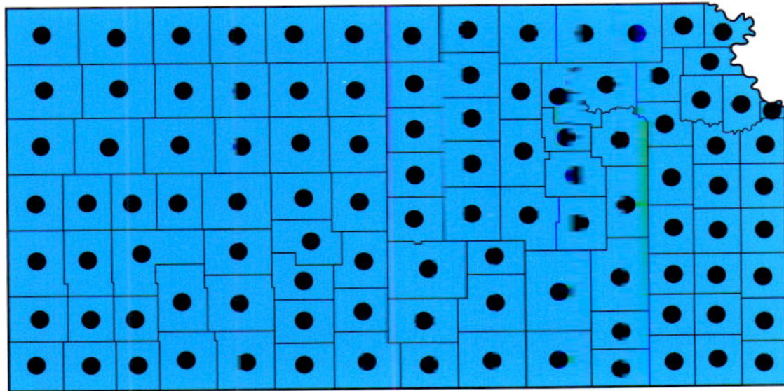

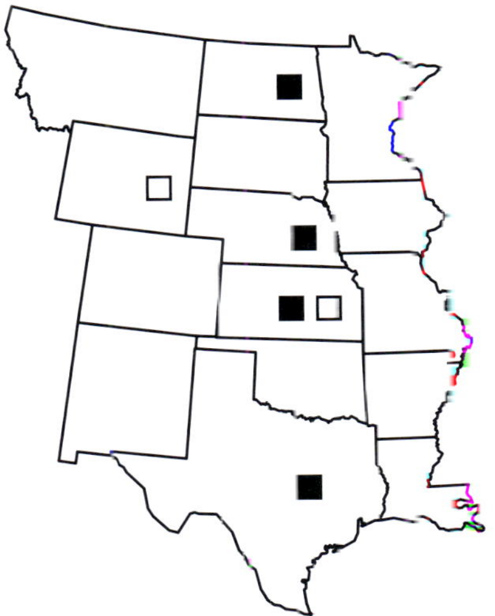

Golden Eagle

Aquila chrysaetos (GOEA)

Status: Rare summer resident in the west, uncommon transient and winter resident from the Flint Hills westward; rare transient and winter resident in the east.

Habitat: Vast open grasslands, especially in the High Plains; frequents prairie dog towns.

Migration: Birds begin leaving the winter roosts by January, and spring migration probably begins soon after. It appears to peak from February through April. Early departure dates include 26 February (Sumner Co.) with unusually late dates of 5 May (Ellis Co.) and 8 May (Cowley Co.). Some later dates may be of vagrants or nonbreeding summering individuals (Ellis Co.). Nonnesting birds usually appear in Kansas in the fall from September through October. The earliest arrival date outside possible breeding areas is 23 August (Cowley Co.). Late arrival dates include 24 October (Greenwood Co.) and 28 October (Pawnee Co.). Most wintering birds are reported from November through February; most common in the west.

Breeding: Nesting occurs along cliffs, especially along eroded canyons, and in isolated trees within shortgrass prairie. All seven nests found in Meade County were in close proximity to prairie dog towns. Eggs have been reported 11 March–3 May; young in nest 4 April–16 July, and fledged young by 22 July. T. Flowers indicated egg-laying begins on or about 1 March and hatching about 1 April in Meade County. Prior to 1891, it may have nested as far east as Comanche County. During the mid-1970s nesting was documented from scattered localities in Cheyenne (since 1975), Logan (since 1975), Meade (since 1974), Hodgeman (1990), Kiowa (1991–1992), and Wallace (1993 and other years) counties, with unverified reports from elsewhere in western Kansas. Verified reports of nesting have declined since the 1990s, and only a single nest, in Clark County, was reported in 2010 (W. Busby, pers. comm.; T. Flowers, pers. comm.; S. Roth, pers. comm.).

Comments: It was formerly more common. Currently, it is listed as a Species in Need of Conservation by KDWP. Local and wintering populations, which were often found at prairie dog towns, have probably declined as a result of the decline of prairie dog communities due to eradication efforts.

See page 494 for banding information.

References: Cable et al., 1996; Flowers, 1992; Jenkins, 2004; Kochert et al., 2002; Seibel, 1978; Thompson and Ely, 1989; Tordoff, 1956; Young, 1993.

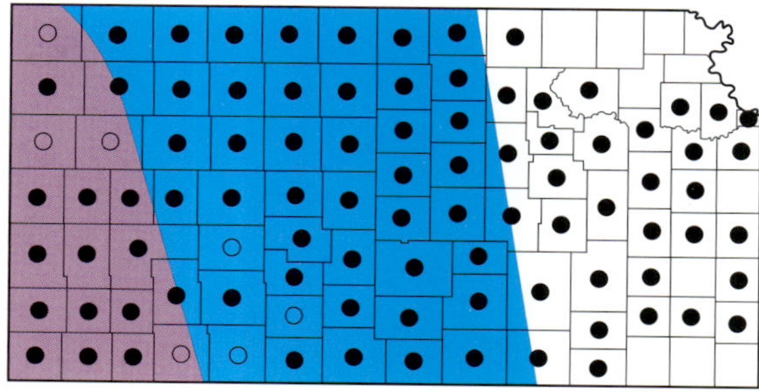

American Kestrel

Falco sparverius (AMKE)

Status: Uncommon permanent resident statewide; common transient; uncommon to common winter resident, becoming rarer in the west during winter.

Habitat: Open areas with scattered trees; frequently nests in parks, towns, and along woodland edges.

Migration: Spring migration peaks from March through mid-April with major movements observed on 12 April (Stanton Co.) and "hundreds" on 16 April (Meade Co.). In fall, migration has been observed 25 August (Meade Co.) and 3 September (Kiowa Co.) through 4 October (Marion Co.), peaking during late September and early October. Local populations in winter are substantially augmented by transients and winter residents from farther north and west.

Breeding: KBBAT reported a fairly even distribution statewide with slightly higher frequencies in the Red Hills and lower in the High Plains. Because kestrels are secondary cavity nesters, they often acquire holes excavated by other animals, or they will use natural holes when available. Nesting occurs in tree cavities, nest boxes, crevices in stone buildings, and nooks and crannies in buildings and bridges. Pairs are investigating nest sites by early March. Copulation has been reported 20 February–28 March, eggs 12 April–24 May, chicks 2 May–28 June, and recently fledged young 11 June–23 July.

Comments: This falcon was formerly known as the Sparrow Hawk. It is often observed hovering in open country in search of prey, which includes insects, small snakes, mice, and other small mammals.

See page 494 for banding information.

References: Busby and Zimmerman, 2001; Cable et al., 1996; Janzen, 2007; Smallwood and Bird, 2002; Thompson and Ely, 1989.

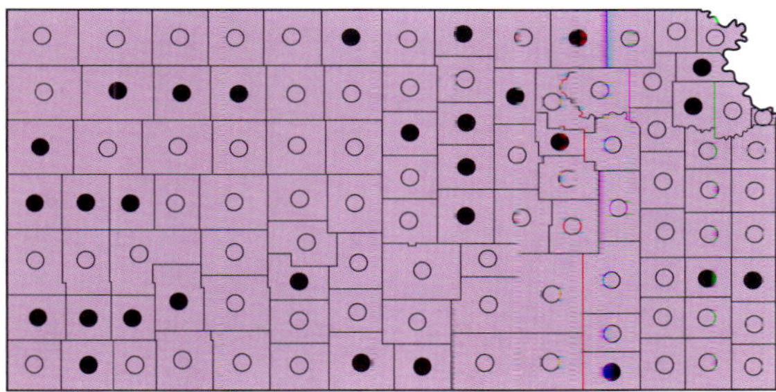

Merlin

Falco columbarius (MERL)

Status: Uncommon transient and rare winter resident.

Habitat: Prefers parks, cemeteries, and towns; often perching on exposed tree limbs, overhead wires, and television antennas; also observed over grasslands, in forested situations, and near marshes, usually where small birds are abundant; in migration found in a wide variety of habitats including open country and woodland edge, often perched on fence posts and utility poles.

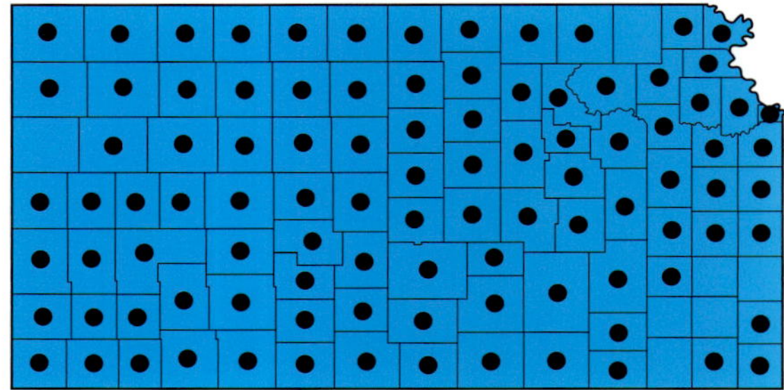

Migration: Recorded from 14 August through 10 June; the few summer sightings are unconfirmed (16 July, Finney Co.). Migration appears to peak in mid-March to early April in spring and mid-September to late October in fall.

Comments: Formerly known as the Pigeon Hawk. Two subspecies regularly occur in Kansas, the pale prairie race, *F. c. richardsonii*, and the darker race, *F. c. columbarius*, which nests in boreal forests.

Banding: One banded (a rehabilitated bird); five encounters. Three banded in Saskatchewan and two banded in Alberta in late June or early July were recovered in Kansas between September (unknown date) and 12 February.

References: Cable et al., 1996; Janzen, 2007; Thompson and Ely, 1989; Warkentin et al., 2005.

Gyrfalcon

Falco rusticolus (GYRF)

Status: Rare winter visitant, primarily in central Kansas. Recorded from 5 November (Russell Co.) to 17 April (Barton Co.); confirmed records through 31 March. Most records are of a single observation with only two records of any duration; one observed at CBWA from 9 to 12 March 1990 (KBRC 92-01) and one in Sedgwick County from 20 to 25 November 2000 (KBRC 2000-71). The paucity of records and short duration of stays indicate high mobility. The species only periodically reaches the state from the main wintering area in the northern United States.

Habitat: Open areas, especially around wetlands where concentrations of passerines and waterbirds occur.

Comments: Kansas appears to be just south of the usual winter range for this species. Although sightings are occasionally reported each year, few records have been confirmed, and many may be confused with similar species. Proof of this is an individual reported from Jefferson County that later proved to be a banded Peregrine Falcon! Arctic populations appear stable. The only specimen from Kansas (KU 34262) was taken in Riley County, 1 December 1880. Although there is a record from Oklahoma of a white individual, this color form has never been observed in Kansas. One trapped by a falconer from Barton County on 17 January 1998, thought to be a white form, was actually a hatching-year gray-phase individual. This bird was photographed by B. Gress on 21 March and subsequently died, but the specimen was not preserved.

References: Baumgartner and Baumgartner, 1992; Booms et al., 2008; Janzen, 1998, 2001; Moore, 2003; Rintoul, 2001, 2003; Thompson and Ely, 1989; Tordoff, 1956.

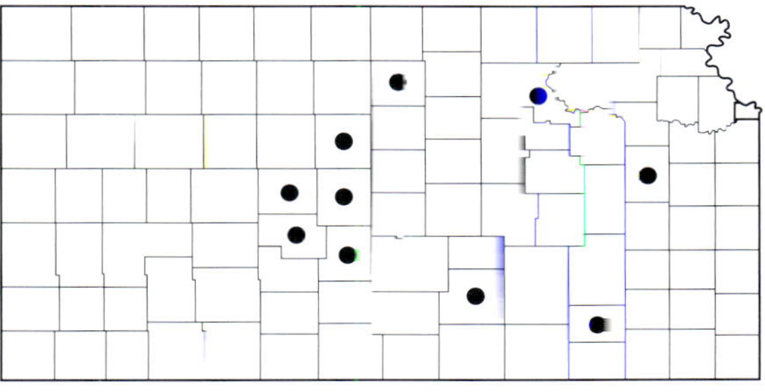

Peregrine Falcon

Falco peregrinus (PEFA)

Status: Uncommon transient statewide; rare winter visitant; recent breeding resident in Topeka (Shawnee Co.); formerly (19th century) bred in Woodson and Ellis counties.

Habitat: Prefers open wetlands, especially around mudflats where shorebirds and waterfowl concentrate; also common in larger cities, for example, Wichita and Topeka; occupies a variety of habitats, especially where cliffs and tall perches are available.

Migration: Usually observed from April through May. Occasional, early transients are observed in March (28 March, Sedgwick Co.) with stragglers into June. Fall migration appears to start by 20 July (Barton Co.), peaks in September, and continues through November (8 November, QNWR). There are scattered winter records for December and January, usually associated with CBCs, with a high total of eight recorded during the 1995–1996 CBC period.

Breeding: Current breeding occurs on tall buildings, with most successful attempts on the Westar Building, Topeka (Shawnee Co.). In 2002 and 2003 birds showed interest in platforms on buildings in downtown Wichita (Sedgwick Co.), but breeding has yet to occur there. Eggs, usually three or four, are laid in early March.

Comments: Formerly known as the Duck Hawk, it was removed from the Endangered Species List in 1994 (*F. p. tundrius*) and in 1999 (*F. p. anatum*).

Banding: 12 banded; six encounters: two banded in Topeka were recovered in Missouri; four encountered in Kansas from: IA (2), MO, YT. The Missouri individual and one of the two Iowa birds were hacked or hand-reared birds. A bird banded in the Yukon Territory on 14 July 1969 was found dead at CBWA on 22 October 1969.

References: Janzen, 2007; Thompson and Ely, 1989; Thompson and Young, 1996; Tordoff, 1956; White et al., 2002.

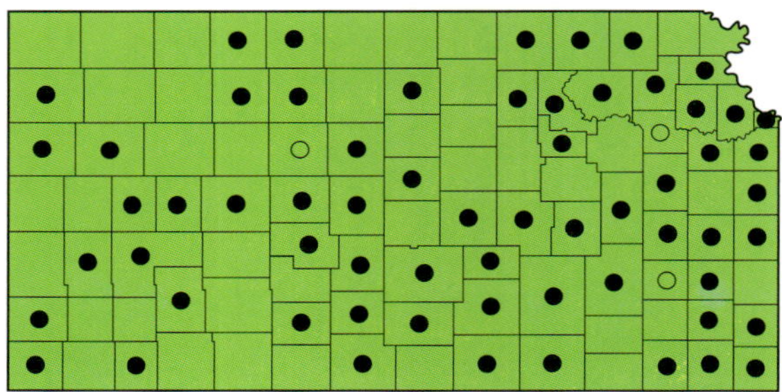

Prairie Falcon

Falco mexicanus (PRFA)

© Judd Patterson

Status: Uncommon transient and winter resident statewide, rarer east of the Flint Hills.

Habitat: Large tracts of open grasslands, especially shortgrass prairies of the High Plains.

Migration: Individuals may occur in western Kansas at any season, but most sightings are early September through late March with extreme dates of 12 July (Finney Co.) and 8 June (Morton Co.). Extreme dates in Ellis County are 8 August–30 March. In eastern Kansas records are 6 November (Coffey Co.) through 14 April (Wabaunsee Co.). A few birds are reported most summers, but breeding has not been confirmed. Two birds defended a territory on bluffs near Scott Lake (Scott Co.) during the summer of 1952 (M. Schwilling). A mummified downy young *Falco* found below bluffs in Gove County during July 1956 (and since lost) may have been this species. Satellite telemetry has revealed that some individuals are from breeding populations in the Snake River Canyon in southwestern Idaho. Seven of 29 females marked with transmitters during the breeding season in Idaho passed through Kansas on their fall migration, and 3 wintered in Kansas.

Comments: Populations appear stable. There is a fossil record from McPherson County. A female banded and equipped with a transmitter by K. Steenhof on 16 April 2000 in the Snake River Canyon, Idaho, and found dead by T. Flowers near Fowler (Meade Co.) provides a brief view of the travels of one bird over an 8-month period. This female laid a clutch of four eggs and successfully fledged at least three young by early June. She remained in the area until 10 July then moved to northwestern South Dakota and eastern Montana (21 July) and by 24 July was in Saskatchewan, where she summered. On 17–18 October she headed south through Nebraska, reaching the Wallace–Logan county line on 28 October and southwestern Kansas on 31 October. She spent 8 November–19 December in the Haskell–Seward–Meade counties area and was electrocuted near Fowler between 20 and 29 December.

See page 494 for banding information.

References: Chandler, 1987; Flowers, 1995a; Janzen, 2007; Rising, 1974; Steenhof et al., 2005; Thompson and Ely, 1989.

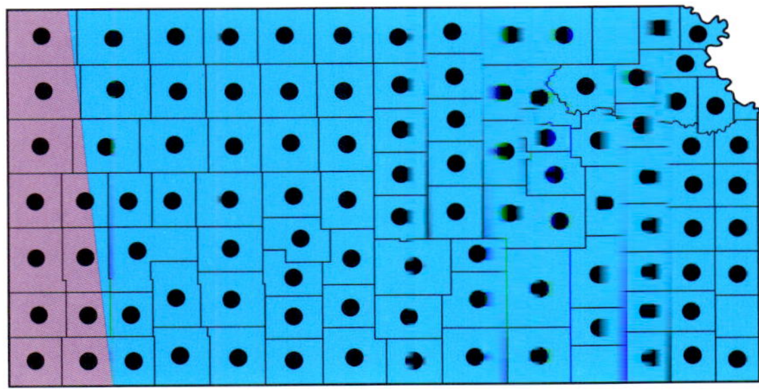

Yellow Rail

Coturnicops noveboracensis (YERA)

© Brian Small

Status: Rare and overlooked transient, primarily in the eastern region, occasionally west to Pawnee County. Prior to 1985 there were only three known specimens: 18 April 1885 (Douglas Co., KU 6901), 1 October 1885 (KU 6903), and 21 October 1933 (Sedgwick Co, KU 20411). The first two were captured by dogs. However, since 1985, at least 33 have been salvaged from television tower kills in the Topeka area.

Habitat: Marshes, especially drier margins, hayfields, grain fields, wet meadows, lowland tallgrass prairie, roadside ditches, and CRP fields.

Migration: Spring transients occur from 5 March and 16 April (both Linn Co.) to 28 May (Barton Co.). Fall transients have been reported from late August (Douglas Co.) to 15 October (Douglas Co., J. King and M. Andersen); tower kills from 25 September to 28 October.

Comments: N. Goss considered it a summer resident but provided no documentation. No evidence or observation of nesting has yet been obtained. Based on numbers killed at night via collisions with transmission towers, it appears to be a nocturnal transient. Known mortality at television towers near Topeka (Shawnee Co.) include 1970 (several), 1985 (3), 1986 (34), 1994 (5), and 2000 (1). An estimated 50–100 rails of probably two species (including Yellow Rail) were flushed from CRP grasslands during a controlled burn in Linn County during mid-April 1992; several were flushed, and one was captured and photographed from the same site in 16 April 1997. At least three were flushed and one captured by W. Counts while mowing lowland alfalfa and clover near Baldwin City (Douglas Co.) during fall 1950 and 1952, and S. Seltman flushed one in Pawnee County on 29 September. It is very difficult to find, even with taped calls, and is probably underreported in Kansas.

Banding: One banded; no encounters. One (rehabilitated) was banded near Perry Reservoir, Jefferson County, April 1985.

References: Alderfer, 2006; Ball et al., 1995; Brookhout, 1995; Goss, 1891; Janzen, 2007; Kluza et al., 2001; Swan and Thompson, 1997; Thompson and Ely, 1989.

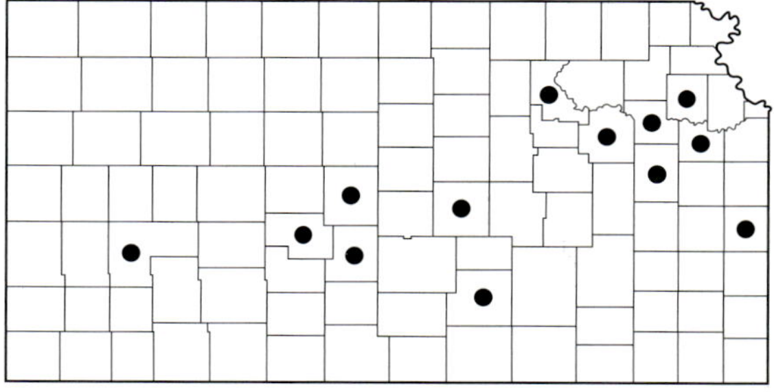

Black Rail

Laterallus jamaicensis (BLRA)

Status: Rare, local summer resident.

Habitat: Wetlands and marshes, almost always in shallow-water environments, including salt marshes, wet meadows, and freshwater marshes.

Migration: Examination of the relatively few data suggests that spring arrival is in late April (21 April, Stafford Co.) and early May (1 May, Comanche Co.), possibly to 13 June (Sumner Co., L. Hicks). At QNWR birds are present by 21 April, and singing continues through 24 July with a high count of six in 1988. Elsewhere fall records are 26 July–31 August (Pawnee Co.) and 17 August (Riley Co.) through 8 September (Barton Co.) with a few October records including 17 October (Morton Co.) and 29 October (Sedgwick Co.).

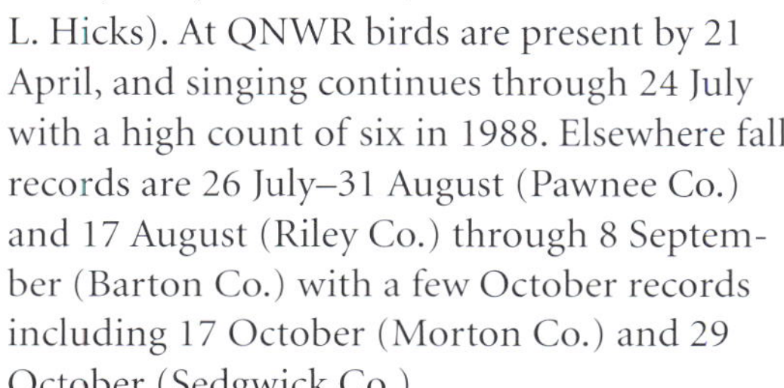

Breeding: The best known and most consistent colony is in a flooded field ("the bobolink field") at the edge of QNWR. Here birders have successfully heard (and occasionally seen) individuals since 1981. Other localities with summering (and probably breeding) birds are CBWA, Coldwater Lake (Comanche Co.), Meade Lake (Meade Co.), and Lake Hargis (Barber Co.). Individuals have been heard recently at numerous tiny marshes statewide—a pattern exhibited since the late 19th century when nests were actually found in Finney, Meade, Franklin, and Riley counties. Preferred nesting sites appear to be marshy areas with stable water levels, a feature not common at most Kansas wetlands. The nest is made of fine-stemmed grasses, rushes, and sedges. Eggs have been reported 6 June–6 July.

Comments: With its tiny size, extremely secretive nature, and dense habitat it is seldom seen even when responding to taped calls. B. Gress and D. Seibel have taken stunning photographs but only after hours of time and effort. At the other extreme, on a few occasions individuals have been captured by hand (Pawnee Co., 26 July, S. Seltman) or nearly captured (Meade Co., 2 September, T. Flowers). The species may be declining like many rail species, but very few data are available on numbers, nesting, or migration activities. The inexperienced observer should remember that the downy young of other (less secretive) rails are also black.

References: Alderfer, 2006; Eddleman et al., 1994; Janzen, 2002b, 2007; Parmelee et al., 1970; Thompson and Ely, 1989; Tordoff, 1956.

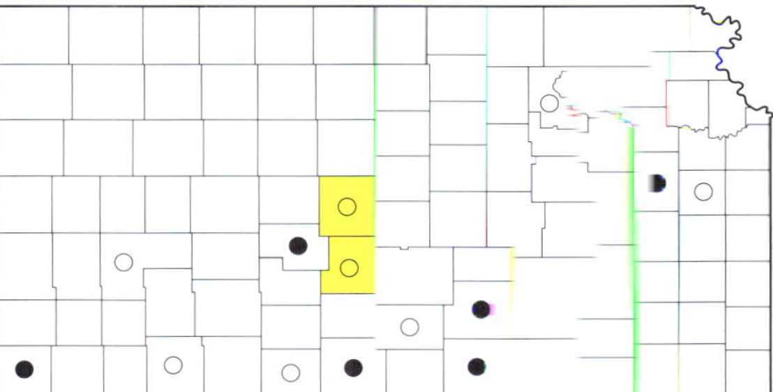

King Rail

Rallus elegans (KIRA)

Status: Local, uncommon summer resident in the central region, occasional in the northeast.

Habitat: Wetlands, salt marshes, even roadside ditches with tall cattails and cordgrass.

Migration: Like other rails it is secretive, making it difficult to assess population size and distribution. It is becoming less often reported at many apparently favorable locations and may be decreasing in numbers. Early March records may be of wintering birds. Presumed transients begin arriving by late March (21 March, Sumner Co.) and early April (4 April, Barton Co.) and continuing into early May or later. Scattered summer sightings, fewer recently, may be transients, nonbreeding individuals, or even local breeders. Fall departure usually begins in September and probably continues through October with a few birds remaining into November. There are at least six December records (to 28 December, Miami Co., KU10412), and four early February records (from 10 February, Barton Co.) suggesting at least occasional overwintering.

Breeding: Available estimates of breeding pairs at CBWA are: 1968, at least 50 pairs (M. Schwilling); 1974, 20–40 pairs; and 1975, 40–80 pairs or more (both R. Tacha). It presumably nests at QNWR. It was a frequent nesting species at SCW, but numbers have declined since 2000 when wetland renovation involved removal of cattails in the north marsh (Winfield Gun Club). A downy chick was collected in Cheyenne County in 1952 (KU 33266). Small numbers were present all summer during 1974 and 1975 in Republic, Kingman, Stafford, and Linn counties, but nests were not found. Nest-building has been reported 4 May, eggs 14 May–27 June, and chicks 31 May–14 August.

Comments: In Woodson County one was found dead, impaled on a barbed-wire fence. Very little is known about its migration. There are only two recoveries of banded birds in North America that moved appreciable distances.

Banding: 208 banded; one encounter: in-state. A bird banded at CBWA on June 1974 was recovered there on 2 August 1975.

References: Alderfer, 2006; Busby and Zimmerman, 2001; Janzen, 2007; Parmelee et al., 1970; Poole et al., 2005; Tacha, 1975; Thompson and Ely, 1989; Wolfe and Wolfe, 1994; Young, 1993.

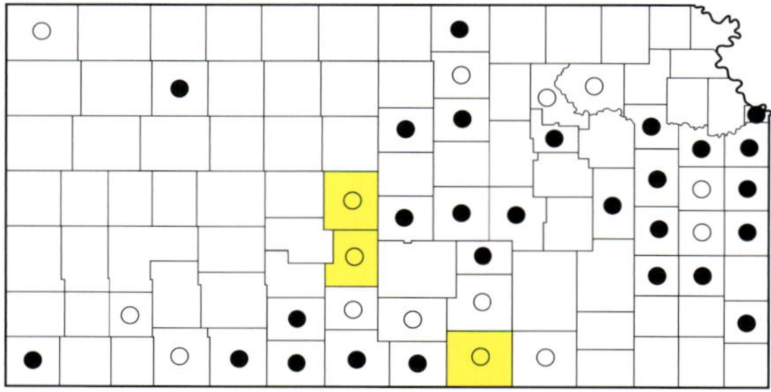

Virginia Rail

Rallus limicola (VIRA)

Status: Locally uncommon summer resident in marshes statewide; casual winter resident; recorded in all months.

Habitat: Frequents wetlands, salt marshes, even uses roadside ditches with tall cattails and prairie cordgrass. More of a generalist than other rails, occurring in a variety of wetlands, including ephemeral wetlands.

Migration: The earliest spring reports (presumed transients) are 10 March (Kingman Co.), 21 March (Barton Co.), and 22 March (Geary Co.). Birds are widespread and actively calling in breeding marshes by mid-April and into May. The fall departure apparently starts in early September continuing into October with most gone by mid-October. There are scattered winter records from November through the CBC period. Small numbers apparently winter at marshes, usually with open, flowing water, during mild winters north to Scott, Trego, Russell, and Geary counties, but there is only one February record. Birds were recently present in Barber County during early January for 3 consecutive years.

Breeding: It was by far the most common rail in 10 marshes sampled by R. Tacha in summer 1974 and 1975 and the only rail to be present at all 10 sites. He estimated 200–400 pairs at CBWA in 1974 and 300 pairs in 1975, using both taped calls and trapping, with much smaller estimates in Seward County (2–25 pairs) and Kingman County (1 or 2 pairs). Statewide, nest-building has been reported 4 May, eggs 23 May–13 July, and chicks 23 May–11 August.

Comments: It has suffered considerable declines in the past, although current populations may be stable. Like most rail species, seasonal changes in habitat use and movement (migration) are probably responses to water availability (flooding), weather patterns, predation pressure, and competition. Vocalizations during fall are apparently less common than spring and should not be used to assess migration chronology. More than 35 have been killed as a result of collisions with transmission towers. It is a game species in Kansas but is not often hunted.

Banding: 1,025 banded; no encounters. Most were banded at CBWA, but also in Wyandotte, Reno, Seward, Ellis, Douglas, Kingman, and Sedgwick counties.

References: Alderfer, 2006; Ball et al., 1995; Busby and Zimmerman, 2001; Conway, 1995; Conway et al., 1994; Janzen, 2002b, 2007; Parmelee et al., 1970; Tacha, 1975; Thompson and Ely, 1989.

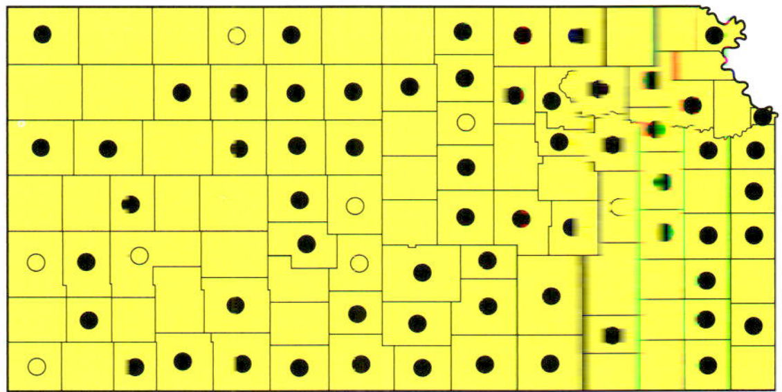

Sora

Porzana carolina (SORA)

Status: Common spring and fall transient statewide; rare summer resident and winter resident recorded in all months.

Habitat: Frequents wetlands and salt marshes, and even uses roadside ditches with tall cattails and prairie cordgrass. Often occurs in the same habitat as the Virginia Rail, in a variety of wetlands, including ephemeral ones.

Migration: Unusually early arrivals are 26 March (Barton Co.) and 31 March (Leavenworth Co.), but arrival is usually mid-April with most migration continuing into mid-May. Late dates for presumed transients include 24 May (Morton Co.) and 27 May (Douglas and Geary cos.). Individuals reported mid-June (Morton Co.) to mid-July may be transients, but some could be local breeders. The fall migration is poorly documented, but reports after early August are probably transients. Migration is definitely under way by 26 August (Leavenworth Co.) and probably peaks during late September and early October. Stragglers remain into early November and occasionally into the CBC period (December, McPherson Co.; 1 January, Seward Co.), and there is an unconfirmed report for 17 February (Haskell Co.).

Breeding: It is an irregular, sometimes abundant summer resident, but few nests have been observed. For nesting it prefers shallow water with emergent vegetation. During mid-July 1967 excessive rains raised the water level at CBWA by 30 inches, flooding thousands of acres of grassland. M. Schwilling noted that thousands of singing males occupied this area in late July and probably nested. R. Tacha reported an estimated 15–25 pairs at CBWA during summer 1975. Nesting probably occurs sporadically elsewhere when local conditions are favorable and has been confirmed or suspected nearly statewide. KBBAT reported only a single confirmed nesting, at Baker Wetlands (Douglas Co.). However, this may not be indicative of breeding in the state because KBBAT observers were restricted to standardized blocks, which rarely supported rail habitat. Eggs have been reported 20 July–21 August and chicks 12 August–5 July.

Comments: It is the most abundant and widely distributed rail in North America.

Banding: 89 banded; no encounters.

References: Alderfer, 2006; Ball et al., 1995; Busby and Zimmerman, 2001; Janzen, 2007; Melvin and Gibbs, 1996; Parmelee et al., 1970; Robbins et al., 2000; Tacha, 1975; Thompson and Ely, 1989; Thompson and Young, 1996; Young, 1993.

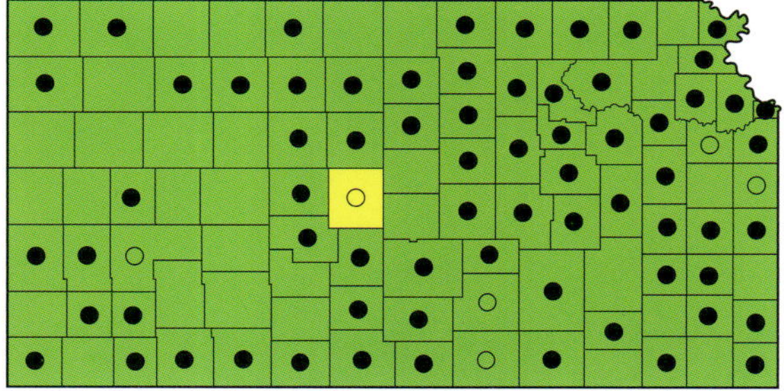

Purple Gallinule

Porphyrio martinica (PUGA)

© Judd Patterson

Status: Occasional summer visitant in the eastern half of the state.

Comments: The first state record was from Douglas County on 26 April 1896. There are specimen records for Sedgwick (KU 20091), Riley (KU 86134), and Douglas (KU 20091, 7777, 15100) counties, and a photo of a bird killed by a thunderstorm, 21 May 2003, Montgomery County (KBRC 2003-49); all others are sight records (Chase, Coffey, Harvey, Johnson, Linn, Lyon, and Wyandotte cos.). All but one record are from the spring to early summer, ranging from 4 April (Wyandotte Co.) to 17 June (Sedgwick Co.). A Purple Gallinule captured by a cat in Haysville (Sedgwick Co.) during the fall, late 1970s, was subsequently released in the "big ditch" in Wichita. The bird was displayed at a Wichita Audubon Society meeting prior to being released. It prefers emergent and floating vegetation and thus is less likely to be found in the west. It nests in southeastern Oklahoma and is known for its vagrancy, including nesting; thus, it may potentially wander into southeastern Kansas more frequently than records indicate.

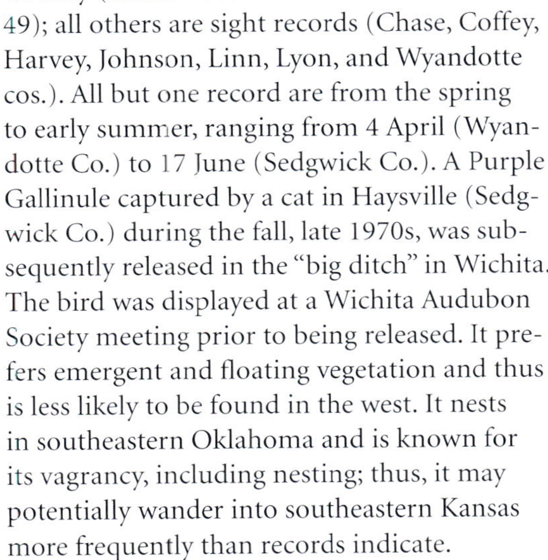

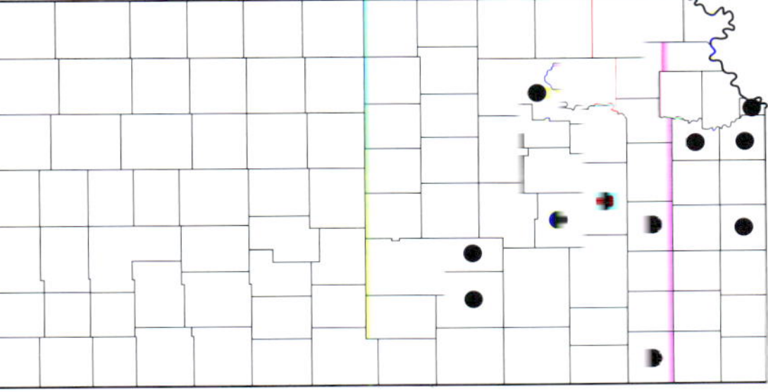

References: Carnes, 2004; Janzen, 2007; Otte, 2004; Thompson and Ely, 1989; West and Hess, 2002.

Common Moorhen

Gallinula chloropus (COMO)

© Judd Patterson

Status: Local, rare summer resident in the northeastern and central region.

Habitat: Wetlands, salt marshes, roadside ditches, and canals; usually associated with submerged or floating vegetation interspersed with emergent vegetation.

Migration: The earliest spring returns are 26 March and 6 April (both Barton Co.) and 7 April (Douglas Co.), but usual arrival is after mid-April with birds well on territory by early May. Fall departure usually begins in September (20 September, Grant Co.) and continues through mid-October with stragglers to 8 November (Barton Co.) and 10 November (Stafford Co.).

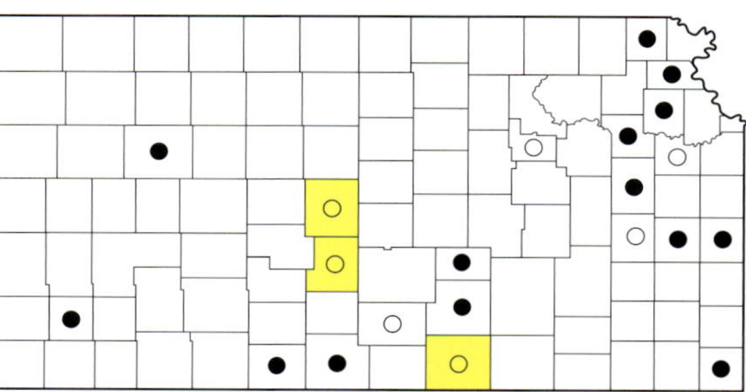

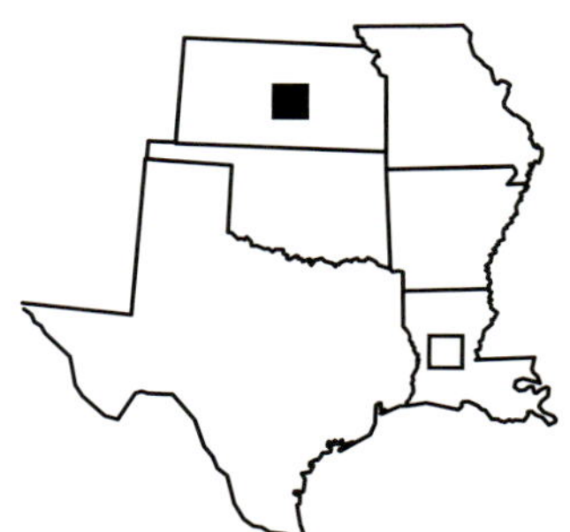

Breeding: It nests most consistently at CBWA and QNWR. KBBAT confirmed nesting at Baker Wetlands (Douglas Co.) and "probable" breeding at Benedictine Bottoms (Atchison Co.) and near Perry Reservoir (Jefferson Co.). Eggs have been reported 22 May–10 July and chicks 13 June–2 September; most young are seen during July and early August. Adults and young remained at SCW until 1 October. It is double-brooded, and females may abandon young after 3–4 weeks to start another brood.

Comments: It was formerly known as the Common (or Florida) Gallinule.

Banding: Three banded; one encounter. One banded near Avery Island, Louisiana, 6 November 1937, was captured by a cat in Coffey County, 2 June 1938. Oldest 7 months.

References: Bannor and Kiviat, 2002; Busby and Zimmerman, 2001; Parmelee et al., 1970; Thompson and Ely, 1989.

American Coot

Fulica americana (AMCO)

© Judd Patterson

Status: Common to abundant transient statewide; uncommon low-density winter resident; local summer resident.

Habitat: Freshwater marshes, brackish marshes, ponds, rivers, and reservoirs.

Migration: At CBWA the earliest arrivals are 7, 20, and 25 February with usual arrival in early or mid-March depending on water conditions. On 28 February 1962, 500 arrived at CBWA, but 100 of these succumbed to a 4-day storm with subzero temperatures. The next group arrived at CBWA on 8 March. In some years, thousands are present at CBWA by early March, with 5,000 reported on 27 March. Elsewhere migration usually begins in early March with flocks of hundreds at many small water bodies and thousands at larger reservoirs and marshes by mid-April. Most have departed by mid-May with small groups or singles remaining into early June (8 June, Ellis Co.; 21 June, Morton Co.). Fall arrival usually begins in September with peak numbers reported from October through November. Flocks of 1,000 are common at most of the larger reservoirs with higher numbers including 9 October (3,000, Douglas Co.), 21 October (10,000+, Cowley Co.), and 24 October (56,000, Barton Co.). Smaller numbers remain, usually on the larger reservoirs, through December and will remain through winter if water remains open.

Breeding: KBBAT demonstrated a wide nesting distribution within the state. Nesting was dependent upon wetlands with abundant emergent vegetation. Nests are usually placed on a mound of old cattails or reeds, usually anchored to new growth, and often placed in open areas. Largest nesting populations are found at CBWA and QNWR. Nesting elsewhere is more variable depending on local water and vegetation conditions. Eggs have been reported 1[illegible] May–18 July and chicks 25 May–17 August. It is sometimes double-brooded.

Comments: It is a game bird in Kansas but is infrequently hunted. Rangewide, populations appear stable.

See page 495 for banding information.

References: Alderfer, 2006; Brisbin and Mowbray, 2002; Busby and Zimmerman, 2001; Janzen, 2007; Parmelee et al., 1970; Seibel 1978; Thompson and Ely, 1989; Young, 199[illegible].

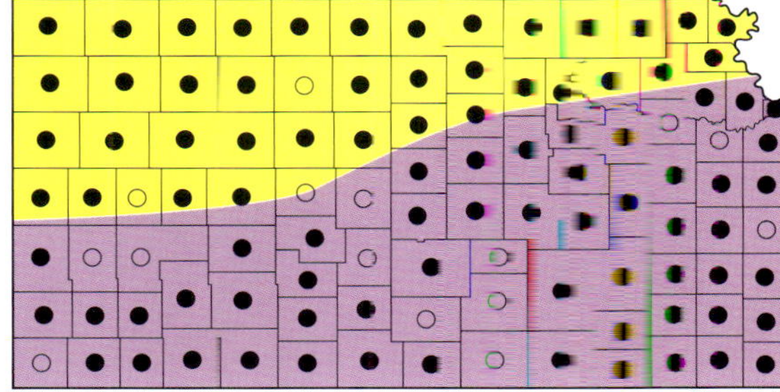

Sandhill Crane

Grus canadensis (SACR)

© Judd Patterson

Status: Common spring and fall transient in central and western Kansas, rare in the east, rare to uncommon local winter resident in south-central Kansas.

Habitat: Wetlands and marshes, from fresh to saline, for roosting and foraging, although most foraging is in a variety of agriculture fields.

Migration: Migration begins by late February or earlier. By early March when winds are favorable, a near constant movement can be seen overhead, and birds can be heard calling across the central part of the state. Among the high estimates are the following: 100,000 on 6 and 14 March (Meade Co.); 50,000, often "horizon to horizon" on 9 March (Rush Co.); 20,000 on 2 March (Stafford Co.); 3,000 on 6 March (Barton Co.); and "thousands overhead" on 4 March (Pawnee Co.). Late migrating flocks include 7 April (Osborne Co.), 4 May (Ford Co.), and 8 May (Barton Co., 30 birds; Cowley Co.). Birds remaining after this time period are likely sick or injured. The fall migration starts slowly with flocks by 14 July (Stafford Co.), 16 July (Finney Co.), 17 August (Sedgwick Co.), and 27 August. The migration peak is typically late October through mid-November and includes high estimates of 24,000 on 24 October, 300,000 on 30 October, and 90,000 on 1 November (all Stafford Co.); 50,000 on 11 November (Meade Co.); 14,000 on 26 October (Barton Co., arrived in one day); and "thousands" on 3 November (Rooks Co.). It has become an increasingly common winter resident from QNWR south through Barber (1,500–2,000, 10 January) and Meade (100,000, 8 December) counties, where birds remain from December through January. The highest CBC counts from QNWR include 48,000 (14 December 2006), 25,002 (19 December 1997), 20,016 (21 December 1995), and 10,505 (18 December 1998). Up to 8,050 were recorded in the Red Hills CBC (Barber Co.) on 2 January 2010, 4,700 on 3 January 2009, and 4,009 on 3 January 2004. The latest date recorded on a CBC is 16 January (Sawyer CBC, Pratt Co.).

Comments: Migration patterns have shifted, and, at least since the 1990s, much larger numbers are wintering in the south-central region more frequently.

See page 495 for banding information.

References: Alderfer, 2006; Cable et al., 1996; Cink and Boyd, 2004; Janzen, 2007; Seibel, 1978; Tacha et al., 1992; Thompson and Ely, 1989; Thompson and Young, 1996, 1998, 1999; Young et al., 2009; Young et al., 2010.

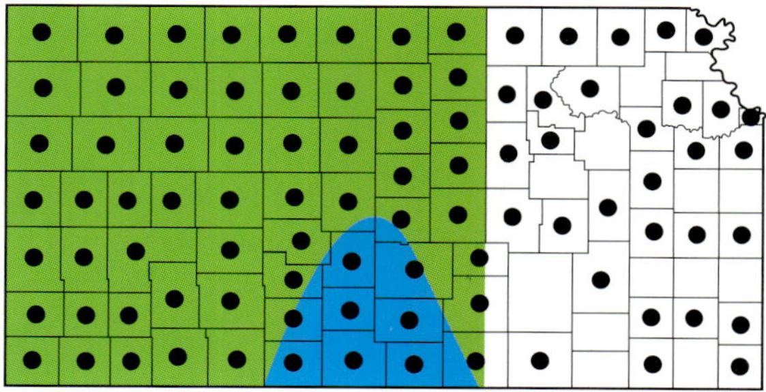

Common Crane

Grus grus (COMC)

© Dave Hutton

Status: Vagrant. This Old World species was photographed by M. Andersen and also seen by P. and H. Owens on 23 March 2008 (KBRC 2008-13) at QNWR, the first state record. This individual, like most records in North America, was associated with a flock of Sandhill Cranes. There are previous records from Alaska; Alberta, Quebec, and Saskatchewan; Phelps, Kearney, and Lincoln counties, Nebraska; Indiana; Texas; and New Mexico.

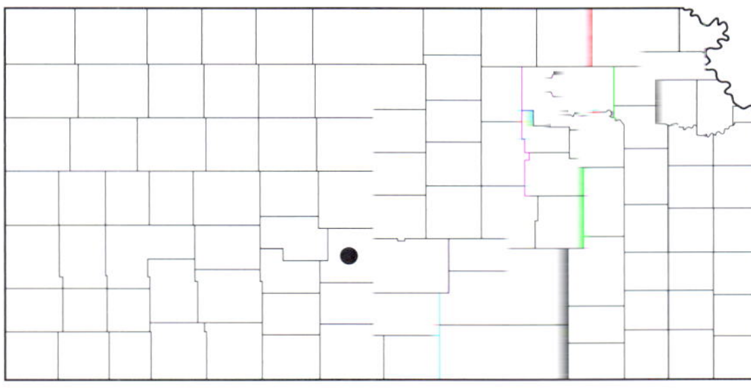

References: Alderfer, 2006; AOU, 1998; Otte, 2009; Tacha et al., 1981.

Whooping Crane

Grus americana (WHCR)

Status: Rare spring and fall transient, primarily in the central region; recorded in most of the state except the very western and eastern tiers of counties.

Habitat: A variety of wetlands and marshes from fresh to saline for foraging and roosting; forages in a variety of agriculture fields. Most records from CBWA and QNWR.

Migration: This species has been recorded from 10 February (QNWR) through 15 May and normally in fall from 5 October through 27 November (QNWR). M. Rader observed 76 at QNWR (highest total ever observed at one time in Kansas) on 1 April 2010. The first CBC record was in 1995 when three were recorded on the Lakin (Kearny Co.) count with 1,721 Sandhill Cranes (16 December). Single individuals also were reported on the QNWR CBC (18 December 1998) and CBWA CBC (20 December 1999). An immature bird that appeared with Sandhill Cranes at QNWR on 10 February 1987 had wintered in Oklahoma. During a cold spell, it retreated back to Oklahoma until 18 March. A number of radiotagged individuals have been followed across Kansas by U.S. Geological Survey researchers. A family left Aransas NWR on 11 April, made three stops in Kansas (near Kingman, Kingman Co., 12–16 April; QNWR, on 17 April; near Beloit, Mitchell Co., on 18 April), and arrived in Wood Buffalo Park about 3 May.

Comments: The Whooping Crane is an endangered species. The only sustaining wild population breeds in Woods Buffalo National Park, Northwest Territories, and adjacent areas of Alberta. They winter along the Gulf Coast, Aransas NWR, Texas. Kansans are fortunate to be geographically located in the center of the main migration corridor, and birds are often observed during both spring and fall migration. Traditional stopover sites such as QNWR and CBWA are of great importance, as are the extensive agriculture fields used to forage in central Kansas during migration.

Banding: None; 138 encounters (individuals with auxiliary markers, usually color bands): all had been banded as young birds in Northwest Territories. About half were reported in spring, 6–20 April (most, midmonth), and half in fall, 11 October–16 November, and singles on 6 and 29 December. The oldest was encountered 15 years, 7 months after banding.

References: Alderfer, 2006; Janzen, 2007; Lewis, 1995; Seibel, 1978; Thompson and Ely, 1989; Thompson and Young, 1996, 1999, 2000.

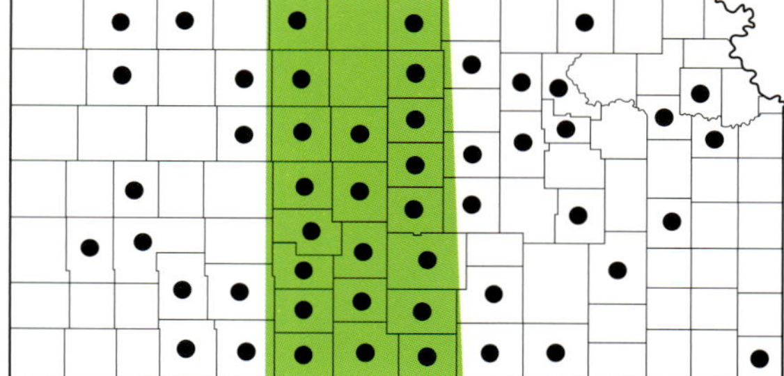

Black-bellied Plover

Pluvialis squatarola (BBPL)

Status: Uncommon spring and fall transient statewide. Greater numbers appear to pass through in spring, often during a short period of time, but they are also known to linger longer in the fall.

© Judd Patterson

Habitat: Marshy areas, sandbars on large rivers, mudflats along reservoirs and ponds, flooded fields, and, less frequently, low-mowed meadows and plowed fields.

Migration: First migratory individuals, usually adults, appear in April with peak numbers occurring during the last 2 weeks of May; stragglers remain through June. Extreme records include 9 April and 19 June, both from CBWA. Usually observed in small flocks of up to 20 individuals, but occasionally larger groups are encountered: 200+ on 17 May 1963 and 22 May 1967, and 500+ on 22 May 1963, all from CBWA; 100 at QNWR, 17–18 May 1997; 94 in Meade County, 17 May 1997; 60 at SCW, 19 May 2008; and 47 in Sedgwick County, 19 May 2008. Nonbreeding birds will occasionally linger into July (31 July, Morton Co.). Most fall migration is mid-August through early November with extreme dates of 2 August (Douglas Co.) and 2 December (Greenwood Co., C. Hall). During fall passage adults migrate first, followed by juveniles. Largest counts include 100+ on 22 August 1968 at CBWA; 36 on 28 August 2008 at SCW; 65 on 3 October 1991 (Harvey Co., G. Friesen); and 150 on 17 October (Stafford Co.).

Comments: A long-distance transient that migrates over a broad front, it is more common along coastal areas. Interestingly, immature birds may not migrate through the interior during the spring.

Banding: 15 banded; no encounters.

References: Janzen, 2007; Parmelee et al., 1969a; Paulson, 1995; Rice et al., 2001; Thompson and Ely, 1989; Young, 1993.

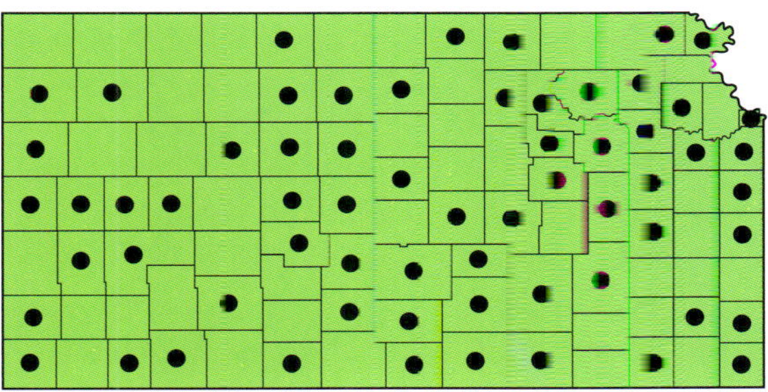

American Golden-Plover

Pluvialis dominica (AMGP)

Status: Uncommon to common spring transient, abundant spring transient in the Flint Hills; rare fall transient in the east and central region, becoming casual westward.

Habitat: Recently burned prairie, native grasslands, sod farms, marshy areas, wet meadows, and less frequently, sandbars on large rivers, and mudflats along ponds and reservoirs.

Migration: Typically, the first transients arrive in late March and are widespread by early April. Peak numbers occur from mid-April to mid-May, with stragglers remaining into early June. Extreme records include 29 February (two, Coffey Co.), 12 March (Linn Co.), and 24 June (Stafford Co.). Nonbreeding birds or failed breeders occasionally summer or return in July and August, but most southbound transients arrive in September and depart by late October, with stragglers (likely juveniles) to 16 November (Stafford Co.). Extreme fall dates include 5 July (SCW and CBWA) and 21 November (Melvern Reservoir, Osage Co.). Vagrants have been reported during the winter months from December through February.

Comments: Large numbers are commonly observed in the central and eastern regions, especially in Flint Hills during spring burning. Large concentrations include: 500, Lyon County, 12 April 1975; 50, Cowley County, 26 March 2000; 100, Chase County, 6 April 2008; several flocks totaling 187 individuals, Cowley County, 6 April 2008, with another 172 on 12 April in the same general vicinity; 200, Anderson County, 19 April 2009; up to 340 in burned pasture in Butler County, with another 173 in Elk County, and 56 in Greenwood County, 11 April 2009; 227 on burned upland surrounding SCW, 17 April 1989; and "several hundred" were observed in Cowley County on 5 May 2008 (B. Sandercock, pers. obs.). In 2010, T. Barksdale (pers. comm.) observed 361 on 16 April and 1,168 on 18 April from Texaco Hill (Chase Co.); and E. Young observed 1,284 on 22 April (Cowley Co.), 2,730 on 25 April (Butler Co.), and 960 on 14 May (Cowley Co.). During fall, large concentrations include 120 on 9 October 2008 (QNWR), 187 on 4 October 2009 (CBWA), 250 on 24 September 2002 (CBWA), and 542 on 27 September 1982 (CBWA).

Banding: 19 banded; no encounters.

References: Alderfer, 2006; Janzen, 2007; Johnson and Connors, 1996; Parmelee et al., 1969a; Rice et al., 2001; Seibel, 1978; Thompson and Ely, 1989; Young, 1993.

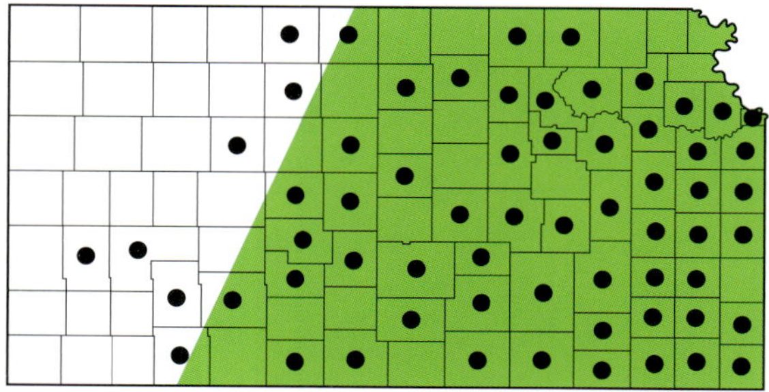

Snowy Plover

Charadrius alexandrinus (SNPL)

Status: Local summer resident in the central and southwestern regions; rare spring and fall transient statewide.

Habitat: Frequents salt marshes, mudflats, and sandbars along rivers.

Migration: First migratory individuals appear during mid-March, earliest record 13 March (QNWR), with an average date around 8 April. Median spring first arrivals include 26 March (Stafford Co.) and 3 April (Barton Co.). Nonbreeding birds have been recorded through 15 June (Douglas Co.). Peak numbers appear in May: 245 on 13 May 1995 and 200 observed on 19 May 2008 (both QNWR). The average fall departure date is 1 September with 18 October (Sedgwick Co.) the latest. Nonbreeding birds are observed as early as 3 July and 17 July (Sumner Co.) and 22 July (Sedgwick Co.). Peak numbers occur in August at QNWR: 300+ on 14 August 1995, 107 observed on 12 August 2004, and 125 on 14 August 2004.

Breeding: It breeds on white saline flats where its pale coloration makes it difficult to see. Colonies recorded in Kansas are 20 nests in Barton County (1969) and 75 pairs in Stafford County (1986), and pairs occasionally nest at nontraditional sites when conditions are favorable. Formerly nested along the Cimarron River in Clark and Meade counties. Such nestings are easily overlooked. Scrape preparation has been reported 28 April–12 June, eggs 24 April–26 July, chicks 18 June–8 August, and recently fledged young by 2 July. Johnston reported an apparent peak of egg-laying around 10 June.

Comments: The subspecies breeding in Kansas is *C. a. nivosus*, a threatened subspecies under the Endangered Species Act. It is a short- to medium-distance migrant that winters coastally along the Gulf Coast.

Banding: 800 banded; 27 encounters, 25 in-state. R. Boyd also observed two color-marked breeding birds from Kansas wintering along the Texas coast. Six of the in-state encounters were birds encountered 5 years to 7 years, 11 months after banding.

References: Alderfer, 2006; Boyd, 1972; Janzen, 2007; Johnston, 1964a; Page et al., 1995; Parmelee et al., 1969a; Rice et al., 200[illegible]; Seibel, 1978; Thompson and Ely, 1989; Young, 1993.

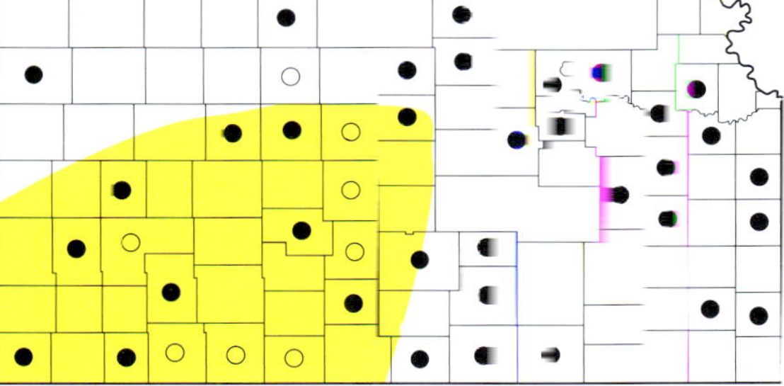

Wilson's Plover

Charadrius wilsonia (WIPL)

© David Seibel

Status: [Hypothetical]. Vagrant with three records. The first was observed by M. Stafford in Pittsburg (Crawford Co.) on 29 March 1995 (KBRC 95-18). The second was observed by R. Highgate and R. Plankenhorn at the Smoky Hills Audubon Pond (Saline Co.) on 1 May 2006 (KBRC 2006-09). The latest record was from QNWR where M. Rogers and P. Haddican observed one on 31 July 2007 (KBRC 2007-26).

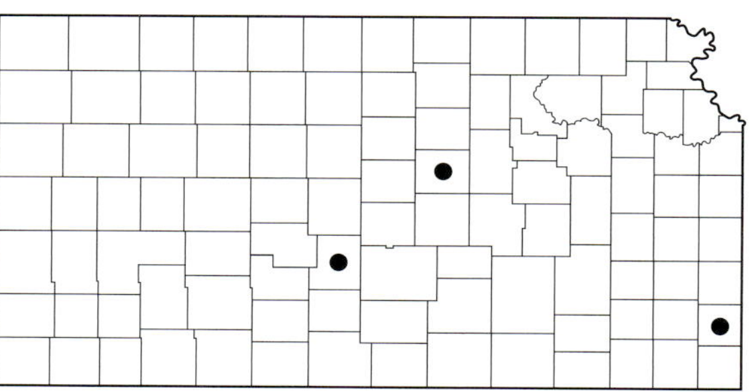

Comments: It usually is found along coastal areas from Virginia to Texas.

References: Alderfer, 2006; Corbat and Bergstrom, 2000; Otte, 2007, 2008; Pittman, 1996.

Semipalmated Plover

Charadrius semipalmatus (SEPL)

Status: Uncommon to common low-density transient statewide; rare summer straggler.

© David Seibel

Habitat: Marshes, sandy riverbanks, mudflats, and temporary water pools.

Migration: During spring it has been recorded from 22 March through 14 June (QNWR) and is most common the last week of April through mid-May with stragglers to 8 June (Barton Co.). High counts include 850 on 10 May and 500+ on 28 April (both at CBWA) and 500 on 7 May (Stafford Co.). Stragglers are often seen from mid-June through July at CBWA, QNWR, and SCW. Fall arrival begins in July (6 July, QNWR) and peaks in early August to mid-September with stragglers into October and exceptionally 6 November (QNWR) and 21 November (Osage Co.). High counts include 310 on 21 September 2008 (QNWR) and 100+ on 10 August (Barton Co.).

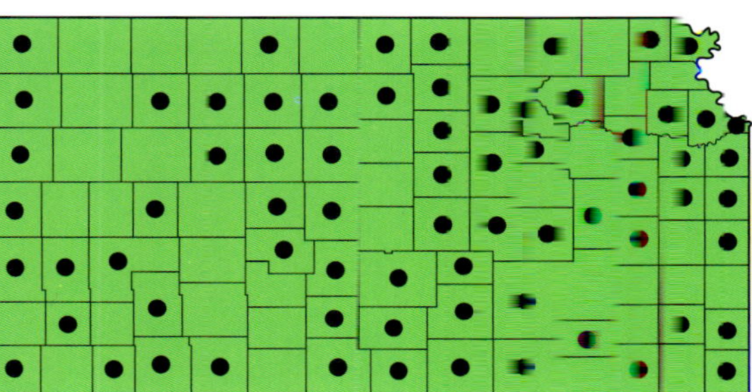

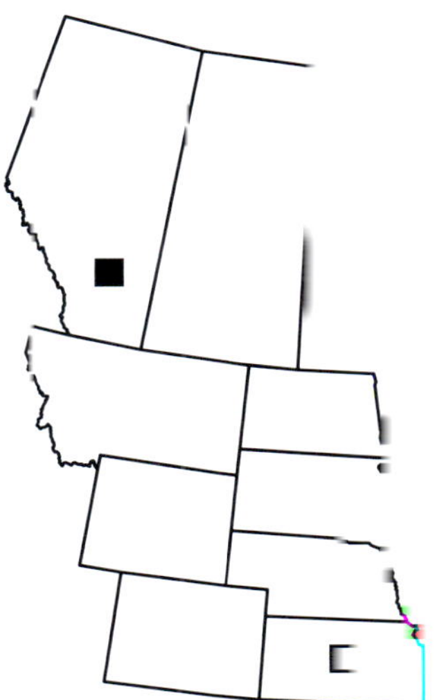

Comments: It is a medium- to long-distance migrant that often migrates alone or in small flocks. Numbers appear to be stable to increasing.

Banding: 779 banded; one encounter. One banded on 27 April 1968 was collected in Alberta on 1 August 1968.

References: Alderfer, 2006; Janzen, 2007; Nol and Blanken, 1999; Parmelee et al., 1969a; Rice et al., 2001; Seibel, 1978; Thompson and Ely, 1989; Young, 1993.

Piping Plover

Charadrius melodus (PIPL)

Status: Rare transient statewide; local summer resident in the northeastern region.

Habitat: Salt marshes, mudflats, and sandbars along rivers.

Migration: The earliest spring records are 21 March (SCW) and 22 March (Finney Co.) with a late date of 14 June (CBWA). High counts include 12 on 26 April and 11 on 27 April (both Stafford Co.). Most migration is mid-April through May. A few June reports are probably fall migrants. Fall departure typically begins about 7 July (Sumner Co.) and lasts through 1 October with stragglers reported to 22 October (Coffey Co.). Most pass through during August.

Breeding: Confirmed breeding is only along the Kansas River in Pottawatomie, Wabaunsee, and Shawnee counties. Breeding should be looked for in southwestern regions during wet years, because it historically bred about 60 miles south of Liberal near Hardesty, Oklahoma (Optima Reservoir now dry, 2010). It should also be looked for in Wichita near Least Tern nesting colonies. Eggs have been reported 11 June–17 July and a chick on 17 July. An egg set (unexamined) taken near Sterling (Rice Co.) and dated 2 June 1893 (MVZ 8118) may actually be of the Snowy Plover.

Comments: The Piping Plover is federally and state listed as an endangered species. All sightings should be made with care—some have been Snowy Plovers.

Banding: 13 banded; no encounters.

References: Alderfer, 2006; Boyd, 1991; Busby et al., 1997; Elliott-Smith and Haig, 2004; Janzen, 2007; Johnston, 1965; Parmelee et al., 1969a; Rice et al., 2001; Seibel, 1978; Thompson and Ely, 1989; Young, 1993.

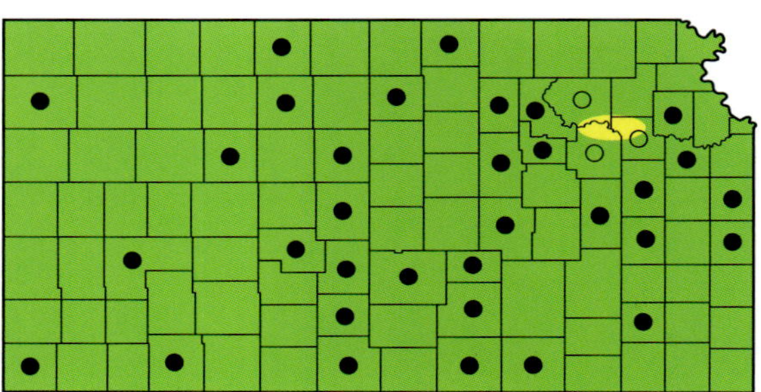

Killdeer

Charadrius vociferus (KILL)

Status: Common summer resident and transient; rare winter resident when open water is available.

Habitat: A variety of open environments including cropland, pasture, hay meadows, burned and unburned grasslands, wetlands, gravel roads, parking lots, rooftops, and river, reservoir, and pond edges with little or no vegetation present.

© David Seibel

Migration: First migratory individuals appear in mid-February to early March with peak numbers occurring from April through May. Median first arrival dates include 24 February (Lyon Co.), 1 March (Russell Co.), 3 March (Ellis Co.), and 6 March (Pawnee Co.). Among the high counts are 1,463 on 25 March (Sumner Co.) and 400 in burned prairie on 26 March (Cowley Co.). Breeding birds frequently begin to stage in July around wetlands, and it becomes difficult to distinguish migrating or nonbreeding individuals. In late July and early August numbers begin to increase with large concentrations observed through October with a sharp decline thereafter. High counts for fall include 2,000+ on 22 and 24 October (Barton Co.). Numbers vary from November through February, dependent on the amount of open water available. As wetlands, ponds, and lake shorelines freeze, remaining birds move to rivers, occasionally concentrating in loose flocks of 10–20 individuals. Few individuals actually winter in the state during most years.

Breeding: Breeding has been documented from all counties except five. The nest is a scrape on bare ground, often associated with gravel. Eggs have been reported 10 March–14 July (two peaks indicating two broods), downy chicks 16 April–30 July, and recently fledged young into September. From 2000 to 2002 a pair successfully nested on the gravel rooftop of the administrative building on the Cowley County Community College campus in Arkansas City.

Comments: It has responded well to anthropogenic changes in habitat, but whether or not this equates to population increases or declines, is unknown. For example, they adapt well to the use of gravel roads, but whether this results in a population source or sink has yet to be ascertained. During 11–13 April [illegible] large numbers were grounded in Rush, Riley, and Pottawatomie counties, and weak and dying birds were observed.

See page 495 for banding information.

References: Jackson and Jackson, 2000; Parmelee et al., 1969a; Thompson and Ely, 1989; Young, 1993.

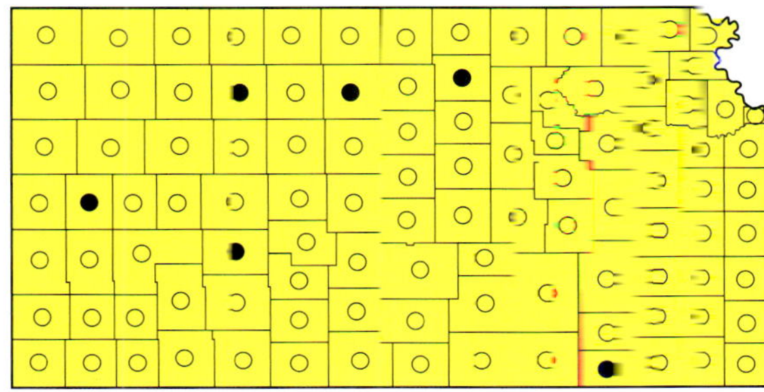

Mountain Plover

Charadrius montanus (MOUP)

Status: A rare transient in the west; rare local summer resident in the southwest from Morton County north to Greeley County; accidental in the east.

Habitat: A specialist of minimally vegetated areas in shortgrass prairie, prairie dog towns, and overgrazed areas of the High Plains; during migration uses wetlands and plowed fields.

Migration: Records range from 30 March (Butler Co., unlikely, see below) and 16 April (Dinsmore) to 6 November (both Morton Co.). Peak migration appears to be in April in the west but most reports from central and eastern Kansas are during spring, 23 March–25 May. T. Cable and others discuss its recent status in Morton County and suggest that the fall migration begins in midsummer and peaks by late August despite records extending into October. Numbers in fall are much larger than those reported in spring: 214 observed on 5 August 1998 (Greeley Co.), 200 on 17 September 1993 (Morton Co.), 100 on 19 September 1999 (Morton Co.), 300 near Ulysses (Grant Co.) on 1 October 2006, and 122 on 24 October 1993 (Kearny Co.).

Breeding: It is now reduced in numbers and quite rare. Birds nest in shortgrass prairie, burned fields with vegetation about 10 cm high, and plowed fields. Reports of nesting in 1993 by M. Schwilling triggered research by S. Fellows and B. Gress resulting in a compilation of 25 confirmed nestings since 1993. Eggs were laid 14 May–2 June, and flightless young were reported 21 May–20 July. They also summarized 54 instances of "possible" breeding.

Comments: It is a short-distance migrant that is currently being considered for listing as a threatened species under the Endangered Species Act. Only an estimated 8,000–10,000 individuals remain. The early record of 30 March (Butler Co.) is considered hypothetical. There are no recent confirmed records from the Flint Hills, and this early date coincides with spring burning and the migration of American Golden-Plovers, which can be quite abundant. Most American Golden-Plovers migrating at this time of year are in winter plumage and can be easily confused with Mountain Plovers.

See page 495 for banding information.

References: Cable et al., 1996; Ely, 1971; Fellows and Gress, 1999; Goss, 1891; Janzen, 2007; Knopf and Wunder, 2006; Ptacek and Schwilling, 1983; Rintoul, 2001, 2003; Rising and Kilgore, 1964; Shackford et al., 1999; Shane and Shane, 1995; Thompson and Ely, 1989; USFWS, 1999.

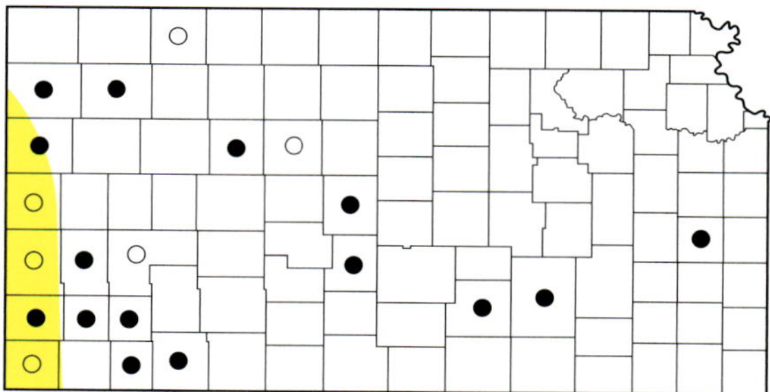

Black-necked Stilt

Himantopus mexicanus (BNST)

Status: Local summer resident in the central and southwestern regions, rare visitant elsewhere; numbers and nesting have increased substantially since the 1990s.

Habitat: Marshes, mudflats, shorelines, and even sewage and evaporation ponds with emergent vegetation when water is sparse.

Migration: The earliest arrival is 21 March (Barton Co., W. Hoffman) with the latest fall departure on 2 October (QNWR). It is most common from April through August. Median first arrivals include 18 April (Stafford Co.) and 20 April (Barton Co.). Confirmed migrants outside of the breeding areas are mostly from spring with dates ranging from 7 April (Russell Co.) to 24 May (SCW). The few fall dates outside breeding areas include 10 September (Linn Co.).

Breeding: Most of the breeding records are from central Kansas, primarily CBWA and QNWR, but since about 1999 the frequency of breeding in the southwest has increased dramatically. They may have bred prior to the first confirmed nesting in the 1960s; a hundred years ago N. Goss stated: "Without doubt the birds occasionally breed in southwestern Kansas." Nesting at CBWA was suspected in the mid-1960s (L. Nossaman) but was not documented until 1974 (M. Schwilling). It has nested there most years since 1978. Unsuccessful nesting was reported from QNWR in 1976 and has been successful most years since 1978. Eggs have been reported 21 May–16 July, chicks 13 June–23 July, and flying young by 10 August.

Comments: It is a short- to medium-distance migrant that winters along coastal areas in the southern United States through Central America.

Banding: One banded; no encounters.

References: Alderfer, 2006; Busby and Zimmerman, 2001; Goss, 1886; Robinson et al., 1999; Thompson and Ely, 1989.

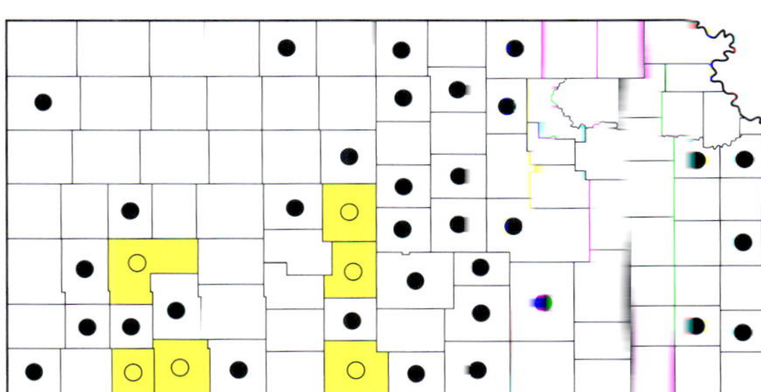

American Avocet

Recurvirostra americana (AMAV)

Status: Common transient and summer resident in western half of the state; uncommon to rare transient from the Flint Hills eastward.

Habitat: Marshes, mudflats, ponds, and shorelines for foraging and resting.

Migration: Most avocets arrive around 1 April and depart by the end of October. Extreme dates are 12 March (Neosho Co.) and 27 December (Barton Co.). The median first arrival date for Barton County is 22 March but is usually about mid-April elsewhere. Outside known breeding areas migration is 12 March (Neosho Co.) to 29 May (Sumner Co.). High counts include 1,300 on 2 May and 1,000 on 22 April (both Barton Co.), 450 on 22 April (Stafford Co.), and 75 on 10 April (Meade Co.). The fall migration begins by at least 7 July (31 individuals, Ellis Co.) and 10 July (SCW) and peaks by early October with small numbers into November. High counts include 2,000 on 14 July and 1,090 on 29 September (both Barton Co.). Late fall dates outside known breeding areas include 14 November (Sedgwick Co.), 16 November (Lyon Co.), and 21 November (Osborne Co.). There are two December records from Barton County.

Breeding: Most breeding takes place at CBWA and QNWR in the central region, extending into the Playa Lake region in the southwest. Both the amount and extent of nesting have increased since the 1950s. Nest-building has been reported on 1 June, eggs 2 May–29 July, and chicks 25 May (day old, Finney Co.).

Comments: On occasion avocets can be observed floating in deep water of reservoirs where they feed in similar fashion to phalaropes, or appear to be resting. It is a short- to medium-distance migrant. However, migration patterns are relatively unstudied compared to other shorebirds.

See page 495 for banding information.

References: Busby and Zimmerman, 2001; Robinson et al., 1997; Thompson and Ely, 1989.

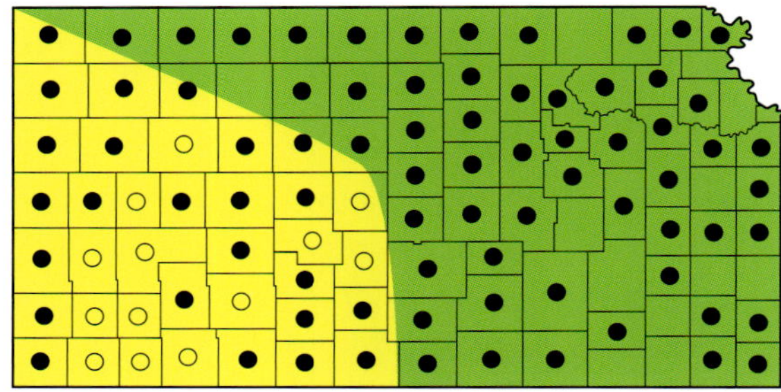

Spotted Sandpiper

Actitis macularius (SPSA)

Status: Common spring and fall transient, rare summer resident throughout.

Habitat: Reservoirs, ponds, streams, rivers, ephemeral pools, and marshes; one of the few sandpipers that occurs along woodland streams.

Migration: The first spring arrivals appear during mid- and late March (earliest, 19 March), but more often by mid-April. Median earliest arrivals include 30 April (Ellis Co.) and 3 May (Russell and Meade cos). Peak migration is early and mid-May with stragglers through 15 June (CBWA). The median spring departure in Ellis County is 23 May. The return movement begins by 3 July (Sumner Co.) and peaks mid-August through mid-September, with stragglers through 4 November (Sedgwick Co.). Median fall arrival in Ellis County is 10 July and median fall departures include 6 September (Ellis Co.) and 17 September (Russell Co.). There are a few midwinter records: 15 December 2001 on the Sawyer CBC (Pratt Co.); 18 December 2004 (Manhattan CBC, Riley Co.); 20 December (Cowley Co.); and one wintered at the Riverton Dam (Cherokee Co.) from December through 6 February.

Breeding: It is a low-density breeder in a variety of wetlands and shores of streams and reservoirs. Suspected breeding has been reported from about 30 counties but confirmation is rarely achieved. Eggs have been reported 11–27 June, dependent young 16 June–4 August, and flying young by 28 July.

Comments: It is one of the most widespread breeding sandpipers in North America. It is also one of the few shorebird species that have reversed sex roles, where the males are responsible for the parental role and females take a more active role in courtship. It typically occurs singly or in small, dispersed groups, rarely in actual flocks. D. Parmelee reported a total of 100+ in small groups at CBWA on 22 May and 12 birds on 5 September. M. Thompson and E. Young observed a small flock flying into a hedgerow at SCW when a severe thunderstorm approached as it started to pour down small hail.

Banding: 275 banded; no encounters.

References: Alderfer, 2006; Busby and Zimmerman, 2001; Cink and Boyd, 2002, 2005; Janzen, 2007; Oring et al., 1997; Parmelee et al., 1969b; Rice et al., 2001; Seibel, 1978; Thompson and Ely, 1989; Young, 1993.

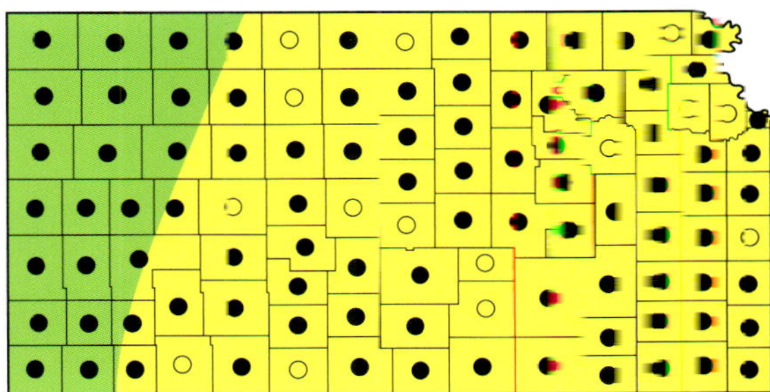

Solitary Sandpiper

Tringa solitaria (SOSA)

Status: Common low-density spring and fall transient statewide; casual summer visitant.

Habitat: Marshes, both fresh and saline, reservoir shores, vegetated river bars, woodland pools, ephemeral pools, and meadows; also sewage lagoons and cattle feedlots.

Migration: Early arrival is in late March with most migration from mid-April through May. Median arrival for Ellis County is 30 April; median departure 16 May. The earliest arrival date is 20 March (Sumner Co.), and late dates include 23 June (Sumner Co.) and 29 June (Lane Co.). The largest concentrations reported are 14 on 11 May and 16 on 9 August (both Barton Co.). The southward migration usually begins by mid-July (earliest 1 July, Trego Co.) and peaks in late August, with most gone by mid-September and with stragglers through 27 October (Barton Co.).

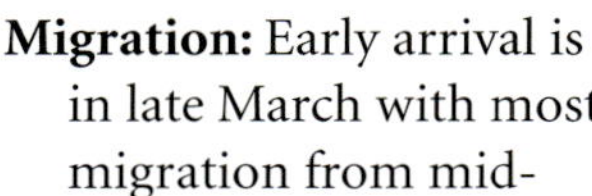

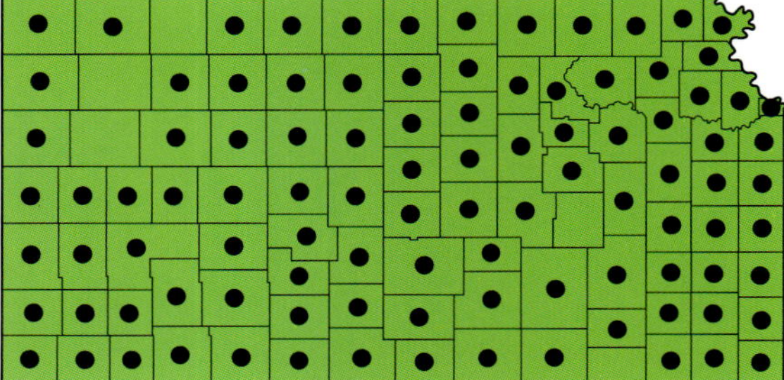

Comments: As the name implies, it is largely a solitary species that only occasionally can be found in true flocks in Kansas. Surprisingly little is known about this species when compared to other North American shorebirds, especially on its breeding grounds.

Banding: 41 banded; no encounters.

References: Janzen, 2007; Moskoff, 1995; Parmelee et al., 1969b; Rice et al., 2001; Seibel, 1978; Thompson and Ely, 1989; Young, 1993.

Spotted Redshank

Tringa erythropus (SPRE)

© Aurélien Audevard

Status: Accidental.

Habitat: Mudflats.

Comments: The only record is an individual in breeding plumage found by D. LaShelle at the Lower Ferguson Marsh, Perry Reservoir (Jefferson Co.), on 1 May 1988. He and numerous others observed the bird on several occasions through 8 May and both photographs and voice recordings were made. It was last seen on 8 May by B. and W. Rose when a hailstorm struck the area and the bird was seen fleeing into the deciduous trees surrounding the marsh. It normally occurs in northern Eurasia and is accidental along both the North Atlantic and North Pacific coasts of North America. This is one of the few interior records.

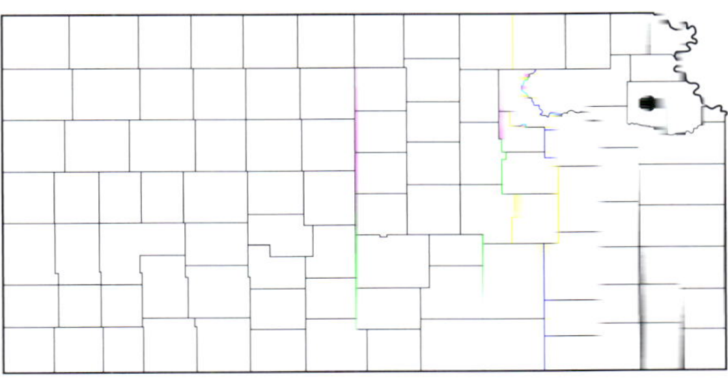

References: Alderfer, 2006; LaShelle, 1988.

Greater Yellowlegs

Tringa melanoleuca (GRYE)

Status: Common spring and fall transient statewide, rare summer and winter visitant; recorded in all months.

Habitat: A variety of wetlands and marshes from fresh to saline, rivers, shorelines of ponds and reservoirs, and ephemeral pools; often wades up to its belly while feeding.

Migration: It is one of the earliest shorebirds to arrive, usually around 21 March, with early records from 17 January (Cowley Co.) and 25 January (Riley Co.) to 8 March (Stafford Co.), but some of these individuals may have overwintered. Median first arrivals include 14 March (Barton Co.) and 5 April (Ellis Co.). Statewide, most migration is during the first 3 weeks of April with most departed by the end of April but with stragglers through 29 June (Stafford Co.). The median late spring departure for Ellis County is 15 May. Large counts include 5,000–6,000 on 31 March and 340 on 14 April (both Barton Co.). There are numerous midsummer reports statewide. The southward migration begins by 7 July (Cowley and Douglas cos.), overlapping the northward movement during some years. The fall migration is well under way by early August, peaks in September, and declines rapidly in early October. Late dates away from areas of concentration include 22 October (Ellis Co.) and 9 November (Trego Co.). Singles and small groups (to 12 individuals) have been reported from early November into the CBC period, 18–26 December (Cowley Co.), 20 December (12, Barton Co.), 21 December (Butler Co.), 22 December (Sumner Co.), 2 January (Barber Co.), and 3 January (Coffey Co.), and some probably overwinter during mild winters. Up to 29 were counted on the QNWR CBC during 14 December 2004, an unusually large number so late in the season.

Comments: Birds recorded during the summer may be first-year nonbreeding birds that move no farther north their first season. Also, shorebirds that nested unsuccessfully or failed to breed sometimes return south soon after reaching the breeding grounds. This may account for the unusual numbers of shorebirds found in Kansas in July and August. It feeds on small invertebrates and fish and one even ate a large frog.

Banding: 38 banded; no encounters.

References: Cink and Boyd, 2005; Elphick and Tibbitts, 1998; Janzen, 2007; Parmelee et al., 1969b; Rakestraw, 1995; Rice et al., 2001; Seibel, 1978; Thompson and Ely, 1989; Thompson and Young, 2000; Young, 1993.

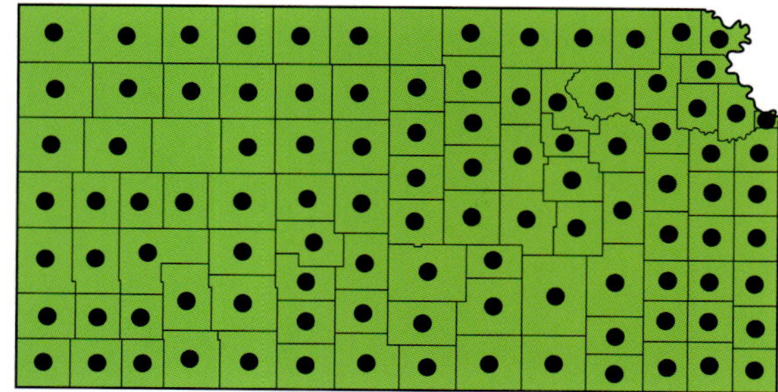

Willet

Tringa semipalmata (WILL)

© David Seibel

Status: Uncommon spring and fall transient statewide, though it can be locally common; rare summer visitant.

Habitat: Marshes, both fresh and saline, reservoir shores, ponds, and ephemeral pools.

Migration: Spring migration is typically about 20 April to mid-May with stragglers into early June (extreme dates, 5 April–16 June). Median first arrivals include 16 April (Barton Co.) and 30 April (Ellis Co.). High counts include 300 on 3 May and 200+ on 30 April (both Barton Co.), 60 on 25 April (Russell Co.), 41 on 28 April (SCW), and 30+ on 30 April (Butler Co.). There are scattered records throughout the summer, and June birds are probably vagrants from breeding areas in the sand hills of Nebraska; there is no evidence of breeding in Kansas. The fall migration begins early, probably by late June, and birds are widespread by late July with most migration during August. High counts include 40 on 18 July (Russell Co.). There are few records after early September but with late dates to 16 October (Stafford Co.), 20 October (Meade Co.), and 12 November (Sedgwick Co.). An extraordinary sighting is one with three Killdeer on the QNWR CBC on 17 December 1999.

Comments: It is a large and a striking shorebird in flight. It appears to be more common in the south-central region in the spring than during the fall, but data are too few to demonstrate a statewide pattern. There are two disjunct breeding populations that may be recognized as distinct species in the near future. The inland or western subspecies (*T. s. inornata*) migrates through Kansas and breeds in nearby Nebraska. There is no physical evidence (specimen, photograph, video, voice recordings, etc.) to indicate that the eastern subspecies (*T. s. semipalmata*) ever ventures into the interior of North America, but it could be easily overlooked. Plumage and size differences are subtle, and, though the vocalizations differ, this can be difficult to perceive and is rarely helpful outside the breeding range.

Banding: 43 banded; no encounters.

References: Alderfer, 2006; Janzen, 2007; Lowther et al., 2001; O'Brien et al., 2006; Parmelee et al., 1969b; Rice et al., 2001; Seibel, 1978; Thompson and Ely, 1989; Thompson and Young, 2000; Young, 1993.

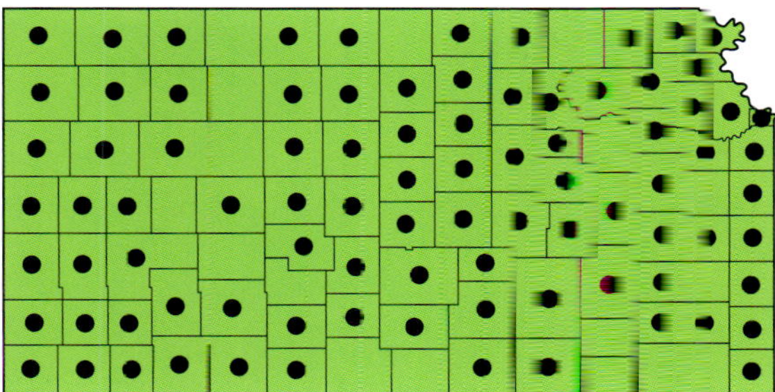

Lesser Yellowlegs

Tringa flavipes (LEYE)

© David Seibel

Status: Common spring and fall transient statewide; casual summer visitant and occasional winter visitant.

Habitat: A variety of wetlands and marshes from fresh to saline, rivers, shorelines of ponds and reservoirs, and ephemeral pools; often wades up to its belly while feeding.

Migration: It is an early migrant, usually arriving in early March, reaches a peak during April and is largely gone by late May except for stragglers into early June. Extreme spring dates are 6 February (Miami Co.) and 28 June (Sumner Co.). Median first arrival dates include 12 March (Barton Co.) and 20 April (Ellis Co.); median spring departure in Ellis County is 10 May. High counts include 850 on 10 May (reduced to 36 two days later; Barton Co.) and "several hundred" on 26 April (Linn Co.). Southbound migrants usually arrive around 12 July but can occur much earlier, as in 1968 when 2,000+ appeared on 28 June (CBWA) and on 1 July (Sumner Co.). Peak migration occurs during August and September with good numbers still present during October (70 at SCW on 15 October) and stragglers through early December. Ten purported Lessers were tallied on the 17 December 1973 CBC at QNWR, and two were present on 23 December 2006 in Arkansas City, Cowley County.

Comments: The largest concentrations pass through the interior of North America in spring and fall, making Kansas wetlands prime feeding sites. Migration in July is dominated by adults, whereas most juveniles don't usually arrive until August. Juveniles can migrate up to 6 weeks later than adults.

Banding: 1,883 banded; three encounters (all banded in fall). One was recovered in central Mexico, one in Suriname, and one in Stephens County in south-central Oklahoma.

References: Cink and Boyd, 2007; Parmelee et al., 1969b; Rice et al., 2001; Seibel, 1978; Thompson and Ely, 1989; Tibbitts and Moskoff, 1999; Young, 1993.

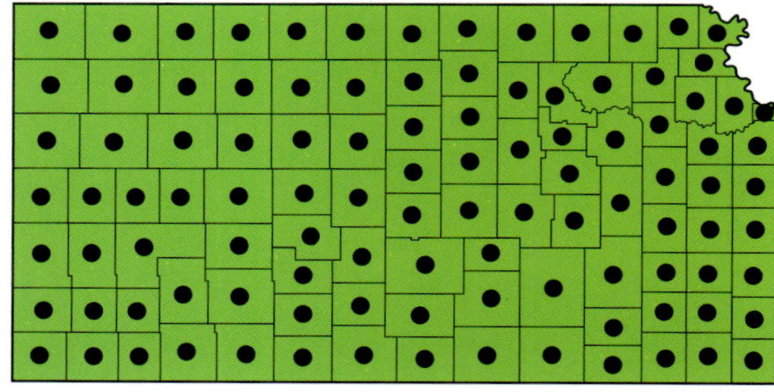

Upland Sandpiper

Bartramia longicauda (UPSA)

Status: Common summer resident in the eastern half of the state, less common westward; common spring and fall transient statewide.

Habitat: Upland prairies, sod farms, and occasionally mudflats. During spring migration, burned pastures are preferred; during fall, recently hayed fields and recently worked cropland are used; sod farms are used during both seasons.

Migration: The earliest recorded arrival date is 6 March, but most birds arrive around 4 April in south-central Kansas, and around 17 April in the northeast. Median first arrivals include 9 April (Cowley and Lyon cos.), 23 April (Barton Co.), and 3 May (Ellis Co.). Arrival at Konza Prairie is in early April. A large nocturnal migration was noted on 7 May (Ellsworth Co.). Large numbers are frequently encountered in burned prairie, especially in the central and Flint Hills regions where hundreds to thousands can be observed. M. Thompson and E. Young observed more than 1,000 in a recently burned field in Sumner County on 19 April 1988. E. Young observed 256 in a burned Flint Hills pasture in Butler County on 11 April 2009, 350 on 22 April 2010 and 480 on 4 May 2010 (Cowley Co.), and 709 on 25 April 2010 (Butler Co.). Birds begin the southward journey in early July, with most birds departing by late August. Typical high numbers are "thousands" on 3 August (southwestern Kansas, S. Seltman), "hundreds" on 22 July (Pawnee Co.), "many flocks" on 5 September (Cowley Co.), "abundant" on 15 August (Seward Co.), and 350 on 9 August 1997 (Stafford Co.). The latest departure dates are 4 October (Pawnee Co.) and 13 October (Shawnee Co.), both highly unusual.

Breeding: Numbers and breeding distribution have probably changed since presettlement days with changes in the prairie ecosystem but these changes have not been well documented. The nest is typically a depression on the ground under a clump of grass. Eggs have been reported 6 May–12 June, small chicks 5–30 June, and nearly fledged young 29 June through August. On Konza Prairie peak nesting begins the last half of May.

Comments: A long-distance migrant that winters in South America where it spends as much as 8 months of the year.

See page 496 for banding information.

References: Alderfer, 2006; Bowen, 19[illegible]; Goering, 1964; Houston and Bowen, 2001; Jensen, 2007; Parmelee et al., 1969a; Seibel, 1978; Thompson and Ely, 1989; Young, 1993; Zimmerman, 1987, 1993.

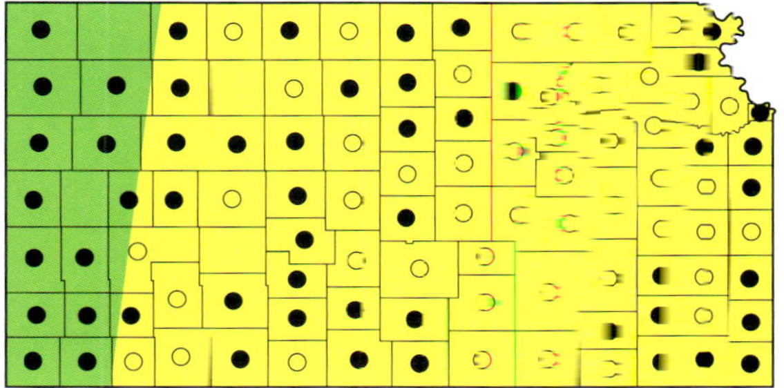

Eskimo Curlew

Numenius borealis (ESCU)

Specimens from the Kansas Museum of Natural History

Status: Probably extinct. Formerly bred in Canada, migrating north through the interior United States in the spring, and offshore along the East Coast in fall (similar to American Golden-Plover). During the 1800s and early 1900s, it was recorded in the spring from March through June, and in September during the fall. It was an abundant migrant, primarily through eastern Kansas, where it was hunted in Sedgwick, Douglas, Lyon, and Woodson counties, with additional records from Riley and Dickinson counties. The last bird taken in Kansas was in 1902. The last Kansas sighting (1982) came from CBWA, Barton County, in central Kansas. However, E. Martinez (pers. comm.) indicated in 2008 that he was uncertain of his sighting, and it may have been another curlew species.

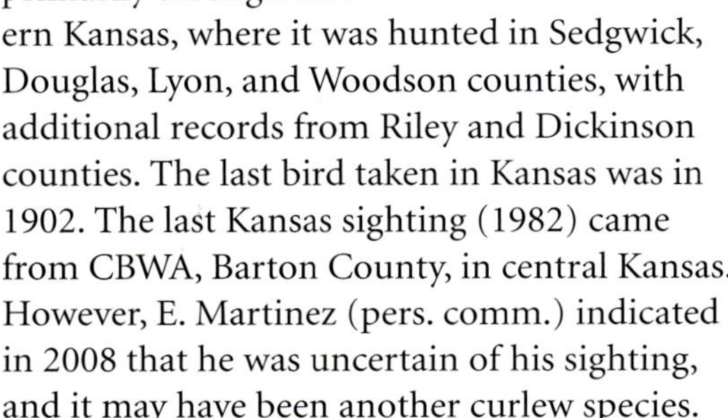

Habitat: Almost exclusively an upland species in the Great Plains. In spring, it preferred burned prairies and newly plowed fields, roosting in bare pastures.

Comments: It was known to feed primarily on insects and berries. Apparently, it followed an elliptical migration and associated with American Golden-Plovers during migration. It also appeared to be both a diurnal and nocturnal migrant. If not extinct, fewer than 100 individuals likely remain. It closely resembles the Old World Little Curlew (*Numenius minutus*), and any sighting should be verified. The most recent sight records for states along the central flyway include 8 birds east of Hastings, Nebraska, on 18 April 1926; 4 on 18 April 1948 in Osage County, Oklahoma; and 23 observed in 1981 in Texas. From 1945 to 1985 they were reported in 23 different years. The latest unconfirmed sightings from Canada were in mid-May 1996. No birds were found in searches conducted on South America wintering grounds in 1992–1993, and the last known specimen was taken in Barbados in 1963. Coordinated efforts since the mid-1980s to locate birds have failed, although isolated unconfirmed reports continue. In Kansas, if the species is extant, the most likely location to find it would be the Flint Hills during the annual spring burning season from March through April. There is a fossil record dating from the Pleistocene in McPherson County.

References: Baumgartner and Baumgartner, 1992; Bent, 1929; Blanco et al., 1993; Bond, 1965; Chandler, 1987; Collins et al., 1995; Ely, 1985; Galbreath, 1955; Gill et al., 1998; Gollop, 1988; Gollop et al., 1986; Goss, 1886; Janzen, 2007; Johnston, 1960, 1965; Sutton, 1967; Swenk, 1926; Thompson and Ely, 1989; Tordoff, 1956; Waldon, 1996.

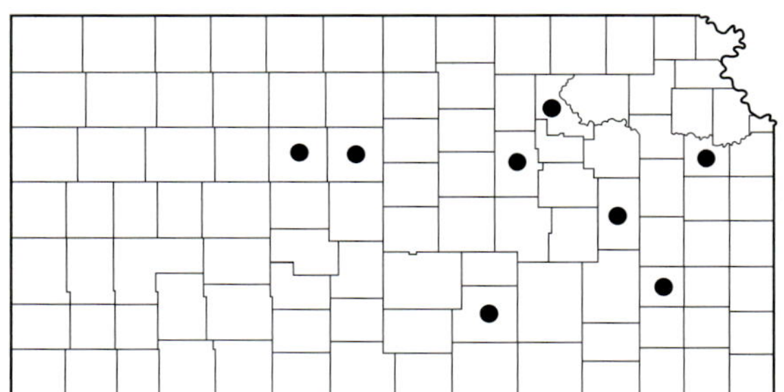

Whimbrel

Numenius phaeopus (WHIM)

Status: Rare spring and fall transient statewide.

Habitat: A variety of wetlands and marshes from fresh to saline, shorelines of ponds and reservoirs, ephemeral pools, and occasionally in upland areas.

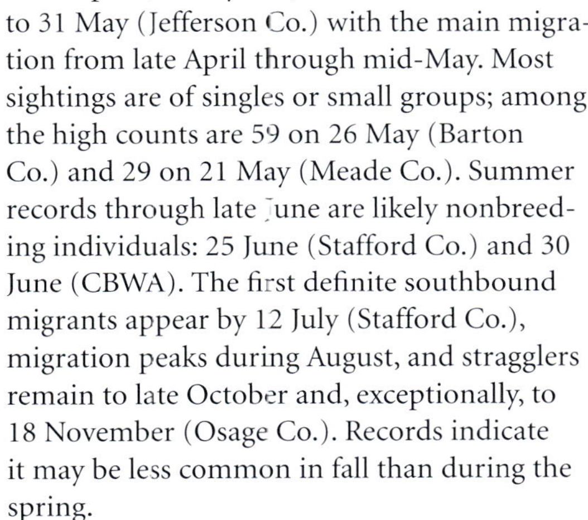

Migration: Most reports are from Barton and Stafford counties. Spring migration dates are 3 April (Finney Co.) to 31 May (Jefferson Co.) with the main migration from late April through mid-May. Most sightings are of singles or small groups; among the high counts are 59 on 26 May (Barton Co.) and 29 on 21 May (Meade Co.). Summer records through late June are likely nonbreeding individuals: 25 June (Stafford Co.) and 30 June (CBWA). The first definite southbound migrants appear by 12 July (Stafford Co.), migration peaks during August, and stragglers remain to late October and, exceptionally, to 18 November (Osage Co.). Records indicate it may be less common in fall than during the spring.

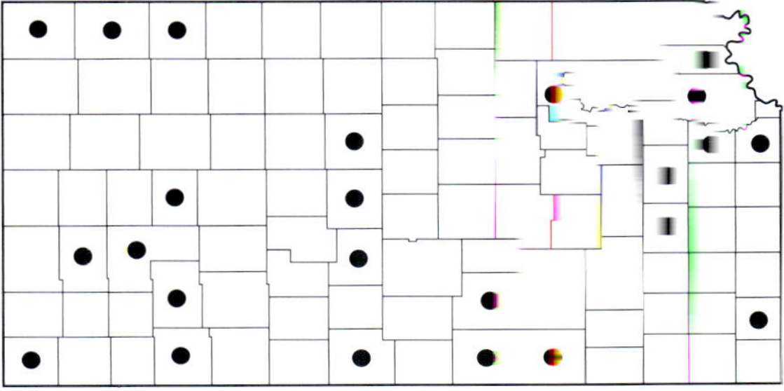

Comments: Although occasionally reported since presettlement days, the first fully documented record is a specimen taken 22 May 1963 at CBWA by H. A. Stephens (ESU B1138). Surprisingly few data exist on the migration of this large shorebird.

References: Janzen, 2007; Parmelee et al., 1969a; Seibel, 1978; Skeel and Mallory, 1996; Thompson and Ely, 1989; Young, 1993.

Long-billed Curlew

Numenius americanus (LBCU)

© David Seibel

Status: Uncommon to common spring and fall transient in western half of the state; rare in the east; rare breeder in the southwest; casual elsewhere in summer.

Habitat: During migration in alfalfa, wheat, recently plowed corn and sorghum fields, and fallow fields; also uses grasslands and prairie dog towns. It is infrequently found on the drier upland areas around CBWA, and QNWR, occasionally along mudflats. For nesting prefers upland shortgrass and sand-sage prairies.

Migration: The earliest recorded arrival date is 21 March (Finney and Kearney cos.), and most depart by 11 June (Sedgwick Co.). One was observed in Cowley County on 26 March (E. Young). Peak migration occurs from the last week of March through the third week of April. The highest counts include 2,838 in 1 day (31 March, T. and S. Shane), 1,144 on 29 March (M. Osterbuhr, T. and S. Shane), 800 on 1 April, 475 on 28 March (M. Osterbuhr, T. and S. Shane), and flocks of 400 and 125 during "late March" all from Finney County; and 110 on 3 April (Seward Co.). There are records for all summer months. Fall migration has been recorded from 21 August to 25 September (CBWA), with an extreme date of 11 November (Morton Co.).

Breeding: During the late 19th century it summered (and probably nested) eastward to Ellis County and probably Riley County, but all confirmed modern records are from Morton, Finney, and Stanton counties. Breeding is also suspected to occur (or have occurred) in Greeley, Hamilton, Logan, Rush, Barton, and Sherman counties. Nests are typically located in arid grasslands usually remote from water. Few data are available for Kansas breeding populations and reproductive biology. Birds are territorial by early May (Morton Co.). Eggs have been reported during June, chicks 22 May–27 June, and recently fledged young by 9 June.

Comments: For this Great Plains endemic, western Kansas serves as an important migration stopover site along the Arkansas River valley in Finney and Kearny counties. Ongoing studies by T. and S. Shane suggest that 5–20 percent of the world population uses these sandhill areas as a stopover point during spring. Flocks forage in irrigated fields and fly to shortgrass areas north of the river to roost.

References: Alderfer, 2006; Busby and Zimmerman, 2001; Dugger and Dugger, 2002; Fellows and Jones, 2009; Morrison et al., 2000; Parmelee et al., 1969a; Shane, 2005; Thompson and Ely, 1989; Tordoff, 1956.

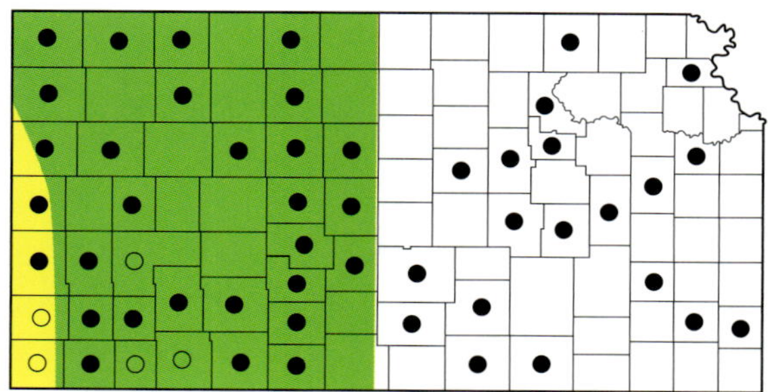

Hudsonian Godwit

Limosa haemastica (HUGO)

Status: Uncommon spring transient in the central region, rare to uncommon elsewhere; rare fall transient.

Habitat: A variety of wetlands and marshes from fresh to saline; occasionally on river mudflats.

Migration: Its northward migration is largely through the interior of the United States, beginning as early as 6 April (Sedgwick Co.) with normal departure by 28 May (Reno Co.) and a late record of 30 June (CBWA). Peak migration occurs from the last 2 weeks of April through May. High counts during the 1960s include 400 on 28 April and 300+ on 23 April; recent counts have exceeded 1,000 individuals on at least five occasions (13–28 April) including 3,000–5,000 on 28 April (all at CBWA, Barton Co.). Elsewhere a sighting of 50 birds would be noteworthy. Most of the few fall records are from CBWA during 19 August–26 September (KU 49855, 49856). Additional sightings (one to six individuals) are 15 July–2 October (an extremely late date, if correct).

Comments: M. Thompson and E. Young, on numerous occasions during spring migration, have observed large concentrations of birds flying over SCW at low altitude, never landing, and continuing their migration to the north. On 12 May 2009, they observed two flocks of 11 and 36 feeding in mudflats at SCW. A thunderstorm occurred in the area, and E. Young continued to survey the area afterwards. Three additional flocks (250, 35, and 20 individuals) were observed heading north over upland and cropland just east of the marsh. Current population size is thought to be stable, but monitoring data are lacking. C. Elphick and J. Klema consider it as one of the most vulnerable shorebird species because of a small global population, fragmented breeding distribution, and high potential for a catastrophic event during the nonbreeding season. Relatively little is known of its biology. In fall birds congregate around James Bay and the Quill Lakes area in Canada. From James Bay they swing eastward out over the Atlantic Ocean enroute to their wintering grounds in southern South America. The western birds from the Quill Lakes area of Saskatchewan possibly take different and currently unknown routes.

Banding: 37 banded; no encounters.

References: Alderfer, 2006; Elphick and Klima, 2002; Helmers, 1991; Janzen, 2007; Morrison et al., 1994; Parmelee et al., 1969; Rice et al., 2001; Seibel, 1978; Thompson and Ely, 1989; Thompson and Young, 1991; Young, 1993.

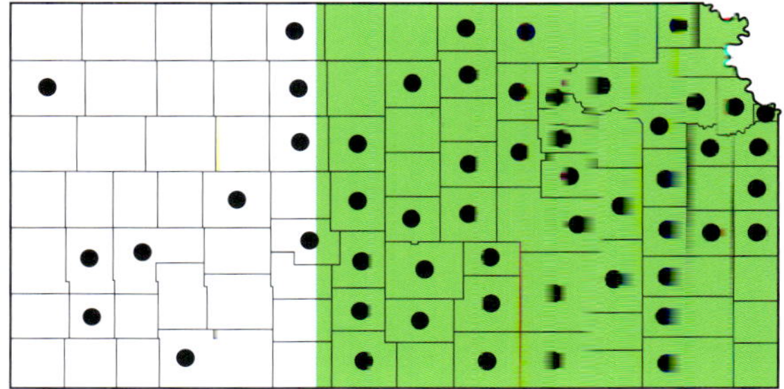

Marbled Godwit

Limosa fedoa (MAGO)

© Judd Patterson

Status: Uncommon spring and fall transient in the central region; rare to uncommon elsewhere.

Habitat: A variety of wetlands and marshes from fresh to saline, especially on mudflats; occasionally along rivers.

Migration: Early arrival dates include 3 April (Barton Co.) and 4 April (Stafford Co.). The median first arrival date is 10 April for CBWA. Statewide, most migration occurs in late April and early May with late departures through 25 June (Stafford Co.). High counts include 180 on 23 April and 200+ on 29 April (both Barton Co.). A few summer but the southward movement is under way by 4 July (Stafford Co.), with most migration in August and stragglers into mid-October and once to 23 November (Barton Co.). High fall counts include 25–30 on 2–9 August (Stafford Co.) and 15 on 5 August (Hamilton Co.). It is less abundant in fall than during the spring.

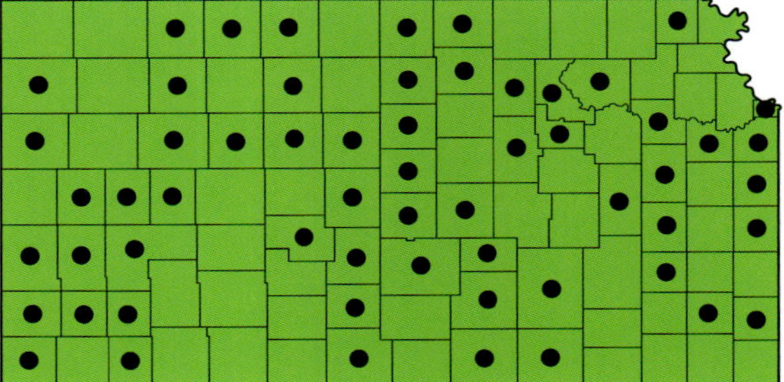

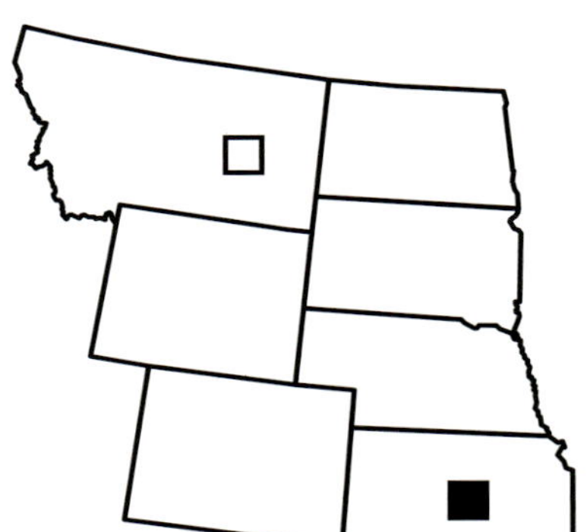

Comments: It breeds in grasslands of the northern United States and southern Canada and winters in coastal wetlands.

Banding: Five banded; one encounter. One bird banded in Montana on 2 August 1939 was shot in Kansas (Sheridan Co.) on 7 October 1940.

References: Alderfer, 2006; Gratto-Trevor, 2000; Janzen, 2007; Parmelee et al., 1969b; Rice et al., 2001; Seibel, 1978; Thompson and Ely, 1989; Young, 1993.

Ruddy Turnstone

Arenaria interpres (RUTU)

Status: Rare to uncommon spring and fall transient statewide; especially the central region.

Habitat: Along shorelines of marshes, reservoirs, and rivers, avoiding vegetated mudflats.

Migration: Occurs in spring from 22 March (Finney Co.) to 12 June. Peak migration occurs from mid-May to early June. Up to 200 have been recorded at CBWA from 18 to 24 May. However, high counts are usually 20–50 individuals or fewer. The fall passage is from 8 July (Sumner Co.) to 8 October (CBWA) with most passing through from mid-September to early October. There is one late date of 11 December (Barton Co.). It appears to be less abundant in fall with a high count of six on several occasions.

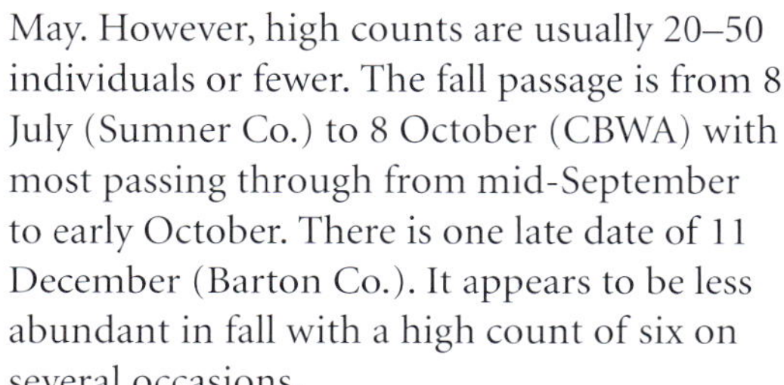

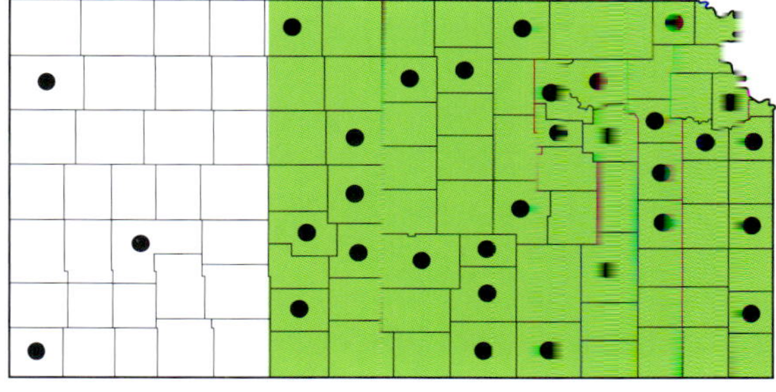

Comments: Perhaps the most striking of shorebirds to pass through Kansas, it is a rare treat when found. It is often observed actively turning over rocks and debris along the shoreline, looking for invertebrates.

Banding: 11 banded; no encounters.

References: Janzen, 2007; Nettleship, 2000; Parmelee et al., 1969a; Rice et al., 2001; Seibel, 1978; Thompson and Ely, 1989; Young, 1993.

Red Knot

Calidris canutus (REKN)

Status: Rare spring and fall transient statewide; most commonly observed in the central region.

Habitat: Mudflats in marshes, but may use flooded fields.

Migration: There are few spring records, although it has been recorded from 9 April (Lyon Co.) and 17 April through 3 June (Barton Co.) with most sightings during the last half of May. High counts include 83 on 19 May (Stafford Co.) and 50+ on 13 May (Barton Co.). The fall passage is from mid-July (banding, 24 July QNWR) to 26 September with an extreme date of 16 October (Jefferson Co.). Mean arrival dates are 2 September (Stafford Co.) and 5 September (Barton Co.). Most pass through from mid-August through September. The high fall count is 11 on 12 July and 14 August (both Stafford Co.).

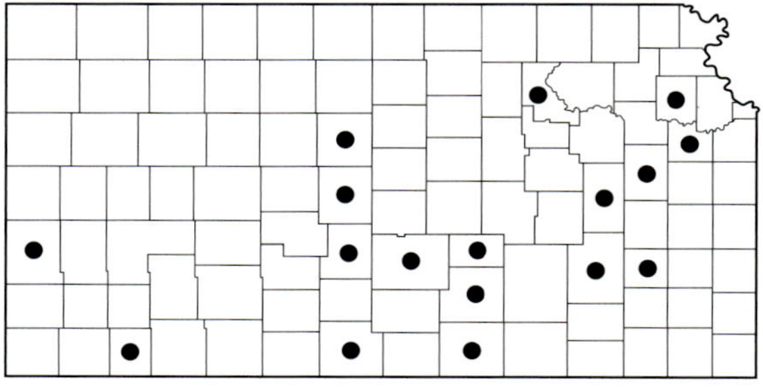

Comments: The Red Knot, formerly known as the Knot, is a long-distance migrant, often remaining for a few days in the same location. One remained from 14 to 16 August 1988 at SCW and several remained near Mulvane (Sedgwick Co.) from 4 to 16 August 1997.

Banding: 19 banded; no encounters. All were banded at CBWA during fall from mid-July through September.

References: Alderfer, 2006; Harrington, 2001; Janzen, 2007; Parmelee et al., 1969b; Thompson and Ely, 1989; Young, 1993.

Sanderling

Calidris alba (SAND)

Status: Uncommon spring and fall transient statewide, most abundant in the central region.

Habitat: Usually mudflats in marshes; also along shorelines of reservoirs, ponds, and rivers, especially if sandy; will use the concrete banks of sewage ponds.

Migration: Normally recorded from 20 April through 8 June (CBWA), with an early record of 14 March (Cowley Co.). Median arrivals include 18 April (Barton Co.), and peak migration is in May. D. Parmelee indicated "thousands of birds" were present at CBWA on 22–24 May 1963, apparently a unique event. The highest count since then is 250 on 19 May (Stafford Co.). The fall passage begins in July, and most have passed by 18 October (Sedgwick and Kearney cos.). Extreme dates are 8 July (Sumner Co.), and 21 November (Phillips Co.) and 14 December (Russell Co.). Peak migration is from August through October. The highest count reported is 300 on 26 September (Barton Co.).

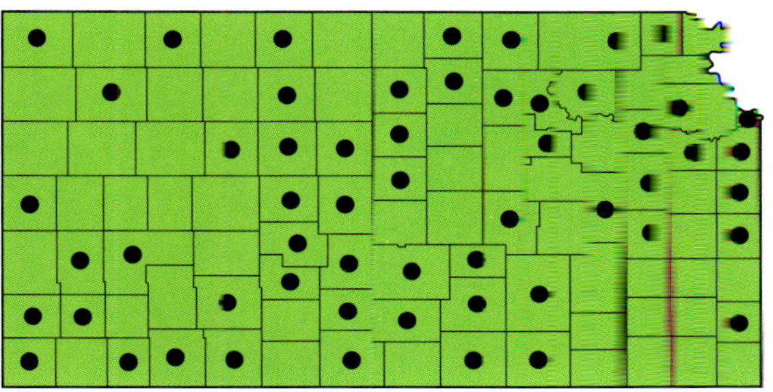

Comments: Although much is known concerning the migration and nonbreeding biology of this species, relatively little is understood about its breeding biology, including its mating system and population dynamics.

Banding: 117 banded; no encounters.

References: Alderfer, 2006; Janzen, 2007; MacWhirter et al., 2002; Parmelee et al., 1969b; Rice et al., 2001; Seibel, 1978; Thompson and Ely, 1989; Young, 1993.

Semipalmated Sandpiper

Calidris pusilla (SESA)

Status: Common spring and fall transient statewide; casual in summer; winter sightings are unconfirmed.

Habitat: Marshes, especially on mudflats, frequently in shallow water, ephemeral pools, sandbars, and pond margins.

Migration: Unusually early arrivals are 2 March (Sumner Co., vocalizations heard) and 8 and 9 April (specimens). Arrival is usually mid-April with the peak migration mid-April through mid-May and with small numbers through 8 June (CBWA). Flocks of tens of thousands have been reported at CBWA during some years. Half of the 30,000+ individuals banded by E. Martinez were during May. There are numerous June records from Barton, Stafford, and Sumner counties. Migration may begin as early as late June (likely unsuccessful breeding birds), perhaps overlapping the last birds moving northward. The fall passage typically begins in July and continues through 25 November (Riley Co.). Peak of migration occurs during July through early September. The main migration in July through August consists primarily of adults. Most juveniles typically arrive during August and remain until September. There are a few December records with a late date of 28 December (Sedgwick Co.), but none have been documented with physical evidence.

Comments: It frequently mixes with other peeps (the nickname for small sandpipers) to form enormous flocks. Kansas hosts the largest concentration of Semipalmated Sandpipers passing through central North America, most using CBWA, QNWR, and SCW.

See page 496 for banding information.

References: Gratto-Trevor, 1992; Parmelee et al., 1969b; Rice et al., 2001; Seibel, 1978; Senner and Howe, 1984; Thompson and Ely, 1989; Young, 1993.

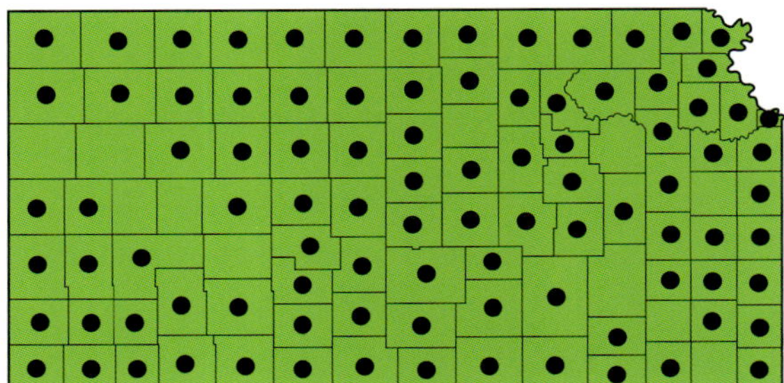

Western Sandpiper

Calidris mauri (WESA)

© David Seibel

Status: Rare spring transient; uncommon to common fall transient statewide; casual in early winter.

Habitat: Marshes, especially on mudflats, frequently in shallow water, ephemeral pools, sandbars, and pond margins; most common at CBWA, QNWR, and SCW.

Migration: The earliest spring arrival is 2 March (SCW, vocalizations heard); more typical arrival is late March with the peak migration during late April and May. June sightings, most from Barton, Stafford, and Sumner counties, have included flocks of 100 or more. The fall passage begins around 4 July (Stafford and Sumner cos.) and peaks during August with declining numbers through September and stragglers through 14 November (Barton Co.). Though there are a few early winter records from 1 December (Marion Co.) through 27 December (Barton Co.), none is documented by physical evidence. Nearly all individuals banded at CBWA were during fall with three-fourths of these during July and August. "Thousands" have been reported at CBWA on several occasions, but these estimates may include other peeps. The July peak is dominated by adults that pass through in large numbers through August and early September. Juveniles begin to arrive in August, and by the latter half of the month they peak and remain through September.

Comments: This species is more abundant in fall due to its elliptical migration pattern where it is more common along the West Coast in spring and more abundant inland during the fall.

See page 496 for banding information.

References: Janzen, 2007; Parmelee [illegible]b; Rice et al., 2001; Seibel, 1978; S[illegible] Martinez, 1982; Thompson and Ely, [illegible] [illegible], 1994; Young, 1993.

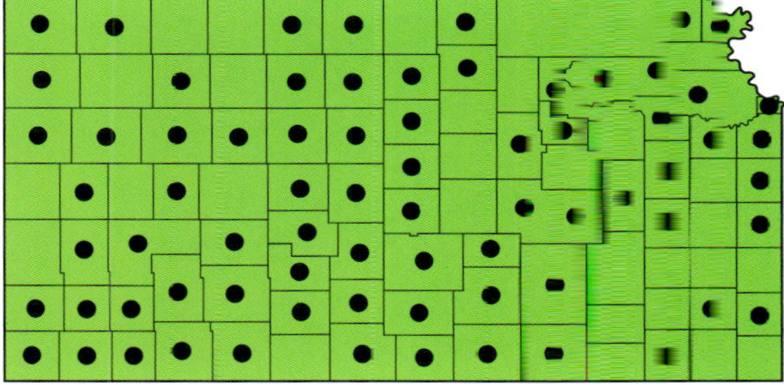

Least Sandpiper

Calidris minutilla (LESA)

Status: Common to abundant spring and fall transient statewide; casual in summer and early winter.

Habitat: Marshes, especially on mudflats, ephemeral pools, sandbars, and pond margins; prefers the wet to moist flats and soils, rather than flooded flats, including moist vegetated areas, similar to what Pectoral Sandpipers prefer.

Migration: Most commonly found from April through May with extreme dates of 22 February (CBWA) and 28 June (Sumner Co.). Peak numbers occur from the last week of April through May. High counts include 4,000 on 2 May (Barton Co.), 2,000 on 2 May (Republic Co.), and 1,000+ on 12 May (Sumner Co.). Birds have been recorded at CBWA, QNWR, and SCW in early July (specimen, 12 July, Stafford Co.) with an extreme late date of 25 November (specimen). Peak numbers occur from mid-July through September and decline rapidly by early October. High counts include 4,500+ on 13 August (Stafford Co.). There are winter records (1–17 individuals) on numerous occasions from 1 December (Marion Co.) through 25 January (Cherokee Co.). Nearly all peeps reported into early winter are thought to be this species, but there is no specimen documentation and little physical evidence for most peeps during winter. Adults dominate the July migration and are slightly more abundant through August. Juveniles begin to migrate in August and remain through September.

Comments: It has been recorded in every month except February. Surprisingly, migratory behavior is not well known for this species.

See page 496 for banding information.

References: Nebel and Cooper, 2008; Parmelee et al., 1969b; Rice et al., 2001; Seibel, 1978; Thompson and Ely, 1989; Young, 1993.

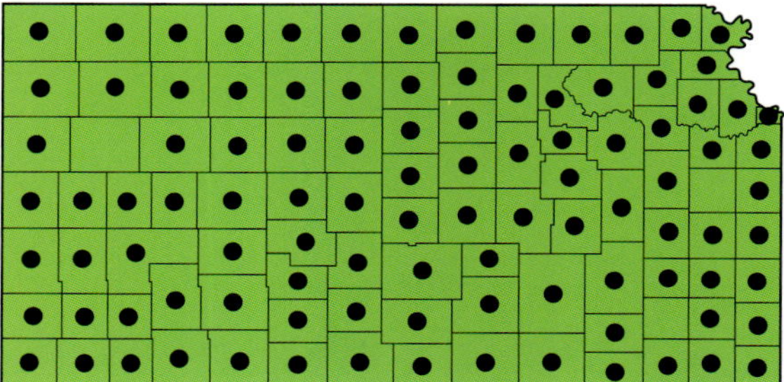

White-rumped Sandpiper

Calidris fuscicollis (WRSA)

© David Seibel

Status: Common to abundant spring transient in the central region, uncommon elsewhere; rare fall transient throughout. There are few summer records.

Habitat: Marshes, especially on open mudflats, ephemeral pools, sandbars, and pond margins.

Migration: It is one of the latest shorebirds to migrate through the region, and often during a brief period. Reports from March, if correct, are exceptional; more typical are arrivals in late April (25 April, Ellsworth Co.; 29 April, Douglas Co., specimen). The migration peak is mid-May to early June. At CBWA estimates of 15,000+ were reported on 10 May, 20,000+ on 16 May 1986, and 12,000 on 26 May 1988. M. Schwilling noted a mass exodus on 28 or 29 May 1968. Smaller numbers have been reported at QNWR (5,000+ on 26 May; 2,500+ on 6 June) and at SCW (1,000+ on 12 May, 2,000 and 2,950 on 19 May [different years], 1,970 on 20 May, "thousands" on 23 May, and 1,374 on 25 May). Late dates include 10 June (Clark Co., specimen, and seven at SCW) and perhaps 29 June (Stafford Co.) if they were not summering birds. The southbound passage is minimal compared to the spring migration as a result of its elliptical migration, where most birds follow the East Coast during fall. Observers in Kansas should use caution when identifying this species in fall migration. At CBWA most migration is the last half of July; elsewhere from late June to late September with stragglers to 16 October (Stevens Co.). Specimen records are 9 July (Stafford Co.) to 29 September (Barton Co.). Large fall counts include 25 on 26 July 1963 (CBWA), 100 on 10–13 August 1987 (SCW), and 42 on 4 September 1989 (SCW).

Comments: Major staging areas in Kansas include CBWA, QNWR, and SCW.

Banding: 5,627 banded; 14 encounters: 1 in-state, 13 from Kansas to: Guyana (8), Argentina, Brazil, NS, ON, unknown. One bird banded at CBWA on 26 May 1970 was recaptured and released in Ontario on 13 August 1975 5 years, 3 months later.

References: Parmelee, 1992; Parmelee et al., 1969b; Rice et al., 2001; Rintoul, 2003; Seibel, 1978; Thompson and Ely, 1989; Young, 1993.

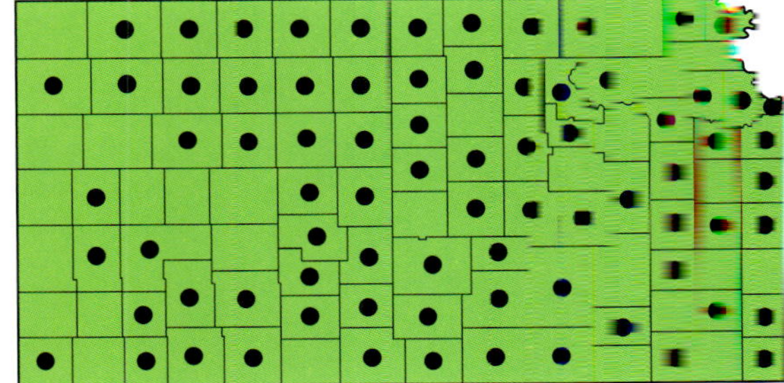

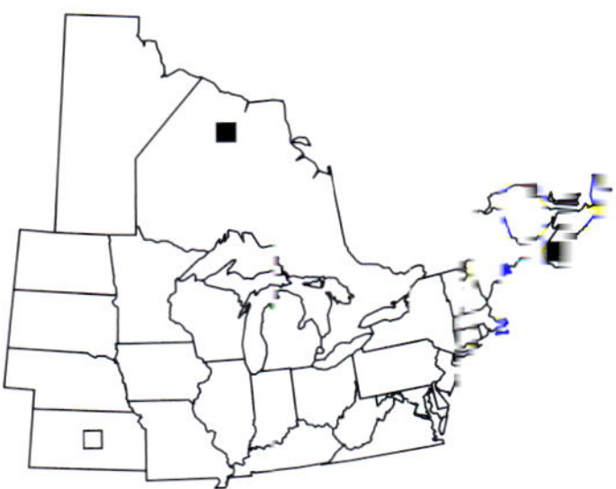

Baird's Sandpiper

Calidris bairdii (BASA)

Status: Common to abundant spring and fall transient statewide; rare summer visitant.

Habitat: Marshes, especially on open mudflats, ephemeral pools, sandbars, and pond margins.

Migration: It is the first peep to arrive in spring with an extreme date of 6 February (Miami Co.) and many reports during late February. Median first arrival dates include 7 March (Barton Co.), 17 March (Russell Co.), and 11 April (Ellis Co.). Peak numbers are mid-April through mid-May with stragglers into early June (17 June, CBWA). High counts include 36,000 on 23 April and 8,000 on 4 May (both Barton Co.), 4,000 on 2 May (Republic Co.), and 3,500+ on 25 April (Stafford Co.). Late June–early July dates may be nonbreeders or early transients. The fall migration begins by at least 10 July (45, Barber Co.). Large numbers arrive in late July–early August. Most migration is during August (adults) and early September (juveniles) but with stragglers into October (specimens to 14 October). The few high fall counts are minimal compared to many of its congeners and include 711 on 23 August (SCW), 200+ on 20 August and 150 on 27 September (both Stafford Co.), 100 on 18 August (Barton Co.), and 50 on 28 July (Russell Co.). Unusually late fall dates include 8 November (Marion Co.), 14 November (Osage Co.), and 25 November and 6 December (both Barton Co.).

Comments: Major staging areas in Kansas include CBWA, QNWR, and SCW. It may be more abundant in spring than fall. Many fall birds appear to overfly Kansas enroute to their wintering grounds in South America, some as far south as Tierra del Fuego. They have one of the longest and most rapid migrations of any bird species. Many arrive in South American within 4–6 weeks of departing the Arctic breeding grounds.

Banding: 537 banded; no encounters.

References: Janzen, 2007; Moskoff and Montgomerie, 2002; Parmelee et al., 1969b; Rice et al., 2001; Seibel, 1978; Thompson and Ely, 1989; Young, 1993.

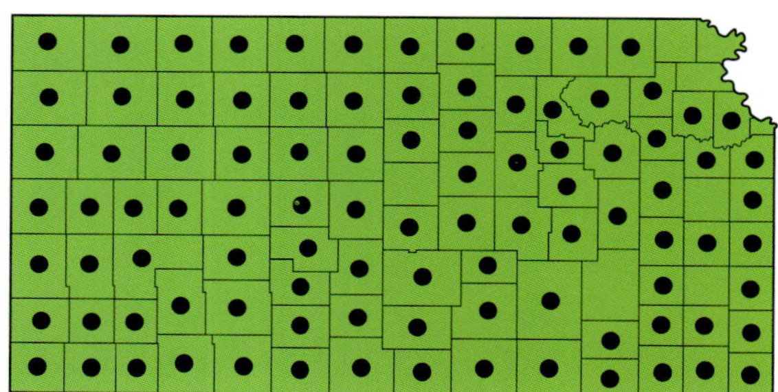

Pectoral Sandpiper

Calidris melanotos (PESA)

Status: Common to abundant spring and fall transient statewide; rare summer visitant.

Habitat: Marshes on open mudflats, ephemeral pools, sandbars, and pond margins; prefers short, wetland grasses and sedges where it can be quite abundant, and is often overlooked.

Migration: Earliest reported arrivals are 6 February (Miami Co., unconfirmed) and 4 March (Douglas Co.) with more typical arrival during late March (16 March, specimen, Douglas Co.). Peak migration is early May through early June with stragglers to 21 June (CBWA) and with occasional birds summering. High counts include 150 on 30 March (Linn Co., early record number), 10,000 during the first week of June 1968 (Barton Co.), and 2,000 on 7 May 1999 (Stafford Co.). In fall adults begin to arrive in July (1 July, Jefferson and Linn cos.), but the main influx is in August (adults) and lasts through September (juveniles) with small numbers remaining into late October and even November (25 November, Coffey Co.). Specimens are available from 9 July to 3 November. High counts include 600 on 11 August, 704 on 23 August, and 405 on 28 August (all Sumner Co.); 600 on 4 September (Barton Co.); 500 on 27 August (Neosho Co.); and 375 on 13 August and "hundreds" on 8–9 August (both Stafford Co.).

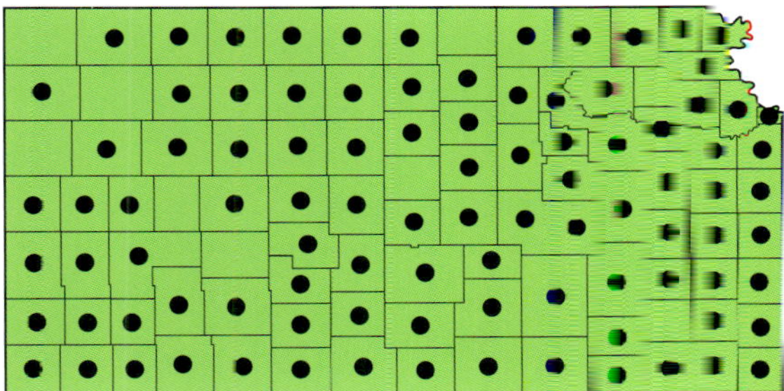

Comments: Major staging areas in Kansas include CBWA, QNWR, and SCW. Numbers may be declining, and the conservation status of this species needs to be studied.

See page 497 for banding information.

References: Holmes and Pitelka, 1998; Parmelee et al., 1969b; Rice et al., 2001; Seibel, 1978; Thompson and Ely, 1989; Young, 1993.

Dunlin

Calidris alpina (DUNL)

© Judd Patterson

Status: Rare to uncommon spring and fall transient; rare winter visitant.

Habitat: Marshes with open mudflats, ephemeral pools, sandbars, and pond margins.

Migration: The earliest sighting is 60 birds in winter plumage on 5 March at CBWA. Other early arrivals include 11 March, 31 March (Stafford Co.), and 4 April (Johnson Co.). Arrival is usually mid-April or later with the peak in late May and stragglers to at least 14 June (Stafford Co.). High counts include 50+ on 23 May, 50 on 18 May, and 127 on 25 May (all in Barton Co.); 48 on 15 May (Stafford Co.); and 33 on 25 May (Sumner Co.). It is a late fall migrant with a few arrivals 12 July–22 September but with most sightings from early October through mid-November and a few extending into the CBC period. The latest specimen is 28 November (Barton Co.). There are five December records: 1 and 19 December (Stafford Co., different years), 8 December (Osage Co.), 12 December (Jefferson Co.), and early December 1977 through 15 January 1978 (Sedgwick Co.). Other late sightings are one on the Liberal CBC (Seward Co.) on 2 January 2000 and one in Coffey County from 3 January through at least 3 February 2003 (KBRC 2003-01, with photographs). Unlike many species of shorebirds, both adults and juveniles migrate together.

Comments: Formerly known as the Red-backed Sandpiper. Its fall migration is unusually late, probably a reflection of it undergoing a premigratory molt. Greater numbers may move through during the spring than fall. Presumably, many of the wintering birds in Texas migrate directly from coastal areas to North Dakota and Winnipeg, Manitoba, overflying Kansas, thus resulting in the relative scarcity of records compared to other shorebirds.

Banding: 63 banded, mostly in spring; no encounters.

References: Alderfer, 2006; Cable et al., 1996; Janzen, 2007; Otte, 2004; Parmelee et al., 1969b; Rice et al., 2001; Seibel, 1978; Steeves and Holohan, 1995; Thompson and Ely, 1989; Warnock and Gill, 1996; Young, 1993.

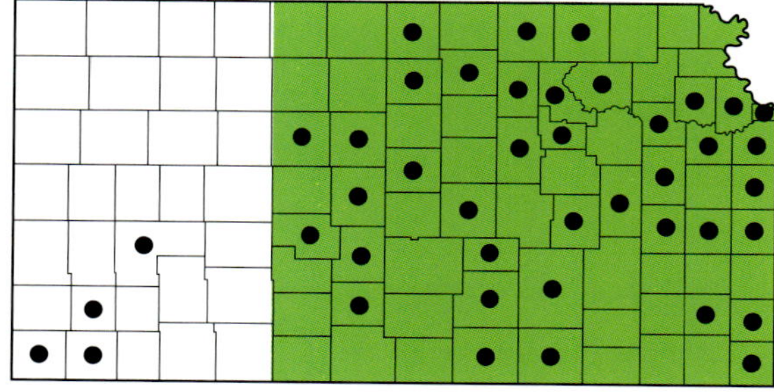

Curlew Sandpiper

Calidris ferruginea (CUSA)

© Aurelien Audevard

Status: Vagrant. There are only seven records for this Old World vagrant, six in fall, 12 July–21 August, and one in spring, 15 May 1971 (CBWA, E. Martinez). Most records are from CBWA, including a specimen from 4 August 1972 (MHP 2585). Two others are from QNWR, 4 August 1991 (KBRC 91-28) and 12 July 2002 (KBRC 2002-04, with photos). The only other record is from Seward County on 21 August 1998 (KBRC 98-55).

Habitat: Open mudflats and ephemeral pools.

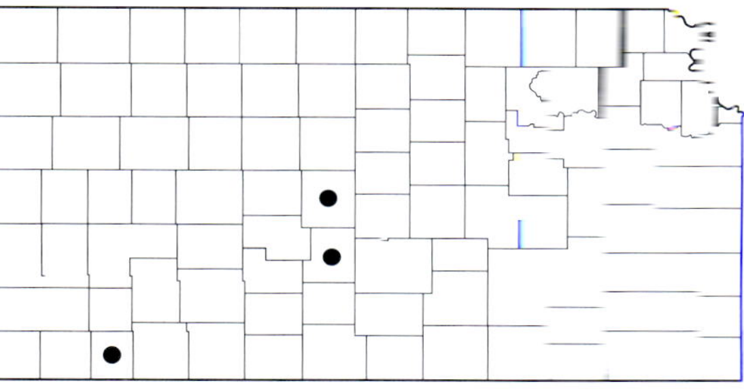

Comments: E. Martinez observed one or two birds at CBWA on three dates between 18 July and 3 August 1975. The individual in 1972 preferred the margin between the shore and shallow water punctuated by clumps of sedge, and spent most of its time there or well up on the shore.

References: Alderfer, 2006; Rintoul, 2003; Thompson and Ely, 1989.

Stilt Sandpiper

Calidris himantopus (STSA)

Status: Common spring and fall transient; most common in central Kansas.

Habitat: Marshes with open mudflats, ephemeral pools, sandbars, and pond margins and occasionally in flooded, vegetated fields. Often feeds in deeper water, often up to its belly, with head submerged, characteristics it shares with dowitchers, with which it frequently associates.

See page 497 for banding information.

Migration: It normally arrives around 6 April and departs by the first week of June. The earliest spring record is 12 March with a late date of 14 June (Stafford Co.). Peak numbers move through from late April through May. High counts include 6,500 on 22 May (Barton Co.), 1,500+ on 26 May (Stafford Co.), and 1,000+ on 12 May and 537 on 19 May (both Sumner Co.). The main fall passage begins in mid-July, with an early date of 3 July (Sumner Co.). Most individuals pass through in September through the first week of October, with a late date of 19 November. Adults begin arriving in July and pass through by mid-August, with juveniles reaching a peak of abundance from late August through September and some lingering into October. Large counts include "thousands" on 22 August and 26 September (Barton Co.) and 3,000–4,000 on 5 October (Stafford Co.).

Comments: Like the White-rumped Sandpiper, it can pass through in large numbers in just a few days. For example in 1968 a mass exodus from CBWA occurred on 28 May. Although it may be difficult to determine just how long the birds had resided at a large wetland like CBWA, in peripheral wetlands it can be quite easy to monitor.

References: Alderfer, 2006; Jehl and Jehl, 1998; Klima and Jehl, 1998; Parmelee et al., 1969b; Rice et al., 2001; Seibel, 1978; Thompson and Ely, 1989; Young, 1993.

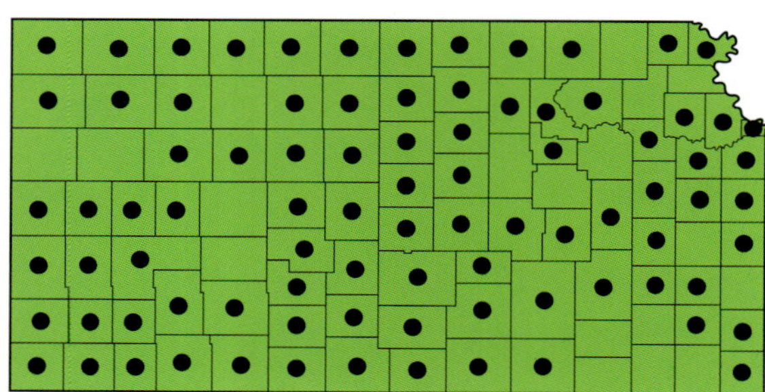

Buff-breasted Sandpiper

Tryngites subruficollis (BBSA)

Status: Uncommon spring and fall transient in the eastern half of the state, rare in the western half.

Habitat: Like the Upland Sandpiper, prefers upland prairies, sod farms, and occasionally mudflats. During spring migration, burned pasture is preferred, and during fall, recently hayed or burned fields and recently worked cropland are used. Sod farms are used during both spring and fall migration.

Migration: Formerly considered rare during the spring, but recent observations within the southern Flint Hills suggest the species may be using burned prairie on a regular basis. Spring records range from 12 April (Cowley Co., 13 individuals) and 14 April (Sedgwick Co.) to 13 June (specimen, Stafford Co.) and 18 June (Seward Co.). Peak migration is late April through the first half of May. In the Flint Hills, E. Young observed 1,095 on 25 April 2010 (Butler Co.), 548 on 4 May (Cowley Co.), 26 flocks totaling 444 individuals on 5 May 2007 (eastern Cowley Co.), 236 (11 flocks, ranging from 9 to 50 individuals) on 3 May 2009 (southeastern Butler Co.), and 122 (5 flocks, ranging from 2 to 68 individuals) on 3 May 2009 (Elk Co.). Other high counts include 100 on 3 May (Stafford Co.), 40–50 on 4 May (Sedgwick Co.), and 56 on 19 May (SCW). Most records are from the fall, when it has been observed from 19 July (Sedgwick Co.) to 11 November (Barton Co.). Migration is under way by mid-August with the peak in August through mid-September and with stragglers into late September, and exceptionally to 11 November (Barton Co.). It usually occurs in small flocks, but high numbers include 500+ on 18 September and 200–300 on 22 August (both Barton Co.). At a sod farm in Douglas County, 200 were observed on 27 August [illegible] and 130 on 2 August 2006. On 22 August [illegible], 355 were observed at a sod farm north of [illegible]wich (Sedgwick Co.), with 100–200 routinely recorded there. On 12 August 2007, [illegible] were present at SCW with another group of [illegible] on [illegible] September 2007.

Comments: The largest concentrations seem to occur on the sod farms of Sedgwick and Douglas counties and in the southern Flint Hills (Butler, Cowley, Elk, and Chautauqua cos.).

Banding: 38 banded; no encounters.

References: Janzen, 2001, 2007; Lanctot and Laredo, 1994; Lanctot et al., 2009; Parmelee et al., 1969b; Robbins, 2007; Seibel, [illegible]; Thompson and Ely, 1989; Young, [illegible].

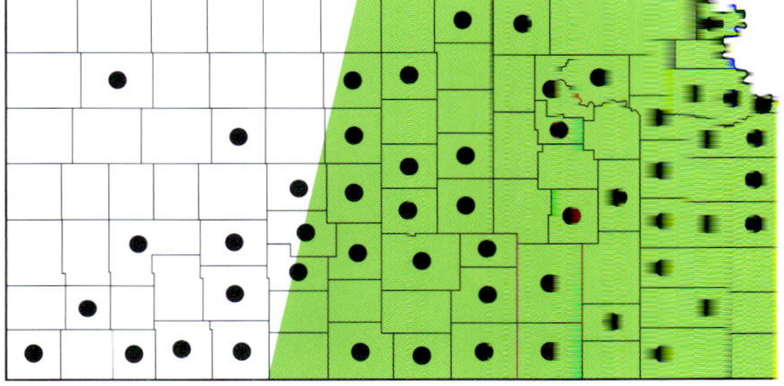

Ruff

Philomachus pugnax (RUFF)

Status: Vagrant in the central and northeastern regions. The only specimen is a bird seen at CBWA by B. Stark and R. Boyd on 21 June 1982. Four additional records have been accepted by KBRC. Most sightings are from CBWA or QNWR. Twelve spring sightings (some unverified) are from 15 April (Barton Co., KBRC 2004-11, with photos) to 22 May (Linn Co.); most are from late April and early May (7 May 2010, SCW, with photos, K. Groeneweg, S. Silliman, E. Young). Six fall sightings (some unverified) are 11 July 2009 (Nemaha Co.) to 5–13 November 2005 (QNWR, KBRC 2005-30); most are late August–early September.

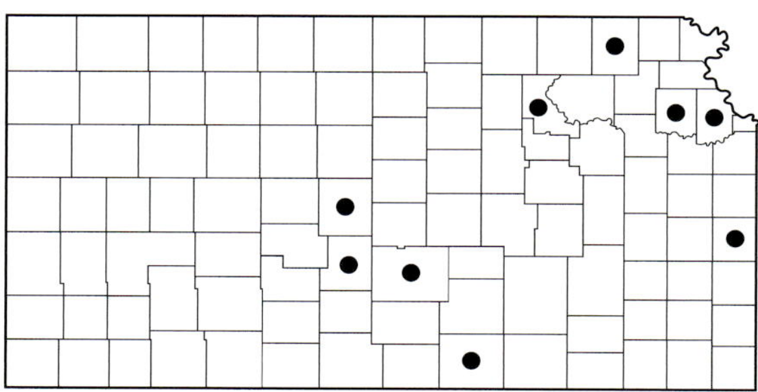

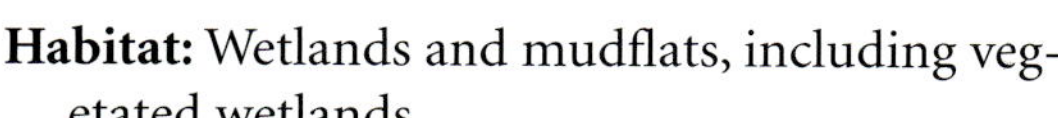

Habitat: Wetlands and mudflats, including vegetated wetlands.

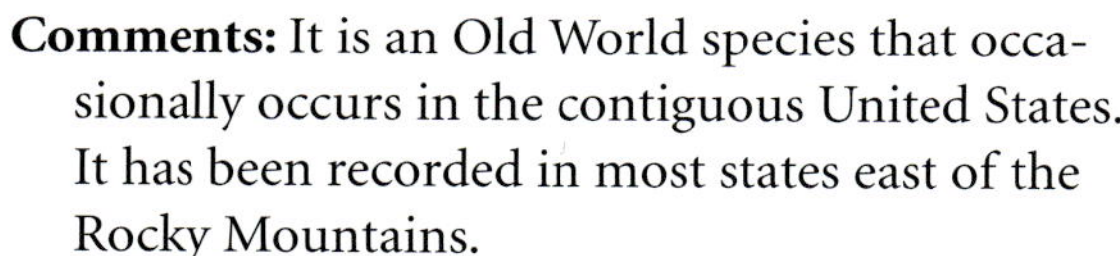

Comments: It is an Old World species that occasionally occurs in the contiguous United States. It has been recorded in most states east of the Rocky Mountains.

References: Alderfer, 2006; Otte, 2005, 2006; Thompson and Ely, 1989.

Short-billed Dowitcher

Limnodromus griseus (SBDO)

Status: Rare spring and fall transient statewide; most records are from CBWA, QNWR, and SCW. Usually appears later in the spring and earlier in the fall than its congener, the Long-billed Dowitcher.

Habitat: A variety of wetlands and marshes from fresh to saline, rivers, shorelines of reservoirs and ponds, and ephemeral pools; often wades up to its belly while feeding with a sewing machine–like motion. It may have a preference for the more saline wetlands.

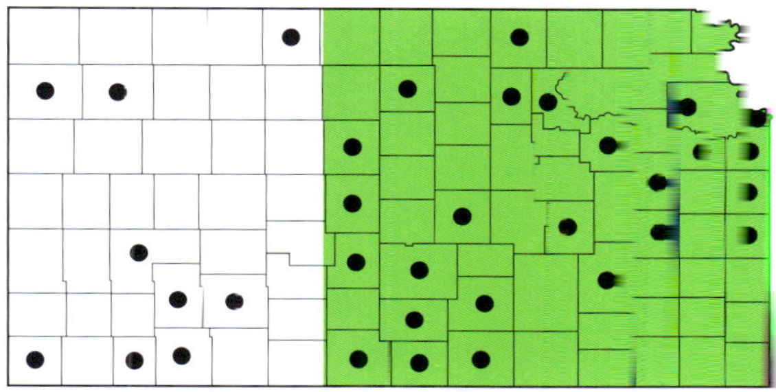

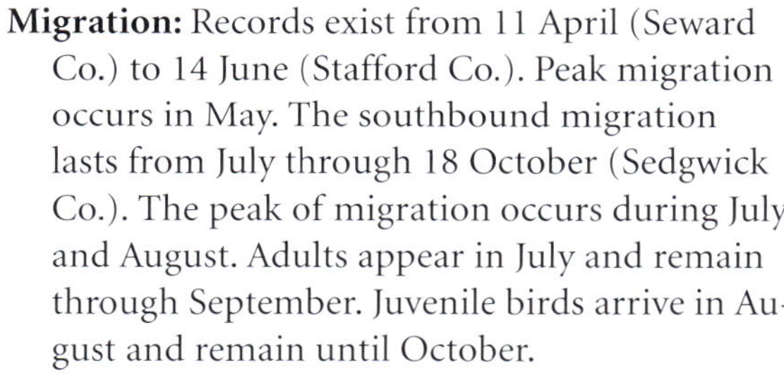

Migration: Records exist from 11 April (Seward Co.) to 14 June (Stafford Co.). Peak migration occurs in May. The southbound migration lasts from July through 18 October (Sedgwick Co.). The peak of migration occurs during July and August. Adults appear in July and remain through September. Juvenile birds arrive in August and remain until October.

Comments: The three subspecies of Short-billed Dowitcher differ subtly in plumage variations and size, but they do have discrete breeding ranges. The western subspecies, *L. g. caurinus*, breeds in western Canada and Alaska and primarily occurs in migration along the West Coast and inland west of the Rocky Mountains. In the interior, *L. g. hendersoni* breeds in central Canada and is the race typically found in Kansas and the Great Plains. Some individuals appear to migrate eastward along the East Coast, and some have even been found along the West Coast. The nominate race, *L. g. griseus*, breeds in northeastern Canada and is the primary subspecies found along the East Coast and down into the Caribbean. Most Kansas specimens are *L. g. hendersoni*, with at least one tentatively referable to *L. g. caurinus*. There is no physical evidence of *L. g. griseus* occurring in Kansas. Of the three subspecies, *L. g. hendersoni* is most similar to the Long-billed Dowitcher during spring, which probably contributes to the relative paucity of verified records at that season. Furthermore, *L. g. hendersoni* has the most variable plumage, at times ranging toward either of the other subspecies. Identification of dowitchers in the Great Plains can thus be particularly difficult; vocalizations and the timing of migration can be helpful clues.

Banding: 59 banded; no encounters.

References: Janzen, 2007; Jehl et al., 2001; Parmelee et al., 1969b; Seibel, 1978; Thompson and Ely, 1989; Young, 1993.

Long-billed Dowitcher

Limnodromus scolopaceus (LBDO)

Status: Common spring and fall transient statewide; abundant at CBWA, QNWR, and SCW; casual summer visitant; recorded in early winter.

Habitat: A variety of wetlands and marshes from fresh to saline, rivers, shorelines of reservoirs and ponds, and ephemeral pools; often wades up to its belly while feeding with a sewing machine–like motion; prefers freshwater wetlands.

Migration: Recorded from 27 February (CBWA) through May, with scattered records until 28 June (Sumner Co.). Median first arrivals include 12 March (Barton Co.) and 30 April (Ellis Co.). Most birds arrive in late March and depart by late May, with a peak of migration during April and mid-May. Tens of thousands have been reported at CBWA during early May and again in early October. The main southbound migration starts in late July and lasts through 15 October. Extreme dates include 1 July (Sumner Co.) and 21 December (Coffey Co.). The peak of migration occurs during August through October. Adults begin movement into the area in mid-July and remain through early October. Most juveniles appear to move through in September and remain through early October. At least some of the unconfirmed sightings during early winter were undoubtedly Wilson's Snipe.

Comments: There are no subspecies of Long-billed Dowitcher; however, it can be confused with the "*hendersoni*" subspecies of the Short-billed Dowitcher due to plumage similarities. Timing of migration can help, along with habitat, but call notes are the best way to separate the two species. Although field guides and some of the literature indicate that there are structural cues that can be used to help in identification, most observations are made while the birds are actively feeding, which can make subtle differences in plumage and gestalt difficult to distinguish. CBWA probably hosts the largest populations of Long-billed Dowitchers in the United States during both spring and fall migration.

Banding: 1,500 banded; four encounters (all banded at CBWA): two in-state including one banded on 12 September 1969 and collected there on 24 October 1976 (7 years, 1 month after banding); an adult banded on 13 October 1982 and shot in central Mexico in February 1983; and an adult banded on 18 August 1971 and shot in northeastern Russia on 26 May 1973.

References: Parmelee et al., 1969b; Rice et al., 2001; Seibel, 1978; Thompson and Ely, 1989; Young, 1993.

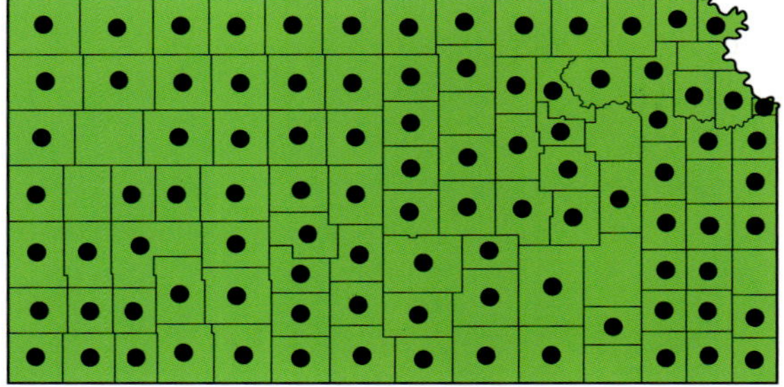

Wilson's Snipe

Gallinago delicata (WISN)

Status: Common spring and fall transient in wetlands statewide; casual in summer, rare in winter; records for all months.

Habitat: A variety of wetlands and marshes from fresh to saline, rivers, and ephemeral pools.

Migration: Early March reports probably include wintering birds. Spring migration begins by at least mid-March with individuals widespread by late March and numbers peaking by mid-April. Most depart by early May with stragglers into mid-June. Because individuals tend to disperse when feeding, few estimates of numbers are made; but reports include 200+ on 23 April (Barton Co.) and 200 on 12–13 April (Lyon Co.). Occasional birds remain all summer, but no nesting has ever been confirmed. The fall movement begins by 13 July (CBWA), with birds widespread by mid-September. The fall migration peak is late September through early November. More than 100 were observed at CBWA on 1 October 1963, with 1,000+ observed there on 14 November 1963. Most birds leave by mid-November, but some remain all winter within larger wetland complexes, near springs, or at wetlands associated with reservoir edges, especially during mild winters when open water remains.

Comments: Formerly known as the Common Snipe, it is a game species in Kansas, though few are harvested. It typically remains motionless until almost stepped upon, then abruptly takes flight. During spring its courtship flight display is sometimes observed over wet meadows and heavily vegetated wetlands. The frequency of summer records suggests that birds may breed locally, so nesting should be looked for in areas where courtship flights are observed.

Banding: 122 banded; seven encounters: all banded at CBWA and recovered there the same year as banded.

References: Mueller, 1999; Parmelee et al., 1969a; Rice et al., 2001; Seibel, 1978; Thompson and Ely, 1989; Young, 1993.

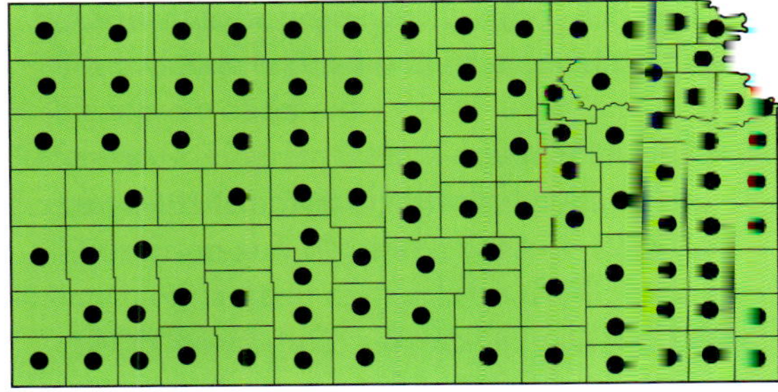

American Woodcock

Scolopax minor (AMWO)

© David Seibel

Status: Uncommon spring and fall transient in the eastern half of the state, becoming rare westward; rare and local in winter. It breeds locally in the east, westward to at least Saline and Reno counties.

Habitat: Unique among Kansas shorebirds in that it is primarily associated with moist soil areas in woodland edge and in early successional woods where it feeds on earthworms.

Migration: February dates may represent early transients. Most records are from April through November. Northbound migrants arrive in late February and early March, and most have departed by mid-April (16 April, Morton Co.). High counts include 10 on 28 February (Johnson Co.). Southbound migrants begin to arrive in late August with most reports during late October and November. Some winter near boggy areas if the ground remains unfrozen during mild winters.

Breeding: The nest is located on the ground in boggy areas where small trees are interspersed with grasslands. Nesting is initiated as soon as the birds return in March, which is very early for a migrant species, and lasts through May. Aerial displays have been reported 20 February–12 May (Ottawa Co.). Eggs have been reported 7 April (Butler Co.) to 28 May (pipped, Jefferson Co.) and chicks 4 April (Cherokee Co.) to 25 May (one-fourth grown, Woodson Co.).

Comments: The American Woodcock is a game species in Kansas, though few hunt them. It normally occurs singly or in dispersed groups. Because of this and its secretive nature, relatively little is known about its migration in Kansas.

Banding: None banded. One purported to have been banded in California on 7 December 1972 and shot in Ottawa County, 11 months later on 18 November 1973, must be an error in the banding record itself. The species is accidental in California.

References: Cable et al., 1996; Janzen, 2007; Keppie and Whiting, 1994; Seibel, 1978; Thompson and Ely, 1989; Young, 1993; Zimmerman, 1987.

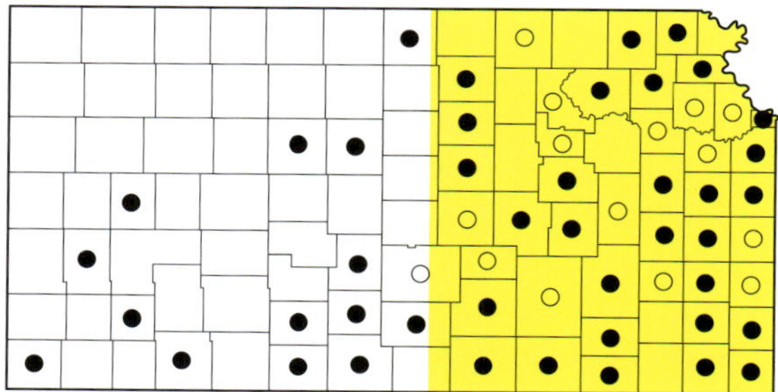

Wilson's Phalarope

Phalaropus tricolor (WIPH)

Status: Common spring and fall transient statewide; local summer resident in central and western regions, primarily at CBWA and QNWR.

Habitat: Marshy areas, inundated mudflats, reservoirs, ponds, and playas.

Migration: Recorded as early as 3 February and as late as 5 December (both CBWA). The 3 February 1974 individual, apparently healthy, was seen on that date, remained for 3 days, and then departed as its feeding area froze over (M. Schwilling). The next report for that season was 5 March (E. Martinez). Although extreme early arrivals include 30 March (Finney and Sumner cos.), usual spring arrival is mid-April with the migration peak during late April to mid-May and with late dates to 31 May (east) and 12 June (west). Median dates of first arrival include 13 April (Barton Co.) and 17 April (Ellis Co.). Flocks of 1,000–2,000 have been reported in Barton, Sumner, and Meade counties, and up to 5,000–10,000 have been observed at QNWR (10 May). Fall arrival probably begins by early July and definitely by the end of the month. Most migration is during August and early September with most birds gone by mid-September and stragglers into late October and, exceptionally, to 5 December (Barton Co.). Adults slightly outnumber juveniles during early fall migration, but there is little difference between the number of adults and juveniles, or in the number of males versus females during the fall migration.

Breeding: Confirmed nesting has occurred in Barton, Stafford, Lincoln, and possibly Meade counties, and behavior of adults suggests at least occasional breeding at other localities, especially at playas in the southwest. The nest, usually in a marshy area, is either a depression in the ground lined with plant material or constructed in dry grass or spike-rush over shallow water.

Comments: Its peculiar habit of spinning in circles as it feeds immediately identifies it as a phalarope. While it rotates, the phalarope kicks up invertebrates with its feet. Phalaropes are among the few species in the avian world in which the females are more brightly colored than the males. This "sex reversal" includes incubation and care of the young by the male.

Banding: 621 banded; no encounters.

References: Busby and Zimmerman, 2001; Colwell and Jehl, 1994; Johnsgard, 1979; Johnston, 1964a; Parmelee et al., 1969b; Rice et al., 20[illegible]; Seibel, 1978; Thompson and Ely, 1989; Tordoff, 1956; Young, 1993.

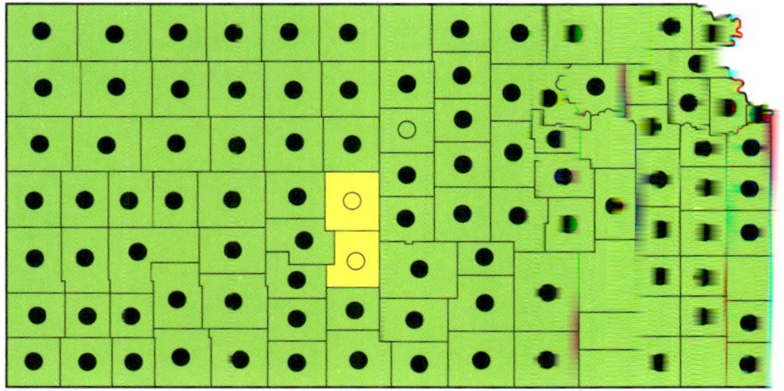

Red-necked Phalarope

Phalaropus lobatus (RNPH)

© James Arterburn

Status: Rare spring and fall transient statewide.

Habitat: Marshy areas, inundated mudflats, reservoirs, sewage lagoons, and ponds.

Migration: During spring recorded from 19 April through 23 June (both Barton Co.) with peak numbers occurring in May: 50+ on 22 May and 30+ on 23 May 1963 (CBWA), and 30 on 22 May 1997 (QNWR). During fall 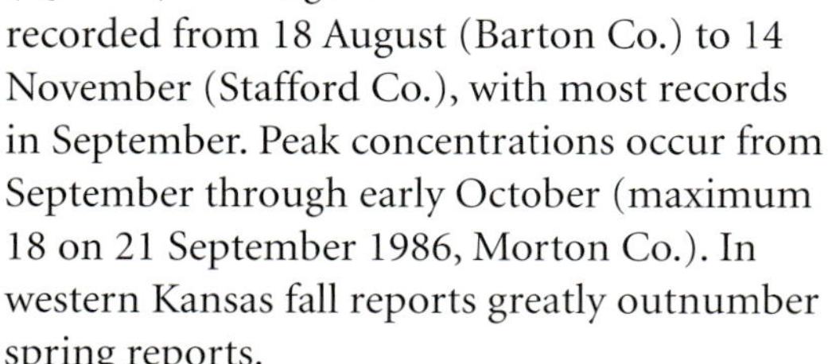 recorded from 18 August (Barton Co.) to 14 November (Stafford Co.), with most records in September. Peak concentrations occur from September through early October (maximum 18 on 21 September 1986, Morton Co.). In western Kansas fall reports greatly outnumber spring reports.

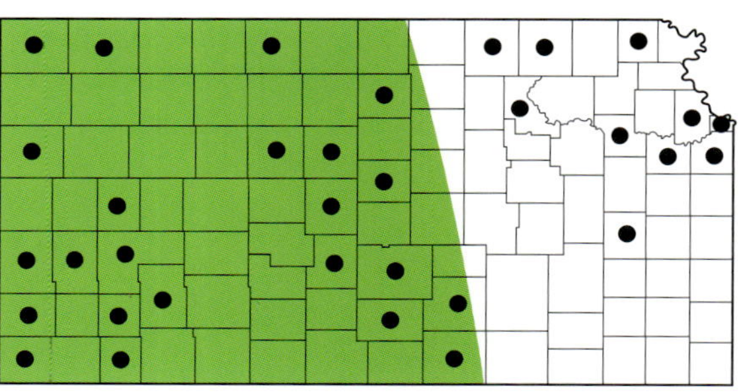

Comments: It was formerly known as the Northern Phalarope. In winter plumage it may be difficult to distinguish from Wilson's Phalarope. The Red-necked Phalarope usually has a darker dorsal pattern, shorter bill, and dark stripe through the eye. During flight it has a definitive white stripe along the wing.

Banding: 90 banded; no encounters. All were banded at CBWA, with most in May and September, indicating peak migration periods.

References: Cable et al., 1996; Parmelee et al., 1969b; Rubega et al., 2000; Thompson and Ely, 1989; Tordoff, 1956.

Red Phalarope

Phalaropus fulicarius (REPH)

© David Seibel

Status: Casual transient with fewer records in spring; most records are from September.

Habitat: Marshy areas, inundated mudflats, reservoirs, sewage lagoons, and ponds.

Migration: The few spring sightings are 1 April (Sumner Co.) to 10 May (CBWA). Most sightings are in fall from 28 August (Barton Co.) and 1 September (Morton Co., KBRC 2005-19, with photos) to 5 November (Stafford Co., video). The latest record is a specimen taken on 5 December (Barton Co., ESU B1224).

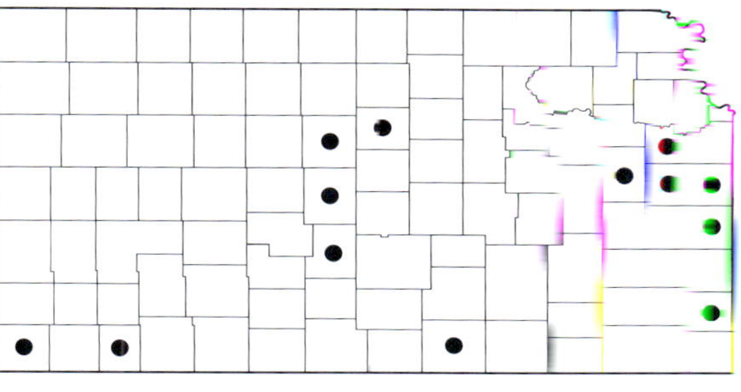

Comments: The rusty reddish spring plumage is unmistakable, but the winter plumage can resemble that of the other two phalaropes. The Red Phalarope differs in having a more uniform gray appearance, a dark gray stripe through the eye, and stouter, more flattened bill. Interestingly, there are two records from 10 May for CBWA. The first, a specimen (10 May 1963, ESU T840), is a male that is gray with only a few reddish feathers, whereas the other, observed on 10 May 1967, was "fairly bright."

Banding: One banded; no encounters.

References: Cable et al., 1996; Otte, 2006; Parmelee et al., 1969b; Thompson and Ely, 1989; Tordoff, 1956; Tracy et al., 2002.

Black-legged Kittiwake

Rissa tridactyla (BLKI)

Status: Rare spring and fall transient, rare summer straggler.

Habitat: Reservoirs and large pools in wetlands; one record from the Arkansas River.

Migration: Records are from 20 March to 5 May (CBWA) with the majority occurring in April. Midsummer records are 27 June–16 July (both Barton Co., M. Schwilling). Fall and winter records are from 26 September (Barton Co.) to 8 January (Miami Co.), with the majority of records in December.

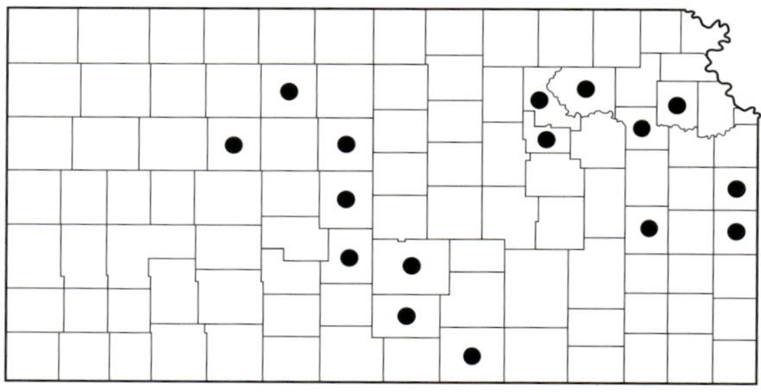

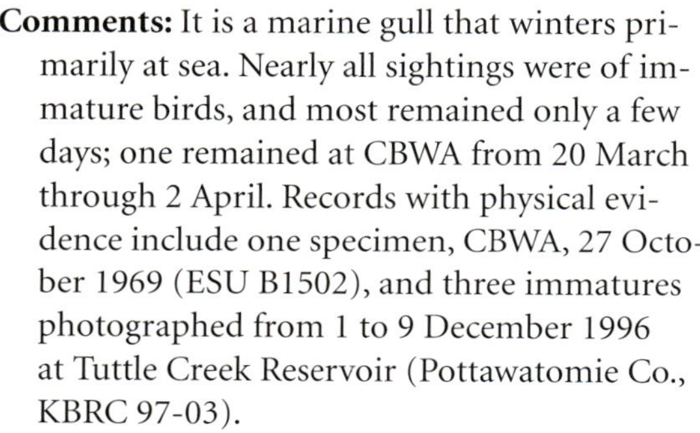

Comments: It is a marine gull that winters primarily at sea. Nearly all sightings were of immature birds, and most remained only a few days; one remained at CBWA from 20 March through 2 April. Records with physical evidence include one specimen, CBWA, 27 October 1969 (ESU B1502), and three immatures photographed from 1 to 9 December 1996 at Tuttle Creek Reservoir (Pottawatomie Co., KBRC 97-03).

References: Hatch et al., 2009; Janzen, 2007; Otte, 2007, 2009; Pittman, 1992, 1995, 1998; Rintoul, 1999; Seibel, 1978; Thompson and Ely, 1989.

Sabine's Gull

Xema sabini (SAGU)

Status: Rare spring and fall transient.

© Linda Williams

Habitat: Reservoirs; large pools in wetlands, and in the west occasionally on sewage ponds.

Migration: Most sightings are in fall, usually of single immatures, but five were present at CBWA on 30 September. The few spring records are 31 March (Barton Co.) to 26 May (Morton Co.). Fall records are from 2 August (QNWR) to 29 November (Sedgwick Co.), with the majority during September and October. Most individuals remain only a few days; but two were at CBWA 10 September–1 October, and one spent 2 weeks on Lake Shawnee (Shawnee Co.) during October 1952. Specimens have been taken from 19 September to 10 October. Two immature birds remained at QNWR (KBRC 97-11) from 27 September through 12 October 1996.

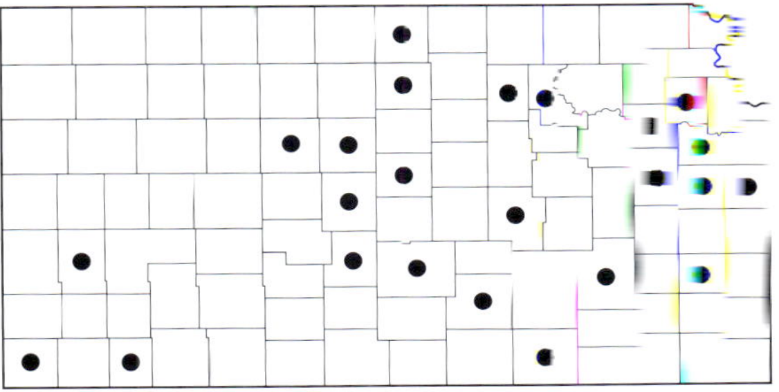

Comments: The first specimen was taken by P. Long at Humboldt (Allen Co.) and reported by N. Goss. Goss stated, "A young male, on the 19th of September, 1876, flew into a billiard saloon in Humboldt, Kansas, at midnight, no doubt attracted there by the light of the burning lamps that brightly reflected out into the darkness."

References: Day et al., 2001; Goss, 1891; Janzen, 2007; Pittman, 1997, 1998; Thompson and Ely, 1989.

Bonaparte's Gull

Chroicocephalus philadelphia (BOGU)

Status: Uncommon to common spring and fall transient; rare winter visitant; recorded in all months.

Habitat: Reservoirs, large pools in wetlands, and major rivers.

Migration: Early migrants usually appear in late March (some may be wintering individuals) with a peak during April and early May and with stragglers through June. Extreme dates include 6 March (Coffey Co.; Douglas Co., specimen) and 27 May (Russell Co.). High counts include 200+ on 25 March (Linn Co.), 200 on 22 April (Douglas Co.), and 100+ on 24 April (Barton Co.).The median arrival for CBWA is 19 April. Fall migration begins in August and continues into December with the peak in October and November. High counts include "several thousand" at Milford Reservoir (Geary Co.), 3,000 on 24 October (JRR), 500 on 8 November (Douglas Co.), and 300 on 12 November (Sedgwick Co.). The earliest fall date is 7 August (Barton Co., 12 individuals); late fall dates outside the main wintering areas include 16 November (Trego Co.), but even in the west occasional birds remain into the CBC period during mild seasons. In recent years increasingly large numbers remain to winter in the east around larger reservoirs and rivers, especially around dams, from December through February. Some of these groups have exceeded 300 individuals including 698+ at Waconda Reservoir (Mitchell Co.) on 19 December.

Comments: It is unique among gulls in that it almost always nests in trees. The bulk of the population winters in the Great Lakes region, Mississippi Flyway, and along the East Coast of North America, so they typically move east of Kansas during migration.

Banding: One banded in May 1978 at CBWA; no encounters.

References: Alderfer, 2006; Burger and Gochfeld, 2002; Janzen, 2007; Rice et al., 2001; Seibel, 1978; Thompson and Ely, 1989; Young, 1993.

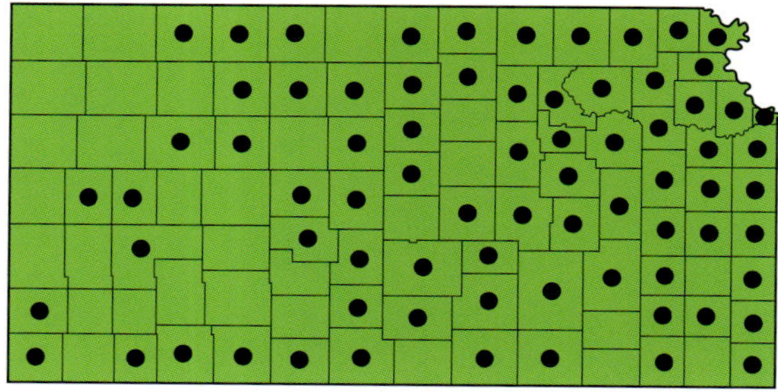

Black-headed Gull

Chroicocephalus ridibundus (BHGU)

Status: Casual spring and fall transient.

Habitat: Large water bodies at reservoirs, rivers, and in wetlands.

Migration: Spring records (most unconfirmed) are 5 March (QNWR) to 25 May (CBWA). Fall records are 5 September (CBWA) to 18 December (Jefferson Co.) with most during October and November.

© David Weible

Comments: The first physical evidence is a video by C. Hobbs from Perry Reservoir (Jefferson Co.) on 8–9 December 1992 (KBRC 92-64). KBRC has subsequently accepted sightings from Douglas, Osage, and Reno counties from the period 6 October–21 November. This is the Old World counterpart of the very similar Bonaparte's Gull, with which it often associates. Identification can be difficult, and spring records may actually pertain to the latter, more common species. Formerly called the Common Black-headed Gull.

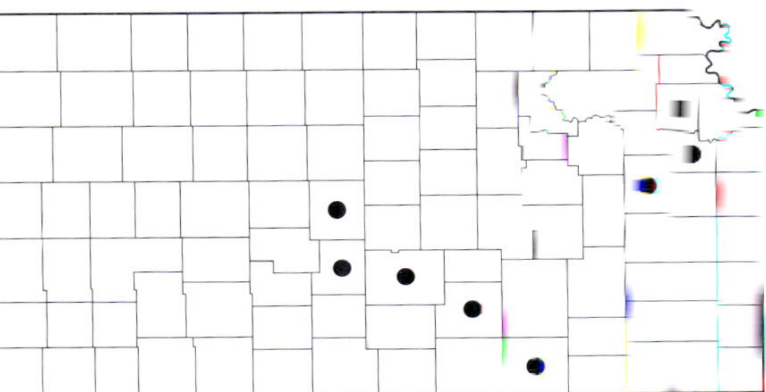

References: Alderfer, 2006; Janzen, 2007; Pittman, 1993, 1995, 1997; Thompson and Ely, 1989.

Little Gull

Hydrocoloeus minutus (LIGU)

Status: Vagrant or casual visitant.

Habitat: Reservoirs, rivers, and wetlands.

© Kevin Groeneweg

Comments: This Old World species has taken up residence around the Great Lakes and southern Minnesota. Although there are no Kansas specimens, photos of one at JRR on 3–4 November 1974 (E. and J. Schulenberg) provided the first physical evidence. The KBRC has accepted 16 records, some with photos. The few records in spring are 13 March (Barton Co.) to 19 May (Pottawatomie Co.). Fall records are more numerous, with most from October through November and with extreme dates of 30 August (Morton Co.) and 3 December (Coffey Co.).

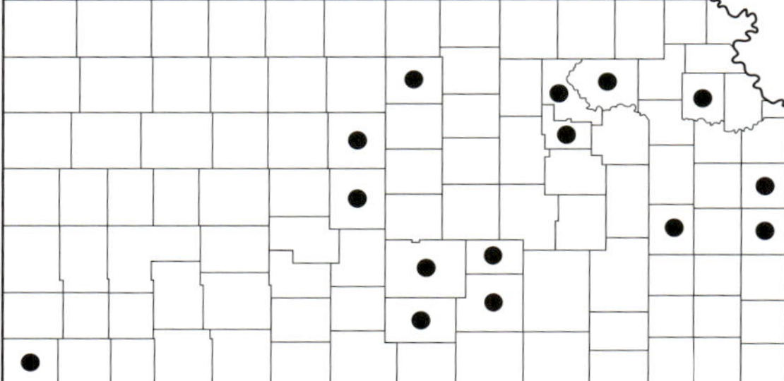

References: Ewins and Weseloh, 1999; Janzen, 2007; Miller, 1975; Otte, 2007; Pittman, 1994, 1995, 1997; Rintoul, 1999, 2002; Thompson and Ely, 1989.

Ross's Gull

Rhodostethia rosea (ROGU)

Status: Accidental. One documented record.

Habitat: Near reservoirs and dam outlets.

Comments: One was observed at the Tuttle Creek Reservoir outlet tubes in Riley County, 14 January 2009, by G. Snyder and T. Cable while taking a lunch break. They immediately called D. Rintoul and J. Shroyer, and the three photographers in the group immediately documented the sighting (KBRC 2009-01). The bird remained for only a short time, departing before other birders arrived and was not seen again. It is a winter vagrant to the lower 48 states and has been previously recorded in the neighboring states of Colorado, Nebraska, and Missouri.

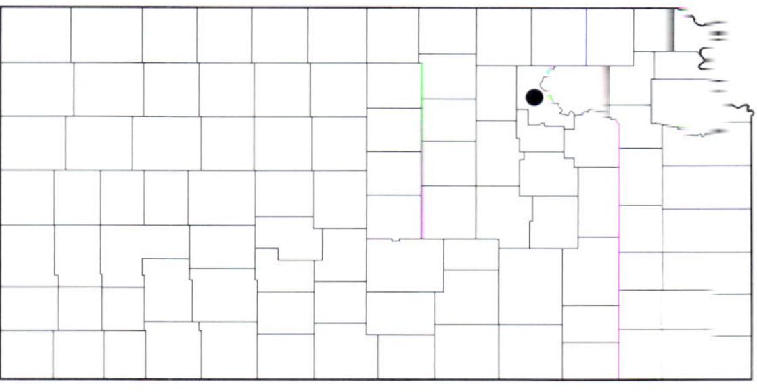

References: Alderfer, 2006; AOU, 1998; Otte, 2009.

Laughing Gull

Leucophaeus atricilla (LAGU)

Status: Rare spring and fall transient; casual summer visitant; primarily in central and northeastern regions.

Habitat: Reservoirs and large pools in wetlands.

Comments: The only specimen was taken in Marion County on 15 May 1933 by R. H. Schmidt. There are numerous sightings from 4 April (Shawnee Co.) through 20 January (Douglas Co.). Most spring sightings are during May, and the number of sightings increases from July into fall. Current records appear to indicate postbreeding dispersal of juvenile or immature birds. M. Thompson and E. Young observed seven or eight individuals at CBWA on 5 October 2008, and E. Young observed an adult and six juveniles at QNWR on 8 November 2009. A few occur in winter if water remains open, for example, one from 4 to 6 January 1994 at Perry Reservoir (Jefferson Co., KBRC 94-09).

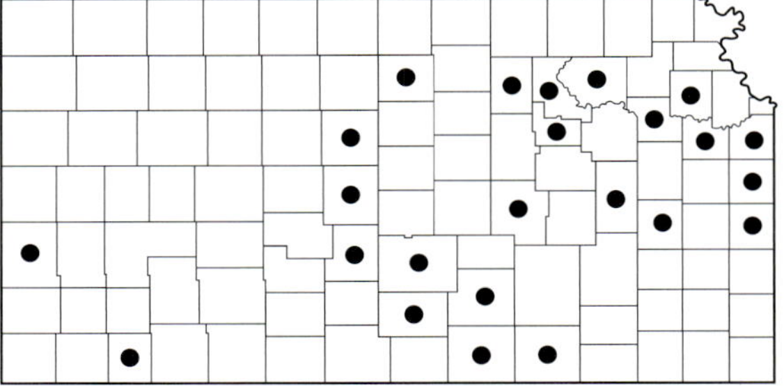

References: Burger, 1996; Janzen, 2007; Otte, 2009; Pittman, 1998; Rice et al., 2001; Rintoul, 2002; Seibel, 1978; Thompson and Ely, 1989.

Franklin's Gull

Leucophaeus pipixcan (FRGU)

© David Seibel

Status: Common to abundant spring and fall transient, rare summer straggler and casual resident (CBWA), and a rare winter visitant; recorded in all months.

Habitat: Follows tractors that are working fields, where they swoop down, or even walk, to grab the insects, worms, and probably small rodents that are uncovered. Otherwise, reservoirs, large pools in wetlands, and large rivers.

Migration: Late January–February birds may have wintered nearby or may be early transients (6 February, Barton Co.). Migration definitely begins by early March with peak numbers present during April and May and stragglers into midsummer (22 July, Sedgwick Co.; 27 July, Cowley Co.; 29 June, Reno Co.). The spring flight (overall) is small compared with the fall movement, but high counts still include 1,500 on 23 April and "thousands" on 21–22 April (both Barton Co.); 6,000 on 6–8 May (Jewell Co.); and 1,275 on 12 May (Sumner Co.). The fall migration begins in late July with peak numbers during late September and October and continues through November with varying numbers remaining around the larger reservoirs (12 January, Riley Co.).

Breeding: There is currently only a single instance of confirmed breeding. KBBAT reported more than 100 birds at CBWA during the summer of 1993 with adults carrying nesting material on 8 July and a flightless juvenile present later in the summer. Other observations included carrying nesting material on 12 June and juveniles begging food from adults in early August (T. and S. Shane); carrying nesting material in pool five on 30 May (L. Moore, G. Pittman); and four juveniles, one begging food on Nature Conservancy property (S. Seltman) and young being fed (D. Rintoul). One dead juvenile (probably flightless) was salvaged and was seen by C. Ely.

Comments: Most of the population appears to migrate through Kansas during the fall en masse. An estimated 500,000 were observed at Cheney Reservoir on 24 October 1997 and at the eastern reservoirs on 16 October 1994. Estimates of 300,000 have been reported from Barton County and the eastern reservoirs during the first half of October. 145,000 at Winfield City Lake (Cowley Co.) on 24 October 2006.

See page 497 for banding information.

References: Alderfer, 2006; Burger and Gochfeld, 2009; Busby and Zimmerman, 2001; [illegible], 1940; Janzen, 2007; Parmelee et al., 1969; Rice et al., 2001; Seibel, 1978; Thompson and Ely, 1989; Young, 1993.

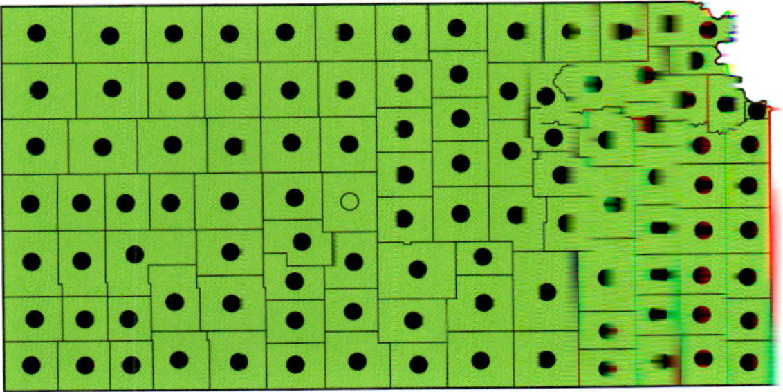

Mew Gull

Larus canus (MEGU)

Status: Casual. Eight records are of wintering birds between 9 November and 13 February (both Sedgwick Co.). The only spring record, a first-year bird observed at CBWA on 24 April 2009 by E. Young, was carefully compared with adjacent Ring-billed Gulls.

Habitat: Reservoirs, large rivers, and large pools in wetlands; landfills.

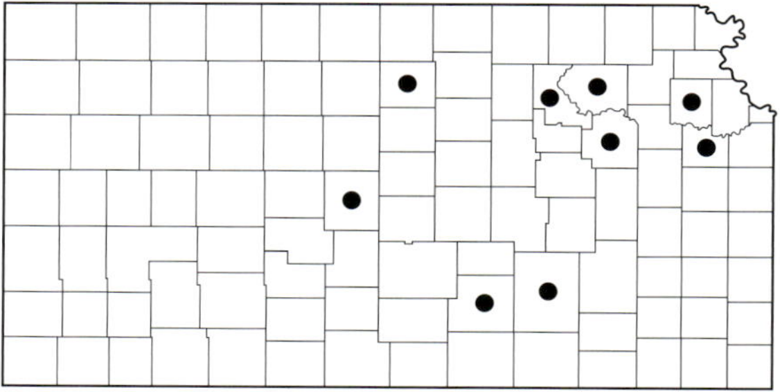

Comments: It was first documented on 17 December 1995 at Tuttle Creek Reservoir (Riley Co., KBRC 97-14) by L. Johnson. No specimen currently exists; physical evidence is based on photos. Most individuals observed appear to be the North American subspecies *L. c. brachyrhynchus*. However, the individual observed by E. Young was a first-winter bird with a black tail band on a completely unmarked white tail and rump giving the appearance of a sharply demarcated black-and-white tail. The back, while gray, was slightly darker than that of the adjacent and slightly larger first-year Ring-billed Gulls. This combination of characteristics indicates that this individual may have been of the *L. c. canus* group and of European origin. The KBRC accepted the record as a Mew Gull without subspecies status (KBRC 2009-19). Few data exist on migratory patterns of this species in North America.

References: Alderfer, 2006; Janzen, 2007; Land, 2010; Moskoff and Bevier, 2002; Otte, 2008; Pittman, 1998; Rintoul, 1999, 2000.

Ring-billed Gull

Larus delawarensis (RBGU)

Status: Common spring and fall transient; uncommon to common winter resident; rare summer visitant; recorded in all months.

Habitat: Reservoirs, large pools in wetlands, rivers, and landfills; occasionally parking lots in urban environments.

Migration: Because large numbers can spend the winter, it is difficult to judge when the spring influx begins. However, numbers increase in March and remain high through April with stragglers remaining through at least 29 May (Phillips Co.). High counts include 1,500 on 8 March (Barton Co.), thousands on 14 March (Mitchell Co.), and 1,000+ on 14 March (Sedgwick Co.). Varying numbers occur during June and July (up to 700 on 9 June and 17 on 18 July, both Barton Co.). The fall migration begins in August (once on 8 July, SCW) and continues into winter with peak numbers from October through November. High counts include 10,000 on 24 October (Coffey Co.), thousands at Cheney Reservoir on 14 November, 1,500 in Butler County on 20 October, and 1,000 on 22 October at SCW. Whether individuals remain for extended periods of time is unknown. Numbers vary in winter, depending on availability of open water. Considerable numbers winter on the larger reservoirs and rivers when there is open water with up to 50,000 at CBWA during some years. More than 10,000 were estimated at Cheney Reservoir on 17 February 2001 and 4,000 along the Arkansas River (Sedgwick Co.) on 17 January 1998.

Comments: Numbers have rebounded to an estimated three to four million individuals in North America in the 1990s, after being decimated from 1850 to 1920 by human persecution and development.

See page 498 for banding information.

References: Alderfer, 2006; Janzen, 2007; Parmelee et al., 1969b; Rice et al., 2001; Rader 1993; Seibel, 1978; Thompson and Ely, 1992; Young, 1993.

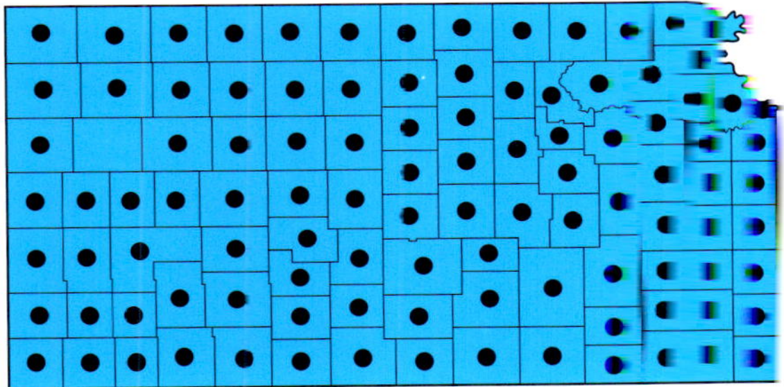

California Gull

Larus californicus (CAGU)

Status: Rare spring and fall transient; rare winter resident.

© Judd Patterson

Habitat: Reservoirs, large pools in wetlands, and rivers.

Migration: Few spring records exist, but extreme dates are from 1 March (Trego Co.) to 19 May (Morton Co.). Main fall migration appears to begin in August and lasts through November. Extreme dates range from 17 July (QNWR) through 28 November (Trego Co.) with most from October. Wintering birds appear from 8 December (Mitchell Co.) to 30 January (Johnson Co.) with most records from January.

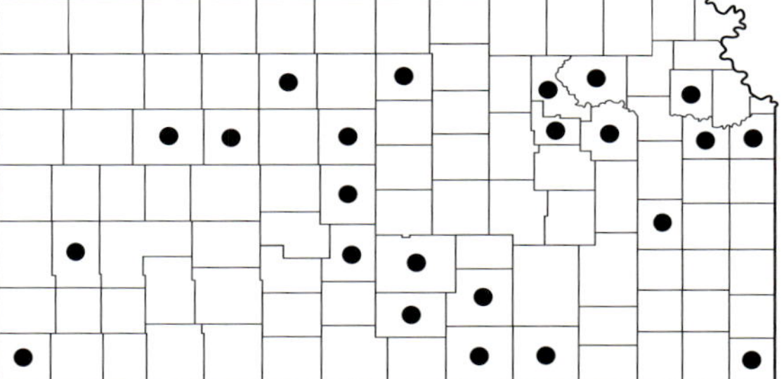

Comments: Most birds migrate to, and winter along, the Pacific Coast, thus bypassing Kansas during migration. The location of the only specimen, taken by N. S. Goss in Reno County on 20 October 1880, is unknown. A photograph does exist of one observed on 16 August 1991 in Morton County by E. McHugh and M. Corder (KBRC 91-31).

Banding: None banded; one encounter. One banded in Saskatchewan on 23 June 1960 was found dead near Stippville, Cherokee County, Kansas, in March 1963.

References: Alderfer, 2006; Janzen, 2007; Thompson and Ely, 1989; Winkler, 1996.

Herring Gull

Larus argentatus (HERG)

Status: Common, low-density transient; uncommon winter resident. There are sight records for every month of the year (few from May through September) with most from counties with large bodies of water.

Habitat: It frequents reservoirs, large pools in wetlands, rivers, and landfills.

Migration: In spring it is most common from 1 March to the end of April with stragglers to at least 4 June. High counts include 200–300 on 14 March (Glen Elder Reservoir, Mitchell Co.) and 100 on 25 February (Cowley Co.). Only a few are found during summer (17 June, Leavenworth Co.; 26 June, Rooks Co., 2; 26 June, Barton Co., 10). The earliest fall date is 6 August (Wyandotte Co.) with most sightings during October and November but with actual numbers low. Largest concentrations are during winter. High counts include 1,645 on 16 December and 1,500+ on 24 January (both Glen Elder Reservoir, Mitchell Co.); 1,000+ on 24 January (Russell Co., unprecedented); and 500 on 17 February 2001 (Cheney Reservoir).

Comments: Large gulls are notoriously difficult to identify, especially those in the large white-headed gull complex, which includes Herring, California, Thayer's, Lesser Black-backed, and Great Black-backed Gulls. Complicating identification are the various plumages (or cycles) the birds molt into before attaining their adult plumage, subspeciation, hybridization among species within the complex, the ability to migrate great distances, and confusing taxonomy. Therefore, care should be made when trying to identify large gulls in Kansas. An attempt should be made to document with photographs and specimens.

Banding: One banded; five encountered in Kansas from: MI (3), OH, WI. At least three were young birds encountered the year after hatching. Oldest 1 year.

References: Alderfer, 2006; Janzen, 2007; Peroni and Good, 1994; Rice et al., 2001; Seibel, 1978; Thompson and Ely, 1989.

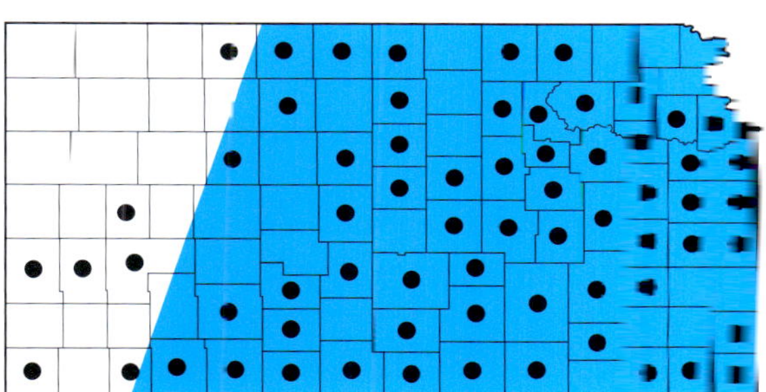

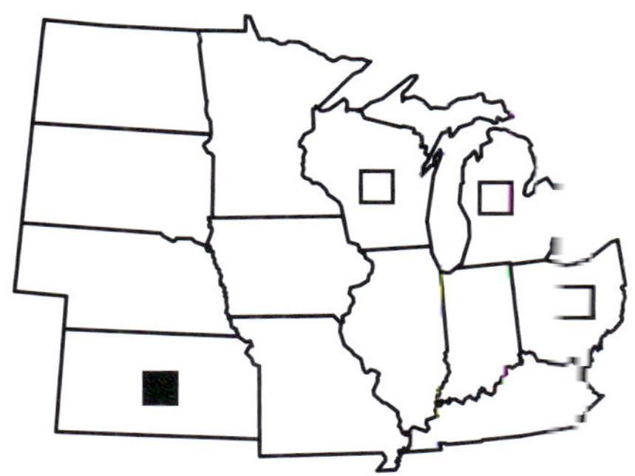

Thayer's Gull

Larus thayeri (THGU)

Status: If a valid taxon, its status is uncertain; probably an uncommon transient and winter resident.

Habitat: Large reservoirs, large rivers, large pools in wetlands, and landfills.

Migration: There are many sight records, with a few confirmed photo-documented records and one specimen (KU 111268; first-cycle male, 8 February 2008, Clinton Reservoir, Douglas Co.). The confirmed records range from 8 November (Douglas Co.) to 8 February (Douglas Co.). There are more than 100 additional sightings (most unverified) ranging in date from 2 September (Barton Co.) to 23 March (Tuttle Creek Reservoir, Riley Co.) and 4 April (two, Jefferson Co.).

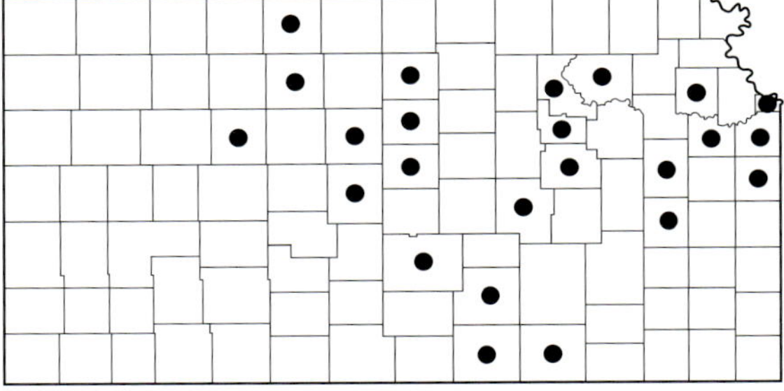

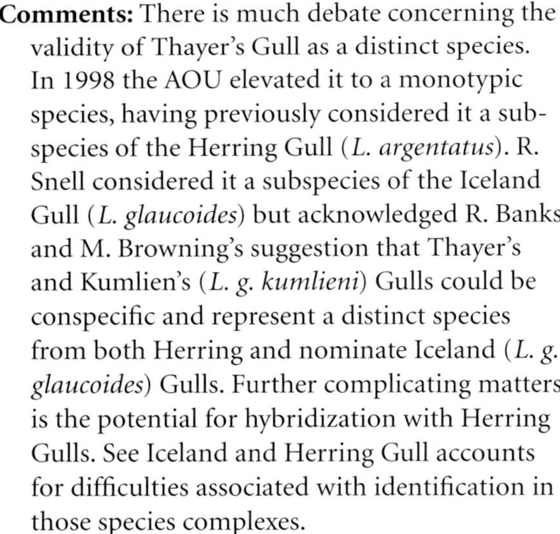

Comments: There is much debate concerning the validity of Thayer's Gull as a distinct species. In 1998 the AOU elevated it to a monotypic species, having previously considered it a subspecies of the Herring Gull (*L. argentatus*). R. Snell considered it a subspecies of the Iceland Gull (*L. glaucoides*) but acknowledged R. Banks and M. Browning's suggestion that Thayer's and Kumlien's (*L. g. kumlieni*) Gulls could be conspecific and represent a distinct species from both Herring and nominate Iceland (*L. g. glaucoides*) Gulls. Further complicating matters is the potential for hybridization with Herring Gulls. See Iceland and Herring Gull accounts for difficulties associated with identification in those species complexes.

References: Alderfer, 2006; AOU, 1998; Banks and Browning, 1999; Cable and Rintoul, 1985; Janzen, 2007; Pittman, 1998; Rintoul, 1999; Snell, 2002; Thompson and Ely, 1989.

Iceland Gull

Larus glaucoides (ICGU)

Status: Status uncertain with records for only five counties. There are no specimens, but two records were confirmed with photographs: 1 March 1997 (Osage Co., KBRC 97-10) and 5 December 2006 (Douglas Co., KBRC 2006-31). Sight records are from 11 December (Sedgwick Co.) to 15 March (CBWA and Sedgwick Co.).

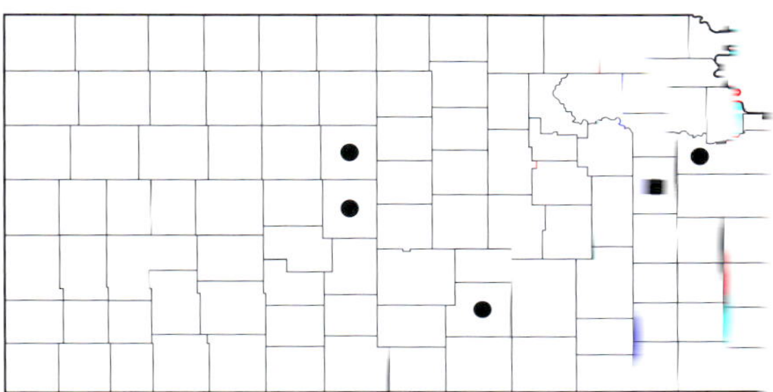

Habitat: Reservoirs, large rivers, large pools in wetlands, and landfills. From 1992 to 2000 most observations were from the Brooks Landfill (Sedgwick Co.). Subsequent to the closing of the landfill most records are from large reservoirs in northern Kansas.

Comments: Separation of purported pale Thayer's Gull from the two subspecies of Iceland Gull (*L. g. glaucoides* and *L. g. kumlieni*) can be very difficult, and the validity of *L. thayeri* has been questioned. For example, plumage states have yet to be determined for the Iceland/Thayer's Gull complex. Therefore, many identifications of the Thayer's/Iceland complex are at best hypothetical.

References: Alderfer, 2006; Janzen, 2007; Otte, 2007; Pittman, 1998; Rintoul, 1999, 2002, 2003; Snell, 2002.

Lesser Black-backed Gull

Larus fuscus (LBBG)

© Linda Williams

Status: Rare winter visitant. It was not recorded in Kansas until 8 February 1996 when M. Thompson observed one at Winfield City Lake (Cowley Co., KBRC 96-11). Subsequently physical evidence (video) was obtained by M. Corder and E. McHugh of a bird observed on 21 December 1996 at Clinton Reservoir (Douglas Co., KBRC 97-01). Current sightings (a few with photos) range from 17 September (CBWA) through 11 March (Douglas Co.) with most from December through February. There is one late record of 5 May (CBWA).

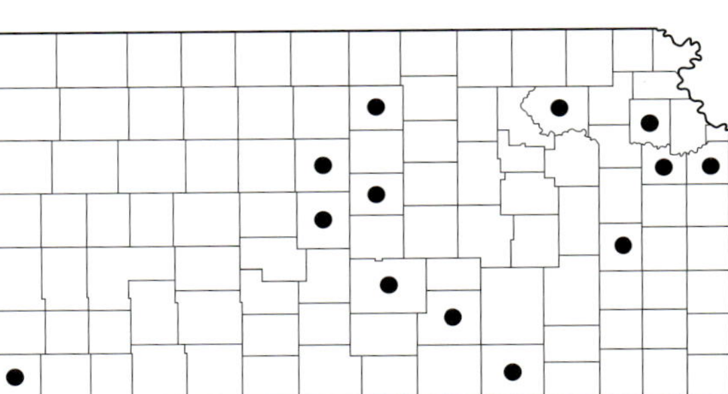

Habitat: Reservoirs, large pools in wetlands, and rivers.

Comments: This Old World species has colonized North America only in the last 60 years since it was first documented in New Jersey in 1934.

References: Alderfer, 2006; Janzen, 2007; Otte, 2006, 2008; Pittman, 1997, 1998; Rintoul, 1999, 2000, 2001, 2002.

Glaucous-winged Gull

Larus glaucescens (GWGU)

Status: [Hypothetical]. Accidental winter visitant. Two of the three records are from the Brooks Landfill (Sedgwick Co.): a second-year bird observed on 24 January 1998 (KBRC 98-14), and another on 12 February 2000. This latter record was rejected due to insufficient details to eliminate other similar species. A third record from Tuttle Creek Reservoir (Riley Co.) observed on 5 February 1998 (KBRC 98-22) was accepted.

Habitat: Reservoirs and landfills.

Comments: This species generally does not migrate, thus there are few accepted interior North American records, although it has been recorded in Colorado and Oklahoma.

References: Alderfer, 2006; Hayward and Verbeek, 2008; Janzen, 2007; Rintoul, 1999.

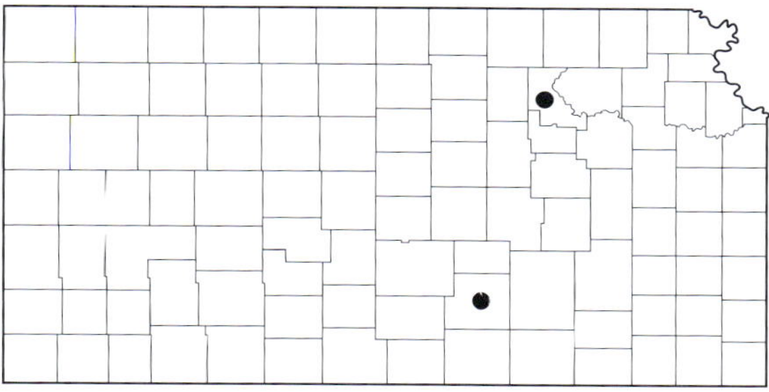

Glaucous Gull

Larus hyperboreus (GLGU)

© David Seibel

Status: Rare winter visitant, casual at other seasons. Most records range from 30 November (Reno Co.) through 6 March (CBWA), with extreme dates of 9 September and 10 April (both Barton Co.) and 23 May (Sedgwick Co.). An adult was at CBWA on 3 July 1967 (M. Schwilling). Although usually occurring as singles, at least nine (and perhaps twice that many) were present at Glen Elder Reservoir (Mitchell Co.) on 24 January 1998. It is the most abundant and widespread of the large "light" gulls.

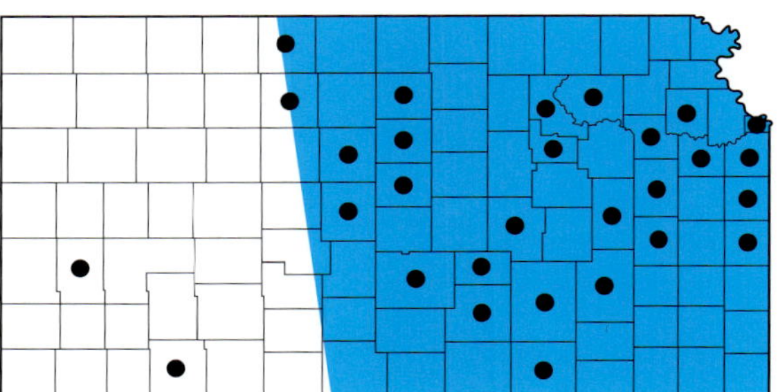

Habitat: Reservoirs, large rivers, large pools in wetlands, and landfills. A bird observed near Udall, Cowley County, was flying over a pond only 10 acres in size.

Comments: Most individuals encountered are immature birds. There are three specimens: an immature female collected on 6 March 1967 (ESU B1406) from CBWA; and two immatures from Clinton Reservoir, Douglas County (KU 111,255, 111,440).

References: Gilchrist, 2001; Janzen, 2007; Thompson and Ely, 1989.

Great Black-backed Gull

Larus marinus (GBBG)

© John Rakestraw

Status: Rare winter visitant. Most records are from December through February with extreme dates from 21 November (Sedgwick Co.) to 25 April (Pottawatomie Co.). The first two records documented with physical evidence are a bird observed by T. Cable and M. Rader at CBWA on 28 December 1999 (KBRC 2003-29), and one observed by K. Kosciuch and D. Rintoul on 25 April 2003 at Pottawatomie State Fishing Lake #2 (KBRC 2003-19).

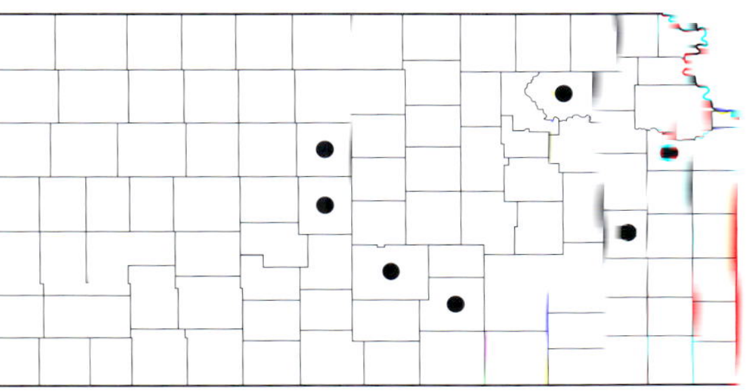

Habitat: Reservoirs, large rivers, large pools in wetlands, rivers, and landfills.

Comments: The earliest sightings were a juvenile at CBWA on 13 April 1973 and an individual in second-year plumage at the same site exactly 1 year later (both by M. Schwilling). Sightings increased markedly during the 1990s. It has not been reported in Sedgwick County since the closing of the Brooks Landfill. Great Black-backed Gulls are equally adept as a predator or a scavenger.

References: Alderfer, 2006; Good, 1998; Janzen, 2007; Otte, 2004, 2006; Pittman, 1997; Rintoul, 1999, 2000, 2002; Thompson and Ely, 1989.

Least Tern

Sternula antillarum (LETE)

Status: Uncommon spring and fall transient, local summer resident in central and northeastern regions.

Habitat: Reservoirs, large pools in wetlands, and rivers during migration; requires saline flats, sandy or small-gravel beaches, and shorelines, either in wetlands or along rivers, using even coal spoil piles for nesting. Nesting is often associated with human recreation areas, residential development, and along rivers where water diversion occurs, which prevent successful nesting. It appears to be most productive at breeding sites such as QNWR that have endured for several years.

Migration: Early arrivals include 15 April (Stafford Co.) and 30 April (Russell Co.) with most migration during May and stragglers into June. In 1989, at SCW, an adult was seen on seven occasions between 22 May and 7 August (nesting not observed), and there are other summer records statewide (pair in Cowley Co., near Arkansas City, 21 June 2008, C. Miller and K. Groeneweg). Whether these are late spring or early fall transients or locally breeding birds is unknown. It appears that fall migration begins in early August and peaks in late August and early September. Late fall dates include 23 September (Barton Co.) and 27 September (Russell Co.).

Breeding: Active colonies exist at QNWR, CBWA, near Wichita (Sedgwick Co.), the Jeffrey Energy Center (Pottawatomie Co.), and on the Kansas River (Wabaunsee and other cos.). Formerly nested along the Cimarron River in Comanche, Clark, and Meade counties, and possibly the SCW. Single pairs and small groups have nested at other localities and are easily overlooked. Eggs have been reported 28 May–16 July and chicks 20 June–27 July. There are two early egg sets from 30 May 1897 taken along the Arkansas River in Rice County (Burke Museum 67292 and 67293).

Comments: This is the smallest tern in Kansas and is listed as an endangered subspecies under the Endangered Species Act. Research by R. Boyd (unpubl. manuscript) and others resulted in the development of habitat manipulation and colony protection, which have been successful in maintaining viable colonies at several sites. Nests are frequently flooded, both on wetland sites as well as along the Arkansas and Kansas rivers.

See page 498 for banding information.

References: Busby et al., 1997; Busby and Zimmerman, 2001; Janzen, 2007; Mulhern and Watkins, 2008; Rice et al., 2001; Seibel, 1978; Thompson et al., 1997; Thompson and Ely, 1989; Tordoff, 1956; Young, 1993.

Gull-billed Tern

Gelochelidon nilotica (GBTE)

Status: Accidental with two records. One adult, documented with photographs, was observed at QNWR on 19 May 1998 (KBRC 98-36) by M. Rader, M. Thompson, and E. Young. A second individual was observed at the Liberal sewage ponds (Seward Co.) on 21 September 2002 by G. Friesen, R. Wedel, and K. Straley (KBRC 2002-07).

Comments: It is considered a vagrant to the interior United States. Unlike most terns, it does not depend on a diet of fish, but frequently consumes insects, small crustaceans, small chicks of shorebirds, Least Tern chicks, and other prey snatched from the ground, air, and bushes.

References: Alderfer, 2006; Molina et al., 2009; Rintoul, 1999, 2003.

© David Welble

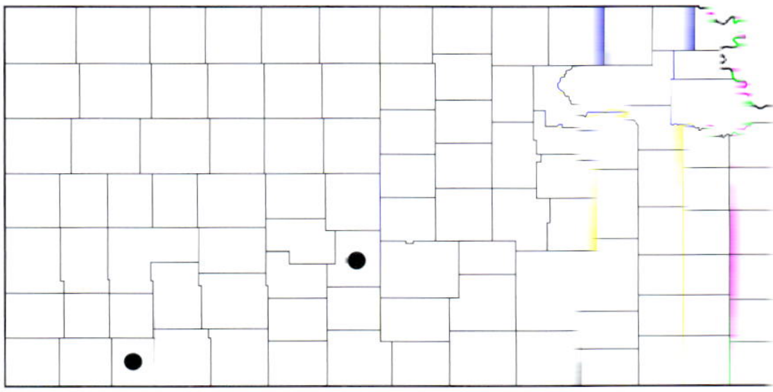

Caspian Tern

Hydroprogne caspia (CATE)

Status: Uncommon to common spring and fall transient, primarily in the eastern and central areas; vagrant in winter.

Habitat: Reservoirs, large pools in wetlands, and larger rivers.

Migration: Smaller numbers appear in spring compared to fall. Recorded from 5 April (Douglas Co.) through 16 June with most sightings mid-May to early June. Scattered records during mid-June and early July are transients or vagrants. The fall migration begins in mid-July (12 July, Geary and Osage cos.) with most sightings in September and with stragglers to 25 October (five, Johnson Co.) and 29 October (Marion Co.). It usually occurs in small groups, but 10–20 individuals are occasionally observed at one location during fall. There is one early winter date of 7 December 1999 (Doniphan Co.). It normally winters along the Gulf Coast; there are few winter inland records.

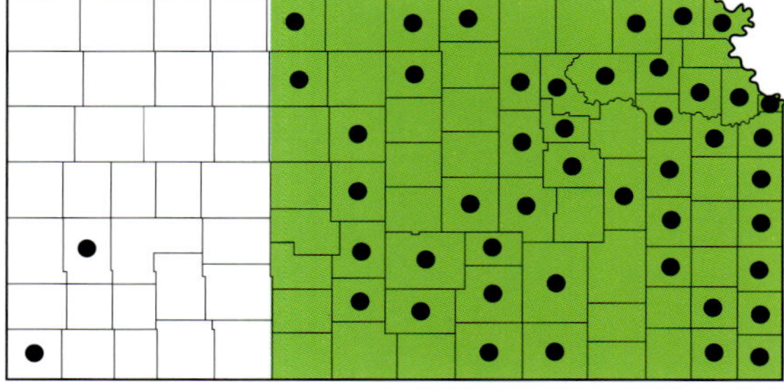

Comments: This is the largest tern found in Kansas. There are three specimens: Douglas County on 27 September 1928 (KU 17147); and two from CBWA on 3 June 1961 (ESU B808) and 22 September 1963 (ESU B1150).

References: Cuthbert and Wires, 1999; Janzen, 2007; Seibel, 1978; Thompson and Ely, 1989; Tordoff, 1956; Young, 1993.

Black Tern

Chlidonias niger (BLTE)

Status: Common spring and fall transient; rare local summer resident in the central region.

Habitat: Reservoirs, large pools in wetlands, ponds, and rivers; forages over grasslands and alfalfa fields during migration in search of insects.

Migration: Usually recorded in spring from late April through June. Extreme dates are 20 March (Harvey Co.) and 21 June (Sumner Co.). Median first arrival dates include 3 May (Barton Co.) and 12–13 May (Rice Co.). Peak numbers occur in May. High counts include 2,000+ on 20 May (Barton Co.); 150 on 19 May 1989 and 450 on 21 May 2008 (both from SCW); 300 on 13 May 2000 and 400 on 16 May 2009 (both Clinton Reservoir, Douglas Co.); 400 on 16–17 May 1996 (Jamestown Wildlife Area, Republic Co.); and 400 on 28 May 1997 (Lovewell Reservoir, Jewell Co.). Small numbers of nonbreeding birds occur at scattered localities during most summers including 25 at SCW during 1958. Fall migration begins in mid-July (155 on 17 July, Osage Co.) and peaks during August and early September with stragglers to 17 October (Stafford Co., five individuals) and 23 October (Barton Co.). High counts include 198 on 26 July 2009 (QNWR); 100 on 14 August 1987 and 141 on 8 August 1988 (both Sumner Co.); 85 on 26 September (Barton Co.); and 60 on 1 August (Reno Co.).

Breeding: For nesting, floating or emergent vegetation is required; thus suitable habitat is restricted, because most wetlands in Kansas are prone to dynamic water fluctuations. It seems to prefer freshwater wetlands. Nesting was confirmed at CBWA in 1961 with at least 11 nests observed 18 June–9 July but destroyed by hail on 19 July. Nesting has been sporadic there since 1968 and was the only confirmed site for KBBAT (1992–1997). Probable breeding occurred in Sedgwick County in 1958. Eggs have been reported 11 June–12 August and chicks on 12 June and 23 July.

Comments: A true prairie tern. Like most terns, young migrate with adults and will beg for food well away from their breeding site. Thus nesting confirmations need to be verified by actually finding nests or flightless young.

Banding: 235 banded; no encounters.

References: Busby and Zimmerman, 2001; S. Heath et al., 2009; Janzen, 2007; Rice et al., 2001; Seibel, 1978; Thompson and Ely, 19[illegible]; Young, 1993.

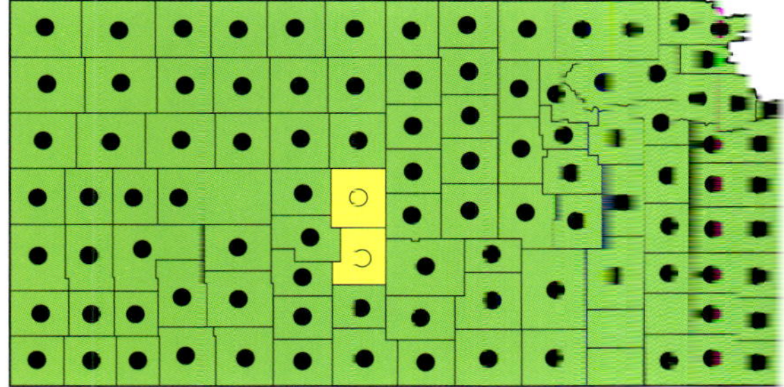

Northern Saw-whet Owl

Aegolius acadicus (NSWO)

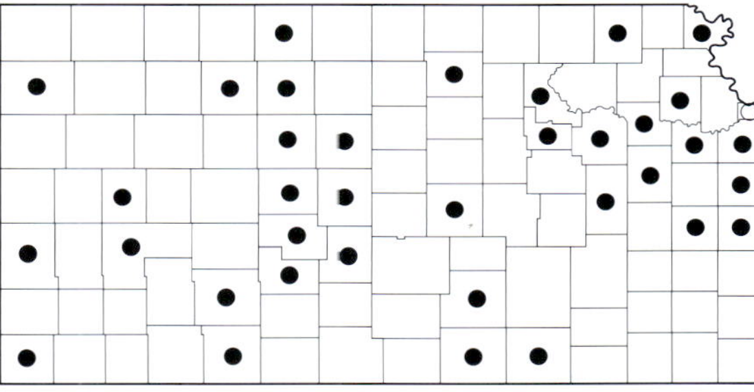

Status: Rare transient and winter resident; one breeding record.

Habitat: Breeds in dense woods and swamps of the northern United States, southern Canada, and in mountainous areas farther south; in Kansas in riparian growth or suburban areas typically roosting in dense conifers or grapevine tangles.

Migration: Fall arrival is 14 October (Ellis Co.) to 28 October (Jefferson Co.) with most sightings from November through January. Late spring dates are 25 March (Johnson Co.) and 7 April (Phillips Co.).

Breeding: A pair found in Kansas City (Wyandotte Co.) during the winter of 1950–1951 remained to nest. Young seen by J. Bishop were present until at least September. Birds responded to a taped call at Hillsdale Reservoir, Miami County, on 27 July 1985 (M. Muehler). A pair visited a yard in Haysville (Sedgwick Co.) on several occasions including 8 August 1977 (D. Vannoy), but there was no evidence of nesting.

Comments: While here, it is completely nocturnal, spends the day roosting in thick vegetation, and is rarely seen. It is probably underreported. It is very tame and can usually be approached very closely and sometimes be captured by hand. One netted in Hays (Ellis Co.) was displayed to a class then spent the remainder of the hour perched on the back of a chair quietly watching the class. Its name comes from the courtship call, which sounds like a saw being sharpened, a call rarely heard in Kansas. It is the smallest owl regularly found in Kansas.

Banding: Four banded (including one "experimental"); no encounters.

References: Janzen, 2007; Thompson and Ely, 1989.

Lesser Nighthawk

Chordeiles acutipennis (LENI)

Status: [Hypothetical]. Vagrant in the southwest. All records are from Morton County. The first report was of one trilling an hour after sunset on 18 September 1993 by S. and D. Seltman and L. Vidal. The observers noted that the call matched a tape of that species. Two subsequent reports were accepted by the KBRC: 30 April 1999, near Elkhart High School (KBRC 2000-14); and 31 August 2002, Elkhart sewage ponds (KBRC 2003-12). The fourth was a possible sighting at the Cimarron River north of Elkhart on 21 September 2006 but was not submitted to the KBRC. A report from Cherokee County was not accepted by the KBRC. The normal range of the species is in the desert southwest from western Texas to California.

References: Cable et al., 1996; Latta and Baltz, 1997; Otte, 2004; Rintoul, 2001.

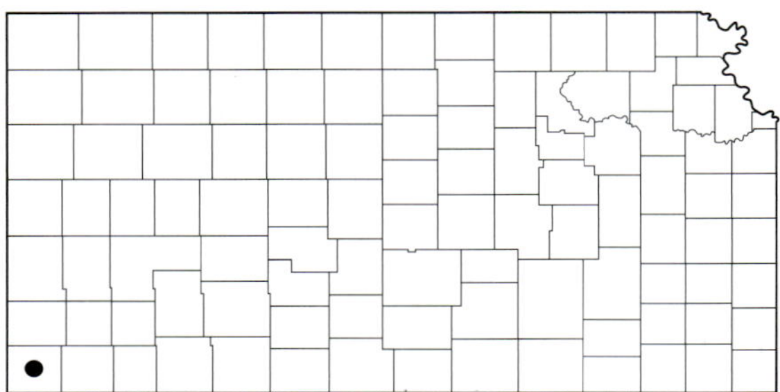

© Jim Burns

Common Nighthawk

Chordeiles minor (CONI)

© Judd Patterson

Status: Common transient and summer resident throughout the state.

Habitat: A variety of open habitats including grasslands and agricultural fields and in towns and cities.

Migration: Early reports before late March cannot be explained and would require physical evidence. Unusually early arrival includes 23 March (Sedgwick Co.) and 29 March (Cowley Co.), but it typically arrives in mid- to late April with birds widespread by 10 May. Median earliest arrivals include 8 May (Ellis Co.), 20 May (Meade Co.), and 13 May (Rice Co.). The fall migration begins in mid-August with most movement during September and early October. Impressive flights include 200+ on 17 September (Ellis Co.), 300+ on 20 September (Sedgwick Co.), and 1,000+ on 5 September (Decatur Co.) and 10 October (Edwards Co.). Median late departure dates include 11 October (Rice Co.) and 13 October (Ellis Co.). Other late dates include 29 October (Johnson and Coffey cos.), 2 November (Cowley Co.), and 4 December (Johnson Co.). The southward migration begins in late August, with most during September and into October. They migrate in fairly large flocks in the evening and at night. When days are cool, large flocks may be seen flying southward, often with 100 or more in the group. Their tendency to fly low makes them vulnerable to being hit by cars, and it may be the species most often brought into rehabilitation centers, usually with broken wings.

Breeding: It is a common breeding bird statewide with highest densities in the Flint Hills and Smoky Hills. It nests on thinly vegetated areas within prairie, gravelly areas, burned-over pastures, and in towns and cities, on rooftops, particularly those that use chat as a covering. Nesting is on the ground, and adults often indulge in broken-wing displays when nest scrapes are approached. Eggs have been reported 10 May–15 August, dependent young 25–26 May, and nearly fledged young 25 May–23 July. The median date for 34 clutches, statewide, is 6 June.

Comments: These goatsuckers forage at dusk, rest during the night (except for courtship), and begin foraging again in the early dawn hours. They find their prey visually. When courting, the male frequently dives toward the ground with the air passing over the wings making a roaring sound, hence the common name "bull bat."

Banding: 402 banded; no encounters.

References: Busby and Zimmerman, 2001; Thompson and Ely, 1989.

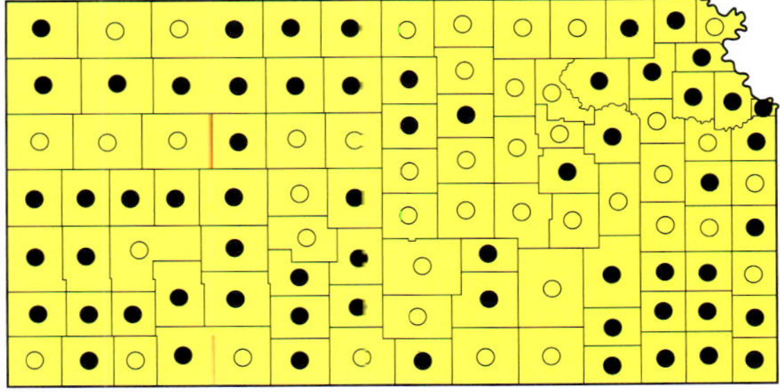

Common Poorwill

Phalaenoptilus nuttallii (COPO)

© Judd Patterson

Status: Locally common transient and summer resident in the west, eastward into the Flint Hills. It may breed anywhere in the state in suitable habitat.

Habitat: Prefers areas with rock and gravel outcroppings; in western Kansas, in areas of open vegetation with a rocky or sandy base.

Migration: The earliest arrivals are 1 April (Sedgwick Co.) and 7 April (Pottawatomie and Riley cos.), but arrival is more typically around 15 April in the east and about 26 April in the west. Most migration is during the last half of April. The fall departure begins by early September and extends into mid-October with stragglers to 2 November ("a frigid night," S. Seltman). Because of its ability to go into torpor on cold nights, the actual departure dates are not well known. One was recorded on a CBC in Barber County on 23 December 1976 by N. Johnson and M. Schwilling. It was flushed from a grassy hillside near a sandhill "seep"; there was no snow cover.

Breeding: Although primarily western, it breeds throughout the state in suitable habitat and is fairly common in the Flint Hills and with nesting records as far east as Anderson, Franklin, and Doniphan counties. Most KBBAT sightings were considered "possible" breeding. Because it is a nocturnal species, the lack of records from western Kansas may reflect when atlas blocks were conducted rather than the lack of Poor-wills. Nesting areas are usually on rocky outcrops with either sand or gravel base. Eggs have been reported 1 May–16 August (Rooks Co.), young 25 May–26 July, and nearly fledged young 25 May–23 July.

Comments: It may have been more common in eastern than in western Kansas during early settlement days. It was "common" at Topeka (Shawnee Co.) during 1871 and was considered "common" in both Riley and Dickinson counties but not reported from specific western localities during that period. They are frequently seen at night sitting on roads. When the headlights of a car shine on them, the eyes take on a red glow. The name comes from the characteristic call, a soft "poor-will," heard at dusk and well into the night.

Banding: 29 banded; no encounters.

References: Allen, 1872; Blachly, 1879–1880; Busby and Zimmerman, 2001; Janzen, 2002b; Lantz, 1901; Thompson and Ely, 1989; Young, 1993.

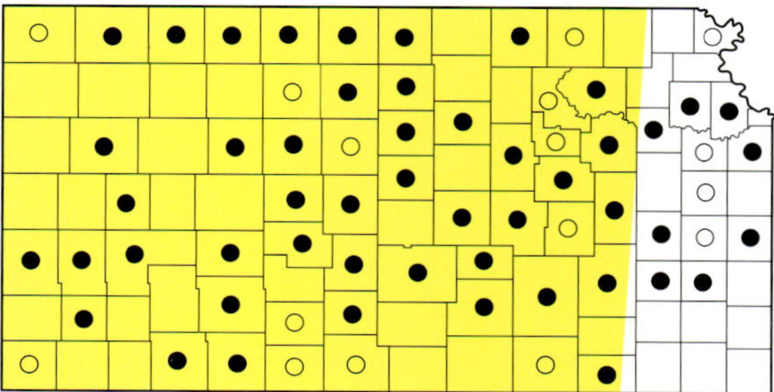

Chuck-will's-widow

Caprimulgus carolinensis (CWWI)

© Judd Patterson

Status: Locally common summer resident in the east, becoming less common westward with confirmed records to at least Meade and Edwards counties.

Habitat: Woodlands, riparian areas, and in the south and southeast, tree-covered hillsides.

Migration: Early spring arrivals include 13 April (Elk Co.) and 19 April (Linn Co.) with most arrivals during late April. Median first arrivals include 24 April (Johnson Co.) and 27 April (Riley Co.). Calling birds are widespread by early May. Late dates outside known breeding areas include 24 May (Thomas Co.) and 16 June (Harvey Co.). Because it is nocturnal, it may go unnoticed unless one listens for its call at dusk, early evening, and again just before dawn. Many more observations are needed to understand the timing and extent of fall migration and breeding. The fall departure is essentially unknown with a few sightings to 16 September.

Breeding: KBBAT found highest frequencies (with confirmed nesting in three blocks) in the Osage Plains. It occurs west to the western edge of the Flint Hills, in the Red Hills, and has bred west to at least Edwards County (egg in oviduct, 19 May 1968). The nest is very difficult to find, and the best indication of probable breeding is when calling continues late into May. The nest is on the ground on leaf litter in forest or forest edge. The young remain in the vicinity of the nest until capable of flight. Copulation has been reported on 9 June, eggs 16 April–14 June, and young 16 June–2 July.

Comments: It appears to be a fairly recent arrival in the state, but see also the paper by M. Jenkinson cited below. The earliest reports are one collected in Chautauqua County on 18 July 1892 (USNM 140355) and one collected in Sedgwick County on 12 June 1898 (specimen lost). Spring migration reports (USNM) indicated presence in Riley County (1913–1915) and Chase County (1916). By 1956, H. Tordoff considered it to be a locally common summer resident. It is now fairly common in the eastern half of Kansas and may be displacing the Eastern Whip-poor-will in areas where they both occur. T. Shane and J. LaShelle obtained densities of 1.80–4.08/square mile along the Republican and Smoky Hill rivers near Junction City. Cink, censusing wooded habitat in the east, obtained densities of 1.2–2.2/square mile in the Cross Timbers and 0.2–2.4/square mile in Oak–Hickory Mosaic.

Banding: 27 banded; no encounters.

References: Busby and Zimmerman, 2001; Cink, 1987; Janzen, 2002b; Jenkinson, 1968; Shane, 1966; Thompson and Ely, 1989.

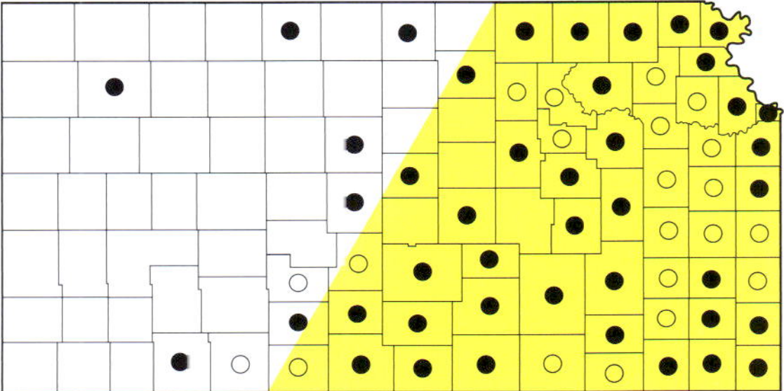

Eastern Whip-poor-will

Caprimulgus vociferus (WPWI)

© Judd Patterson

Status: Locally common transient and summer resident in the east; breeds west to Pottawatomie, Wabaunsee, and Chautauqua counties; rare farther west.

Habitat: Woodlands; resides and breeds in deeper forest than the Chuck-will's-widow.

Migration: The earliest arrival date is 3 April (Johnson Co.) but is usually late April; median first arrival is 20 April (Johnson Co.) and "very large numbers" on 15 April (Jefferson Co.). Most migration is from mid-April through early May. Late dates include 9 May (Scott Co.), 21 May (Pawnee Co.), and 9 June (Ellis Co.). Very few data are available for the fall migration, which appears to be from late August (Reno Co.) through September with unverified reports to 14 October (Ellis Co.) and one heard in Barton County on 4 November. Clearly more study is needed.

Breeding: There are very few actual breeding records. Like most caprimulgids, it nests on the ground among fallen leaves in wooded areas, and the nests are extremely difficult to find. Most breeding surveys are based on calling during the breeding season. KBBAT confirmed nesting in only two blocks, listing 49 blocks as "probable," and 46 as "possible." "Nesting" has been reported 1 May–6 July, and eggs have been reported 30 April–3 July.

Comments: Its range seems to be shrinking as the Chuck-will's-widow continues to expand its distribution. Studies in Douglas County confirmed that when Chuck-will's-widows moved into an area, Eastern Whip-poor-will numbers tended to decrease, but KBBAT found many areas where the two species were coexisting. Most KBBAT records were in the eastern two tiers of counties with clustering in the northeast. It has declined markedly in some areas. For example, it bred in Harvey County through the 1980s but not since. C. Cink censused 30 sites in wooded habitats in the eastern one-third of Kansas during 1983, reporting singing (territorial) males in most counties west to Chautauqua and Pottawatomie counties. *C. vociferus* outnumbered *C. carolinensis* except in the Cross Timbers and a few upland riparian sites. Highest densities were in Oak Hickory Forest (2.1–2.8/square mile) and the Oak–Hickory Mosaic (0.6–2.8/square mile).

See page 499 for banding information.

References: Busby and Zimmerman, 2001; Cink, 1987, 2002; Thompson and Ely, 1992.

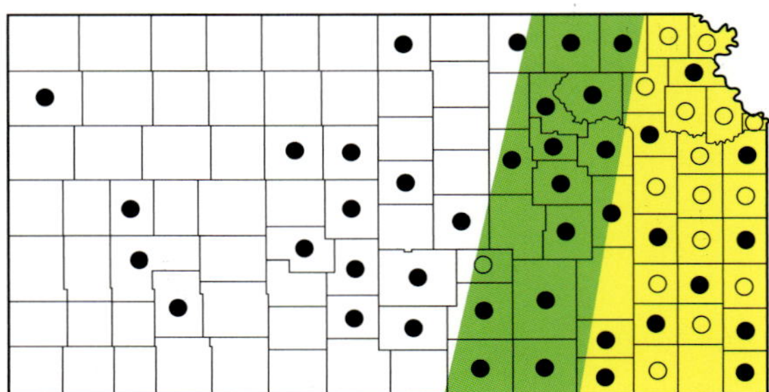

Chimney Swift

Chaetura pelagica (CHSW)

Status: Common transient and breeder in eastern and central regions, becoming less common and local westward.

Habitat: Usually observed flying high over towns, cities, or open country, often near water.

Migration: The earliest birds may arrive by 7–10 March (Douglas Co.), but most arrival is in mid-April with a peak in early May and most transients gone by mid-May. Median first arrivals include 13 April (Cowley Co.), 15 April (Rice Co.), and 18 April (Ellis Co.). The highest spring count reported is 6,000 on 25 April (Riley Co.). Concentrations may appear by mid-August with significant movement through mid-October. Movements are affected by weather and may vary as much as 3 weeks from year to year. Median last departure dates include 11 October (Rice Co.) and 12 October (Ellis Co.). Significant migrations have been noted on 25 September and 10 October. High counts include 5,000 on 27 September and "thousands" on 20 September (both Cowley Co.), 200 on 19 August (Barton Co.), and 100 on 20 September (Sheridan Co.). Late dates include 24 October (Shawnee Co.) and 30 October.

Breeding: As its name implies, it nests mainly in chimneys, less often in deserted farm buildings and silos. Prior to settlement it nested in tree hollows and in caves, but no such nestings have been reported in Kansas in modern times. The nest is a flat platform of dead twigs, broken from trees while in flight, held together and stuck to the chimney wall by the bird's saliva. The young flutter up the chimney and depart in about 4 weeks. Nests are difficult to access, and contents are rarely reported. Nest-building has been reported 23 May, eggs 15 June–5 July, young 25 June–3 August, and recently fledged young by 2 July.

Comments: Courtship also takes place in the sky. As chimney design has changed, there are fewer nest sites, and this may be causing a reduction in populations. Many people cap their chimneys in the mistaken belief that the swifts bring biting insects into the chimney and subsequently into the house and on to people. Some large chimneys are used for staging in migration with thousands of migrating swifts using one chimney. The swifts start flying in circles about dusk and, resembling a miniature tornado, flutter into the chimney and cling to the sides to roost. One chimney in Winfield hosted an estimated 10,000 birds during migration.

© David Seibel

See page 499 for banding information.

References: Busby and Zimmerman, 2001; Cink and Collins, 2002; Thompson and Ely, 1989.

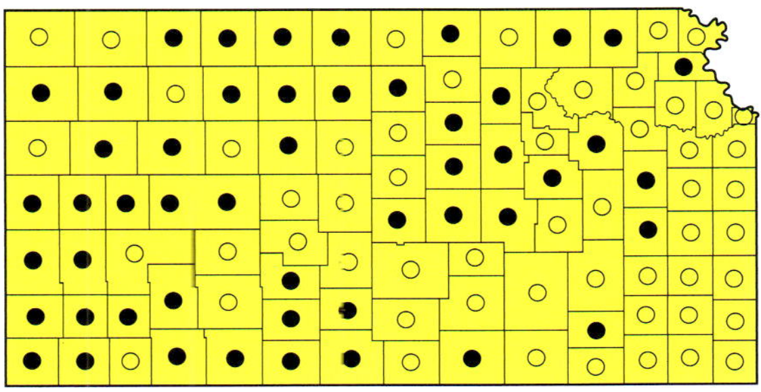

White-throated Swift

Aeronautes saxatalis (WTSW)

© Gerald Wiens

Status: Casual visitant. There are eight records for the state. The first record was of two birds seen repeatedly at Point of Rocks (Morton Co.), on 9–11 June 1972, by S. Patti. The second, on the Kansas State University campus in Manhattan (Riley Co.), on 2 November 1978, was observed by S. Fretwell and four others for 20 minutes. It fed from near ground level to high overhead as it hawked for insects with starlings and gulls and finally attempted to roost by clinging high on the side of the biology building. The third sighting was one observed on 24 November 1990 at Junction City (Geary Co.), by L. Moore. On 17–18 April 1992, another was seen at the University of Kansas, Lawrence (Douglas Co.), by C. Burris and S. Frantz. It too clung to the side of a building and was photographed. One captured inside a grain elevator in Arkansas City (Cowley Co.) on 8 April 1993 was photographed by G. Wiens and released. Another, trapped in a building on 23 April 2001 (Ford Co.), was identified and released by M. and K. Sexson. One reported on 1 October 2005 near Tuttle Creek Reservoir by M. Mayfield, in both Riley and Pottawatomie counties, was probably the same individual seen in the area on 6 October.

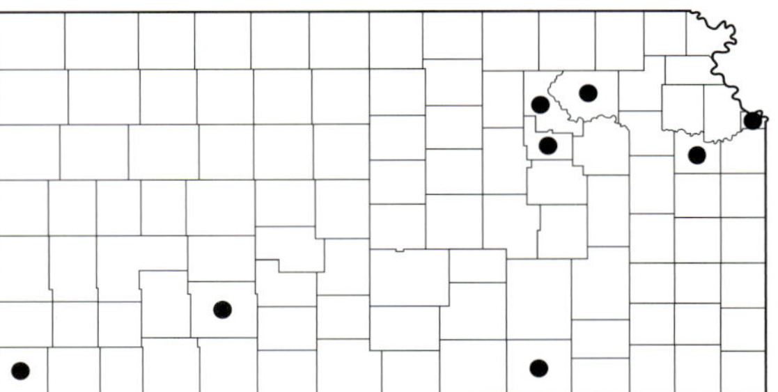

Comments: It will undoubtedly continue to visit the state and should be looked for around buildings or rugged cliffs, which are its favorite nesting and roosting sites.

References: Thompson and Ely, 1989; Wiens, 1993.

Broad-billed Hummingbird

Cynanthus latirostris (BBLH)

Status: Vagrant. Two confirmed records. An immature male first appeared at a feeder of P. Rich in Garden City (Finney Co.) on 10 October 2004. It moved two blocks to the T. Shane yard on 7 November 2004, where it stayed until over-stressed by a snowstorm on 29 November 2004. It was found hanging upside down shaking about 45 minutes after sunset and was slightly injured with feathers missing on the neck from probable House Sparrow and/or House Finch attack. It was revived with sugar water and later moved to the Garden City Zoo where it was an extremely popular exhibit until it died on 18 May 2005. The bird, now in definitive alternate plumage, was preserved as a specimen (KU 97178). The second record, also a male, was photographed in Shawnee (Johnson Co.) on 26 April 2006 by C. Hobbs (KBRC 2006-07).

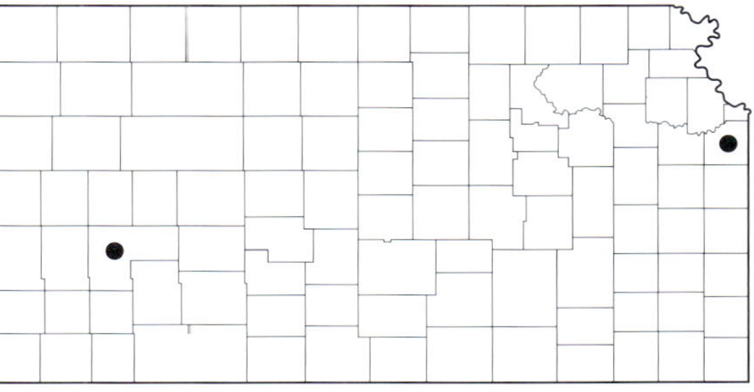

Comments: This hummer typically breeds in the southwestern United States into Mexico.

References: Powers and Wethington, 1999; Terres, 1980.

Magnificent Hummingbird

Eugenes fulgens (MAHU)

Status: Vagrant. The first report was by O. Rice who described a large hummer coming to a feeder in Topeka (Shawnee Co.) in 1965. A Magnificent Hummingbird appeared at the feeder of H. Town in Boicourt (Linn Co.) on 18 April 1977 and remained until 29 May. Photos of this bird by M. Pressgrove were identified by A. Phillips. On 11 July 2004, M. Corder discovered a large hummer at a feeder in Chautauqua County. It was identified as a Magnificent Hummingbird and was seen by numerous persons. A large hummer with a turquoise throat was reported by K. Harden at a feeder near Winfield (Cowley Co.) during late summer 2008. Although not photographed or seen by an experienced ornithologist, it was presumed to be this species.

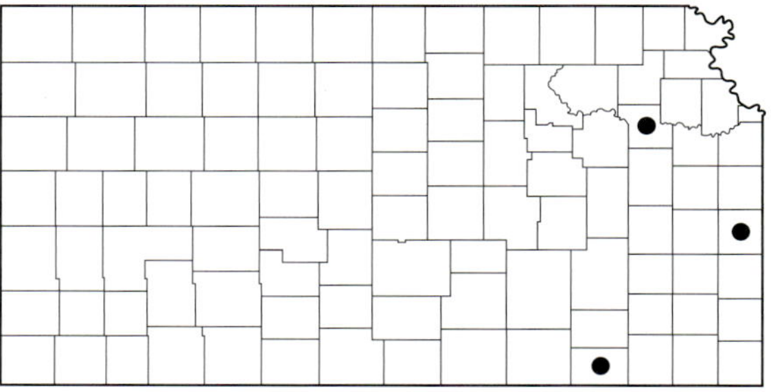

Comments: "Large hummers" also were reported at feeders in Riley and Chautauqua counties in 1990 and in Pawnee County in 1991. This is another hummingbird of the southwestern United States with a history of vagrancy. It breeds in the mountains of southern Arizona, possibly New Mexico, and the Chisos Mountains of Texas. There are numerous records for Colorado including one breeding record.

References: Powers, 1996; Thompson and Ely, 1989.

Ruby-throated Hummingbird

Archilochus colubris (RTHU)

© Judd Patterson

Status: Common transient and summer resident in the eastern half of the state; rare transient and casual summer resident westward.

Habitat: Riparian areas and in cities and towns with sufficient trees for nesting.

Migration: The earliest spring arrival dates are 2 April and 10 April (Harvey Co.) with usual arrival during mid- and late April. R. Johnston gave 6 May as the median earliest arrival for eastern Kansas. Most migration is during mid-May. Late spring dates include 24 May (Ellis Co.). Fall migration begins in July, is widespread by mid-August, probably peaks by mid-September, and continues into October with stragglers to 24 October (Lyon Co.) and 8 November (Harvey Co.). The number of late sightings is expected to increase as more monitoring of feeders occurs. As expected, there are no winter records from the state, but all "late" hummers should be carefully studied and their identities carefully determined.

Breeding: This minute bird breeds in riparian areas, cities with trees, parks, and other types of woody situations. Most breeding records are from Wichita eastward and KBBAT reported most records east of a line from Cowley County northward to Washington County largely east of the Flint Hills and with 60 percent of them from the Osage Plains. KBBAT also reported possible nesting as far west as Morton and Seward counties. These would be very rare events and could involve Black-chinned Hummingbirds. Nest-building has been reported 4 June–2 July, eggs 14 June–10 August, and nestlings 26 June–27 August.

Comments: It is the only truly eastern hummingbird in the United States, reaching its western limits in Kansas. Hummingbird feeding is gaining in popularity, and large numbers may be attracted to favorable, well-maintained sites. One such site at the Dailey residence in the Cross Timbers (Chautauqua Co.) commonly attracts 50–100 hummers daily during mid-July and once hosted a Magnificent Hummingbird (see that account). Westward, numbers decrease and transients of more western species predominate. These minute birds winter in Mexico southward through Costa Rica and Panama with many performing the amazing feat of flying nonstop across the Gulf of Mexico, some 500 miles.

See page 499 for banding information.

References: Busby and Zimmerman, 2001; Johnston, 1964a; Thompson and Ely, 1992.

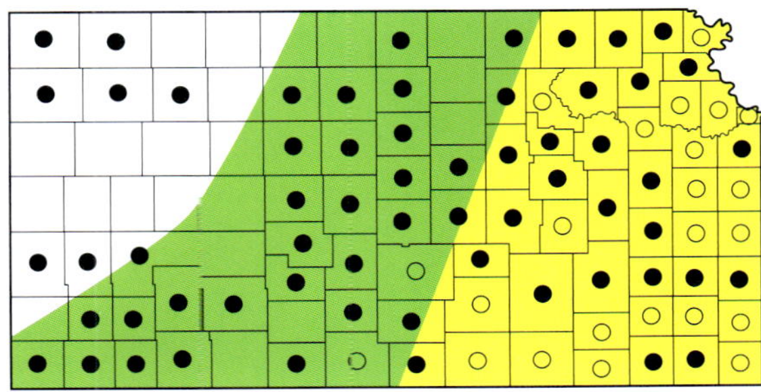

Black-chinned Hummingbird

Archilochus alexandri (BCHU)

Status: Rare visitant and possible summer resident; regular in Garden City (Finney Co.) and in Morton County; casual eastward. Only adult males in spring can be positively identified in the field.

Habitat: Usually observed in suburban areas associated with feeders.

Migration: The few spring sightings (all males) are 22 April–20 May. Late summer–fall sightings, including one adult male, are from 26 July–3 October and 5 November (Johnson Co., banded). Six of these sightings were accepted by KBRC.

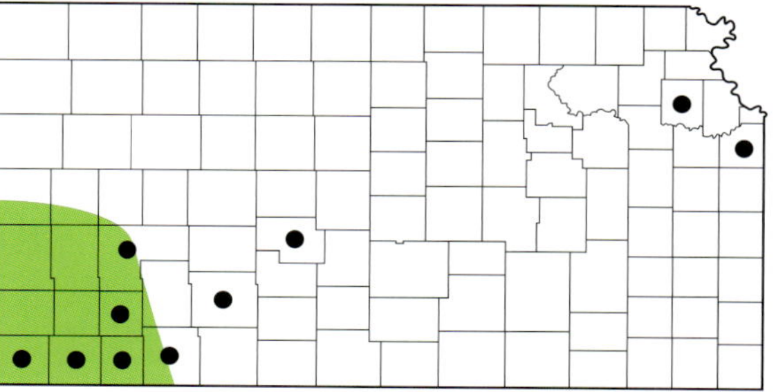

Breeding: KBBAT reported a probable breeding record from Garden City (Finney Co.), and an unidentified *Archilochus* built a nest and incubated one egg (unsuccessfully) in Elkhart (Morton Co.) 12 July–10 August 1996 (L. and R. Smith). The few spring records and the apparent nesting attempts suggest that it may breed, at least casually, in the southwest, so any summer sighting of a hummingbird should be investigated.

Comments: The Black-chinned Hummingbird and the Ruby-throated Hummingbird are closely related. Females and fall immatures closely resemble the other *Archilochus* occurring in Kansas (Ruby-throated), and identification often requires experience, precise measurements, or extensive observation; all reported sightings should be fully documented.

Banding: One banded; no encounters.

References: Baltosser and Russell, 2000; Thompson and Ely, 1989.

Anna's Hummingbird

Calypte anna (ANHU)

© Jim Burns

Status: Casual in fall and winter. There are at least 12 records for the state, 6 of which have been accepted by the KBRC. All were during the time period "August" and 15 September–25 January. The first individual, a male on 21 September 1990 at the J. and N. Dennett residence, Oxford (Sumner Co.), remained until 23 November (by now in full adult plumage). Originally identified by W. Champeny, it was ultimately observed by more than 200 people with numerous photos and video. It may have arrived in August, but video taken 2 September was inconclusive. The next record by J. Steiner, Winfield (Cowley Co.), on 21 November 1994, involved at least three and perhaps four different individuals as determined by plumage differences. A second bird (by plumage) appeared at the same feeder on 24 November 1994, disappeared, and was replaced by a third individual several days later. This male remained until mid-February when it came to the feeder in the morning, was last seen around 9:00 a.m. and did not return. The temperature that day reached into the 70s and it is surmised that the bird departed for its breeding grounds. All observations at the Steiner residence were verified by M. Thompson. Other sightings include 6 October–11 November (immature male, Finney Co., T. and S. Shane), "August" (immature male, Morton Co., L. and R. Smith), 15–25 January (female, Saline Co., D. Rudick), 29 October (Ellis Co., G. Farley), and 18 September (Sedgwick Co., P. Griffin). Most were documented with photos. Most Kansas records have been of females or young males.

Habitat: All of the Anna's Hummingbirds in Kansas were observed at feeders. It seems to be extremely hardy with records into January and February. One of the males in Cowley County survived temperatures of 4°F and was observed coming to the feeder during a snowstorm!

Comments: Females and immature males of many hummingbird species are exceedingly difficult to identify, and photographs, a specimen, or detailed measurements and direct comparisons are usually needed for an unequivocal identification.

Reference: Pittman, 1992; Thompson and Young, 1995; Varnoy, 1991.

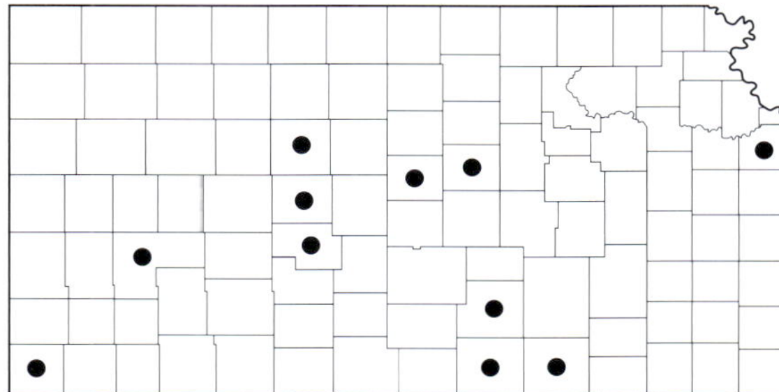

Costa's Hummingbird

Calypte costae (COHU)

Status: Vagrant. Three of four records have been accepted by the KBRC. The first specimen, a male found dead in his yard by S. Chisum, a rancher near Sharon Springs (Wallace Co.), was given to J. D. Dick and J. Rising, who were visiting the ranch. It was undated but was retrieved on 1 June 1990 (KBRC 93-22) and is preserved at KUMNH (85990). The second record (KBRC 94-01), from Lawrence (Douglas Co.), on 5 November 1993 was captured, photographed, banded, and released. The third at the D. Kazmaier residence in Larned (Pawnee Co.) on 12 August 2005 was reported by P. Janzen and S. Seltman. The latest record (KBRC 2005-35), a subadult male, was seen and photographed by T. Cable on 27 September 2005 in Manhattan (Riley Co.). It remained until 7 November.

© Jim Burns

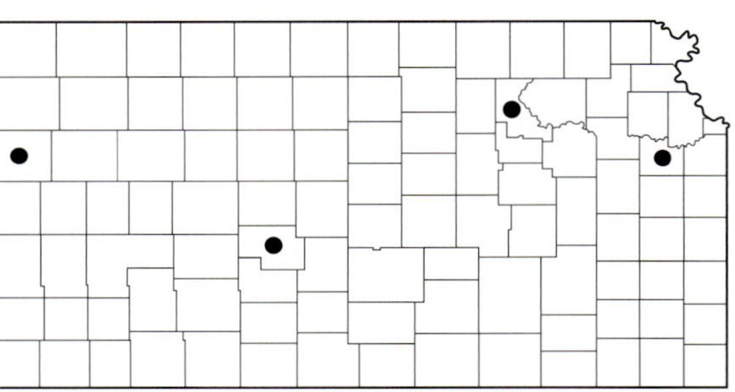

Comments: Kansas and central Texas are the usual eastern limits of vagrancy for this species. It is interesting to note that it does not favor urban settings in Arizona and uses feeders sparingly. Females are easily confused with other hummingbirds in the field.

Banding: One reported but not in the current BBO database as this species; no encounters.

References: Baltosser and Scott, 1996; Otte, 2006; Pittman, 1994, 1995.

Calliope Hummingbird

Stellula calliope (CAHU)

Status: Rare, mostly fall transient in the west, rarely in eastern or central Kansas.

Migration: Nearly all documented records are from fall, most during August and early September and with extreme dates of 15 July and 19 October. The only spring sighting is 4 April 2003 from Garden City (Finney Co., M. Osterbuhr).

Comments: The first (and currently only) specimen (KU 71266) was an immature female taken by R. Graber on 3 September 1952, on the Cimarron River, southeast of Richfield in Morton County. It was next reported on 15–18 August 1992 when an immature or female was observed in Rush County (S. Seltman). Beginning in 1994, T. and S. Shane and others in Garden City began maintaining and carefully monitoring feeders and were soon recording western species of hummingbirds. T. Shane (pers. comm.) provided the following details. During the period 1994–2009 the Shane yard produced 196 observations of Calliopes involving 89 different individuals. Four were adult males (15–29 July), 25 were immature males (8 August–22 September), and 60 were adult females, immature females, or immature males that did not show magenta gorget spots or extremely heavy throat spots (20 July–19 October). Major migration was 7 August–22 September (peak 25 August–9 September) with individuals remaining from 1 to 4 days (mean, about 2 days). The mean number of individuals observed per year was 5.6 with a range of 0 (3 seasons) to 29 (2002). Three-day clusters for observations of arrivals were 15, 20, and 26 July; latest departures were 22 and 27 September and 19 October. The numbers of individuals for each 10- to 11-day period were highest for the first one-third of September (55) and the second one-third (51) and first one-third of August (30). Similar attempts to attract and identify "western" hummers begun by D. Kazmaier in Larned (Pawnee Co.) also have been very successful with regular sightings (including Calliope) since 2000. As more birders became familiar with this and other species, the number of Calliope sightings increased throughout the southwest and elsewhere, including Sedgwick County (KBRC 2001-39), Pratt County (adult male, photo), Ellis County (photos), Ellsworth County (photos), and Miami County (KBRC 2009-35). At least 100 sightings have been recorded since 1992. Most of these records were not submitted to the KBRC. The fact that it occurs regularly in western Kansas during fall migration and is a vagrant there during spring and vagrant elsewhere in the state is no longer debated.

References: Land, 2010; Rintoul, 2002; Thompson and Ely, 1989.

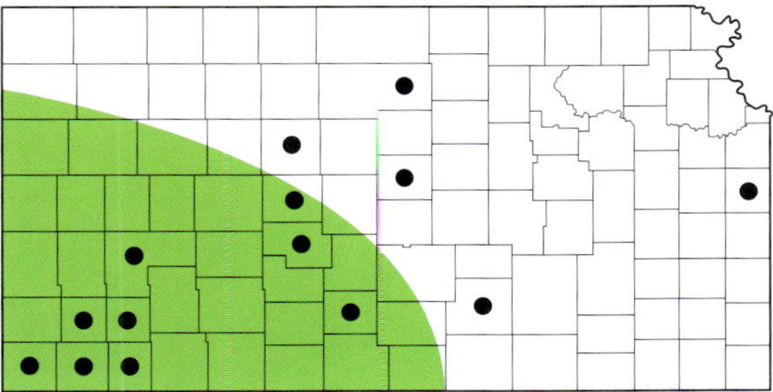

Broad-tailed Hummingbird

Selasphorus platycercus (BTLH)

Status: Rare transient in the western half of the state.

Habitat: The first record for the state was feeding on black locust flowers on the North Fork of the Cimarron River. Subsequent sightings were mainly in residential areas at feeders or gardens that have been planted to attract hummingbirds.

Migration: Most records are from feeders during fall. The few spring records (most were males) are 26 April–18 May and 3–9 June. Fall records are 26 July–30 September, with most records during August.

Comments: The first record was a male (KU 102803) collected by M. Thompson on 18 May 1978 in Morton County. Another adult male was observed in Sumner County by W. Champeny on 13 August 1979. The wing sounds were heard distinctly. Two additional males were seen and heard in Garden City (Finney Co.) on 27 July–4 August 1991 (L. and B. Rich and others) and 26–28 July 1992 (L. and B. Rich and T. and S. Shane). As mentioned under Calliope Hummingbird, a concentrated effort has been made to document hummingbird migration, especially in Finney and Pawnee counties. These efforts have resulted in dozens of reports since 1992 with reports north and east to Decatur, Reno, Sedgwick, Riley, Cowley, and Sumner counties. Most have been immatures or females and were often unverified; however, some were confirmed by photos or video and submitted to KBRC, which currently accepts 15 records. Great care should be taken in making identifications; at least one identified by an experienced observer proved to be a Rufous Hummingbird.

References: Calder and Calder, 1992; Thompson and Ely, 1989.

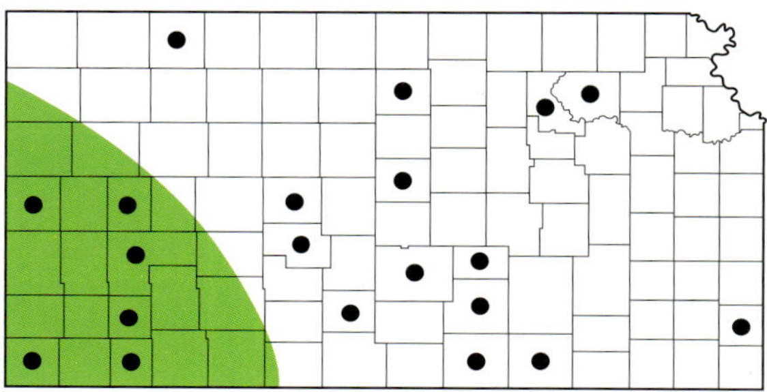

Rufous Hummingbird

Selasphorus rufus (RUHU)

Status: Rare transient statewide, more common in the central and western regions.

Habitat: Usually found in urban or rural yards and gardens, often at feeders.

Migration: The only spring record is 26 April (Finney Co.). The earliest fall arrivals are 13 July (Finney Co.) and 16 July (Morton Co.), with most sightings in August and early September with a few birds remaining until at least 6 December. In the southwest (primarily Finney Co.) there seems to be a continual movement of birds through the area (up to six at one time) during the fall migration period, with individuals remaining only a few days. Elsewhere some individuals have remained at feeders for extended periods, including one in Sedgwick County that stayed until 9 December, was captured and placed in the Sedgwick Co. Zoo where it died (specimen saved, KU 108916); and 10 November–1 December (Sumner Co.). Other late fall dates include 4–9 October (Shawnee Co.) and 20 November–6 December (Johnson Co., to rehabilitation for winter). We do not recommend "rehabbing" healthy birds "for the winter."

Comments: Although not reported until the 1960s, it is now the most widely reported and widespread of the western hummers visiting Kansas. This is undoubtedly due to a greatly increased awareness and interest in hummingbirds and the concomitant placement and monitoring of feeders and cultivation of "hummer" plants in gardens. This is especially true in the southwest but is increasing statewide. The earliest confirmed reports were by W. Champeny in Sumner County in 1964, and they still continue to show up during most falls. There were a few scattered reports during the 1970s and 1980s including the first specimen by M. Schwilling on 23 August 1973 in Barton County. The number of sightings increased dramatically beginning in the 1990s in Finney and later Pawnee counties. Alerted to the existence of a sizable migrant population, birders began erecting more feeders and

monitoring them later in the season throughout the state. It is not a species monitored by KBRC, which has, nevertheless, accepted eight of the records submitted since 1990. Many of the hundreds of additional sightings are unverified, and some are undoubtedly Broad-tailed and Allen's Hummingbirds, and perhaps other species. Nevertheless, a migration pattern has emerged, and the number of birds remaining into early winter and perhaps overwintering is sure to increase. How the Kansas birds relate to transients in other states and to birds wintering in the southeastern states can be determined only by a banding study. Many hummers are aggressive at feeders, but the Rufous is more aggressive than most and typically drives off other hummingbirds that try to feed.

See page 500 for banding information.

References: Schneider, 1996; Thompson and Ely, 1989.

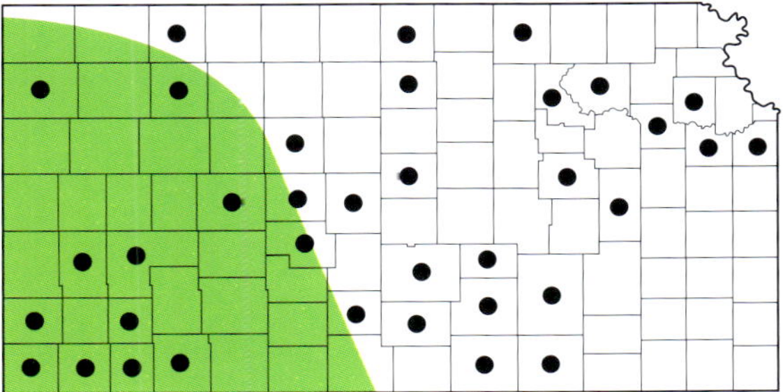

Allen's Hummingbird

Selasphorus sasin (ALHU)

© Mark Chappell

Status: Vagrant. The only verified record for Kansas (KBRC 92-56) is an immature male observed by C. Hobbs and L. Moore at Bonner Springs (Wyandotte Co.) on 25 August 1992 and banded by J. Hall. Photographs and selected rectrices (KU 85903) were sent to J. V. Remsen, who, with S. Cardiff, confirmed the identification. In recent years the number of extralimital reports of this and other western hummers has increased dramatically due, at least in part, to the increased availability of hummingbird feeders.

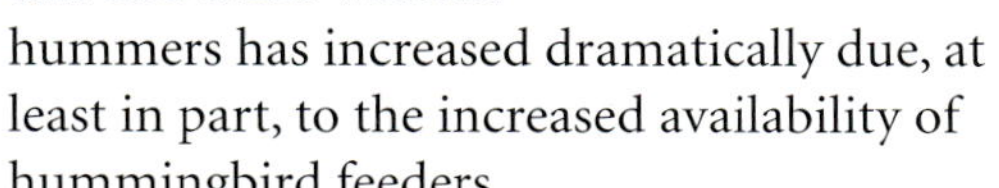

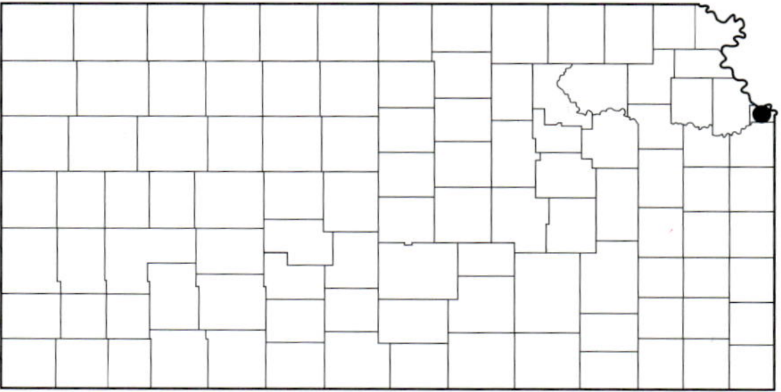

Comments: Allen's and Rufous Hummingbirds are nearly identical in appearance, and examination of the rectrices is necessary for positive identification. Typically, males of Allen's have a green back contrasting to the rusty back of a male Rufous. However, immature Rufous and some adult male Rufous may retain a varying amount of green. Allen's has a very narrow outer rectrix (R 5), and R 2 is not notched. Females and immature males of both species are not safely distinguishable in the field.

Banding: One banded; no encounters.

References: Pittman, 1993; Williamson, 2001.

Belted Kingfisher

Megaceryle alcyon (BEKI)

Status: Uncommon summer resident and transient; rare in winter.

Habitat: Open water from farm ponds to reservoirs and rivers.

Migration: There are very few actual dates of arrival, because transients overlap wintering individuals. Early arrivals follow open water, and arrival may vary considerably from year to year. Presumed transients are present by 20 February (Sumner Co.), 7 March (Sheridan Co.), and 11 March (Washington Co.) and are widespread by early April. Most migration is probably mid-March through mid-April. The fall departure is even less understood. Birds are present at most sites until water freezes, but whether these are local breeding birds or from points farther north is unknown. In Morton County, where no breeding has ever been reported, presumed transients have been reported 3 April–16 May and 31 August–20 October. In general the number of fall sightings is high in September, declines in October, and drops dramatically in November. The increase in numbers during the CBC period is undoubtedly the result of increased birder activity and concentration of birds to conspicuous open-water sources. Actual migration data are few but include 18 recorded in 1 day during fall migration at Winfield City Lake in Cowley County (early October).

Breeding: It is a low-density breeder west through the Flint Hills and Red Hills wherever perennial streams, ponds, or reservoirs provide a dependable supply of small fish. Westward, it occurs irregularly, wherever local conditions provide an adequate food supply. Many streams and playas, especially in the southwest, are ephemeral and lack suitable food items. It typically excavates a burrow in a stream bank but may also nest some distance from water. There are nesting records from 21 April into May, but few nest contents have been reported. The nest is usually 2–6 feet deep but can be as deep as 15 feet. Females have been flushed from burrows 19 May–17 June, eggs reported on 3 May, adults carrying food into burrows 31 May–4 July, and recently fledged young 8–29 June. The young remain in the nest around 1 month.

Banding: 53 banded; one encounter. One banded at Seney NWR on Michigan's Upper Peninsula on 13 July 1939 was shot in Kansas during September 1939, on or enroute to its wintering ground.

References: Busby and Zimmerman, 2001; Janzen, 2007; Thompson and Ely, 1989; Young, 1993.

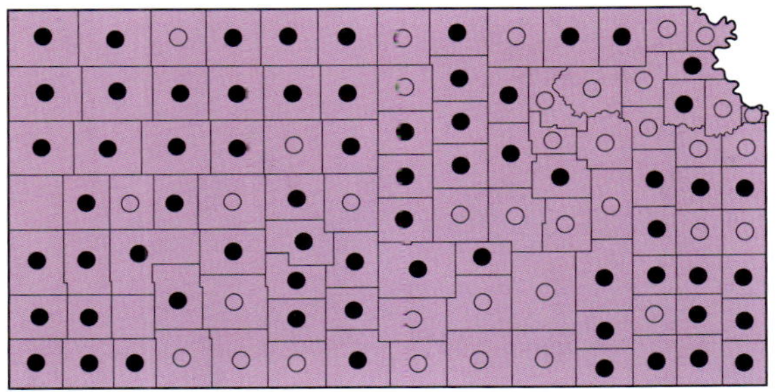

Lewis's Woodpecker

Melanerpes lewis (LEWO)

© Mark Chappell

Status: Casual visitant. There are three specimens: Ellis County, 6 May 1878 (KU 11954); Douglas County, 7 November 1908 (KU 7890); and Morton County, 4 July 1927 (KU 16647). A fourth specimen, reportedly collected by H. Menke in Finney County on 23 April 1893, is apparently lost. Most modern records are from western Kansas during the period 23 April–6 June but with sightings east to Pottawatomie County (10 April–10 May) and Ellsworth County (9–11 May). Additional sightings include 4 July (Morton Co.), 31 August–16 September (southwest), 28 October–4 November (Ellis Co.), and 7 November (Douglas Co.).

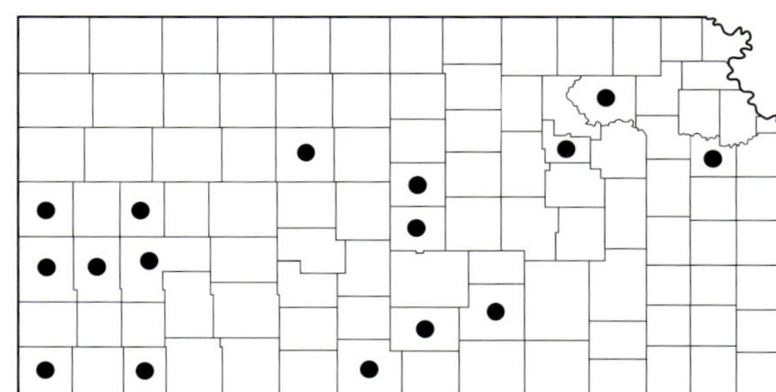

Comments: Past speculation that it may nest in western Kansas is not supported by evidence. All observations were single birds except the one collected in Ellis County (1878) that was taken from a flock of six to eight birds.

Reference: Thompson and Ely, 1989.

Red-headed Woodpecker

Melanerpes erythrocephalus (RHWO)

Status: Common summer resident statewide; local and irregular winter resident in the eastern one-third of the state.

Habitat: Woodlands and locally in open-country woodlots as a result of various land uses. It is often seen some miles from trees but needs them for nesting. In lieu of a tree, it may excavate a cavity in a utility pole. Fence posts are frequently used as perches while hunting in the open. The few that winter in Kansas utilize forest with oak, hickory, and pecan, especially in the eastern half.

Migration: Some records as early as 7 April may be new arrivals or overwintering birds. Most arrive apparently in late April with peak movement during early May. Median first arrivals include 2 May (Ellis Co.) and 3 May (Rice and Meade cos.). "Woods" (unpubl. manuscript, 1976) reported presumed transients after 16 April and a marked increase in numbers around 1 May (Shawnee Co.). Considering the conspicuousness of the species, the relatively few reports of fall departure are surprising. The southward migration starts in early September, peaks in late September and early October, and may continue into November. The median departure date for Ellis County is 26 September; other late dates for central and western Kansas include 18 September (Graham Co.), 4 October (Finney and Harvey cos.), and 9 November (Morton Co.). Many late dates are of immature birds. Late dates for Meade County are 19 September–5 October. Several hundred, in groups of two to six, were "migrating" along the Smoky Hill River on 28 August. The few counts include 63 on 6 September (Cowley Co.) and 100+ "apparently migrating" on 27 November (Linn Co.) but were probably already in their wintering area. Most winter concentrations are in eastern Kansas, but occasional birds are reported west to Russell, Pratt, and Trego counties. Significant overwintering was reported in Johnson County in 1970–1971, 1973–1974, and 1979–1980.

© David Seibel

Breeding: KBBAT reported confirmed or probable nesting in 43 percent of all blocks surveyed with lowest frequency in the High Plains. It seems to be quite common in central Kansas and riparian areas in the west where the lack of water has caused a major die-off in cottonwoods. Statewide, nest excavation has been observed 2 May–21 June, eggs 1–30 June (median, 8 June), young in nest 13 May–21 August, and recently fledged young 9–21 July.

Comments: In winter it should be looked for in pecan groves or oak–hickory forest where mast production has been strong.

See page 500 for banding information.

References: Busby and Zimmerman, 2001; Thompson and Ely, 1992.

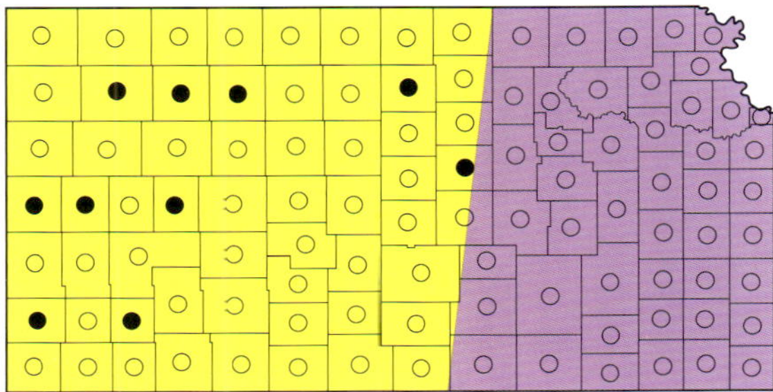

Red-bellied Woodpecker

Melanerpes carolinus (RBWO)

Status: Common resident in the eastern half of the state, uncommon in the central region, and rare in the far west. It has recently moved westward along streams and into towns and cities where adequate trees are available for nesting and feeding.

Habitat: Riparian and upland forest and suburban areas with mature trees.

Migration: Though generally sedentary in eastern Kansas, seasonal fluctuations in both numbers and local distributions (Shawnee Co., "Woods," unpubl. manuscript, 1976) suggest some movement of transients or extensive dispersal. It was not reported from western Kansas by any 19th- or early 20th-century researchers. The earliest reports from the west are from Comanche and Cloud counties in 1911 and "occasional in winter" during 1933–1936 (Rooks Co.). In Ellis County only occasional, widely scattered individuals were reported prior to 1960. It was reported during 9 of the next 11 years with only one report outside the time period 9 October–28 April, most during midwinter, and often at feeders. The first nesting was suspected in 1973 and then documented in 1974. Earliest reports from the southwestern counties include 1953 (Finney Co.) and 1954 (Morton Co.). Rising considered it an "uncommon and local resident" in the west during the 1960s.

Breeding: It currently breeds nearly statewide and continues to expand its range in the west. The nest cavity is in a dead trunk or often underneath a tree limb. Nest-building has been reported 6 April–4 May, eggs 14 April–22 June, young in nest 5 May–22 June, and recently fledged young 3 June–21 July.

Comments: It is one of the most common woodpeckers found in cities in eastern Kansas. Attracted to feeders, it eats both suet and seeds, and adults frequently bring their young to feeders soon after fledging. It is a vociferous species frequently heard before it is seen. The male is frequently confused with the Red-

headed Woodpecker despite its light face, throat, and breast. The red belly from which it gets its name is not usually visible while it is perched on the side of a tree.

Banding: 722 banded; 30 encounters: all in-state. Banding shows that it is sedentary with all but one of the encounters within the same 10-minute block in which it was banded. One individual was encountered 7 years, 1 month after banding.

References: Busby and Zimmerman, 2001; Janzen, 2007; Thompson and Ely, 1989.

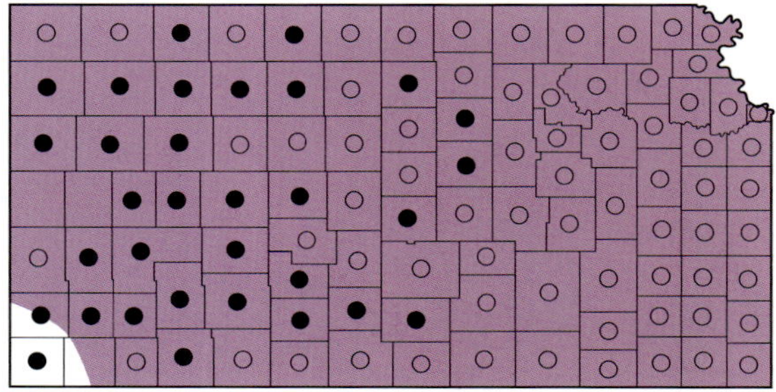

Williamson's Sapsucker

Sphyrapicus thyroideus (WISA)

Status: Vagrant. There are four, possibly five records. J. M. Porter reported a male in Concordia (Cloud Co.) on 4 April 1935. M. Thompson read Porter's journal (on file at KUMNH) and found little more than his statement of finding the bird and no description of plumages. Porter was a competent birder who had stated that the identification was made after viewing skins sent to him by W. Long. The second record was an adult male from Elkhart (Morton Co.) on 22 September, observed and photographed by several people (KBRC 2000-65). The third record, a bird at a feeder in Manhattan (Riley Co.) on 5 January 2004, was observed briefly by L. Johnson, and identification was tentative. A female first observed in Garden City (Finney Co.) on 9 October 2009 by T. Shane remained through 26 October and was seen and photographed by numerous others. It had a particular tree in the cemetery where it could be reliably found. On 5 December 2009, D. Klema found an adult male at Wilson State Park, Wilson Reservoir (Russell Co.). Numerous observers saw and photographed this individual, which was still present on 26 January 2010.

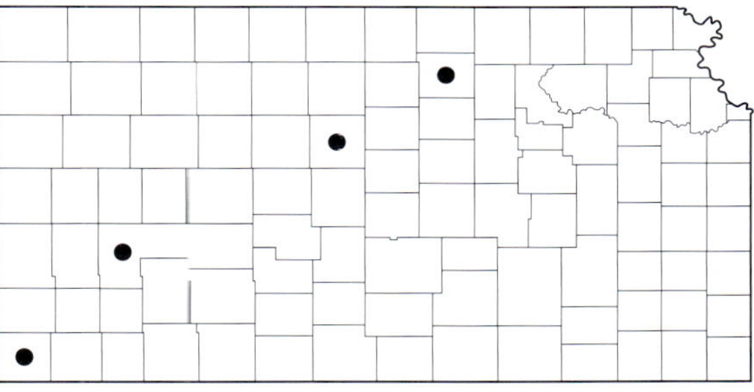

Comments: This species is rare outside the Rocky Mountains, rarely straying out of its native habitat.

References: Rintoul, 2001; Thompson and Ely, 1989.

Yellow-bellied Sapsucker

Sphyrapicus varius (YBSA)

Status: Uncommon transient and winter resident statewide.

Habitat: Prefers conifers in winter but has been recorded using more than 246 species of trees.

Migration: Early dates, for example, 10 March (Ellis Co.) and 23 March (Barton Co.), may have been wintering birds. Most migration is during April, with stragglers to 18 May (Shawnee Co.). The median departure date for Ellis County is 7 April. Unusually early fall arrivals include 29 August (Johnson Co.) and 4 September (Pawnee Co.), but usual arrival is not until early October (3 October, Douglas Co., and 4 October, Harvey and Ellis cos.). The peak migration, statewide, is mid- to late October with numbers declining through November and into the CBC period. Wintering individuals are most often seen in residential areas west to Ellis and Phillips counties. There are few reports after the CBC period, probably because it is such a secretive species (except occasionally at feeders).

Comments: Sapsuckers receive the name from their habit of making rows of small rectangular to semicircular holes through the bark and into the vascular tissue of trees and feeding on the sap. The holes, often in parallel rows, are usually more conspicuous than the birds themselves. R. Imler reported 816 feeding holes in a 3-foot segment of a pine on which a bird had fed for 8 days. These excavations rarely kill a tree and are often visited by other species such as warblers (and in the southern United States, overwintering hummingbirds). It is wary and usually tries to avoid being seen, often by swinging around to the other side of the tree when approached. Many of the sapsuckers in Kansas are in immature plumage and do not attain the breeding plumage until late in the winter or early spring. The white slash in their wings is an identification aid along with the presence of feeding holes. There is one record (near Lawrence, Douglas Co., 15–21 December 2000; KU 92332) of an apparent Yellow-bellied × Red-breasted (*S. ruber*) hybrid. This is certainly the first evidence of *S. ruber* genes in or near Kansas! See Red-naped Sapsucker for more details.

Banding: 54 banded; no encounters.

References: Imler, 1937; Robbins et al., 2005; Thompson and Ely, 1989.

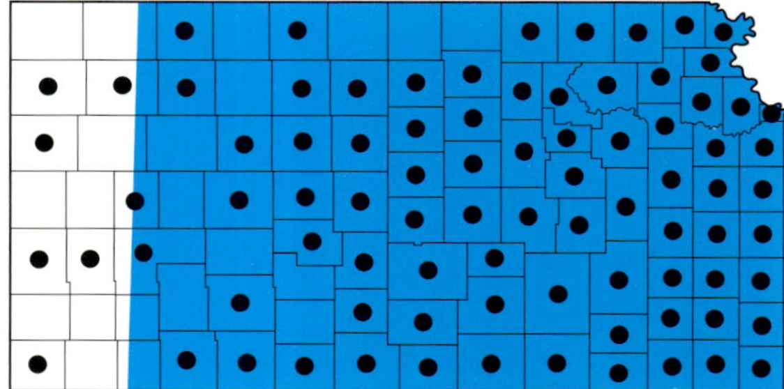

Red-naped Sapsucker

Sphyrapicus nuchalis (RNSA)

Status: Rare transient in extreme western Kansas. Nearly all records are from Morton County. The earliest record is a specimen taken by N. Goss on 14 October 1883 in Wallace County (KU 72136). This specimen is in poor condition but thought to be this species. Two other specimens at KUMNH originally identified by H. Tordoff were reexamined by M. Thompson and M. Robbins and determined to be Yellow-bellied Sapsuckers. Other specimens of *S. nuchalis* were taken on 21 September 2000 (KU 91177) and 24 September 2004 (KU 93303-05). Spring records include 17 March (Scott Co.), 23 March (Thomas Co.), and 1 and 26 April (both Morton Co.). An adult female sapsucker collected near Lawrence (Douglas Co.), on 21 December 2000 (KU 92332), first thought to be a male of this species, was determined using DNA techniques to be a likely Yellow-bellied × Red-breasted Sapsucker (*S. ruber*) hybrid. Red-naped × Yellow-bellied hybrids, frequent in some areas, can further confound field identification. All three sapsuckers were considered conspecific until 1983; nine prior sightings of "Yellow-bellied Sapsuckers" from Barber, Ellis, and Thomas counties westward, during the period 16 September–29 December, should now be considered "unidentified sapsuckers." Included is a male banded in Hays (Ellis Co.) on 4 December 1977 that had an extensive red nape.

Comments: The Red-naped Sapsucker begins molting into an adult plumage prior to migration, whereas the Yellow-bellied Sapsucker migrates in immature plumage. Clearly, the best time to find this bird in western Kansas is in mid-September to early October.

References: AOU, 1998; Robbins et al., 2005; Walters et al., 2002.

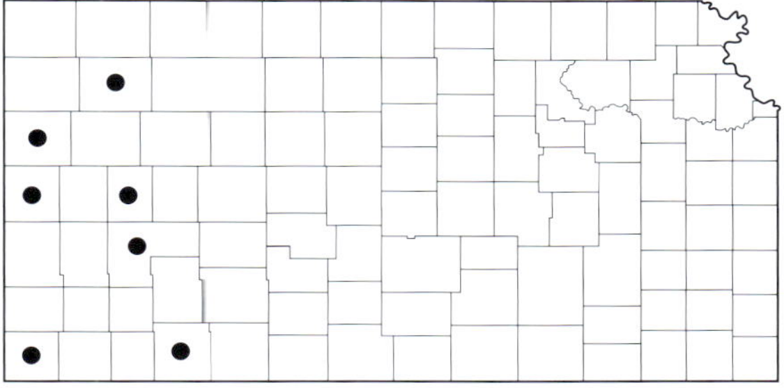

Ladder-backed Woodpecker

Picoides scalaris (LBWO)

Status: Irregular resident in Morton County, rare elsewhere in extreme southwestern Kansas; accidental to casual eastward.

Habitat: Open riparian growth bordered by prairie in the southwest.

Migration: Although considered resident, it is also a vagrant northward and eastward, perhaps following river systems. Most records are from the CNG (Morton County), with scattered records from elsewhere in the southwest. An extraordinary example of vagrancy is the female first observed in Riley County on 30 September 2001 by L. Johnson. He, and occasionally others, observed this individual in essentially the same location on numerous occasions through at least 11 January 2009, nearly 8 years! An observation by L. Mallonee from Sedgwick County was substantiated by a video of a bird at a feeder on 17 January 1991. A third record from Linn County about 10 May 1998 was not submitted to the KBRC and could not be assessed.

Breeding: Three of the breeding records are from Morton County. An active nest was found on 2 June 1968. J. and R. Graber reported a female exhibiting nesting behavior on 9 May 1950, and M. Schwilling had a pair entering a nesting cavity on 1 May 1983. In Hamilton County, a female with a brood patch was collected on the Arkansas River on 28 April 1967, but neither a male nor a nest cavity could be found. No nests contents have been observed to date.

Comments: The woodpecker appears to be an irregular visitant and breeder, particularly along the Cimarron River (Morton Co.). Some years it is present in such low densities that it is extremely difficult to find.

References: Johnson, 2008; Thompson and Ely, 1989.

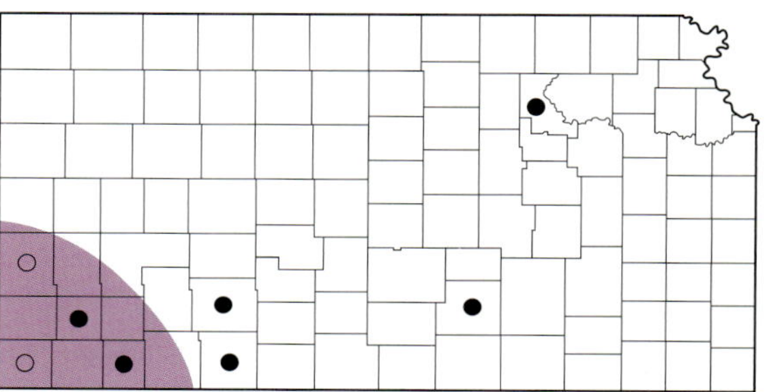

Downy Woodpecker

Picoides pubescens (DOWO)

Status: Common permanent resident in the east, becoming irregular in the far west.

Habitat: Woodlands and cities in the east; follows riparian corridors and occurs in cities with trees.

Migration: Though largely sedentary some movement does occur during fall and winter from the north and/or west. A specimen of *P. p. leucurus* (see Comments below) collected on the Cimarron River (Morton Co.) on 29 December is such an example.

Breeding: KBBAT reported the highest percentages of confirmed nestings east of the Flint Hills and in the Smoky Hills with lower frequency in the Red Hills. Frequencies declined further as riparian growth decreased westward, especially in the southwest. Like other woodpeckers, it utilizes dead trees or dead limbs in which to excavate its nest cavity, usually underneath a limb, and uses hollow limbs to drum during courtship or territorial defense. Nests are most easily found during late May and early June when the incessant calling of the young can be heard from a considerable distance. Eggs have been reported 7 April–3 June, "incubation/brooding" 23 April–14 May, young 9 May–29 June, and recently fledged young 27 May–15 July.

Comments: It has increased in numbers in parts of the west since the 19th century when it was a "rare winter visitant" (Finney Co.) or "rare resident" (Decatur Co.). It is the smallest woodpecker in the state except for the Ladder-backed Woodpecker (largely restricted to the southwest). It can be confused with the Hairy Woodpecker, which is larger and lacks black barring in the tail. This is the only woodpecker that has three subspecies occurring in the state. The subspecies *P. p. medianus* occurs in most of Kansas, *P. p. pubescens* in the southeast from Montgomery County eastward, and *P. p. leucurus* in Morton County (winter). While trees are preferred for foraging, it also extracts insects from stems of old sunflowers, giant ragweed, and yucca flower stalks. It readily visits feeders for suet and sunflower seeds.

Banding: 2,530 banded; 90 encounters: all in-state; all encounters were in the same area as banded. Oldest 3 years, 10 months.

References: Busby and Zimmerman, 2001; Jackson and Ouellet, 2002; Thompson and Ely, 1989.

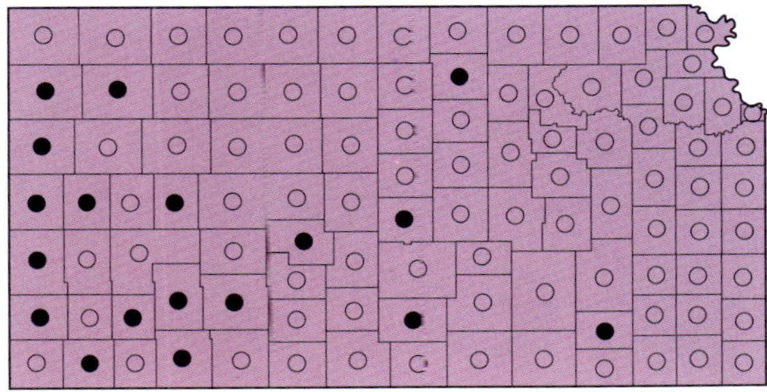

Hairy Woodpecker

Picoides villosus (HAWO)

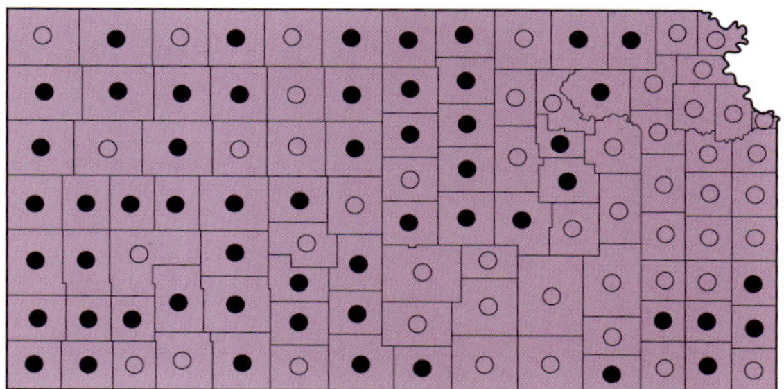

Status: Common resident in eastern and central Kansas; irregular and local in the southwest.

Habitat: Riparian woodlands, mature upland forest in the east, and towns and cities with mature trees. Westward, as riparian forest gives way to the High Plains, its numbers dwindle.

Migration: Though generally considered sedentary, there is some movement into Kansas from the west, and probably north, during winter. Specimens of the Rocky Mountain race *P. v. monticola*, collected on the Cimarron River (Morton Co.) on 15 and 28 April 1967, indicate an eastern incursion, probably from the previous winter. The breeding birds in the southwest are *P. v. villosus.*

Breeding: It prefers mature woodlands. The nest cavity is usually excavated on the underside of a limb. The male drums on hollow trees or other vibrating surfaces that will make his drumming echo through the forest. Like other woodpeckers, the drumming sequence is unique to the species. The young clamor from the nesting cavity making the nest easy to find. Copulation has been reported 16 April, nest cavity excavation 4 March–7 May, eggs 10–14 May, young in nest 29 April–21 June, and recently fledged young 21 May–21 July.

Comments: It closely resembles the Downy Woodpecker but is larger and lacks the barring on the outer tail feathers. It also has a longer, heavier bill and different vocalizations.

Banding: 486 banded; 27 encounters: all in-state. Oldest 9 years, 3 months. Examination of these data indicates that, like most woodpeckers, it is largely sedentary.

References: Busby and Zimmerman, 2001; Thompson and Ely, 1989.

American Three-toed Woodpecker

Picoides dorsalis (ATTW)

Status: Vagrant. The only record (KBRC 2005-06) is an adult male found by A. Mitchell, M. Gearheart, and W. Chatfield-Taylor on 3 July 2005 at the picnic grounds near the Cimarron River, in the CNG north of Elkhart (Morton Co.). It remained in the area until at least 13 July. It was seen by many birders and was probably the most photographed American Three-toed Woodpecker in history! It rarely leaves the mountains, and its presence in a prairie region was totally unexpected.

References: Leonard, 2001; Otte, 2006.

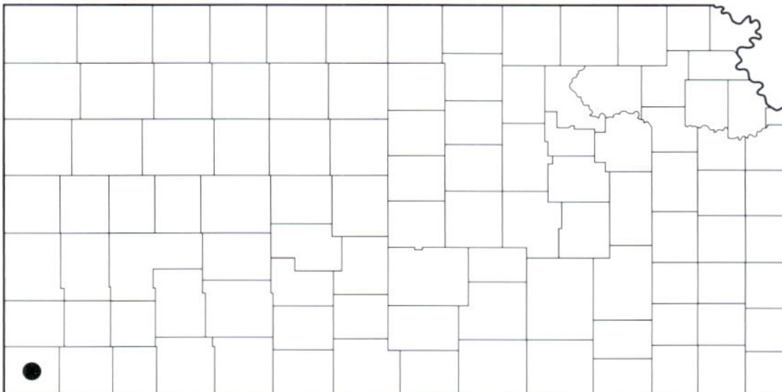

© Judd Patterson

Northern Flicker

Colaptes auratus (NOFL)

Status: Common transient and summer resident statewide; locally common winter resident. Although a few red-shafted flickers (or near phenotypes) occur during summer there is presently no confirmed evidence of breeding in western Kansas. However a mixed pair was observed entering a cavity on 1 May 1983 (Morton Co.).

Habitat: Woodlands and open areas with few trees. Unlike most woodpeckers, it is not confined to foraging in trees but spends much of its time on the ground hunting for ants. If ants are unavailable, it will consume vegetable matter.

Migration: Migrations of the yellow-shafted form are difficult to follow, because both breeding and transient birds are involved. Some breeding birds probably move southward in winter. Large numbers of transients from farther north move into the state or through the state, and some probably winter. Large numbers of red-shafted birds, probably from the northwest, visit the state during fall and winter, and their movements are better documented. In Ellis County, mean earliest fall arrival is 25 September; the median spring departure is 6 April. High percentages are intermediates. In the extreme east smaller numbers are noted from mid-September through early November with some wintering through March. Fall movements of yellow-shafted birds have been observed 19 September and 10 October (each 100+, Morton Co.) through 24 October (40+, Morton Co.) and 1 November (30, Wyandotte Co.). Although most migration is at night, there is considerable daytime movement, and it is common to see 20–30 in a flock moving through the open plains. It winters locally, usually in residential or wooded areas, throughout the south and east. The spring movement is primarily during March and April.

Breeding: It is much less confined to woodland than other woodpeckers. Although it nests in tree cavities, it may utilize a stump in the middle of a field, far from trees. Unlike typical

woodpeckers, some nests are used during multiple years.

Comments: Close examination of flickers in winter reveals that many are intermediates or hybrids between the two races.

See page 500 for banding information.

References: Thompson and Ely, 1989; Wiebe and Moore, 2008.

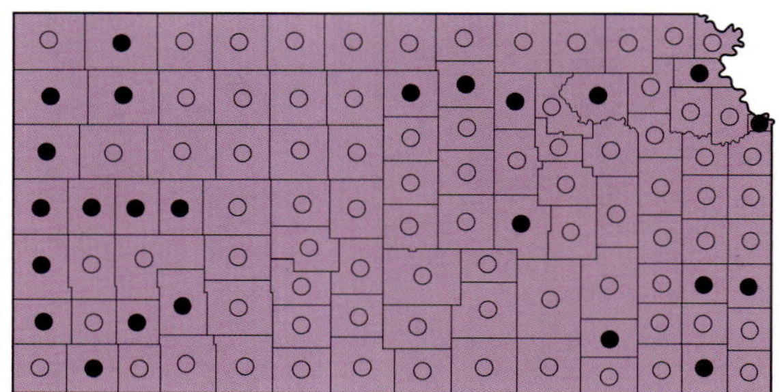

Pileated Woodpecker

Dryocopus pileatus (PIWO)

© Judd Patterson

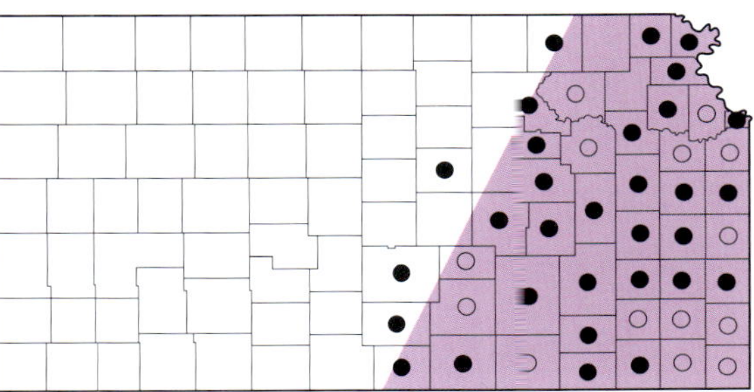

Status: Uncommon resident of eastern Kansas.

Habitat: Riparian and upland forest with mature trees; occasionally moves into edge habitat.

Breeding: The largest of Kansas woodpeckers, it probably nests wherever it regularly occurs. Its loud and characteristic drumming can be heard in early spring. The nest cavity is excavated in a large dead tree, usually 30–40 feet above the ground. The cavity entrance, a large oval, is diagnostic of the species. The earliest nesting records were by N. Goss in 1886. Courtship has been reported 18–29 April, nest excavation 3–30 April, eggs 11 May, young 8 May–6 June, and recently fledged young 31 May–29 June. The young become quite noisy as they mature and can be seen with their heads sticking out of the nesting cavity, calling for food from the adults.

Comments: Considered "rare and local" in the extreme east as late as 1960, it has gradually expanded its range along the riparian corridors of the Arkansas River west to Harper, Reno, and Kingman counties in the south and along the Kansas River tributaries in the north to Saline, Riley, and Marshall counties. As it has become more common, it is increasingly seen in mature trees in some towns and cities. This handsome woodpecker is the size of a crow. When it flies, it does not have the typical undulating flight of a woodpecker but instead a straight, direct flight. For such a large bird, it can be inconspicuous because it is extremely wary of humans and may silently depart without alerting a human of its presence. However, in the spring, its raucous call can be heard for quite a distance. It frequently feeds in dead stumps and fallen logs near the ground where it searches for ants and grubs.

References: Busby and Zimmerman, 2001; Goss, 1886; Thompson and Ely, 1989.

Olive-sided Flycatcher

Contopus cooperi (OSFL)

© David Seibel

Status: Uncommon transient statewide.

Habitat: It occurs mainly in coniferous forest and mixed forest north and west of Kansas. In Kansas, it is nearly always found sitting on high, dead branches where it sallies forth to catch insects, usually returning to the same branch.

Migration: The earliest arrival is 20 April; the latest departure 21 June. Median spring arrival in Ellis County is 17 May. It is most numerous during the last 2 weeks of May. Extreme fall dates are 6 August and 31 October. Median fall arrival in Ellis County was 4 September with most migration from mid-August to mid-September. Statewide, most migration is during September. The largest number reported is 15–20 on 28 September (Morton Co.).

Comments: N. Goss reported it nesting based on a specimen (KU 72365) collected on 27 May 1883. He states that it was one of a pair nesting near the top of a tall cottonwood, on the South Fork of the Solomon River near Wallace (Wallace Co.). This is certainly an erroneous report that has never been satisfactorily explained. Appearing in August it is one of the earliest fall arrivals. The habit of sitting in the top of a tree on a dead branch is characteristic of the species. The large bill and head and short neck give this species a "bull-headed" appearance. The white breast contrasting with dark olive flanks is unique among Kansas flycatchers. Although also diagnostic, the two white tufts of feathers on the back above the tail that help to identify the species are difficult to see high overhead.

Banding: 10 banded; no encounters.

References: Cable et al., 1996; Janzen, 2007; Thompson and Ely, 1992.

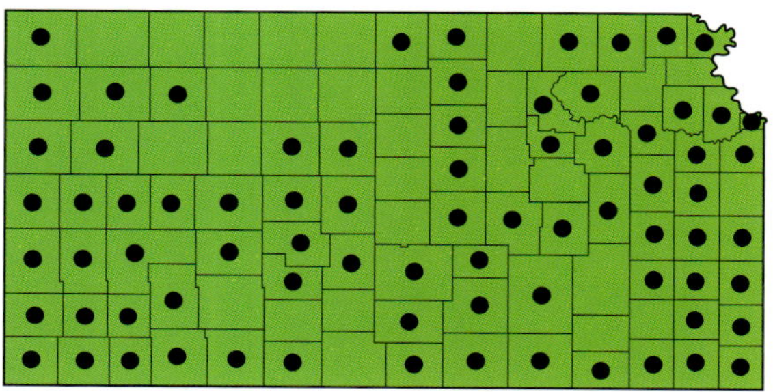

Western Wood-Pewee

Contopus sordidulus (WEWP)

Status: Uncommon but regular transient in the extreme west, vagrant eastward; probably breeds locally in small numbers along rivers in the extreme west.

Habitat: Riparian habitat and towns with numerous trees; in Morton County along the Cimarron River and the North Fork of the Cimarron River.

Migration: Specimens have been taken 29 April–11 June. Sight records extend this period to 19 April and 12 June. Specimens from Ellis County (16 May–1 June) were definite transients; others farther west (6 May–8 June) could be transients or breeders. Singing males in proper habitat 6 May–24 June were probably breeding. The fall migration begins by 6 August. Specimens from 30 August to 14 September (Ellis Co.) are definitely transients. Sight records extend this period to 1 August (unconfirmed) and 19 September.

Breeding: There are no confirmed breeding records for the state. KBBAT reported three possible and one probable nesting records but no confirmed nesting. Singing males on territories and in proper habitat are probably breeding and have been reported from Cheyenne, Morton, Rawlins, Seward, and Wallace counties.

Comments: It may sit low if there is no obstructing vegetation or higher in open canopy. Eastern and Western Wood-Pewees can be reliably distinguished in the field only by song. Museum specimens are sometimes misidentified, as are handheld birds. Further complicating matters are the findings of J. Barlow and J. Rising: out of eight specimens collected in southwestern Kansas, 7 June–6 August, they considered one to be *C. virens*, five *C. sordidulus*, and two intermediates but nearest *C. sordidulus* on the basis of coloration. They postulated that the specimens from southwestern Kansas were intermediate in physical characteristics. Clearly, more work needs to be done on the actual breeding range in Kansas.

Banding: Three banded in Barton, Meade, and Ellis counties. The bird banded in Barton County may have been misidentified.

References: Barlow and Rising, 1965; Busby and Zimmerman, 2001; Cable et al., 1996; Thompson and Ely, 1992.

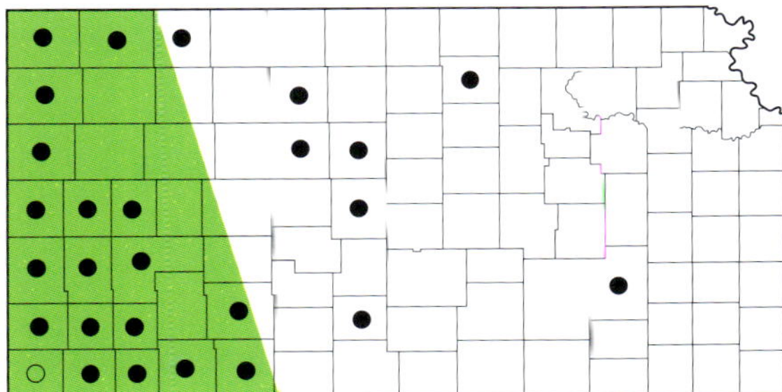

Eastern Wood-Pewee

Contopus virens (EAWP)

Status: Common transient and summer resident in the east, breeding westward locally to Osborne and Stafford counties; uncommon transient and breeder in central Kansas and along riparian corridors to the west.

Habitat: Wooded areas in the east; also cities with mature woodlands and along rivers and streams with woods.

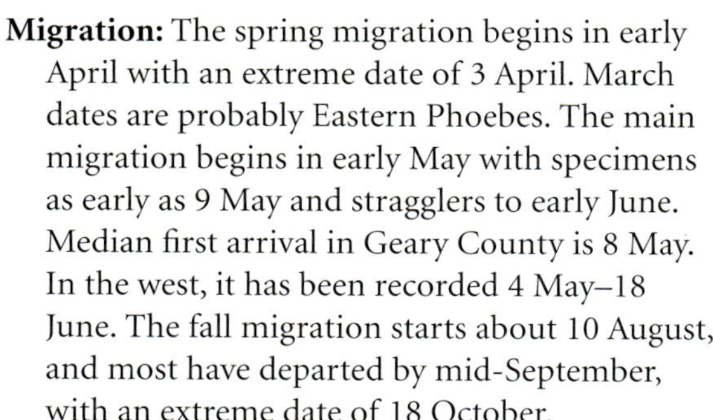

Migration: The spring migration begins in early April with an extreme date of 3 April. March dates are probably Eastern Phoebes. The main migration begins in early May with specimens as early as 9 May and stragglers to early June. Median first arrival in Geary County is 8 May. In the west, it has been recorded 4 May–18 June. The fall migration starts about 10 August, and most have departed by mid-September, with an extreme date of 18 October.

Breeding: It breeds in woodlands in eastern Kansas and west through the Flint Hills into central Kansas where it occurs along riparian corridors. KBBAT showed most breeding east of the Flint Hills, becoming sparser west. The preferred breeding habitat is contiguous forestlands. On the KBBAT block encompassing Timber Creek in Cowley County, it was the most common breeding bird. Statewide, nest-building has been reported 4 June–20 July, eggs 26 May–8 July, nestlings 2 June–24 July, and recently fledged young 28 August–10 September. Johnston gave 15 June as the modal date for completion of clutches with more than half of the eggs laid 11–20 June.

Comments: See comments on Western Wood-Pewee.

Banding: 256 banded; one encounter. A bird banded on 4 July 2001 at Fort Riley was recovered in a banding operation near Killeen, Texas, on 2 July 2002.

References: Busby and Zimmerman, 2001; Cable et al., 1996; Janzen, 2007; Johnston, 1964a; Thompson and Ely, 1992.

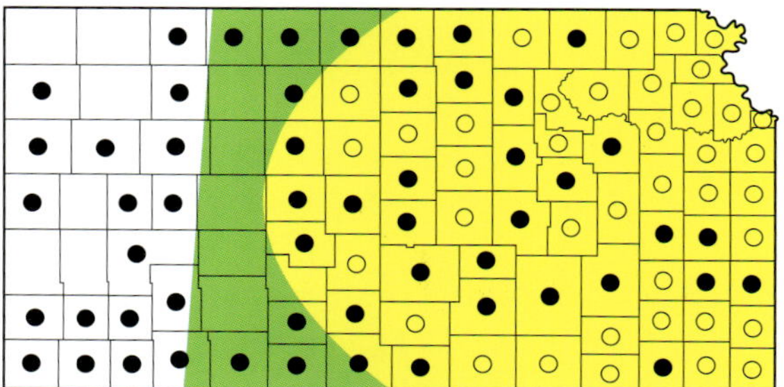

Yellow-bellied Flycatcher

Empidonax flaviventris (YBFL)

© David Seibel

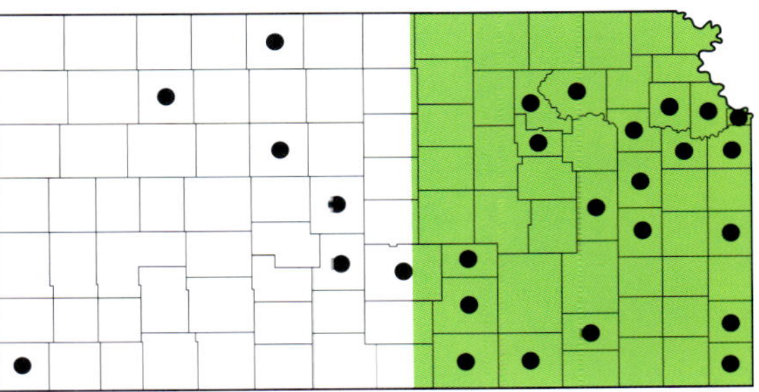

Status: Rare to uncommon transient in the eastern one-third of the state; casual in the west.

Habitat: Riparian forest where it usually feeds in the open understory.

Migration: Confirmed reports (handheld birds, specimens, singing males) are 4 May–5 June. The usual migration period is around 2 May–5 June with the peak during the last half of May. April records are probably in error. Like many *Empidonax* flycatchers, its fall return starts in early August (1 August, specimen) and continues through 7 October with unconfirmed sightings to 21 and 24 October.

Comments: The genus *Empidonax* is a confusing group of nine very similar species that can be reliably identified in the field only by voice (songs of most species are usually discernible with practice; call notes tend to be less distinctive). Visually, even handheld individuals require careful examination. Most species require use of measurements and characters not included in standard field guides; two can be reliably distinguished only by direct comparison with known specimens (if then). No matter how well seen, it is not possible to identify every individual in the field. Birders attempting to identify *Empidonax* flycatchers should study both the descriptions and the cautions given by K. Kaufman. The following comments on periods of occurrence and, to a lesser extent, status are based largely on specimens, handheld birds, bandings, and singing males and may require future modifications. The same is true for each species of *Empidonax*.

Banding: 72 banded; no encounters. The banding records show a very narrow migration period. Spring bandings were from 4 to 6 May and one on 1 June. In fall, bandings were 4 August (one bird) to 1–3 September when the majority were banded.

References: Kaufman, 1990; Thompson and Ely, 1992.

Acadian Flycatcher

Empidonax virescens (ACFL)

Status: Uncommon transient and summer resident in the eastern one-third of the state; casual elsewhere; rarely found outside of riparian forests.

Habitat: Confined to riparian woodlands while breeding; also upland deciduous forest during migration.

Migration: The earliest spring arrival date is 30 April with most movement during May and possibly extending into early June. Johnston gave the median arrival as 9 May. During May 1976 it was the most abundant of four species of *Empidonax* banded in Johnson County (M. L. Myers). Like many of the *Empidonax* flycatchers, the southward migration begins in early August with the peak in early September. The few fall records (to 30 September) suggest that either departure is by mid-September or that birds are overlooked among the various migrating *Empidonax*. A specimen from Ellis County on 27 July 1971 is an unusual vagrant.

Breeding: Its breeding range in Kansas is very local in appropriate habitat and confined to the eastern one-third of the state. It nests regularly west to south-central Cowley County and in the northeast to Atchison County. The KBBAT study found scattered midsummer records from throughout its summer range, probably of nesting birds, but not confirmed. Eggs have been reported 25 May–16 July (median 14 June) and nestlings 6 June–21 July. The nest is usually built in shady, bottomland deciduous forest, usually near water.

Comments: See comments on *Empidonax* identification under Yellow-bellied Flycatcher.

Banding: 150 banded; no encounters.

References: Busby and Zimmerman, 2001; Johnston, 1965; Thompson and Ely, 1992.

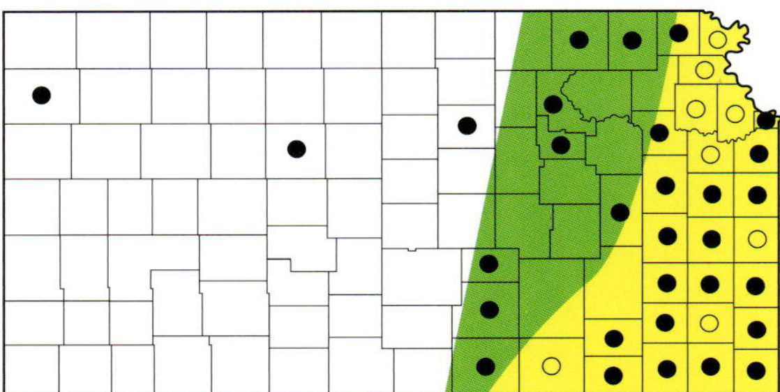

Alder Flycatcher

Empidonax alnorum (ALFL)

© David Seibel

Status: Probably a common transient statewide; generally more numerous than the Willow Flycatcher in the eastern counties.

Habitat: Riparian deciduous woods, edge areas near water, and parks.

Migration: Specimens and singing males have been reported 4–29 May and, exceptionally, to 10 June, with most confirmed records between 21 and 29 May. In fall, specimens are available for the period 29 July–12 September, with most from 14 to 21 August. The migration is probably completed around 15 September (unconfirmed).

Comments: Many details are unclear because of similarity to other *Empidonax* species, especially the Willow Flycatcher with which it was formerly considered conspecific. Many records, even now, are lumped as "Traill's Flycatcher," the combined name for both of these sibling species. The two can be reliably distinguished only by voice or, with difficulty, by direct comparison of handheld individuals. The typical song of the Alder Flycatcher, often heard during spring migration, is a burry "wee-BEE-o" or "ree-BEE-er" with the second syllable ascending and the third syllable abruptly dropping in pitch and volume (and often indistinct). "Traill's Flycatchers" occur statewide with confirmed migration records from 28 April through 12 June and 3 July through 28 September. The Alder Flycatcher nests only north of Kansas, where it prefers less-open, wetter habitat than the Willow Flycatcher (which does nest in Kansas in small numbers).

Banding: Most bandings are included under the combined "Traill's Flycatcher" because of the difficulty in distinguishing this flycatcher from the Willow Flycatcher. Banded (including "Traill's"): 1,019; two encounters: one in-state, and an adult "Traill's" banded at Hays (Ellis Co.) on 24 May 1970 was found dead in Lincoln, Nebraska, on 29 May 1975.

References: Busby and Zimmerman, 2001; Janzen, 2007; Thompson and Ely, 1992.

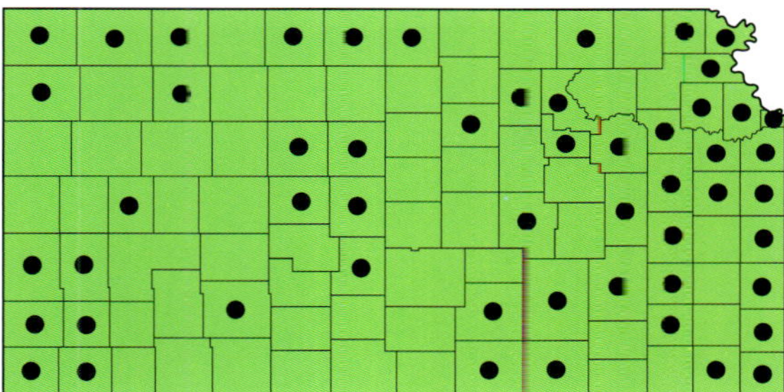

Willow Flycatcher

Empidonax traillii (WIFL)

Status: Uncommon to common transient statewide, more common in the west; rare local summer resident in the northeast; casual in summer elsewhere in the east. Formerly considered conspecific with Alder Flycatcher and still often combined as "Traill's Flycatcher" when indistinguishable.

Habitat: During migration found in all wooded and edge habitats, usually perching low in undergrowth. Its behavior is essentially like that of the Alder Flycatcher.

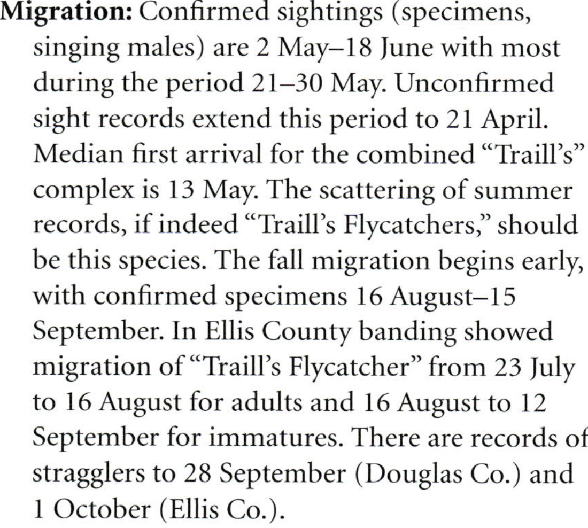

Migration: Confirmed sightings (specimens, singing males) are 2 May–18 June with most during the period 21–30 May. Unconfirmed sight records extend this period to 21 April. Median first arrival for the combined "Traill's" complex is 13 May. The scattering of summer records, if indeed "Traill's Flycatchers," should be this species. The fall migration begins early, with confirmed specimens 16 August–15 September. In Ellis County banding showed migration of "Traill's Flycatcher" from 23 July to 16 August for adults and 16 August to 12 September for immatures. There are records of stragglers to 28 September (Douglas Co.) and 1 October (Ellis Co.).

Breeding: T. Anderson found seven nests in willows near the Missouri River in Wyandotte and Doniphan counties in 1963. Nesting has been documented from Marshall County (1886), and KBBAT reported confirmed breeding in Douglas and Miami counties and a possible nesting record from Sedgwick County. Eggs have been reported 17–29 June, nestlings on 7 July, and recently fledged young on 17 July.

Comments: Early and late dates are tentative, because current records are inadequate to distinguish breeding from transient individuals. Additionally, most early sightings were lumped into the composite "Traill's Flycatcher," and silent birds cannot be safely distinguished from other *Empidonax* species except in the hand (if then). The typical song of the Willow Flycatcher is often described as a burry or sneezy "FITZ-bew," usually descending and always accented on the first syllable.

Banding: As with the Alder Flycatcher (which see), most bandings are under the composite "Traill's Flycatcher." Only 14 bandings of known Willow Flycatcher, with no encounters recorded.

References: Busby and Zimmerman, 2001; Cable et al., 1996; Janzen, 2007; Johnston, 1964a, 1964b; Thompson and Ely, 1992.

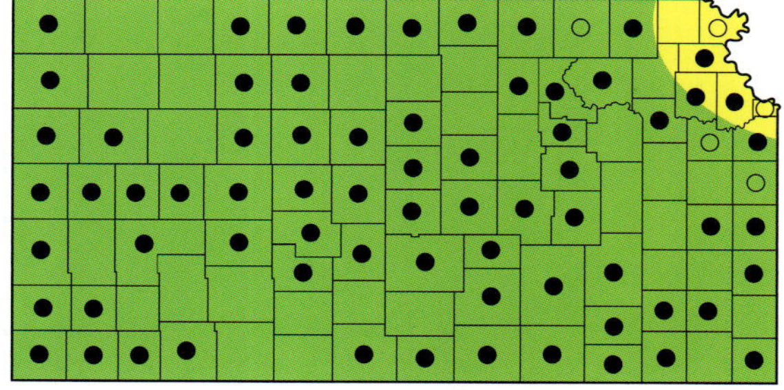

Least Flycatcher

Empidonax minimus (LEFL)

Status: Common transient statewide; one probable breeding record for Brown County.

Habitat: Riparian forest, patches of forest, parks, and shrubbery.

Migration: This is the earliest of the *Empidonax* flycatchers to transit the state. There are sight records from 5 April (singing, Rooks Co., M. Rolfs) through 6 June. Median first arrival in Ellis County is 1 May. Migration usually begins in late April and peaks by mid-May. Singing males are occasionally found during midsummer. Fall migration begins early with postbreeding (or nonbreeding) adults arriving by mid-July (earliest 6 July, Cheyenne Co.), with peak numbers by mid-September and stragglers into October (latest 20 October, Ellis Co.). Median fall arrival was 7 September in Rice County. In Ellis County adults passed through 16 July–23 August, overlapping briefly with immatures, which were present 15 August–24 September.

Breeding: The nearest known breeding areas are in eastern Nebraska. KBBAT reported one probable breeding pair (6 June 1996) in Brown County, but no nest was found and these could have been late migrants.

Comments: It is a ubiquitous flycatcher during migration, and its distinctive call (a two-note "che-BECK" accented on the second syllable) can be heard almost anywhere in the state during spring migration. It is mostly silent during the fall passage. See comments on *Empidonax* identification under Yellow-bellied Flycatcher.

Banding: 2,092 banded; one encounter. One bird banded in Kansas on 21 September 1972 was "caught by hand" in Manitoba during May 1974.

References: Busby and Zimmerman, 2001; Cable et al., 1996; Janzen, 2007; Thompson and Ely, 1992.

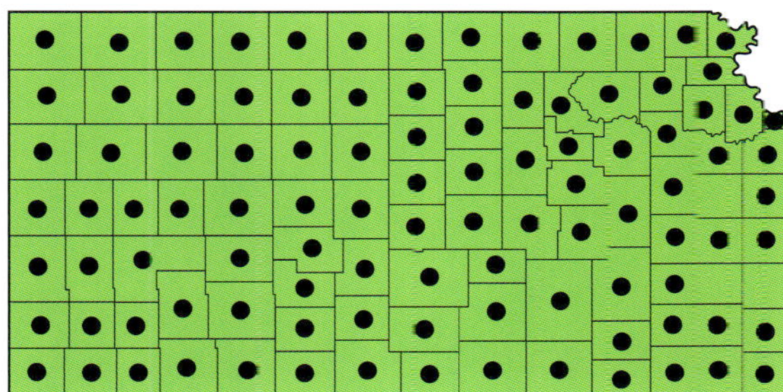

Hammond's Flycatcher

Empidonax hammondii (HAFL)

Status: Casual transient in fall in the extreme west; casual eastward.

Habitat: Riparian woodlands.

Migration: All eight confirmed records are from fall between 4 September and 4 October (median date 15 September). The only spring record (unverified) is one banded in Barton County on 1 June 1968.

Comments: See comments on *Empidonax* identification under Yellow-bellied Flycatcher. The first record for the state was brought in by a cat at Hays (Ellis Co.) on 15 September 1961. Extreme dates are 25 August (Morton Co., unconfirmed) and 4 October (Ellis Co.). Most of the sightings are from Morton County, 25 August–28 September, and most of these are during early September. The identities of two birds banded in Barton County (22 September and 1 June) and one in Meade County (late August) were unverified. The 1 June individual is likely in error. There are five fall specimen records from Ellis County (MHP 297, 1139, 2317, 2350, 2379) and one fall specimen from Morton County (KU 91184). Two additional sightings supported by photos have been accepted by the KBRC: Tribune (Greeley Co.), 4 September (KBRC 2005-17); and Leoti (Wichita Co.), 4 September (KBRC 2006-19).

© Jim Burns

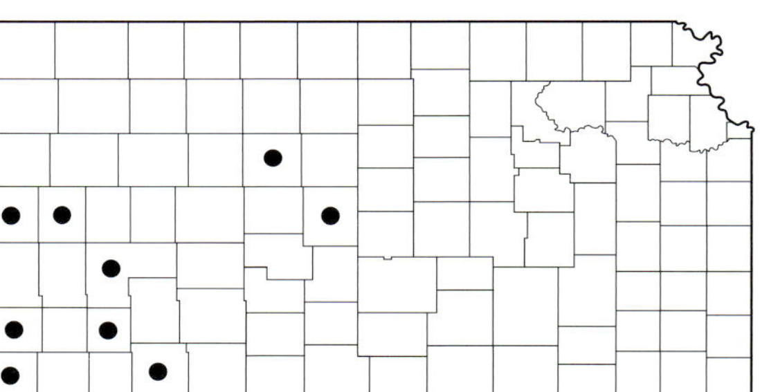

Banding: Three banded; no encounters.

References: Cable et al., 1996; Otte, 2006, 2007; Thompson and Ely, 1992.

Gray Flycatcher

Empidonax wrightii (GRFL)

Status: Casual transient in extreme southwestern Kansas. All reports are from Morton County with nearly all from fall. The only specimen record is in the Sternberg Museum (MHP 1555) taken on 29 April 1967. Five of 10 sight records have been accepted by the KBRC. Accepted spring reports are 29 April–26 May with unverified reports extending this period to 20 April. Confirmed fall records are 5–21 September with unverified sightings extending this period to 28 August and 30 September. A sighting from 7 July 1989 may have been a vagrant.

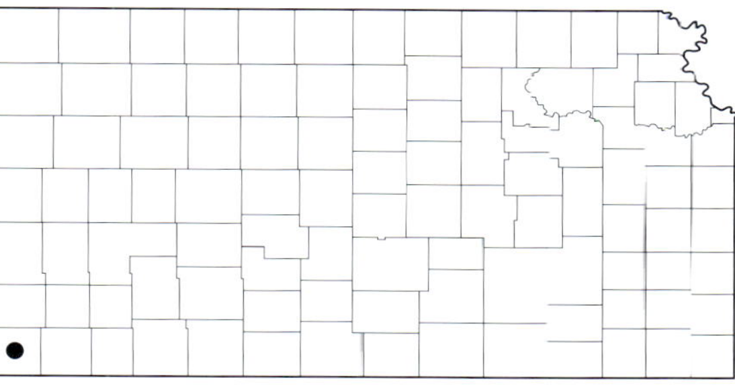

Comments: See comments on *Empidonax* identification under Yellow-bellied Flycatcher.

References: Cable et al., 1996; Thompson and Ely, 1992.

Dusky Flycatcher

Empidonax oberholseri (DUFL)

Status: Rare transient in the southwest with one record (specimen) from Trego County.

Habitat: Riparian woodlands, usually in cottonwood groves or in salt-cedar thickets. On the breeding grounds it occurs in relatively arid habitats.

Migration: Considered irregular in occurrence until the 1990s, recent evidence indicates a more regular status in at least Morton County. It is interesting that all specimens are from spring, whereas the bulk of sightings are during fall. Specimen records are 29 April–23 May and 22 June (Trego Co.). Sight records extend this period to 17 April (Scott Co.). Recent fieldwork indicates a regular fall movement, 6 August–27 September, with most during the first week of September.

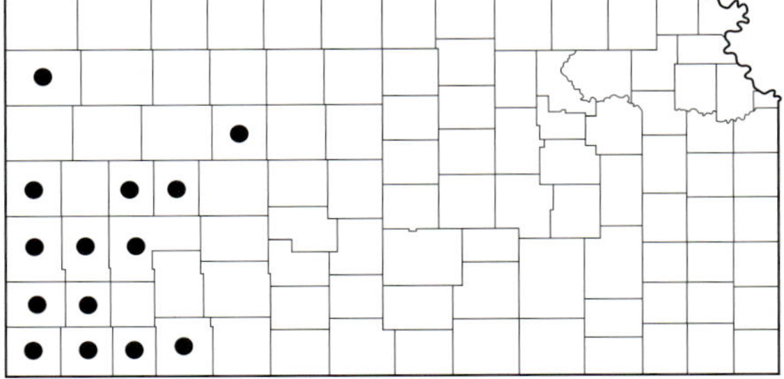

Comments: See comments on *Empidonax* identification under Yellow-bellied Flycatcher. The Dusky Flycatcher is probably the most regular of the "western" *Empidonax* species to transit western Kansas, moving eastward along the Cimarron and Arkansas rivers.

References: Cable et al., 1996; Thompson and Ely, 1992.

Cordilleran Flycatcher

Empidonax occidentalis (COFL)

Status: Casual spring transient and rare fall transient in the southwest; casual eastward to Ellis County.

Habitat: Riparian woodlands along the Cimarron River and North Fork of the Cimarron River in Morton County; also suburban yards and cemeteries.

Migration: All confirmed records are from Morton County (specimen; singing) except for a specimen from Ellis County (5 September 1971) and perhaps one banded near Meade (Meade Co., unverified). The only two spring records are 11 May (unconfirmed) and 26 May (singing, S. Seltman), both Morton County. Fall sightings, most from Morton County and unverified, are 24 August–26 September and 2 October (Finney Co.).

Comments: It is usually found in the lower understory of trees from which it dashes out to hawk insects. Most recent sightings are of silent birds identified only by plumage characteristics, particularly the teardrop-shaped eye-ring. Some of these are undoubtedly correct; subsequent collecting, however, has shown that some were "yellowish" individuals of other *Empidonax* species. The possibility that the Cordilleran's sibling species, the Pacific-slope Flycatcher (*E. difficilis*), could stray into Kansas makes field identification of this species particularly tenuous, as argued for Colorado by T. Leukering. See additional comments on *Empidonax* identification under Yellow-bellied Flycatcher.

Banding: One banded (Meade Co., 2 September 2006, unverified); no encounters.

References: Cable et al., 1996; Leukering, 2000; Thompson and Ely, 1992.

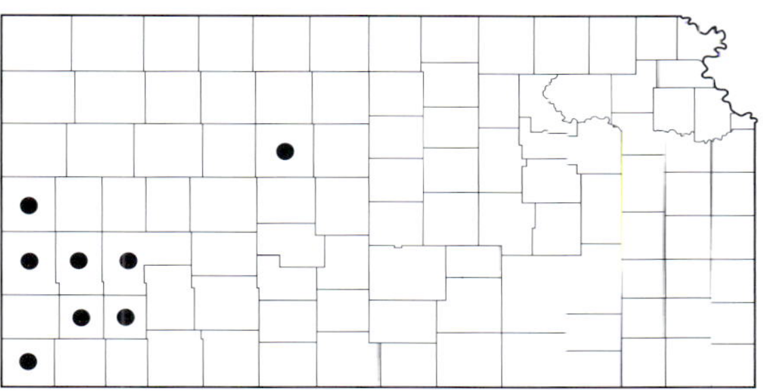

Black Phoebe

Sayornis nigricans (BLPH)

Status: [Hypothetical]. Vagrant. There is one accepted sighting by T. Shane on 16 March 1976 (KBRC 2001-5). The bird was seen 8 miles north of Elkhart, CNG (Morton Co.). There is a recent sighting of a bird in the same area on 13 September 2009. The bird was observed for 2 minutes, but no photographs were taken. The KBRC reviewed the record (2009-29) but did not believe that the description ruled out a hybrid.

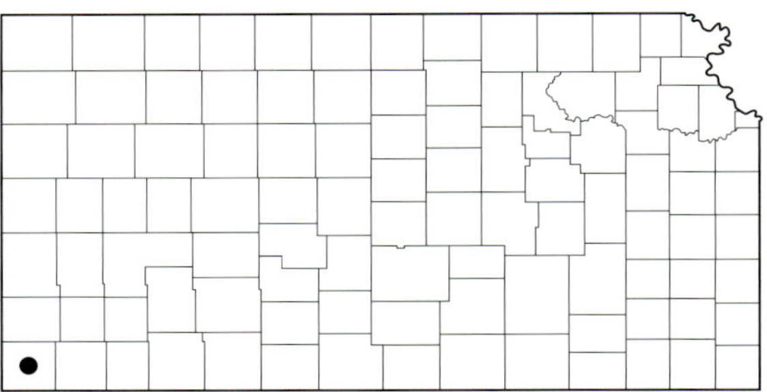

Comments: This species should be watched for in southwestern Kansas. The usual habitat is around water. It has nested in nearby Colorado.

References: Land, 2010; Rintoul, 2002; Thompson and Ely, 1992; Wolf, 1997.

Eastern Phoebe

Sayornis phoebe (EAPH)

Status: Common transient and summer resident in the east, becoming progressively less common westward where it is rare and local in summer and casual in winter; a few may overwinter during mild winters.

© Judd Patterson

Habitat: Usually near water; requires some vegetation in the vicinity of its nest site; often near human habitation.

Migration: Very early arrivals include 28 February (Cherokee and Douglas cos.) and 1 March (Johnson Co.) but is usually mid-March in the east and a week later in the west. Median first arrivals include 17 March (Johnson Co.), 22 March (Russell Co.), and 30 March (Ellis Co.). Most migration is mid-March into April. The fall migration begins in September and lasts through November. There are several records on CBCs, and one lingered until 4 January.

Breeding: It usually nests near water, often placing its nest on a ledge or girder under a bridge. Natural sites such as cliffs and rocky outcrops and outbuildings are used less frequently. The nest is made of mud, plant stems, moss, algae, rootlets, and fine grasses. Nest-building has been reported 19 March–10 May, eggs 21 March–4 July, nestlings 26 April–8 July, and recently fledged young 14 May–29 June. It is typically double-brooded. John Schukman reported the peaks for first and second clutches in Ellis County were 29 April and 10 June in 1973 and 15 April and 27 May in 1974, respectively.

Comments: This is the most common of the phoebes in Kansas and one of the earliest passerines to arrive, often arriving with snow still in the area. None of the 19th century ornithologists reported the species from western Kansas, leading J. Rising to suggest that breeding there is of recent origin. It was considered "uncommon" in Rocks County prior to 1937 and reported in Ellis County by L. Wooster by 1941.

Banding: 1,963 banded; five encounters: three in-state. Two nestlings banded near Baldwin City (Douglas Co.) were encountered on or near their wintering grounds: one banded 28 June 1982 was recaptured and released near Jay, Oklahoma, on 10 October 1982; one banded 26 June 1986 was found dead near Bay City, Texas, on 3 February 1987. Oldest 2 years, 2 months.

References: Busby and Zimmerman, 2001; Cink, 2006; Janzen, 2007; Rising, 1974; Schukman, 1993; Thompson and Ely, 1992.

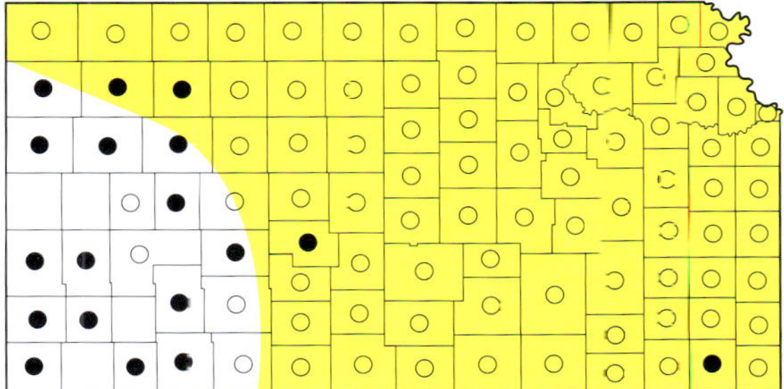

Say's Phoebe

Sayornis saya (SAPH)

Status: Common transient and summer resident in the western half of the state; rare to absent in the eastern half.

Habitat: Dry open country of the west, rarely noted near trees except at isolated farmsteads. It is the ecological replacement of the Eastern Phoebe, with Eastern typically nesting along streams with near continuous woody vegetation, and Say's in areas with spotty or no vegetation.

Migration: The earliest spring arrival is 19 February (Gove Co., possibly wintered) with a few in early March (2 March, Pawnee and Ellis cos.). More usual arrival is mid-March with most migration probably in early to mid-April. Recent median first arrival for Ellis County is 3 April; in 1884 the bulk arrived on 18 April. Fall departure is poorly documented but probably begins in late August or early September with few reported after mid-September. In 1952, Seltman reported that individuals were still present in the upper Smoky Hill River valley on 23 September despite deep snow cover. One remained at SCW from 28 August to 16 October 2005. Late dates include 15 November (Russell Co.), and a few occasionally remain into the CBC period including five individuals on 30 December 1979 and two on 31 December 1982 (both Morton Co.). The latter two birds were along the cliffs west of Point of Rocks where the sun warmed the cliffs and provided a wind shield.

Breeding: KBBAT confirmed nesting in the western half of the state with the highest number of blocks reporting its presence in the High Plains, most frequently in topography dissected by stream channels with little or intermittent stream flow and usually sparse vegetation in the nesting area. Breeding records are from Cloud, Ellsworth, Reno, and Kingman counties westward. Nests are placed under bridges, on rocky outcrops, and in caves along streambeds and in man-made structures such as sheds. Mud is rarely used in nest construction. Nest-building has been reported 23 April–29 June, eggs 30 April–17 July (once 7 August), and nestlings 30 May–18 July. In Ellis County, J. Schukman noted that nesting began about 2 weeks later than for the Eastern Phoebe with the peak for initiation of clutches on about 6 May and 24 June for first and second clutches, respectively. It often uses old Barn Swallow nests and on occasion Eastern Phoebe nests.

Banding: 127 banded; one encounter: in-state, same site, 2 years, 10 months after banding.

References: Busby and Zimmerman, 2001; Cable et al., 1996; Schukman, 1993; Thompson and Ely, 1989.

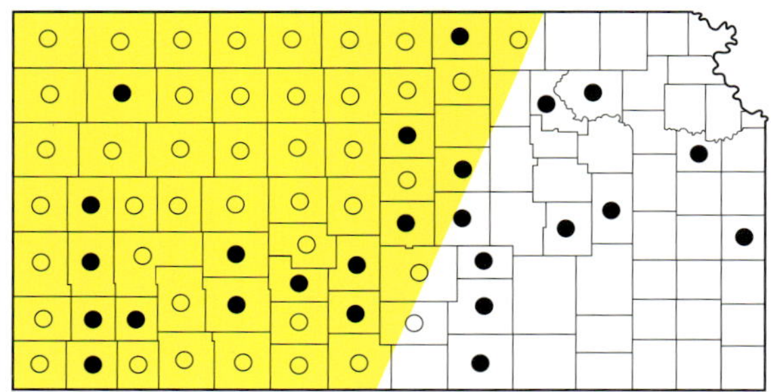

Vermilion Flycatcher

Pyrocephalus rubinus (VEFL)

© David Seibel

Status: Casual visitant in the southwest; vagrant in the east.

Habitat: Semiarid portions of the state, straying eastward in open areas.

Migration: Most records are from spring, 12 from April alone. The other spring records are 14 March 2001 (Barton Co.), 4 May (Shawnee Co.), and 19 May 2002 (Leavenworth Co.). The two fall records are 11 September 2006 (Washington Co.) and 1 November 2000 (Pratt Co.).

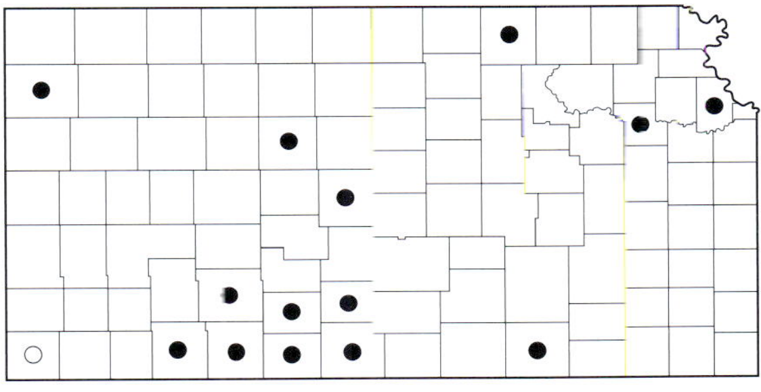

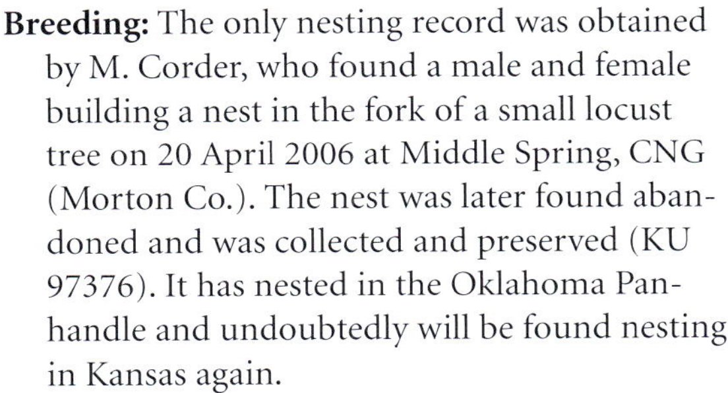

Breeding: The only nesting record was obtained by M. Corder, who found a male and female building a nest in the fork of a small locust tree on 20 April 2006 at Middle Spring, CNG (Morton Co.). The nest was later found abandoned and was collected and preserved (KU 97376). It has nested in the Oklahoma Panhandle and undoubtedly will be found nesting in Kansas again.

Comments: There are three specimens from Kansas. The first specimen (MHP 1396) was collected on 15 April 1967 at Middle Springs (Morton Co.). The second was salvaged from a group of five that died in a snowstorm in Coldwater (Comanche Co.) on 4 April 1973. M. Swisher sent one of the birds to KUMNH (KU 67614). The third (KU 97190) was taken on 3 April 2006, the same year that nesting was documented in Morton County.

References: Cable et al., 1996; Corder, 2006; Land, 2010; Thompson and Ely, 1992.

Ash-throated Flycatcher

Myiarchus cinerascens (ATFL)

Status: Rare nesting species in Morton, Meade, and Seward counties; probably transient in the west; vagrant elsewhere.

Habitat: It occurs in riparian woodlands in arid areas. Most Kansas records are from woodlands along the Cimarron River (Morton Co.).

Migration: Sight records and specimen records from Morton County are mainly in April, with an early date of 20 April. Outside the breeding range spring dates are 26 April (Clark Co., singing) and 14 May (Comanche Co.). Most of the other southwestern Kansas records are in April–June. The fall migration is poorly known, but transients (perhaps including local nesting birds) have been reported 7 August (Sedgwick Co., vagrant) and 22 August (Meade Co.) through 19 September (Morton Co.), with a vagrant in Miami County on 30 September.

Breeding: Recently, it has become more common and may have become established as a regular nesting species. It has been recorded nesting in Morton, Meade, and possibly Seward counties. In Morton County it breeds sympatrically with the Great Crested Flycatcher. Like other *Myiarchus* flycatchers, it nests in old woodpecker holes in trees and has utilized bluebird nest boxes in Morton County (as have birds nesting nearby in adjacent Oklahoma and Colorado). The nest is composed of mostly plant material, usually with shed snake skins, plastic bags, and bits of cellophane. Eggs have been reported 21 May–22 July and young 5 June–22 July.

Comments: It replaces the Great Crested Flycatcher in the southwestern United States. Both occur together in southwestern Kansas, and care must be taken when identifying them in the field. It was first reported in Kansas by R. and J. Graber in Morton County in May 1950 and reported irregularly through the 1980s. The first nesting was in Wolf Canyon just inside the Meade County line in 1983. The first reported nesting in Morton County was in 1986, and it has occurred regularly since 1991 when nest boxes were erected along the Cimarron River by M. Schwilling.

References: Boyd, 1985; Busby and Zimmerman, 2001; Cable et al., 1996; Graber and Graber, 1950; Thompson and Ely, 1992.

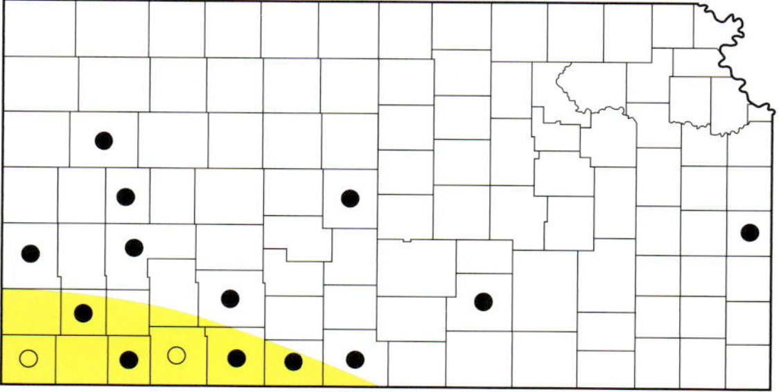

Great Crested Flycatcher

Myiarchus crinitus (GCFL)

Status: Common transient and summer resident in eastern and central Kansas; rare westward where it is restricted to riparian habitats and occurs very locally.

Habitat: Wooded habitats from deciduous forests to towns and riparian woodlands.

Migration: The earliest spring dates are 28 March and 3 April (both Cowley Co.), but typical arrival is mid-April with peak migration during the first half of May. Median earliest arrivals include 28 April (Rice Co.), 28 April (Johnson Co.), and 2 May (Ellis and Meade cos.). Departure of spring transients is masked by the presence of local nesting birds. The fall migration is poorly documented, because birds are largely silent during this period; probably starts in mid-August and is largely finished by early September. Median departure from Ellis County is 6–9 September. Unusually late dates are 12 October (Rush Co.) and 19 October (Ellis Co.). The latest record is 3 November 2006 in Morton County by J. Shroyer, who noted that it was clearly a *Myiarchus* flycatcher with a bright yellow belly.

Breeding: It nests in natural cavities or woodpecker holes in trees. One famous pair built their nest in a cannon on the state house grounds in Topeka in 1887. The nest was destroyed when the cannon was fired! Great Crested Flycatchers are known to use snake skins or the modern equivalent, cellophane and plastic, to line the nest. Nest-building has been reported 12 May–2 June, eggs 21 May–31 July, young 29 May–27 July, and recently fledged young 1 July–10 August (Morton Co., S. Seltman). Nesting sites can be used in successive years. An egg set at the California Academy of Science dated 1 April 1906 is likely an error in labeling.

Comments: It is a very vocal species in the spring with a very distinctive call and is often heard but not seen.

Banding: 432 banded; no encounters.

References: Busby and Zimmerman, 2001; Cable et al., 1996; Janzen, 2007; Thompson and Ely, 1992.

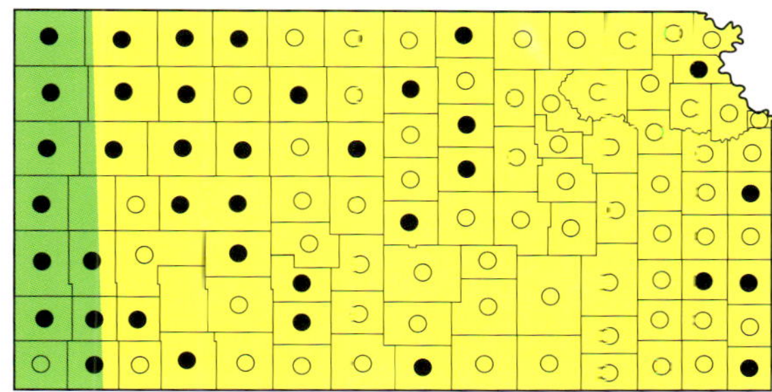

Great Kiskadee

Pitangus sulphuratus (GKIS)

Status: Accidental. There is one record from Morton County (KBRC 95-22, 95-20). H. McFadden found one at Middle Spring, CNG, on 18 May 1995. It remained until 31 May; and, though it was difficult to observe, numerous birders saw it, photos and video were taken, and the distinctive call was heard.

Comments: The normal range of this species is southern Texas south into South America. There are extralimital records from New Mexico and Oklahoma.

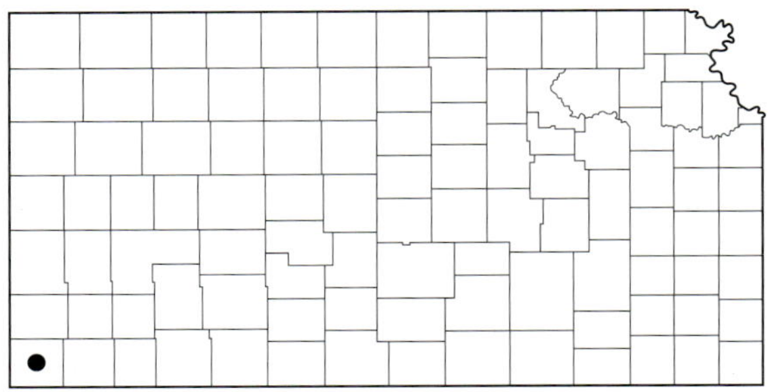

References: Brush and Fitzpatrick, 2002; Pittman, 1996.

Cassin's Kingbird

Tyrannus vociferans (CAKI)

Status: Uncommon transient in the southwest; vagrant elsewhere. It may become a casual nesting species, because it does nest close to the Kansas border in Colorado.

Habitat: Open areas or in areas with many dead trees such as along the Cimarron River in Morton County; utilizes barbed-wire fences and dead limbs as perches while looking for insects.

Migration: Spring sightings fall within the period 10 April–15 June. The number of fall sightings has increased in recent years concomitant with an increase in birding activity in the area, and these now comprise a majority of sightings. The fall passage begins around 29 August with a late date of 30 September. It was formerly considered an uncommon migrant, but on 22 September 2005, S. Patti and M. Thompson counted around 100 in Morton County; next day only 4 or 5 birds were seen. Whether this was an indication of migration in larger numbers than previously recorded or an anomaly remains unclear. Most sightings outside of Morton County have been scattered sightings in the west but with a notable observation from QNWR on 10 May 2008 by S. Seltman and D. Kazmaier (with photos).

Comments: It was first reported by R. and J. Graber, who reported up to two pairs along the Cimarron River near the KS 27 bridge north of Elkhart and collected a specimen on 26 May 1950. Their sightings were in open, weedy areas on the dry riverbed itself, not in the nearby cottonwood groves. It is easily confused with the Western Kingbird, and observers outside of southwestern Kansas should be careful to note all identification marks and the call before making a definitive identification.

References: Cable et al., 1996; Graber and Graber, 1951; Thompson and Ely, 1992.

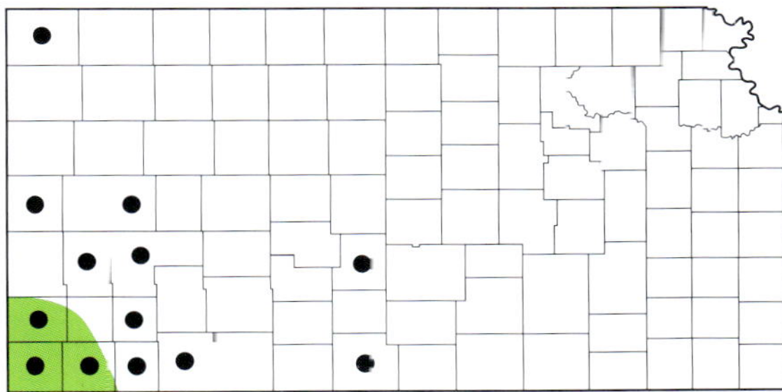

Western Kingbird

Tyrannus verticalis (WEKI)

Status: Common transient and summer resident; uncommon and local in the extreme east.

Habitat: Edge riparian growth, shelterbelts, farmsteads, and residential areas with extensive lawns with trees to nest in. Often seen feeding around sport complexes and other open areas with lights during the evening.

Migration: It usually arrives in late April with a very early date of 21 March (Dickinson Co.). Median earliest arrival dates include 20 April (Cowley Co.), 21 April (Rice Co.), 22 April (Barton and Meade cos.), 23 April (Pawnee Co.), and 26 April (Ellis Co.). Large diurnal movements have been noted on 25–26 April (Meade Co.). The fall migration begins in late August and is usually finished by 25 September with an extreme date of 19 October (Montgomery Co.). Median departure is about 10 September (Ellis Co.). Unlike other members of the genus *Tyrannus*, the Western Kingbird does not seem to form large groups before migration begins. High counts include 65 on 17 August (Sumner Co.), 50+ on 8 September (Barton Co.), 49 on 22 August (Sumner Co.), 43 on 13 August (Edwards Co.), and 45 on 27 August (Douglas Co.). However, 300+ in Morton County on 30 August had all departed by the next day, and there are sightings of up to 250 birds in Morton County on 4 September 1999 and 200 birds on 22 September 2005.

Breeding: It breeds statewide but is more sparsely distributed in the eastern one-fourth. The nest is usually placed on a horizontal branch, utility pole, or other man-made structures. Nest-building has been reported 12 May–31 July, eggs 8 June–2 July, nestlings 1 June–21 July, and fledging mid-June through mid-July.

Comments: J. Porter, in speaking of north-central Kansas in 1951, noted a steady eastward range expansion "over the last 60 years" and L. Carson noted a "continued increase" in numbers in 1950 (AFN 4(4):250).

Banding: 186 banded; two encounters: both in-state.

References: Busby and Zimmerman, 2001; Cable et al., 1996; Janzen, 2007; Porter, 1951; Thompson and Ely, 1992.

Eastern Kingbird

Tyrannus tyrannus (EAKI)

Status: Common transient and summer resident statewide, more common in the east.

Habitat: Open fields and woody edge habitats.

Migration: Very early dates include 21 March (Cowley Co.), 10 April (Ford and Morton cos.), and 12 April (Sumner Co.), with most migration during late April through mid-May. Median first arrival dates include 24 April (Cowley Co.), 24 April (Lyon Co.), 25 April (Ellis Co.), and 29 April (Rice Co.). High counts include 188 on 13 May and 220 on 21 May (2010, both Sumner Co.), 200 on 12 May (Sumner Co.), 35 on 30 April (Ellsworth Co.), and 2 flocks of 10 each on 8 May (Doniphan Co.). Migration continues through May. The fall migration is preceded by flocking. These congregations are often feeding on dogwood berries (500+ on 2 September [Harvey Co.], and regularly on Konza Prairie [Geary and Riley cos.]), less often on sand plums (21 August, Stafford Co.). Among the large flocks observed on wires were 470 on 11 September (Kingman Co.), which were gone the next day. More incredible was a flock of 5,000–10,000 individuals on 30 August 1994 (Sumner/Cowley county line) feeding over a field of sorghum. Most were gone with a cold front the next day (M. Thompson, E. Young). T. Cable reported a "steady stream" of migrants following the shore of Tuttle Creek Reservoir (Riley Co.) on 30 August. The median departure date for Ellis County is 10 September. It would appear that most migration is during late August and early September. The few reports after mid-September include 28 September (Morton Co.) and 8 October (Sedgwick Co.).

Breeding: Nest-building begins shortly after arrival. M. Thompson saw one placed on a snag projecting out of the water on a farm pond. Nest-building has been reported 1 May–29 June, eggs 2 May–12 July, chicks 25 May–5 August, and recently fledged young 1 July–12 August. Johnston reported 15 June as the modal date for completion of clutches, with 70 percent of all eggs laid during June.

Comments: It feeds on both insects and berries; among their favorite fruits are rough-leaved dogwood and pokeberry. Flocks in April and May in Sumner County are often observed foraging over alfalfa fields.

See page 500 for banding information.

References: Busby and Zimmerman, 2001; Cable et al., 1996; Janzen, 2007; Johnston, 1964a; Thompson and Ely, 1992; Young, 1993; Young and Thompson, 1995.

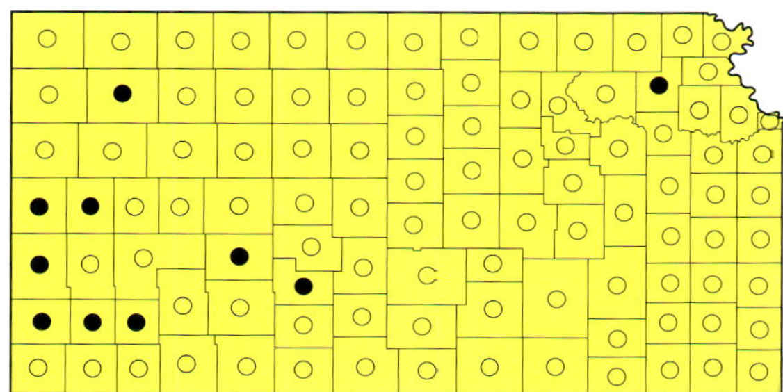

Scissor-tailed Flycatcher

Tyrannus forficatus (STFL)

© David Seibel

Status: Common to uncommon summer resident in the east and south; uncommon to rare in the west.

Habitat: Open spaces with isolated or widely dispersed trees.

Migration: This one of the earliest flycatchers to arrive in the spring with early dates, all from south-central Kansas, of 6 March (Sedgwick Co.), 11 March (Sumner Co.), 14 March (Cowley Co.), and 2 April (Harvey Co.). Median first arrival dates include 10 April (Cowley Co.), 12 April (Lyon Co.), and 26 April (Ellis Co.). Most migration is late April to early May. High counts include 35 on 21 May (Sumner Co.) and 20 on 1 May (Cherokee Co.). It is one of the last flycatchers to migrate south, with most migration during September and early October and with one extreme date of 23 November (Geary Co., M. Corder). Prior to migration, flocks develop with high counts including 100+ on 6 October (Barber Co.) and 40–50 on 24 September (Ellis Co.). M. Thompson reported more than 1,000 in one flock in the nearby Oklahoma Panhandle.

Breeding: KBBAT documented breeding south and east of a diagonal line from Morton to Russell and Washington counties. North and west of this line breeding birds are fewer and more widely dispersed and easily missed during sampling. It prefers to nest in open spaces in isolated trees such as at golf courses and is less likely to nest in riparian habitats and along residential streets than the other kingbirds. Nest-building has been reported 1 May–16 June, eggs 20 May–23 July, young 17 June–26 July, and recently fledged young 24 June–16 September. R. Johnston gave 25 June as the modal date for egg-laying.

Comments: Originally considered common in southern Kansas, it undertook a major range expansion during the 1940s and was nesting in southwestern Missouri by 1957 and southeastern Nebraska by 1959. In 1957 T. Pucci noted four pairs in the Kansas City area "whereas even one would recently have been a rarity" and E. Cole noted more than 12 pairs in the Kansas City area by 1964. J. Zimmerman mapped the Kansas distribution in 1978 using BBSs and found it most abundant in the south with smaller numbers present in the north and east but none in the southwest. This is one of the most beautiful birds in Kansas. In the fall, they share a common roosting area, which may contain hundreds of birds.

Banding: 43 banded; no encounters.

References: Busby and Zimmerman, 2001; Janzen, 2007; Johnston, 1964a; Thompson and Ely, 1992; Zimmermann, 1978.

Fork-tailed Flycatcher

Tyrannus savana (FTFL)

© David Seibel

Status: Accidental. There is one record. R. Mengel observed a single bird 2 miles east and 3 miles south of Hoisington on 13 May 1979. He noted characteristics in the field and later sketched the bird from memory. The record was accepted by the KBRC (at the initial meeting of the committee) from these sketches.

Comments: It has been recorded numerous times in the United States, and its presence was not unexpected.

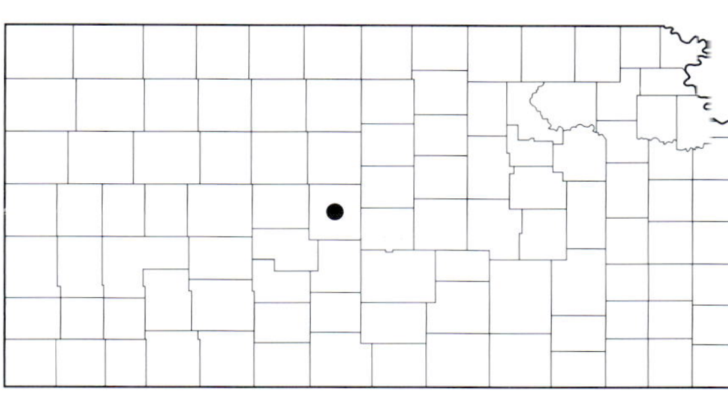

Reference: Jenkinson, 1991.

Loggerhead Shrike

Lanius ludovicianus (LOSH)

© Judd Patterson

Status: Formerly common transient and summer resident; less common in the far west; rare in winter.

Habitat: Open country with small stands or scattered trees. Pastures, hedgerows, and fence lines in prairie or cultivated areas are favored.

Migration: Data are inadequate to confidently distinguish wintering individuals from transients. Migration is probably under way by mid-March, certainly by late March and early April, and probably completed by late April. Johnston gave a median arrival of 21 March (8–31 March). Active migration was observed in the Pawnee County area from about 13 March to 9 April. Numbers of summer residents appear to be highest in late August and September with a gradual withdrawal during October. Peak passage of transients is probably October with return of wintering birds continuing into November. Examination of CBC data shows a gradual decrease in numbers of wintering shrikes since 1950 with two sharp declines during 1956–1969 and 1988–1997. This decline is still occurring, though at a slower pace.

Breeding: Breeding Bird Surveys show it to be declining in the Great Plains, but KBBAT conducted from 1992 to 1997 failed to confirm this for Kansas. KBBAT recorded it occurring in the highest number of blocks in the Flint Hills eastward and lowest in the High Plains. Nest-building occurs as early as 20 March in the southeast and 7 April westward. Johnston reported a modal date of 15 April (1 April–30 June) for egg-laying. The median for 43 clutches statewide is 27 April (5 April–1 June). Recently fledged young have been reported 21 May–29 June with most in mid-June.

Comments: Adults and young remain together as a tight family group after fledging and are conspicuous, active, very vocal components of the windbreak and roadside fauna at this time. Shrikes are commonly called "butcher birds" for their habit of impaling uneaten food (large insects and small vertebrates, including birds and mammals) on spines of Osage orange (*Maclura pomifera*) and other thorny trees and barbed-wire fences.

See page 500 for banding information.

References: Busby and Zimmerman, 2001; Janzen, 2007; Johnston, 1964a, 1965; Sauer et al., 2008; Thompson and Ely, 1992; Thompson and Young, 1998.

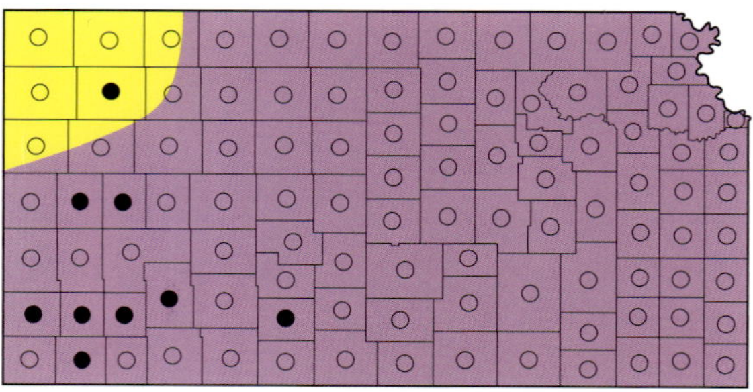

Northern Shrike

Lanius excubitor (NSHR)

© David Seibel

Status: Irregular, rare, winter visitant, chiefly in western and central Kansas.

Habitat: Open areas with scattered perches such as isolated trees, power lines, and fence lines.

Migration: Arrival is typically in late October continuing into early November. N. Goss reported arrival in early November, and R. Johnston gave a median arrival of 2 November (5 October–6 November). Early dates include 5 October and 15 October with most around 24 October. The increase in sightings during the CBC period probably results from increased observer activity. It was considered especially "common" during the winters of 1888–1889, 1889–1890, and 1985–1986. Departure is poorly documented, but most birds are gone by February with a few sightings through late March. N. Goss reported departure in March and Johnston a median departure of 9 March (3–23 March). Late dates include 24 March (Lane Co.), 29 March (Riley Co.), and 5 April.

Comments: It was considered quite common in winter by some 19th-century and early 20th-century observers including F. Snow, D. Lantz, and C. Bunker, but many of these records are dubious because of a long tradition of considering all wintering shrikes to be of this species. Subsequently it has been uncommon to rare and usually occurring north of a line from southeastern to northwestern Kansas. It is very similar in appearance to the Loggerhead Shrike, sharing the big-headed appearance and powerful beak but can be distinguished by the narrower mask, paler gray coloration, and often heavier barring underneath. Some individuals are nearly brown in color. It is most frequently seen perched on an open, elevated perch, then drops low to the ground and with a "buzzing" flight moves to the next perch where it rises sharply to a similar perch. Food includes large insects, small mammals, and small birds. Food not eaten immediately may be impaled on thorns of Osage orange (*Maclura pomifera*) trees or barbed-wire fences.

Banding: Probably two banded; no encounters. Two of four reported bandings were out of season and undoubtedly were Loggerhead Shrikes. One banded at Ellinwood by G. Ernsting returned so regularly to attack netted birds that banding operations were suspended for several days.

References: Bunker, 1913; Goss, 1891; Johnston, 1965; Snow, 1903; Thompson and Ely, 1992.

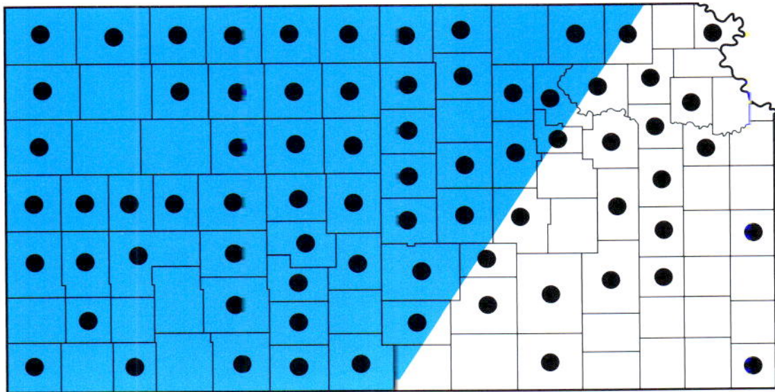

White-eyed Vireo

Vireo griseus (WEVI)

© Judd Patterson

Status: Uncommon transient and rare summer resident in the eastern one-third of the state; casual westward.

Habitat: Prefers thickets near riparian woods. This habitat is available only in the eastern part of the state from Cowley County and Sedgwick County eastward.

Migration: The earliest date of arrival is 3 April (Cowley and Linn cos.) but is usually around 15 April. Most migration is during late April through 10 May with most transients departed by 21 May. The fall departure usually begins in late August but is clouded by the presence of local breeders. Most have departed by the end of September with extreme dates of 14 October and 7 November (Ellis Co.) and 23 November (Grant Co.).

Breeding: It is presumed to breed in the three eastern tiers of counties. KBBAT confirmed breeding in Labette, Montgomery, and Douglas counties. It has bred west to Sedgwick County where P. Janzen and B. Gress observed adults feeding a recently fledged young on 4 July, and J. Calhoun has recorded them through the summer (presumed breeding) in southern Sedgwick County along the Arkansas River. Some of the additional reports of "breeding" are based on the presence of adults in proper habitat during summer or of adult specimens showing reproductive activity. The nest is usually placed in a shrub or low tree within 3 feet of the ground. Eggs have been reported on 26 May, adults carrying food on 12 June, young on 29 June, and recently fledged young (one, actually a cowbird) on 4–6 July.

Comments: Nineteenth-century reports (e.g., "common" at Topeka, May 1871) suggest that it has declined in numbers during the 20th century, as does the finding by J. Linsdale of 15 breeding pairs near Geary (Doniphan Co.) during 1921–1925. The decline may be caused by a significant reduction in habitat due to succession and agricultural development. It is easily overlooked when not singing and is probably underreported. The best way to find the bird is by its call. It can easily be attracted by a squeaking noise or playing a tape of its song.

Banding: 12 banded; no encounters. This supports the observation that it is not a common bird in Kansas.

References: Allen, 1872; Busby and Zimmerman, 2001; Janzen, 2007; Linsdale, 1933; Thompson and Ely, 1992.

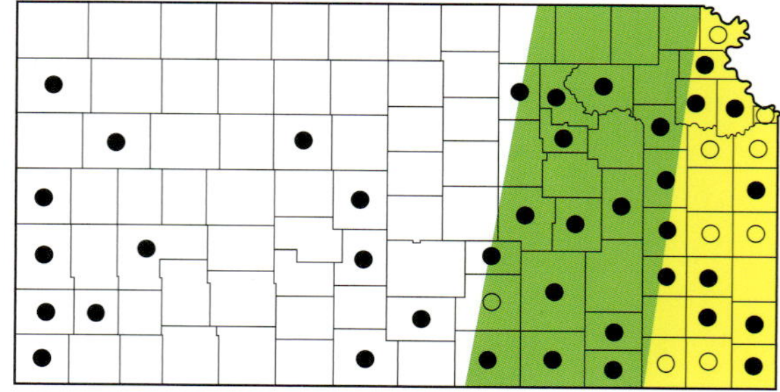

Bell's Vireo

Vireo bellii (BEVI)

Status: Common transient and summer resident in the eastern half of the state, less common westward.

Habitat: Thickets and scrub vegetation, preferring the more upland areas along roadsides and isolated patches of dense vegetation in grasslands.

Migration: The earliest reported arrivals are 15 April (Kiowa Co.) and 19 April (Lyon Co.), but more typically arrival is late April and early May. Most migration is during mid-May with stragglers to early June. Fall departure starts in August and is largely completed by 15 September with stragglers into late September, including 27 September (Grant Co.) and 29 September (Ellis Co., banded). Unusually late reports are from 11 October (Shawnee Co.) and 23 October (Elk Co.). The only report from a fall tower kill is a single bird at the Topeka KTKA television tower (Shawnee Co.) on 11–12 October.

Breeding: It breeds statewide with lowest densities in the southern High Plains. Preferred nesting sites are dense thickets of dogwood, coralberry, willow, plum, and other shrubby vegetation. Roadside thickets of rough-leaved dogwood will nearly always produce this vireo in the east; sandhill plums in the west. The nest is woven in the fork of a plant about 1–5 feet above the ground (typically lower). Nest-building has been reported 21 May–6 June, eggs 17 May–17 July (median 4 June, 28 clutches), young 23 June–26 July, and recently fledged young 28 June–9 July. Egg sets were taken as early as 1883 from Riley County. The Brown-headed Cowbird is a serious parasite on this species.

Comments: This is the smallest of the Kansas vireos and one of the easiest to find during the breeding season. Playing its song will almost always bring it out into the open.

Banding: 546 banded; four encounters: all in-state, at banding site.

References: Ball et al., 1995; Busby and Zimmerman, 2001; Janzen, 2007; Thompson and Ely, 1992.

Black-capped Vireo

Vireo atricapilla (BCVI)

Status: Once a summer resident of the Red Hills in south-central Kansas; now a vagrant, if it occurs there at all. Recent attempts to find the species have all ended in failure.

Habitat: It was confined to the Red Hills in the south-central part of the state. In this area, small oaks and other low, shrubby plants supplied the nesting habitat that it prefers. The habitat is still available in the area, but it is likely that the Brown-headed Cowbird has prevented the Black-capped Vireo from reoccupying it.

Breeding: The only confirmed nesting records are from Comanche County. Purported nesting in Cowley and Hodgeman counties are assumed to be in error as are sight records from Doniphan and Gray counties. These records were from observers who contributed sightings to the former U.S. Biological Survey, which was then collecting data on bird migration. The Hodgeman County record is based on a set of eggs in the Baylor University egg collection. We have not examined these eggs, but they are undoubtedly misidentified because Hodgeman County has not had proper habitat within historical times. N. Goss collected three pairs in southeastern Comanche County, 7–18 May 1885 (three extant specimens: KU 2472, 72557, 72558), and found a nest under construction 11 May 1885. He considered these vireos to be quite common.

Comments: The Black-capped Vireo still nests in Oklahoma. In the areas where it occurs, removal of the Brown-headed Cowbird has kept the bird from being extirpated.

References: Grzybowski, 1995; Thompson and Ely, 1992.

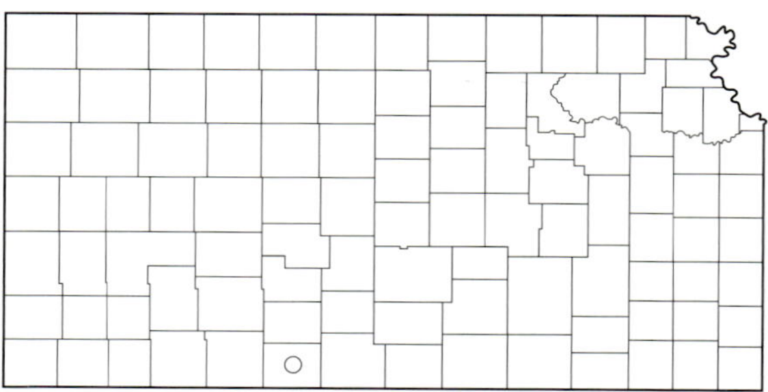

Gray Vireo

Vireo vicinior (GRVI)

© Jim Burns

Status: Vagrant. The only record is one observed on 5 May 1996, in the shelterbelt north of the Elkhart cemetery (Morton Co.). It was observed by 13 birders for 30 minutes and was photographed by T. Cable, M. Rader, and S. Seltman (KBRC 96-39).

Comments: It is a bird of montane and arid habitats in Colorado and the southwestern United States. A breeding population occurs in southeastern Colorado in northern Las Animas and southern Otero counties, and it may have bred in Oklahoma, near Kenton, Cimarron County.

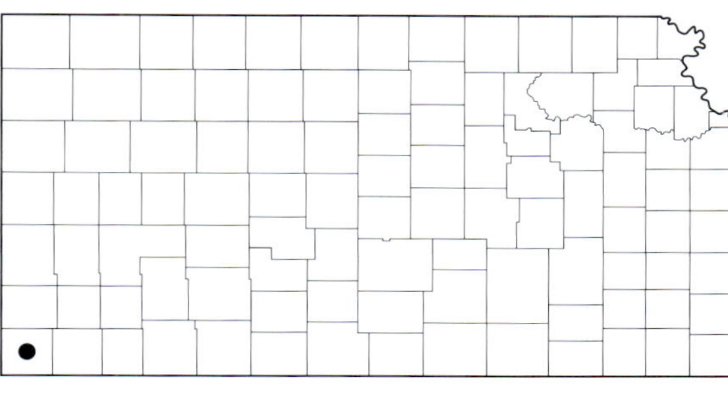

References: Barlow et al., 1999; Pittman, 1998.

Yellow-throated Vireo

Vireo flavifrons (YTVI)

Status: Uncommon transient and summer resident in the east; casual or rare in the west.

Habitat: Deciduous forest in the east, riparian growth westward; during migration, also in wooded parks and yards.

Migration: Early spring arrival is 18 April (Douglas Co.) with most migration during early May. In nonbreeding areas late spring dates are 18 May (Geary Co.) and 29 May (Stafford Co.) with stragglers to 16 June (Morton Co.). The fall migration is poorly documented with no fall records west of Rice County. It probably starts in mid- or late August and continues to about 10 September with stragglers to 2 October (Coffey Co.) and 17 October (Rice Co.).

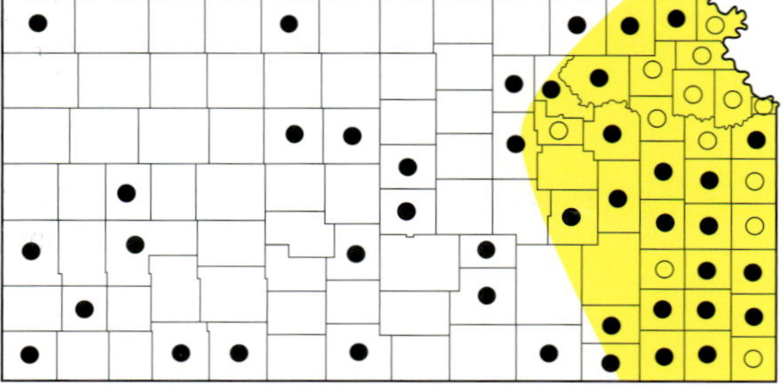

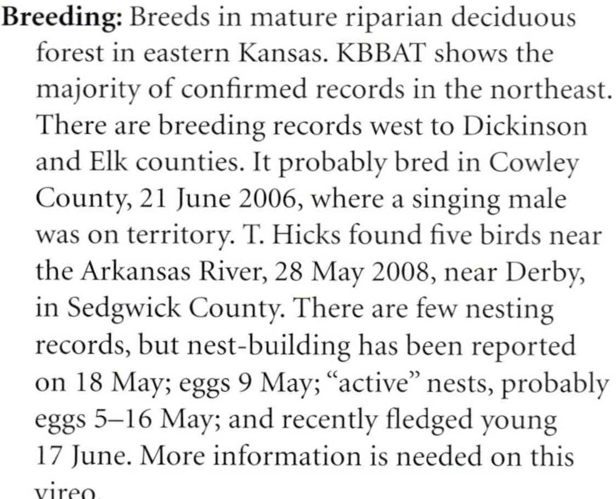

Breeding: Breeds in mature riparian deciduous forest in eastern Kansas. KBBAT shows the majority of confirmed records in the northeast. There are breeding records west to Dickinson and Elk counties. It probably bred in Cowley County, 21 June 2006, where a singing male was on territory. T. Hicks found five birds near the Arkansas River, 28 May 2008, near Derby, in Sedgwick County. There are few nesting records, but nest-building has been reported on 18 May; eggs 9 May; "active" nests, probably eggs 5–16 May; and recently fledged young 17 June. More information is needed on this vireo.

Banding: Eight banded; no encounters.

References: Busby and Zimmerman, 2001; Cable et al., 1996; Janzen, 2007; Thompson and Ely, 1992.

Plumbeous Vireo

Vireo plumbeus (PLVI)

Status: Casual transient in Kansas; one unconfirmed report of nesting (Decatur Co., 1912). Most sightings are from the southwest during fall, but with two unconfirmed reports from Sedgwick County (23–26 September 2001 and 16 May 2002). Spring records include five from the southwest and vagrants on 7 May (Ellis Co., C. Ely) and 16 May (Sedgwick Co., T. Hicks). The Ellis County individual was compared directly with known specimens of *V. plumbeus*, but its current location is uncertain. Specimens include three from Morton County taken by R. and J. Graber on 8–10 May 1950, and one from Finney County on 7 May.

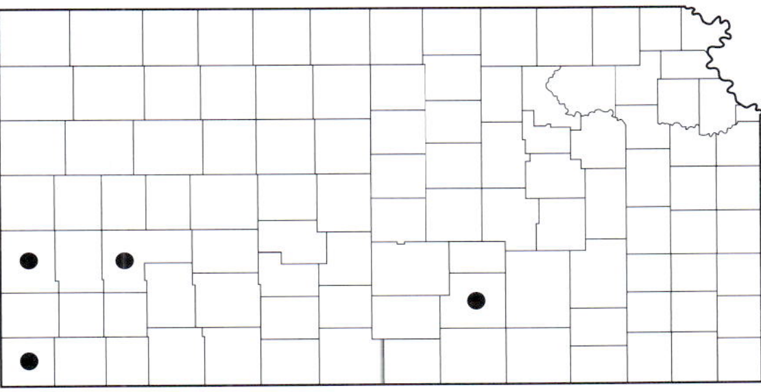

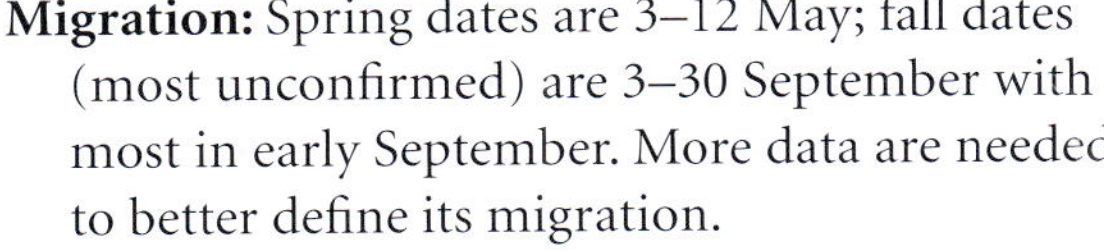

Habitat: Riparian woodlands.

Migration: Spring dates are 3–12 May; fall dates (most unconfirmed) are 3–30 September with most in early September. More data are needed to better define its migration.

Breeding: A clutch taken 16 June 1912 in Decatur County by G. Love is now in the Field Museum of Natural History (12567). Its identity should be confirmed.

Comments: This western species was, until recently, part of the Solitary Vireo complex, and the correct determinations of some sightings remain in doubt. However, many Plumbeous Vireos can be distinguished in the field. All vireos in the Solitary Vireo complex should be carefully identified to permit accurate determination of ranges and migration periods.

References: Cable et al., 1996; Graber and Graber, 1951; Janzen, 2007.

Cassin's Vireo

Vireo cassinii (CAVI)

Status: Casual migrant. There are four specimen records in KUMNH; two collected 8 May and 11 May 1950 (KU 78487, 78491) and two 3 September 1952 (KU 31904, 31905). There are 15 sight records, but, because this species and the Solitary Vireo are very difficult to distinguish in the field, most sight records are open to question.

© Jim Burns

Habitat: Shelterbelts, riparian growth, and residential areas with mature trees.

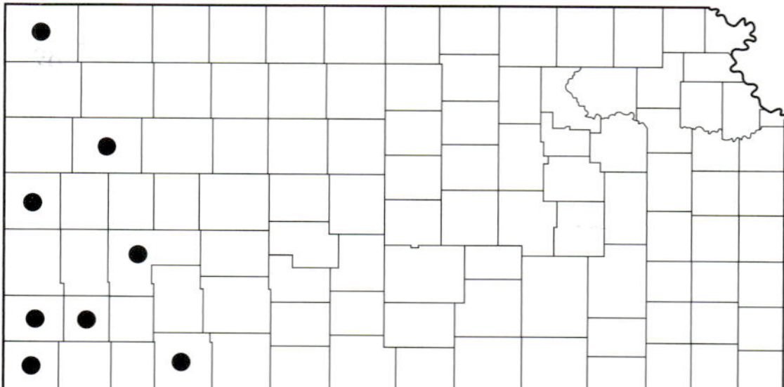

Migration: Most sightings are from Morton County: in spring, 3–11 May; in fall, when more numerous, 29 August–20 October. The higher incidence in fall may be an aberration, because more birders visit Morton County during that season.

Comments: The Solitary Vireo complex was recently split into three species. Field identification of *V. cassinii* is extremely difficult. Several specimens identified as *V. cassinii* proved to be *V. solitarius* when compared directly with other museum specimens.

References: Cable et al., 1996; Land, 2010.

Blue-headed Vireo

Vireo solitarius (BHVI)

Status: Common transient in the east and rare in the west. Most records from western Kansas are in the fall.

Habitat: Woodlots of a few acres to heavy forest; occasionally in conifers; westward in shelterbelts, riparian growth, and residential areas with mature trees.

Migration: The earliest arrival is 21 April (Harvey Co.) but is usually late April through the third week of May with a straggler to 15 June (Cowley Co.). Median first arrival is 2 May (Johnson Co.). The peak migration is in mid-May. A report from 16 July is probably a vagrant. The fall migration is gradual. The earliest reports are 4 August (Ellis and Geary cos.) but with arrival usually in early September, with the peak from September through mid-October and stragglers to 11 November (Ellis Co.) and 26 November (Geary Co.). Median dates of first arrivals are 9 September (Ellis Co.) and 28 September (Johnson Co.); median departure in Ellis County was 7 October. There are two CBC sightings in 1968 and 1977 (both Cowley Co.). Television tower kills in Shawnee County suggest the majority pass through in mid-September to mid-October. Forty-nine were salvaged from four kills during the period 25 September–12 October.

Comments: Until recently this beautiful vireo was considered a single, variable species, the Solitary Vireo. It was split into three species, making it difficult to correctly place many older sightings. The Blue-headed Vireo is still the most common of the three to pass through Kansas. Not all vireos in this group can be positively identified. Separating the Blue-headed Vireo from Cassin's Vireo is extremely difficult and should be left to expert observers. Some specimens collected in Morton County, thought to be Cassin's Vireo, upon comparison with known specimens, proved instead to be the Blue-headed Vireo.

Banding: 186 banded (most entered as "Solitary Vireos"); no encounters.

References: Cable et al., 1996; Janzen, 2007; Thompson and Ely, 1992.

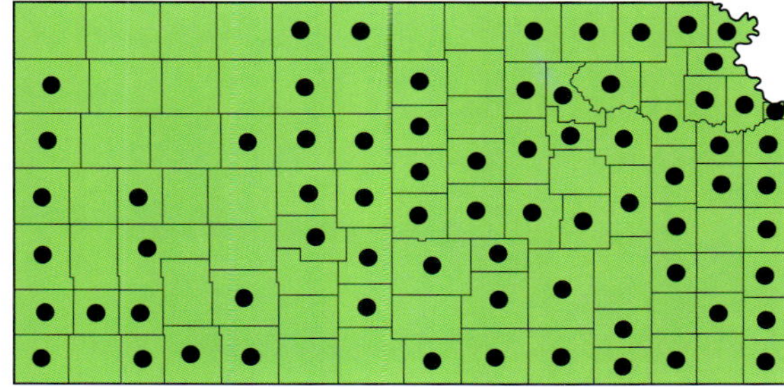

Warbling Vireo

Vireo gilvus (WAVI)

Status: Common transient and summer resident statewide.

Habitat: Woodlands, preferring edges, and in towns, especially those with well-spaced, mature cottonwood trees.

Migration: Earliest spring arrivals are 6 April (Cowley Co.), 15 April (Wyandotte Co.), and 18 April (Geary Co., numerous), but arrival is more often the last week in April with birds widespread by the first week of May. Median first arrival dates include 28 April (Rice Co.), 29 April (Ellis Co.), and 3 May (Johnson Co.). Spring departure is masked by the presence of local breeding birds. The fall migration begins in early September (median departure, Ellis Co., 12 September) and continues into early October (8 October, Harvey Co.). At least 56 were recovered from tower kills in Shawnee County and three others from a kill in Goodland (Sherman Co.). The majority were killed during late September with a late date of 11–12 October.

Breeding: KBBAT documented nesting statewide with highest number of blocks recording it in the Smoky Hills and Arkansas Lowlands and fewest reports in the southwest. It is an easy bird to find during the breeding season, but the nests are placed high making them difficult to find. One pair was found nesting in a grape arbor in Winfield (Cowley Co.). Nest-building has been reported on 1 May–10 June, eggs 29 May–20 June, young 7 June–26 July, and recently fledged young 6–26 July.

Comments: The Warbling Vireo is a relentless singer from early spring to midsummer, and can be heard almost any place with a lot of tall trees. It is probably a composite species, but only typical *V. gilvus* has been collected in Kansas. However, observers should listen for different vocalizations.

See page 500 for banding information.

References: Busby and Zimmerman, 2001; Cable et al., 1996; Janzen, 2007; Thompson and Ely, 1992.

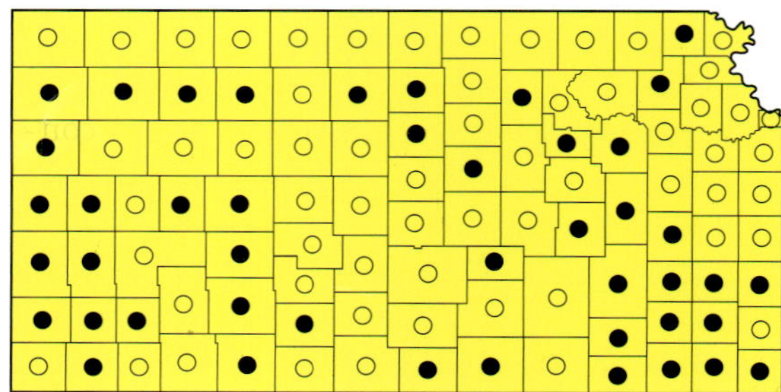

Philadelphia Vireo

Vireo philadelphicus (PHVI)

© David Seibel

Status: Uncommon transient in the east; rare transient in the west.

Habitat: Woodland edges and in towns with mature trees.

Migration: Reports of spring specimens and handheld birds are from 5 to 30 May. Earliest reported sightings are 19 April (Linn Co.) and 21 April (Johnson Co.), but most arrivals are very late April to early May with most gone by late May. Specimens and handheld birds from fall are from 2 September to 15 October. Mid-August sightings are suspect. Migration probably begins in very late August and is largely over by early October. However, tower kills (22 individuals) are later—25 September–12 October—and there is a specimen from 15 October (Douglas Co., KU 79051).

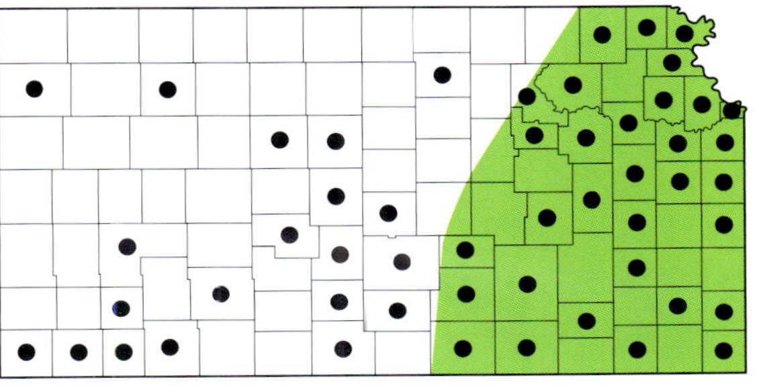

Comments: Television tower kills near Topeka (Shawnee Co.) seem to indicate it is more common in migration than previously thought. It is not a prolific singer during migration, which may be another reason it is overlooked. Inexperienced observers should remember that it is easily confused with several warblers and with the Warbling Vireo.

Banding: 55 banded; no encounters.

References: Ball et al., 1995; Busby and Zimmerman, 2001; Janzen, 2007; Thompson and Ely, 1992; Tordoff and Mengel, 1956.

Red-eyed Vireo

Vireo olivaceus (REVI)

© David Seibel

Status: Common transient and summer resident in the eastern one-third of the state; uncommon transient and summer resident in the west.

Habitat: Riparian forest, woodlands, and towns with mature trees.

Migration: Earliest spring arrivals are 16 April (Douglas Co.), but arrival is usually the last week of April with birds widespread by early May. Median first arrival dates include 4 May (Johnson Co.) and 6 May (Ellis Co.). About 100 were reported at Wyandotte County Lake on 15 May. Most migration is during early to mid-May with stragglers into early June. A few occur in summer in areas where breeding has not been reported, but whether these are vagrants or from very local nesting areas is unknown. Earliest fall migrants appear in early August (4 August, Scott Co.; 9 August, Ellis Co.), but migration probably peaks in mid-September with most birds gone by mid-October (17 October, Ellis Co., banded). An unusually late date is 6 November (Riley Co.). It was one of the most common species recovered from television tower kills in the 1980s with at least 142 recovered from towers in the Topeka area (Shawnee Co.) and 3 from Goodland (Sherman Co.). Most were killed in late September.

Breeding: Most of the breeding records are from the eastern one-third of Kansas, occurring with some regularity west to the Flint Hills. It breeds in woodlands in the east and follows riparian corridors into the west. Breeding records are sparse west of line from Sumner County to Republic County with KBBAT showing only a few blocks recording it west of that line. The nest is placed from 2 to 60 feet above the ground. Active nests have been reported 7 June–23 August, but there are few reports of nest contents. Nest-building has been reported 19 June, eggs 7–28 June, young 2 June–23 August, and recently fledged young 22 August–15 September.

Comments: It is a persistent singer, even singing during the heat of the day. It usually sings from the top of the tree canopy, making it difficult to observe.

Banding: 608 banded; no encounters.

References: Ball et al., 1995; Busby and Zimmerman, 2001; Thompson and Ely, 1992.

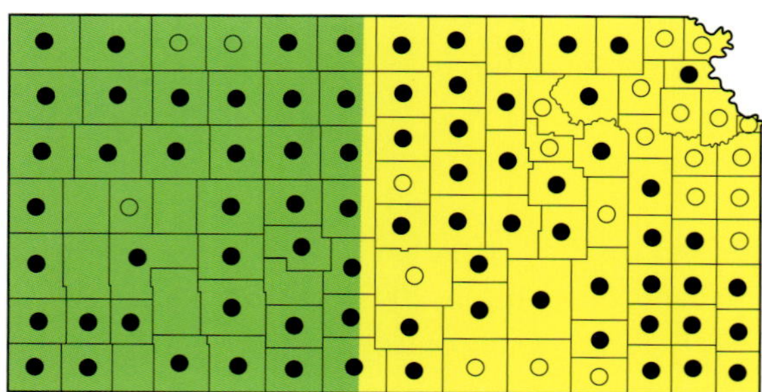

Pinyon Jay

Gymnorhinus cyanocephalus (PIJA)

Status: Irregular fall and winter visitant to the western part of the state; casual elsewhere.

Habitat: Usually along river courses, but also in towns at feeder stations.

Migration: Extreme dates of occurrence are 31 July–18 May, but more than three-fourths of all dated sightings are from fall and early winter. The few spring sightings are 10 March (Cheyenne Co.) to 18 May (Comanche Co.). Most sightings have been of short duration, but a number have spent extended periods at feeders, including in Kingman County (31 July–8 August 1966), Ford County (winter 1975 through early May 1976), Pratt County (23 October 1976–15 March 1977), and Saline County (5 January–9 February 2009). It is a very gregarious bird often occurring in large flocks. On two occasions (12 September 1982 and 22 September 2000) flocks of 100+ birds were observed along the Cimarron River in Morton County.

Comments: Its appearance in Kansas is very erratic. The first 30 sightings, for example, occurred during 20 different winters with few multiple sightings in a given winter. The number of sightings has increased dramatically in recent years with increased birding activity in the southwest. The presence of these birds in Kansas may be related to pinecone crop failure within the species' breeding range. On 18 November, two birds were watched at close range in Leoti Park (Wichita Co.) as they collected grasshoppers and wedged them into bark crevices (C. Ely, R. Lohoefener). It breeds regularly in small numbers within 75 air miles of Kansas in the Black Mesa, Cimarron County, Oklahoma.

References: Balda, 2002; Cable et al., 1996; Thompson and Ely, 1992; Wiggins, 2005b.

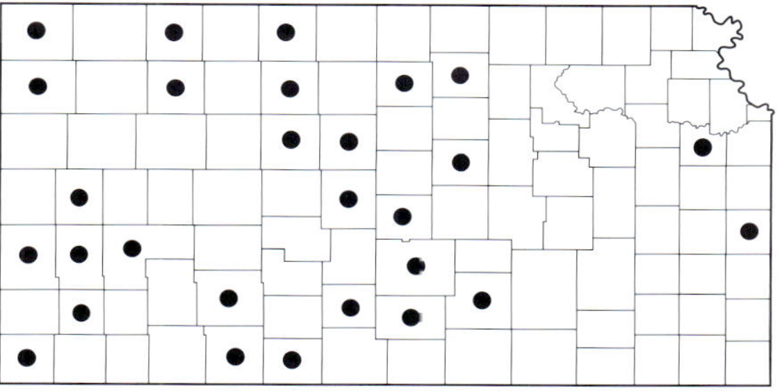

Steller's Jay

Cyanocitta stelleri (STJA)

© Judd Patterson

Status: Casual, irregular, and irruptive visitant in the southwest.

Habitat: Along river courses and in cities and towns.

Comments: Although generally thought of as resident at high elevations, individuals descend to lower elevations during the winter months. Many of the individuals that irrupt into habitats not typically occupied (such as Kansas) are believed to be young birds. Recorded dates of occurrence are between 11 September and 5 May during the following years: 1916, 1934, 1953–1954, 1964, 1973, 1978, 1989–1990, and 2002–2003. Most visits are of short duration, but one was present in Meade (Meade Co.) from 26 January to at least 24 April. The 1989–1990 invasion into southwestern Kansas was particularly widespread and apparently involved a large number of individuals. Up to 10 birds were seen together in Morton County between 13 October and 9 May. Two specimens taken in Morton County during the 1989 irruption represent *C. s. macrolopha*, the subspecies found in Colorado. Two specimens from the eastern part of the state (Riley and Douglas cos.) represent the northwestern subspecies *C. s. annectens*. This remains puzzling, because one would expect the southern Rocky Mountain race to be the one visiting Kansas.

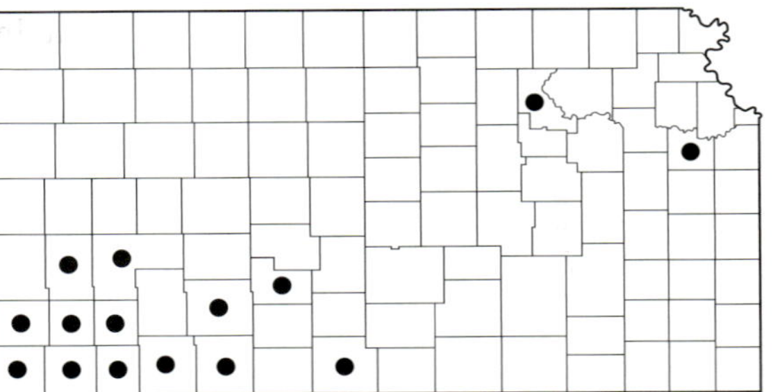

References: Cable et al., 1996; Cink and Boyd, 2003; Greene et al., 1998; Thompson and Ely, 1992.

Blue Jay

Cyanocitta cristata (BLJA)

Status: Common transient and summer resident becoming less common westward, especially in the southwest; common in winter in the east during years of good mast production; rare and irregular westward.

Habitat: Urban environments and riparian woodlands, especially in the west. Eastward it also occurs in upland woodlands and woodlots.

Migration: It is a conspicuous diurnal migrant. In Ellis County a few arrive in April with major flights between 23 April and 3 May. "Woods" (unpubl. manuscript, 1976) reported migration in Shawnee County 18 April–4 May. Reported arrivals in other areas include 19 April (Barton Co.), 24 April (Russell Co.), and 26 April (Finney Co.). Records of actual movements include 24 April ("a mass, all day movement, involving individual flocks of 50–100 individuals," Riley Co.) and 2 May ("unending stream," Wyandotte Co.). The fall migration is better documented. In Ellis County migrating flocks have been observed 30 August–16 October with the major movement 25 September–4 October and including "a few thousand in flocks of 10–80" on 27 September. In Shawnee County migration was 15 September–4 October. Statewide most migration is during late September and early October. Other large movements include 12 September ("large flocks," Meade Co.), and 7 October ("thousands" each, in Pawnee, Reno, and Rush cos.). Examination of CBC data indicates highest early winter densities in the northeast, west to Riley County. It is local and often sporadic in the west. For example, birds were present throughout the winter in Ellis County during only 12 of 35 winters (1960–1995). During a comparable period it was recorded on 12 of 24 counts in Morton County.

Breeding: Breeding densities are highest in the east, westward through the Flint Hills. Westward it occurs in gradually declining numbers in riparian habitat and urban areas and is nearly absent from the southwest. Statewide, nest-building has been reported 16 April–9 July, eggs 4 April–10 July (median for 48 clutches, 25 May), young in the nest 10 May–31 July, and recently fledged young 1 June–27 July.

Comments: The species was known to have been affected by West Nile virus as early as 1999, but population levels seem to have rebounded by the early to mid-2000s.

See page 500 for banding information.

References: Busby and Zimmerman, 2001; Jackson and Rising, 1968; Tarvin and Woolfenden, 1999; Thompson and Ely, 1992.

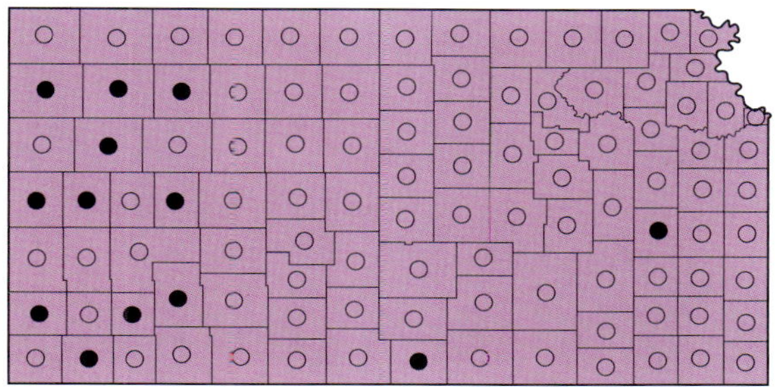

Western Scrub-Jay

Aphelocoma californica (WESJ)

Status: Irregular, low-density visitant to the southwest during fall and winter; casual elsewhere.

Habitat: It occurs singly or in small groups along river or stream courses in the southwest; in winter also at feeding stations in cities and towns.

Migration: It usually occurs during fall through early winter with extreme dates of occurrence of 16 September and 14 May. A few wintered at a feeder in Dodge City (Ford Co.) during at least five winters during the period 1970–1978. Extended stays include 16 September–6 May (Morton Co.) and 28 October–10 February (Stevens Co.). High counts are 25+ on 12 September 1989 (Morton Co.) and 24 on 4 October 1989 (Seward Co.). Vagrants have apparently followed river systems eastward to Stafford (1970), Barton (1971, at least 4 birds), and Cowley (1976) counties.

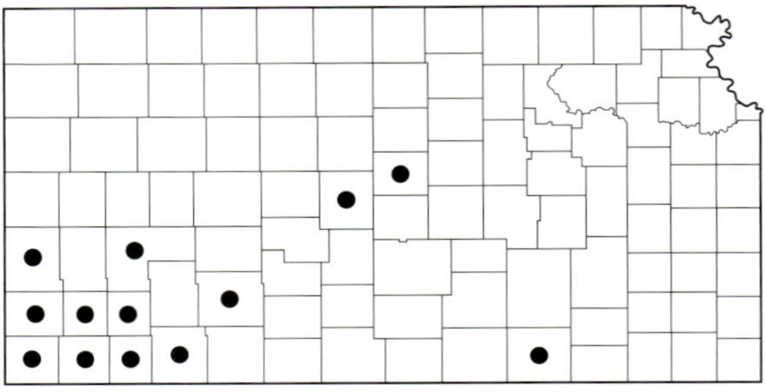

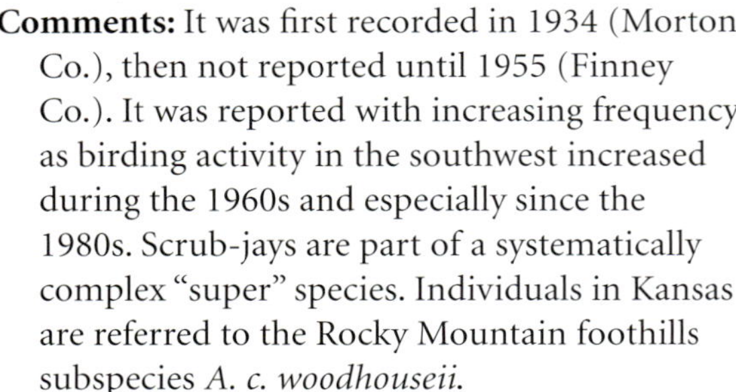

Comments: It was first recorded in 1934 (Morton Co.), then not reported until 1955 (Finney Co.). It was reported with increasing frequency as birding activity in the southwest increased during the 1960s and especially since the 1980s. Scrub-jays are part of a systematically complex "super" species. Individuals in Kansas are referred to the Rocky Mountain foothills subspecies *A. c. woodhouseii.*

Banding: One banded; no encounters.

References: Cable et al., 1996; Curry et al., 2002; Thompson and Ely, 1992; Wiggins, 2005a.

Mexican Jay

Aphelocoma ultramarina (MEJA)

Status: Accidental. The only record is of a specimen (now lost) taken near Mt. Jesus (Clark Co.) by A. Keith in March 1906.

Comments: The presence of the Mexican Jay (formerly Gray-breasted Jay) in Kansas is curious, and it has confounded ornithologists for years. The species is "extreme" in its sedentary nature, and there are only three extralimital records of the species, including the Kansas record. The two other records are from Texas. Although the specimen has been lost, the measurements of it would seem to confirm the specific identity. A. Wetmore and L. L. Dyche examined the specimen and made the identification.

References: McCormack and Brown, 2008; Thompson and Ely, 1992.

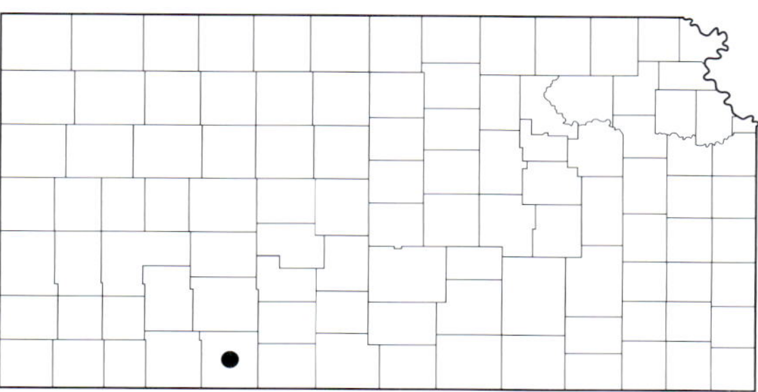

Clark's Nutcracker

Nucifraga columbiana (CLNU)

Status: Casual and irruptive; nearly statewide.

Habitat: Can appear almost anywhere; usually in open riparian woodlands (southwest), stands of cone-bearing conifers, or at feeders in cities and towns.

Migration: Individuals have been reported from 13 August to early May. A significant incursion into the Great Plains occurred during 1972–1973. In Kansas, the first individuals were reported along the Smoky Hill River (Logan Co.) in October followed by sightings in Johnson County on 19 October, Ellis County on 19 October, and Shawnee County on 31 October. By late April it had been reported from 10 counties statewide. A smaller invasion confined to the southwest occurred in 1996–1997. The latest spring dates are 20 April (Marshall Co.) and 5 May (Finney Co.).

Comments: A handsome bird, Clark's Nutcracker is a tricolored species named after the famous explorer, William Clark.

Banding: Two banded; no encounters.

References: Thompson and Ely, 1992; Tomback, 1998.

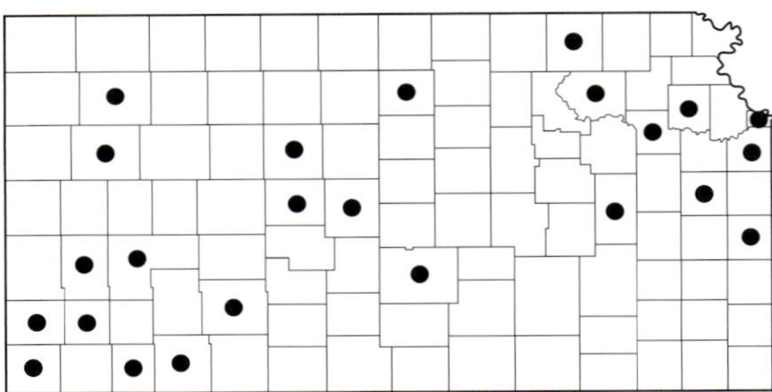

Black-billed Magpie

Pica hudsonia (BBMA)

Status: Resident in central and western Kansas; fairly common west of the Flint Hills, and generally west of a diagonal line through Republic, Stafford, and Comanche counties. Casual in fall and winter in the northeast; absent from the southeast.

Habitat: Open country with scattered trees: hedgerows, windbreaks, and open riparian woodland.

Migration: It is generally sedentary, but records from the northeast suggest postbreeding dispersal during fall and winter. Flocking in late summer, fall, and winter is common, with high counts of 100+ on 30 July (Norton Co.) and 100 on 10 November (Morton Co.). Eastward, the largest flocks have been 50 in December 1934 (Rooks Co.) and 25 August (Pawnee Co.) and 40 on 30 August (Rush Co.).

Breeding: The large, domed stick nest, placed in a tree usually at a low to medium height in a relatively open area, is easily located. Active nests have been observed 9 March–24 June. Eggs have been reported 22 March–10 May, nestlings 7 May–15 June, and recently fledged young 18 May–24 June. The median date for 17 observed clutches is 26 April.

Comments: The few 19th-century reports suggest that it occurred primarily as a winter visitant. In fact, breeding may be a 20th-century phenomenon. The earliest report of breeding is of a report along Brush Creek (Graham Co.) in 1873 or 1874. J. Linsdale had only two sightings along the Arkansas River (Hamilton Co.) in 1921, but it was "abundant" at the same ranch in 1934. In Morton County, one was collected in 1934. R. and J. Graber found a few in 1950, and until the recent West Nile virus outbreak it was "abundant" there. Likewise it was absent from Decatur County in 1908, arrived there about 1918, and nested regularly by 1921. A similar pattern is shown throughout western and central Kansas. By 1954 nesting had been reported east to very near the present breeding range. Expansion continues with recent nesting in Marshall County (1999) and Dickinson and Riley counties (both 2000). It is a bird that is easily recognized and appreciated. Recently, magpies, as other corvids, were severely impacted by West Nile virus. Although no specific data have been gathered in Kansas for the Black-billed Magpie, some anecdotal information suggests that a slow recovery may be under way.

See page 500 for banding information.

References: Busby and Zimmerman, 2001; Cable et al., 1996; Koenig and Reynolds, 2009; Linsdale, 1927; Thompson and Ely, 1992; Trost, 1999; Young et al., 2009.

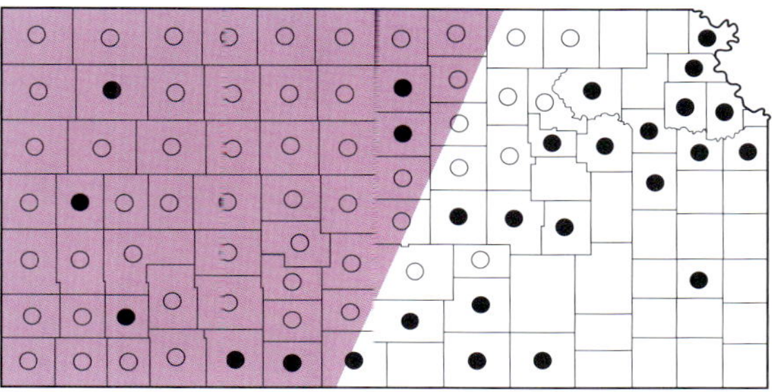

American Crow

Corvus brachyrhynchos (AMCR)

Status: Common to abundant transient statewide; common resident in eastern and central Kansas; uncommon in the extreme west and southwest.

Habitat: Wide variety of habitats, nesting and roosting in woodlands, riparian growth, and parks and residential areas.

Migration: Although some local populations are

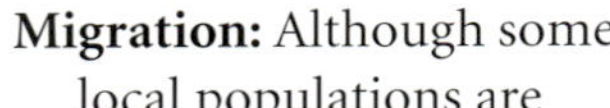

believed to be resident, it is a conspicuous diurnal migrant. The northward flight is smaller than the fall passage. Many residents are already nesting when the major flight (typically mid-March to early April) occurs. Reported movements include 18 March ("thousands moving all day," Russell Co.), and 7 April ("steady stream of flocks," Ellis Co.). The fall movement is much larger, and W. Long reported migration involving "untold millions" of birds through the central part of the state. Migration begins by 15 September, peaks about 10 October in most years, and continues through early November ("large flocks," Barton and Ellis cos.). Reports include 11 October (80–100,000, "flocks from horizon to horizon," Russell and Ellis cos.), and 20 October (3,000, Barton Co.). Large numbers winter in central Kansas. The huge flocks formerly roosting in catalpa groves in Harvey and McPherson counties now occur in reduced numbers.

Breeding: J. Rising noted that nesting in the west was confined to river valleys. Its status is similar today but with significant numbers nesting in parks and wooded residential areas throughout the west. Statewide nest-building has been reported 17 February–9 May, eggs 10 March–7 June, young in nest 14 April–15 June, and recently fledged young 18 May–19 July. A. Bent gave dates for 22 clutches as 3 March–15 May with half of them 3–19 April. The median date for 41 recent clutches statewide is 7 April.

Comments: Only H. Menke, who considered it a "common migrant" in Finney County, specifically reported it in western Kansas during the 19th century. L. Wolfe noted that it was rare in Decatur County until about 1909 or 1910 but became very common by 1915 (first nest, 1908). Although crows were particularly susceptible to West Nile virus, that disease has apparently run its course, and population levels seem to have rebounded.

See page 501 for banding information.

References: Bent, 1946; Busby and Zimmerman, 2001; Janzen, 2007; Langley, 2000; Long, 1940; Menke, 1894; Rising, 1974; Thompson and Ely, 1992; Verbeek and Caffrey, 2002; Wolfe, 1961.

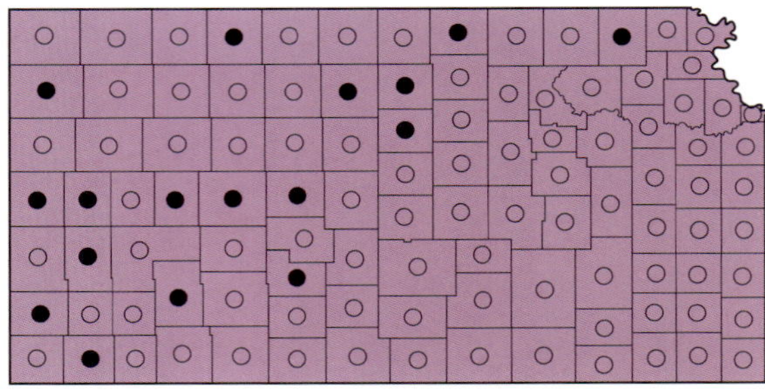

Fish Crow

Corvus ossifragus (FICR)

© Judd Patterson

Status: A relatively recent addition to the Kansas avifauna, it was first reported 30 September 1984, from Linn County. There are currently more than 20 records for the state, including video recordings with accompanying sound recordings but no specimen.

Habitat: Generally restricted to river courses in the southeast.

Migration: An unusually early sighting is 3 February 2002 (Douglas Co., M. Robbins), and one was observed at SCW (E. Young) on 20 March. Most sightings have been in spring between 4 April and 4 May with summer records (most from Cherokee, Cowley, and Sedgwick cos.) through 31 August and once 30 September. The largest numbers reported to date are 35–40 (multiple locations) on 1 May, 40–50 on 1 June, and 20 on 27 July (all Cherokee Co.).

Breeding: In Cherokee County, three nests were found on 4 May 1991, a bird was observed on the nest on 19 June (G. Horak), and two nests were reported on 25 April 1998 (E. McHugh and others). T. and L. Hicks observed nest-building in Sedgwick County in 2007 that was associated with a Great Blue Heron colony. Five pairs were observed nesting on the Arkansas River (Sedgwick Co., T. and L. Hicks) on 25 May 2008, and J. Calhoun observed a colony near Wichita during 2008 and 2009 (up to 10 birds) and observed nest-building on 22 April and completed by 6 May.

Comments: Following the first sighting in Linn County in 1984, it next appeared near Galena (Cherokee Co.) on 3 May 1986 and has been regular there since 1990 on and near Shoal Creek and Spring River. By 1999, it was found in Montgomery, Labette, and Neosho counties and by 2003 was found also in Chautauqua, Greenwood, and Cowley counties. The northernmost locality is currently Douglas County (several records since 2002); the most westerly are Sumner and Sedgwick counties with numerous sight and call records since 2006 and observed breeding in 2009–2010 in the latter (J. Calhoun). Care should be exercised in separating the Fish Crow's "car" call from an almost identical call of young American Crows. The species has undergone dramatic population growth within the last decade, with a commensurate range expansion. T. Hicks postulated the expansion was the result of the recovery of heron populations, with which they frequently nest, from the millinery trade; the increase in heronries and cormorant colonies associated with construction of reservoirs; and global warming.

References: Hicks, 2009; Janzen, 2007; McGowan, 2001; Thompson and Ely, 1992.

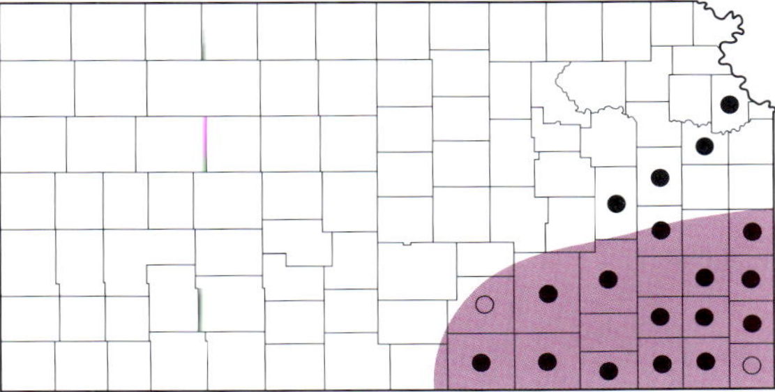

Chihuahuan Raven

Corvus cryptoleucus (CHRA)

© Brian Small

Status: Uncommon, local resident in the extreme southwest.

Habitat: Arid grasslands and nearby agricultural areas.

Migration: It was considered "resident" during the 19th century but without documentation. Spring arrival in breeding areas is from early March through 2 April with most birds present by mid-April. A flock of "hundreds" at a gas plant in Liberal (Seward Co.) on 24 April seems late to be locally breeding birds. Flocking occurs in August through late September (Stevens Co.), but M. Schwilling considered this not a migration but rather a drifting to various feeding sources. It is occasionally reported on the CNG CBC. Winter reports include 100–150 on 3 December 1952 (Finney Co.) and 300 at a municipal dump on 21 January 1968 (Seward Co.). S. Patti and M. Thompson noted large concentrations at Liberal (Seward Co.) from November through January in 1979–1980 and 1984 feeding on offal from the slaughterhouses.

Breeding: M. Schwilling surveyed extreme western Kansas during the summers of 1951–1952, finding nesting birds in the two westernmost tiers of counties and east to Gray and Hodgeman counties. KBBAT established confirmed breeding in Stevens and Seward counties and probable breeding in Morton and Stevens counties. Nest-building has been reported 12 May, eggs 26 March–19 May (median 24 April), and young 15 April–17 June.

Comments: There is little firsthand information on the two ravens from presettlement days, and the two species were often confused. This was probably the species most closely associated with bison herds. J. Allen did not report it at Fort Hays during the summer of 1871 or later that winter in northwestern Kansas. N. Goss considered it "rare" in the west, and W. Long considered it extirpated in 1930. However, it was present in at least Kearny and Hamilton counties in the 1940s and possibly in 1932. If we assume that events in Kansas paralleled the much better documented situation in nearby Colorado, we can assume that numbers increased during the years of bison slaughter and that upon its conclusion the major raven range withdrew to the south and west. The reason for the later decline is unknown.

See page 501 for banding information.

References: Allen, 1872; Bednarz and Raitt, 2002; Busby and Zimmerman, 2001; Cable et al., 1996; Goss, 1883; Herbert, 1980; Janzen, 2007; Nelson, 1998; Patti, 2004; Thompson and Ely, 1992.

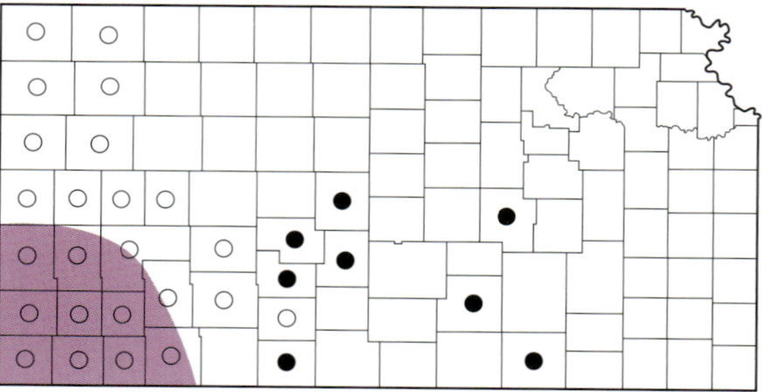

Common Raven

Corvus corax (CORA)

Status: Currently a rare visitant to Morton County with one nesting attempt; vagrant elsewhere.

Habitat: Canyons, arid grasslands, and riparian growth (largely cottonwood groves).

© Judd Patterson

Breeding: The unsuccessful nesting attempt in Morton County during early May 2006 and recounted in considerable detail by M. Robbins and others is the first known attempt in more than a century. As a nest site, the pair had selected a large cottonwood just below the Point of Rocks, which is arguably the "roughest" area in extreme southwestern Kansas. One bird (male?) had lost a secondary from the left wing, a characteristic noted in one bird of a pair seen on all visits from 4 April through 13 June strongly suggesting that all sightings were of the same pair. The female was believed to have been incubating on 6 May with nest desertion occurring between 11 and 22 May.

Comments: As a species it is actually fairly accommodating in its habitat tastes and requirements, which range from boreal, conifer, and deciduous woodlands to tundra, prairies, and grasslands, and in some areas towns and cities. It does seem to need dramatic contours in the landscape that provide thermals for foraging over long distances. During early settlement (1871) it was reported as resident at Fort Hays eastward to Leavenworth. By the late 1890s, however, it was considered only a visitant, and by the 1930s, was considered to have been extirpated from the state. At least one author related the disappearance to the disappearance of the vast bison herds from the central plains. In fact, there were no unequivocal records between the collection of an individual in Jewell County on 8 November 1916, and the observation of two birds at the Point of Rocks in Morton County on 8 November 1997 (KBRC 1997-50). Thereafter, an extraordinary 45+ individuals were reported flying along the Cimarron River on 20 September 2003 by four observers. Interestingly, although the species is considered to be largely sedentary, there are many sporadic reports (outside of Kansas) of large groups of juvenile Common Ravens ranging in number from a few birds to "thousands" of individuals

References: Allen, 1872; Boarman and Heinrich, 1999; Moore, 2004; Pittman, 1998; Robbins et al., 2006; Thompson and Ely, 1992.

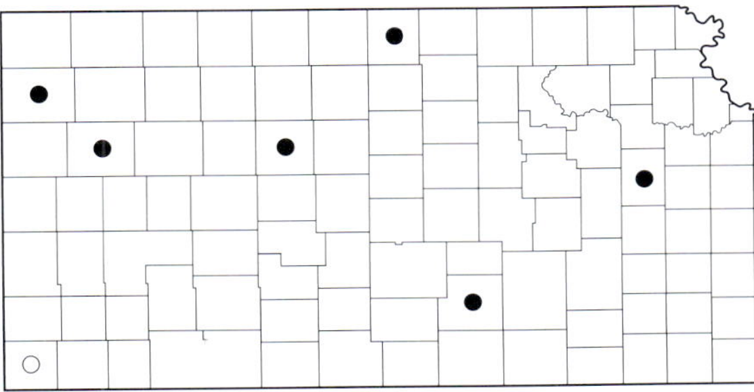

Horned Lark

Eremophila alpestris (HOLA)

Status: Statewide all year; widespread and abundant during winter in the west; less common eastward. The breeding population may be resident, but numbers are augmented greatly by transients and wintering birds statewide.

Habitat: Primarily mid- and shortgrass prairie, overgrazed pastures, and cultivated land; locally in disturbed areas such as sand dunes, lake margins, unpaved roads, and fallow ground.

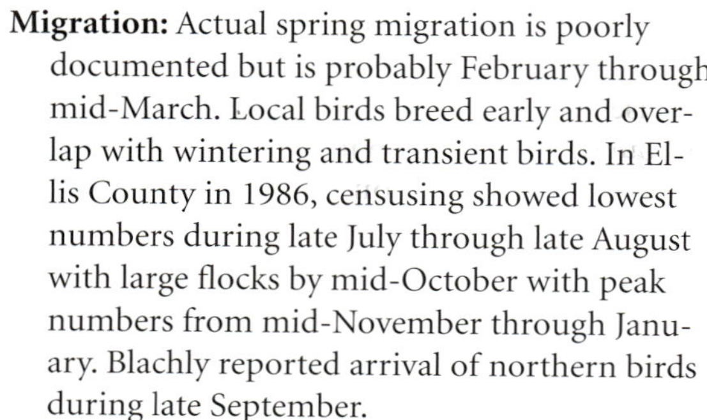

Migration: Actual spring migration is poorly documented but is probably February through mid-March. Local birds breed early and overlap with wintering and transient birds. In Ellis County in 1986, censusing showed lowest numbers during late July through late August with large flocks by mid-October with peak numbers from mid-November through January. Blachly reported arrival of northern birds during late September.

Breeding: Breeding densities are highest in the High Plains, decrease eastward through the Flint Hills (where local), and drop dramatically eastward. Allen considered it by far the most numerous species in the vicinity of Fort Hays (Ellis Co.) in 1871. Displaying and pair formation may begin by early January. The nest is placed in a depression near a grass clump; tall, dense vegetation is avoided. Extreme dates for 44 clutches, most from the west, are 3 March and 23 June with most from 18 March to 19 April and 20 May to 19 June, indicating two broods. It may be single-brooded in the east. Recently fledged young have been reported from 18 April through 10 August. Young birds begin flocking soon after fledging.

Comments: The early beginning of nesting has been suggested as a means of avoiding cowbird parasitism. Numbers from CBCs vary greatly within and between years and are not a good indicator of numbers. Weather and the great variation in numbers of observers and the amount of time spent in windswept habitat vary significantly statewide. More than 270,000 individuals (by far the highest count ever) were reported on the 1992–1993 CBCs with 86 percent on a single count (Sawyer) in south-central Kansas. During periods of heavy snowfall, flocks may congregate along newly opened roads, where many are killed by passing vehicles. Under such conditions flocks also move into the immediate vicinity of farm buildings and even towns.

Banding: 58 banded; no encounters.

References: Allen, 1872; Blachly, 1879–1880; Busby and Zimmerman, 2001; Thompson, 1993; Thompson and Ely, 1992.

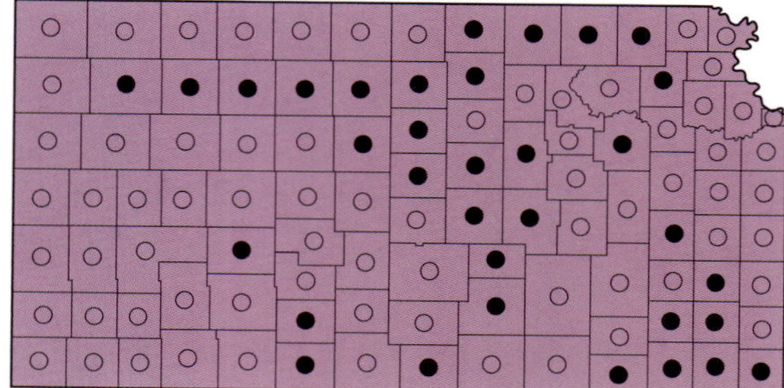

Purple Martin

Progne subis (PUMA)

Status: Common transient and summer resident in the east becoming uncommon in central Kansas and rare and local in the west. It is most abundant in fall.

© David Seibel

Habitat: Nests primarily near human habitations; at other seasons usually open country, often near water.

Migration: It is often the first swallow to arrive, usually later in the west. Typically, one or a few males (scouts) arrive at a nest site up to 2 weeks before the main group. Median dates of first arrivals include 14 March (Cowley Co.), 25 March (Ellis Co.), and 30 March (Rice Co.). First arrivals include 19 and 28 February and 3 March. Most migration is during April. Migrating flocks are much smaller in spring than in fall, rarely more than 100 birds (23 May). The actual fall departure is poorly documented but is most probably late August through mid-September. Breeding birds depart nesting colonies soon after the young fledge and join postbreeding flocks, often by mid-July. In the west birds are nearly absent after early August. Postbreeding flocking is well documented and often spectacular. Flocks of 1,000 birds have been reported by 12 July in Wichita, and these roosting aggregations have grown to 20,000–50,000 birds in some recent years. C. Blachly noted this behavior in the late 19th century in Manhattan. A steady stream of migrants was observed flying southward along the shores of Tuttle Creek Reservoir on 31 August. J. Linsdale reported a loose flock 0.5 mile long and nearly as wide roosting in cattails in Doniphan County on the late date of 23 September. Other late dates include 28 September and 23 October. Extremely late dates (10 and 14 November in different years) and winter reports are likely errors in identification.

Breeding: Its habit of nesting colonially in secondary cavities probably limits its overall distribution and abundance. Currently, nearly all nesting is in human-constructed "martin houses." L. Wolfe reported nesting in crevices of buildings in Oberlin in the early 1900s as did R. Imler at Stockton in the 1930s. R. Johnston gave 5 June as the modal date of egg-laying, with 57 percent of all clutches during the period 1–10 June. Statewide, eggs have been observed 8 May–21 June and recently fledged young 7–29 July.

Comments: M. Thompson noted Purple Martins in Belize the first week of August.

See page 501 for banding information.

References: Blachly, 1879–1880; Busby and Zimmerman, 2001; Imler, 1937; Janzen, 2007; Johnston, 1964a; Linsdale, 1927; Thompson and Ely, 1992; Wolfe, 1961.

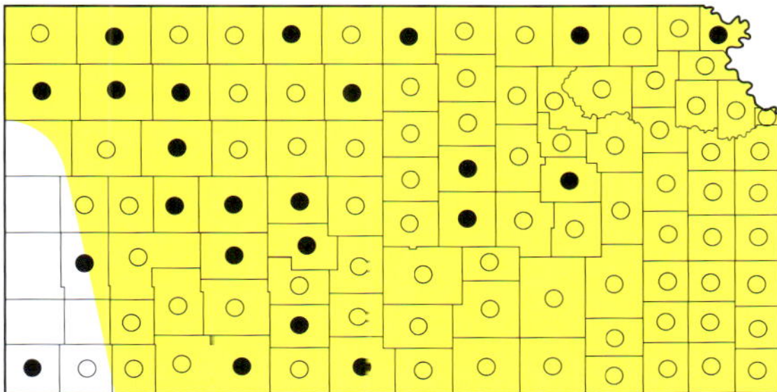

Tree Swallow

Tachycineta bicolor (TRES)

Status: Uncommon transient in the east, less common and more local in the west; local breeder in the northeast and south, becoming more scattered westward.

Habitat: Near water; in breeding season at reservoirs, ponds, or rivers where suitable nesting cavities occur.

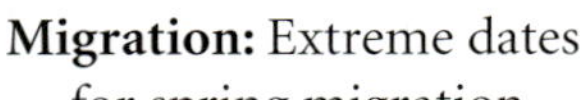

Migration: Extreme dates for spring migration are 1 March and 19 May with most from mid-March through April in the east; mid-April through early May in the west. Median arrival dates include 20–24 March (Linn Co.), 9 April (Russell Co.), and 22 April (Ellis Co.). Large numbers include 100+ on 16 April and 150+ on 3 May. Extreme dates for fall migration are 22 July and 24 October with stragglers to 10 November and occasionally into midwinter (four records, 15 December–31 January). Most migration is during September with flocks through mid-October. J. Linsdale reported thousands along the Missouri River during late August and early September with small flocks through 11 October. Any wintering swallow is likely to be this species. One on 15 December 1970 was plucking insects from a completely frozen surface at CBWA; the other three winter birds were feeding over patches of open water.

Breeding: Clutches have been reported 11 May–12 June and recently fledged young 12 June to 2 and 18 July. The earliest documented nestings (1922–1940) were along the Missouri River. Nesting was occasionally reported elsewhere in the east, and in the 1980s a major increase in populations and range occurred, perhaps the result of an increase in primary cavities in drowned trees at new reservoirs and a marked increase in the placement of artificial nest boxes. By 1993 nesting had occurred in 20 counties west to Pratt and Russell counties and more recently in Clark, Meade (for about 10 years), and Logan counties.

Comments: It has clearly benefited from human activity. Nesting is clearly dependent on water and a nest site. J. Linsdale reported a colony that moved 4 miles to a flooded site when the original site dried up, then returned the following season when water was present. The Linn County population grew from 19 nests to about 100 individuals in 11 years, declined, and then disappeared, possibly because of the appearance, then loss, of drowned trees.

Banding: 37 banded; no encounters.

References: Brumwell, 1951; Busby and Zimmerman, 2001; Linsdale, 1927; Rice, 1980; Thompson and Ely, 1992.

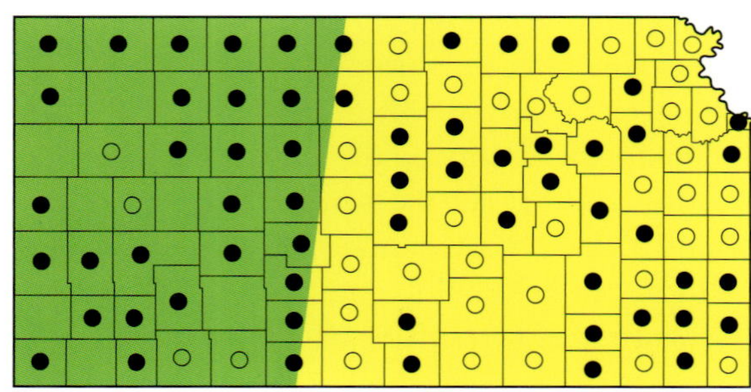

Violet-green Swallow

Tachycineta thalassina (VGSW)

© Judd Patterson

Status: Rare visitant in western and central Kansas, usually in fall; casual eastward.

Habitat: Open country near water, often in flocks of mixed swallows.

Migration: The four spring records (three from the east and none verified) are 28 March, 14 April, and 5 and 29 May. Most sightings have been during fall. Seventeen sightings from CBWA (some unverified) are between 8 August and 9 October with one on 1 November. Thirteen of these sightings were in September. Seventeen additional sightings from throughout the state (most unverified) were between 3 July and 15 October.

Breeding: The single known nesting was in a sandstone bluff along Goose Creek, 5 miles east of the Colorado line in Wallace County on 3 June 1987. S. Roth and four students saw two males and a female and obtained photographs. One male was carrying nesting material into a cavity of the rock face. On 17 and 18 June M. Schwilling visited the site and observed a female foraging over the valley and making regular visits to the cavity, apparently feeding newly hatched young. The outcome of the nesting is unknown.

Comments: Although on the hypothetical list since 1956 and reported more than 20 times subsequently, no physical evidence was obtained until the nesting in 1987. Most sightings have been of single birds, often in mixed flocks of swallows on dirt roads or utility lines, and on several occasions individuals were studied by multiple observers at close range.

References: Cable et al., 1996; Schwilling, 1972; Schwilling and Roth, 1987; Thompson and Ely, 1992; Tordoff, 1956.

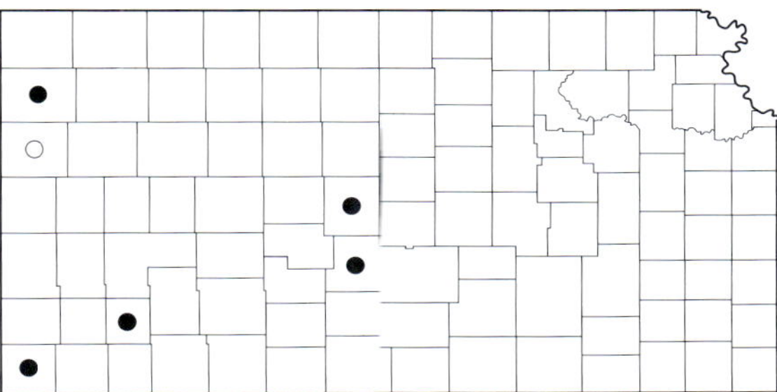

Northern Rough-winged Swallow

Stelgidopteryx serripennis (NRWS)

Status: Common transient and summer resident statewide.

Habitat: Usually near streams, ponds, or reservoirs; also at road-cuts and rock outcrops; postbreeding birds congregate (often with other swallow species) at marshes and roadsides.

Migration: Usually begins in April but with very early dates including 11 March (Sumner Co.). Mean arrival dates include 8 April (Ellis and Russell cos.) and 10 April (Cowley Co.). Most migration is mid-March through mid-May. At Hays (Ellis Co.) nearly 60 percent of 245 individuals banded were between 11 and 21 May. Few high counts are available, but 200 were reported on 11 April (Russell Co.). Most birds depart nest sites soon after the young fledge, forming flocks of hundreds by mid-July (358 at SCW, 26 July) and up to 5,000 by late September (Linn Co.). Most migration is during the last half of September with stragglers to 20 October and 9 November. R. Johnston gave a median departure date of 10 October for northeastern Kansas. Individuals reported 19 December and 26 December of different years were probably Tree Swallows. One reported 7 February 2009 in Jefferson County was not verified.

Breeding: KBBAT found them in the largest number of blocks in the northeast and very few blocks in the southwest. Dominant vegetation at nest sites ranged from closed canopy along streams to open prairie. Nesting is either in a burrow excavated in a vertical bank, in a rocky crevice, or in a drain pipe or similar artificial structure. R. Johnston reported 14 instances of breeding between 11 May and 30 June with a modal date of egg-laying of 3 June and with 70 percent of all eggs laid between 21 May and 10 June. Nest-building has been observed 18 May–10 June and nestlings 11 June–20 July.

Comments: It is still confused with the very similar Bank Swallow. This confusion extends back to the 19th and early 20th centuries when C. Blachly considered the Bank Swallow to be a common summer resident in Riley County, as did O. Tiemeier in Rawlins County, while not reporting rough-wings. Many early descriptions of Bank Swallow nesting sites in Ellis County and elsewhere are obviously of rough-wings.

See page 501 for banding information.

References: Blachly, 1879–1880; Busby and Zimmerman, 2001; Ely, 1971; Janzen, 2007; Johnston, 1964a; Johnston 1965; Thompson and Ely, 1992; Tiemeier, 1938; Young, 1993.

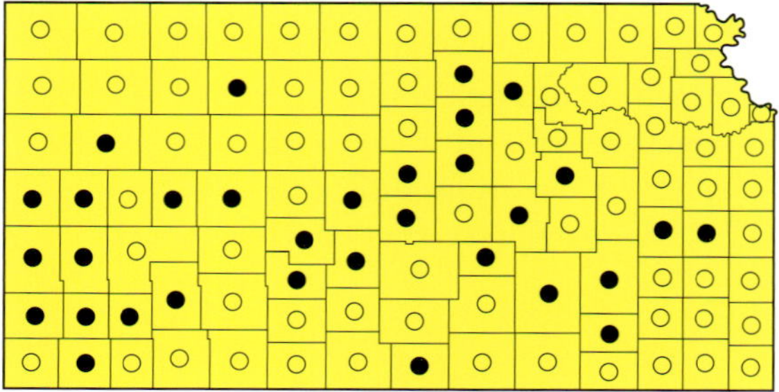

Bank Swallow

Riparia riparia (BANS)

Status: Uncommon transient statewide; common transient at CBWA; breeds locally along rivers in the northeast and at scattered sites westward through central Kansas.

Habitat: Breeding usually along a few major rivers; at other seasons flocks with other swallows near marshes and shorelines.

Migration: Extreme spring dates are 26 March and 9 June but usually mid-April through mid-May with the peak during late April and early May. Small flocks may appear outside breeding areas by 25 July (Finney Co.) with large flocks appearing by early to mid-August. Peak migration is mid-August through early September with most departing before 20 September. Late dates include 3 October (Linn Co.) and 18–19 October (Stafford Co., unconfirmed). Largest numbers are reported at CBWA; for example, 7,000+ on 2 August 2000 and 3,000+ on 21 August in 1993 and 1994. Thousands were reported in the Mulvane area (Sedgwick Co.) on 16 August.

Breeding: It is a colonial nester, excavating burrows in vertical banks, usually along rivers but occasionally along smaller streams, in sand pits, and even in sawdust piles. Few nesting data are available, but R. Johnston reported the completion of 60 clutches between 11 May and 20 June (mode, 5 June). Nearly 75 percent of all eggs were laid 21 May–10 June, but in 1 year high water delayed egg-laying until 12 July.

Comments: Early accounts considered the species "common," even "abundant" in suitable localities, with small colonies reported westward to Decatur County. Presently most breeding is in the extreme northeast and at scattered localities along the Kansas and Republican rivers. It is interesting that it was not reported breeding in either Doniphan (1921–1925) or Leavenworth (1939–1940) counties, as would be expected. The apparent decline in breeding populations may be due to alteration of river channels by human activities. Early reports of nesting in Ellis County and probable numerous others were actually of the more widespread Northern Rough-winged Swallow, which at times may nest in small colonies. Nests of the Bank Swallow are usually close together near the top of a bank; rough-wing nests (where colonial) are more randomly placed and often utilize natural "cavities."

Banding: 554 banded; no encounters.

References: Brumwell, 1951; Busby and Zimmerman, 2001; Ely, 1971; Janzen, 2007; Johnston, 1964a; Lindsdale, 1927; Thompson and Ely, 1992.

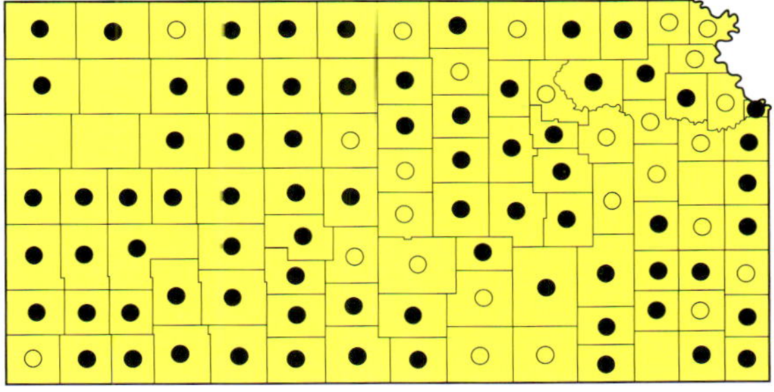

Cliff Swallow

Petrochelidon pyrrhonota (CLSW)

© Judd Patterson

Status: Common transient statewide; common but often local summer resident, chiefly in western and central Kansas.

Habitat: Usually near water; breeds chiefly on cliff faces, under bridges and overpasses, in highway box culverts, and under eaves of buildings.

Migration: Arrival dates vary considerably with extremes of 26 March (Cowley Co.) and 27 May (Sumner Co.), but most arrival is in mid-April with peak numbers in mid-May. Median arrival dates include 13–16 April (Russell Co.). Premigratory flocking begins soon after fledging with flocks of 100–200 reported by 7 July and flocks of 1,000 or more by mid-July. Such flocks gather near water, resting on wires and on roadways. Migration may begin by late July or early August (9 August, roosting in a cornfield near Topeka). Most depart during September with flocks of several hundred reported through 7 October. Late dates include 15 October (Barber Co.) and 19 October (Stafford Co.).

Breeding: The timing and actual location of colonies may vary from year to year, probably dependent on availability of proper mud, local food supply, and amount of disturbance. A few colonies may reach 5,000 pairs, for example, the Elkader Bridge in Logan County. R. Johnston reported 610 records of breeding with 85 percent of all eggs laid between 21 May and 10 June. Young in the nest have been reported 29 May–17 August with fledging reported as early as 6 June 2010, when E. Young observed 24 locations with a total of 340 fledglings being fed by adults in Barber County. In one case (1971) a flock of several hundred birds arrived at a vacant bridge and began building on the late date of 6 July, more than a month after a nearby colony had completed nest-building. This late attempt, however, was not completed.

Comments: Since presettlement days large colonies have used natural sites in the rugged outcrops bordering the Smoky Hill River and tributaries in the west and in the Red Hills. Many soon took advantage of man-made structures. E. Fleharty reported an account from the *Dodge City Times* dated 31 May 1879 that stated "an army of swallows settled under the eaves of the courthouse at Great Bend suddenly migrated in a body to the Catholic church. The noise of the lawyers was too much for them." By the late 1960s an increasing number of birds began using box culverts under highways, sometimes replacing Barn Swallow colonies.

See page 501 for banding information.

References: Busby and Thompson, 2001; Fleharty, 1995; Johnston, 1964a; Thompson and Ely, 1992; Young, 1993.

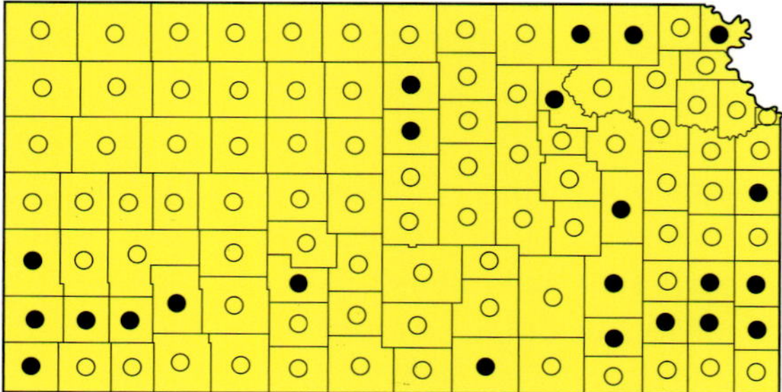

Cave Swallow

Petrochelidon fulva (CASW)

Status: Currently a rare, irregular immigrant, especially in fall; one probable nesting record.

Habitat: Vicinity of water or marshes.

Migration: Spring dates are between 4 April and 28 May (some unverified). Most reports are for the period 17 June–27 September, often in large flocks of mixed species of swallows. Most Kansas records are probably postbreeding dispersals from elsewhere. The presence of individuals far north and east of the breeding grounds suggests the effect of weather patterns on dispersal, for example, a major influx into New York State in November 2005.

Breeding: R. Penner reported a pair carrying mud to a box culvert on Shop Creek, The Nature Conservancy preserve (Barton Co.), 2 July 2009. One bird continued to sit on the nest while the second continued bringing mud. The nesting attempt was not monitored, and its outcome is unknown. However, young birds of the year were found at CBWA on 29 July 2009, along with adults.

Comments: It formerly nested in caves north to Arizona, southeastern New Mexico, and southern Texas. In the 1980s it began a rapid range expansion northward with an increase in population size and a shift in nesting sites as it began utilizing culverts and began nesting with Cliff Swallows and Barn Swallows. It was first reported in Nebraska in 1991 and in Oklahoma in 2000. The first Kansas report was of an immature and a molting adult at CBWA on 13 July 2001 by S. Patti and C. Hobbs. The birds alternated between foraging over the marsh and resting on a water-control structure along a dike road. Five other species of swallows (largely Bank Swallows) were present. One bird remained through 16 July, was seen by numerous observers, and was videotaped by T. Cable on 14 July. M. Thompson compared images from this film with specimens at the University of Kansas, concluding that the birds were from the southern Texas population *P. f. pelodona* (= *P. f. pallida*). A different adult (not molting) was reported on 26 July, as were two adults and an immature on 29 July, but neither sighting was confirmed. On 27 September 2001 T. Shane and M. Osterbuhr saw two adults with a small flock of Bank Swallows and Barn Swallows at Ackley Lake (Finney Co.), and obtained one photo. These individuals were not found the next day. Subsequent sightings include reports from Stafford (2003, 2004), Hamilton (2005), Ford (2005), Johnson (2005), and Barton counties.

References: Grzybowski and Fazio, 2004; Land, 2010; Patti and Shane, 2001; Spahn and Tetlow, 2006.

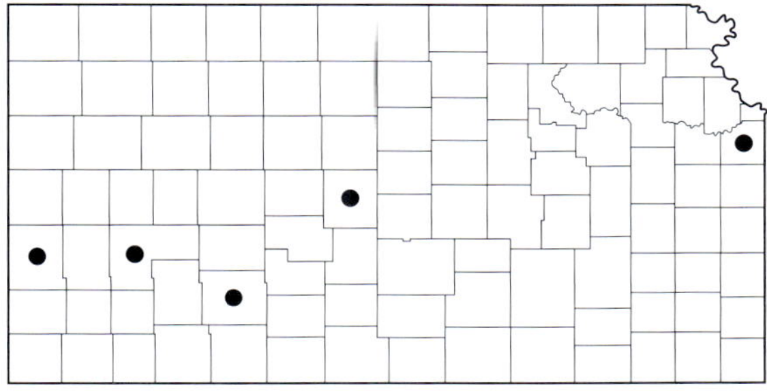

Barn Swallow

Hirundo rustica (BARS)

© David Seibel

Status: Common transient and summer resident statewide; less common and local in far west. It may be locally abundant during migration.

Habitat: Nearly all open areas. During migration may congregate along roadsides and near marshes and shorelines.

Migration: Extreme spring dates are 11 March (Sumner Co.) and 6 May with peak migration during the last half of April and early May. Median arrival dates include 4 April (Cowley Co.), 10–12 April (Russell Co.), and 14 April (Ellis Co.). Migrating flocks are usually small (<50 birds). Departure from nesting areas may occur weeks before actual fall migration, and thousands may be in favored feeding and roosting areas by early September. These staging areas are typically near water with power lines for diurnal resting. Actual roosting is often in marshes. Earliest dates of actual or presumed departure are 4 and 8 September in the west and 15 September in central Kansas. Late migration dates include 11 October ("sky filled," Stafford Co.) and 22 October ("large migration," Rush Co.). Most migration is mid-September through mid-October with stragglers (usually in staging areas) through 21 November (CBWA) and 24 November (Milford Reservoir). In August 1994 birds began staging near SCW and built to a peak of 21,700 on 27 September. About 2,020 remained on 19 October. Exceptionally, an estimated 35,000–40,000 were still present at Melvern Reservoir (Osage Co.) on 2 October 1985. Whether such aggregations include both summer residents and transients is unknown. There are no confirmed winter records.

Breeding: Originally a solitary nester on rock outcrops and similar sites, it increased greatly in numbers with the arrival of settlers and now uses man-made structures almost exclusively. It has recently become a colonial nester in highway culverts and highway overpasses. It is typically double-brooded. In Ellis County, the first brood is mid- or late May through mid-June, the second mid-June through early August. Extreme nesting dates are 1 and 11 May (earliest clutches) and 28 August (young in nest, Shawnee Co.). Recently fledged young were reported in Ellis County on 11 September.

Comments: It is ubiquitous in Kansas with confirmed breeding records in every county and was found nesting on 87 percent of KBBAT blocks, the highest for any species.

See page 501 for banding information.

References: Anthony and Ely, 1976; Busby and Zimmerman, 2001; Lohoefener, 1977; Thompson and Ely, 1992; Young, 1993; Young and Thompson, 1995.

Carolina Chickadee

Poecile carolinensis (CACH)

Status: Common permanent resident in southern tier of counties west to Clark County. It overlaps and interbreeds with the Black-capped Chickadee in the northern part of its range.

Habitat: Woodlands, parks, and suburban yards; readily visits feeders.

Migration: It is largely sedentary with a few individuals wandering north and west during the nonbreeding season. A specimen from Ellis County is believed to be mislabeled.

Breeding: KBBAT documented breeding north to central Crawford, extreme southern Allen and Woodson, northern Harper, and western Comanche counties with "possible" breeding in Pratt and Clark counties. It may have nested in Meade and Seward counties in the recent past. Examination of the scanty data indicates eggs on 1 May (Neosho Co.), nearly fledged young between 30 April (Cowley Co.) and 7 May (Crawford Co.), and recently fledged young on 25 May (Wilson Co.).

Comments: The Carolina Chickadee was apparently overlooked by all 19th-century ornithologists, though it is possible, as suggested by J. Rising, that its occurrence in Kansas is a 20th-century event. It was considered a "common resident" in southern Kansas by C. Long. J. Rising studied the area of overlap between the two species, marking its northern limit by a line from northern Bourbon County westward through central Sedgwick County to extreme southeastern Clark County. Nearly one-third of the 44 specimens within the zone of contact (Neosho, Woodson, Chase, and Comanche cos.) were phenotypically intermediate to varying degrees. An apparent mixed pair was collected in Seward County on 6 May. The female (*P. carolinensis*) had laid eggs, but no young were found. More recently, M. Thompson studied the area of overlap in Cowley County by using song type and concluded that the present line of overlap was south of the J. Rising line. Wherever the two species overlapped, both song types (often by the same individual) and intermediate or aberrant songs occurred. Its range expands and contracts at the western edge of its range, usually during winter. Specimens, banded birds, and individuals of the normal song type indicate presence in Meade County during at least 1950, 1965–1967, 1988, 1995, and 1997 (T. Flowers, pers. comm.). Some of these were apparent hybrids. None has been noted there since the outbreak of West Nile virus.

See page 501 for banding information.

References: Busby and Zimmerman, 2001; Long, 1940; Rising, 1974; Thompson and Ely, 1992.

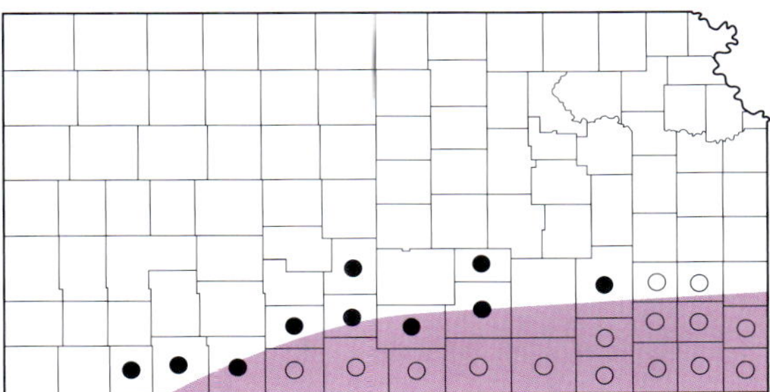

Black-capped Chickadee

Poecile atricapillus (BCCH)

Status: Common permanent resident in eastern two-thirds of state, becoming less common in the northwest; rare and local in the southwest.

Habitat: Woodlands, parks, and urban areas with mature trees; readily visits feeders.

Migration: Most individuals are sedentary, but the appearance of birds outside the normal breeding range indicates some movement, usually during winter. Most of these individuals probably move in from the west and north. At SCW individuals heard and observed were recorded on 20 February, 29 September–29 October, and 7 December (all in 1988), and wintering birds were heard on 7 December 1988, and from 26 December 1990 to 5 January 1991. Thompson observed the species there four times in 4 years from 3 to 28 March (1968–1971).

Breeding: R. Johnston reported 51 records of breeding (21 March–10 June) with 15 April as the modal date of egg-laying and with 64 percent of all eggs laid between 11 and 30 April. Bent reported that half of 16 clutches were from 21 April through 14 May. More recently, the median date for 27 clutches statewide was 27 April (25 March–8 June). Nest-building has been reported between 23 March and 19 May and recently fledged young from 3 May through 30 June. Hybridization occurs where Carolina Chickadees and Black-capped Chickadees occur together.

Comments: Numbers become progressively smaller westward along the various river systems. It is apparently cyclical in the southwest, occurring chiefly in fall and winter but with a few observations during the breeding season (in Meade Co., 5 of more than 23 recent sightings). It breeds regularly westward along the Arkansas River to Pawnee and Ford counties with additional sightings in Hamilton County. Since 2002 there are no sightings from Meade County and few elsewhere in the southwest. CBCs showed a healthy population at Scott Lake during the period 1988–1999 (mean 66 individuals) with a sharp decline in 2000–2001 (13), a total of 11 birds on three of four counts through 2005, and none since. Where the two species occur together, hybridization produces a mixture of physical characteristics and a variety of call notes including both two-note and four-note calls often given by the same individual! Banded individuals and several specimens suggest that the Meade County population included such hybrids.

See page 501 for banding information.

References: Bent, 1946; Busby and Zimmerman, 2001; Flowers, 1995a; Johnston, 1964a; Thompson and Ely, 1992; Young, 1993.

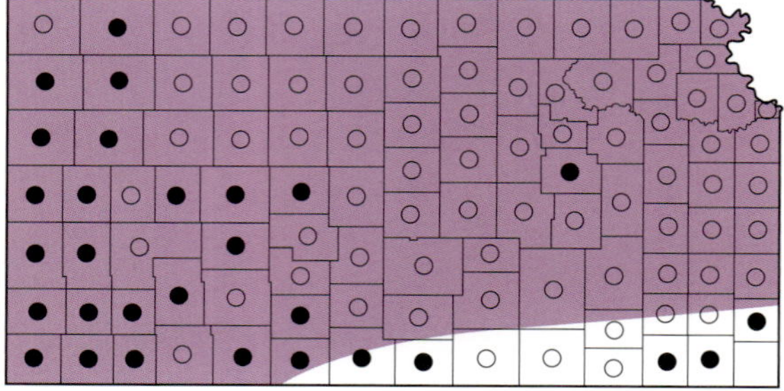

Mountain Chickadee

Poecile gambeli (MOCH)

Status: Rare to uncommon vagrant in the southwest, especially along the Cimarron River.

Habitat: Riparian woodlands, parks, and ornamentals in yards; also visits feeders.

Migration: The spring departure is poorly documented, in part because few observers visit the area during those months. The five available spring dates are between 4 March and 5 May. Earliest fall reports are 21 October–12 November in various years. The great majority of sightings are late November through 6 February, especially during the CBC period. Overall dates for individual seasons are 23 November 1987 through 27 March 1988 (Morton Co.), 21 October 1989 through 5 May 1990 (Morton Co.), and 20 November 2000 through 4 May 2001 (Finney Co.).

Comments: M. Schwilling reported the first sighting in 1951, an individual that spent most of the winter in a Garden City park (Finney Co.). At least 13 individuals were reported at several localities in Morton County during the period 28–31 December 1978. It was next reported on the 1982–1983 CBC (12 birds in Morton Co.) and 1 bird remained until 1 May. It subsequently appeared on 8 of the next 25 CBCs in Morton County. During most of these seasons it was accompanied by other montane species, especially in 1987–1988, 1989–1990, 1992–1993, and 2000–2001. It has also appeared in other areas north and east to Scott, Ford, and Meade counties. The largest and most widespread occurrence was in 2000–2001 with at least 41 individuals appearing on seven CBCs, including 23 at the CNG. It usually occurs singly or in small flocks and is similar to other chickadees in behavior. It can be identified by the white line over the eye and a call different from that of the Black-capped Chickadee, which occasionally occurs along the Arkansas River and rarely along the Cimarron River.

Banding: Two banded (Meade Co., T. Flowers); no encounters.

References: Cable et al., 1996; Schwilling, 1951; Thompson and Ely, 1992; Thompson and Young, 2001.

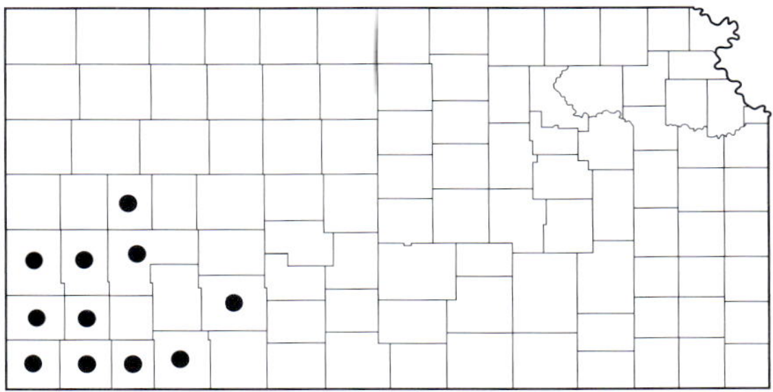

Juniper Titmouse

Baeolophus ridgwayi (JUTI)

Status: [Hypothetical]. Vagrant to extreme southwestern Kansas in fall.

Habitat: Riparian woodlands along Cimarron River.

Migration: No spring sightings; three fall records range from 30 September to 31 December.

Comments: The KBRC (KBRC 2000-68) added the Juniper Titmouse to the state list on the basis of three sightings along the Cimarron River in Morton County during 2000. S. Seltman reported one near the Boy Scout area, 2 miles north and 5 miles east of the K-27 bridge on 30 September, and S. Patti reported one at the same locality on 7 October. The third was reported by J. Runco west of the Point of Rocks waterfowl ponds (about 7 miles upriver) on December 31. The first two sightings and probably the third may be independent sightings of the same individual. The species is considered nonmigratory, but G. Sutton noted an influx into the Black Mesa during fall and winter, presumably from Colorado and New Mexico. During winter it may descend to lower elevations and probably on occasion follows river systems eastward. Other montane species were found in southwestern Kansas during the winter of 2000–2001.

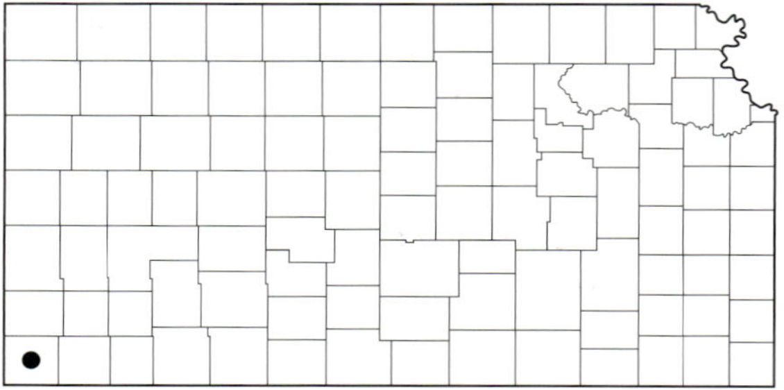

Banding: Five reported banded by one individual, but dates and coordinates indicate error in identification.

References: Rintoul, 2001; Sutton, 1967.

Tufted Titmouse

Baeolophus bicolor (TUTI)

Status: Common permanent resident in east, regularly west to Barber and Cloud counties; casual westward.

Habitat: Woodland, parks, and residential areas; prefers areas with midlevel understory.

Migration: Generally resident with occasional wandering during nonbreeding season.

Breeding: Nesting is poorly documented. R. Johnston reported 21 records of nesting with a modal date for egg-laying of 25 April and with 54 percent of all clutches laid 11–30 April. Statewide, nest-building has been reported on 19 April, eggs 29 March–16 June, nestlings 23 April–28 June, and recently fledged young 20 May–11 July. It occasionally nests outside the core range, most notably once in Finney County during the 1950s.

Comments: Like chickadees, it travels in small flocks, often of mixed species, and with its loud, distinct call ("peter-peter-peter") is easily located. It is attracted to bird feeders but is usually shier and less confiding than chickadees. It nests in secondary tree cavities and often makes use of bird boxes. KBBAT found it in more blocks in the Glaciated Region and Osage Plains and fewer blocks in the Flint Hills, and it occurs regularly westward to the eastern edge of the Red Hills. Northward, it breeds locally along river systems to Saline and Cloud counties and occurs sporadically westward. A small population occurs in the magnificent old-growth oak grove at Camp Webster in Saline County. This is a western outpost for a group of species from the closed-canopy eastern deciduous forest.

Banding: 2,624 banded; 197 encounters: all in-state (local or short-distance movements). Oldest 5 years.

References: Busby and Zimmerman, 2001; Thompson and Ely, 1992.

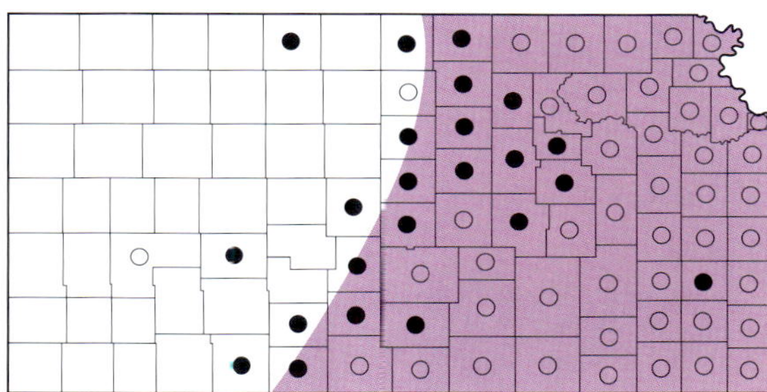

Bushtit

Psaltriparus minimus (BUSH)

Status: Rare and irregular winter visitant to the southwest; vagrant eastward.

Habitat: Riparian woodlands, parks, and residential yards.

Migration: Fall dates range from 5 September (Morton Co.) to 10 November (Morton Co.). However, the great majority of reports are during the CBC period (mid-December to early January), a period of heavy birding in the west. The latest date is currently 12 January (Finney Co.) with no late winter or spring records.

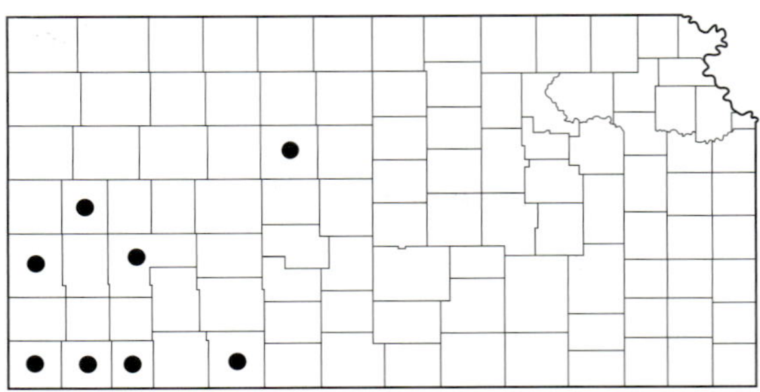

Comments: It was first documented at Hays (Ellis Co.), when C. Ely netted a flock of four along Big Creek on 16 November 1968. The next report was of four individuals along the Cimarron River (Morton Co.) on 31 December 1976. It has been reported on five subsequent counts in Morton County but remains a rare visitant even there. However, the area is rarely birded during late winter and early spring. It has recently been reported at other localities in the southwest. Most sightings have been in open deciduous growth along the Cimarron River or in cemeteries, yards, and similar residential situations. Although it typically occurs in small groups, flocks of 20 (Morton Co.) to 30 (Seward Co.) birds have been observed on several occasions, and 34 individuals (several groups) were observed on the CBC in Morton County on 1 January 2005. These flocks are very active and appear constantly on the move. Whether these flocks remain in an area for an extended time or leave and then return is currently unknown.

References: Cable et al., 1996; Cink and Boyd, 2005; Ely, 1969; Thompson and Ely, 1992.

Red-breasted Nuthatch

Sitta canadensis (RBNU)

Status: Uncommon transient and winter resident throughout the state; late spring or summer records in at least five counties (Geary, Sedgwick, Cowley, Douglas, and Finney), with confirmed breeding in Sedgwick and Geary counties.

Habitat: Primarily in areas with stands of large conifers, such as parks, campuses, cemeteries, shelterbelts, or farmsteads with junipers or pine; frequents feeders in towns and rural areas, especially during invasion years.

Migration: In Ellis County spring numbers peak during April with stragglers through mid-May and once to 15 June. Wintering birds typically depart by 11 May with some dates after late May likely representing breeding birds. Early fall arrivals might actually be lingering summer residents; 12 August is the normal arrival date, with numbers at numerous sites by mid-September. Departure dates for fall transients are unknown, because many birds appearing in fall remain throughout or well into winter.

Breeding: Although its normal breeding range is in northern or montane coniferous forests, it has nested at least twice. In Geary County, an adult was seen feeding three juveniles during June 1974, and pairs probably nested in 1975, 1976, and 1999 as well. In Sedgwick County, a pair nested in a wren house made from a pine log in 1982, and in 2000 a pair was feeding recently fledged 28 May–27 June. Breeding is also suspected in Cowley County (1978 and 1979), Finney County (KBBAT), and Russell County (excavating a cavity on 6 April 1984).

Comments: This is an irruptive species that can be quite common when its food is scarce in the more northerly or mountainous portions of its range, for example, 1949–1950, 1968–1969, 1993–1994, and 1999–2000.

Banding: 170 banded; one encounter: in-state.

References: Busby and Zimmerman, 2001; Gress, 1982; Janzen, 2007; Shane and LaShelle, 1974; Thompson and Ely, 1992.

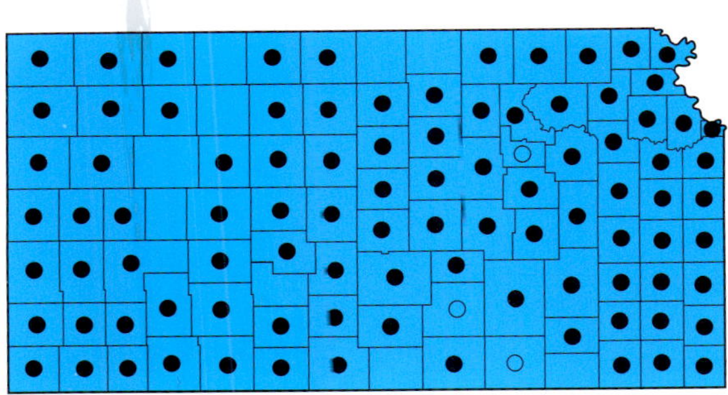

White-breasted Nuthatch

Sitta carolinensis (WBNU)

Status: Uncommon to fairly common medium-density resident and winter visitant in the east; less common in the west (especially the High Plains), particularly during summer.

Habitat: Deciduous woodlands, and riparian and urban areas with mature trees. This is one of the few birds found in deep forest in the winter.

Migration: Spring passage of migrants is obscured by presence of resident populations in the east. In Ellis County, most numerous during April and early May with a few probably remaining to breed. Present in southwestern Kansas to 13 May. Again, in eastern Kansas, fall arrival of transients is obscured by presence of resident populations, but numbers do appear to increase in winter. In Ellis County, it becomes more widespread beginning in late August and early September. Arrives around 14 September in southwestern Kansas, with low numbers remaining into winter.

Breeding: Actual nest records are few because of the difficulty in accessing nests that are usually in natural cavities or old woodpecker excavations 15 feet or more above the ground. Nest-building has been reported on 1 April, eggs 17–25 March, nestlings 9 March–18 May, and recently fledged young 13 June–29 July. Breeds most commonly in the eastern one-third of the state, declining across the central counties to almost no records in the western one-third, where it is very local. This distribution reflects the abundance of trees; for example, KBBAT reports confirmed breeding in 19 of the 25 heavily wooded counties east of the 96th meridian, progressively diminishing to only 3 of the 24 nearly treeless counties west of the 100th meridian. However, BBS data do not reflect such a clear correlation, showing very similar relative abundances throughout all but the High Plains of far western Kansas.

Comments: Although some fall and winter movement undoubtedly occurs, it is currently not well documented. Specimens taken in Morton County and originally thought to be of the western form *S. c. nelsoni* could not be verified as to race. Like other nuthatches, this species goes down the tree headfirst, gleaning the bark for arthropods or plant material. It readily comes to feeders, where it prefers sunflower seeds and sometimes suet. It is not averse to feeding on the ground, where it probes among leaves and bark looking for insects and seeds.

Branding: 512 branded; three encounters: all instate.

References: Busby and Zimmerman, 2001; Cable et al., 1996; Sauer et al., 2008; Thompson and Ely, 1992.

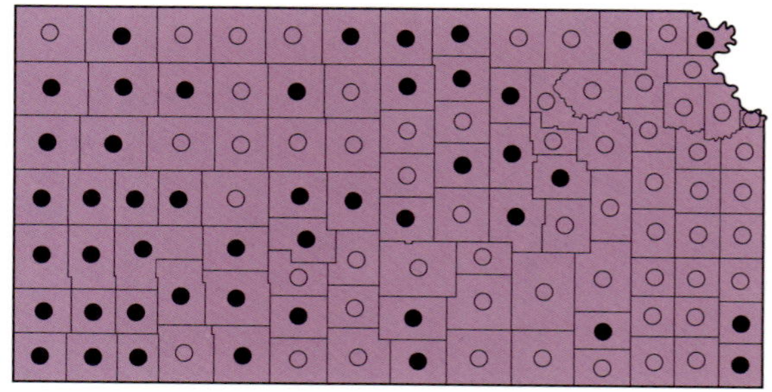

Pygmy Nuthatch

Sitta pygmaea (PYNU)

Status: Vagrant in at least the western two-thirds of the state; casual winter visitant or winter resident in the extreme southwest. First state record was on 23 November 1961 at Sim Park in Wichita (Sedgwick Co.), where C. Holmes and others observed a flock of 10 birds through 13 January 1962. One seen by M. Schwilling in Linn County on 30 March 1956 may have been a Brown-headed Nuthatch. There are two specimen records: one taken on 30 December 1961 in Sedgwick County (KU 40762); one on 13 May 1967 in Morton County (MHP 1393).

Habitat: It breeds in long-needled pine forests in montane regions of the western United States, Mexico, and the southern edge of Canada. In Kansas, it is generally found in stands of conifers, for example, in parks or cemeteries. The flock in Sim Park (Sedgwick Co.) was associated with Scotch pine.

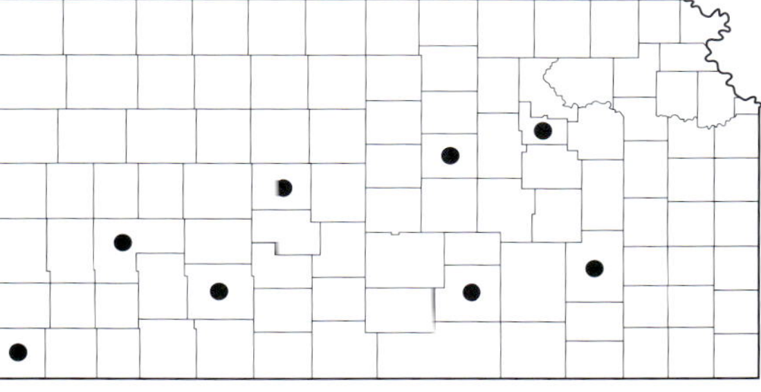

Migration: Most records from 10 September through 13 January; only two spring records, 27 April and 13 May. All have been of single birds except for the flock of 10 in Wichita in 1961–1962.

Comments: This species is common in mountainous regions to the west of Kansas. It is nonmigratory, but some populations wander irregularly, and at times widely, after the breeding season. Flocks and individuals stray sporadically into Kansas, seemingly following river courses.

References: Cable et al., 1996; Schwilling, 1956; Thompson and Ely, 1992; Thompson and Holmes, 1963.

Brown-headed Nuthatch

Sitta pusilla (BHNU)

© David Seibel

Status: Accidental. One well-documented record in Johnson County, and one possible sighting in Linn County.

Habitat: Within its normal range in the southeastern United States, found mostly in mature pine forests and rarely venturing from pine-dominated areas. In Kansas, the only confirmed record was in an urban residential area with numerous large deciduous trees and some conifers. The possible Brown-headed Nuthatch in Linn County was feeding in cottonwoods and elms along the south bank of the Marais des Cygnes River.

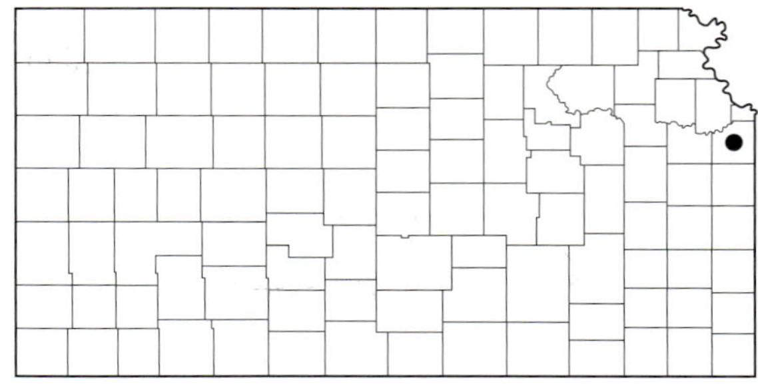

Migration: The only confirmed record was a single bird first observed by E. McHugh at his feeder in Mission Hills (Johnson Co.), 25 December 1997. Numerous other observers saw and photographed the bird in the same neighborhood through 24 January 1998. The possible record at MDCWA on 30 March 1956 was originally reported as a Pygmy Nuthatch, but that identification has subsequently been questioned.

Comments: Although significantly declining throughout its range, it is still common in much of the southeast, with populations as far northwest as west-central Arkansas. However, it is nonmigratory and almost entirely sedentary, so extralimital records are rare.

References: Schwilling, 1956; Thompson and Ely, 1992; Withgott and Smith, 1998.

Brown Creeper

Certhia americana (BRCR)

Status: Uncommon transient and low-density winter resident.

Habitat: Woodlands, riparian areas, parks, cemeteries, and residential areas with numerous trees.

Migration: Its low density and inconspicuous nature make it difficult to note any significant peak migration periods, but spring migration is probably mid-March to early April with few after 20 April. A distinct movement was noted in Ellis County on 17 April, but the median late spring date there is 5 April. Late spring dates include 5 and 10 May. The earliest fall arrival is 20 August but is usually about October 1, with birds widespread by midmonth. Median dates for first arrival include 10 October (Ellis Co.), 14 October (Johnson Co.), and 22 October (Rice Co.). Although there is no obvious peak, most migration is probably late October through early November.

Comments: It is a nonflocking species, but total numbers in an area may be surprisingly high; as, for example, 70 on the Emporia CBC on 16 December. One of the smallest of Kansas birds, the Brown Creeper can nonetheless withstand the harshest of winters. It spends most of its time foraging on tree trunks and limbs, usually beginning at the base and creeping upward as it scrutinizes the bark for food. It then flies to the base of a nearby tree and repeats the process again and again. Its thin, high-pitched call is frequently the first clue to its presence, thanks to its exceptional camouflage, diminutive size, and slow movements. In the winter, creepers roost behind loose bark on a tree.

Banding: 380 banded; two encounters: both in-state.

References: Hejl et al., 2002; Thompson and Ely, 1992.

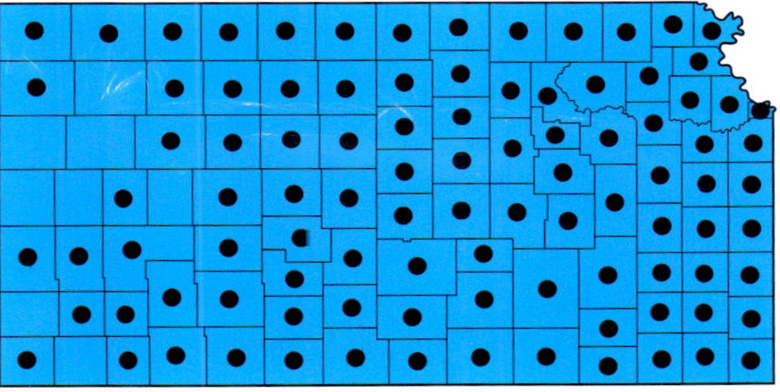

Rock Wren

Salpinctes obsoletus (ROWR)

Status: Common transient and local summer resident in west becoming less common and local eastward; casual, chiefly during fall and winter, to Douglas and Cowley counties.

Habitat: Large rocky outcrops in grassland, also large artificial "rock piles," and road-cuts with rock.

Migration: Actual arrival dates within the breeding range are few, the earliest being 3 March (Russell Co.) and 17 March (Trego Co.), but usually late March or early April. Spring dates outside the breeding range are between 3 April (Cowley Co.) and 28 April (Pottawatomie Co.). The spring migration peak is probably mid-April. Late dates from the breeding range are typically to 27 September (Lane Co.) and 13 October (Finney Co.) with stragglers to 15 November and 18 December and a few into the CBC period. Peak migration is probably mid-September through mid-October. More than 80 individuals were reported in Morton County on 19 September. Recent sightings between 10 January and 13 February suggest overwintering in the far west. East of the main breeding range fall dates are between 11 September (Stafford Co.) and 24 November (Douglas Co.), again with a few into early January.

Breeding: R. Johnston reported 16 records of breeding (10 May–20 July) with a modal date of 15 June for egg-laying. Actually breeding begins earlier. Seven of 10 clutches (1892–1913) from Decatur County, 8–23 May and 11 and 24 June, were fresh, and three others (8–20 May) were slightly incubated. Recent (1997–1998) egg dates from Logan and Scott counties were 8 May–5 July (43 records), and in 60 nests fledging occurred from 27 May to 4 August.

Comments: The Rock Wren is aptly named, occurring in large or small rock outcrops within the breeding range and selecting similar substitute sites when visiting eastern Kansas. Here, most individuals are found on the riprap below dams, at abandoned stone buildings, or along road-cuts. At least one spent several days around the stone steps of a building at a university campus. The length of time individuals remain at a given locality is currently unknown. A few birds present during midsummer east of the known breeding range may be breeding outliers or nonbreeding individuals.

Banding: Three banded; no encounters.

References: Busby and Zimmerman, 2001; Cable et al., 1996; Johnston, 1964a; Lowther et al., 2000; Matiasek, 1998; Thompson and Ely, 1992.

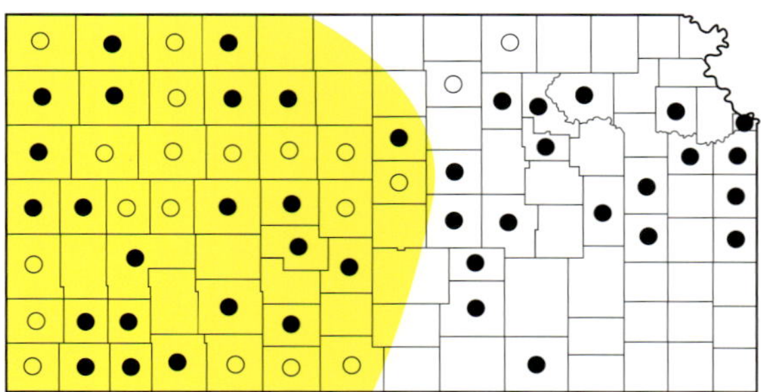

Canyon Wren

Catherpes mexicanus (CANW)

Status: Casual visitant to the southwest.

Habitat: Escarpments and rocky outcrops of steep, arid canyons.

Migration: Generally sedentary but with some postbreeding dispersal. Recent Kansas sightings are between 6 September and 14 February. An earlier series of intriguing sightings was reported 15 October 1944 to 8 April and 10 June 1945.

Comments: The first physical evidence of its occurrence in Kansas was of an immature reported on the sand cliffs north of the Boy Scout Camp, Cimarron River (Morton Co.), 6 September 1992, by R. Parker, S. Crawford, and T. Shane and supported by a photo (KBRC 92-500). It was seen on 7 September and again on 6 February 1993 (now in adult plumage) by S. Seltman. Sightings from Point of Rocks by M. Rader occurred on 25 November and 27 December 1995 and on 14 September 1997 (KBRC 96-04). A single individual photographed south of Scott State Lake on 30 December 1993 by R. Rucker (KBRC 94-07) was subsequently observed on 3 January and 13 February. A series of early sightings of a Canyon Wren at the Warkentine Mill at Halstead (Harvey Co.) were well documented by E. Ruth, whose notes describe the bird, its song, and its very close association with the stone buildings at the mill. Her yearly list for 1942 lists a Canyon Wren for 19 May as does her life list, the latter with a notation that it was seen in their yard. Although there is no description of the bird, and there seems to be an unexplained discrepancy in the date, the description of the song is intriguing (D. Platt). In March 1943, there are several notes about a new wren (unidentified), and the year list for 1943 includes a "new wren" for 26 March. In a letter to F. Baumgartner in 1950, E. Ruth states: "canyon wrens wintered here for several winters (in the mill buildings) 1943 and 1944." The more detailed (and convincing) reports for 1944 and 1945 were reviewed and accepted by the KBRC in 1998 (posthumously, KBRC 98-39). Unfortunately the KBRC report gives incorrect years—29 October 1945 [sic] through 8 April 1946 [sic] rather than 1944 and 1945. The bird was noted on 15, 18, and 29 October 1944 and on at least six dates between 8 March and 10 June 1945. Additional unconfirmed reports include one singing from tall, eroded dirt cliffs on the Delbert Davis ranch in southeastern Meade County on 22 August 1986 by T. Flowers.

References: Cable et al., 1996; Pittman, 1993, 1995, 1997; Rintoul, 1999.

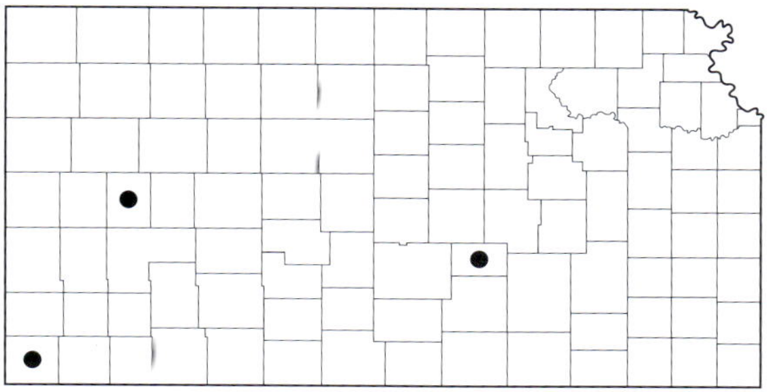

Carolina Wren

Thryothorus ludovicianus (CARW)

© David Seibel

Status: Common permanent resident in the east becoming less common and local in the Flint Hills and casual westward.

Habitat: Preferred habitat is mesic woodland with well-developed understory, similar riparian growth, and urban and suburban areas with abundant shrubby vegetation.

Migration: Permanent resident with occasional vagrancy. Postbreeding dispersal is widespread from midsummer through the next spring. Singing birds may occur during midsummer almost anywhere west of the normal range, but such individuals usually depart after a short visit. Most records for the west are during fall between 26 August and 11 November, but a few overwinter successfully. Breeding may occur at such sites for a few years as at Garden City (Finney Co.) in July 2001.

Breeding: The breeding season is extended with at least two, perhaps three, broods. Johnston reported 14 records of breeding between 11 April and 10 August with 15 April as the modal date for egg-laying. More recent data for the first brood include nest-building 6 March–28 April, eggs 17 March–3 April, and recently fledged young 13 April–14 May. A second brood is begun by early May with young fledged by 9 July. Reports of late nesting (renestings, or third broods) include nest-building 3 July, eggs 20 August, and recently fledged young 15 and 19 September.

Comments: Within its normal breeding range it is susceptible to dramatic changes in numbers resulting from severe winters with heavy snow cover. Recovery is often slow as in the Kansas City area and throughout eastern Kansas following massive mortality during 1961–1962 and 1976–1977, respectively. In Cowley County, it was nearly absent in 1978, still scarce in 1980–1981, and did not return to normal numbers until 1986. Examination of KBBAT data suggests that populations were close to normal levels during 1992–1997. It is a very vociferous bird and sings most of the year. In residential areas it becomes very accustomed to humans, often entering outbuildings where it may nest on a shelf, in a hanging pot, an old boot, a hanging glove, a half-opened drawer, or perhaps, inside a partially opened sack of fertilizer. The nest proper is a large bulky affair of stems and partially skeletonized leaves lined with rootlets, and often with a tapered opening.

See page 501 for banding information.

References: Busby and Zimmerman, 2001; Janzen, 2007; Johnston, 1964a; Thompson and Ely, 1992.

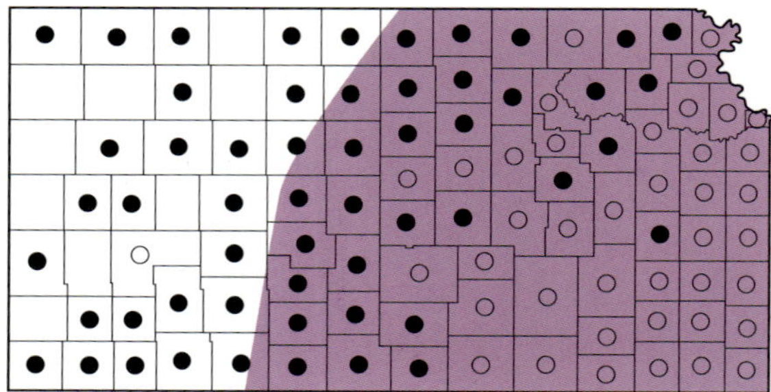

Bewick's Wren

Thryomanes bewickii (BEWR)

Status: Transient and low-density resident from the Flint Hills eastward and in the south, west through the Red Hills.

Habitat: Open woodland with well-developed brushy understory, forest edge, and open riparian woodland; less common in residential areas.

Migration: The few records, though insufficient to document the extent of migration, suggest a movement from at least mid-March through early April. Extreme dates of sightings outside the breeding range are 9 March through 13 May and 4 June (Decatur Co.). In Ellis County, four of five records were in spring (12 April–17 May), and the fifth bird, which wintered, was last seen on 4 April. Individuals occur frequently but erratically during fall and winter in areas where they do not breed, suggesting considerable dispersal during late summer with a noticeable movement in mid-October through mid-November. Wintering has been documented north to Ellis and Russell counties.

Breeding: Contents of only a few nests have been reported. Johnston reported 21 records of breeding (21 March–10 July) with modal dates of 15 April (first clutches) and 15 June (second clutches). Nest-building has been reported 22 March–22 May, eggs 12 April–8 June, and recently fledged young 15 May–15 July.

Comments: Breeding occurs regularly south of a line from Riley to Seward counties with highest populations in the Flint Hills. Populations in the eastern United States have declined in recent decades. Competition by House Wrens that puncture the eggs of this species and other hole-nesting species has been blamed. However, M. Robbins and D. Easterla consider the southern expansion of House Wrens and the decline in Bewick's Wrens in Missouri to be coincidental and likely related to cultural changes such as clearing of brushy habitats.

Banding: 464 banded; one encounter. One banded in Arkansas on 27 December 1964 was found dead in east-central Kansas in April 1965.

References: Busby and Zimmerman, 2001; Johnston, 1964a; Kennedy and White, 1997; Robbins and Easterla, 1992; Thompson and Ely, 1992.

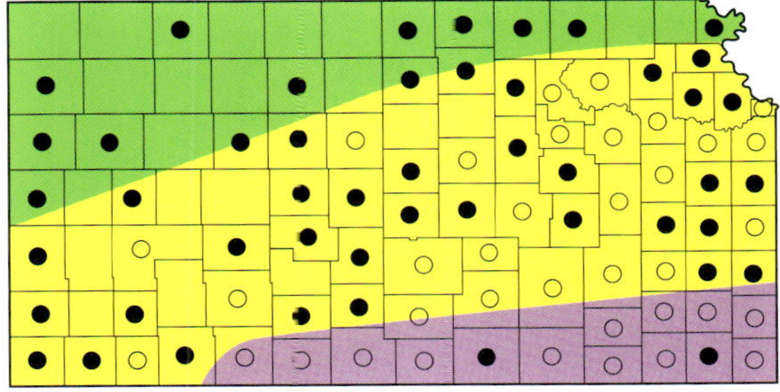

House Wren

Troglodytes aedon (HOWR)

Status: Common to abundant transient and summer resident statewide; local and less common westward during breeding season; casual in winter.

Habitat: Urban areas, open woodland, forest edge, riparian and brushy fields, windbreaks, and farmsteads.

Migration: Arrival is usually in mid-April with extremely early dates of 4 March and 16 March. Median arrival dates include 15 April (Franklin Co.), 17–18 April (Rice and Ellis cos.), and 22 April (Pawnee Co.). Migration peaks in early May and is over by 20 May. The fall migration is poorly documented. In Ellis County numbers were decreasing by mid-August. Most migration is during September with most gone by 1 October. R. Johnston reported median departure of 30 September (10 September–13 October). Typical late dates are 15 and 19 October, exceptionally to 29 November and with scattered individuals (usually in residential areas) remaining into the CBC period. However, there are no records between 3 January and 4 March.

Breeding: Highest frequencies are in the northeast (Glaciated Region) westward through the Flint Hills and in the Red Hills. It also occurs commonly in riparian woodlands westward through the High Plains, especially in the northwest. It uses a great variety of secondary cavities, both natural and man-made. R. Johnston reported 110 records of breeding (11 April–31 July) with 20 May the modal date of egg-laying and 45 percent of all clutches laid during 11–31 May. Statewide nest-building has been reported 30 April–12 June, eggs 1 April–11 July, and recently fledged young 16 June–31 July. It is double-brooded.

Comments: It is a persistent singer and a very popular yard bird wherever it occurs. It is one of the species that has benefited by human activity, readily accepting birdhouses. During the 19th century, in the west, it was considered a rare summer resident in Finney County but was abundant along Big Creek in Ellis County in 1871.

Banding: 4,276 banded; nine encounters: eight in-state. One banded 21 May 1976 was shot in South Dakota on 26 July 1977.

References: Allen, 1872; Busby and Zimmerman, 2001; Janzen, 2007; Johnston, 1964a, 1965; Menke, 1894; Thompson and Ely, 1992.

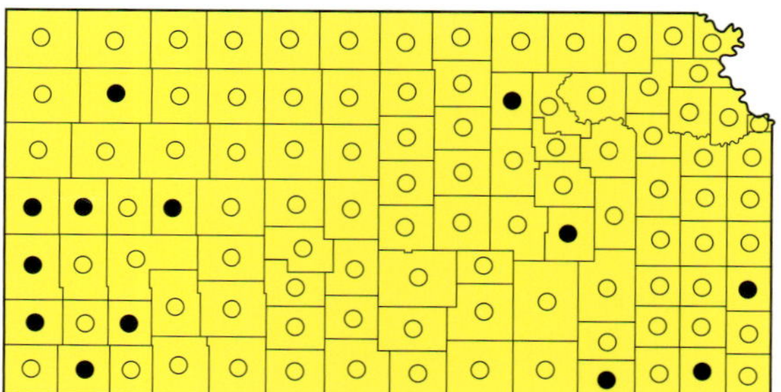

Winter Wren

Troglodytes troglodytes (WIWR)

Status: Regular, rare transient and low-density winter resident; chiefly in the east.

Habitat: Usually found in woodland or riparian with areas of dense undergrowth, parks, and residential areas.

Migration: Few spring records; none from the west. Extreme dates for presumed transients are 23 March and 7 May. Migration is probably mid-March through early April with a few through early May. Late February and early March reports are probably of wintering birds. In 2002 a cluster of reports during late March suggests migration. Fall migration is probably early September through early November with the peak during mid-October. The earliest reported arrivals include 4 and 9 September (Shawnee and Russell cos., respectively). Five were salvaged from a tower kill near Topeka on the late date (for a tower kill) of 28 October. Late arrival dates include 2 and 16 November (Finney and Ness cos., respectively). Most reports are during December and January, especially the CBC period. Late January to early February reports of presumed wintering birds occur west to Norton, Ellis, and Meade counties. The few sightings are insufficient to establish migration periods and extent of wintering. Unusually large numbers were reported during 1974–1975 and 1976–1977.

Comments: Probably underreported. The Winter Wren is shy, usually difficult to observe, and occurs in very low densities. It is a small, dark wren with heavily barred abdomen and a very short tail that is usually cocked upward. It is usually secretive, remains close to the ground, and scurries to cover when alarmed. But if the observer is quiet and patient, individuals often reemerge after a few minutes. Its song, a beautiful series of high-pitched trills, is occasionally heard even during midwinter.

Banding: 62 banded; no encounters. More than 90 percent were banded during fall; half during October.

References: Janzen, 2007; Kluza et al., 2001; Thompson and Ely, 1992.

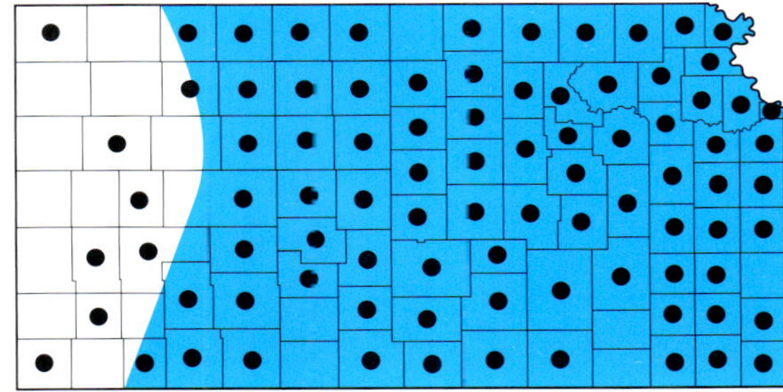

Sedge Wren

Cistothorus platensis (SEWR)

Status: Uncommon transient and local summer resident in the east; casual westward; probably often overlooked.

Habitat: Tall, dense vegetation, wet meadows, sedge marshes, and tall-grass prairie; frequently uses CRP land.

Migration: Three reported 30 March at CBWA were probably overwintering. Typical dates outside the breeding areas are 16 April through 18 May. The highest count recorded is 20+ on 21 April (Stafford Co.). Individuals begin arriving in breeding areas by mid-July, and most have arrived by mid-August. Outside breeding areas early dates for fall departure include 11 September (Shawnee Co.), 12 September (Crawford Co.), 15 September (Lyon Co.), and 19 September (Morton Co.) with regular movement by mid-September. Migration probably peaks in October with stragglers through 14 November and rarely through the CBC period. Tower kills near Topeka (Shawnee Co.) between 25 September and 28 October include 56 individuals on 11–12 October.

Breeding: Statements by N. Goss that eggs were laid during the last of May and first of June are surprising. Johnston stated that eggs were laid in late July and early August. Singing males have been reported as early as 13 July (Barton Co.), nest-building 10–24 August, eggs 24 August–7 September, and recently fledged young 20 August. Recent breeding has been documented from Coffey County (six singing males, 4 August), Atchison County (22+ at Muscotah Marsh, 10 August), Jefferson County (13 at three localities, 10 and 25 August), and Stafford County (recently fledged young, M. Robbins, pers. comm.). KBBAT surveys found singing males between 18 July and 15 August but, because of the lateness of nesting, may not be representative of the actual breeding areas.

Comments: Midsummer arrival followed by late-summer nesting has been noted throughout other central plains states including eastern Nebraska. Dual nesting areas have been proposed, because some populations, unable to complete (or even initiate nesting), moved to alternative, more desirable, localities. However, K. Hobson and M. Robbins report that even when conditions in Kansas are favorable for nesting during May and June, the breeding population still arrives in mid-July. This population, including birds of both sexes, is believed to arrive from farther north.

Banding: Three banded; no encounters.

References: Ball et al., 1995; Bedell, 1996; Busby and Zimmerman, 2001; Hobson and Robbins, 2009; Johnston, 1964a; Kluza et al., 2001; Thompson and Ely, 1992; Tordoff and Mengel, 1956.

Marsh Wren

Cistothorus palustris (MAWR)

Status: Uncommon transient; rare but regular in winter; rare, very local breeder.

Habitat: Usually in cattail marshes.

Migration: Some of the early spring dates (29 March–4 April) are probably overwintering birds. R. Johnston gave median arrival as 22 April (19–29 April). Typical arrival dates include 15 and 17 April with presumed departure dates of 10–16 May. Usual arrival is probably mid-April with most migration between 20 April and 15 May. Very early fall dates (9 and 10 September) may be of summering birds or early fall arrivals; 48 have been salvaged at tower kills near Topeka (Shawnee Co.) 30 September–28 October and 3 at Goodland (Sherman Co.) on 12–16 September. R. Johnston gave 8 October (26 September–31 October) for median departure in the northeast. Most migration is apparently late September through mid-October with stragglers into early winter. During late December through February individuals may be found statewide wherever patches of cattails occur. A few overwinter most years most regularly at CBWA, QNWR, Wilson Reservoir, and in Sedgwick County. High CBC counts include 16 and 30 at QNWR in different years, 12 at Scott State Lake, and 8 in the Red Hills.

Breeding: Preferred nesting habitat is cattail marshes. Singing males have been reported from a number of marshes statewide during the breeding season, but confirmation of breeding is rare. Eggs have been reported 30 May–4 July and recently fledged young 21–31 August in Barton and Doniphan (1921–1925) counties; breeding also was reported from Republic County in 1981. KBBAT produced a single attempted nesting record at CBWA. During the breeding season additional "dummy" nests are constructed but never completed or used.

Comments: It is very sporadic in occurrence and is often absent from what appears to be suitable breeding habitat.

© David Seibel

Banding: 13 banded; no encounters.

References: Ball et al., 1995; Barkley et al., 1977; Busby and Zimmerman, 2001; Johnston, 1965; Kluza et al., 2001; Thompson and Ely, 1992; Tordoff and Mengel, 1956.

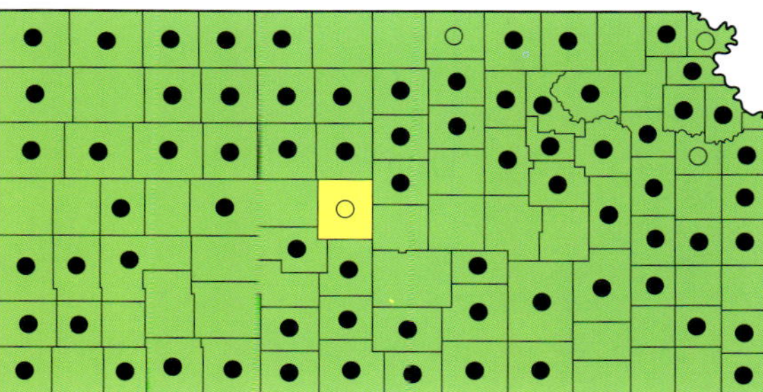

Blue-gray Gnatcatcher

Polioptila caerulea (BGGN)

Status: Uncommon transient in western and central regions, becoming more common eastward. It breeds regularly from the Flint Hills eastward and in the Red Hills; rare and local elsewhere.

Habitat: All types of wooded areas including parks and residential areas; preferred breeding habitat is deciduous forest, scrubby oak woodland, thin riparian woodland, and grassland overgrown with low oaks and juniper.

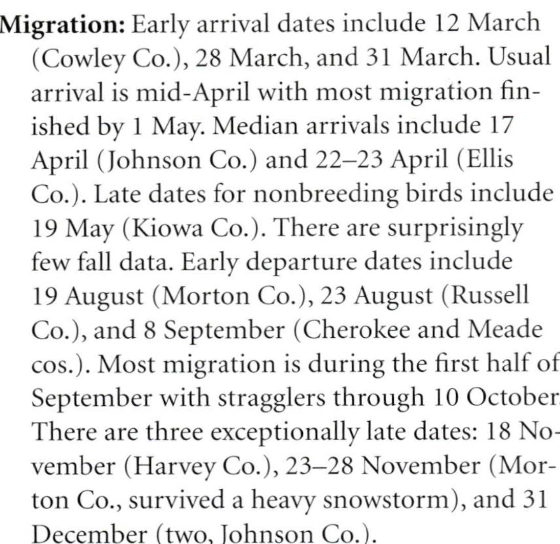

Migration: Early arrival dates include 12 March (Cowley Co.), 28 March, and 31 March. Usual arrival is mid-April with most migration finished by 1 May. Median arrivals include 17 April (Johnson Co.) and 22–23 April (Ellis Co.). Late dates for nonbreeding birds include 19 May (Kiowa Co.). There are surprisingly few fall data. Early departure dates include 19 August (Morton Co.), 23 August (Russell Co.), and 8 September (Cherokee and Meade cos.). Most migration is during the first half of September with stragglers through 10 October. There are three exceptionally late dates: 18 November (Harvey Co.), 23–28 November (Morton Co., survived a heavy snowstorm), and 31 December (two, Johnson Co.).

Breeding: Although nest-building is commonly observed, there are few records of actual nest contents. Nest-building has been reported 17 April (Riley Co.) through 14 June (Doniphan Co.), eggs 24 April–30 May, and recently fledged young 10 June–17 August. Johnston reported 12 records of breeding between 20 April and 20 June with 10 May as the modal date for egg-laying.

Comments: Highest breeding frequencies are in the open woodlands and mosaic of scrubby trees and prairies present throughout much of the eastern one-third of Kansas with an outpost in the Red Hills cedars. It breeds regularly east of a line from Jewell and Barber counties and appears during the breeding season at scattered localities westward. A breeding pair was collected on the Cimarron River (Morton Co.) on 11 June 1965, and Rising considered it a low-density, possibly irregular summer resident in the west. Examination of recent data suggests a gradual expansion of range westward as has been proposed by Sharpe in Nebraska. However, it was not found in summer in Ellis County during the period 1960–1995.

Banding: 82 banded; no encounters.

References: Busby and Zimmerman, 2001; Cable et al., 1996; Janzen, 2007; Johnston, 1964a; Rising, 1974; Sharpe et al., 2001; Thompson and Ely, 1992.

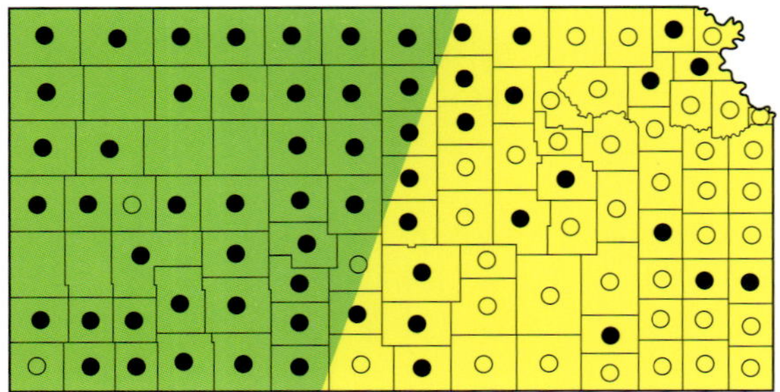

Golden-crowned Kinglet

Regulus satrapa (GCKI)

Status: Regular transient, uncommon in the west, common in the east; regular but low-density winter resident in the east; rare and irregular in the west.

Habitat: Wooded habitats, showing a decided preference for conifers; often in plantings such as cemeteries, parks, and suburban yards.

Migration: There are few early spring reports, probably because birds begin drifting northward by early March. Sightings increase by 24 March (Osage Co.), and most have departed by 22 April (Geary Co.) with stragglers through 5 May (Douglas Co.). Most migration is late March through April. The median late date for Ellis County is 1 April (10 March–18 April). Statewide, only six were banded during the spring. It is much more numerous during fall than during spring. Early arrival dates include 22 September (Morton Co.) but are usually in early October (2 October, Jefferson Co.; 8 October, Ellis Co.). Median arrival dates include 24 October (Ellis Co.) and 31 October (Rice Co.). Most migration is during mid-October through mid-November with declining numbers into early December. Seventy-eight were salvaged at television tower kills near Topeka (Shawnee Co.) between 10 and 28 October. High numbers include "hundreds" on 5 November (Meade Co.) and 62 on 28 October (tower kill, Shawnee Co.).

Comments: Birds are more local and annual numbers fluctuate more in western than in eastern Kansas. More than half of the 116 birds banded at Hays were during two fall seasons—1969 and 1972. Statewide, the number of individuals overwintering fluctuates widely from year to year. It was unusually abundant in Kansas during early December 1970, 1979–1980 (east and central), and early December 1990 (west). A high of 53 was reported on the Meade CBC during 1991–1992 and 168 on the 2002–2003 Wichita count.

Banding: 237 banded; two encounters: both in-state (at banding site within 1 month of banding).

References: Ball et al., 1995; Janzen, 2007; Kluza et al., 2001; Thompson and Ely, 1992; Tordoff and Mengel, 1956.

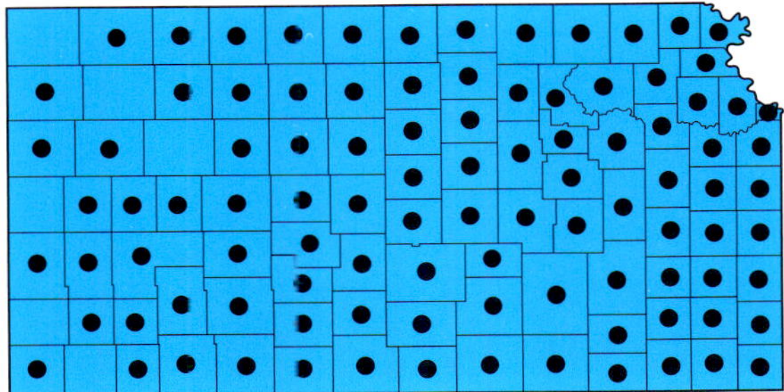

Ruby-crowned Kinglet

Regulus calendula (RCKI)

Status: Common transient statewide; rare winter resident, chiefly in the east.

Habitat: Woody or brushy areas including riparian woodlands, windbreaks, ornamental plantings such as cemeteries, and parks and suburban areas.

Migration: Early spring dates (some perhaps wintering individuals) have been reported from 21 March (Morton Co.) to 24 March (Osage Co.). Arrival is usually during early April and peaks after midmonth. Most have departed by early May but with lingering individuals to 27 May and exceptionally 6 June (Finney Co.). Median arrival dates include 4 April (Ellis Co.) and 10 April (Johnson Co.). Median late departures include 7 May (Ellis Co.). Large counts include 25 on 11 April and "many" on 13 April, both Linn County. Extreme early arrivals include 19 August (Cowley Co.) and 29 August (Harvey Co.), but arrival is usually early to mid-September. Median arrivals include 19 September (Johnson Co.) and 24 September (Ellis Co.). Peak migration is usually mid-October with numbers gradually declining into the early winter CBC period. The median late departure date of presumed transients in Ellis County is 7 November. Large counts include ca. 50 on 9–11 October (Harvey Co.), 50+ on 10 October, and ca. 30 on 3 October (Harvey Co.).

Comments: A few remain through at least early January during most winters, and overwintering has been documented from at least Cowley, Douglas, Ellis, Finney, and Morton counties and is suspected from numerous others.

Banding: 1,105 banded; one encounter. One banded in Kansas on 1 November 1973 was found dead in Texas on 21 November 1973.

References: Swanson et al., 2008; Thompson and Ely, 1992.

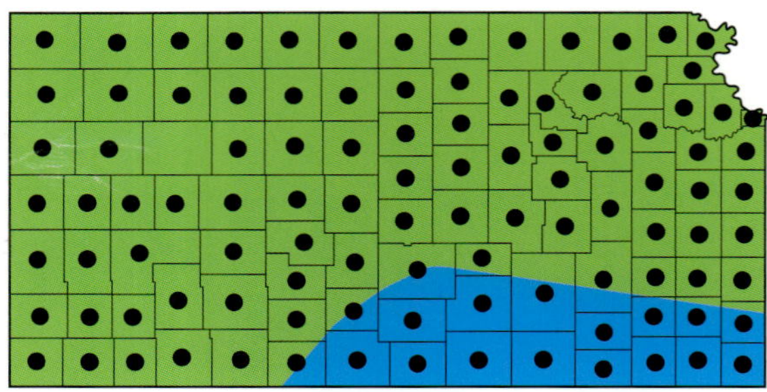

Northern Wheatear

Oenanthe oenanthe (NOWH)

© Aurélien Audevard

Status: [Hypothetical]. Vagrant. Added to the Kansas list on the basis of an adult male observed in Cheyenne County on 5 April 1997 by D. and L. Busse and D. Henderson (KBRC 97-19). A previous report of a single bird in Ottawa County on 7 November 1995 was rejected by the KBRC (95-35) for insufficient evidence.

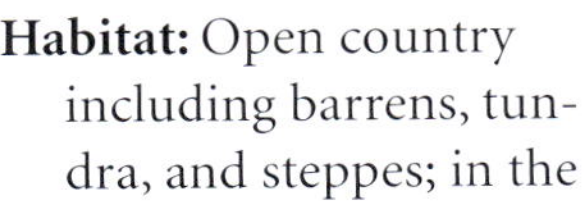

Habitat: Open country including barrens, tundra, and steppes; in the United States, overgrazed pastures, cultivated fields, and similar open areas.

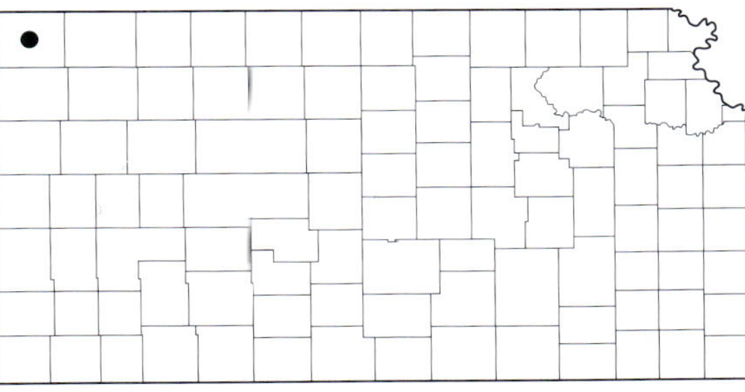

Migration: Elsewhere usually first half of May and in fall, mid-September to mid-October.

Comments: There are about seven reports from the Great Plains including South Dakota and Nebraska (both hypothetical) and southern Texas. In the United States, casual, usually during fall or early winter. It occurs most frequently in the northeast and along the Atlantic coast but casual to northern California and Virginia with vagrants to Bermuda and the West Indies. It breeds over much of the High Arctic, including Canada and Alaska, typically migrating (via presumed ancestral routes) to Asia (western population) or via Greenland and Europe to northern India and northern Africa. It resembles a bluebird in shape and habits but spends most of its time on the ground. It was presumably named for its white rump ("white arse" of old Anglo-Saxon). The white rump together with its white tail with inverted black "T pattern" is distinctive.

References: Pittman, 1996, 1998; Sharpe et al., 2001; Terres, 1980.

Eastern Bluebird

Sialia sialis (EABL)

Status: Common transient and summer resident in the east; uncommon in winter; uncommon and local in the west where rare in winter.

Habitat: Open woodlands, dispersed trees in grassland, orchards, suburban plantings, and farmsteads; westward usually riparian growth or cedar woodlands.

Migration: The timing and extent of migration are not well understood. Statewide, individuals appear at potential nest sites by mid-February to early March, but some may have wintered nearby. "Woods" (unpubl. manuscript, 1976) reported arrivals in Shawnee County from mid-February through 7 March. Obvious transients have been reported 8–25 March. As in spring, the fall migration is poorly documented. Flocking begins by 14 July ("large flock," Doniphan Co.) through September and continues into winter with most migration probably in October, including 7–8 October ("good flight," Johnson Co.) and 18 October ("many migrating," Morton Co.). Other large counts include 75 on 28 October (Douglas Co.) and 40+ (4 October, Crawford Co.). Wintering birds often occur in sheltered areas near open water or near fruiting trees and shrubs.

Breeding: Nest-building has been reported as early as 14 March (Cherokee Co.). "Woods" (unpubl. manuscript, 1976) summarized results of 256 nests from boxes established by L. Dittemore in Shawnee County during the 1960s. The earliest clutch was on 30 March, the latest 30 July. R. Johnston reported 54 records of breeding between 1 April and 20 July with modal dates of 25 April and 5 June for first and second clutches, respectively. Other dates of late nesting include 11 August (newly hatched young) and 23 August (nestlings). M. L. Myers reported an unusual fourth brood on 6 September and L. Dittemore reported a female carrying nesting material on 13 October. KBBAT found confirmed nesting in 378 blocks, due to the use of nest boxes that bluebirds readily utilize.

Comments: The establishment of "bluebird trails" (lines of nest boxes) can make a noticeable difference in local populations.

See page 501 for banding information.

References: Allen, 1872; Busby and Zimmerman, 2001; Cable et al., 1996; Johnston, 1964a; Menke, 1894.

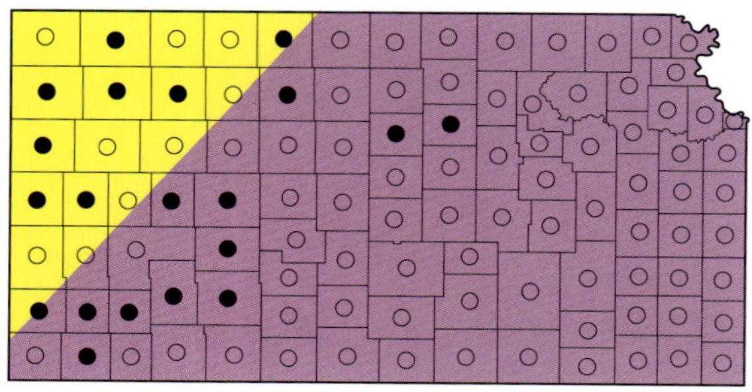

Western Bluebird

Sialia mexicana (WEBL)

Status: Casual visitant to the extreme west.

Habitat: In Kansas, in riparian woodlands and ornamental plantings.

Migration: The few spring reports, most unconfirmed, are between 4 March and 14 May. Except for the 26 September report all fall reports are during the period 18 October–3 January. Most reports from the east are from CBCs.

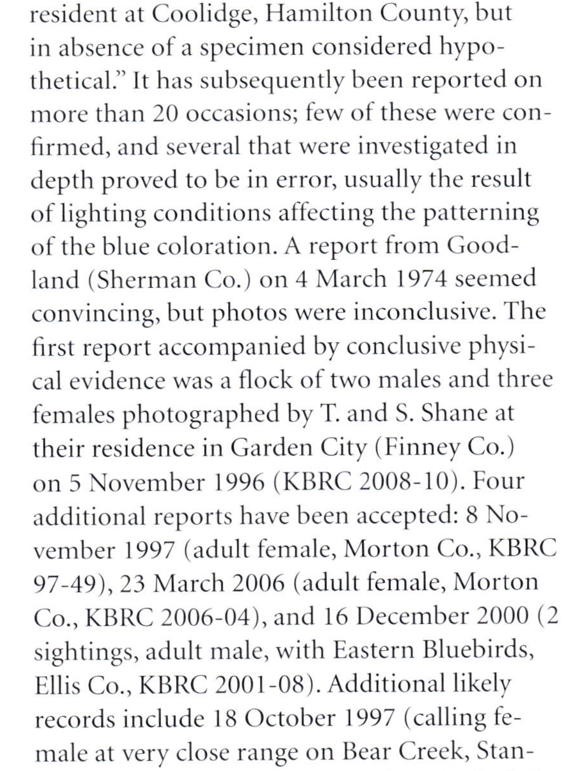

Comments: It was first reported from Kansas by C. Long who stated "reported as a winter resident at Coolidge, Hamilton County, but in absence of a specimen considered hypothetical." It has subsequently been reported on more than 20 occasions; few of these were confirmed, and several that were investigated in depth proved to be in error, usually the result of lighting conditions affecting the patterning of the blue coloration. A report from Goodland (Sherman Co.) on 4 March 1974 seemed convincing, but photos were inconclusive. The first report accompanied by conclusive physical evidence was a flock of two males and three females photographed by T. and S. Shane at their residence in Garden City (Finney Co.) on 5 November 1996 (KBRC 2008-10). Four additional reports have been accepted: 8 November 1997 (adult female, Morton Co., KBRC 97-49), 23 March 2006 (adult female, Morton Co., KBRC 2006-04), and 16 December 2000 (2 sightings, adult male, with Eastern Bluebirds, Ellis Co., KBRC 2001-08). Additional likely records include 18 October 1997 (calling female at very close range on Bear Creek, Stanton Co.). Several recent reports have included reports of call notes, including one "heard only" on 26 September 2008 (Morton Co.). The species is probably overreported in Kansas.

Banding: One reported but probably an error.

References: Long, 1940; Otte, 2007, 2009; Pittman, 1998; Rintoul, 2002; Thompson and Ely, 1992.

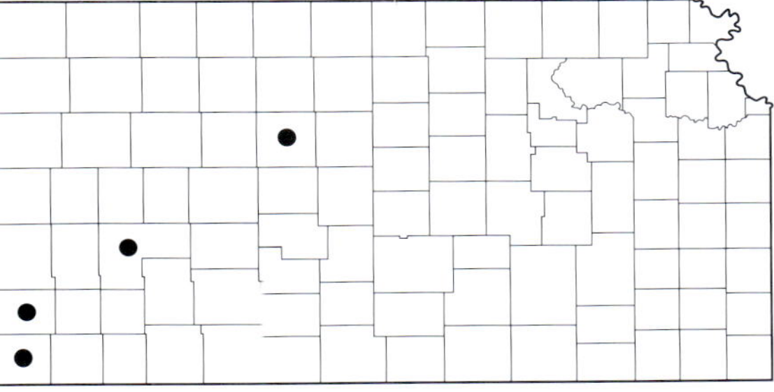

Mountain Bluebird

Sialia currucoides (MOBL)

Status: Regular but uncommon transient and winter resident in the west; usually common in the Red Hills in winter and uncommon to rare eastward during winter.

Habitat: Open country with scattered trees, especially conifers; also windbreaks, cemeteries, parks, cultivated fields, and, rarely, residential areas.

Migration: Spring migration in the west is apparently 5 March through mid-April but with stragglers through 5 May. The typical median date for Ellis County is 27 March. Individuals reported 23 May through 10 June (Ellis and Finney cos.) may have been summering. Eastward, wintering birds depart by 31 March (Russell Co.). The earliest modern report is 6 October in Barton County. In the west, birds are widespread by midmonth with a median arrival in Ellis County of 21 October. Eastward, early dates include 16 October (Harvey Co.) and 22 October (Chase Co.) with most arrivals in early November. Large numbers include highs of 100+ on 21 October (Morton Co.), 100+ on 28 October (Trego Co.), and "hundreds" in windbreaks in west-central Kansas on 24–25 November in 1998. In most areas numbers decrease by early December.

Breeding: Occasional breeding is suggested by the observation of four fledged young on 8 June 1986 (Wallace Co.), a fledged juvenile collected on 20 June 1911 in Hamilton County (not Greeley Co., KU 5900), and an adult in breeding condition taken on 5 June 1950 in Finney County (not Stanton Co., KU 32576). The only confirmed breeding is of a mixed pair that nested on the Konza Prairie (Riley Co.) in 1997. Cavitt and others reported that a male mated with two different female Eastern Bluebirds, producing two hybrid broods, one fledging 26 May and the second (presumably) after 12 July.

Comments: Recently, the largest numbers of wintering birds have been in the Red Hills. Highest numbers on CBCs have been in the Red Hills (Barber County; 1,440 in 1996); 234 at Wilson Reservoir (Russell County; 1995); and 179 in Trego County (1993). Other large counts include 500+ in a 17-mile stretch in the Red Hills on 6 December and 200 in Sedgwick County during 1988–1989. At the other extreme, only 21 were recorded in the entire state on the 2001–2002 CBC with 20 of these in the Red Hills.

See page 501 for banding information.

References: Busby and Zimmerman, 2001; Cable et al., 1996; Cavitt et al., 1998; Goss, 1891; Thompson, 1997; Thompson and Ely, 1992; Thompson and Young, 1996.

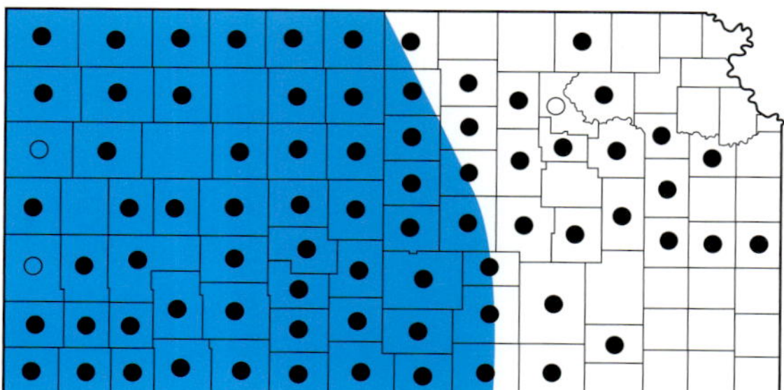

Townsend's Solitaire

Myadestes townsendi (TOSO)

Status: Uncommon transient and low-density winter resident in western and central Kansas; rare to casual in the east, usually during winter.

Habitat: Found in riparian woodlands, cedars, parks, cemeteries, and suburban areas where fruit-bearing trees (especially cedars) are present.

Migration: Most birds depart by mid-March with stragglers into April. Median departure for Ellis County is 5 April. Four unusually late dates include 24 April (Cowley Co.), 29 April (Stafford Co.), 10 May (Cheyenne Co.), and 15 May (Morton Co.). Usually arrives in late September and early October with early dates of 5 September (Morton Co.) and 17 September (Harvey Co.). The median arrival date in Ellis County is 16 October. The highest fall count is of 20+ scattered individuals in Morton County on 28 September. It is most numerous and widespread during December and January.

Comments: Wintering birds are typically solitary with higher densities in areas with abundant cedars or other fruiting trees and shrubs. It is sporadic at most eastern localities, usually in suburban parks or cedar groves. For example, it was reported on only 18 CBCs in Harvey County during the period 1949–1998. Statewide, high CBC totals include 16 in Scott County, 14 in Morton County, and 13 in Finney County. Unusually large numbers were reported during early winter 1996–1997 with 92 individuals reported east to Riley and Sumner counties on 20 of the 54 CBCs.

Banding: 19 banded; no encounters.

References: Cable et al., 1996; Graber and Graber, 1951; Platt, 2002; Thompson and Ely, 1992.

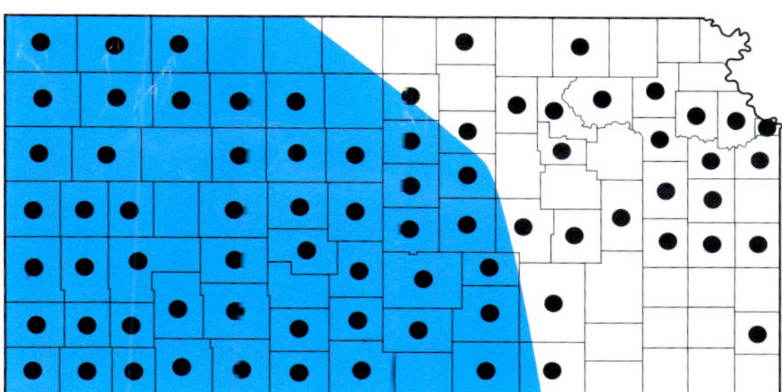

Veery

Catharus fuscescens (VEER)

© David Seibel

Status: Regular but low-density transient, especially in the east; rare in fall.

Habitat: Wooded habitats, including riparian, parks, and residential areas with understory, often near water.

Migration: Specimens are available for the period 5–29 May, and sightings extend this period from 20 April and possibly to 6 or 9 June (unconfirmed). Median arrival statewide is about 9 May (22 April–20 May). Median arrival for Ellis County is 12 May; median departure is 24 May. At Hays (Ellis Co.), 86 percent of the 94 Veerys banded were during spring (5–31 May), and more than 75 percent of these were banded during the period 12–24 May (median 19 May). It is much less common in fall than in spring with about one-fourth as many sightings. Specimens are available for the period 5–28 September (median 16 September). Sight records extend this period to 27 August (banded) and perhaps 30 September. The median fall arrival date at Hays, 6 September, coincided with the median banding date of the 13 individuals handled.

Breeding: Although N. Goss stated that it "probably" bred in Kansas, there is no evidence to support this.

Comments: Comments by H. Tordoff and R. Johnston that the Veery is "fairly common" or "more numerous," respectively, in the west are either a "lapsus" or the result of confusion with other *Catharus* species. Banding and collecting, since at least 1960, clearly show that it is the least common *Catharus* in the state. Western Veerys are darker than eastern ones and can easily be confused with western races of both Swainson's Thrush and Hermit Thrush.

Banding: 165 banded; no encounters.

References: Goss, 1886; Johnston, 1965; Thompson and Ely, 1992; Tordoff, 1956.

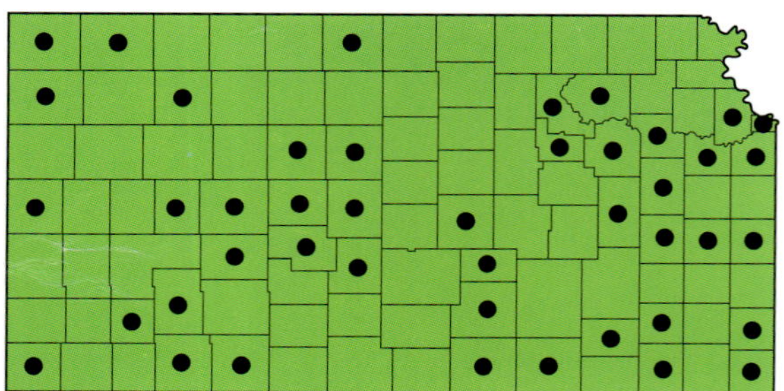

Gray-cheeked Thrush

Catharus minimus (GCTH)

Status: Regular but low-density transient, especially in the east; rare in fall.

Habitat: Wooded habitats, including riparian areas, parks, suburban areas, windbreaks, and farmsteads; prefers shady woods with understory.

Migration: Specimens are available for the period 25 April–15 June, and sight records extend this period to 19 April (Johnson Co.) and 27 June (Wallace Co.). The main migration occurs during a brief period. At Hays (Ellis Co.) 158 birds were banded between 2 May and 3 June with nearly 75 percent banded between 8 and 15 May. Median arrival dates include 2 May (Johnson Co.) and 7 May (Ellis Co.). In 1949, the peak in Shawnee County was 5 May. The median departure for Ellis County is 20 May. It has recently been considered a rare but regular transient in Morton County based on singing birds. In 1973, it was said to have been "very numerous" and to have outnumbered the Swainson's Thrush in Johnson County and during 1976 was "very abundant" in Johnson County and "above average in numbers" in Cowley County. Very few are reported in fall. N. Goss reported migration during "September," and H. Harris reported it in the Kansas City area in "late September." However, there are no fall specimens, and only three have ever been reported as banded in the state during fall. The 14 fall reports (none confirmed and many probably in error) have a median date of 17–18 September (1 September–24 October). In Missouri, most fall data are from tower kills, but none were found at tower kills near Topeka, perhaps because all major tower kills reported have been from 25 September or later.

Comments: The species continues to pose identification problems, especially in the west, and great care should be used in the identification of any nonsinging individuals. Any birds found dead, especially in fall, should be preserved.

Banding: 586 banded; no encounters.

References: Ball et al., 1995; Cable et al., 1996; Goss, 1891; Harris, 1919; Robbins and Easterla, 1992; Thompson and Ely, 1992; Tordoff and Mengel, 1956.

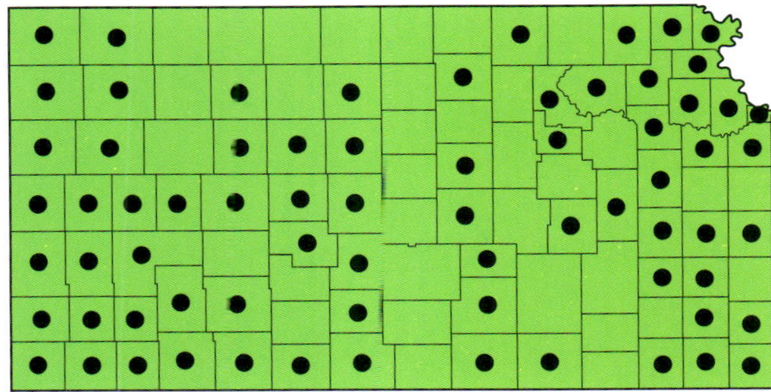

Swainson's Thrush

Catharus ustulatus (SWTH)

Status: Common transient statewide; by far the most common *Catharus* occurring in the state.

Habitat: Widespread in wooded habitats, including riparian areas, parks, residential areas, windbreaks, and farmsteads.

Migration: Very early arrivals include 3 April (Cowley Co.) and 5 April with most during late April. Specimens are available from 24 April to 11 June (Rawlins Co.). Median arrival dates include 30 April (Johnson Co.), 3 May (Ellis Co.), and 9 May (Rice Co.). Most migration is during May with large movements reported on 11 May (Johnson Co.), a "peak" on 11 May (Shawnee Co.), a "heavy migration" on 23 May (Morton Co.), and stragglers through 13 June (Douglas Co.). Median departure dates include 28–29 May (Ellis Co.) and 31 May (Johnson Co.). High counts include 82 on 17 May 1910 (Sedgwick Co.). The fall migration is poorly documented. Specimens are available 3 September–7 October, and sight records extend this period to 2 August (Sedgwick Co.) and 31 October (Harvey Co.). Median arrival for Ellis County is 9 September. Most migration is during September and October. In Ellis County, fall numbers are much lower than in spring, and the peak banding was between 16 and 23 September. A sight report from 15 November (Morton Co.), if accurate, is exceptional. Occasional reports during the CBC period need confirmation and are more likely Hermit Thrushes.

Comments: Although not mentioned by H. Menke in the 19th century, it is now the most common *Catharus* in western Kansas. Eastward, in spring it is often one of the dominant transients in open undergrowth beneath taller trees in parks and residential areas. At such times singing is frequent.

Banding: 4,613 banded; four encounters. Of the three banded in Kansas, two individuals banded during May were recovered on or near the breeding areas the same season in Alaska and British Columbia during July and August, respectively. The third, a young bird banded 12 May 1979, was shot on or near its wintering area in El Salvador in June 1984. One found dead in southeastern Kansas on the late date of 14 June 1985 was probably returning from its second winter in the tropics. It had been banded as a young bird in Pennsylvania on 13 September 1983. Oldest 3 years.

References: Cable et al., 1996; Janzen, 2007; Menke, 1894; Thompson and Ely, 1992.

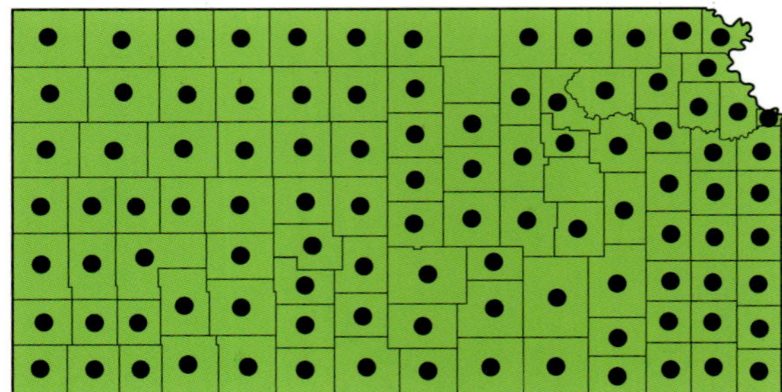

Hermit Thrush

Catharus guttatus (HETH)

Status: Regular but uncommon transient in the west and east, less common in the central portion; low-density winter resident, chiefly east of the Flint Hills.

© David Seibel

Habitat: Any wooded habitat, riparian woodlands, woodland with understory, parks, and suburban areas.

Migration: Dates of early arrival of presumed transients include 1 April in the east and 10 April and 27 April in the west. Most migration is from mid-April through mid-May with stragglers through 8 June (Morton Co.) and 10 June (Jewell Co.). In Ellis County, the median of 10 spring records is 4–5 May. There are few dated fall records. In the east, extreme dates are 8 September and 9 November; in the west 4 September (Stanton Co.) and 28 November (Russell Co.). Sightings peak in mid-October then decline by mid-November. Data are inadequate to confidently distinguish between transient and wintering individuals. Reports from December through March are probably overwintering individuals. Although most midwinter reports are east of the Flint Hills, a few occur each year farther west. One banded 16 November in Ellis County and recaptured in the same yard on 12 April probably overwintered. It has been reported on roughly one-fourth of the 500+ CBCs during the last 10 years with totals ranging from 8 to 65 individuals. The maximum on any individual count was 13 at Arkansas City in 2008–2009.

Comments: Highest densities occur in eastern and far western Kansas. This was the least common *Catharus* banded in Ellis County (1960–1995), composing less than 1 percent of the *Catharus* thrushes handled during that period. Identification is made easier if an individual lifts its tail abruptly then allows it to drop slowly downward or if the bird is from a population in which the reddish tail contrasts markedly in color from the rump and back. The problems of accurately identifying *Catharus* in the field are compounded in the Hermit Thrush by the variability among the various races reaching the state. Through fading of its freshly molted fall plumage and loss of feather edges by wear, an individual can look very different by the end of the spring migration. Comparison with museum specimens is tricky because of the effects of foxing (change of color) and postmortem aging. The entire group remains a challenge.

Banding: 114 banded; no encounters.

References: Cable et al., 1996; Thompson and Ely, 1992.

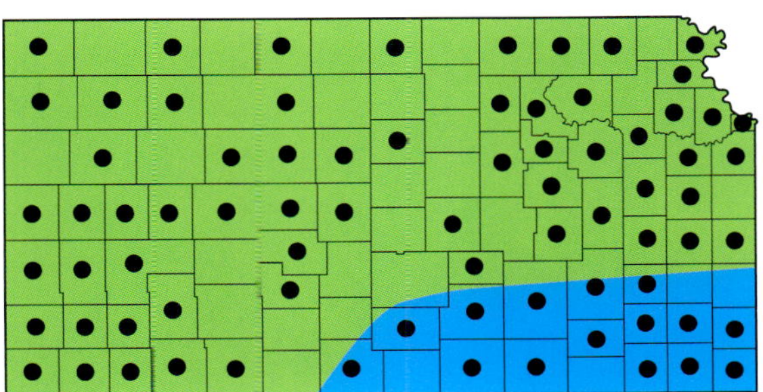

Wood Thrush

Hylocichla mustelina (WOTH)

Status: Uncommon transient and summer resident east of the Flint Hills; locally along river systems into central Kansas.

Habitat: Woodlands and riparian and residential areas with a well-developed understory.

Migration: Earliest arrival dates are 19 March and 3 April, but arrival is usually late April or early May. Johnston reported a median arrival of 9 May (19 April–20 May). Late dates in nonbreeding areas include 10 May (Edwards Co.), 11 May (Morton Co.), and 25 May (Ellis Co.). There are few documented records after mid-August, and most migration appears to be during September and early October. R. Johnston gave 15 September (3 September–1 October) for median departure. Late fall dates include 18 and 29 October. In the west, dates from Ellis County are 4 September–22 October with a very late date of 6 November. Elsewhere dates are 8 September (Russell Co.) through 2 October.

Breeding: Once breeding locally along streams northwestward to Decatur County, its westward limit is currently east of a line from Sumner, Saline, and Cloud counties. Actual nesting data are few. Johnston reported the modal date for laying (first clutches) as 5 June with 55 percent of all eggs laid between 21 May and 14 June. Statewide, nest-building has been reported 13 May–4 July, eggs 20 May–9 August, and recently fledged young 9 June–8 July.

Comments: The core breeding range during the late 19th century was apparently in the northeast, west, and south to at least Marshall, Dickinson, and Cowley counties. In Shawnee County, it was considered "exceedingly abundant" in 1871, was "most common of the thrushes" in 1909, but was "rare" before 1976. Near the turn of the century, it was "common in summer" in Riley and Cowley counties, then disappeared until recently, when it seems to be making a comeback in Cowley County. A survey of isolated remnants of good habitat along streams in north-central Kansas in 1981 and 1983 found singing males west to Republic, Cloud, Lincoln, and Saline counties with confirmed nesting in Saline County. More recently, KBBAT confirmed breeding at only five sites, all along the Missouri River or in Douglas County. The westernmost "probable" reports were in Sumner, Dickinson, and extreme southeastern Riley counties.

Banding: 318 banded; no encounters.

References: Allen, 1872; Busby and Zimmerman, 2001; Johnston, 1964a, 1965; Lohoefener et al., 1983; Thompson and Ely, 1992; Wolfe, 1961.

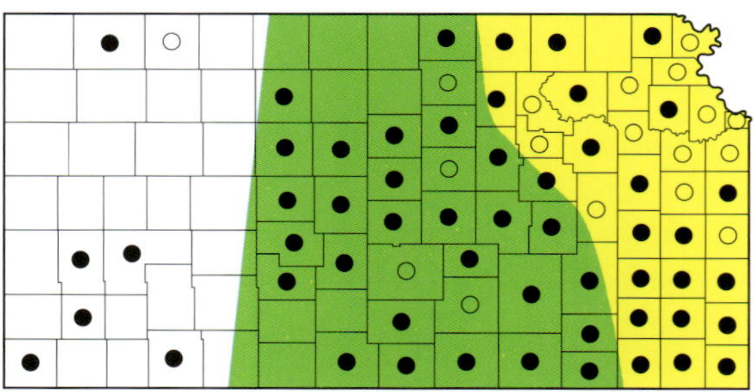

American Robin

Turdus migratorius (AMRO)

© Judd Patterson

Status: Present statewide all year; common transient statewide; most common in the east during summer; variable numbers during winter.

Habitat: All wooded habitats, especially open woodlands and riparian and residential areas.

Migration: Migratory movements are often confused by local movements of wintering flocks. In Ellis County, individuals of the breeding population return by late February or early March and are common by midmonth. Large flocks of presumed transients are present through at least 21 March, and most transients are probably gone by early April. In the west, migration continues into early May (Morton Co.). Flocks of 1,000 or more presumed transients have been reported 3 October–1 November. Summering birds and most transients probably leave by early November. During some winters large numbers remain and form large roosting flocks, often with various species of blackbirds.

Breeding: R. Johnston reported 334 records of breeding between 1 April and 20 July. The modal date for the laying of first clutches was 25 April with nearly half of all eggs laid during the period 11–30 April. "Woods" (unpubl. manuscript, 1976) gave egg dates (150+ active nests) between 27 March and 29 May in Shawnee County. Statewide, nest-building has been reported 3 April–10 July, eggs 27 March–9 August, and recently fledged young 4 May–20 July.

Comments: During presettlement days it apparently bred only in extreme eastern Kansas, appearing westward during migration and less often in winter. For example, Allen saw only two birds, both in Shawnee County, during a 2-month visit to Kansas during May and June 1871. By the 1920s, it was a common breeder in Decatur, Finney, and Hamilton counties, where it had previously been primarily a transient or winter visitant. It remains an uncommon breeder in the extreme southwest. Impressive roosting congregations occur some years. The largest reported to date, in Arkansas City (Cowley Co.), built up rapidly to 50,00–100,000 birds, peaked on 21 February 1974 at an estimated 250,000–500,000, then declined to several thousand during the first half of March, probably as transients moved northward.

See page 502 for banding information.

References: Allen, 1872; Betts, 1958; Busby and Zimmerman, 2001; Rising, 1974; Thompson and Ely, 1992; Thompson and Young, 1998, 1999; Young and Thompson, 1995.

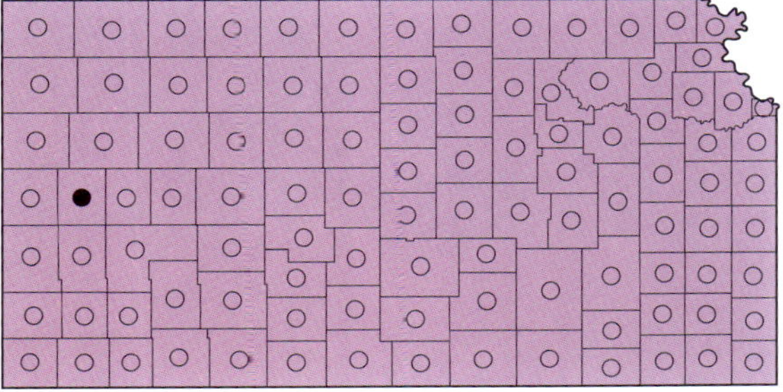

Varied Thrush

Ixoreus naevius (VATH)

© Judd Patterson

Status: Casual winter visitant, chiefly in the west.

Habitat: Riparian growth or residential yards.

Migration: The earliest fall arrivals are 22 September (Morton Co.) and 9 October (Finney Co.), with most appearing between 21 October and 23 November, or during the CBC period. The eight late winter–spring sightings were between 7 February and 5 April with a single sighting on 9 May (Wallace Co.).The most extended stays, presumably the same individuals, are 21 October 1992–14 January 1993 (Finney Co.), December 1988–23 March 1989 (Sedgwick Co.), and 23 December 1974–5 April 1975 (Sherman Co.).

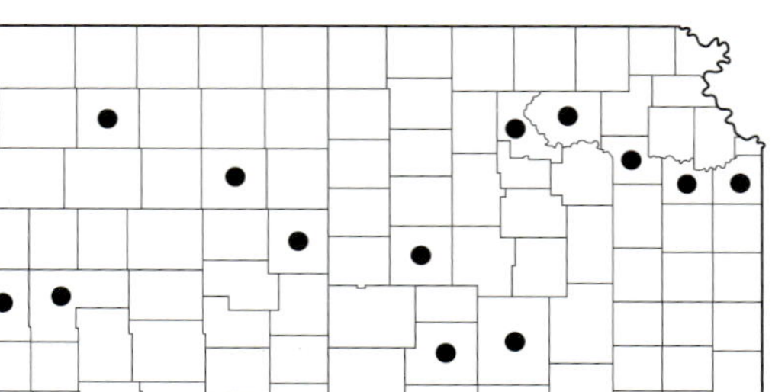

Comments: It was first reported in Kansas by H. Menke from a specimen taken 17 October 1891 in Finney County and subsequently lost. It was not reported for another half century but has since been reported with increasing frequency. The second and third reports were during the winter of 1956–1957 in Douglas and Pottawatomie counties. It was reported 3 times during the 1970s, 7 times during the 1980s, 10 times during the 1990s, and 6 times during the 2000s. Multiple sightings occurred during six of these winters. All sightings were of single birds and were either in riparian woodlands or in residential areas, often at or near feeders. A number of individuals were first reported by nonbirders as "funny-looking robins." It typically forages on or near the ground and is generally silent.

References: Cable et al., 1996; Menke, 1894; Thompson and Ely, 1992.

Gray Catbird

Dumetella carolinensis (GRCA)

© Judd Patterson

Status: Common transient and summer resident in eastern and central Kansas, becoming progressively less common westward.

Habitat: Thickets in woodland edge and riparian and residential areas.

Migration: Early dates include 12 April (Cowley Co.) and 21 April (Douglas Co.), but most early arrivals are during late April or early May. The median date of early arrival is 7 May for Ellis, Rice, and Russell counties. Late dates for presumed transients include 13 June (Morton Co.). Most fall migration is during September with movements reported 21–30 September (Shawnee Co.) and a flock of 12 on 20 September (Reno Co.). Most banding at Hays was during 10–20 September. The median late date for Rice County was 25 September and for Ellis County, 1 October. Other late dates include 14 October (many, Geary Co.) with stragglers to 2 November (Morton Co.), 16 November (Douglas Co.), and a few lingering into the CBC period, chiefly in residential yards.

Breeding: KBBAT failed to confirm any nesting west of a line from Norton and Comanche counties. R. Johnston reported 77 records of breeding, 11 May–31 July, giving 25 May as the modal date for egg-laying and with 57 percent of all clutches laid 21 May–10 June. In Shawnee County eggs were observed 10 May–8 July and young in the nest 16 June–23 July. Statewide, nest-building has been reported 4 May–29 June and newly fledged young 14 June–29 August.

Comments: Catbirds require dense shrubby thickets for nesting and are more secretive than other Kansas mimids. One of its calls, a cat-like "meeeaah," is often the best indication of its presence. However, birds frequently occur in residential areas, and some wintering individuals have been associated with feeders. Survival through the winter has not yet been documented, but individuals have survived through at least 26 January; one seen on 1 April in Hays (Ellis Co.) may have survived the previous winter.

Banding: 3,545 banded; 29 encounters: 26 instate; 2 from Kansas to: Mexico, MN. The first, banded 2 October 1971, was found dead in Mexico on 20 August 1973; the other, banded 17 May 1980, was killed by a cat in Minnesota during July 1980. One found dead in Kansas on 24 October 1956 had been banded in New York on 21 September 1956. Oldest 8 years, 9 months.

References: Busby and Zimmerman, 2001; Cable et al., 1996; Thompson and Ely, 1992.

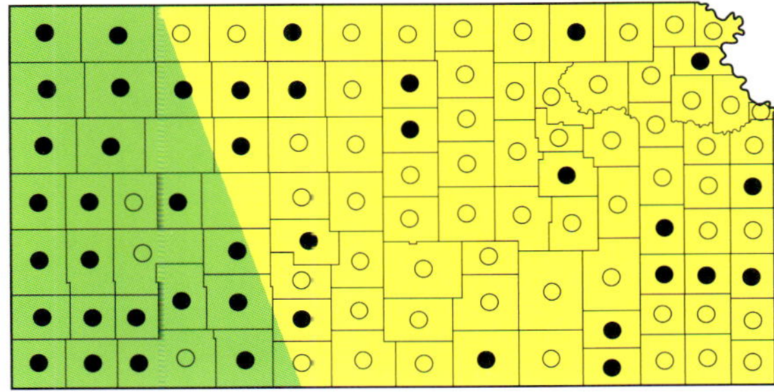

Northern Mockingbird

Mimus polyglottos (NOMO)

Status: Common resident, partly migratory in the east; uncommon transient and summer resident in the west.

© Judd Patterson

Habitat: Riparian areas, open areas with scattered thickets, windbreaks, hedgerows, and residential areas.

Migration: Individuals identified as spring arrivals are reported from 4 March through 23 April. Examples of median arrival include 14 April (Ellis Co.) and 4–20 April (Rice Co.). Apparently most migration is during April. At Hays (Ellis Co.), wintering birds departed about 31 March (24 March–4 April), but whether they continued northward or dispersed locally is unknown. Present data are too few to document the fall movement. The number of sightings decreases rapidly after early October in open areas and 20 October in urban areas. It is present all year in much of the state but is greatly reduced in numbers during winter. Wintering birds appear to be "in place" by mid-November, occasionally late October, to be most obvious from December through mid-February, and to leave in late March.

Breeding: R. Johnston reported 5 June as a modal date for first clutches; more recently the median date (41 clutches) is 29 May (20 April–1 July). Statewide, nest-building has been reported 28 April–17 June and recently fledged young 10 June–30 July. KBBAT reported it most frequently in the eastern Flint Hills and eastward. Westward its distribution was reduced by lack of breeding habitat in areas of extensive agriculture. But even here it nests successfully at farmsteads and in gullies and windbreaks. It commonly nests in suburban yards, and its loud and persistent singing make it a familiar bird throughout most of the state.

Comments: It was common in summer along Big Timber Creek (Rush Co.) and in Riley County, "plentiful" in Finney County during the 19th century, and a "very common summer resident" in Decatur County at the turn of the 20th century. More recently, it has been considered resident at least in southern Kansas. Wintering birds, often in towns, are highly visible and confuse the migration picture. Such individual birds frequently defend fruiting trees and shrubs from birds of other species.

Banding: 259 banded; five encounters: all in-state. Oldest 5 years.

References: Allen, 1872; Blachly, 1879–1880; Busby and Zimmerman, 2001; Johnston, 1964a; Menke, 1894; Thompson and Ely, 1992.

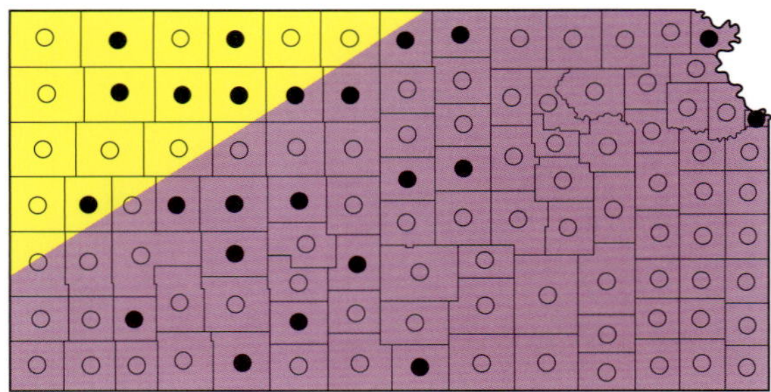

Sage Thrasher

Oreoscoptes montanus (SATH)

© Judd Patterson

Status: Rare visitant to the southwest, usually in fall and winter; probably nested at least once; vagrant eastward.

Habitat: Sand-sage grassland and associated riparian growth, windbreaks, and ornamental plantings.

Migration: Four of the five spring sightings are from the southwest, 23 March–23 April; the fifth is 4 March from Trego County. Most sightings have been in September. Fall dates for Morton County are 10 August through 17 October and 1 November. Usually only a few individuals are seen, but T. Cable and S. Seltman reported a high of 18 on 27 September 1986. Elsewhere in the southwest, sightings were between 12 August (Grant Co.) and 11 October (Gove Co.). CBC reports suggest at least occasional wintering in the southwest. An individual wintered in Rush County from 6 November 1982 to 22 January 1983. Other peripheral sightings (21 September–9 February) were likely vagrants.

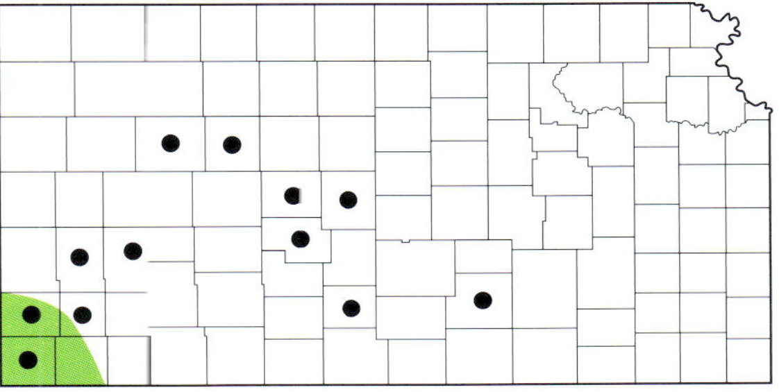

Breeding: An immature in juvenal plumage (KU 41709) taken from a family group on 17 July 1963 in Morton County strongly suggests breeding. The only other summer report is 11 June.

Comments: Although considered a "rare transient" by H. Tordoff and R. Johnston, most sightings are probably of vagrants or transients displaced eastward by weather. Most sightings are from Morton County with reports from all months except May.

References: Cable et al., 1996; Janzen, 2007; Johnston, 1963, 1964a, 1965; Thompson and Ely, 1992; Tordoff, 1956.

Brown Thrasher

Toxostoma rufum (BRTH)

© David Seibel

Status: Common transient and summer resident statewide; a few overwinter.

Habitat: Thickets at woodland edge, riparian woodland, windbreaks, parks, and residential yards.

Migration: Early arrival dates are usually about 1 April in the east and much later westward. March reports may be of overwintering birds. Median first arrivals include 7 April (Cowley Co.), 15 April (Rice Co.), 20 April (Ellis Co.), and 26 April (Finney Co.). Large numbers or peak movements have been reported between 19 April and 5 May, and most transients have probably departed by mid-May. Numbers decline after mid-September. R. Johnston gave 28 September as the median departure date in the northeast and "Woods" (unpubl. manuscript, 1976) reported a fall peak on 12–25 September in Shawnee County. Departure is usually later with normal departure of 14 October for Cowley and Sumner counties and stragglers to 3 November. Westward, median late departure dates include 16 October (Ellis Co.) and 24–25 October (Rice Co.). Small numbers occur through the CBC period with a high of 6 on the Halstead–Newton count in 1996. Individuals are known to have survived the winter north and west to Meade and Sherman counties. In winter it is usually solitary, but a flock of 12 was reported from Decatur County on 25 December 1977.

Breeding: R. Johnston reported 72 records of breeding near Concordia (Cloud Co.) during 1930–1936 by J. Porter, with the earliest clutch on 3 May. He later reported 237 records of breeding (most from northeastern Kansas), between 1 May and 20 July, with 15 May as the modal date for egg-laying and with one-third of all eggs laid 11–20 May. Statewide, nest-building has been reported 1 April–29 June, eggs 1 May–15 July, and recently fledged young 16 May–30 July. It is apparently single-brooded but with much renesting after nest failures.

Comments: Lowest densities are in the southwest where T. Cable noted that at times it can be scarce or even absent in Morton County. It is much more common in the northwest. It is often conspicuous when singing (typically from the top of a tall tree) or feeding on a lawn with robins. It is also fearless in defending its nest or young. At other times it is more secretive and best found by its loud call, a smacking "spuck."

See page 502 for banding information.

References: Busby and Zimmerman, 2001; Cable et al., 1996; Johnston, 1958, 1964a; Thompson and Ely, 1992; Young, 1993.

Curve-billed Thrasher

Toxostoma curvirostre (CBTH)

Status: Regular visitant and sporadic resident in the southwest; casual eastward, usually along rivers during fall and winter.

Habitat: Shrub-dotted, sand-sage grassland in sandhills near rivers; winters in sheltered ravines, cemeteries, and suburban yards.

Migration: Breeding birds are presumed to be resident. Most reports of nonbreeders are between 28 August and 20 April with most during fall. Although many reports are from the CBC period, sightings from Barton and Norton counties were 27 May and 24 June, respectively.

Breeding: M. Schwilling, in reviewing all Kansas records through 1979, reported at least six active nests from Gray, Hamilton, and Morton counties during 1976–1986. Interestingly, nearly all were associated with the few, scattered clumps of cholla cactus (*Opuntia* sp.) known in the area. More recent nests have been in residential yards in Elkhart and in the Richfield (Morton Co.) and Hugoton (Stevens Co.) cemeteries. The last nesting example in Stevens County is especially remarkable in that it involved three active nests spaced about 75 m apart in "sculptured" junipers with all feeding young on the extremely early date of 18 May. Data from 1977 and 1978 indicate double broods. Nest-building has been reported 14 April–26 June, eggs on 24 June, and recently fledged young on 19 July.

Comments: It was first reported from Kansas on 1 May 1950 by R. and J. Graber, a sight record during their 3.5-month study in the southwest. There are a few scattered records during the next two decades, and a small nesting population was present during at least 1976 (probably 1974) through 1979. Scattered nesting was reported through the 1980s, but M. Schwilling, in a survey of all known nesting areas during 1991 and 1993, could find only one pair of nesting birds (Elkhart, Morton Co.). He concluded that its expansion into Kansas as a breeding species was a natural but temporary event. S. Seltman (pers. comm.) found three pairs nesting in Stevens County in mid-May 2009; with at least two birds there on subsequent visits, this event may be repeated. It is interesting that one spent the summers of 1996 and 1997 in a dense salt-cedar thicket near the CBWA, and one in Cowley County was in a dense multiflora rose thicket.

© Jim Burns

Banding: Three banded; no encounters.

References: Busby and Zimmerman, 2001; Cable et al., 1996; Schwilling, 1980; Thompson and Ely, 1992.

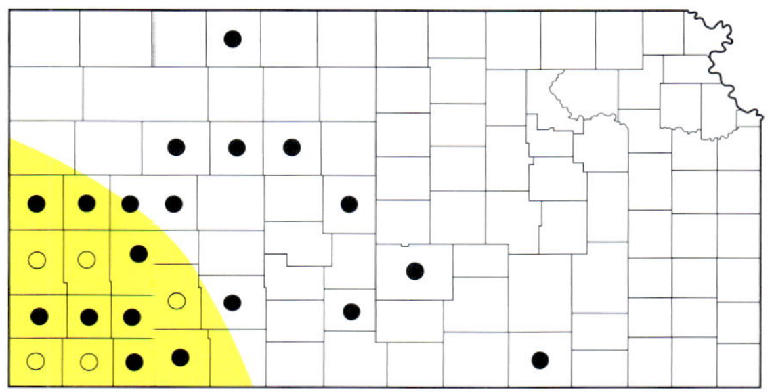

European Starling

Sturnus vulgaris (EUST)

Status: Introduced. Common permanent resident statewide.

Habitat: During the breeding season, wherever potential nest cavities exist; at other seasons, favors cultivated areas, feedlots, and residential areas.

Migration: The breeding population is apparently resident. Migration, though poorly documented, is probably late September into November and from February through mid-March. In most years CBC totals are in the tens of thousands but exceeded 1 million birds on the 1999–2000 and 2000–2001 counts, largely due to a "winter roost" in Arkansas City (Cowley Co.).

Breeding: Nesting was documented in 1940 (Doniphan Co.) but probably occurred by 1935 or 1936, because it was by then well established at Lawrence and Wichita. R. Johnston gave 15 April and 5 June as modal dates for egg-laying for first and second broods, respectively. Statewide, nest-building has been reported 18 March–28 August, eggs 25 March–22 July, young in nest 30 April–19 June, and recently fledged young 2 May–9 July.

Comments: O. Smock reported the species in Arkansas City in 1926, but L. Goodrich claimed the first arrivals were during the winter of 1929–1930. Winter specimens (KU) indicate presence in several southeastern counties by 1930 (Allen, Anderson, and Labette cos.), 1933 (Sedgwick and Sumner cos.), 1934 (Greenwood Co.), and 1936 (Osage Co.). Flocks appeared in the Wichita area on 28 February 1932 and near Lawrence on 25 December 1933. It was soon "quite common" at Wichita, had been documented at Manhattan, and reached Topeka by 1936 (28 March). Flocks were in Leavenworth by fall 1939, Ellsworth by 1938, Hays by 8 February 1940, and Cheyenne County by November 1956 (common by 1976). Expansion through southwestern Kansas was slower. It was not seen there by R. and J. Graber and rarely by M. Schwilling through the 1950s. M. Schwilling's notes have entries for Finney (1951, 20 May, nest), Kearny (1951, 22 April, nest), and Morton (1954, 27 September, ca. 25) counties. In 1965, J. Rising found starlings only in Meade, Finney (common), and Hamilton (common) counties.

See page 502 for banding information.

References: Busby and Zimmerman, 2001; Cable et al., 1996; Janzen, 2007; Johnston, 1964a; Seibel, 1978; Sharpe et al., 2001; Sutton, 1967; Thompson and Ely, 1992; Thompson and Young, 2000, 2001.

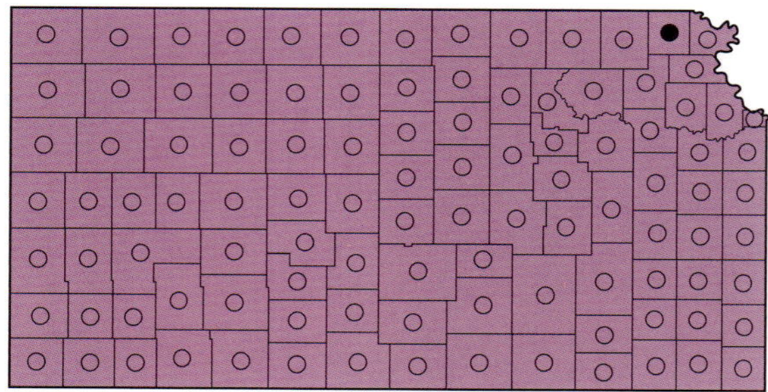

American Pipit

Anthus rubescens (AMPI)

Status: Common transient statewide; casual in winter.

Habitat: Moist areas with low or sparse vegetation such as muddy fields and reservoir margins, and burned prairie in spring.

Migration: Early March dates may include wintering birds. Usual extreme dates for spring in the west are 18 March–21 May with most migrating during April. Large numbers include "thousands" on 13 April (Sumner Co.), 1,000+ on 9 April as floodwaters receded from cultivated fields (Butler Co.), and 500+ on 15 April (Sedgwick Co.). A few summer reports (14 June through late July) are inexplicable. Usual extreme dates for fall in the east are 25 September–20 November, with most migration during October. Large numbers include "hundreds" on 19 October (Pawnee Co.), 200+ on 5 November (Stafford Co.), and 100+ 11 November (Barton Co.). In Ellis County (14 years) migration was 20 September–3 November, with most sightings in mid-October. Smaller numbers occur through the CBC period, especially in the southeast, including 200 on 1 January in Cherokee County and 50 in Cowley County. One on a CBC in Finney County was unexpected. Late January through early March reports are probably wintering birds, though actual wintering at any site has not yet been documented.

Comments: Birds feed on the ground, usually in small, loose flocks and run rapidly about picking up insects. Edges of sewage ponds, freshly plowed fields, and recently burned prairie are popular feeding sites. Occasional tail wagging and a characteristic flight call aid in identification. The species is probably underreported in open grassland and cultivated areas where less birding occurs.

Banding: Six banded; no encounters.

References: Janzen, 2007; Thompson and Ely, 1992; Young, 1993.

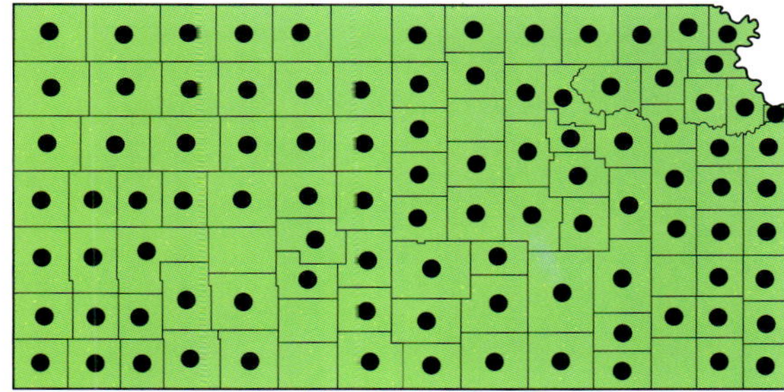

Sprague's Pipit

Anthus spragueii (SPPI)

Status: Uncommon transient in Flint Hills and High Plains; formerly in winter in the west.

Habitat: Short- and mid-grass prairie, low grass or eroded areas within tallgrass prairie, pastures, and fallow cropland.

Migration: It is much more abundant and widespread in spring than in fall. Extreme spring dates are 13 March (east) and 21 May (west) with most sightings during the last half of April. High spring counts are 75 on 11 April, 30 on 8 April, and 16 on 25 April (all Butler Co.); 10 on 25 April (Cowley Co.); and 10 on 3 May (Rush Co.). Extreme fall dates are 23 September (east) and 16 November (west) with peak migration during the first half of October. The highest fall reports are "common" on 11 October (Pawnee Co.) and 100 on 24 October (Linn Co.). Single birds reported on CBCs in Cowley County and a specimen (KU 37971) from 20 January, also Cowley County, may have been wintering birds.

Comments: In November 1877 L. Watson reported it as "not rare in Ellis County—present every winter, and in company with shore larks and longspurs." There were few reports from the west during the next century and none later than 20 November. N. Goss considered it a transient in the east but "quite common" in middle and western Kansas, a status continued by C. Bunker and W. Long. Other late 19th-century reports are from the "high prairie" east to Anderson, Woodson, and Douglas counties, all during mid-October. It has been reported regularly in west-central Kansas, especially during the fall migration, since the 1980s. Seltman regularly reported flocks of up to 50 birds while preparing ground and planting wheat between late September ("arrived early and in large number") and mid-October. In the Flint Hills flocks of 10 birds are more likely. It prefers native grassland, feeds in dispersed flocks, and is extremely well camouflaged. As a result many sightings are made only after a deliberate search or by flushing individuals and noting the characteristic call and undulating flight. Only when birds follow farm machinery are they easy to observe.

References: Bunker, 1913; Goss, 1891; Long, 1940; Snow, 1878; Thompson and Ely, 1992.

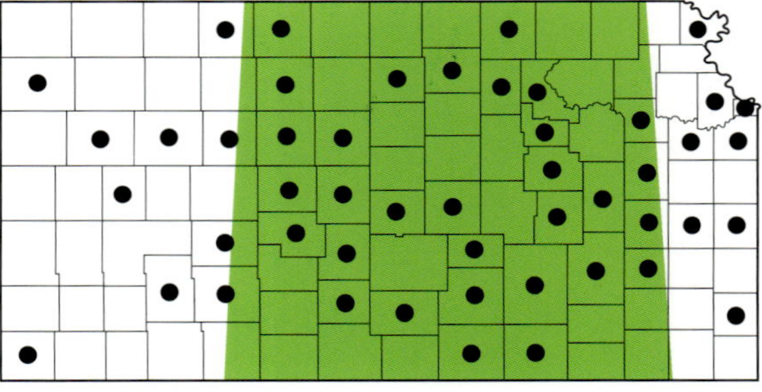

Bohemian Waxwing

Bombycilla garrulus (BOWA)

© Brian Small

Status: Irregular winter visitant statewide.

Habitat: Usually near fruiting trees and shrubs, often in cedars, in parks and residential yards.

Migration: Earliest dates for fall arrival are 29 September and 4 October, but arrival is more typically in mid-November. Late dates for spring departure are 30 March (west) and 16 April (east). Statewide, most reports are between late November and late January. High counts in the east are 1,000 during the period 21 December–15 April (Kansas City area) and 150 on 23 January (Sedgwick Co.). The high count for the west is 45 on December 28 (Ellis Co.).

Comments: During the 19th century it was considered rare, though a large flock was reported in Riley County in 1879. It has been very irregular since. For example, in Ellis County it was reported once in 1926–1927, most of the winter during five winters from 1960–1962 through 1972–1973, and not at all from 1980 to 1995. A similar pattern has been reported from Shawnee County. Statewide, it was reported during at least 38 winters during the period 1879–2008. The largest and most extensive invasion was in the winter of 1961–1962 (also in Missouri and Oklahoma) with smaller but notable invasions in 1972–1973, 1986–1987 (chiefly in the west), and 2004–2005 (chiefly west). It usually occurs in small flocks but with large flocks reported during irruption years. It is occasionally found in flocks of Cedar Waxwings and may join American robins, European starlings, and other species when feeding.

Banding: 23 banded; no encounters.

References: Ely, 1971; Janzen, 2007; Seibel, 1978; Thompson and Ely, 1992.

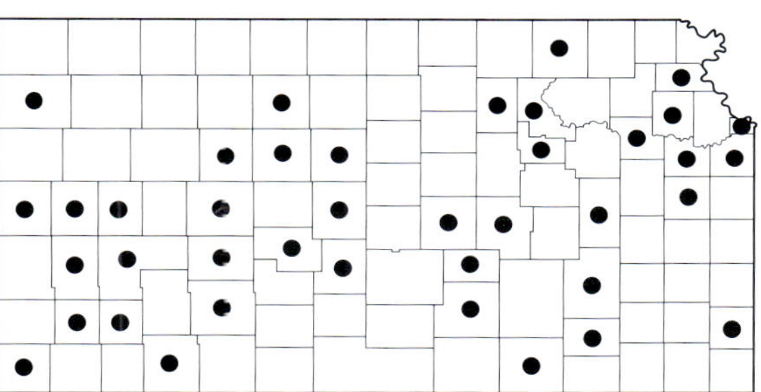

Cedar Waxwing

Bombycilla cedrorum (CEDW)

© Linda Williams

Status: Common transient; common but irregular in winter; local summer resident.

Habitat: Near fruiting trees and shrubs in woodland edge, parks, cemeteries, and residential yards.

Migration: It is irregular in distribution and numbers, at least in part depending on the local food supply of berries, including cedar, hawthorn, hackberry, and other types. Usual extreme dates for fall arrival are 24 August (east) and 9 October (east) with major arrivals in September during most years. Usual extreme dates for spring departure are 3 May (west) and 13 June (east) with most birds gone by mid-May. In Ellis County, the median arrival date is 20 September, and the median departure date is 26 May with most birds gone by mid-April. "Woods" (unpubl. manuscript, 1976) noted three periods of peak numbers in Shawnee County: early November, late January, and mid-April. Large numbers include 1,000+ on 21 May (Douglas Co.), 1,000 on 26 February (Wyandotte Co.), and 973 on 1 January (Morton Co.).

Breeding: KBBAT reported that the breeding range in Kansas was more extensive than expected. Confirmed nesting was found at 32 sites, mostly in the northeast but extending southward to Neosho County and westward along rivers to Lyon, Geary, and Norton counties. R. Johnston reported six nests from Shawnee and Wyandotte counties during the period 1949–1961, with egg-laying in June and early July. Nest-building has been reported on 6 June (Osage Co.), eggs on 3–16 June, young in the nest 29 June, and recently fledged young 15 June–23 September. Nesting in Kansas tends to be earlier than reported in other parts of its range. Nesting was not documented until 1947 in Johnson County (H. Hedges [AFN 2(1):18]). Five additional nests and recently fledged young were found in Johnson, Shawnee, and Wyandotte counties during the early 1950s. All subsequent sightings were in the northeast until an adult with dependent young was observed in Cowley County in 1961. T. and S. Shane photographed a fledged young at Scott State Park (Scott Co.) on 6 July 1986 and summarized nesting in the west (Smith, Wichita, Morton, and Norton cos.) through 1998.

See page 502 for banding information.

References: Busby and Zimmerman, 2001; Janzen, 2007; Johnston, 1964a; Menke, 1894; Shane and Shane, 2000; Thompson and Ely, 1992.

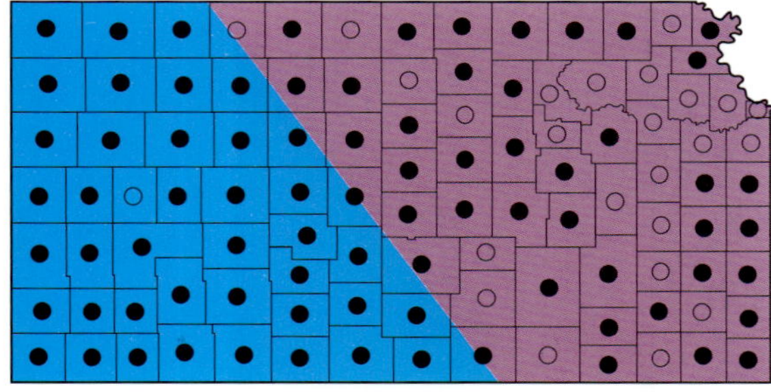

Phainopepla

Phainopepla nitens (PHAI)

Status: Casual winter visitant in the southwest.

Habitat: Riparian habitat in sand-sage prairie and residential yards.

Migration: There are no spring records from Kansas. The four confirmed records are 3–23 September.

Comments: The Phainopepla was first reported from Kansas by L. and B. Rich when one appeared in their yard in Garden City (Finney Co.) on 8 and 9 September 1993. It next appeared at Middle Springs (Morton Co.), where J. Rakestraw saw a female on 3 September 1994. Next day it was seen by six additional observers. Later that season a male appeared in the Rich's yard from 25 to 30 September 1994. All three birds were photographed. It was not reported again until 22 September 2005 when S. Patti found one east of the K-27 bridge across the Cimarron River north of Elkhart (Morton Co.). Two sightings were in a residential yard; two were in riparian growth along the Cimarron River. One, in Garden City, was observed flycatching from a perch in a tree and flying down to elderberries, which it was apparently eating. Two additional reports, along the Cimarron River (Morton Co.) on 10 September 1987 and in Haskell County on 3 October 1994, were not verified.

References: Cable et al., 1996; Rich and Rich, 1994.

© Jim Burns

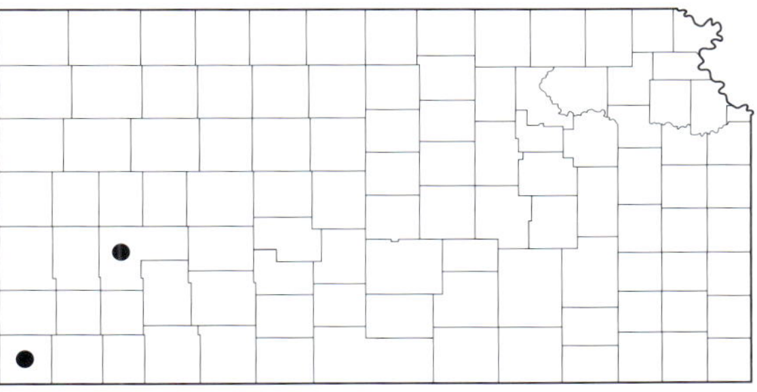

Lapland Longspur

Calcarius lapponicus (LALO)

Status: Common to abundant transient and winter resident in western and central Kansas; uncommon to common and often erratic transient and winter visitant in the east.

© David Seibel

Habitat: Irrigated cropland, stubble fields, prairies, and wheat fields; during periods of heavy snowfall, large flocks may concentrate along recently cleared roads, and even in farmyards.

Migration: Current data do not allow a clear distinction between winter "movements" caused presumably by snow cover within and beyond Kansas and true spring migration. The northward migration may begin by early or mid-February. Although the number of sightings during March is relatively small, flocks of up to 10,000 have been reported on a few occasions. Late spring dates include 11 April (Ness Co.), 12 April (Pawnee Co., several hundred), and 17 April (Johnson Co., 40). Early fall dates include 8 October (Gove Co.) and 9 October (Douglas Co.), but arrival is usually around 5 November with thousands present by mid-November and huge numbers by late November. Numbers fluctuate wildly depending, in part, on local snow cover, but typically remain high through early winter.

Comments: In some years the species is so abundant that dense flocks may literally cover many acres, and hundreds of thousands can be seen in an hour. C. Ely reports having seen more than a million birds in one day. A dense concentration covering 100+ acres on 19 January 2000 may have held an astounding four million birds (Pawnee Co., S. Seltman). O. Rice (*in* "Woods," unpubl. manuscript, 1976) described the erratic movements of this species during an invasion of the Kaw River valley near Topeka during the winter of 1970–1971. Two hundred were noted on 26 December with thousands, perhaps even millions, present by 23 January, yet 2 days later not a single bird could be found. Huge numbers are sometimes destroyed by natural disasters. Terres described the widespread mortality over a three-state area on the night of 13–14 March 1904 when migrating flocks were forced down by inclement weather (sticky snow). As many as five million may have crashed into the ground and perished on that one night. A smaller disaster occurred on the night of 25 January 1998 in Hamilton County when an estimated 20,000 were killed hitting fences, power lines, and three small radio towers during a snowstorm.

Banding: 50 banded; no encounters.

References: Cable et al., 1996; Janzen, 2007; Terres, 1948; Thompson and Ely, 1992.

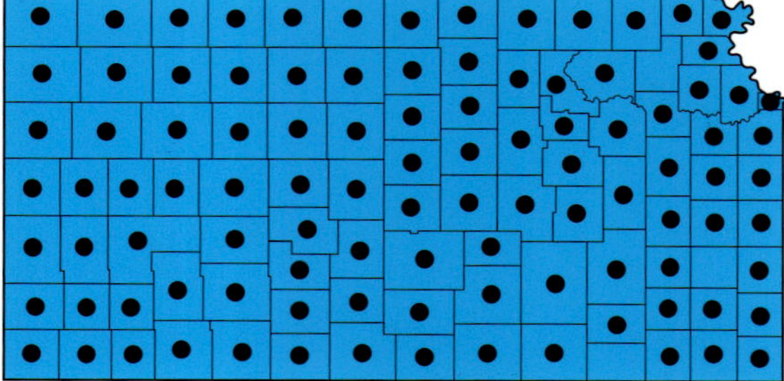

Chestnut-collared Longspur

Calcarius ornatus (CCLO)

Status: Uncommon transient and winter resident in central and western Kansas; rare and sporadic in the east; formerly nested in Ellis County (June 1871) and probably elsewhere in the northwest.

Habitat: Prefers taller vegetation than other longspurs (with the possible exception of Smith's), and favors native prairie during migration; also, especially in winter, occurs in a variety of crop and stubble fields.

Migration: Spring migration is better documented than fall. Presumed transients have been reported from 5 March (Sedgwick Co.) and 9 March (Rush Co.) to 23 April (Morton Co.) and 5 May (Barton Co.) with the peak during mid-March to early April. Large counts include "thousands" during mid-March to mid-April (Pawnee Co., S. Seltman), "several thousand" on 30 March (Barton Co., M. Schwilling), and 1,000+ on 3 April (some in breeding plumage, Ness Co., S. Seltman). Unusually early fall arrivals include 5 September (1, Norton Co.), 21 September (Pawnee Co.), and 25 September (30, Morton Co.). Usual arrival is about 2 October (Ellis Co.) with "good numbers present" by 24 October. A nocturnal movement was reported over Stanton County on 18 October. Migration extends through mid-November. Its winter status is uncertain. Menke considered it an "abundant" winter resident near the end of the 19th century. There are occasional reports of large flocks during midwinter (11 January, Cheyenne Co., S. Seltman), but in most areas where it occurs regularly during migration (Ness, Pawnee, and Rush cos.) there are few reports. Some reports of large flocks, especially in cropland, were undoubtedly of Lapland Longspurs.

Breeding: J. Allen reported nesting at Fort Hays (Ellis Co.) during June 1871. He noted that they "were only met with on the high ridges and dry plateaus, where they seemed to live somewhat in colonies. At a few localities they were always numerous, but elsewhere were often not met with in a whole day's drive." He collected a series of 30 adults and at least three clutches of eggs (specimens at MCZ). Clutches were completed about 3 June.

Comments: It may occur in mixed flocks of longspurs and/or Horned Larks especially during winter in stubble fields and along recently snowplowed roadsides. Its breeding range has been greatly reduced by the plowing and overgrazing of native prairie.

References: Allen, 1872; Cable et al., 1996; Janzen, 2007; Menke, 1894; Thompson and Ely, 1992.

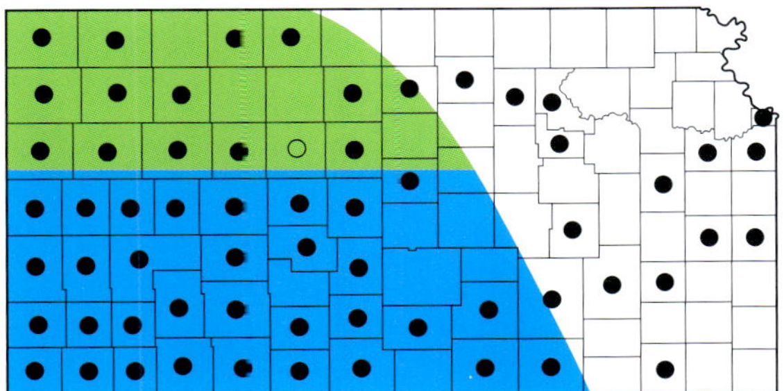

Smith's Longspur

Calcarius pictus (SMLO)

Status: Uncommon transient and rare, local winter resident, principally in the Flint Hills and very locally eastward; perhaps casual in central and western Kansas.

Habitat: Tallgrass prairie but within this habitat it prefers areas of short, thick grass. In other states, it occurs regularly in grassy fields at airports. In Kansas, it is most often recorded from pastures in the Flint Hills, often but not always in close-cropped grass. Taller grasses may allow the birds to escape detection more readily and may be used more frequently than realized. Small flocks are sometimes found in stubble fields, where birds will literally crouch behind single stalks while a passerby walks within a foot or two.

Migration: Its actual status in much of Kansas is uncertain. The earliest fall sighting is 26 September (Geary Co.). Otherwise the median arrival date is 24 October with most sightings during late October and November. Wintering occurs locally in the Flint Hills. Reports of winter flocks in central and western Kansas are suspect; transients have been reported in Morton County on several occasions. Sightings increase during late winter as transients arrive from the south, with most migration occurring between early March and 26 April. It usually occurs in small flocks of 40–70 individuals but with 500 on 22 February (Butler Co.), 500 on 25 February (Lyon Co.), and 400 on 9 November (Wabaunsee Co.). Specimens have been taken between 4 November and 23 April.

Comments: Although considered "common" to "fairly common" by authors as recent as H. Tordoff, the number of sightings does not support this. For example, there were only five sightings in 25 years in Shawnee County ("Woods," unpubl. manuscript, 1976). It breeds near tree line from central Alaska to north-central Canada. It usually occurs in pure flocks, rarely with other longspurs. Such birds should be documented with particular care. A. Wetmore, in describing the activity of a flock in close-cropped pasture near Independence (Montgomery Co.), noted that birds sat so closely and were so well camouflaged that he could pass within a dozen feet without seeing them. Unless disturbed repeatedly, individuals usually fly only a short distance with a zigzag flight and then drop back into the vegetation, because birds generally prefer to rely on camouflage rather than fleeing.

References: Cable et al., 1996; Janzen, 2007; Peterson, 1980; Thompson and Ely, 1992; Tordoff, 1956; Wetmore *in* Bent, 1968.

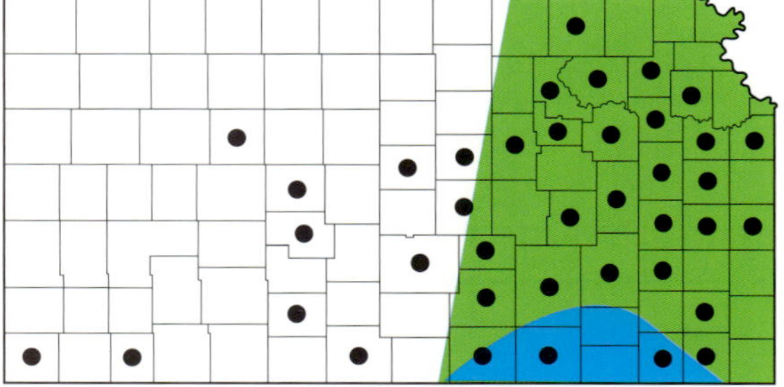

McCown's Longspur

Rhynchophanes mccownii (MCLO)

Status: Uncommon to rare transient and sporadic (sometimes abundant) winter visitant or winter resident in the west; casual in the east.

Habitat: Shortgrass prairies and overgrazed rangeland.

Migration: Presumed transients have been reported from 2 March (Douglas and Pawnee cos.) to 21 April (Stafford Co.) with most in late March. The highest modern counts are 1,000 concentrated in a wheat stubble field on 23 March–3 April and a flock of 100 on 29 March (both Pawnee Co., S. Seltman). The few fall sightings include an extremely early date of 7 September (Norton Co., S. Seltman) with most sightings during mid-October. High fall counts include 400 along the Arkansas River near the Colorado border on 1 November (D. Seibel and G. Pittman), flocks of "hundreds" in Hamilton County, and "many" from Morton County (both 17 October, different years). There is one early fall specimen from the east (Anderson Co., 21 October 1879, KU 72865). Most winter records are during the CBC period with specimens through 24 February (Douglas and Ellis cos.), and a sight record from Linn County on 22 February. Several hundred were gathered along recently snowplowed roads in Morton County on 31 December.

Comments: Overall, its breeding range (and perhaps total numbers) has decreased considerably since settlement of the Plains. During the late 19th century it was considered "abundant" during winter in Finney County and "abundant" during migration in Ellis County, but this is no longer true. During migration it usually occurs in pure flocks, but during winter it may occur with Lapland Longspurs and less often with Chestnut-collared Longspurs. When feeding, birds are often scattered, and individuals may crouch motionless until approached very closely. The tail pattern, when visible, is distinctive, but other identifying marks are more subtle; it can be easily confused with other longspurs.

References: Cable et al., 1996; Janzen, 2007; Thompson and Ely, 1992.

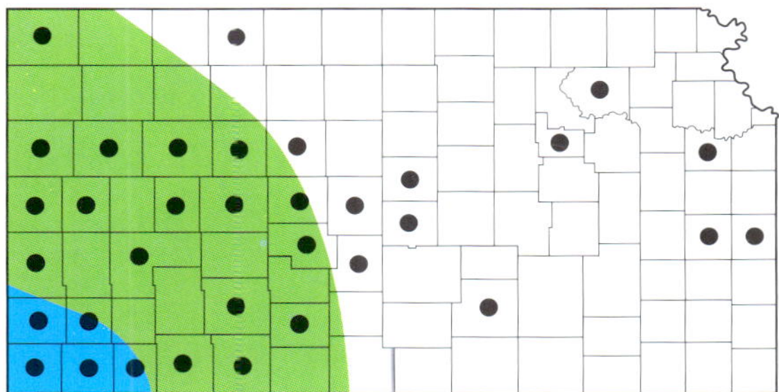

Snow Bunting

Plectrophenax nivalis (SNBU)

© Chris Valentine

Status: Rare and irregular winter visitant, mostly in central and eastern Kansas.

Habitat: Bare areas near reservoirs, including riprap along the dam face, roadways, and even in parking lots; also along rural roads or in cultivated fields; and on sandy shores and sandbars along rivers.

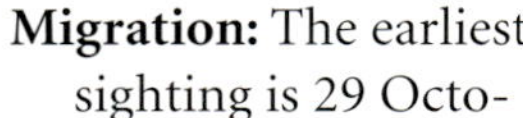

Migration: The earliest sighting is 29 October (Barton Co.) with most arrivals in mid-November. Most reports are during the CBC period through 20 February. Individuals rarely remain at one location for more than a few days; the longest reported stay is 24 January–12 February (Pottawatomie Co.).

Comments: It was considered very rare and sporadic in occurrence prior to about 1965. A specimen taken 29 December 1965 (Barton Co., M. Schwilling) and three sightings (Douglas and Trego cos.) were the only records since the 1870s. Subsequently the number and frequency of sightings have increased dramatically, and it now occurs during most winters. This increase probably reflects both an increased effort by observers and increase in habitat. In Kansas, it usually occurs singly or in very small groups usually near the larger reservoirs. In the northern states it often arrives with winter storms, and large flocks swirl from field to field (much as Lapland Longspurs do in Kansas), hence the early vernacular name, "snowflake." It is a bird of open country, feeding and roosting on the ground, sometimes in soft snow. It is attracted to recently manured fields, where it feeds on weed seeds and waste grain. In the northeastern United States flocks also frequent ocean beaches, lake margins, and salt marshes. This is the most northerly breeding songbird in North America, and its bill and toes are disproportionately short, adaptations for reducing heat loss. Its call is a short, descending whistle.

References: Janzen, 2007; Thompson and Ely, 1992.

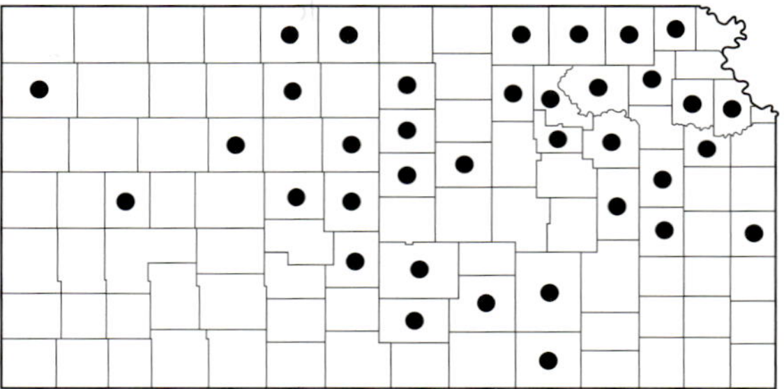

Blue-winged Warbler

Vermivora cyanoptera (BWWA)

Status: Very rare transient and summer resident in extreme eastern Kansas; casual visitant elsewhere.

Habitat: Woodland edge, brushy fields, and thickets, often near water; also in parks and residential areas during migration.

Migration: Sightings of presumed spring transients are 18 April to at least 2 June; specimen records from 1 May to 2 June. Most sightings are during the first half of May. Dates for presumed fall transients are 10 August–10 October with most during mid-September. Midsummer records may be breeding birds or vagrant unmated males.

Breeding: There are no fully documented accounts of breeding in Kansas, although both N. Goss and F. Snow considered it a "rare summer resident," and a singing male in suitable habitat in rural Bonner Springs (Wyandotte Co., C. Hobbs) on 11 May 1999 almost certainly nested there. That spring at the same site, a singing male (presumably the same bird) was observed repeatedly through at least 21 May, and on 2 July, D. Henness found an adult with two fledged young. A singing male was again found near the same site from 6 May to 15 June 2000. The species regularly breeds in several locations in nearby western Missouri. Historically, it apparently bred as near as Swope Park in Kansas City, Missouri, and more recently a breeding population has been present in Weston Bend State Park, just across the Missouri River from Fort Leavenworth (Leavenworth Co.) for several years. In southwestern Missouri the species breeds regularly within 35 miles of the Kansas border.

Comments: Except when singing its relatively weak, buzzy song from the open top of a low tree, this species generally stays near the ground, where it forages for small beetles, ants, caterpillars, and spiders. Its movements are slow and deliberate, reminiscent of a vireo. It frequently interbreeds with the closely related Golden-winged Warbler where the two ranges overlap, producing two very distinct hybrids and numerous intermediate types.

References: Cable et al., 1996; Goss, 1891; Parkes, 1951; Robbins and Easterla, 1992; Shirling, 1920; Snow, 1903; Thompson and Ely, 1992.

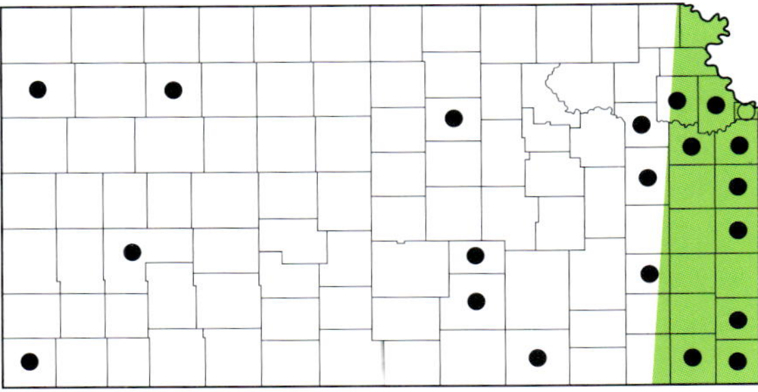

Golden-winged Warbler

Vermivora chrysoptera (GWWA)

© David Seibel

Status: Rare to uncommon transient in eastern Kansas; casual westward.

Habitat: Occurs in deciduous woods, especially second growth, and in overgrown pastures, various riparian habitats, and especially parks and residential areas.

Migration: About three-fourths of all sightings have been in spring, most during the period 2–10 May. Spring dates in the east are 28 April–28 May; westward 17 April–26 May. Fall reports are 15 August (Miami Co.) to 20 September and 3 October with a straggler to 23 October; westward 30 August–29 September.

Comments: It was not reported from Kansas until 1921 and has been reported regularly only since the 1970s. It is usually difficult to find, but in northeastern Kansas it is periodically much more numerous (or at least vocal and visible) during spring migration. It was noted as "common" in Johnson County in spring 1972 and has been reported in relatively high numbers in surrounding counties every few years since. In May 2009, there were several reports of multiple individuals at single sites in Johnson and Wyandotte counties. Early arrivals often feed high in leafless trees and actively search terminal buds for insects, vaguely resembling chickadees in both habits and appearance. From directly below, this resemblance can be surprisingly strong. As mentioned in the previous account, the Golden-winged Warbler hybridizes readily with the Blue-winged Warbler, and its breeding range is gradually shrinking as a result of replacement by that species. A hybrid of the "Lawrence's" phenotype was reported in Barton County on 9 September 1978.

Banding: Five banded; no encounters.

References: Parkes, 1951; Thompson and Ely, 1992.

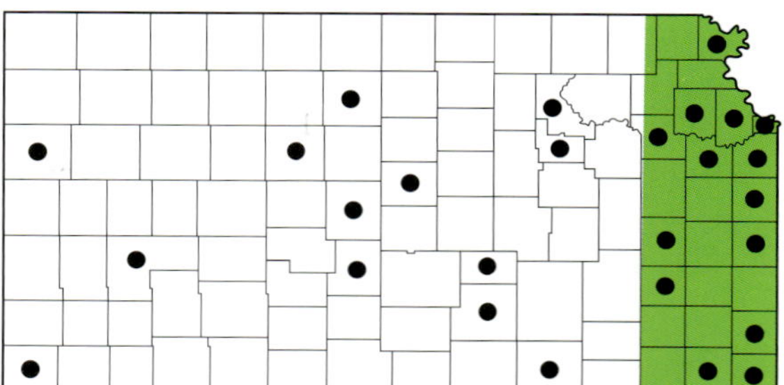

Tennessee Warbler

Oreothlypis peregrina (TEWA)

Status: Transient statewide, less numerous in the west. In the east, common in spring and uncommon in fall; in the west, uncommon in spring and rare in fall.

Habitat: Deciduous trees in almost any setting, feeding primarily in treetops, usually within foliage; on occasion may drop down to lower vegetation.

Migration: Much more common in spring than in fall. Spring specimen records are from 23 April to 9 June, and sight records extend this to 18 April. It is most common in the east during the first half of May with most gone by 30 May; westward it is most common 15–25 May. Median first arrival dates include 11 May (Ellis Co.) and 10–13 May (Sherman Co.). Fall specimen records are 20 September–22 October, and sight records extend early dates to 15 August. One found dead on 30 November 1972 (Ellis Co.) is exceptional. It is most common during late September and early October with stragglers to 24 October.

Comments: This treetop species is easily overlooked when not singing, but difficult to miss in the spring when the males sing their amazingly loud, distinctive song incessantly. At such times it is often surprisingly common along tree-lined streets in towns. More than 100 were reported on 13 May (Leavenworth Co.), 60 on 15 May (Wyandotte Co.), and 60 were banded on 26 May (Ellis Co.). Especially in the fall, it is easily confused with similar species such as the Orange-crowned Warbler, which passes through Kansas in greater numbers and is more likely to linger during migration. Fall birds are duller in pattern, silent, and difficult to identify in treetops. All sightings after 10 October need verification.

Banding: 391 banded; no encounters.

References: Cable et al., 1996; Janzen, 2007; Thompson and Ely, 1992.

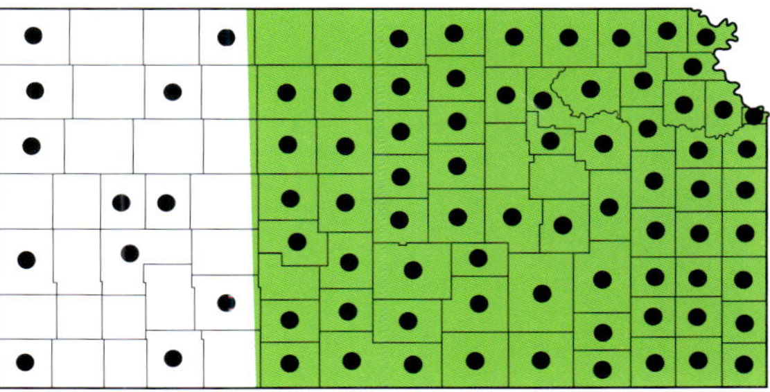

Orange-crowned Warbler

Oreothlypis celata (OCWA)

Status: Common transient in western and central Kansas, usually less common in the east; casual in winter, chiefly in the east.

Habitat: During migration, all types of shrubby or woody vegetation and nearby weed patches. It forages at all heights from near ground level in weeds to high in trees, where it feeds chiefly at the tips of branches and within the canopy.

Migration: Extreme spring dates for presumed transients are 28 March (probably overwintered) to 29 May (Ellis Co.) and one found dead on 3 June (Meade Co.). Specimen records are 13 April–20 May. Median first arrivals include 21 April (Ellis Co.), 22 April (Sherman Co.), and 25 April (Barton Co.). It is most common from late April through early May; most have departed by late May. The median late departure for Ellis County is 15–17 May. Unusually high numbers were reported, independently, in both Ellis and Shawnee counties during 1972. Extreme fall dates for presumed transients are 19 August and 23 November; specimen records are 7 September–19 October. Median fall first arrival in Ellis County is 18 September; median departure, 21 October. More than two-thirds of the 1,500+ individuals banded in Ellis County (1966–1973) were during fall with the peak during the last half of September. Large numbers include 200+ on 7 October (Butler Co.), "large numbers" on 1 October (Cowley Co.), and 76 and 63 killed at the Topeka KTKA television tower on 11–12 October 1986 and 8–9 October, respectively. It ranked third among species of warblers recovered at television tower kills during 1954–1994, comprising 14 percent of the 1,755 warblers recovered. Stragglers occur into the CBC period during most years, and a few have remained into early February (at least 11 counties) including 7 February (Saline Co.). One visited a suet feeder in Pottawatomie County for 6 weeks or longer during the winter of 2002 and might have remained until mid-March (K. With).

Comments: In early spring it is conspicuous as it feeds actively, often with Yellow-rumped Warblers, among developing buds and flowers of tall deciduous trees. Other than the Yellow-rumped Warbler, this is one of the most likely warblers to remain in Kansas in winter, usually at feeders, where it replaces its usual diet of insects with suet, peanut butter, and fruit as available.

See page 502 for banding information.

References: Ball et al., 1995; Cable et al., 1996; Janzen, 2007; Thompson and Ely, 1992; Tordoff and Mengel, 1956.

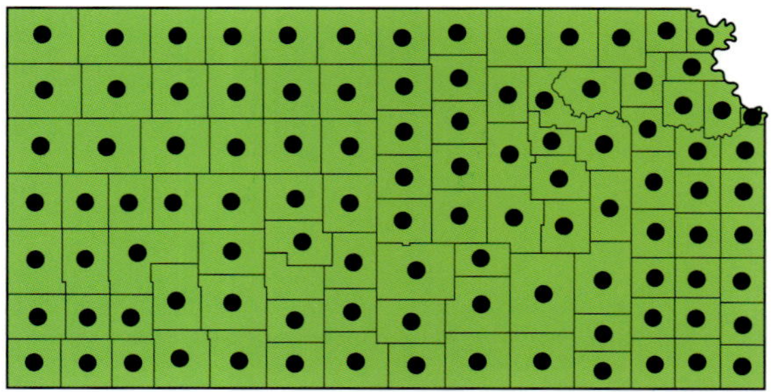

Nashville Warbler

Oreothlypis ruficapilla (NAWA)

Status: Common transient statewide.

Habitat: During migration all wooded areas, preferring the interior parts of leafy trees. Feeds at all heights from ground level in weeds (chiefly in fall) and bushes to tall trees, but mostly at low to moderate heights.

Migration: Specimen records are from 25 April to 20 May; sight records extend these to 12 April and 27 May. Usually arrives the last of April with a peak during the last half of May. Median first spring arrivals include 25 April (Sherman Co.) and 27 April (Ellis Co.); median late departure is 17 May (Ellis Co.) with a straggler to 2 June (recapture of a banded bird). It is usually much more common during fall. In Ellis County, more than 95 percent of the 500+ individuals banded were in fall, usually the last half of September. Specimen records are 24 August–12 October; sight records extend these to 9 August and 11 November (three banded, Ellis Co.). Median first fall arrivals include 12 September (Ellis Co.); median late departure is 19 October (Ellis Co.). R. Johnston reported a median arrival of 3 September for the northeast. It was the most common victim salvaged from five tower kills in the Topeka area between 25 September and 17 October during four different seasons. Just over 27 percent of the recoveries (499) were this species. There is a single well-documented winter record (7 January–15 February 1983, fide M. McHugh, photo) and two unconfirmed reports (15 December–15 February).

Comments: During the 19th century it was considered a "rare" transient, but now it is often one of the most abundant species, especially during fall. "Woods" (unpubl. manuscript, 1976) called it the "most common" warbler during some years (Shawnee Co.), and J. Linsdale considered it the "most common small transient" on 13 September (Doniphan Co.). Like many warblers, it is usually heard before it is seen in the spring. It usually occurs in mixed flocks with other warblers. It feeds almost entirely on insects such as caterpillars, leafhoppers, and aphids as well as spiders gleaned from twigs, buds, and leaf surfaces.

See page 502 for banding information.

References: Ball et al., 1995; Johnston, 1965; Linsdale, 1928; Snow, 1903; Thompson and Ely, 1992; Tordoff and Mengel, 1956.

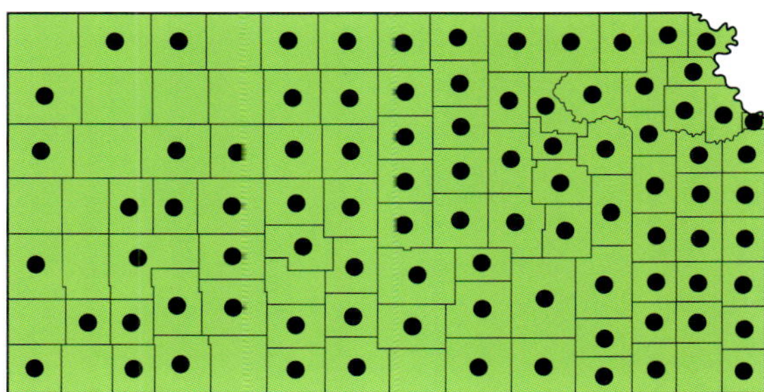

Virginia's Warbler

Oreothlypis virginiae (VIWA)

Status: Rare transient in the southwest; vagrant elsewhere.

Habitat: Normally scrubby brush land, in pinyon–juniper forest, and under open pines. In Kansas, cottonwoods along the Cimarron River, in shelterbelts in Elkhart, and residential yards.

Migration: There were very few records for the state prior to 1992, including three specimens, and perhaps six additional sight records. Since then, there have been at least 10 more sightings, mostly from the southwestern corner of the state (Morton Co.), as expected, but with three individuals straying well eastward. Spring records are all within the short period of 4–14 May, including the only two from Johnson County; fall records, nearly all from Morton County, range from 24 August to 20 September. The single record of summer vagrancy, an adult male captured and banded in Geary County on 8 July 1999 by A. McAndrews and Z. Meissner (KBRC 99-29), is completely unexpected.

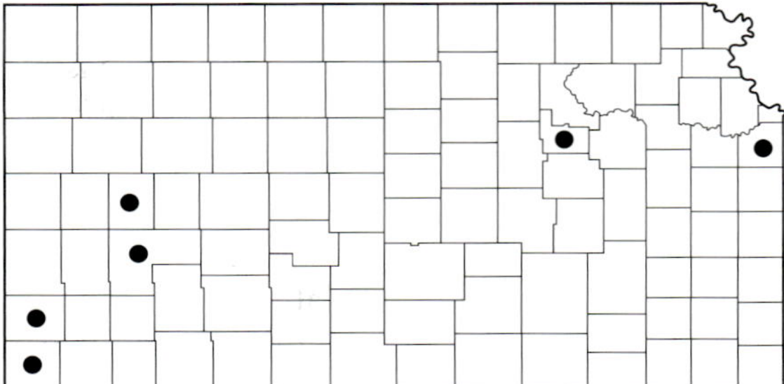

Comments: Large numbers of Virginia's Warblers nest at lower elevations in the mountains of Colorado and migrate through the foothills near Trinidad, making this a likely species to stray into southwestern Kansas during migration. It is a shy species that feeds near the ground, often in dense vegetation, making it very difficult to observe. It twitches its tail frequently.

Banding: One banded; no encounters.

References: Cable et al., 1996; Rintoul, 2000; Thompson and Ely, 1992.

Northern Parula

Parula americana (NOPA)

Status: Uncommon to common transient and summer resident in the east; rare transient in central and western Kansas. Probably breeds locally west to Sumner and Riley counties.

Habitat: During migration, any wooded habitat from deciduous woods to tree-lined city streets; during the breeding season restricted to riparian woodlands, with a distinct preference for large sycamores.

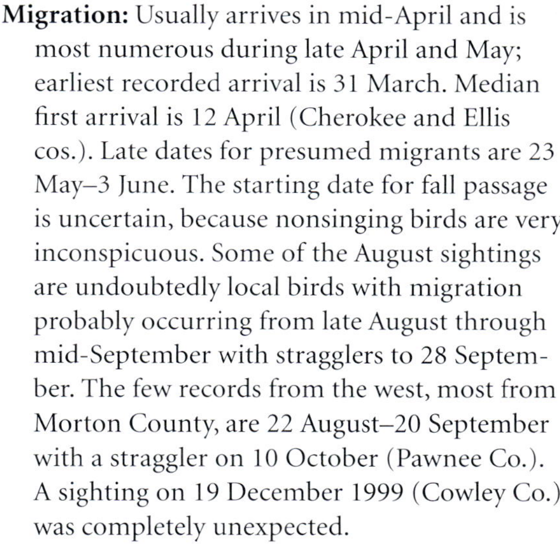

Migration: Usually arrives in mid-April and is most numerous during late April and May; earliest recorded arrival is 31 March. Median first arrival is 12 April (Cherokee and Ellis cos.). Late dates for presumed migrants are 23 May–3 June. The starting date for fall passage is uncertain, because nonsinging birds are very inconspicuous. Some of the August sightings are undoubtedly local birds with migration probably occurring from late August through mid-September with stragglers to 28 September. The few records from the west, most from Morton County, are 22 August–20 September with a straggler on 10 October (Pawnee Co.). A sighting on 19 December 1999 (Cowley Co.) was completely unexpected.

Breeding: Nests are extremely difficult to find, but KBBAT and BBS data reveal populations of likely breeders in the eastern one-fourth of the state, primarily in the Osage Plains but with smaller numbers in the Glaciated Region and the Flint Hills. In Kansas the nest is usually placed in a hanging cluster of leaves or other debris on a horizontal branch. E. and J. Schulenberg watched a pair completing a nest in a thick clump of dead leaves, about 10 feet above the ground in an oak tree, in Cherokee County, 2 May 1980. The nest is constructed of grass and plant tendrils and lined with plant down and hair. Nest-building has been reported 2–21 May, eggs 11 May, young 14 June, and recently fledged young 17 June to late July.

Comments: Recently, territorial males have been observed at many locations in proper habitat along numerous streams within its summer range. It occurs most often in treetops, especially when singing and during the breeding season, but may occur at lower heights. The song is a characteristic ascending buzzing trill, usually with a very abrupt ending that drops slightly in pitch. The call note, a sharp chip, is surprisingly loud for such a small bird.

Banding: 25 banded; no encounters.

References: Busby and Zimmerman, 2001; Janzen, 2007; Moldenhauer and Regelski, 1996; Schwilling et al., 1981; Thompson and Ely, 1992; Thompson and Young, 2000.

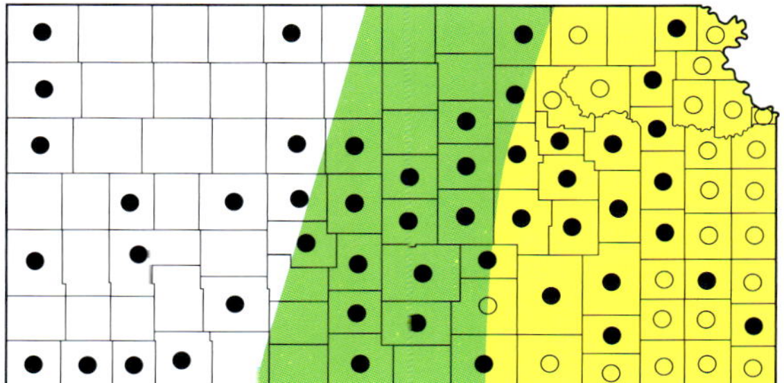

Yellow Warbler

Dendroica petechia (YWAR)

© David Seibel

Status: Common transient statewide, breeding in the east, very locally westward. Current distribution in summer is patchy; possibly much more common and widespread in the past.

Habitat: On migration, woodlands, parklands, forest edges, brushy or weedy fields (especially in fall), and shady or shrubby areas in towns; in the breeding season, most common in riparian edge habitats, preferring willows and cottonwoods.

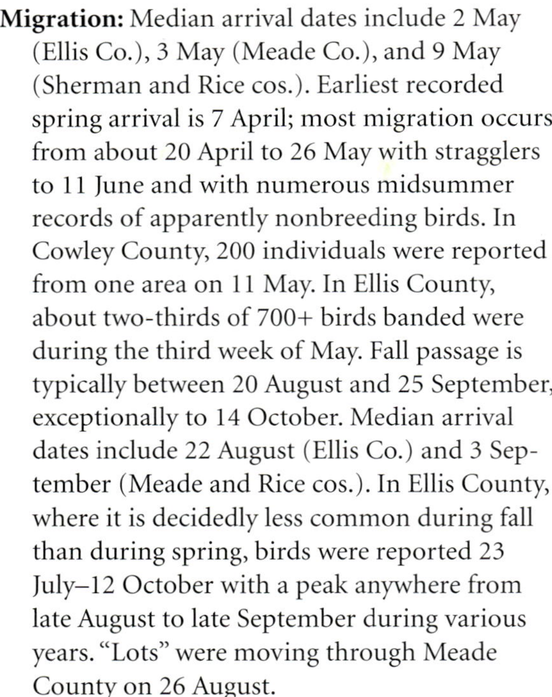

Migration: Median arrival dates include 2 May (Ellis Co.), 3 May (Meade Co.), and 9 May (Sherman and Rice cos.). Earliest recorded spring arrival is 7 April; most migration occurs from about 20 April to 26 May with stragglers to 11 June and with numerous midsummer records of apparently nonbreeding birds. In Cowley County, 200 individuals were reported from one area on 11 May. In Ellis County, about two-thirds of 700+ birds banded were during the third week of May. Fall passage is typically between 20 August and 25 September, exceptionally to 14 October. Median arrival dates include 22 August (Ellis Co.) and 3 September (Meade and Rice cos.). In Ellis County, where it is decidedly less common during fall than during spring, birds were reported 23 July–12 October with a peak anywhere from late August to late September during various years. "Lots" were moving through Meade County on 26 August.

Breeding: The breeding range in much of Kansas is unclear. Nest-building has been reported 10 June, eggs 25 May–17 June, and recently fledged young 30 June–18 July. It was considered an "abundant summer resident" in both Finney and Decatur counties before and at the turn of the 20th century. A definite population decline was reported for Shawnee County by E. Heywood (*in* "Woods," unpubl. manuscript, 1976), and M. Schwilling (pers. comm.) reported a similar decline in Chase County since the 1930s. KBBAT reported scattered records, only 5 percent of which represent confirmed nesting, with an additional 34 percent "probable." The distribution declined from a high of 42 percent of blocks surveyed in the Glaciated Region to only 6 percent in the more-arid High Plains.

Comments: The wood-warbler is probably the most familiar to Kansans.

Banding: 1,734 banded; no encounters.

References: Ball et al., 1995; Bent, 1953; Busby and Zimmerman, 2001; Godfrey, 1979; Thompson and Ely, 1992; Tordoff and Mengel, 1956.

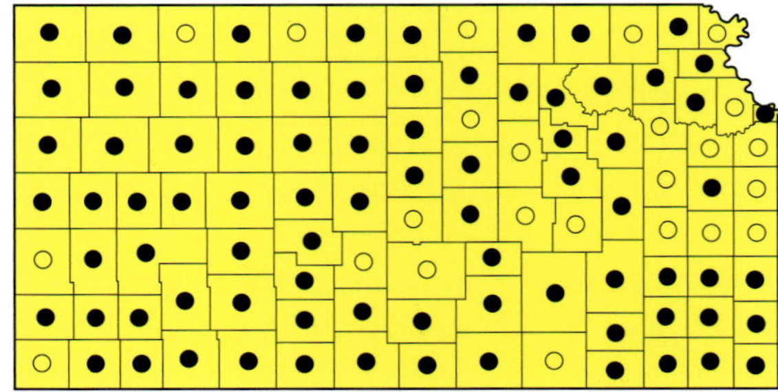

Chestnut-sided Warbler

Dendroica pensylvanica (CSWA)

Status: Uncommon but regular transient in the east; casual in the west.

Habitat: In migration almost any wooded area including mature upland forests, riparian woodlands, hedgerows, urban parks, and yards with large trees.

Migration: It is much more frequently recorded during spring than during fall. Most frequently observed during May with extreme dates of 26 April–13 June (Kiowa Co., singing). It was reported in "unprecedented numbers" in the Kansas City area 18–26 May 1961, but is never really common. The highest individual count is six on 10 May (Douglas Co.). In fall it occurs from mid- to late September with stragglers to mid-October; extreme dates are 3 August–20 October. On 11 October 1970, several were with a wave of transients observed in Ford County following the first snow of the year.

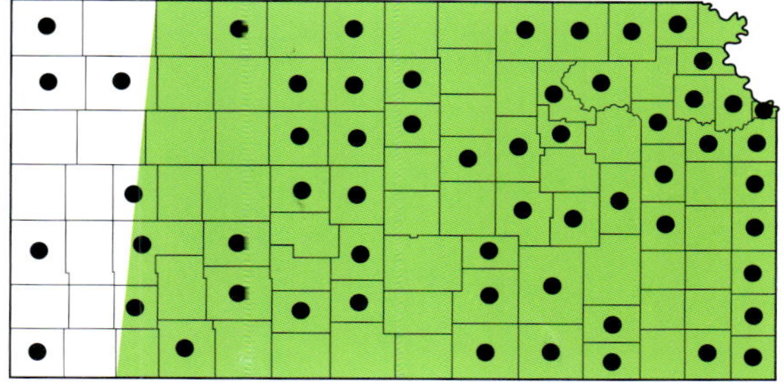

Comments: A published nesting record by P. Lowther was later found by L. Kiff to be in error and was corrected by M. Jenkinson. According to J. Terres, this was a very rare species during the early 19th century but became one of the most abundant wood-warblers in the northeastern quarter of the United States and Canada after the original forests were cleared. It gleans insects in typical warbler fashion and also flutters near foliage to snatch insects from exposed surfaces, mostly within 7 feet of the ground. Males sing from within or from the tops of small shrubs and low trees.

Banding: 26 banded; no encounters.

References: Jenkinson, 1984; Lowther, 1977; Terres, 1980; Thompson and Ely, 1992.

Magnolia Warbler

Dendroica magnolia (MAWA)

Status: Uncommon transient in the east; rare or casual in the west.

Habitat: During migration all types of woody habitats from riparian growth to shrubbery in yards.

Migration: Extreme dates in spring are 26 April (Sedgwick Co.) and 6 June (singing male, Johnson Co.). Usual arrival is around 6 May with the peak during mid-May, and most are gone by 20 May. "Woods" (unpubl. manuscript, 1976) gave the peak for Shawnee County as 12 May, unusually early. A singing male on 25 June 1968 (Ellis Co.) is exceptional. The high count recorded is 11 on 8 May (Linn Co.). Extreme fall dates are 28 August (Linn Co.) and 15 October (Geary Co.). Arrival is usually around 10 September with the peak during the last one-third of September into early October. Sightings after 15 October need verification. A CBC report for 14 December was most likely another species, perhaps a Yellow-rumped Warbler.

© David Seibel

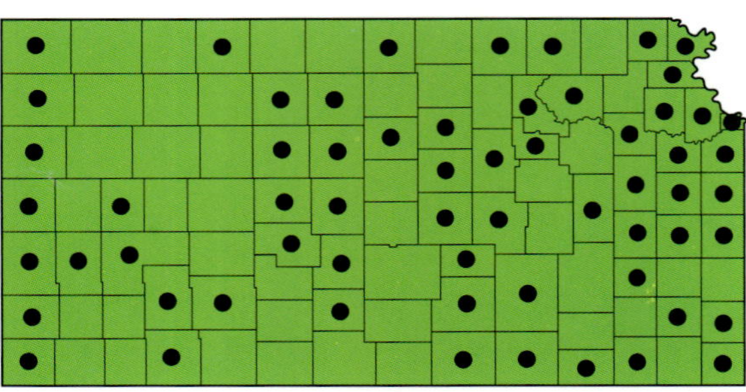

Comments: It is a very active species, hopping around with drooping wings and partly spread tail, usually at low heights. On its wintering grounds, from southern Mexico to Costa Rica, it is very common in disturbed habitats such as forest edges and brushy fields.

Banding: 57 banded; no encounters.

References: Cable et al., 1996; Janzen, 2007; Thompson and Ely, 1992.

Cape May Warbler

Dendroica tigrina (CMWA)

Status: Rare transient; vagrant in winter in the east. Most records during spring.

Habitat: During migration, in any woody vegetation, often high in trees such as oaks. One was found by Seibel in Cowley County in arborvitae in winter.

Migration: Spring sightings are 30 April–27 May. Nearly three-fourths of the 34 dated records are during 7–14 May. There are currently only five fall records, all between 31 August and 25 September, with a late date of 18 October (Johnson Co.). There are seven early to midwinter records during the period 1 December–1 February from Cowley (three) and Douglas (four) counties. The most extended stay was 16 December 1970–28 January 1971 in Winfield (Cowley Co.). This individual visited a feeder for suet. One, thought to be a first-winter male, visited a heated birdbath at the residence of J. Conrad in Lawrence (Douglas Co.), 29 January–1 February 2000; an adult male was seen at the same location 11–17 January 2002!

Comments: On its breeding grounds, it may become very numerous locally in response to outbreaks of forest caterpillars, particularly the spruce budworm. In Missouri, the springs of 1966, 1968, and 1982, following such outbreaks, produced relatively high numbers of Cape May Warbler sightings, but this did not occur in Kansas. It sometimes associates with foraging flocks of chickadees in the fall. Despite its scarcity, in general, this is one of the warblers most likely to occur at feeders in Kansas in midwinter.

Banding: Two banded; no encounters.

References: Cable et al., 1996; Janzen, 2007; Robbins and Easterla, 1992; Thompson and Ely, 1992.

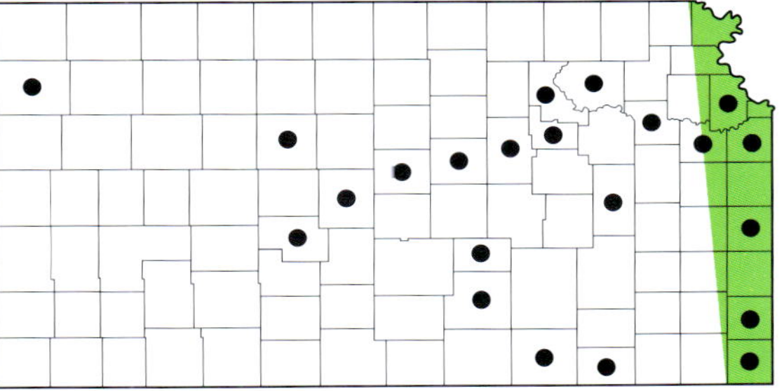

Black-throated Blue Warbler

Dendroica caerulescens (BTBW)

© Judd Patterson

Status: Rare transient statewide.

Habitat: In migration any type of wooded area, usually at low heights and with other warblers.

Migration: Extreme spring dates (chiefly sight records) are 16 April (Pottawatomie Co.) to 4 June with most 5–15 May. Extreme dates for fall are 3 September–8 November (Ellis Co.). Most fall sightings are mid-September to early October with median fall dates of 28 September in the west and 3 October for the east. At least six have been salvaged from tower kills in the Topeka area on 10 September and five to eight on 23 October. The high count is five on 22 October (Kearny Co.).

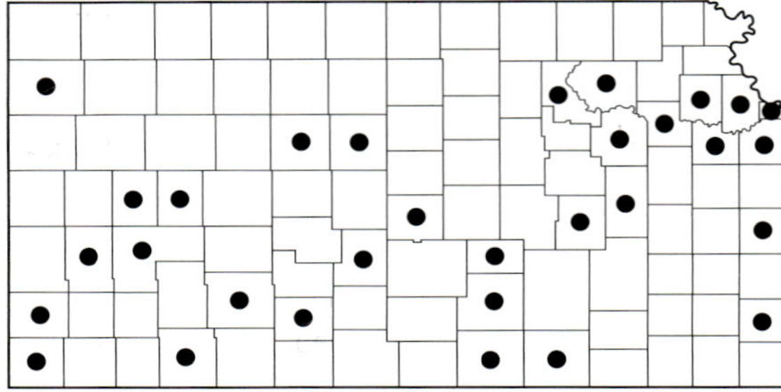

Comments: This is one of the few "eastern" wood-warblers for which a high proportion of records are from the western half of the state, and most of these are during fall. A similar pattern occurs in Oklahoma, Nebraska, and, to some degree, Missouri. It is an eastern wood-warbler and rarely reaches Kansas. It is an active feeder, gleaning insects from twigs, snatching those flying nearby, or fluttering against foliage. It also eats spiders and occasionally seeds and fruits.

Banding: Seven banded; no encounters.

References: Ball et al., 1995; Cable et al., 1996; Robbins and Easterla, 1992; Sharpe et al., 2001; Thompson and Ely, 1992; Tordoff and Mengel, 1956.

Yellow-rumped Warbler

Dendroica coronata (YRWA)

Status: Two distinctive subspecies groups, formerly considered separate species, largely overlap in Kansas but have different spatial and temporal limits. "Myrtle Warbler" (*D. c. coronata* group) is a common transient and an occasional winter resident, especially in the east. "Audubon's Warbler" (*D. c. auduboni* group) is an uncommon transient and rare winter resident in the far west and a rare to casual transient in the central and eastern portions of the state.

Habitat: Any woody or shrubby habitat, including residential yards.

Migration: Early arrival begins during the first week of April, and birds are most numerous during late April and early May. Most have departed by mid-May with stragglers to 28 May. Extreme spring dates for presumed transients are 5 March (Ellis Co.) to 28 May (Morton Co.). Median first arrivals include 10 April (Sherman Co.), 16 April (Ellis Co.), and 21 April (Barton Co.). High numbers include "abundant" on 28 April (Morton Co.) and "numerous" on 5 May. Early fall arrivals are 18 August–11 September, but most arrival is from late September to a peak in October. Numbers decline rapidly by early November, and nonwintering birds are gone by mid-November (Kingman Co.). Extreme dates for presumed transients are 18 August–18 November. High numbers include 800 on 2 October (Russell Co.), 200+ on 28 September (Morton Co.; both forms), and 100+ on 23 October (Johnson Co.). Report of a single bird in a windbreak near CBWA on 30 July (if accurate) may have been a vagrant. Extreme spring dates for "Audubon's Warbler" in the west are 23 March–21 May and once to 16 June (Morton Co.). Median arrival in Hays is 16 April. It is most common during the last half of April through mid-May with migration observed 28 April–24 May. M. Schwilling reported "thousands" (probably both forms) at Buffalo Park (Finney Co.) during 10–14 May 1953. Farther east reported through 17 April (Shawnee Co.), 29 April (Sumner Co.), and 20 May (Pawnee Co.). Extreme fall dates for presumed transients are 11 September (Haskell Co.) to 23 November with a few remaining through at least 18 February (Ellis Co.) and 2 March (feeder, Douglas Co.).

Comments: As a whole, the species is one of the most common wood-warblers in the state.

See page 502 for banding information.

References: Cable et al., 1996; Hunt and Flaspohler, 1998; Sibley, 2000; Thompson and Ely, 1992; Young, 1993.

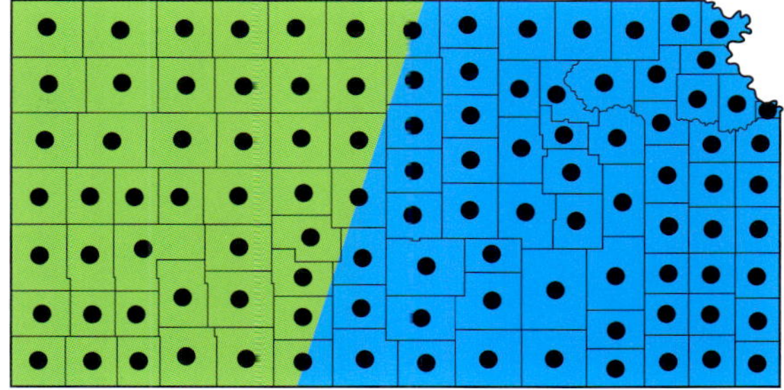

Black-throated Gray Warbler

Dendroica nigrescens (BTYW)

Status: Rare but probably regular transient in the far west; occurs casually elsewhere.

Habitat: In migration, deciduous growth, often riparian, usually at low to moderate heights.

Migration: As of 1992 there were seven specimen records from Finney and Morton counties, taken between 28 April and 13 May. Sight records, mostly from western and north-central Kansas, extend this period from 18 April to 17 May with most during late April and very early May. More than 30 birders observed one during a KOS field trip to CBWA on 2 May 1982. Extreme fall dates are 3 August and 17 October. Most of the few fall sightings are from Morton County, but with recent sightings north to Decatur County (9 September) and east to Harvey County (16–17 October). Nearly all recent sightings are of single individuals.

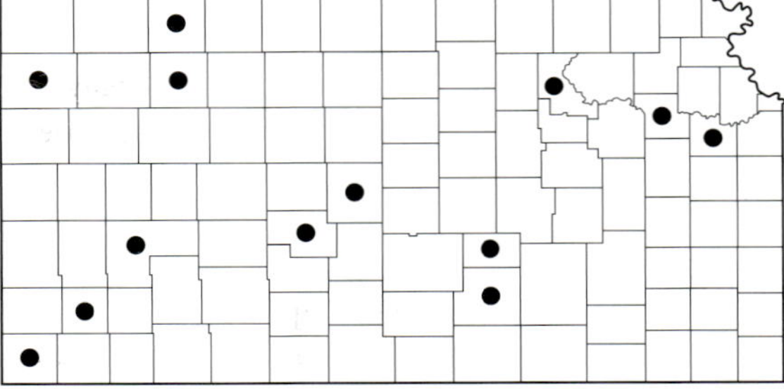

Comments: It is usually shy and retiring and is deliberate in its actions. It was considered "quite common" in Morton County during the second week of May 1950 by R. and J. Graber but has been rare there since that time.

References: Cable et al., 1996; Graber and Graber, 1950; Janzen, 2007; Thompson and Ely, 1992.

Black-throated Green Warbler

Dendroica virens (BTNW)

Status: Uncommon transient in eastern Kansas, becoming progressively less common westward; casual in winter.

Habitat: Stands of large conifers (e.g., in cemeteries) and deciduous forest or large deciduous trees in urban yards and parks.

Migration: Extreme spring dates are 1 April and 5 June (Sedgwick Co.). Arrival is usually late April, and about half of all spring sightings are during 1–10 May. Most of the remainder are gone by 20 May with stragglers to 26 May and once to 5 June. Extreme fall dates are 3 August (Sedgwick Co.) to 11 November. Arrival usually begins in late August and continues into mid-October with stragglers to 11 November. Typical sightings are of 1–5 individuals but 25+ were reported in Sedgwick County on 24 September. One was observed in Cowley County from 16 December 1970 through 5 January 1971, and there is an unconfirmed report (Sumner Co.) on 1 December 1998. A vagrant, 29 July 2007 (Sedgwick Co., P. Janzen), was completely unexpected.

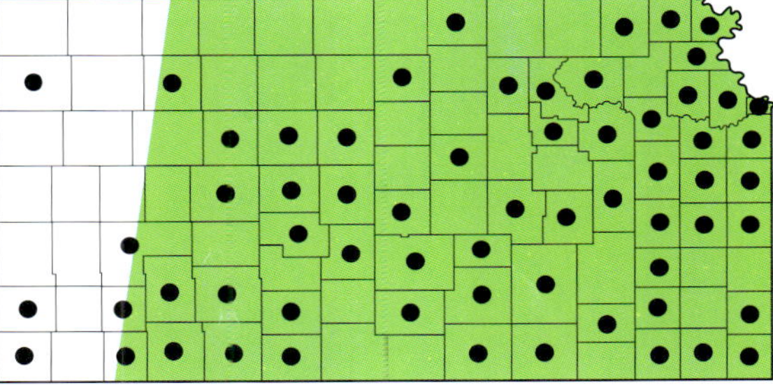

Comments: It can be relatively tame during migration, but males sing persistently from within foliage and are often difficult to observe in tall trees. Typical of wood-warblers, it eats small arthropods, including beetles, flies, moths, and caterpillars, and occasionally berries of poison ivy.

Banding: 26 banded; no encounters.

References: Bent, 1953; Janzen, 2007; Thompson, 1971; Thompson and Ely, 1992.

Townsend's Warbler

Dendroica townsendi (TOWA)

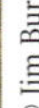

© Jim Burns

Status: Rare but regular transient in the west; vagrant in the east.

Habitat: During migration uses a wide range of habitats, including deciduous riparian woodlands, usually at moderate heights.

Migration: Most records are from the southwest, especially Morton County where it has been regular (chiefly in fall) since at least 1986. Extreme spring dates are 14 April (Ellis Co.) and 20 May (Morton Co.). Statewide, most spring sightings are 29 April–10 May (median date, 4 May). Extreme fall dates are 17 August–18 October (Trego Co.) with most during mid-September (median date, 19 September). Up to five individuals have been seen at one time. There are specimen records from 25 August to 25 September and 3 to 8 May from Ellis, Trego, and Morton counties at KUMNH (seven), DMNH (one), and MHP (one). There is also a photographic record from Rush County on 27 April.

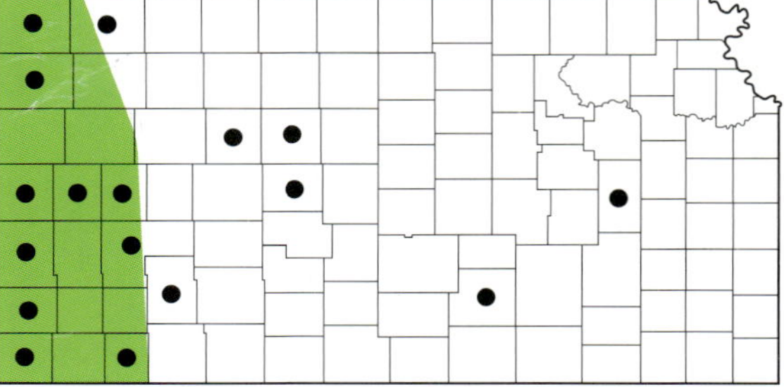

Comments: This is the western counterpart of the Black-throated Green Warbler, which it closely resembles in behavior and song; of the two, T. Cable and others consider Townsend's Warbler "much more likely to be encountered" in southwestern Kansas. It feeds primarily on beetles, true bugs, leafhoppers, caterpillars, and spiders. At feeding stations (outside of Kansas) it has been reported to eat peanut butter and cheese. It has also been observed taking spiders from under the eaves of buildings. It hybridizes with the Hermit Warbler where the two meet in Oregon and Washington.

References: Cable et al., 1996; Thompson and Ely, 1992.

Hermit Warbler

Dendroica occidentalis (HEWA)

Status: Accidental. The only record is one collected on the Arkansas River near Holcomb (Finney Co.), 7 May 1964, by J. Davis (MHP 925).

Habitat: The Kansas specimen was feeding in salt cedar on the riverbank.

Comments: It flits about gleaning insects from branches, trunks, terminal twigs, and the tips of conifer needles, sometimes hanging chickadee-fashion. It eats small arthropods, including beetles, caterpillars, flies, aphids, and spiders.

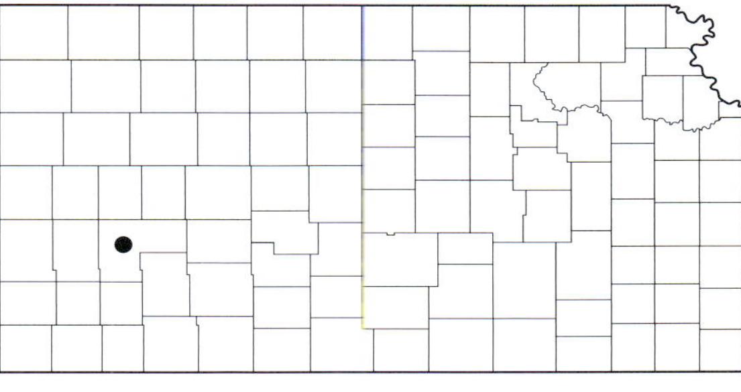

References: Pearson, 1997; Thompson and Ely, 1992.

Blackburnian Warbler

Dendroica fusca (BLBW)

Status: Uncommon transient in eastern tier of counties, diminishing westward; rare in the west.

Habitat: Dense riparian woodlands, city parks, and residential neighborhoods with large deciduous trees.

Migration: Extreme spring dates are 25 April–6 June. Arrival is usually early May with the peak in midmonth and few remaining after 25 May but with stragglers into early June. Typically no more than one to three birds are seen at one time but with a high of nine on 24 May. It occurred in "unprecedented numbers" in the Kansas City area on 18–26 May 1961 (T. Pucci and J. Rising [AFN 15(4):5]). Extreme fall dates are 21 August–21 October (exceptionally to 7 November). Median fall arrival is 15 September with most reported during the first 3 weeks.

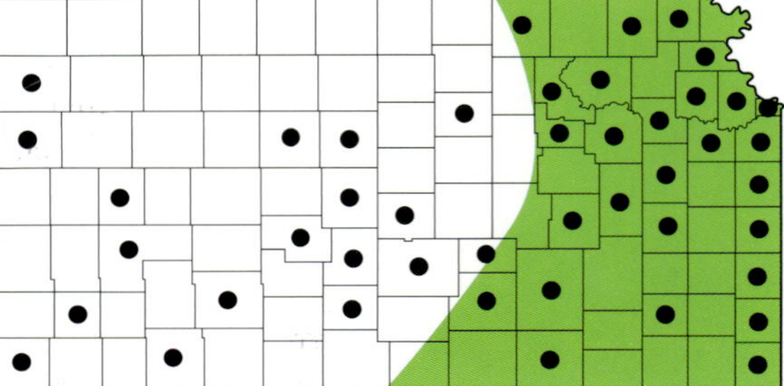

Comments: This beautiful species is normally a very low-density transient, but a few individuals can usually be found each spring in eastern counties, especially if one recognizes the song as it rises, steplike, to end almost above the range of human hearing. Always a treat for a bird-watcher to see even a lone bird, imagine the thrill of seeing a true fallout as described by E. H. Forbush in Massachusetts: "swarms moving through treetops, low shrubs, and even grassy areas and plowed fields." It winters primarily in northern South America.

Banding: Four banded; no encounters.

References: Bent, 1953; Cable et al., 2007; Janzen, 2007; Thompson and Ely, 1992.

Yellow-throated Warbler

Dendroica dominica (YTWA)

Status: Uncommon transient, rare to uncommon and very local summer resident, mostly in the easternmost tier of counties; scattered records westward through the central one-third of the state; accidental in southwestern corner.

Habitat: Strongly associated with large sycamores, usually along streams or rivers but also in city parks.

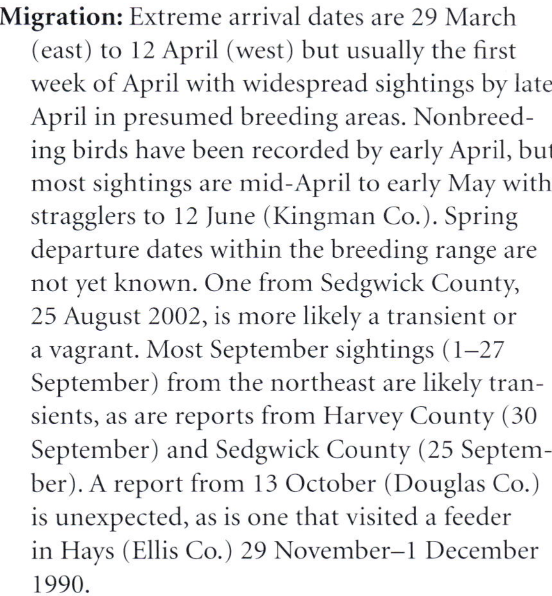

Migration: Extreme arrival dates are 29 March (east) to 12 April (west) but usually the first week of April with widespread sightings by late April in presumed breeding areas. Nonbreeding birds have been recorded by early April, but most sightings are mid-April to early May with stragglers to 12 June (Kingman Co.). Spring departure dates within the breeding range are not yet known. One from Sedgwick County, 25 August 2002, is more likely a transient or a vagrant. Most September sightings (1–27 September) from the northeast are likely transients, as are reports from Harvey County (30 September) and Sedgwick County (25 September). A report from 13 October (Douglas Co.) is unexpected, as is one that visited a feeder in Hays (Ellis Co.) 29 November–1 December 1990.

Breeding: M. Schwilling found the state's first nest on 2 May 1980 in Schermerhorn Park (Cherokee Co.) and observed a total of 11–14 birds in the area. The continued reporting of territorial males and pairs at the same location strongly suggests annual breeding. Nesting also has been confirmed in Geary and Linn counties (recently fledged young). Two birds (presumably adults) seen in Riley County on 8 July 1994 were possibly breeding. E. McHugh found a recently fledged young along the Marais des Cygnes River in Linn County on 29 July 2002 and multiple territorial males. Other evidence of possible or probable breeding includes multiple sightings of territorial males and pairs in Johnson and Wyandotte counties each spring since 2001; a juvenile in Johnson County on 29 August 2007; "very vocal young" at Perry Reservoir (Jefferson Co.) on 4 August 2001.

Comments: Numbers may have increased dramatically in eastern Kansas during recent years, though the increased numbers of observers who recognize its song and increased searching also play a part.

Banding: Seven banded; no encounters.

References: Busby and Zimmerman, 2001; Goss, 1891; Janzen, 2007; Robbins and Easterla, 1992; Schukman, 1996; Schwilling et al., 1981; Sharpe et al., 2001; Thompson and Ely, 1992.

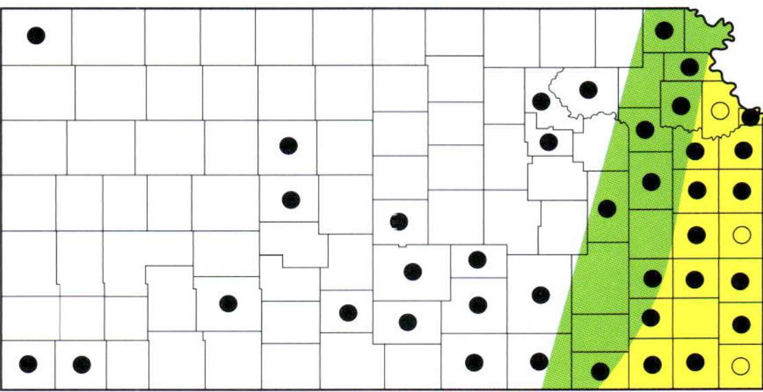

Pine Warbler

Dendroica pinus (PIWA)

Status: Casual transient in the extreme east; vagrant elsewhere; stragglers linger into late fall or winter, especially around feeding stations.

Habitat: Any wooded habitat during migration but seems to prefer large conifers. During winter, conifer stands or even one large pine tree can provide shelter for individuals that linger around feeding stations.

Migration: Nearly three-fourths of all sightings are during fall or winter. Extreme dates for spring (some probably wintering individuals) are 19 March–23 May with most during late April to mid-May. Observations of birds during March are probably of birds already moving northward to nearby breeding areas. Extreme dates for fall are 1 August–29 October with others extending into early winter. Most fall sightings are mid-September to early October. There are numerous sightings during December and January during at least 16 winters since 1964, mostly lone birds visiting feeders for a few days to a few weeks. Most reports are from Sedgwick County eastward but have included Ellis (4 December) and Meade (29 December–16 January) counties. The latest date for an overwintering bird is 20 February (Johnson Co.), a male that had been present since at least 12 January. It (presumably the same bird) was seen with a second bird nearby on 16 February.

Comments: This is a hardy species, nesting early and wintering over much of its breeding range. It feeds at any height in trees and shrubs, and in the east, during fall and winter, even feeds on the ground with bluebirds and sparrows. Early ornithologists called it the "Pine Creeping Warbler" because of its habit of feeding about the trunks of pines in nuthatch fashion. In the fall, adult females and immatures can be incredibly drab and devoid of field marks and can easily be confused with other species, especially when observed from below. Singing males are usually distinctive when seen, but one song type can be confusingly similar to that of Chipping Sparrows, which often occur in the same habitat. In fact, the birds themselves are sometimes attracted to recordings of the other species' songs. Males sometimes sing during warm days in late winter.

References: Cable et al., 1996; Janzen, 2007; Sharpe et al., 2001; Thompson and Ely, 1992.

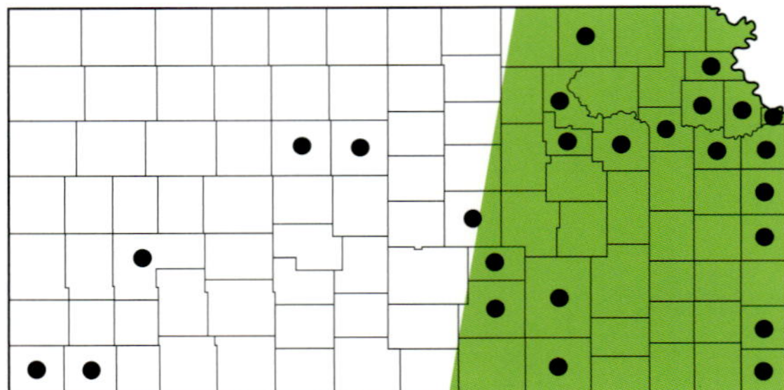

Prairie Warbler

Dendroica discolor (PRAW)

© Judd Patterson

Status: Rare transient and casual local summer resident in the eastern tier of counties; vagrant elsewhere and in winter.

Habitat: Confined almost entirely to scrubland or vegetation that is not over 10–15 feet high.

Migration: Extreme spring dates for presumed transients 20 April–23 May and exceptionally to at least 5 June (Ellsworth Co., singing male, near Kanopolis Reservoir, C. Smith). Most sightings are early to mid-May. Departure dates of spring transients are confounded by the possible presence of breeding birds (and in some cases apparently unmated territorial males) that remain through the summer. On at least two occasions, territorial males have been observed for extended periods, but no females were seen, including 14 May–2 July 1988 (Point of Rocks, Morton Co., P. Janzen and J. Yoder) and 31 May–16 June 1997 (Camp Horizon, Cowley Co., T. Hicks). A singing male was observed repeatedly at a site in western Douglas County from 8 to 15 May 1999 and again on 13 May and for several days in early June 2000 (probably the same individual) by P. Wedge and others, but no mate was seen. A lone bird reported by R. Field from Clinton Reservoir (Douglas Co.) on 8 August 1999 was an extremely early transient, a postbreeding vagrant, or else an undocumented breeder. Otherwise, the extreme dates for presumed transients are 2 and 23 September. One winter record, an adult male observed in Wichita (Sedgwick Co.) from 30 October to 19 December 2004 was videotaped by P. Griffin.

Breeding: Although considered a "rare summer resident" and "rather frequent" (Shawnee and Leavenworth cos., 1871) during the late 19th century it is now one of the rarest warblers in Kansas. There are no recent breeding records in Kansas, and it was not reported by KBBAT. H. Hedges reported a small colony (13+ singing males) near Lake Quivira (Johnson and Wyandotte cos.) from at least 1941 to 1953, and J. Rising reported breeding in Cherokee County in 1964. Recent midsummer sightings in Linn County (10 July 1977, J. Parrish) and Johnson County suggest possible breeding. The latter involved a singing male on 16 May 1998 (C. Hobbs) and an accompanying female on 19 May (D. Seibel), but no nest was found.

Comments: It rarely ventures westward beyond the eastern tier of counties and is seen very infrequently even there. The territorial male in Morton County in 1988 is thus extraordinary.

References: Busby and Zimmerman, 2001; Cable et al., 1996; Goss, 1891; Hedges, 1953; Janzen, 2007; Rising and Kilgore, 1964; Thompson and Ely, 1992.

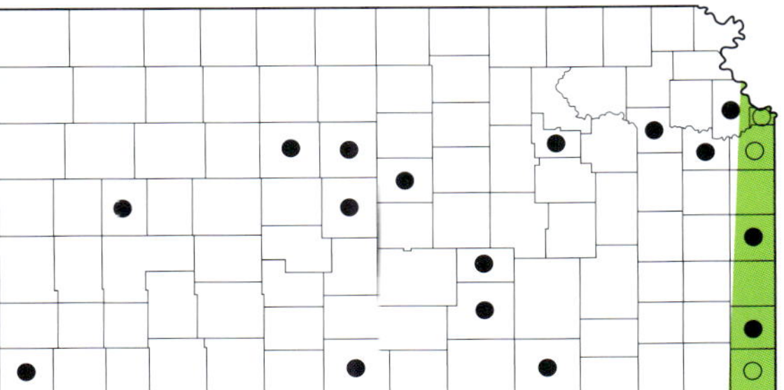

Palm Warbler

Dendroica palmarum (PAWA)

Status: Rare to uncommon transient in the east, casual in the west; occasional into midwinter.

© David Seibel

Habitat: Deciduous forest as well as open parkland or grassy areas at the edges of ponds or marshes, often near hedgerows; westward in open riparian vegetation (and along dikes at CBWA); winter stragglers may visit feeding stations.

Migration: Currently nearly three-fourths of all sightings are during spring. Extreme spring dates are 10 April–27 May with three-fourths of these during the period 27 April–10 May. It usually occurs singly or in small groups of three to five individuals. Extreme dates for fall are 4 September–29 October with most sightings 23 September–16 October. Stragglers have been reported on 15 and 22 November and into the CBC period, usually in the east. One visited a feeder during December–January 1975 (Elk Co., S. Albright); another was reported in Morton County on 30 December.

Comments: It usually feeds on or near the ground in relatively open or scrubby areas. Although not a common species, at least 10 individuals have been recovered from tower kills near Topeka during late September and late October. Behavior is a good clue to this species' identity. It tends to walk on the ground or along a low branch and bob its tail.

Banding: Four banded; no encounters.

References: Ball et al., 1995; Cable et al., 1996; Janzen, 2007; Thompson and Ely, 1992; Tordoff and Mengel, 1956.

Bay-breasted Warbler

Dendroica castanea (BBWA)

© Jim Burns

Status: Rare transient in the eastern tier of counties; casual in the west.

Habitat: Riparian woodland and wherever mature trees are found, for example, windbreaks, city parks, and residential areas.

Migration: Extreme spring dates are 2 and 27 April to 10 June (Morton Co.) and 13 June (Johnson Co., M. Cooper). Usual arrival is around 6 May with a median date of 12 May and usual departure about 20 May. Most migration is 10–20 May. A high of six birds was reported on 15 and 19 May. T. Pucci and J. Rising reported "unprecedented numbers" in the Kansas City area 18–26 May 1961 (AFN 15(4):5). Fall sightings are many fewer. Confirmed records (specimens, tower kills, and banded birds) are from 20 September to 7 November. Sight records (most unconfirmed) extend this to 30 August and 28 November. Most fall sightings are 19 September–3 October.

Comments: In Nebraska and Missouri it is reported to be more common during fall than during spring, but the reverse is true in Kansas. The few fall reports may be due, in part, to confusion with the very similar Blackpoll Warbler. Although the spring male is unmistakable, both sexes in fall plumage, and especially immature females, can be confusingly similar to the Blackpoll Warbler. D. Sibley gives an excellent synopsis of distinguishing characters and concludes that "all birds should be readily identifiable" if seen well. However, some individuals, such as a bird photographed on 5 September 2006 in Wyandotte County, show a thorough mix of these characters and may defy identification in the field and possibly even in the hand. Such individuals might be hybrids. Birders use the nickname "Baypoll Warbler" for indistinguishable individuals.

Banding: 13 banded; no encounters.

References: Cable et al., 1996; Sibley, 2000; Thompson and Ely, 1992; Tordoff and Mengel, 1956.

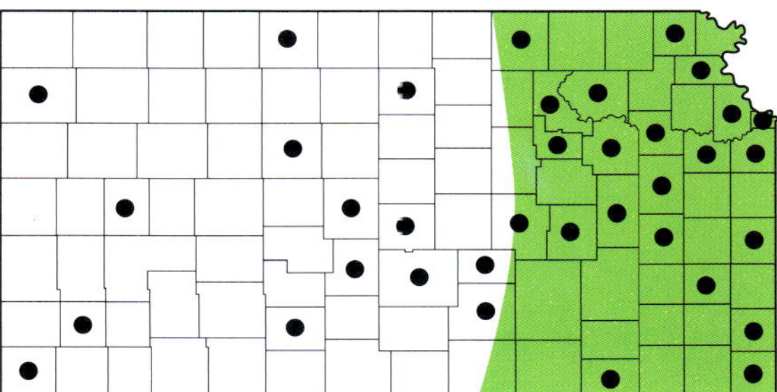

Blackpoll Warbler

Dendroica striata (BLPW)

© Judd Patterson

Status: Uncommon spring transient throughout the state; rare in the fall (more sightings in western Kansas at this season than in the east).

Habitat: During migration any wooded area, including riparian growth, parks, residential yards, cemeteries, and shelterbelts.

Migration: Extreme dates are 15 April (Cowley Co.) and 28 April (Johnson Co.) to 3 June (Ellis Co.) and 11 June (Rawlins Co.). Median arrival dates include 2 May (Johnson Co.), 6 May (Sherman Co.), and 11 May (Ellis Co.); median departure dates include 23 May (Ellis Co.). Statewide, most migration is about 5–21 May. Numbers may vary widely at a locality from year to year. Waves were reported on 5 May 1965 and 18 May 1974 (Johnson Co.) and "Woods" (unpubl. manuscript, 1976) reported peak migration on 12 May 1972 (Shawnee Co.). A fallout at Hays (Ellis Co.) brought birds down to net level on 20 May 1967, resulting in the banding of 38 individuals, 56 percent of the total banded there in 30 years. The fall migration is via the northeastern United States, the East Coast, and directly over water to its wintering grounds in South America, thus missing Kansas and the other central states except for small numbers that stray westward regularly. Confirmed records (specimens, tower kills, and banded individuals) are from 27 August through 7 October. Sight records, most unconfirmed, extend this period to 9 August (Sedgwick Co., T. Hicks) and 1 November (Morton Co.). November sightings are more likely Bay-breasted Warblers.

Comments: Its migration has been studied more thoroughly than most. Moving northward slowly at first, by the time it reaches Kansas it may be covering several hundred miles a night until it reaches its breeding grounds in the coniferous forests from Alaska to Labrador. It has the largest breeding range of any wood-warbler except that of the Yellow-rumped Warbler. Fall birds of either sex can be confusingly similar to the Bay-breasted Warbler and may even hybridize; both species are rare in Kansas at that season, and all records should be carefully documented.

Banding: 148 banded; no encounters.

References: Cable et al., 1996; Janzen, 2007; Thompson and Ely, 1992.

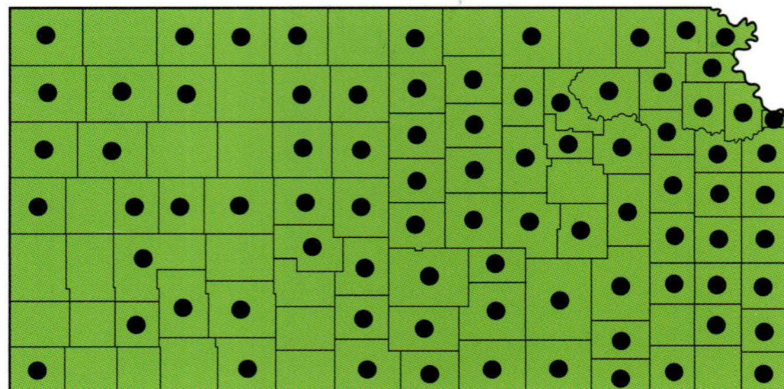

Cerulean Warbler

Dendroica cerulea (CERW)

Status: Rare transient and summer resident in the east; casual transient in the west; never common in Kansas, numbers seem to be declining as they are elsewhere.

Habitat: Mature deciduous forest; in eastern Kansas, canopies of tall trees along rivers or in the few places with large stands of upland forest; westward in shelterbelts, riparian growth, and in towns.

Migration: The earliest recorded arrival date in eastern Kansas is 23 April with most early arrivals by early May, a migration peak in mid-May, and a (presumed) transient on 9 June (Douglas Co., specimen). Westward, sightings are 25 April (Stafford Co.) to 22 June (Morton Co.) with most around mid-May. It is rarely recorded in the fall in Kansas. Nesting birds probably depart in August; the only records of presumed transients are a specimen for 13 September (Doniphan Co.), a "September" sighting from Sumner County, and an unconfirmed sighting on 21 September (Linn Co.).

Breeding: N. Goss and F. Snow considered this species a rare summer resident during the late 19th century, but the nearest specific evidence is of two birds collected by Goss in Woodson County on 30 July and 11 August. The first actual nest was found on 26 May 1985 near MDCWA (Linn Co.) by R. Boyd. It was placed about 40 feet high in a silver maple (*Acer saccharinum*). The nest was successful, and the adults were seen feeding young on 19 June. E. McHugh reported an immature near the same site on 22 August 1997 and territorial males at MDCWA on 30 June and 4 and 14 July 2002. J. Schukman reported probable nesting activity (up to five singing males on 5 July 2003) in bottomland forest on Fort Leavenworth (Leavenworth Co.) during most years since 1991–1996. One reported near Wathena (Doniphan Co.) by G. Pittman suggests another possible breeding area, as does a singing male at Schermerhorn Park (Cherokee Co.) on 2 July 2000.

Comments: It has never been found on a BBS in Kansas, and the only sightings by KBBAT (1992–1997) were in 4 of the 745 atlas blocks, all along the forested eastern edge of the state in Labette, Anderson, Leavenworth, and Doniphan counties.

Banding: 16 banded; no encounters.

References: Boyd, 1986; Busby and Zimmerman, 2001; Cable et al., 1996; Goss, 1891; Janzen, 2007; Rosenberg et al., 2000; Sauer et al., 2008; Schukman, 1996; Snow, 1903; Thompson and Ely, 1992.

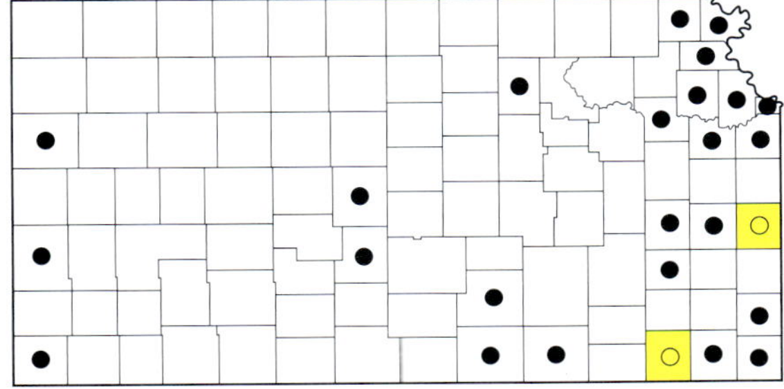

Black-and-white Warbler

Mniotilta varia (BAWW)

Status: Common transient; uncommon to rare summer resident in the east; uncommon transient in the west.

© David Seibel

Habitat: Eastern deciduous and riparian gallery forests; during migration any large stands of deciduous trees, including heavily wooded urban parks or yards and rural shelterbelts.

Migration: Early dates for spring arrival include 18 March (Geary Co.) and 25 March (Rice Co.), but arrival is usually in early April with the peak in early to mid-May and with stragglers to 2 June and 12 June. Median first arrival in Ellis County is 25 April; mean late departure is 13 May. Statewide, individuals after early June may be breeding birds rather than transients. Fall passage occurs primarily between 10 September and 6 October. The earliest reported fall occurrence, on 10 August, might have been a summer resident. Some individuals linger much later in the fall, with at least five November records through 29 November and two early winter reports from Cowley County on 1 December (E. Young) and 14 January (male at feeder, A. Barnard).

Breeding: Its breeding status and habits remain poorly documented, but it probably nests in patches of appropriate habitat, especially oak woodlands scattered throughout much of the eastern one-third of the state. KBBAT produced records of actual or potential nesting in a total of 50 study blocks (28 possible, 14 probable, and 8 confirmed), of which only 2 were west of the Flint Hills: 1 "probable" record in Reno County and 1 "possible" in Seward County. The highest frequency of records (19% of 176 blocks) was in the Osage Plains. M. Thompson and C. Ely report breeding records at least west to Sedgwick County, and there is at least one confirmed nesting in southern Cowley County (D. Herrin and D. Seibel, pers. comm.). It nests on the ground, requiring a relatively undisturbed stratum on the forest floor. This may limit its success in Kansas, where burning and grazing practices routinely involve wooded areas. Breeding pairs are also easily overlooked by traditional survey techniques, because the males often stop singing entirely as soon as pair-bonds are formed.

Comments: It was apparently more widespread and more regular in the late 19th and early 20th centuries, because both N. Goss and F. Snow considered it "quite common" and "not uncommon," respectively.

See page 503 for banding information.

References: Busby and Zimmerman, 2001; Cable et al., 1996; Goss, 1891; Janzen, 2007; Snow, 1903; Thompson and Ely, 1992.

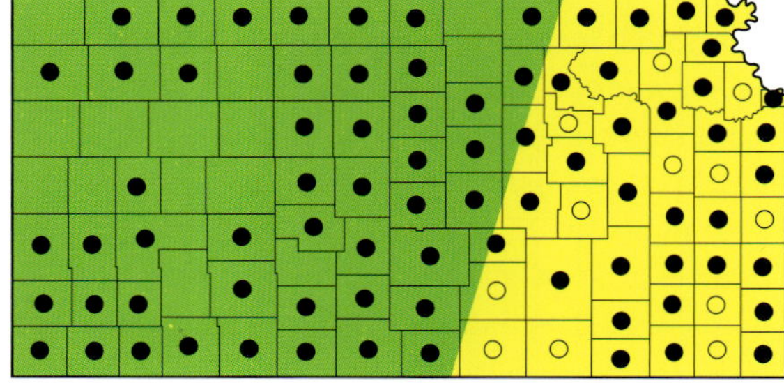

American Redstart

Setophaga ruticilla (AMRE)

Status: Common transient and very local summer resident in the eastern one-third of Kansas; uncommon transient elsewhere.

Habitat: Humid deciduous woodlands, from mature hardwood forest, successional forest, to open forest edge; westward in shelterbelts, riparian woodlands, and wooded parks and residential areas.

Migration: The earliest arrival is 15 April (Cowley Co.) but is usually around 30 April. Median early arrivals include 10 May (Ellis and Sherman cos.) and 13 May (Johnson Co.); mean spring departure in Ellis County is 26 May with stragglers through 13 June. Peak migration is usually mid-May but was on 24 May (unusually late) in Shawnee County in 1969. T. Cable reported 100+ at Fort Leavenworth on 17 May 1992, and J. Schukman reported the same number during June 2000 at the same location where it is a common breeder; in the west, 13 to 18 May is more usual. Exact departure dates are confounded at both seasons by the continuing presence of breeding birds. Fall passage probably begins in late August, peaks by mid-September, and is largely finished by 20 September but with stragglers into late September and once to 12 October (Douglas Co.). The median fall arrival date for Ellis County is 28 August and is 30 August for other sites west of probable breeding areas.

Breeding: Breeds primarily in the northeastern counties, where summer residents are uncommon to rare overall but can have large local populations, notably in the Missouri River bottomland forest on Fort Leavenworth (Leavenworth Co.). Here, J. Schukman has consistently found a large breeding population during most years since 1993, including at least 30 territorial males, probably on territories on 29 May, and females with brood patches during June and on 2 July. Singing males are occasionally found in midsummer in areas where they do not nest, such as on 24 July (Ellis Co.). The nest is placed in a tree from 6 to 30 feet high.

Comments: Breeding is consistent only on the eastern periphery of Kansas in the first one to two tiers of counties next to Missouri. KBBAT project yielded no confirmed nesting records except in the special block on Fort Leavenworth (Leavenworth Co.). Possible breeding also was reported for Saline County in central Kansas; this was by far the westernmost record.

Banding: 386 banded; no encounters.

References: Busby and Zimmerman, 2001; Cable et al., 1996; Janzen, 2007; Sauer et al., 2008; Schukman, 1996; Thompson and Ely, 1992.

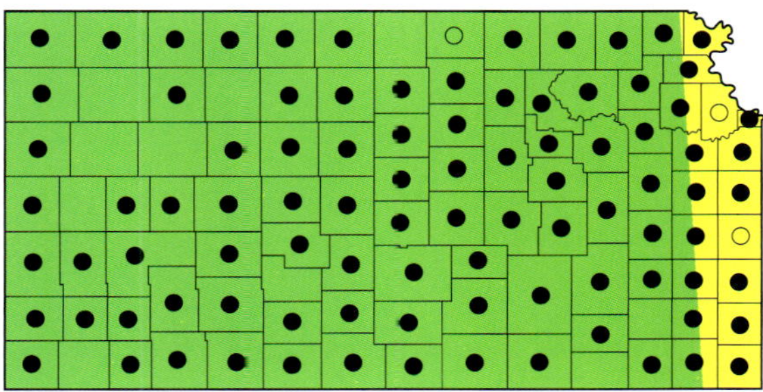

Prothonotary Warbler

Protonotaria citrea (PROW)

Status: Uncommon transient and rare summer resident in eastern one-third to half of state; may be fairly common locally in proper habitat (particularly at MDCWA); rare transient elsewhere.

Habitat: Swampy woodlands, mature forest at water edge, and dense willow stands along rivers; occasional in residential areas. Inundation of wooded valleys around the edges of reservoirs has increased the available habitat for the species in scattered locations, for example, in the Flint Hills and Osage Plains.

Migration: The earliest arrivals are 8 April (Montgomery Co.) and 10 April (Linn Co.) but are usually about 25 April, with most migration during the first half of May. West of the breeding range, first arrivals are late April (Finney Co.) to 21 May (Ellis Co.) with most during early May. The latest passage of spring migrants and earliest fall arrivals are clouded by the lingering presence of breeding birds. N. Goss states that most individuals leave the state in August; J. Linsdale reported migration in Doniphan County from 3 August to 10 September; R. Johnston lists the median departure date as 22 August (6 August–10 September). Latest confirmed dates are 8–10 October (Sedgwick Co., P. Briggs), with an unconfirmed record on 10 November (Kearney Co.). One reported at Middle Springs (Morton Co.) on 5 July (K. Hart and S. Guy) must have been a vagrant.

Breeding: Typically nests in cavities of trees (old woodpecker holes or tops of broken stumps) standing in still or slow-flowing water. The cavity entrance ranges from 0.5 to 10.0 m above the ground or water surface, with a mean height of about 2 m. It may use nest boxes or other man-made structures. N. Goss reported two instances of a pair nesting in a sawmill (the second time, in a tin cup sitting on a beam near the roof); more recently, a pair used a wren house in Winfield (Cowley Co.), and in 1978 one nested unsuccessfully in an old bluebird box standing in flooded timber. Eggs have been reported 19 May–1 July (median, 12 clutches, 15 June), young in nest 9 June–11 July, and recently fledged young 9 June–23 July.

Comments: This is one of the most striking wood-warblers, and the only eastern species that nests in cavities.

Banding: 18 banded; one encounter: in-state.

References: Busby and Zimmerman, 2001; Goss, 1891; Janzen, 2007; Johnston, 1965; Linsdale, 1928; Petit, 1999; Thompson and Ely, 1992.

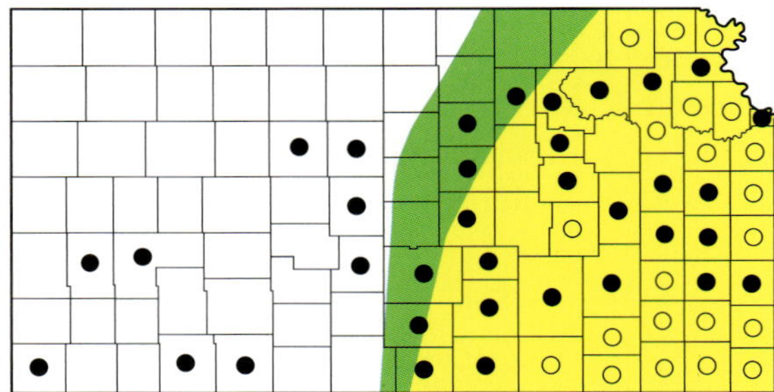

Worm-eating Warbler

Helmitheros vermivorum (WEWA)

© Judd Patterson

Status: Rare transient and possible summer resident in the extreme east; casual westward.

Habitat: Dense understory of wooded slopes, generally in large tracts of deciduous forest; in western and central Kansas, in shelterbelts, trees with undergrowth, or residential yards.

Migration: The earliest arrival dates are 9 and 10 April (Harvey Co.), but arrival is typically about 16 April with peak movement 20 April–15 May and with stragglers to 28 May and rarely early June. Median first arrival dates include 2 May (Sedgwick Co.) and 5 May (Ellis Co.). It is typically found singly or in very small groups. Some late May to early June reports may be of breeding individuals. There are only eight fall records on 29 August (Johnson Co.) and 2–14 September. Only one of these (Ellis Co., 5 September) is from western Kansas.

Breeding: Like several other wood-warblers it nests on the ground. It was reported as "breeding" by N. Goss without any supporting details. D. C. Hilton reported a newly fledged young with an adult at Fort Leavenworth (Leavenworth Co.) on 7 June 1919, and J. Linsdale reported a singing bird on 11 July 1923 in Doniphan County. There are at least four recent records during the breeding season: 1 June 1997, Schermerhorn Park (Cherokee Co., A. Swalwell); 21–27 May 1993, Nelson Environmental Study Area (Jefferson Co., G. Pittman); 9 July 1994, adult (KBRC 94-14) near MD-CWA (L. Moore); and 1 June 1995, one mist-netted in Missouri River bottomland forest on Fort Leavenworth (Leavenworth Co.). Three of them may have been late transients.

Comments: Citing a known population just across the Missouri River, W. Busby and J. Zimmerman hypothesize that the June 1995 record (and perhaps others) might have been a stray from Missouri. In spring 1990, a single Worm-eating Warbler was observed by several members of the KOS in a now-famous shelterbelt in Elkhart (Morton Co.). With subsequent records from the same vicinity, this species has likely been seen more often in extreme southwestern Kansas than in parts of the state much closer to its normal range in eastern deciduous forest. The nearest breeding population to Kansas is in the Missouri Ozarks.

See page 503 for banding information.

References: Busby and Zimmerman, 2001; Cable et al., 1996; Goss, 1891; Hilton *in* Tordoff, 1956; Janzen, 2007; Linsdale, 1928; Pittman, 1995; Thompson and Ely, 1992.

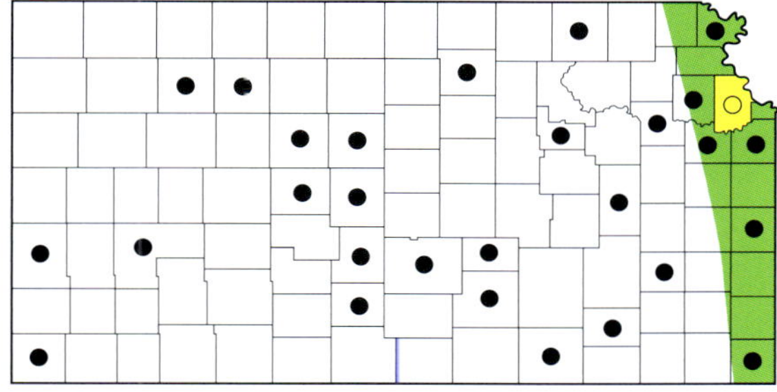

Swainson's Warbler

Limnothlypis swainsonii (SWWA)

Status: Vagrant, mostly in the extreme eastern part of the state.

Habitat: Prefers dense thickets in river-edge habitat, especially in stands of cane (outside of Kansas).

Migration: Of the nine Kansas records, all but one are from the period 4–23 May; five are from the easternmost tier of counties, and four of these are from Johnson County. There are two specimen records: Johnson County, 11 May 1957 (KU 33464); and Cherokee County, found dead at a television tower, 16 May 1965 (ESU B1327). In addition, there are three sightings from Johnson County by M. L. Myers: 23 May 1969, 4 May 1973, and 13 May 1980. The three most recent sightings have been farther west. A singing male was seen by many observers at Elk City Reservoir (Montgomery Co.) from 14 to 25 June 1992 (KBRC 92-38, photograph). There is no evidence that this bird found a mate. Breeding was documented along the Little Caney River in Washington County, Oklahoma, near the Kansas border in 1914 and 1917, close to the area where the Montgomery County bird was found. A. J. Kirn reported nests with eggs during the period 29 May–27 June. The three remaining sightings were even farther west: one bird was seen and videotaped in Rush County, 9 May 1994; another was seen in Wichita (Sedgwick Co.) on 7 May 1996 (KBRC 97-08); M. Osterbuhr observed another on 5 May 2009, and photographed this warbler in Finney County (submitted to KBRC).

Comments: Kansas birds have probably "overshot" their destinations during migration. This warbler is plain brownish above and white below, with no distinctive field marks, but like most wood-warblers, it has a distinctive song.

References: Busby and Zimmerman, 2001; Janzen, 2007; Land, 2010; Pittman, 1993, 1998; Sutton, 1967; Thompson and Ely, 1992.

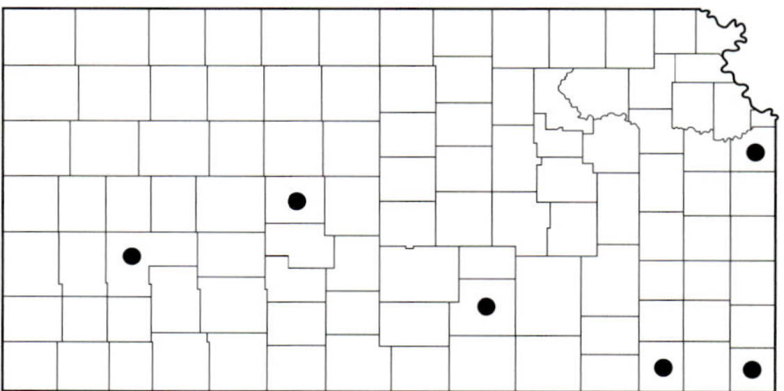

Ovenbird

Seiurus aurocapilla (OVEN)

Status: Common transient and rare summer resident in the eastern one-third; uncommon transient westward.

Habitat: Mature deciduous forest in the east and along wooded rivers and in shelterbelts or quiet, wooded residential areas farther west.

Migration: The earliest arrival dates are 19 and 23 April. More typically arrival is in late April with most migration during mid-May and with most departed by mid-May but with stragglers to 4 June (Ellis Co.) and 6 June (Osage Co.). Median earliest arrival includes 8 May (Ellis Co.); median last departure is 24 May (Ellis Co.). Some late May and early June reports in the east are undoubtedly of local breeders. Extreme dates for transients are 2 August (Ellis Co.) and 23 October (Topeka area). Typical fall arrival is early September with most migration during mid- and late September and stragglers into October. Median first fall arrival is 12 September (Ellis Co.) with additional reports from 16 September (Cheyenne Co.) to 6 October (Barton Co.); late dates in the west are 2–20 October. It ranks seventh in numbers of individuals (96+) recovered at tower kills in Rawlins County and the Topeka area.

Breeding: J. Linsdale found none in Doniphan County during 1921–1925, and M. Brumwell reported single nesting pairs at Fort Leavenworth (Leavenworth Co.) in 1939 and 1940. More recently, C. Cink and R. Boyd provided the first fully documented evidence, in Douglas County in 1979. Following observations of an Ovenbird in suitable habitat in 1978, they found 10 adults and one nest with young in the same woods in 1979, and another nest with four eggs in the same area in 1980. D. Seibel observed an extremely territorial male feigning injury in an apparent distraction display at the Nelson Environmental Study Area (Jefferson Co.) in late May or early June. Similar behavior was observed in Doniphan County. The only confirmed breeding record was a female with a brood patch captured at Fort Leavenworth (Leavenworth Co.) on 6 June 1994. Actual breeding data (all by C. Cink and R. Boyd) are scant: eggs were probably laid in early May, and one clutch was recorded on 24 June; young fledged prematurely on 19 June; and recently fledged young were seen 3–19 June.

See page 503 for banding information.

References: Ball et al., 1995; Barkley et al., 1977; Brumwell, 1951; Busby and Zimmerman, 2001; Cink and Boyd, 1982; Linsdale, 1928; Thompson and Ely, 1992; Tordoff and Mengel, 1956.

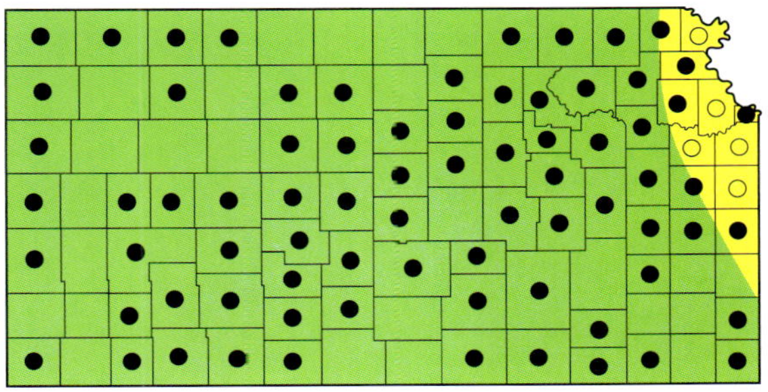

Northern Waterthrush

Parkesia noveboracensis (NOWA)

© Alfredo D. Colon

Status: Uncommon transient throughout the state.

Habitat: Around pools of standing water in wet deciduous woodland, riparian undergrowth, and suburban yards.

Migration: It migrates later in spring than the very similar Louisiana Waterthrush, for which early April reports are typical. Extreme arrival dates are 7–15 April (doubtful) and more typically 20 April–26 May (later sightings need confirmation). Median first arrivals are 5–6 May (Sherman Co.) and 9 May (Ellis Co.). Most migration is during late April to about 25 May. Late departures from the west are 24–26 May. The high count is 12 on 4 May (Douglas Co.). Extreme fall dates are 7 August (doubtful) to 23 October. Arrival is typically about 20 August, with birds widely distributed by early September. Most migration is 20 August to mid-September with stragglers into October. Most reports during late September to mid-October have been of birds (at least 26) recovered at tower kills near Topeka during the period 1954–1994. The current late date of 30 November 2009, QNWR (S. Seltman), is exceptional.

Comments: Waterthrushes are wood-warblers, not thrushes, but they receive their name from their superficially thrushlike appearance and habits. Like thrushes, both the Northern Waterthrush and Louisiana Waterthrush are denizens of dark woodland floors, where they walk along the ground, fallen logs, and low branches. They more nearly resemble the otherwise dissimilar pipits and wagtails (family Motacillidae) in their habit of pumping their tails up and down vigorously as they walk or even stand. It is much less tied to wooded streams than the very similar Louisiana Waterthrush and is thus more widespread in the state during migration. In western Kansas it can be found in any area with trees (such as shelterbelts), especially if there are at least ephemeral pools nearby. The two species of waterthrush differ only subtly in appearance, but the song of each is distinctive, which helps to distinguish the two during spring migration. Their call notes are more similar but also separable with practice.

Banding: 252 banded; no encounters.

References: Ball et al., 1995; Cable et al., 1996; Janzen, 2007; Thompson and Ely, 1992; Tordoff and Mengel, 1956.

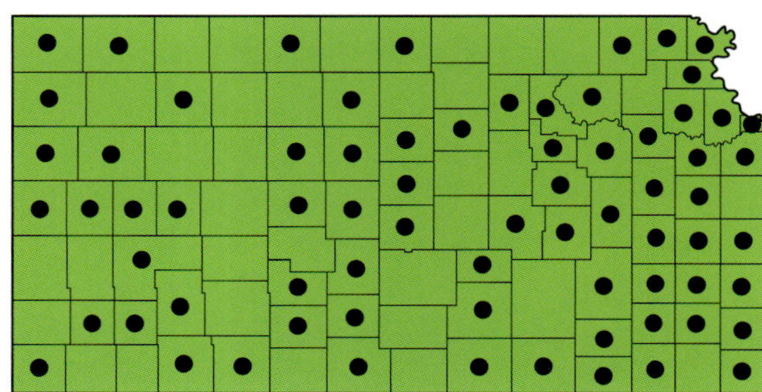

Louisiana Waterthrush

Parkesia motacilla (LOWA)

Status: Uncommon transient and summer resident, mostly in the eastern one-third of the state; uncommon to casual transient in the west.

Habitat: Perennial streams in mature deciduous forest.

Migration: In eastern Kansas, this is one of the earliest spring warblers, arriving as early as 25 March. Usual arrival is early April with individuals widely dispersed by midmonth. Farther west, it arrives much later (17 April–9 May) and with departure dates to 14 and 24 May (Ellis Co.). Early June records are probably local breeders. Rarely seen in fall, the 18 records are within the period 1 August–21 September (Ellis Co., unconfirmed, M. Rolfs). Some of the early August records are probably local breeders (singing birds on 12 and 17 August). Sightings outside the breeding range are 5 August (banded, Meade Co., T. Flowers) to 21 September. Most migration is probably mid-August to early September as in nearby Missouri. Actual fall departure may be even earlier than shown by Kansas records. A specimen (KU 94150) collected in El Salvador on 24 July 2001 was a young of the year.

Breeding: It breeds along fast-flowing streams in hilly country in the eastern one-third of the state and, apparently, in the few pockets of such habitat that still exist farther west. L. Wolfe found a nest near Oberlin (Decatur Co.) in 1910. Several recent records from the Red Hills suggest that a few pairs have nested there since at least 1998. P. Janzen reports sightings from 1998 to 2002 in Schwartz Canyon (Comanche Co.) including apparent nest-building on 1 May and a singing male as late as 8 July. More recently, on Thompson Creek in nearby Kiowa County, an adult was observed carrying a fecal sac on 18 May 2007 and another was seen in Barber County on 27 May 2009, well into the nesting season for this species. Recent records in late spring and summer from Sedgwick County (Chisholm Creek Park, Wichita, 29 May 2007; and Crane Park, Derby, 12 June 2009) likewise suggest breeding. Eggs have been reported 9 May–18 June, young in nest 18 May–17 July, and recently fledged young 31 May, making June migration south plausible.

Comments: W. Busby and J. Zimmerman note that this species is ecologically the "sandpiper" of the wood-warbler family.

Banding: 82 banded; no encounters.

References: Busby and Zimmerman, 2001; Cable et al., 1996; Colvin, 1936; Janzen, 2002b, 2007; Robbins and Easterla, 1992; Thompson and Ely, 1992; Wolfe, 1961.

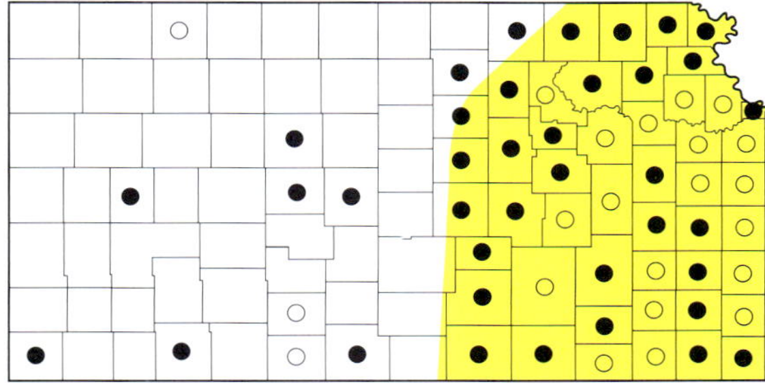

Kentucky Warbler

Oporornis formosus (KEWA)

Status: Uncommon but conspicuous transient and local summer resident in the eastern one-third of the state; rare transient in the remainder of state.

© David Seibel

Habitat: Lush understory of mature oak–hickory forest and riparian hardwoods; during migration a wider variety of wooded habitats including hedgerows and wooded thickets in urban parks.

Migration: Extreme early arrivals are 21 April (Douglas Co.) and 25 April (Ellis and Johnson cos.), but usual arrivals are late April and early May with most migration during the first half of May. Counts are typically low, but "lots" were moving through Wyandotte County on 26 May (C. Hobbs). Late departures for birds west of the Flint Hills include 17 May (Ellis Co.) and 31 May (Sherman Co.). In the east, actual late departure of spring migrants and early arrival of fall transients are confused by the presence of local breeders. Examination of the few data suggests that fall migration probably begins in early August and peaks in late August with stragglers into mid-September and rarely October.

Breeding: In Kansas, it nests primarily in hardwood forest east of the Flint Hills but may breed sporadically west to the 97th meridian (Cowley Co. in the south and Clay Co. in the north). Along the eastern edge of the Flint Hills its breeding distribution becomes very patchy (found in only 8% of 74 study blocks surveyed by KBBAT) and is limited to protected riparian gallery forest with dense understory vegetation. There are few documented nest records, none west of the Flint Hills. Eggs have been reported 16 May–23 June, young in nest 3 June–6 July, and recently fledged young 5 June–19 July. The Kentucky Warbler builds its nest on the ground or in low shrubs.

Comments: It tends to skulk in the dense understory of dark woods and can be difficult to see, but its loud, distinctive song readily reveals its presence. At times, however, the song can sound surprisingly like that of the Carolina Wren, Ovenbird, or even the Northern Cardinal.

Banding: 309 banded; one encounter: in-state, at banding site.

References: Busby and Zimmerman, 2001; Cable et al., 1996; Janzen, 2007; Thompson and Ely, 1992.

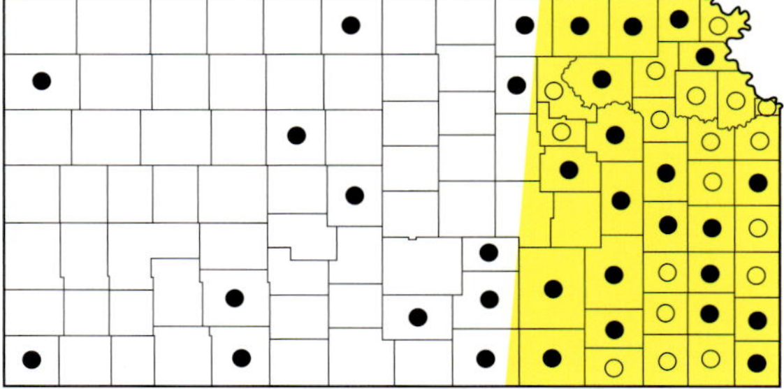

Connecticut Warbler

Oporornis agilis (CONW)

© Brian Small

Status: Casual transient in eastern Kansas; vagrant elsewhere.

Habitat: Dense understory or woodland edge, riparian undergrowth, and parks and residential areas with sufficient shrubbery.

Migration: Most migration is east of Kansas. The few documented spring records are during the period 11 May (Douglas Co., R. Antonio) to 24 May (Jefferson Co., C. Hobbs and D. LaShelle) and involve singing males. Other sight records extend this period to 6 May (Ellis Co., M. Rolfs), and 28 May (complete eye-ring and no black on chest, but diagnostic measurements not taken). Most migration is probably during the last half of May. In fall, sight identification is even more difficult, because males are silent and the distinguishing characteristics are even more subtle. Specimens are available for 23 September (Shawnee Co., KU 32622) and 28 September (Ellis Co., MHP 4221). Sight records (none confirmed) extend this period to 3 September. A report for 22 October is in error.

Comments: The closely related Connecticut, Mourning, and MacGillivray's Warblers form a difficult complex for field identification, because their habits are elusive (skulking in dense undergrowth) and immatures and adult females of the three species are very similar in appearance. All three are relatively heavy, slow-moving warblers that walk on the ground or along low branches. The Connecticut Warbler is the largest and most thrushlike of the three, and the only one with a *complete* white eye-ring (all ages and at all seasons) that can be very difficult to discern, especially in the fall. The smaller, more arboreal Nashville Warbler is superficially similar in coloration but differs in many details of plumage and soft-part color, structure, behavior, and voice. The loud, distinctive song of the male Connecticut Warbler—a staccato, accelerating series of notes sometimes described as "trick-or-treat … trick-or-treat … trick-or-TREAT! trick-or-TREAT!" is most often the clue to both its presence and its identity.

Banding: Six banded; no encounters.

References: Janzen, 2007; Thompson and Ely, 1992.

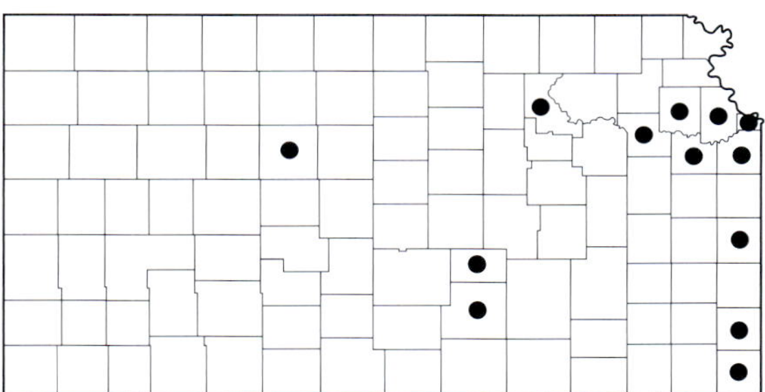

Mourning Warbler

Oporornis philadelphia (MOWA)

Status: Common but largely overlooked transient in the eastern half of the state; uncommon transient in the west.

Habitat: Dense thickets in deciduous forest and woodland edge, usually skulking near the ground; in the fall, also in residential yards and stands of giant ragweed with other migrating warblers.

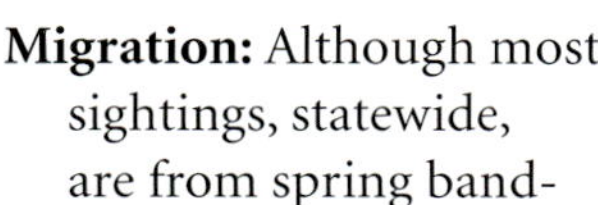

Migration: Although most sightings, statewide, are from spring banding studies, tower kills suggest it is equally and perhaps more common during fall. The earliest spring arrivals are 22 April (Sumner Co., banded) and 27 April, but arrival is usually early to mid-May. Peak migration is during the third week of May (Ellis and Johnson cos., bandings; and Shawnee Co.). J. Linsdale considered it the most common transient warbler on 20 May (Doniphan Co.). Migration is largely finished by 25 May but with stragglers to 6 June (Sedgwick Co.). Confirmed fall records (specimens, tower kills, and handheld individuals) are 23 August (Doniphan Co.) to 16 October (Ellis Co.), and sight records extend this period to 19 August (Morton Co.). Median first fall arrival is 9 September (Ellis Co.), and most migration is during September. High counts include 25+ on 5 September (Cowley Co., E. Young), and M. Thompson banded 46 individuals in Cowley County during the first week of September in 1969. Very late sightings of *Oporornis* include 26 October (Harvey Co.) and 4 November (Ellis Co.), but the actual species were not confirmed.

Comments: Like its congeners, this relatively slow-moving warbler is often difficult to see because of its retiring habits and affinity for dense cover. Even when large numbers are present most go unnoticed, especially in the fall when they are largely silent. In the spring, singing males are more readily detected, but this species is not as vocal as many warblers during migration. It ranked fourth, with 159 individuals (9% of all individual warblers) salvaged at tower kills in the Topeka area during the period 1954–1994, and numerous others were found during unreported kills in various other years (E. and E. Lewis). The Mourning Warbler can be confusingly similar to the much rarer Connecticut Warbler and more western MacGillivray's Warbler, especially in basic (fall) plumages.

Banding: 397 banded; no encounters.

References: Ball et al., 1995; Cable et al., 1996; Janzen, 2007; Linsdale, 1928; Thompson and Ely, 1992; Tordoff and Mengel, 1956.

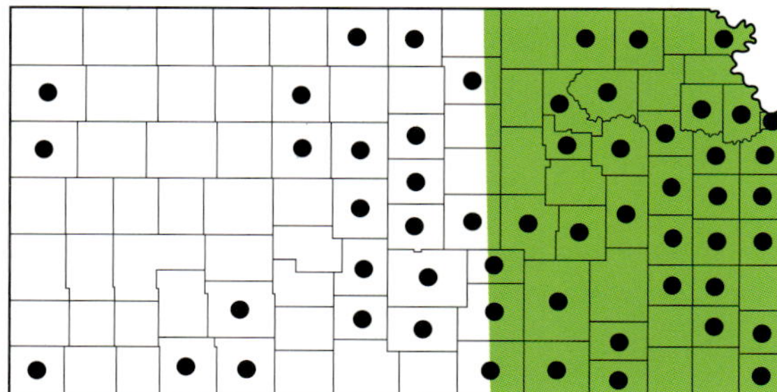

MacGillivray's Warbler

Oporornis tolmiei (MGWA)

Status: Uncommon transient in the western one-third of the state; vagrant eastward.

Habitat: Dense undergrowth in woodlands, windbreaks, parks, and residential yards.

Migration: It is more common during spring than fall. Extreme dates are 1 May (Cowley Co.) to 6 June (Ellis Co.) with most migration during 15–25 May. Median first arrival is 13 May (Ellis Co.) and 13–14 May (Sherman Co.). In Ellis County half of all bandings were 21–31 May. Two summer records are unexpected: 20 June (Grant Co., C. Ely) and 17 July (singing male, Cheyenne Co., S. Patti). Confirmed fall records (specimens and handheld individuals) are 27 August–30 September, and sight records extend this period to 18 August (M. Schwilling) and 12 October (both Morton Co.). Median first arrival in Ellis is 9 September. Most migration is mid-September. An individual *Oporornis* with light gray hood and faint eye-ring visited a feeder in Hays (Ellis Co.) on 2 December 1972 (M. Rolfs).

Comments: In appearance and habits MacGillivray's Warbler closely resembles its eastern congeners, the Connecticut Warbler and, especially, the Mourning Warbler; even some spring adults are difficult to identify by sight. As usual, the song of the male is a helpful clue. Thompson and Ely considered measurements necessary to safely separate fall MacGillivray's Warblers from Mourning Warblers; although subsequent advances in field identification techniques may soften this argument, it is a good reminder of how similar in appearance the two species can be, even in the hand.

Banding: 59 banded; no encounters.

References: Cable et al., 1996; Graber and Graber, 1951; Janzen, 2007; Thompson and Ely, 1992.

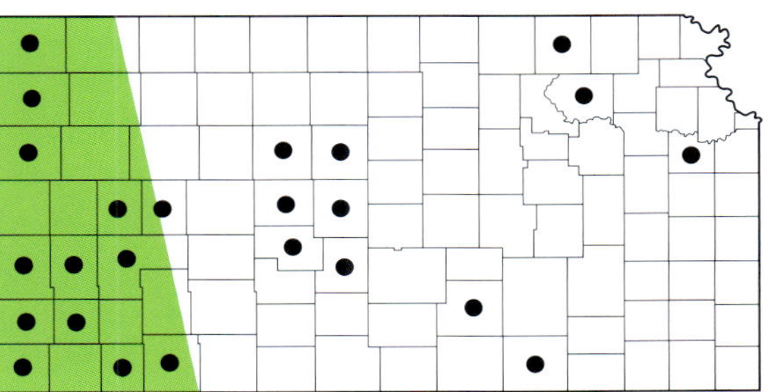

Common Yellowthroat

Geothlypis trichas (COYE)

Status: Common transient and summer resident in favorable habitat statewide; most abundant east of the Flint Hills and in large marshes elsewhere; occasional winter straggler or resident.

Habitat: Nesting is primarily in cattail and sedge marshes, moist overgrown fields or brushy edges with an extensive litter layer, tallgrass prairie, and wet hay meadows. Transients occur in marshes and riparian growth and commonly occur in thickets and ragweed patches, sometimes far from water.

Migration: The earliest arrivals are 3 April (Pawnee Co.) and 4 April (Finney Co.); arrival is usually late April and early May with the peak migration during mid-May. The mean earliest arrival dates include 3 May (Ellis and Sherman cos.), 3–4 May (Russell Co.), and 5 May (Johnson Co.). In Ellis County, peak migration ranged from 7–15 May (1972) to 20–24 May (1969). It was unusually abundant during May 1935 in Rooks County. Statewide most transients have probably departed by 20 May. Early June reports are a mixture of stragglers and local breeders. Numbers are much smaller in fall than during spring. Only 20 percent of 600+ individuals banded in Ellis County were during the fall. Transients probably begin arriving by late August, peak by mid-September, and continue passage through early October with stragglers to 29 October and 29 November (Barton Co.). The median fall arrival date for Ellis County is 14 September, and half of the fall bandings were during the period 21 September–2 October. During mild winters a few individuals have remained through the CBC period in Cowley, Geary, Harvey, Scott, and Linn counties (3 years). There are reports to at least 7 January (Barton Co.), 12 January (Stafford Co.), and 26 January (Douglas Co., A. Powell).

Breeding: It is likely the most numerous breeding wood-warbler in the state. It is abundant in larger marshes such as CBWA, QNWR, and SCW, but even small marshes of 1 acre or less will sometimes have one or two breeding pairs. Completed but empty nests have been reported 18 May–25 June, eggs 29 May–25 June, young in nest 6–16 June, and recently fledged young 20 June–10 July. The nest is placed about 2 feet high in cattails, sedges, or other herbaceous ground cover.

Comments: It is the only warbler in Kansas regularly found in cattails.

See page 503 for banding information.

References: Busby and Zimmerman, 2001; Imler, 1937; Janzen, 2007; Sibley, 2000; Thompson and Ely, 1992.

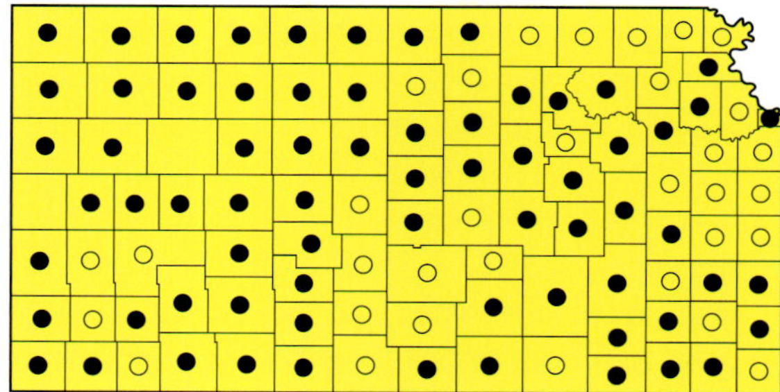

Hooded Warbler

Wilsonia citrina (HOWA)

Status: Rare transient and casual summer resident in the extreme east; casual transient elsewhere. Most records are during spring migration.

Habitat: Mature hardwood forest with well-developed understory; during migration also in riparian growth, woodland edge, parks, residential areas, and occasionally even shelterbelts.

Migration: Earliest spring arrivals are from western Kansas: 10 April (Ellis Co., G. Farley) and 14 April (Finney Co., photo, T. Shane). Most arrivals are around 30 April with most migration during the first half of May and with stragglers through late May to 5 June (Cowley Co.). Median early arrival is 4 May (Johnson Co.). Most of the few fall sightings are 4–23 September with one to 1 October (Finney Co., M. Osterbuhr).

Breeding: It was considered a "summer resident" in the east during the late 19th century but without any supporting evidence. The only direct evidence of nesting is a single nest (W. R. Breicheisen) near Welda (Anderson Co.) in 1959. That clutch was presumably completed about 23 May with a young fledgling being banded on 22 June. Probable breeding is suggested by an immature female seen near Perry Reservoir (Jefferson Co.) on 20 July and an immature male seen there on 9 August (E. McHugh). One singing at Scott Lake (Scott Co., M. Corder) on 23 June 1996 was most likely a vagrant. Only one record was obtained by KBBAT, a singing male, with no evidence for nesting, at Fort Leavenworth, Leavenworth County. It nests in dense understory of wet, mixed deciduous forest, typically where a gap in the canopy allows light to filter through to the lower vegetation; in the southern United States it is a bird of wooded swamps.

Comments: Territorial males are vocal and conspicuous, but the species can be secretive during fall migration. Typical of its family, it eats insects, but it is a more aerobatic forager than most, often snatching its prey out of the air like a flycatcher. Like some other wood-warblers, it frequently fans its tail showing its conspicuous white tail pattern.

Banding: 26 banded; no encounters.

References: Busby and Zimmerman, 2001; Cable et al., 1996; Janzen, 2007; Thompson and Ely, 1992.

Wilson's Warbler

Wilsonia pusilla (WIWA)

Status: Common spring and fall transient statewide.

Habitat: Dense undergrowth in second-growth woodland and woodland edge, shelterbelts, thickets, overgrown fields, and even shrubbery in towns.

Migration: The earliest arrivals are 7 April (Sedgwick Co.) and 12 April (Hamilton Co.), but first arrival is usually during late April with most migration during mid-May and stragglers to 22 May. Median first arrivals include 1 May (Ellis Co.), 5 May (Sherman Co.), 6 May (Harvey Co.), and 8 May (Johnson Co.). Late departures include 26 May (Morton and Wyandotte cos.) and 27 May (Cowley Co.). One reported 12 June (Jefferson Co., D. Larson) is unusually late. It is much more common during fall than during spring, and numbers fluctuate greatly from year to year, especially in the west. Earliest arrivals include 5 August (Sedgwick Co.) and 25 August (Pawnee Co.), but during typical years arrival is late August and early September. Median first arrivals include 1 September (Rice Co.) and 2 September (Ellis Co.), with most migration during the last half of September. In Ellis County, 95 percent of the 654 individuals banded were during the period 11–20 September, often during weather-induced fallouts. Two such incidents resulted in the banding of 71 (13 September) and 42 (16 September) individuals, respectively (different years). Comparable numbers have been reported in Morton County with estimates of 300+ on 21 September and 200+ on 14 and 28 September, again during different years. Elsewhere numbers are usually smaller with 15 on 6 September (Linn Co.) and 20 on 2 September (Sedgwick Co.). Median departure for Ellis County is 30 September with stragglers into mid-October. It was among the warbler species present during a fallout following the first snow of the season in Dodge City on 11 October 1970 (Ford Co., J. Challans). Stragglers include 20 October (Meade Co., banded) and 27 October (Morton Co.). It ranked fifth among species of warblers salvaged from tower kills during the period 1954–1994.

Comments: This species is one of the most common transient warblers in Kansas, particularly in the fall in western Kansas, where it may outnumber even the abundant Yellow-rumped Warbler. Occasionally feeds high in trees, but usually stays relatively low in the vegetation.

Banding: 1,493 banded; no encounters.

References: Ball et al., 1995; Barkley et al., 1977; Cable et al., 1996; Janzen, 2007; Thompson and Ely, 1992; Tordoff and Mengel, 1956.

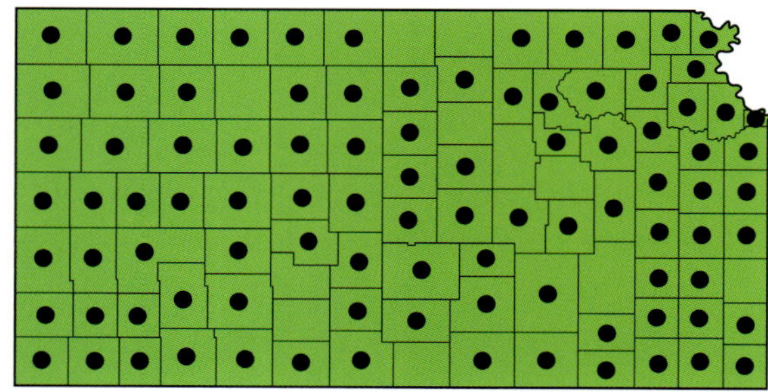

Canada Warbler

Wilsonia canadensis (CAWA)

Status: Uncommon transient in eastern Kansas; casual in the west.

Habitat: Dense understory or edges along riparian or upland deciduous forest; also in parks and suburban yards with well-developed, dense understory.

Migration: The species migrates northward through the eastern United States so it is less commonly reported during spring than fall. The earliest reported arrival is 6 April (Harvey Co.), but more typically arrival is 20 April to early May with most migration 10–25 May and with stragglers to 4 June. The median earliest arrival is 6 May (Johnson Co.). Sightings for 15 June (Geary Co., C. Otte) and 8 July (Riley Co.) are probably summer vagrants. The earliest fall arrivals are 17–18 August (Greenwood Co., C. Hall) with usual arrival 23–27 August and most migration during the first half of September with stragglers into early October, once to 11 October (Sedgwick Co., D. Kilby). A few have been salvaged from tower kills in Goodland (Sherman Co.) and the Topeka area 12 September–1 October.

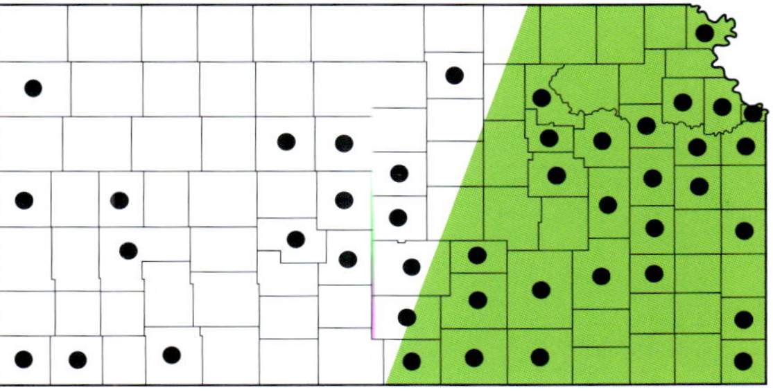

Comments: The name Canada Warbler is misleading, because this species nests south along the Appalachians into northern Georgia. It is not particularly shy but is easily overlooked, because it tends to be relatively quiet during migration and often stays hidden in dense vegetation.

Banding: 43 banded; no encounters.

References: Ball et al., 1995; Barkley et al., 1977; Carson, 1954; Janzen, 2007; Thompson and Ely, 1992; Tordoff and Mengel, 1956.

Painted Redstart

Myioborus pictus (PARE)

Status: Accidental. Two records. A single adult was seen west of the refuge headquarters at QNWR on 5 April 2000 by C. F. and M. Zeillemaker (KBRC 2000-15). Another adult was discovered at the Lake Coldwater campground (Comanche Co.) on 23 June 2003 by P. Seibert and others. This bird was photographed and seen by many observers through 28 June (KBRC 2003-39).

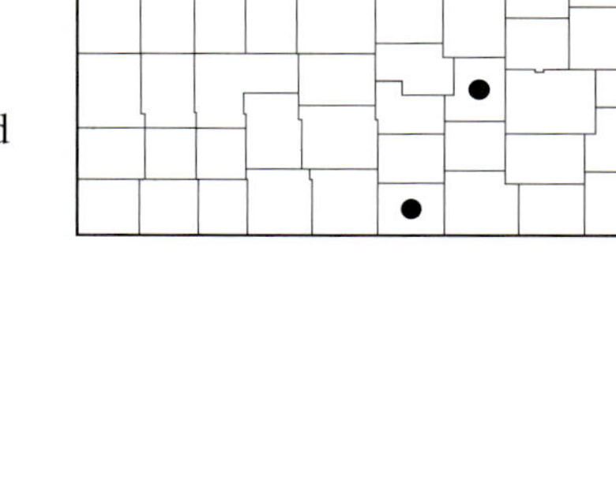

Habitat: It normally inhabits open pine–oak or oak woods in the mountains of southern Arizona and New Mexico. Both Kansas birds were in open deciduous woods in rural settings near standing water. The Comanche County bird was in a rustic campground with numerous willows and large cottonwoods, where the bird foraged among the treetops.

Comments: The Comanche County bird was observed and photographed by many birders during the 6 days that it was present. Almost every time it flew from one tree to another it gave its characteristic sharp "scree" call. It also sang repeatedly, but at fairly wide intervals. Oddly, it appeared to have a patch of feathers missing from the abdomen, reminiscent of a brood patch.

References: Barber et al., 2000; Otte, 2004; Rintoul, 2001.

Yellow-breasted Chat

Icteria virens (YBCH)

Status: Uncommon transient and rare to uncommon summer resident statewide.

Habitat: Riparian woodlands, usually in dense shrubbery; also thickets in old fields and grassland.

Migration: The earliest arrivals are 17 April (Finney Co.) and 20 April (Harvey Co.) with typical arrival during late April, most migration during mid-May, and stragglers through early June. Median first arrivals include 6–7 May (Johnson Co.) and 10 May (Ellis Co.). Half of the individuals banded in Ellis County were during 15–19 May. Late spring departures and early fall arrivals are uncertain due to the presence of local breeders. Migration probably begins late August, peaks in mid-September, and is largely over by late September with stragglers into early October. Half of individuals banded in Ellis County in fall were during the last half of September. Late dates include 12 October (Ellis Co., banded) and 23–24 October (Harvey Co.). One was reported at Dodge City (Ford Co.) during winter 1968–1969 (J. Challans [AFN 23(3):493]).

Breeding: KBBAT found higher frequencies in eastern and western Kansas (although always less than 10% of the blocks) than in the central one-third of the state, where it was nearly absent during the breeding season. However, at least a few individuals were found in every physiographic region. It nests low in thickets of dogwood, willow, rose, or other types of low-growing shrubs or trees. Eggs have been reported between 19 May and 23 July (median 11 June), young in nest 12–23 June, and recently fledged young 17 August. Nearly all reported nests were prior to 1950, 10 of them from Doniphan County (1922–1923).

Comments: It was considered a common summer resident and breeder throughout the late 19th and early 20th centuries. It was so common at Topeka in May 1871 that J. Allen reported seeing three or four males hovering in the air and singing at the same time. I. Boyd reported declining numbers in the east by 1955. It was common along the Arkansas River in Cowley and Sumner counties as recently as 1960 but apparently has not bred there since at least 1992. BBS data had few records to evaluate population trends.

Banding: 330 banded; no encounters. Oldest 2 years (T. Flowers).

References: Allen, 1872; Busby and Zimmerman, 2001; Cable et al., 1996; Janzen, 2007; Thompson and Ely, 1992; Tordoff and Mengel, 1956.

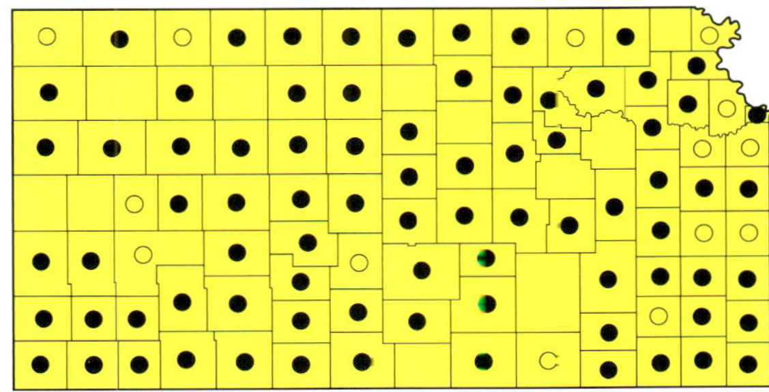

Green-tailed Towhee

Pipilo chlorurus (GTTO)

Status: Rare to uncommon transient in the west; vagrant eastward.

Habitat: Thickets in ravines, riparian growth, sagebrush, and, eastward, thickets and residential yards.

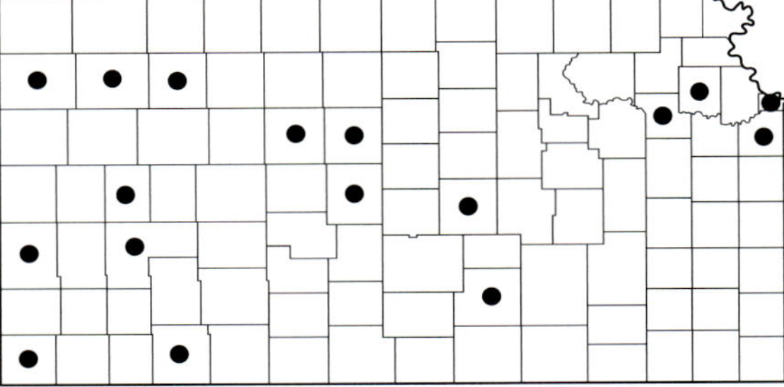

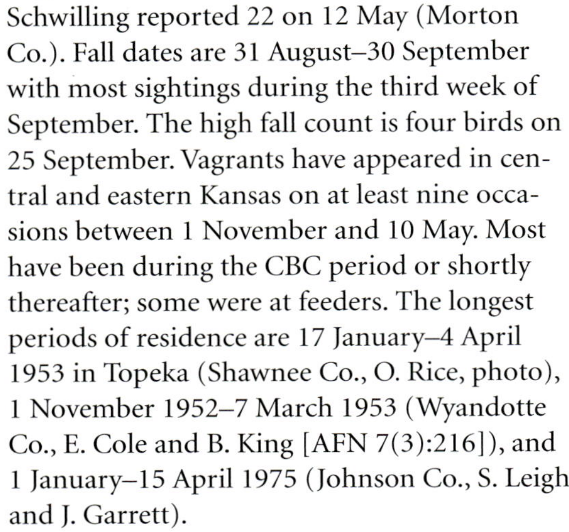

Migration: In the southwest, spring records are 25 April–23 May with most reports during the first half of May. Most sightings are of single birds, but M. Schwilling reported 22 on 12 May (Morton Co.). Fall dates are 31 August–30 September with most sightings during the third week of September. The high fall count is four birds on 25 September. Vagrants have appeared in central and eastern Kansas on at least nine occasions between 1 November and 10 May. Most have been during the CBC period or shortly thereafter; some were at feeders. The longest periods of residence are 17 January–4 April 1953 in Topeka (Shawnee Co., O. Rice, photo), 1 November 1952–7 March 1953 (Wyandotte Co., E. Cole and B. King [AFN 7(3):216]), and 1 January–15 April 1975 (Johnson Co., S. Leigh and J. Garrett).

Comments: In Kansas it tends to be furtive, yielding only brief glimpses as it flits from one patch of cover to the next. Its primary food is seeds and fruits, for which it typically forages on or near the ground.

References: Cable et al., 1996; Janzen, 2001, 2007; Thompson and Ely, 1992.

Spotted Towhee

Pipilo maculatus (SPTO)

Status: Common transient and uncommon winter resident in central and western Kansas; less common in east; summer resident in the northwest and perhaps the southwest. Some historical records are ambiguous, because the Spotted Towhee and Eastern Towhee were considered conspecific from 1983 to 1995.

Habitat: Areas of dense brush, often in or near riparian woodland, hedgerows, and along dry riverbeds; occasional in parks and residential areas.

Migration: Migration probably begins in March. Most migration is in late April and early May with stragglers to 11 June. Some June sightings may be summer vagrants or, in the northwest, isolated breeders. Median first arrivals in the west include 20 April (Ellis Co.) and 21 April (Meade Co.); median late departure is 9 May (Ellis Co.). In the east it is essentially gone from most localities by early May, but a few (perhaps hybrids) have been reported during midsummer (see Breeding). The fall migration is better documented than the spring passage. First arrivals, some of which may be locally raised birds, appear by 3 September (Greeley Co.), but most early arrivals are in late September with birds becoming common by mid-October. Median early fall arrivals include 28 September (Meade Co.) and 2 October (Ellis Co.); median last departure is 1 November (Ellis Co.). Most migration is during early October. Small numbers remain into the CBC period, and wintering has been documented.

Breeding: J. Rising and T. Anderson collected a male (KU 41508, hybrid) feeding a fledged young in Decatur County on 27 July 1963, and S. Seltman reported a nesting pair (not described) near Lenora Lake (Norton Co.) on 16 June 1997. Five pairs were reported by S. Patti (KBBAT) on 10 and 11 June 1996 (Cheyenne and Rawlins cos.). Seven "probable" nesting records and one "confirmed" record (Seward Co.) were reported. The easternmost report was in Dickinson County. Whether or not these were hybrids is unknown.

Comments: Hybridization occurs with the Eastern Towhee in at least northwestern Kansas. Such intermediates occur throughout the state during migration and especially in winter. The songs and calls of nonhybrid Spotted Towhees are usually distinct from those of Eastern Towhees.

See page 503 for banding information.

References: AOU, 1998; Busby and Zimmerman, 2001; Cable et al., 1996; Janzen, 2007; Johnston, 1964a; Rising, 1983; Thompson and Ely, 1992.

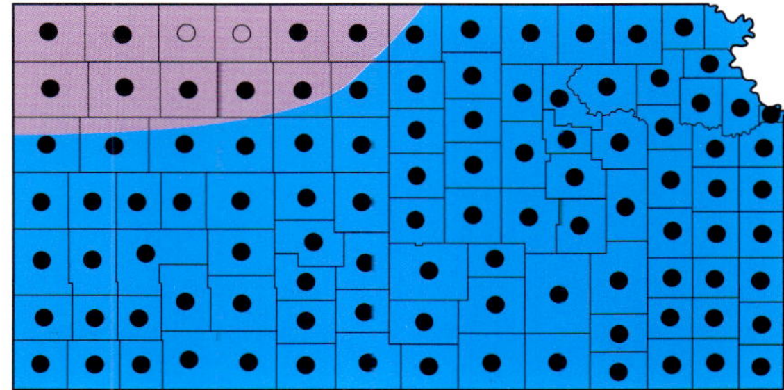

Eastern Towhee

Pipilo erythrophthalmus (EATO)

Status: Occurs in the eastern one-third of the state, where it is a common transient, uncommon to rare summer resident, and rare winter resident; status in the west is uncertain.

© David Seibel

Habitat: Successional thickets, brushy woodland edge, riparian growth, and dense undergrowth in disturbed areas of mature deciduous forest; also in scrubby stands of eastern red cedar.

Migration: Migration probably begins in early April, peaks by late April to early May ("good numbers," Sedgwick Co.), and is largely over by mid-May, by which time residents are nesting. Median earliest arrivals, outside suspected breeding areas, include 20 April (Rice Co.) and 21 April (Barton Co.). Arrival dates within breeding areas include 25 March (Johnson Co.) and 8 April (Harvey Co.). Fall migration is probably late September through mid-October with small numbers remaining into the CBC period and, locally, throughout the winter.

Breeding: The breeding status of this species in Kansas is uncertain. Only during the last year of the KBBAT project did participants attempt to separate records of Eastern Towhees and Spotted Towhees. The westernmost record that season (1997) was a "probable" nesting in Smith County. In earlier years nesting was documented west to Lyon and Riley counties and considered probable west to Cloud and Marion counties. Additional midsummer sightings between 18 June (Pawnee Co.) and 14 August (Stafford Co.) may have been transients or summer vagrants. A male seen throughout the summer of 1999 (Sedgwick Co., P. Janzen) and a juvenile in the same area on 14 August suggest possible breeding, but no female was ever seen. Eggs have been reported 22 May–14 July and recently fledged young (hybrid) 27 July.

Comments: This species replaces the Spotted Towhee in eastern North America, and its range corresponds with the eastern deciduous forest. C. Ely saw none during 35 years of study and banding at Hays (Ellis Co.); his westernmost sighting was a single male in Barton County. T. Flowers has seen none in 20+ years of banding in Meade County. It has been reported in Morton County on three occasions: 21 September, 23 October, and 4 May, all presumable transients. Whether these were intermediates is unknown. See also Spotted Towhee.

See page 503 for banding information.

References: AOU, 1998; Busby and Zimmerman, 2001; Cable et al., 1996; Janzen, 2007; Johnston, 1964a.

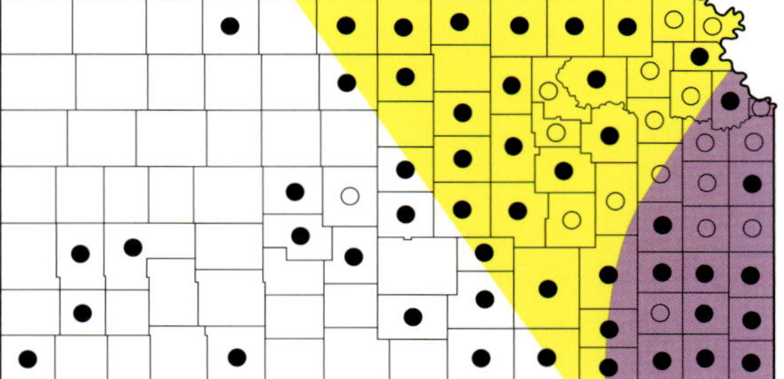

Rufous-crowned Sparrow

Aimophila ruficeps (RCSP)

Status: Casual at all seasons along the southern border of the state from the 99th meridian westward; local summer resident in the western Red Hills near the Oklahoma border; vagrant elsewhere.

Habitat: In Comanche County, the territorial males were in a steep, rocky canyon in mixed-grass prairie interspersed with patches of woodland. Most sightings in Morton County have been in rock outcrops and steep, shrub-filled gullies near sand-sage grassland.

Migration: The few spring records from Morton County are 21 April–3 May (and 11 June, if not summer vagrants). The breeding population in Comanche County apparently arrives by 23 April. Fall reports from Morton County are 1 September–12 November with some remaining into the CBC period and with birds reported on the count day or during count week during 9 different years. The latest winter date is 13 January. Vagrants have been reported on 29 May and 6 June (among rocks near the Tuttle Creek dam, Riley Co.), 6 October (Ellis Co., banded, G. Farley), 27 November (below spillway, Clark Co. State Lake, G. Pittman), and 26 December 1982 (Junction City CBC, Geary Co., "excellent details").

Breeding: Small numbers apparently breed regularly in Schwartz Canyon. In May 2002 a family group with two or three juveniles was videotaped; on 6 May 2004 an adult was observed feeding young. On 21 October 1989, at least two juveniles were videotaped in Comanche County, about 1 mile west of Schwartz Canyon. A singing male was observed in a similar site on the south side of the Salt Fork near the scenic outlook (on U.S. 160, 10 miles west of Medicine Lodge) in adjacent Barber County on 18 May 2002 (S. Patti) and 23–24 April 2005 (P. Janzen and others).

Comments: The first specimen for the state was collected on 7 June 1936 (KU 29222) in Schwartz Canyon on the Merrill Ranch in Comanche County. Nearly 60 years later, on 6 June 1996, S. Patti and M. Rader heard a singing male at the same location, and B. Busby found two territorial males there on 3 July 1997. From 1998 to 2007, numerous spring and summer sightings were reported here and in the surrounding Red Hills. Only one of the singing males reported outside the Red Hills is likely to represent a locally breeding population—13 June 1990, Point of Rocks (Morton Co.; P. Lehman and S. Finnegan).

References: Busby et al., 1999; Busby and Zimmerman, 2001; Cable et al., 1996; Janzen, 2002a, 2002b; Thompson and Ely, 1992.

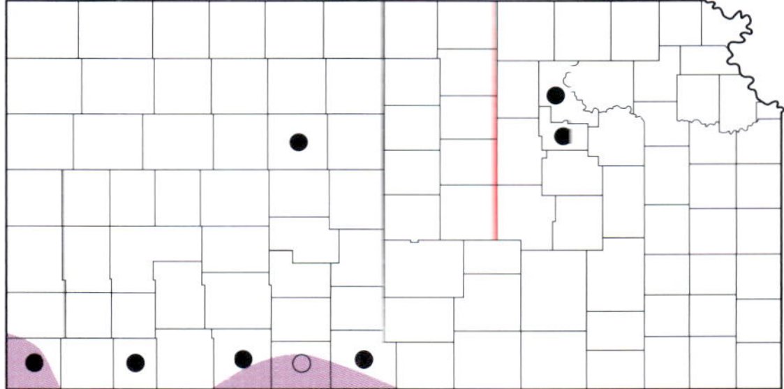

Canyon Towhee

Melozone fusca (CANT)

Status: Casual visitant at any season, almost exclusively in Morton County. Possible summer resident.

Habitat: Patches of dense arid scrub.

Migration: All accepted records are from Morton County. Spring sightings are 14 April and 15 May through 11 June; fall records are 2 August and 7–15 October through the CBC period. Most records are during midwinter (late December to early January). It usually occurs singly, but there are two records of three birds. Most appearances are brief, though two birds remained at Point of Rocks from 15 October to 30 December 1989 and possibly 14 April 1990 (one bird, same spot).

Breeding: The behavior of one of two birds observed on 11 June 1972, a sighting on 11 June 1978 (A. White), and the 2 August sighting suggest the possibility of summer vagrancy. There is currently no evidence of nesting. However, the presence of breeding birds within 30 miles of this site suggests the need to monitor the area for future breeding.

Comments: It can be extremely difficult to see unless it ventures out to forage on the ground nearby. The first report in Kansas, of two birds seen by S. Patti and E. Cole on 10 and 11 June 1972, is also significant in that two individuals, one possibly carrying "grass," were observed. However, they were unable to find a nest, and their photos were unsuitable for publication. The first adequate photos were taken by E. McHugh on 4 January 1975. It has been reported during 11 years, most since the mid-1990s, presumably in part due to the increased amount of birding in the area. The only sighting outside Morton County (Gove Co., 7 May 2007) by an experienced birder was rejected by the KBRC due to inadequate documentation. The most likely place to observe the Canyon Towhee is in CNG north of Elkhart (Morton Co.) in brushy washes below Point of Rocks overlooking the Cimarron River. It was split from the "Brown Towhee" in 1989.

References: AOU, 1998; Cable et al., 1996; Otte, 2008; Patti, 1972; Thompson and Ely, 1992.

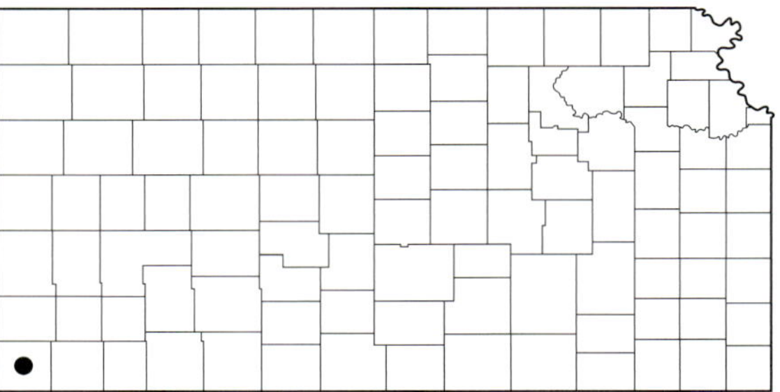

Cassin's Sparrow

Peucaea cassinii (CASP)

Status: Common transient and summer resident in sand-sage in the west, chiefly south of the Arkansas River, but regularly north to Wallace County and farther east during irruption years.

Habitat: Sand-sage grassland; during expansions, into other grasslands, yucca patches in shortgrass prairie, and wheat fields.

Migration: Early spring arrivals include 2 and 4 April (Morton Co.) and 4 May (Hodgeman Co.). Most migration is probably the last half of April through the first half of May. Singing and territorial displays are intense through mid-June, after which birds are inconspicuous and difficult to find. The few fall dates suggest departure by late September. One on 10 November (Morton Co.) is exceptional.

Breeding: It nests regularly in sand-sage prairie in the southwest and has nested east to Rice County. KBBAT reported it as "present with high frequency of occurrence" in the western Red Hills. Eggs have been reported 24 May–10 July, young in nest 24 May–10 June, and recently fledged young 11–29 June. It is an irruptive species, much more numerous and widespread in some years. Nests are placed either on the ground or in a small bush (usually sage) a few inches above the ground and are extremely well hidden.

Comments: A major irruption occurred in 1974 with increased numbers at established localities and displaying males observed at numerous localities north and east of the usual range, often in atypical habitats. A BBS route in Wallace County had 87 birds on 21 stops versus the previous high of 24 on 17 stops. Males displayed over grassland and wheat fields eastward to Ellis (nine males at six sites), Barton (two males at two sites), Stafford (five males at two sites, sand hills with plum thickets), Rice (15 males at nine sites), and Barber (five males at two sites, two nests) counties. J. Allen had found it "rather common along the streams" in Ellis County during the summer of 1871, but most modern records there have been during irruptive years. Nesting is in loose colonies. Each male spends most of each morning, from before sunrise until the day becomes hot, repeating its conspicuous flight song—a form of "skylarking." He flies up from one tall shrub, sets his wings, and with head up and tail spread glides to a second shrub 20–36 feet distant. Except for singing males, birds are usually on the ground.

Banding: 10 banded; no encounters.

References: Allen, 1872; Busby and Zimmerman, 2001; Cable et al., 1996; Janzen, 2002b; Thompson and Ely, 1992; Williamson, 1974.

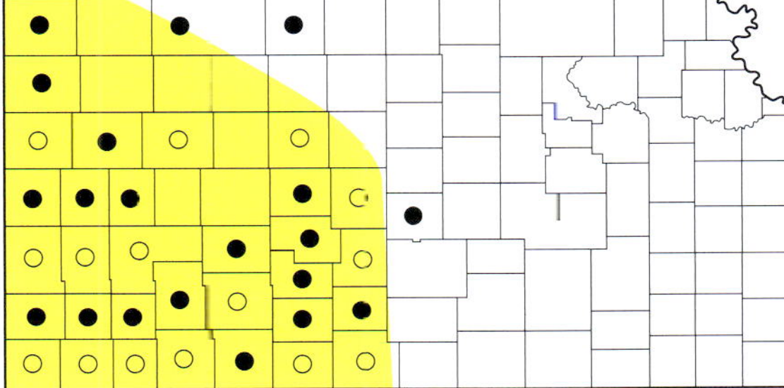

Bachman's Sparrow

Peucaea aestivalis (BACS)

© Judd Patterson

Status: Formerly a casual visitant in northeastern Kansas.

Habitat: Open pinewoods with abundant grass cover and only moderate hardwood shrubbery; in Missouri (and Kansas) also in brushy fields on hillsides.

Migration: The only two sightings are 24 and 26 April.

Comments: There are only two records, a specimen from Lake Quivira (Wyandotte Co.), 24 April 1949 (KU 32377), and a sighting from Johnson County, 26 April 1948, both by H. C. Hedges. The preferred habitat does not occur in Kansas. The nearest nesting localities are in the Ozarks of Missouri, where it occurs in glades and in overgrown fields with scattered trees and shrubs and has apparently been in decline since the 1960s. It is interesting that the Kansas sightings closely followed the logging of the last extensive stand of shortleaf pine in Shannon County (Missouri) in 1946. It is a habitat specialist and very sensitive to natural forest succession. In Arkansas it is one of the first species to leave as successional hardwood shrubs and saplings dominate over tall grass on the forest floor. Accordingly, it responds positively to a regime of regular burning. This species is sometimes called the "Pine-woods Sparrow" in reference to one of its preferred habitats. It is often difficult to observe or flush. The song, a clear, whistled note followed by a trill, is usually delivered from a tall bush or a tree branch. It also has a flight song.

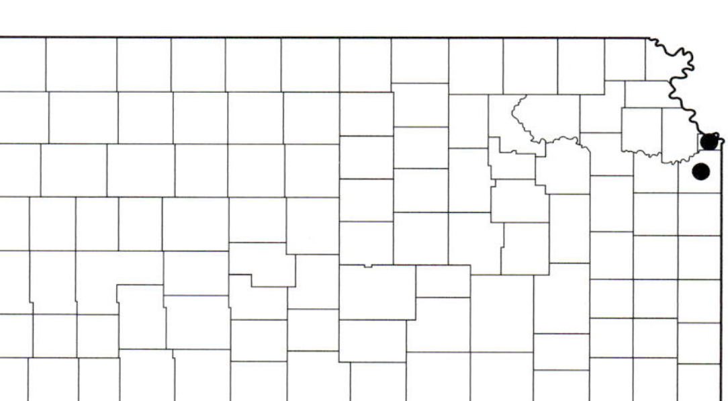

References: Fredrickson, 1951; Robbins and Easterla, 1992; Thompson and Ely, 1992.

American Tree Sparrow

Spizella arborea (ATSP)

Status: Common to abundant transient and winter visitant statewide.

Habitat: A wide variety of weedy habitats from old fields to woodland edge, hedgerows, and riparian situations; in the west the greatest concentrations are in weedy draws within grassland or cultivated areas, with patches of native sunflowers and ragweed being favored.

Migration: Early fall and late spring dates need confirmation. Sightings for 16–18 August (Sherman Co.) are probably misidentifications, and an 8 September report (Morton Co.) is (if correct) extremely early. Early arrivals include 2 October (Meade Co.) and 4 October (Russell Co.), but typical arrival is mid-October or later (16 October, Pawnee Co.; 18 October, Harvey Co.). The median earliest arrival in Ellis County is 1 November. It is widespread by early November with peak migration occurring through the month. There is some winter movement, and statewide numbers vary with severity of winter and distribution of snow cover but usually peak during midwinter. Birders rarely record numbers for common species except on CBCs. Such counts frequently exceed 1,000 individuals, for example, 5,100 (Glen Elder Reservoir, 2004–2005), 3,000 (Glen Elder Reservoir, 2005–2006), and 2,723 (Morton Co., 1976). Numbers decline by mid-March with the onset of the northward movement. The median last departure in Ellis County is 2 April with a few stragglers to 15 April. Elsewhere last reported dates range from 8 April (Meade Co.) to 24 April (Reno Co.) and 5 May (Morton Co.). Some reports from mid-May through July may be of vagrants, but most are misidentifications.

Comments: In Kansas, this is a highly gregarious bird, usually occurring in flocks of from six to eight individuals to as many as several hundred in good feeding areas. The constitution of such flocks changes constantly as some individuals leave and wander to join other flocks. The birds feed by scratching on the ground, by jumping up at overhanging seed heads, and by alighting on the seed heads directly. Birds frequently sing during the warm days of late winter. During winter, nocturnal flights can frequently be heard just prior to heavy snows or during ice storms. During particularly inclement weather some individuals move into towns and visit feeders.

See page 503 for banding information.

References: Bent, 1968; Cable et al., 1996; Cink and Boyd, 2004, 2005, 2006; Ely, 1977; Janzen, 2007; Thompson and Ely, 1992; Thoreau, 1910.

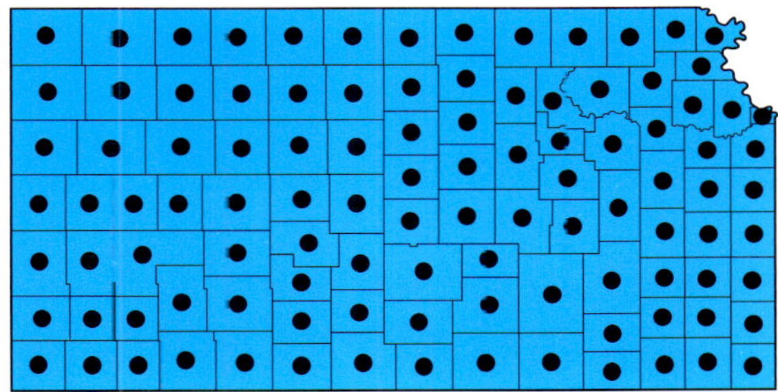

Chipping Sparrow

Spizella passerina (CHSP)

Status: Common transient statewide; local summer resident in the east, casual westward. In winter, casual in the east and accidental in the west.

Habitat: Nests in residential areas, especially with conifers, and open wooded areas; during migration, semiwooded habitat including roadsides and lawns.

Migration: Early arrival dates include 13 March (Clark Co.) and 15 March (Ford Co.), but first arrival is usually in early April with most migration during the first half of May and with most transients gone by late May. Median earliest spring arrival dates include 12 April (Johnson Co.), 18 April (Ellis Co.), and 24 April (Meade Co.). Peak migration in Ellis County has varied from late April through mid-May in various years, often with early and late peaks. Late dates for individuals outside presumed breeding areas include 26 May (Morton and Wallace cos.) and 2 June (Ellis Co.). Early fall dates, outside breeding areas and presumably early transients, include 19 August (Morton Co.) and 27 August (Scott Co.). Sightings increase during early September, and movement is widespread by midmonth. In Ellis County, the earliest record is 28 July, but the median earliest arrival is 27 September; the latest departure is 21 November (median 28 October). Statewide, it is most abundant during October, but "thousands" were reported in Cowley County on 3 November (T. Hicks). There are a few winter records (December–8 February) from at least 11 counties, some documented by photographs or specimens. However, it remains a rare bird in winter.

Breeding: Frequencies are highest in the Glaciated Region. Appropriate habitat is much patchier to the south and west, and the percentage declined accordingly in the Osage Plains and in the Flint Hills. There were additional scattered sightings statewide but no nesting confirmed south or west of Jewell County. The few documented nesting records include eggs 7 May–8 July, young in nest 21 May–6 July, and recently fledged young 23 July.

Comments: It was considered a common summer resident in the east during the late 19th and early 20th centuries. Fall and winter birds can be difficult to distinguish from other *Spizella* species. The distinct rufous cap is lost in winter; note instead the distinctive gray rump often difficult to see, and dark eye-line that always extends forward into the lores.

Banding: 3,808 banded; no encounters.

References: Busby and Zimmerman, 2001; Cable et al., 1996; Janzen, 2007; Thompson and Ely, 1992.

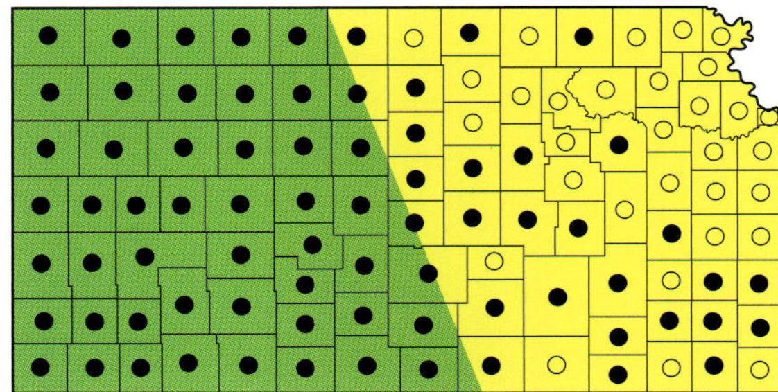

Clay-colored Sparrow

Spizella pallida (CCSP)

Status: Common transient statewide, at times abundant in the west; may have nested in the extreme west; perhaps casual into midwinter.

Habitat: Brushy fields and such semiopen areas as forest edges, parks, and roadsides.

Migration: Early arrivals include 9 April (Morton Co.), 12 April (Ellis Co.), and 13 April (Barton, Johnson, and Lyon cos). Earliest median arrival dates include 26 April (Ellis Co.) and 27 April (Barton Co.); the median departure date for Ellis County is 17 May. Most migration is during late April through mid-May with late dates of 5 June (Ellis Co.), 12 June (Cheyenne Co.), and 15 June (Morton Co.). Peak bandings in Ellis County were during the first half of May. Other high numbers include "mass flight" in Riley County on 4 May and "thousands" in Ellis County on 6 May. In the west it frequently outnumbers the Chipping Sparrow with which it associates. Early fall arrivals include 12 August (Morton Co.) and 15 August (Jefferson Co.). The median earliest arrival for Ellis County is 12 September; the median latest departure is 12 October. Most migration is mid-September (peak in Ellis Co.) through mid-October (numerous on 1 October, Butler Co.) with stragglers into November (14 November, Riley Co.; 23 November, Cowley Co., specimen). It has been reported from several tower kills including 46 in Goodland (Sherman Co.; 12–16 September) and 28 in the Topeka area (25 September–9 October). Few midwinter reports, to 5 February (most on CBCs), were confirmed, but there is a specimen from 9 December (Crawford Co.) and recent sightings through 2 January (Rooks Co.).

Breeding: It may have nested in extreme northwestern and southwestern Kansas on two occasions. A male with enlarged gonads (KU 31950) was collected in Cheyenne County on 12 June 1954, and two adults were seen feeding three fledged young in Morton County on the very late date of 4 September 1964. It was not found by KBBAT.

© David Seibel

Comments: Records in summer and winter need to be carefully documented and distinguished from other *Spizella* species, especially Brewer's Sparrow. During migration, it usually feeds in flocks on the ground, often with other sparrows, especially the Chipping Sparrow, flying up into low trees or shrubs when disturbed.

Banding: 2,795 banded; no encounters.

References: Ball et al., 1995; Cable et al., 1996; Janzen, 2007; Thompson and Ely, 1992; Tordoff and Mengel, 1956; Trautman, 1964.

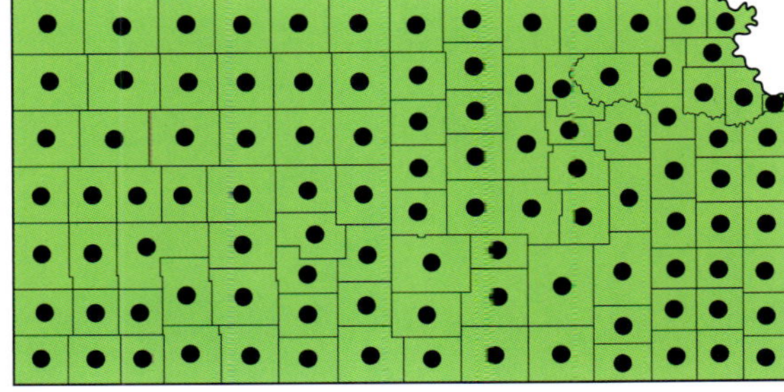

Brewer's Sparrow

Spizella breweri (BRSP)

Status: Rare transient in western Kansas; very local summer resident in the extreme southwest; vagrant elsewhere.

Habitat: Sand-sage grassland; during migration also in low riparian growth, windbreaks, and weed patches.

Migration: Sight records of nonsinging birds need careful verification, especially in fall when they closely resemble immature Clay-colored Sparrows. Spring sight records from Morton and Finney counties (some unverified) are from 8 April to 30 May with most May dates involving breeding colonies. There are five records from Ellis County during 5–17 May (specimens and banded individuals) and scattered records westward from 9 May (Seward Co.) through 3 June (singing, Gove Co.). A vagrant was observed in Shawnee County on 30 April 1961 by many observers. These birds are secretive and very difficult to observe after the nesting season. The relatively few fall records are 19 August–1 October (Finney Co.), with most during the last half of September and most from Morton County. The highest count during migration is 20+ on 19 September (S. Seltman). The single winter record (visual but carefully described) is one on the CNG CBC on 31 December 1988.

Breeding: Most nesting is from mid-May to mid-June. Up to 23 singing males were reported by M. Ports in Morton County in 1979. Other colonies probably exist; KBBAT reported one additional confirmed nesting in Morton County on 19 June (a bird carrying nesting material) and a possible nesting in Stevens County. The nest, extremely well hidden, is concealed in sagebrush, usually within 3 feet of the ground. Eggs have been reported 18–27 May, young in nest 26 May–2 June, and recently fledged young 6–9 July.

Comments: R. and J. Graber reported it as "quite common" in the sand-sage grassland of Morton County in April and May 1950. Subsequently, small breeding colonies were discovered in Morton County (1978, M. Thompson, M. Schwilling, and A. White) and Finney County (1984, C. Ely). Most recent reports have been from Morton County. Singing males are easily found and identified by their remarkable song. During migration, occasional individuals are discovered in large flocks of other *Spizella* species.

© Jim Burns

Banding: 11 banded; no encounters.

References: Busby and Zimmerman, 2001; Cable et al., 1996; Graber and Graber, 1950; Ports, 1978; Thompson et al., 1980; Thompson and Ely, 1992.

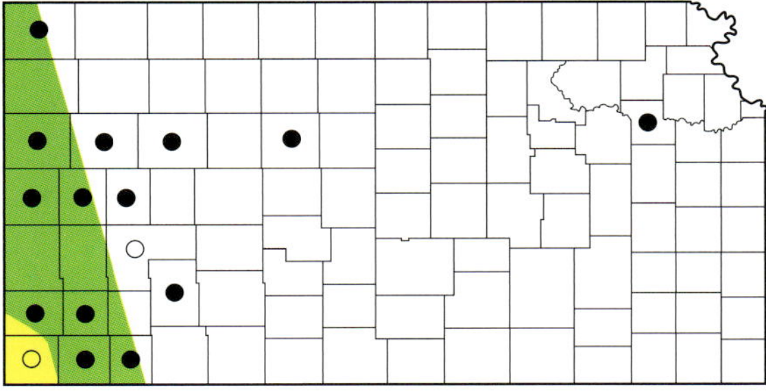

Field Sparrow

Spizella pusilla (FISP)

Status: Common transient and summer resident in the east; uncommon transient and local summer resident in the west; generally rare in winter but may be locally common in the south.

Habitat: Nests in old fields and prairies with shrubs or thickets but is local in distribution with much seemingly appropriate nesting habitat in central and western Kansas not utilized; during migration occurs in any brushy or edge habitat or open woodland.

Migration: Many early March sightings, at least in the south-central region, are probably of wintering individuals; numbers increase by mid-March ("common," 12 March, Coffey Co.), and the species is common and widespread by mid-April. Singing males on territories may be active by 2 April (Stafford Co.). In Ellis County, median first arrival is 16 April (once on 28 March), and median last departure is 17 May with the peak migration during late April. Fall arrival is clouded by the continued presence of local breeders. In Ellis County the median first fall arrival is 4 October; median last departure is 29 October, and peak migration is 10–20 October. Statewide, most migration is during October. November sightings may be late transients or wintering individuals. It winters in small numbers statewide most commonly in the south and east.

Breeding: Nest-building has been reported 4–28 June, eggs 5 May–4 August (median of 43 clutches 24 June), young in nest 25 May–15 August, and recently fledged young 7 June–2 October. Individuals are strongly territorial. The nest, usually well concealed, is placed on the ground or in a shrub within 3 feet of the ground. If the nest is destroyed by predation or weather, additional nesting attempts may be made.

Comments: Even during migration it rarely occurs in flocks of more than a few individuals. There is some evidence that it increased its original range following the clearing of virgin

forests by early settlers, and that subsequently its numbers have declined as many small abandoned farms have been lost to succession or urban development. Wintering individuals are common in mixed flocks of other species and occasionally visit feeders.

Banding: 1,488 banded; nine encounters: all in-state.

References: Busby and Zimmerman, 2001; Cable et al., 1996; Janzen, 2007; Thompson and Ely, 1992.

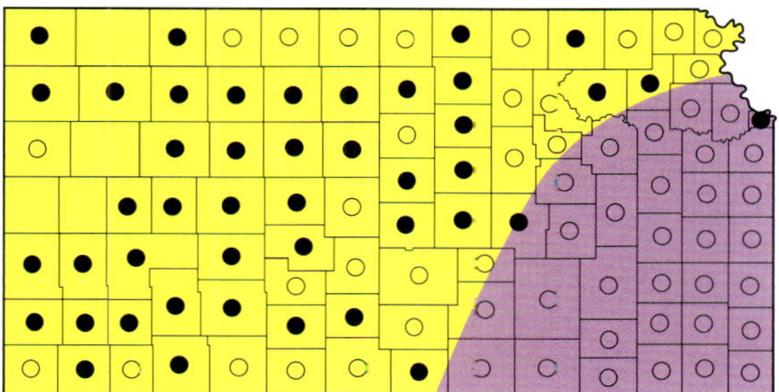

Vesper Sparrow

Pooecetes gramineus (VESP)

© David Seibel

Status: Common to abundant transient statewide; rare and local summer resident in the southwestern and northeastern corners of the state; casual in winter.

Habitat: Transients prefer fallow fields, stubble, and overgrazed pastures. In spring, flocks are common, even abundant, along roadsides, often with Savannah Sparrows. The eastern population nests in overgrown fields and forest edge with scattered trees and shrubs; the western, in sand-sage prairie.

Migration: February and early March reports may be of wintering birds. Early dates for presumed transients include 10 March (Osage Co.), 11 March (Sumner Co.), and 14 March (Cowley Co.). It is widespread and common by late March to early April (255 on 11 April, Butler Co.) with high numbers through early May and stragglers through 22 May (Phillips Co.). The median first arrival for Ellis County is 4 April; the median late departure is 8 May. Midsummer records from central Kansas, outside known breeding areas, may be vagrants, local breeders, or even misidentifications. Some of the early August reports are probably of local breeding birds, including 1 August (Russell Co.), 9 August (Morton Co.), and 10 August (Jefferson Co.). Transients begin arriving by at least 18 September (100, Morton Co., E. Young) and are widespread and abundant from late September to mid-October: large counts include Morton County, 20 September (thousands, "clouds all day," P. Janzen) and Pawnee County, 16 October (1,000+, S. Seltman). Small numbers have been reported into at least midwinter in 22 counties. The number of mid-February records suggests actual overwintering.

Breeding: KBBAT (1992–1997) obtained three confirmed reports of breeding and several additional observations during the breeding season in opposite corners of the state. In the northeast, Brown County was the site of two separate confirmed breeding records, with six "probable" and five "possible" records in the same and adjacent counties. In the southwest, one confirmed, two "probable," and one "possible" breeding record were reported from Morton County.

Comments: It feeds on the ground in open areas, often alighting on a fence wire or post when alarmed. Males commonly sing during early morning, usually from a fence post, overhead wire, or tree.

See page 503 for banding information.

References: Busby and Zimmerman, 2001; Cable et al., 1996; Janzen, 2007; Thompson and Ely, 1992.

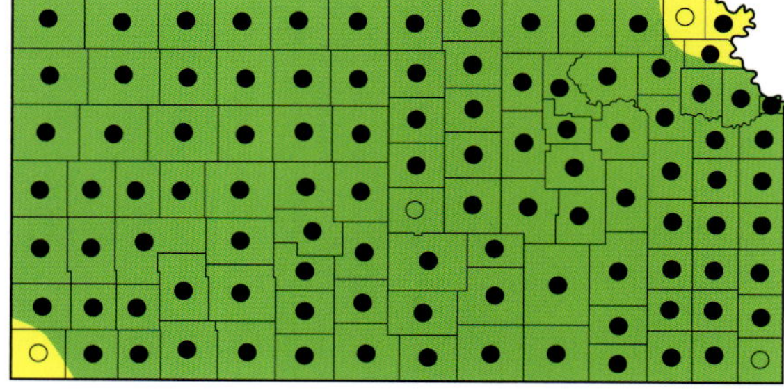

Lark Sparrow

Chondestes grammacus (LASP)

Status: Common transient and summer resident statewide, most numerous in the western half of the state; casual in winter.

Habitat: Low or sparse vegetation interspersed with bushes including large lawns, golf courses, edges of fields, ravines in grasslands, heavily overgrazed prairie, and rural roadsides.

Migration: Early spring arrivals include 24 March (Rush and Johnson cos.), but first arrival is usually early April (7 April, Rush Co.) with birds widespread and often common by 21 April. Median first arrivals include 10 April (Meade Co.), 17 April (Ellis Co.), 19 April (Lyon Co.), 21 April (Johnson Co.), and 22 April (Barton Co.). Peak migration is late April through early May. The fall migration is poorly documented but is early. A flock of 100+, largely juveniles, was reported on 4 August (Norton Co., S. Seltman), and there are few records after 15 September. Large flocks in Meade County 25 September–7 October (T. Flowers) and 100 in Morton County on 28 September (E. Young) were obvious transients. Late dates include 10 October (Seward Co.), 13 October (Sedgwick Co.), and 29 October (Cowley and Sumner cos.). It is rarely found during winter (specimen, KU 37973, 19 January 1957, Cowley Co., M. Thompson). It has also been reported 18 February in Stafford County and on CBCs at eight localities in extreme southern and eastern Kansas, but not all were verified.

Breeding: Although not uniformly distributed, KBBAT found it potentially breeding in all physiographic regions with the highest frequency of confirmed breeding in the Red Hills. Small patches of proper habitat in otherwise unfavorable areas attract birds. Nest-building has been reported 1 May–21 July, eggs 22 April–21 July, young in nest 16 May–27 July, and recently fledged young 25 May–28 July. Statewide, the median date for 66 clutches is 9 June.

Comments: During migration it occurs in smaller flocks than most common sparrows, but it is an active, conspicuous species and is one of the better-known sparrows in Kansas. D. Baepler reported active nests of a Lark Sparrow, an Orchard Oriole, and a Scissor-tailed Flycatcher in the same tree, and L. Wooster found a nest with eggs within the base of a Swainson's Hawk nest in Ellis County.

Banding: 372 banded; no encounters.

References: Baepler *in* Bent, 1968; Busby and Zimmerman, 2001; Cable et al., 1996; Janzen, 2007; Thompson and Ely, 1992; Wooster *in* Ely, 1971; Young, 1993.

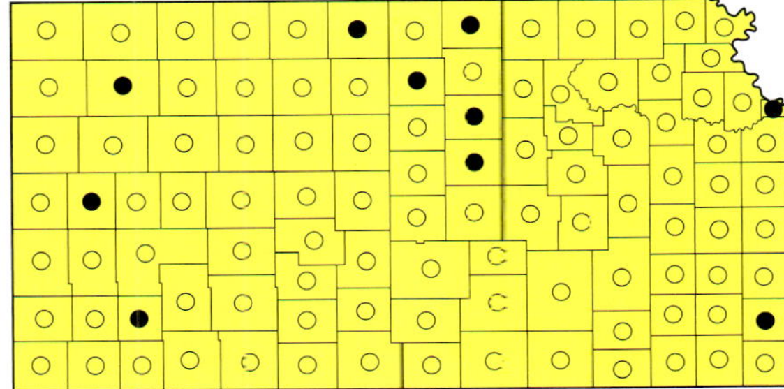

Black-throated Sparrow

Amphispiza bilineata (BTSP)

Status: Vagrant.

Habitat: Riparian growth bordering sand-sage grassland, parks, and residential yards.

Migration: The three spring records are 10 March–4 May; the two late summer records are 1 and 22 July; the five fall records are 13 August–31 December.

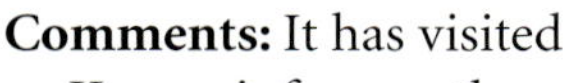

Comments: It has visited Kansas infrequently with most reports during the 1990s. All but one of the sightings were of single birds with two seen on the Cimarron River (Morton Co., 4 May). The first report was of one captured in a garage 5 miles northeast of Garden City (Finney Co., M. Schwilling) on 25 November 1952; the second was one seen in extreme southwestern Morton County on 1 July 1969 (E. Martinez). The number of sightings increased with an increase in birding activity in the southwest during the 1990s. However, only in 1992 has there been more than one report in a single year. The only known extended stay is one at Overland Park (Johnson Co., P. and B. Rhudy) from at least 30 November through 31 December 1992. Multiple sightings have occurred only in Morton, Finney, and Sedgwick counties. It typically forages on or near the ground, often flying up into low bushes when approached. It eats seeds, various plant parts, and insects such as grasshoppers and aphids. It forms small flocks in winter.

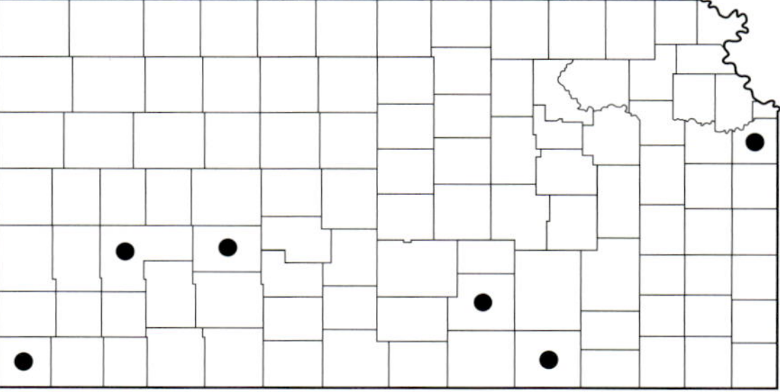

References: Cable et al., 1996; Janzen, 2007; Schwilling, 1954; Thompson and Ely, 1992.

Sage Sparrow

Amphispiza belli (SAGS)

Status: Vagrant in the southwest.

Habitat: Sand-sage grassland on sand hills near the Cimarron River.

Migration: Specimen records are 1 November and 10–11 January. Two sight records from Morton County fall within this period. Additional sight records for 13–14 May and 1 and 5 July are probably in error. An April report from Morton County was actually of Lark Buntings in winter plumage. The highest number reported is six on 8 January 1974 (Morton Co., S. Patti).

Comments: This is a shy species that often occurs in small flocks within its normal range, although in Kansas, it has been reported only as single individuals. It forages mostly on the ground under sagebrush and similar vegetation, gleaning its food from the surface of the ground rather than by scratching. It has the unusual habit of cocking its tail upward while running across the ground, and it flicks its tail frequently while perched. It may fly to the top of a bush when alarmed, in response to "pishing," or while singing.

References: Cable et al., 1996; Thompson and Ely, 1992; Tordoff and Alcorn, 1957.

© Jim Burns

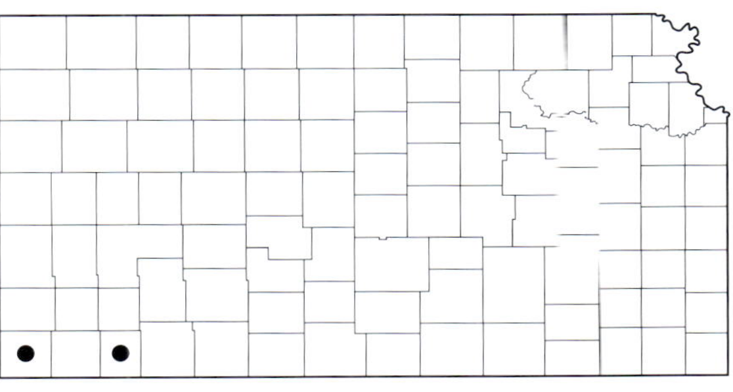

Lark Bunting

Calamospiza melanocorys (LARB)

Status: Common transient and summer resident west of the 99th meridian; casual to locally uncommon in winter; vagrant eastward.

Habitat: Stubble fields, wheat and alfalfa fields, midgrass prairie, and sand-sage grasslands.

Migration: Flocks of hundreds in Meade County on 25 March and 150 on 3 April probably wintered nearby. Known transients begin arriving by mid- to late April. The earliest for Ellis County is 10 April (median 30 April). Heavy migration occurs into at least mid-May, including 12 May ("large flocks," Finney Co.). Flocking begins by early July soon after young fledge and is conspicuous through early September (Meade Co.). The median fall departure for Ellis County is 31 August. The number of sightings decreases sharply in most of Kansas by early September. However, S. Seltman reported flocks of up to 1,000 in Morton County on 3 August 1991 and estimated more than 10,000 in the county that day. Vagrants have been reported from Jewell County (26 December, specimen) and Sedgwick County (18 October, 25 November, and 11 May). T. Shane and S. Seltman concluded that the establishment of wintering populations in Kansas since the mid-1970s occurred simultaneously with those established in adjacent states. After a lull in 1980–1987, both the number of sightings and size of wintering flocks increased dramatically. Its current winter status there is unclear.

Breeding: It is the ecological counterpart of the Dickcissel west of the Flint Hills, but chooses nest sites with sparser vegetation. Populations vary considerably (e.g., a 10-fold increase in 1969 in Ellis Co.), with breeding populations sometimes expanding eastward during peak years. "Vagrant" nesting has been documented in Riley, Shawnee, and Franklin counties. J. Wilson studied Lark Buntings near the eastern edge of the normal breeding range (Ellis Co.), reporting that birds nested singly or in loose colonies in fallow fields with low, sparse, emergent weeds as well as prairie. Farming activities, especially disking of stubble fields, and predation caused most nest failures. Eggs have been reported 11 May–7 June (median 9 June), young in nest 27 May–19 July, and recently fledged young 8 June–23 July.

Comments: Males deliver their flight song from spring arrival into mid-July.

Banding: 219 banded; no encounters.

References: Busby and Zimmerman, 2001; Cable et al., 1996; Cink and Boyd, 2003; Janzen, 2007; Rice, 1965; Shane and Seltman, 1995; Thompson and Ely, 1992; Wilson, 1976.

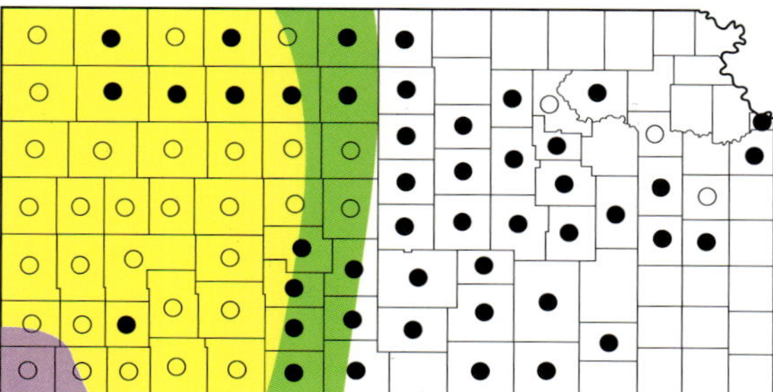

Savannah Sparrow

Passerculus sandwichensis (SAVS)

Status: Common transient statewide; casual in winter; vagrant during summer.

Habitat: Variety of grasslands, from overgrazed prairies to wet meadows and marshes, stubble fields, and roadsides.

Migration: Spring arrival is apparently early, perhaps starting in late February (20 February, Russell Co.; 22 February, Rush Co.), but these may be local movements of wintering birds. Numbers increase markedly by mid-March with a few visiting feeders during this period. The peak is usually April ("abundant," Riley Co., 11 April; and 1,550 on 11 April and 3,925 on 25 April, both in Butler Co., E. Young) through early May (1,850 on 4 May, Cowley Co., E. Young) with stragglers to early June. The few summer sightings (Stafford Co., 17 July, one "territorial," J. Schulenberg; Woodson Co., 28 July 1926, specimens, KU 15535, 15538) are probably vagrants or very early transients. The fall migration probably begins in August (6 August, Jefferson Co.; 21 August, Morton Co., if not summering birds). It becomes widespread in September (3 September, Ellis Co.; 7 September, Meade Co., banded; 12 September, Douglas Co., specimen). Most migration is during October ("thousands" in October in Flint Hills, E. Young) with smaller numbers into November, although M. Thompson and E. Young observed several hundred in Sedgwick and Sumner counties on 28 November 2000. S. Seltman reported 100+ on 15 January (Montgomery Co.). It overwinters, especially in the south during mild winters where flocks of 20+ can be found, and is probably often overlooked in this season in open country.

Comments: There is currently no evidence of breeding in Kansas. All summer sight records should be carefully documented, because it could easily be confused with the much more likely Grasshopper Sparrow in juvenal plumage (which also has a streaked breast). Typical of migrating grassland sparrows, they spend most of their time on the ground under or near dense vegetative cover and are often difficult to see. When approached on foot, they usually run rather than fly, but when they do flush, they tend to fly farther than most small grassland sparrows before diving back into dense cover. Along roadsides, Savannah Sparrows frequently afford the best views by flying up to fence wires or posts when disturbed by a passing vehicle.

Banding: 173 banded; one encounter: in-state.

References: Cable et al., 1996; Janzen, 2007; Thompson and Ely, 1992; Young, 1993.

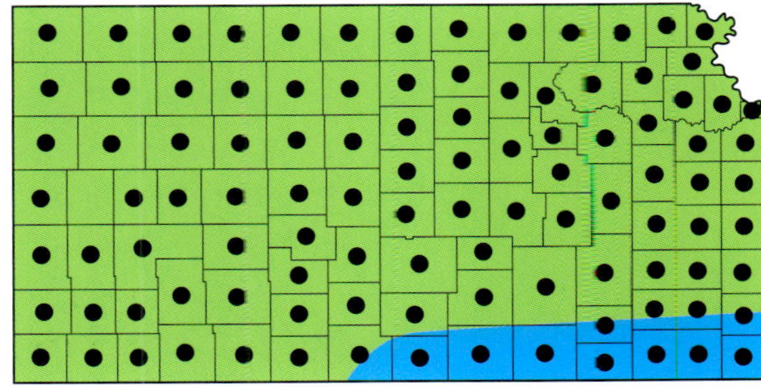

Grasshopper Sparrow

Ammodramus savannarum (GRSP)

Status: Common transient and summer resident statewide; vagrant in winter.

© Judd Patterson

Habitat: Natural grasslands or patches of grass in or near small grains for nesting and more diverse habitats, including brushy fields and roadsides, during migration.

Migration: The earliest arrivals are 6 March (Coffey Co.) and 25 March (Linn Co., specimens), but usual first arrival is about 10 April with individuals widely distributed by 21 April. Median first arrivals include 12 April (Rush Co.) and 26 April (Ellis Co.). In Morton County, R. and J. Graber reported the first individual on 4 April, but the species was not "regularly seen" until after the 24th. Most migration is during the last half of April through the first half of May. Flocks are forming by mid-August, and in Ellis County numbers declined sharply soon after. Migration begins in September and is largely finished by early to mid-October but with stragglers through 5 November (Meade Co.) and 28 November (Comanche Co., specimen). It is a common victim of tower collisions, with 22 recovered near Goodland on 12–16 September and 72 near Topeka on 25 September–28 October during various years.

Breeding: KBBAT found it to be one of the most widespread species nesting in Kansas, occurring in all regions but with highest occurrence in central and western Kansas. The nest is on the ground in a depression, typically very well concealed under a clump of grass or forb and often domed. Nests are most easily found by following adults carrying food to the young. Eggs have been reported 14 May–24 August (median 4 June), young in nest 2 June–27 August, and recently fledged young 6 June–23 August.

Comments: In recent years has shown a gradual decline in numbers, including in Kansas. It is by far the most familiar of the small, flat-headed, short-tailed grassland sparrows of the genus *Ammodramus*. All are secretive and similar in appearance, but each has a distinctive song and diagnostic, though subtle, plumage differences. At close range, note the yellow lores and yellow on the bend of the wing of the Grasshopper Sparrow. There is an extensive prebasic (fall) molt that may leave the birds almost flightless. S. Seltman observed a flock of more than 100 birds in such condition in Pawnee County on 7 October 1988.

Banding: 551 banded; one encounter: in-state.

References: Busby and Zimmerman, 2001; Cable et al., 1996; Janzen, 2007; Thompson and Ely, 1992.

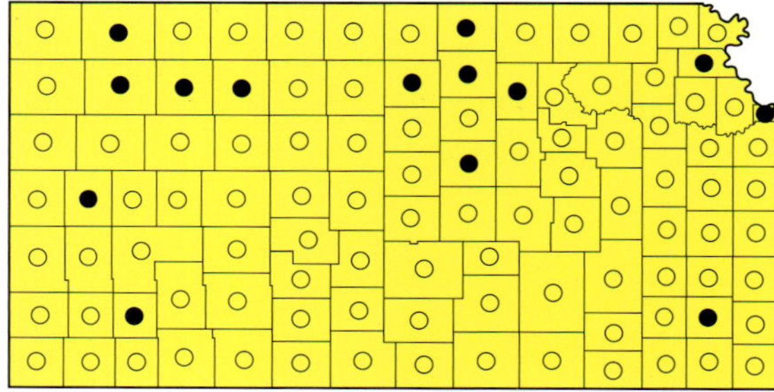

Baird's Sparrow

Ammodramus bairdii (BAIS)

© David Seibel

Status: Rare transient with scattered reports statewide; possibly more common than reflected by current records.

Habitat: Variety of prairie types, from tallgrass in the Flint Hills to shortgrass in the western High Plains and sandsage grassland in Morton County. It seems to prefer relatively undisturbed native grassland.

Migration: Both rare and elusive, it is difficult to identify when not singing, and most sightings are unconfirmed. Specimens from spring are 25–28 April, and sight records (most unconfirmed) extend this period from 2 April to 9 May. Fall specimens were taken 25 August–11 October, nearly all at television tower kills. Sight records (most unconfirmed) extend this period to 30 October. Summer sightings (excluded here) are undoubtedly in error, and a November sighting is highly unlikely. All sight records need verification.

Comments: It is an extremely elusive species, migrating individually or in small flocks, essentially silent and typically staying hidden at all times in dense (even if very short) grass. Its secretive habits, excellent camouflage, and similarity to other grassland sparrows make it very difficult to see or identify. Given that it is a relatively common breeder in grasslands of the northern Great Plains, it is reasonable to speculate that many birds pass through Kansas unnoticed. Because most of the well-documented records are of birds killed by striking guy wires at television towers in the dark, it is also possible that most individuals overfly the state at night. Ten of 12 fall specimens were recovered from such kills, from Goodland (Sherman Co., 11–16 September, 9 birds, 3 years) and near Topeka (Shawnee Co., 11 October, 1 bird). Fall birds can be particularly challenging to identify because some in juvenal plumage migrate before molting, making them especially resemble Grasshopper Sparrows. However, Baird's Sparrow generally has lighter edges to the feathers on the back, giving it a "scaly" appearance, and the tail is longer and blunter. On the breeding grounds its behavior changes dramatically through the early part of the nesting season as males tirelessly sing their beautiful, distinctive song from the highest shrub or blade of grass available.

References: Ball et al., 1995; Barkley et al., 1977; Cable et al., 1996; Janzen, 2007; Thompson and Ely, 1992.

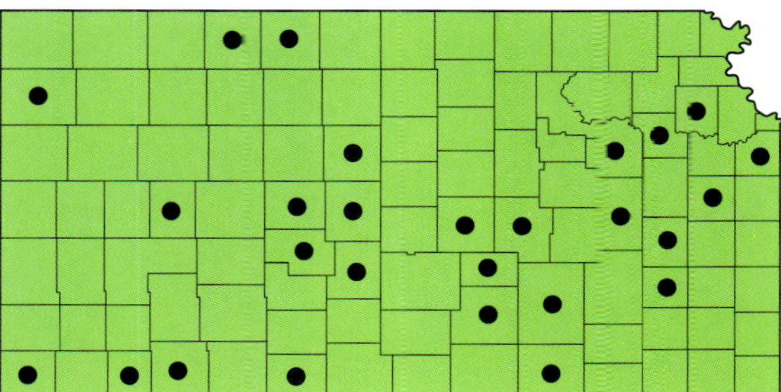

Henslow's Sparrow

Ammodramus henslowii (HESP)

© David Seibel

Status: Uncommon transient and local summer resident in the eastern one-third of the state.

Habitat: Tallest, densest grasslands available, breeding in tallgrass prairie and planted grasslands such as uncut brome pasture with forbs; requires a dense litter layer; in many areas outside of Kansas it prefers moist areas, but in others (Konza Prairie, Riley and Geary cos.) it occurs in dry upland prairie.

Migration: Too few data are available to adequately define migration. The earliest reports are 3 March (Crawford Co.), 26 March (Linn Co.), and 9 April (Anderson Co.). More usual are reported arrivals in mid-April with widespread singing males by 19 April and continuing into May. Most migration is probably late April to early May. Breeding individuals may be on territories by 24 April or earlier. Few fall dates are available. Migration is probably early September (12 September, Woodson Co.) through early October with stragglers to 26 October. Winter sightings need verification.

Breeding: Nesting has been documented in 10 counties, mostly east of the 97th meridian, with the largest number at Fort Riley, Geary County (>1,000 in 1 year, J. Keating), but not as stable as a population present at the Konza Prairie (Riley Co.). Nests are extremely difficult to find, and the species is probably underreported. Nest-building has been reported on 22 June, eggs 24 May–27 June, young in nest 13 June–5 July, and recently fledged young 13 June–22 July. KBBAT reported more than 30 "probable" and "possible" breeding records. The nest is well hidden on the ground, covered by an overhanging grass clump. In some areas (including Shawnee Mission Park, Johnson Co.) the species is at least semicolonial. Late breeding records (recently fledged young, 22 July) indicate that birds either renest after a failed attempt or are double-brooded.

Comments: It requires unburned, idle, or lightly grazed grasslands for successful nesting, and proper grassland management will control its future in Kansas. Grazing and burning practices that destroy the litter layer render large expanses of prairie in the Flint Hills (and elsewhere) unusable to the Henslow's Sparrow. A secretive ground dweller, it is probably more widespread than current records indicate, especially as a transient.

Banding: 51 banded; no encounters.

References: Busby and Zimmerman, 2001; Janzen, 2007; Schulenberg et al., 1994; Thompson and Ely, 1992; Zimmerman, 1993.

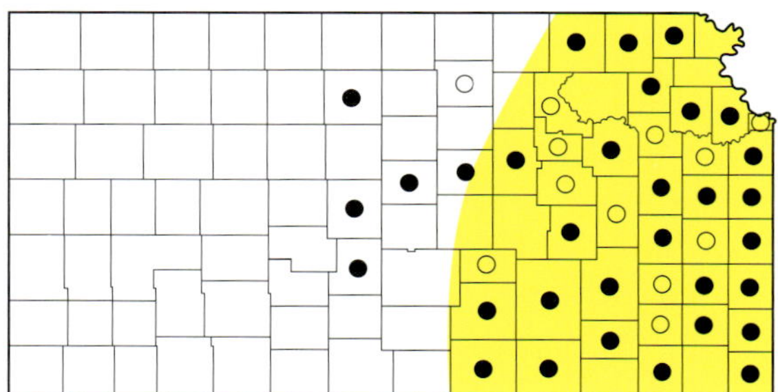

Le Conte's Sparrow

Ammodramus leconteii (LCSP)

© David Seibel

Status: Uncommon or overlooked transient and rare to uncommon winter resident in the east; casual westward.

Habitat: Variety of grassland habitats but appears to favor old fields and weedy areas.

Migration: Some early March dates are probably of overwintering birds. Early arrivals include 6 March (Sumner Co., "numerous," M. Thompson) and 8 March (Harvey Co., G. Friesen). Presumed transients arrive by mid-March (20 March, Montgomery Co.), peak during April (median arrival 17 April), and become uncommon through mid-May with stragglers to 16 May (Lyon Co.) and 17 May (Douglas Co.). A report of several in Riley County on 23 June, if correct, is exceptional. It is reported more often in fall than during spring. Early fall dates include 18 September (Kingman Co.) and 30 September (Lane Co., specimen; Finney Co.), with most arrivals during early October and with the peak migration 10–31 October and smaller numbers occurring into late November. Large counts include 50–100 on 30 October (Barton Co.) and 64 on 19 October (Sumner Co.). Twenty-eight were salvaged at three tower kills near Topeka (Shawnee Co.) 11–28 October. It has wintered locally in low numbers in at least 14 counties in the south and east. Specimens have been taken between 30 September and 10 May.

Comments: Although easily identified in spring, fall birds, especially immatures, can be very confusing. Even museum specimens have been originally identified as Baird's Sparrows or Nelson's Sparrows. In the fall, it can be extremely elusive (and shabby in appearance) during an extensive prebasic molt that apparently occurs during an extended stopover after the first leg of its southward migration. When carefully sought, it often proves to be much more numerous than generally believed, at least in the east. It is usually quite tame, but its camouflaged plumage and quiet skulking habits make it extremely easy to overlook. When alarmed it prefers to run rather than fly. When flushed it flies weakly for a short distance before diving back into heavy cover. Like many grassland sparrows, it rarely responds to "pishing," but will often approach or call in response to recordings of its song, even during migration or winter. The best way to see one well is to stand or sit quietly in its habitat and let it approach you.

Banding: 39 banded; no encounters.

References: Ball et al., 1995; Cable et al., 1996; Janzen, 2007; Kluza et al., 2001; Sibley, 2000; Thompson and Ely, 1992; Tordoff and Mengel, 1956.

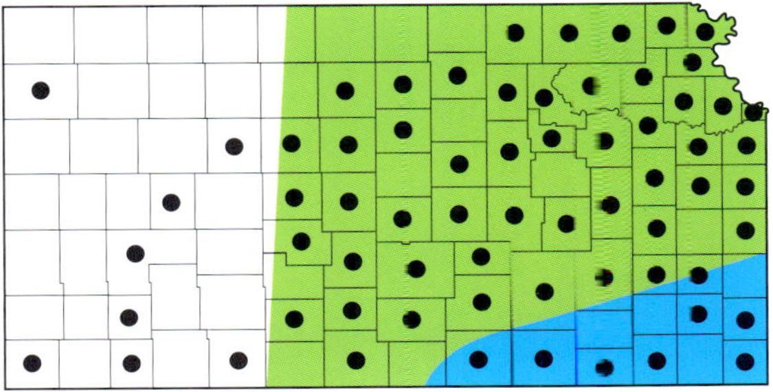

Nelson's Sparrow

Ammodramus nelsoni (NESP)

Status: Rare or overlooked transient in eastern and central Kansas.

Habitat: Freshwater and salt marshes and meadows; most consistently in islands of prairie cordgrass and inland salt grass within areas of shorter grasses and sedges.

Migration: The few confirmed spring sightings are 25 March (Stafford Co.) and 4 April (Chase Co.) through 8 May (Shawnee Co., 20, "Woods," unpubl. manuscript, 1976) and 22 May (Jefferson Co., singing). June records are suspect. There are no spring specimens. The report by N. Goss of nesting in Kansas is almost certainly in error. It is recorded much more frequently in fall. The earliest dates (3 September, Lyon Co.; 9 September, Osage Co.) are unconfirmed. Statewide, most fall sightings are between 29 September and 8 November, with most during October (median date 18 October) and with more than half during the period 13–26 October. At least 10 have been salvaged at tower kills near Topeka (Shawnee Co.) 25 September–10 October. Specimens have been taken between 6–10 October (Shawnee Co.) and 26 October (Sumner Co.).

Comments: All sight records need careful documentation. It is often difficult to observe, especially during migration. It tends to stay well hidden in tall grasses, but will sometimes respond to quiet "pishing" and will often allow close approach if a person is lucky enough to see it before it flushes. In recent years, several observers, notably M. Thompson, E. Young, and A. Powell, have systematically searched prime habitat at Baker Wetlands (Douglas Co.), SCW, and marshes in Jefferson County, consistently finding up to eight individuals in clumps of prairie cordgrass during mid-October and early November. Although perhaps easiest to find in tiny patches of prairie cordgrass at the edges of ponds or in wet ditches, numbers of individuals are almost certainly higher in larger marshes. It was split from the very similar Saltmarsh Sparrow (*A. caudacutus*) in 1995. Before that time, the two had been considered a single species, the "Sharp-tailed Sparrow," and until 2009 each had retained "Sharp-tailed" as part of its common name. Ironically, among the *Ammodramus* sparrows, these two have relatively broad tails, although the tips of the individual feathers are indeed pointed.

© David Seibel

References: AOU, 1998, 2009; Ball et al., 1995; Goss, 1891; Janzen, 2007; Thompson and Ely, 1992; Tordoff and Mengel, 1956.

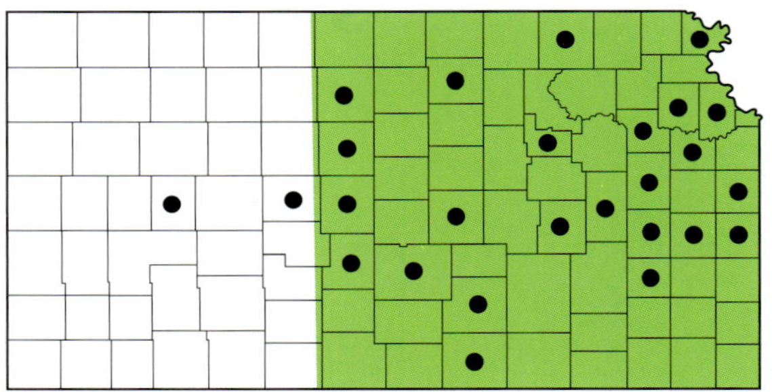

Fox Sparrow

Passerella iliaca (FOSP)

Status: Common transient and uncommon winter resident in the east; rare transient and casual winter resident westward.

Habitat: Deciduous woodlands with a brush component, woodland edge, fencerows, or brush piles in eastern and central Kansas; westward, any area with a mix of brush and trees; visits feeding stations, especially in rural areas.

Migration: Migration is under way by mid-March (10 March, Harvey Co.), peaks in mid-March and early April, and is largely complete by mid-April. Late dates include 22 April (Russell and Geary cos.), 28 April (Ellis Co.), and 2 May (Wilson Co.), with an unlikely sighting on 24 May. More than 100 were observed on 30 March in Leavenworth County (J. Schukman). Sightings from 28 August and 22 September are unverified. Usual arrival is early October (3–4 October, Douglas Co., specimens; and 5 October, Morton Co.) with most migration during mid-October and early November and with stragglers and wintering birds into the CBC period. At least 12 were salvaged at two tower kills near Topeka (Shawnee Co.) on 23 (1) and 28 October (11). Most wintering birds (late December through early March) are in eastern and southern Kansas with probably a few during some winters west to Ellis, Scott, and Morton counties.

Comments: It characteristically feeds on the ground under dense vegetation or brush piles, scratching through leaves and litter with both feet simultaneously like a towhee. Two subspecies may be expected in Kansas. Most are of the eastern race, *P. i. zaboria*, characterized by a rusty face contrasting with a gray crown and collar, rusty wings and back, and a reddish brown tail. Unverified sightings of the Rocky Mountain race, *P. i. schistacea*, have been reported in Scott (December–January), Pawnee (10 March), and Sedgwick (24 March) counties but have not yet been documented by physical evidence. It is considered one of the finest singers among sparrows, delivering a series of clear, melodious, flutelike notes from within undergrowth. This can be heard occasionally in Kansas, especially during spring migration.

Banding: 399 banded; no encounters

References: Janzen, 2007; Kluza et al. 2001; Thompson and Ely, 1992; Tordoff and Mengel, 1956

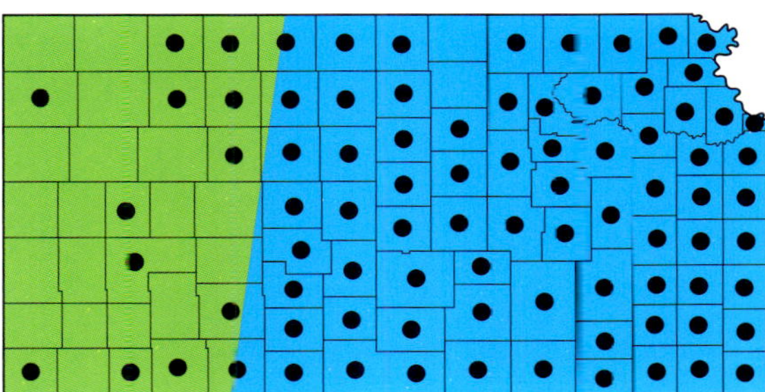

Song Sparrow

Melospiza melodia (SOSP)

Status: Common transient statewide; common winter resident in east, uncommon in west. Local summer resident in the northeast.

Habitat: Brushy cover near water, woodlands, roadsides, and residential gardens; in winter also cattail marshes; in summer woody edge habitats around water.

Migration: Migration is probably mid-March to early May with the peak during April. Median first date for Ellis County is 20 March; median departure is 18 April. Extreme spring dates include 24 May. The highest count reported is a flock of 50 on 13 March (Pawnee Co., following a snow). Late summer records outside known breeding areas (20 August, Stafford Co.; 28 August, Ellis Co.) may be vagrants, early transients, or from a still unknown breeding site. Early fall dates for presumed transients include 2 September (Shawnee Co.), but arrival is usually early to mid-October. Median first fall arrival for Ellis County is 14 October. Most migration is during October and early November. Numbers decrease into December, but many remain through the winter especially in the east. Actual departure and arrival dates of wintering birds are unknown.

Breeding: The first confirmed nest records for Kansas in recent times were in 1966 and 1967 in Wyandotte County by T. Anderson, who found four nests in a willow thicket bordering the Missouri River near Wolcott. He had found territorial birds at the same site in 1965. Birds were present during the breeding season in a total of 47 KBBAT blocks in 14 northeastern counties, extending westward to Jewell County and diagonally southeast to Anderson and Linn counties. P. Janzen reported breeding near Cheney Reservoir in 1998 (also singing at the site on 6 August 2000). T. Hicks observed adults feeding young on the Arkansas River near Mulvane (Sedgwick Co.) on 18 July 1999. Eggs have been reported 30 April–15 May, young 20 May–18 June, and recently fledged young 23 May–19 July. O. Smock found an active nest in southern Cowley County around 1929.

Comments: It usually occurs singly or in small, loose flocks outside the breeding season.

Banding: 2,734 banded; 14 encounters: all in-state.

References: Anderson, 1982; Busby and Zimmerman, 2001; Cable et al., 1996; Janzen, 2007; Kluza et al., 2001; Seibel, 1978; Thompson and Ely, 1992.

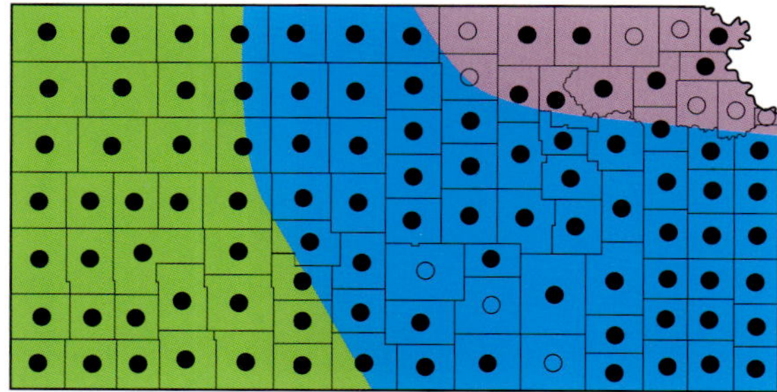

Lincoln's Sparrow

Melospiza lincolnii (LISP)

Status: Common transient statewide; rare and local winter resident.

Habitat: Brushy habitats, especially riparian situations, and in brushy tangles in fields and woodlands; occasionally at feeder stations, where it tends to feed on the ground.

Migration: Early March birds are probably overwintering individuals. More typical arrival is 23 March (Geary Co.) with peak migration from mid-April through early May and with stragglers to 31 May (Morton Co.), 5 June (Ford and Morton cos.), and 16 June (in 1885, N. Goss). Median first arrival in Ellis County is 20 April. Earliest fall arrivals are 6 September (Stafford Co.) and 13 September (Meade Co., banded) with more typical arrival in late September, the peak in October, and stragglers to 3 November (Doniphan Co.) and 30 November (Lyon Co.). Median first arrival in Ellis County is 21 September; median late departure is 31 October. High counts include 30+ on 28 September (Morton Co.) and 20+ on 29 October (Sedgwick Co.). A total of 174 individuals were recovered from six tower kills near Topeka (Shawnee Co.), most of them, by far, during 1–12 October. Small numbers regularly winter in eastern and southeastern Kansas and rarely elsewhere. Presumed wintering birds are present mid-December through early March.

Comments: It passes through Kansas enroute to wintering areas on the Gulf Coast and in Central America. It is usually a shy species, but it will often respond to "pishing" by hopping into the open for a brief look, then darting back into cover. It feeds on the ground under vegetation by scratching like a towhee, kicking backward with both feet at once. It is probably more common than many birders realize, with large numbers having been killed at television towers on single nights during migration.

Banding: 3,117 banded; one encounter. One banded in Kansas on 24 October 1974 was captured and released in Tennessee on 26 March 1975, presumably migrating on both occasions.

References: Ball et al., 1995; Cable et al., 1996; Janzen, 2007; Kluza et al., 2001; Thompson and Ely, 1992; Tordoff and Mengel, 1955.

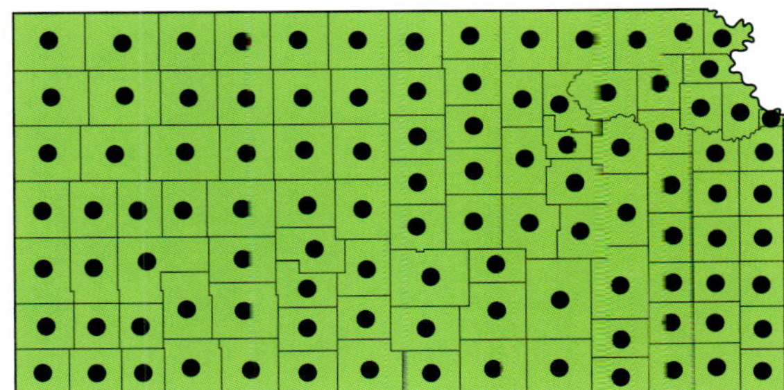

Swamp Sparrow

Melospiza georgiana (SWSP)

Status: Common transient and locally uncommon winter resident in the east; uncommon to rare transient and rare winter resident in the west.

Habitat: Dense cover in marshy areas or in riparian habitat; in winter marshy areas near open water.

Migration: March observations may be of wintering individuals or early transients. Numbers begin increasing in early April with most migration mid-April ("large numbers," Coffey Co., L. Moore) through early May. High numbers include 20+ on 3 April (Stafford Co.). Arrival is later in the west, usually late April and early May. Most have departed by 6 May but with stragglers to 13 May (Sedgwick Co.) and 21 May (Douglas Co.). The earliest fall date is 25 August (Pawnee Co., S. Seltman), but first arrival is usually in late September or early October (mid-October, Ellis Co.). It is most numerous and most widespread during October and becomes largely restricted to marshy areas by late November. Twenty-six have been salvaged from tower kills near Topeka (Shawnee Co.) on 1–8 October (4) and 28 October (22). Small numbers are commonly recorded through mid-January statewide. Reports through 28 February, usually at prime marsh habitat (Barton, Douglas, Linn, Jefferson, Russell, Sedgwick, and Sumner cos.), suggest successful overwintering, but there are few actual reports for late winter.

Comments: Individuals may occur in very small patches of cattails in seepage areas as long as standing water remains unfrozen. It typically remains under cover but often responds to "pishing" or recorded calls. The call is distinctive and once learned is the easiest way to locate the species. According to J. Terres it does much of its feeding in shallow water, where it picks up floating insects. Individuals may join flocks of mixed sparrows and occasionally visit feeders.

Banding: 503 banded; no encounters.

References: Cable et al., 1996; Janzen, 2007; Terres, 1980; Thompson and Ely, 1992.

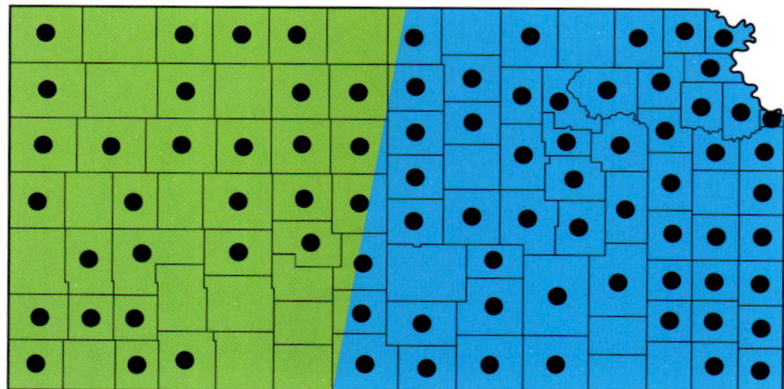

White-throated Sparrow

Zonotrichia albicollis (WTSP)

© David Seibel

Status: Common transient and uncommon winter resident in the east; uncommon transient and rare winter resident in the west.

Habitat: Various shrubby situations such as woodlands, roadsides, hedgerows, parks, and residential areas.

Migration: Early dates for presumed transients include 12 March (Coffey Co.) and 16 March (Harvey Co.), but most arrivals are in April with peak migration during mid-April through early May. Median first arrival dates include 21 April (Rice Co.) and 23 April (Ellis Co.). Median departure in Ellis County is 8 May. Late dates include 12 May (Ellis Co.) and 13 May (Doniphan Co.). Stragglers are reported to 6 June (Leavenworth Co.). Early fall arrivals include 5 September (Trego Co.), 6 September (Stafford Co.), and 16 September (Finney Co.), with most arrivals by mid-October and the migration peak from late October to mid-November. At least 27 were salvaged from tower kills near Topeka (Shawnee Co.) on 8–12 October (12) and 28 October (15). A few remain through at least early December in the west and winter during some mild years. It is regular in winter in eastern Kansas.

Comments: It winters in the southeastern and south-central United States. It sings occasionally in winter and commonly during spring migration. The song is a series of high, clear, whistled notes often transliterated as "Old Sam Peabody, Peabody, Peabody."

Banding: 1,951 banded; four encounters: three in-state. The fourth, banded 5 November 1978, was killed flying into an object in Minnesota on 11 May 1979 either during migration or on its breeding grounds.

References: Ball et al., 1995; Cable et al., 1996; Janzen, 2007; Kluza et al., 2001; Thompson and Ely, 1992.

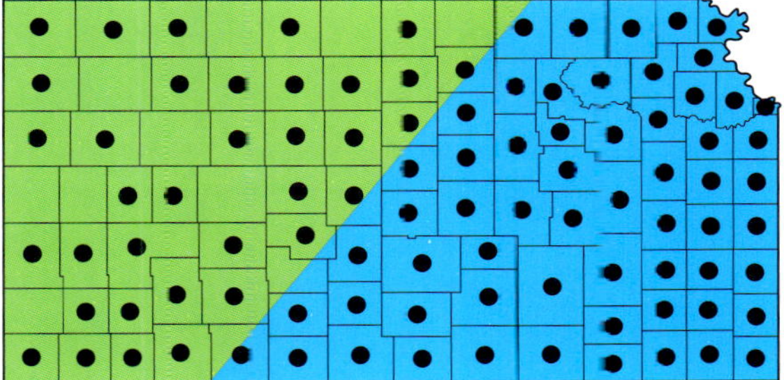

Harris's Sparrow

Zonotrichia querula (HASP)

Status: Common transient in eastern Kansas and an abundant winter resident in south-central Kansas; rare to uncommon in the far west, occasionally during summer.

© Judd Patterson

Habitat: Woodland edges, brushy fields, streamside thickets, hedgerows, sunflower patches, and feeding stations in suburban areas.

Migration: Very early fall arrivals include 26 September (Greeley Co.) and 29 September (Harvey Co.). Median first arrival dates include 19 October (Ellis Co.) and 1 November (Rice Co.); median departure dates include 1 May (Rice Co.) and 10 May (Ellis Co.). Up to 1,000 individuals have been reported in a single roosting flock (Pawnee Co.). Arrival is usually mid-October with most migration through November. Five were salvaged from a tower kill near Topeka (Shawnee Co.) on 28 October. Spring departure is usually mid-April through mid-May with stragglers into early June (2 June, Osborne and Smith cos.), exceptionally to 30 July (Sumner Co., L. Hicks). High counts include 200+ on the late date of 10 May (Pawnee Co.). There are scattered summer records from 17 June through 28 August from at least nine counties from Russell and Sumner counties eastward. Many of these were singing, in full breeding plumage, and identification was positive.

Comments: Numbers seem to fluctuate with the severity of winter weather and the availability of seed crops. At least through early January, Kansas hosts a major portion of the species' total wintering population, as demonstrated by data from CBCs. During the 50 years from 1957 to 2006, an average of only 138 (of 1,146) counts in the United States reported any Harris's Sparrows. Of these, a mean of 20 (i.e., 14.5% of all counts reporting the species) were from Kansas, but these counts compiled an average of 51.0 percent of the total number of individuals nationwide. The Udall/Winfield CBC (Cowley Co.) has reported the highest numbers in the nation on several occasions and has averaged 22.4 percent of the total Kansas count during the 45 years it has reported. The highest count for Kansas was 14,366 in 1986 (a low year for Udall/Winfield, with only 913 reported); the highest count for Udall/Winfield was 5,073 in 2003, representing 49.8 percent of the Kansas total and 31.2 percent of the national total for that year.

See page 503 for banding information.

References: Cable et al., 1996; Janzen, 2007; Johnston, 1960, 1965; Kluza et al., 2001; National Audubon Society, 2007; Norment and Shackleton, 1993; Seibel, 1978; Thompson and Ely, 1992.

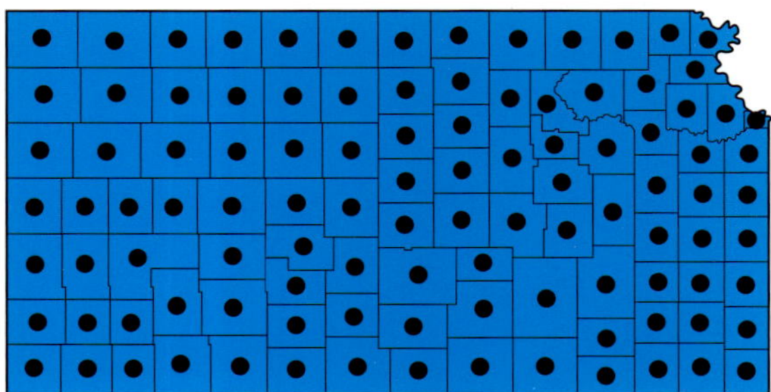

White-crowned Sparrow

Zonotrichia leucophrys (WCSP)

Status: Common transient and winter resident, especially in the west; local in winter in much of the central region, rare in the east.

Habitat: Brushy fields, woodland-edged roadsides, riparian situations, yards, and parks; during winter locally common in riparian habitats and hedgerows in the west.

Migration: Early fall arrivals include 1 September (Coffey Co.), 19 September (Morton Co.), and 21 September (Meade Co.), but arrival is usually early October with peak migration during late October and November. Median first arrival in Ellis County is 1 October. High numbers include 160+ on 24 October (Morton Co.) and 150+ on 28 November (Finney Co.). Sixteen were salvaged from tower kills near Topeka (Shawnee Co.) on 8–12 October (14) and 28 October (2). The late dates for fall transients and arrival of early spring transients are masked by large numbers of wintering birds, especially in the west. Spring transients are present by at least mid-April and widespread by the end of the month. Median date for spring arrival in Ellis County is 24 April; median date for spring departure is 13 May. Late spring dates include 21 May (Meade Co.) and 11 and 12 June (Ellis Co., different years). Large counts include "abundant" on 28 April (Morton and Hamilton cos.) and "abundant" on 4 May (Riley Co.). One (with dark lores) on 18 July 1994 in Russell County was probably a vagrant.

Comments: It is a conspicuous transient because of its choice of habitats. Its song is often heard on warm winter days and during spring migration. It can often be induced to hop into view by imitating its song or by "pishing." Typical of its genus, it feeds on the ground, vigorously scratching through leaf litter. Its diet includes willow catkins and tree buds in spring and seeds of various weeds and grasses all year. In winter some individuals visit feeders for chicken feed grains, cracked corn, and ground sorghum.

Banding: 3,043 banded; three encounters: two instate. The third, banded in Ellis County on 16 March 1973, was shot at Yellowknife in Northwest Territory on 25 June 1975 on its breeding grounds. Oldest 4 years, 1 month.

References: Cable et al., 1996; Janzen, 2007; Thompson and Ely, 1992.

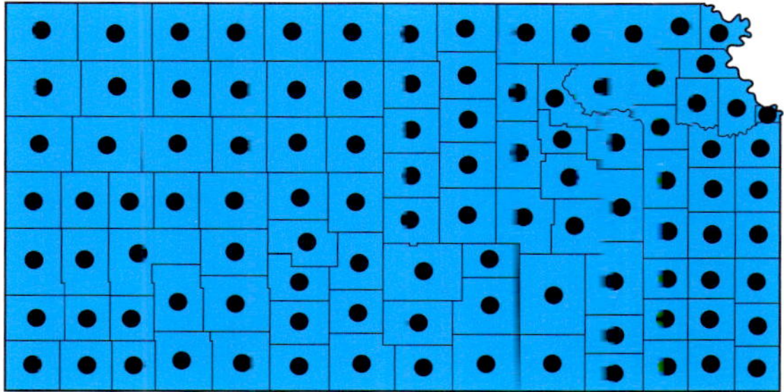

Golden-crowned Sparrow

Zonotrichia atricapilla (GCSP)

© Mark Chappell

Status: Winter vagrant, with scattered sight records statewide.

Habitat: Dense brush, overgrown fields, brushy riparian habitat, and feeding stations, especially in rural settings.

Migration: There are at least 24 records, two-thirds of them since 1990. Extreme dates are 20 October (Phillips Co., R. Rucker) to 13 May (Harvey Co.) with most sightings during or near the CBC period. In two instances birds remained at feeders for extended periods, including 3 January–29 March 1998 (two individuals, Finney Co., photos, M. Osterbuhr) and March and April 2008 (Sumner Co., W. Champeny). Most records are of single birds, but two were present in Finney County in 1998, and three were reported in Morris County on 3 December 2003 (R. Japuntich, KBRC 2003-66).

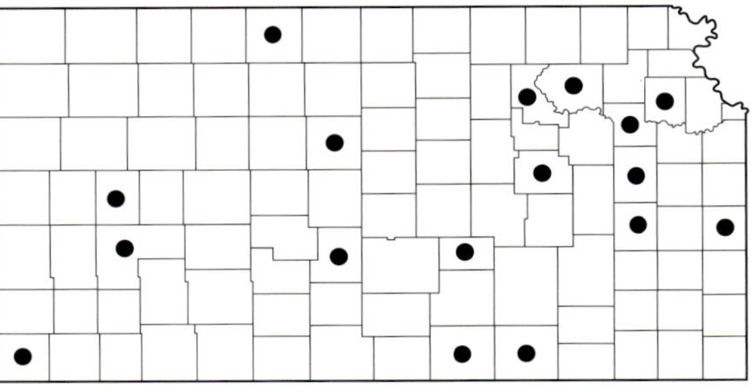

Comments: The first report for Kansas was of one visiting a feeder at Halstead (Harvey Co.) on 13 May 1957 and carefully described by E. Ruth. It was followed by sightings from Pottawatomie County (L. Edmunds) on 14 April 1965 and Cowley County on 15 and 17 February 1982 (J. Barnes). Beginning in 1987–1988 one or more were reported during most winters and from localities across the state. The first sighting verified by physical evidence (photos, KBRC 93-01) was on 10 January 1988 (Scott Co., T. Shane). Often found in association with White-crowned Sparrows, it forages chiefly on the ground. It is most likely to be seen in late fall or winter around a feeder with other sparrows.

References: Hardy, 1957; Otte, 2004, 2008; Pittman, 1994; Thompson and Ely, 1992.

Dark-eyed Junco

Junco hyemalis (DEJU)

© David Seibel

Status: Common to abundant transient and winter resident statewide; vagrant in summer.

Habitat: Various brushy habitats from riparian growth and woodland edge to parks and gardens; often along roadsides, especially in wooded areas; frequently visits feeders.

Migration: Early arrivals include 29 August (Douglas Co., KU 17494) and 19 September (Cheyenne and Sumner cos.), with most arrivals during early October and a migration peak during the last half of October and first half of November. Median dates for first arrivals include 7 October (Ellis Co.) and 10 October (Rice Co.). High counts for fall include 200 on 25 October (Wyandotte Co.) and 175+ (Morton Co.). Spring migration is masked by the presence of wintering birds but probably begins in March, peaks from early to mid-April, and is largely over by early May. Median last departures include 16 April (Ellis Co.) and 21 April (Rice Co.) with stragglers to 19 May (Norton Co.). There are three summer records, all Slate-colored, all single birds, on 6 June (Wyandotte Co., feeder, L. Moore), 21 June (Nemaha Co., T. Shane), and 27 July (Riley Co., birdbath, T. Cable). The various forms typically occur in mixed flocks. White-wings are more often seen during late fall and early winter; Gray-headed during spring. T. and S. Shane reported median arrival dates by subspecies in Finney County: Slate-colored, 18 October; Oregon, 17 October; Pink-sided, 16 October; and White-winged, 8 November. They observed the Gray-headed race only twice in 18 winters, two individuals in spring (24–25 March and 6–12 April) and one overwintering (28 October–6 April). The known date span for Gray-headed in Kansas is 23 October–12 April.

Comments: Five subspecies have been reported, and intergrades are so common that many individuals cannot be safely distinguished in the field. Nonetheless, there are fairly pronounced distributional differences. In decreasing order of abundance: Slate-colored (*J. h. hyemalis*) predominates eastward; Oregon (*J. h. oreganus*) predominates westward; Pink-sided (*J. h. mearnsi*) and White-winged (*J. h. aikeni*) winter primarily in the west; and Gray-headed (*J. h. caniceps*) strays nearly statewide but probably occurs most often in the extreme southwest. Of these races, all except *J. h. mearnsi* were considered separate species until 1973. This is the familiar "snowbird" of Kansas. The various races are similar in habits.

See page 504 for banding information

References: AOU, 1998; Cable et al., 1996; Janzen, 2007; Shane and Shane, 2008; Thompson and Ely, 1992.

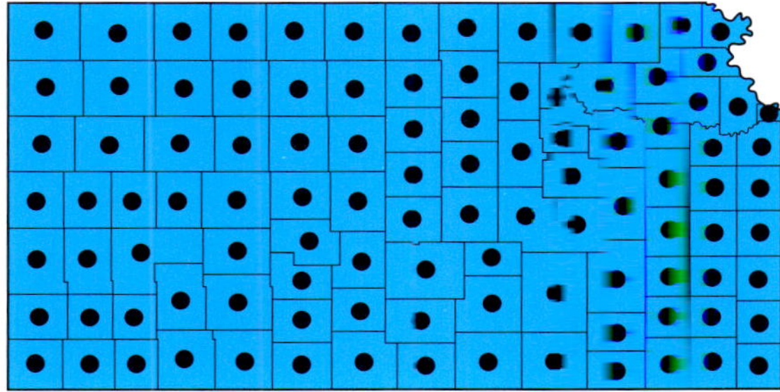

Hepatic Tanager

Piranga flava (HETA)

Status: [Hypothetical]. Vagrant.

Habitat: Normally in montane pine–oak forests.

Comments: The only sighting is of an adult male observed in Morton County by P. Janzen, J. Cornelius, and J. Martin on 22 April 2006 (KBRC 2006-05). It was in the shelterbelt just north of the Elkhart cemetery. KBRC accepted this record, but without any physical documentation it remains "hypothetical" on the state checklist. It is reported regularly in southeastern Colorado and may be expected again in Kansas.

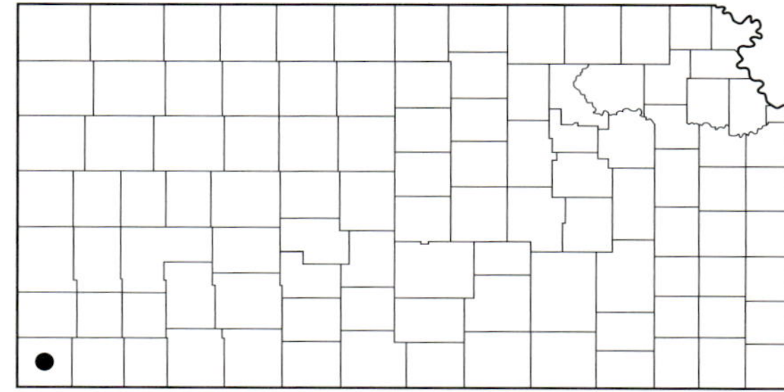

Reference: Otte, 2007.

Summer Tanager

Piranga rubra (SUTA)

Status: Uncommon transient and summer resident in the eastern one-third of the state; rare to casual transient westward.

Habitat: Riparian and upland hardwood forest, especially oak woodland in the Osage Plains and Glaciated Region, riparian gallery forest in the Flint Hills, and in almost any wooded area (cottonwood and locust groves) farther west.

Migration: Usually arrives around 25 April (extreme date 18 April); median first arrivals include 25 April (Johnson Co.) and Johnston gave 29 April for median arrival. The spring departure is uncertain because of the presence of breeding birds. Outside the breeding range late dates are 28 and 29 May. Fall departure generally begins in early September, with most gone by early October and with stragglers to 27 October (Lyon Co.).

Breeding: It reaches the northwestern limit of its breeding range in Kansas. It nests west to Sumner County in the south and probably Saline County in the north (possibly northward to Cloud Co.). Although regularly reported during the breeding season in the eastern one-third of the state, few nests have been discovered. M. Schwilling found eight nests in Linn County during 1956. Nest-building has been observed 14–19 May, eggs 18–26 June, and recently fledged young 25 July–22 August. The nest is usually placed about 20 feet high in deciduous forest.

Comments: All of the tanagers (genus *Piranga*) that occur in Kansas have recently been reclassified as members of the family Cardinalidae, removing them from the family Thraupidae, which includes the tanagers of Central and South America. Male Summer Tanagers typically sing from the tops of trees, where the dense foliage and their habit of remaining motionless for long periods often make them very difficult to locate despite their intense color. Young males may breed while in a mixed red and yellow plumage but achieve the full red plumage by their second autumn. Unlike the Scarlet Tanager, male Summer Tanagers do not lose their bright color in the winter. This species eats mostly insects and has a particular appetite for bees and wasps, especially the larvae. It will also consume fruit when available.

Banding: 61 banded; one encounter. A young male banded on 1 October 1977 was captured by hand in Belize on 29 December 1980 on its wintering grounds.

References: AOU, 2009; Bent, 1958; Busby and Zimmerman, 2001; Cable et al., 1996; Janzen, 2007; Thompson and Ely, 1992.

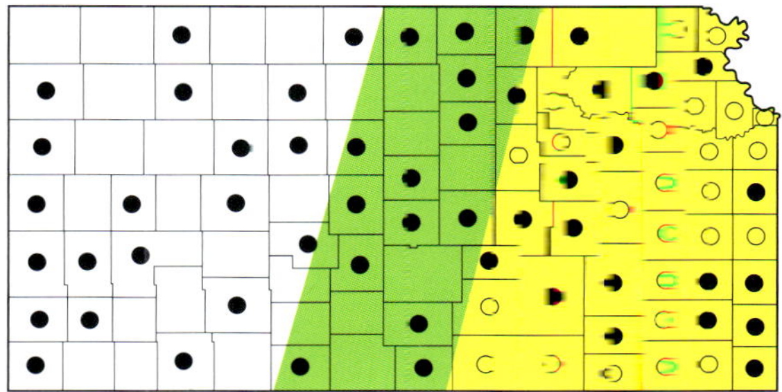

Scarlet Tanager

Piranga olivacea (SCTA)

Status: Uncommon transient and rare to uncommon (very local) nesting species in the eastern one-third of the state, rare to casual westward.

Habitat: A specialist of mature eastern deciduous forest and mixed oak forests in upland or more often riparian situations; in migration, in less mature deciduous woods, parks, and residential areas.

Migration: Transients usually arrive around 28 April with an extreme date of 10 April. Median early arrival dates include 1 May (Johnson Co.); usual departure is by 18 May with stragglers to 7 June. Dates of fall arrival are obscured by the presence of nesting birds in the east, and there are few records elsewhere. Fall departure is typically during September and early October (television tower kills, 5–7 October, Shawnee Co.). The few fall dates outside the breeding range are 2 September–14 October with a late date of 10 November 1996 (Finney Co.).

Breeding: "Active nests" have been reported 3 June–15 July, nest-building 4–24 May, and young 15 July. However, if summer records are taken into account, the Scarlet Tanager has likely nested as far west as Saline and Ottawa counties in the north and Sumner County in the south. M. Thompson banded a pair in western Cowley County that was apparently utilizing oak trees for a nest site. The pair returned to the same site a second year, but the trees were cut before the third nesting season and the birds were not seen afterward. KBBAT reported a total of two "confirmed," seven "probable," and eight "possible" breeding locations in the easternmost two tiers of counties (1992–1997), with another possible site each in Woodson and Ottawa counties.

Comments: It was considered a "common summer resident" in Dickinson County about 1900 and "common" in Riley County about 1880. Recently, it was largely absent from pockets of apparently suitable habitat in central Kansas, the western edge of its range. C. Ely and R. Lohoefener surveyed remnant riparian oak habitat during June 1979 and July 1981 and found only a single territorial male each year at a single locality in Saline County and a single female in Clay County. It is difficult to observe because of its habit of remaining relatively motionless while singing from dense foliage in the treetops in mature hardwood forest. The best area to find this species is along the Missouri River.

Banding: 41 banded; no encounters.

References: Busby and Zimmerman, 2001; Cable et al., 1996; Janzen, 2007; Thompson and Ely, 1992.

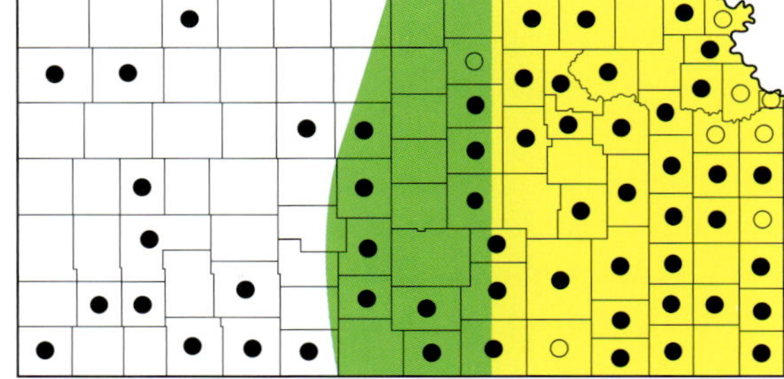

Western Tanager

Piranga ludoviciana (WETA)

Status: Casual to rare transient in the extreme west and a vagrant eastward.

Habitat: Riparian growth along dry riverbeds in western Kansas, shelterbelts, and residential areas with trees; occasional at feeders.

Migration: The earliest arrivals are 27 April (Morton Co.) and 30 April (Ellis Co.) with most sightings during the first half of May and with stragglers through 1 June. Midsummer vagrants include 24 June (Chase Co.) and 8 July 1969 (Sumner Co., W. Champeny). Early fall arrivals include 4 August (Chautauqua Co.) and 17 August (Morton Co.). Most migration is during the first half of September with stragglers to 23 September (Morton Co.) and 24 September (Sedgwick Co., P. Janzen). There are three early winter records: one near Lawrence (Douglas Co.) on 18 December 1982 (R. Boyd and C. Cink), one at Manhattan on 31 January 1933 (D. Rintoul, photo), and one that arrived near Larned (Pawnee Co., S. Seltman) on 7 December 2009 and survived severe winter conditions until 24 December. It can be quite common in Morton County, where S. Patti and M. Thompson saw 30 on 22 September 2005.

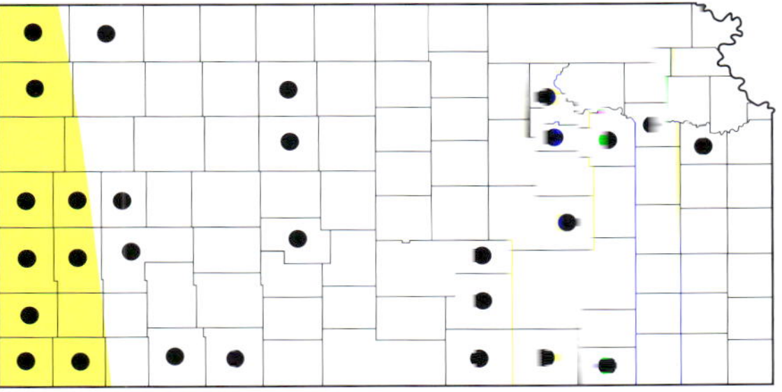

Comments: Most records are from Morton County since 1992, probably because of the increased numbers of birders visiting that corner of the state. It is unusual among vagrants in that sightings statewide have been at all seasons.

Banding: Four banded; no encounters.

References: Cable et al., 1996; Janzen, 2007; Thompson and Ely, 1992.

Northern Cardinal

Cardinalis cardinalis (NOCA)

Status: Common permanent resident in the east becoming uncommon to rare in the west.

Habitat: Second-growth woods, riparian areas, brushy areas, parks, and residential yards.

Migration: Banding has shown that it is nonmigratory though some local movement occurs during the nonbreeding season. In the west, some short-range dispersal occurs.

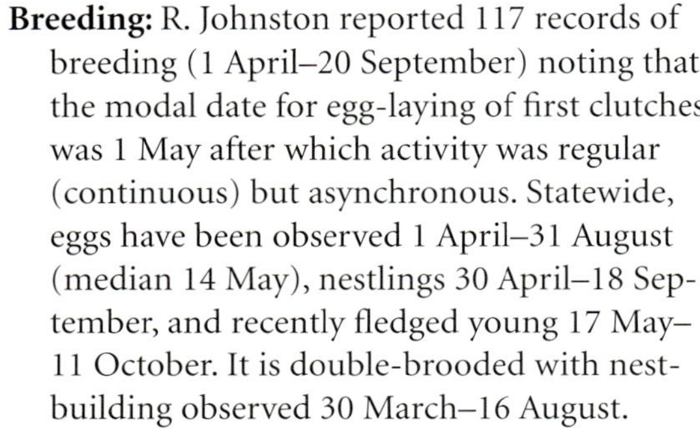

Breeding: R. Johnston reported 117 records of breeding (1 April–20 September) noting that the modal date for egg-laying of first clutches was 1 May after which activity was regular (continuous) but asynchronous. Statewide, eggs have been observed 1 April–31 August (median 14 May), nestlings 30 April–18 September, and recently fledged young 17 May–11 October. It is double-brooded with nest-building observed 30 March–16 August.

Comments: This is clearly a species that has benefited from human settlement and the increase in edge habitat, from the planting of trees and shrubs in windbreaks and at farmsteads in the west to the degradation of closed forest in the east. Its brilliant plumage and song and confiding nature also made it a favorite of humans, who since pioneer days have noticed it and often provide food and shelter in parks and residential areas. During the presettlement period, cardinals were common to abundant in the east but absent from the far west. In Ellis County, L. Watson noted that it was rare in Ellis (1888), and L. Wooster had only scattered records from Hays as late as 1927–1955. In the southwest W. Long saw only two during November 1934 (Seward Co.), and in 1950 R. and J. Graber considered it "not very common" in any locality but saw "several" in Meade and Hamilton counties. By 1974, J. Rising considered it "moderately common" in much of the southwest. In well-birded Morton County it remains an "uncommon resident from late summer into spring" with no summer records.

Banding: 8,547 banded; 176 encounters: 174 in-state, local and short distance, 1 to Kansas from nearby Missouri; 1 from Kansas to New Jersey is an error. Oldest 8 years, 1 month.

References: Busby and Zimmerman, 2001; Cable et al., 1996; Cooke, 1888; Graber and Graber, 1951; Janzen, 2007; Johnston, 1964a; Long, 1940; Rising, 1974; Thompson and Ely, 1992; Watson *in* Ely, 1971.

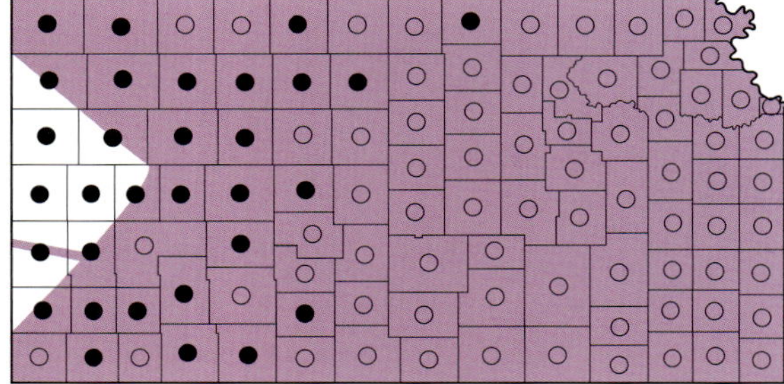

Pyrrhuloxia

Cardinalis sinuatus (PYRR)

Status: Irregular visitant to the southwest, usually in winter.

Habitat: Riparian vegetation in sand-sage prairie, windbreaks, and residential yards.

Migration: Extreme dates of sightings are 25 October and 19 May.

Comments: The first sighting, initially by S. Patti and M. Thompson, was a female at the CNG Tunnerville Work Center north of Elkhart (Morton Co.) observed on several occasions between 28 October and 11 November 1989. They were unable to find the bird on 9 December, but on the 30th, in the "hawk [rehabilitation] barn," they found and preserved feathers that had been clipped from its wings and tail. A male was observed by many observers in the shelterbelt north of the Elkhart Cemetery between 1 January and 25 March 1993, followed by one in Hamilton County on 9–16 January 1994. Unexpected were single birds at the MDCWA on 1 and 22 April 1994, and one photographed in Wichita (Sedgwick Co.) on 3 February 1995. Other confirmed sightings were a male on 25 April 2000 (Ford Co.) and a female on 19 May 2000 (Stafford Co.). A sighting from Kearny County on 25 October 2000 was not confirmed.

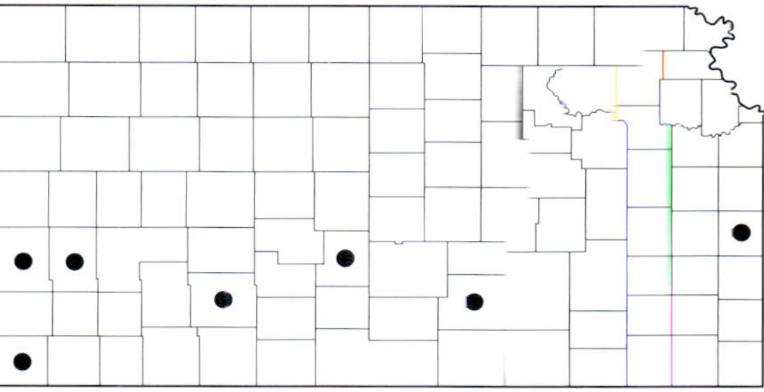

References: Cable et al., 1996; Janzen, 2007; Thompson and Ely, 1992.

Rose-breasted Grosbeak

Pheucticus ludovicianus (RBGR)

Status: Common transient and summer resident in the east; uncommon to rare transient westward.

Habitat: Woodlands, riparian areas, parks, and residential areas during migration.

Migration: Extreme dates for spring transients are 22 April and 22 June with most migration during May. The median earliest date for arrival in Ellis County is 4 May; the latest median departure of presumed transients is 21 May. Extreme dates for fall migration are 11 August and 19 October with a late straggler on 4 November. About half of all fall sightings are during 10–25 September. An occasional bird is reported during the CBC period, usually at a feeder in the east but once in Ellis County.

Breeding: Few data are available. Active nests have been reported 11 May–17 July with nest-building 12–23 May, eggs 26 May–6 June, young in nest 1–17 June, and recently fledged young 6 June–14 July. KBBAT found it most common in the Glaciated Region with scattered confirmed nestings south to Coffey, Harvey, and northern Sedgwick counties and westward along the Republican River drainage to Smith County.

Comments: During the early settlement period it was common only in the east. Near the turn of the century N. Goss had not seen it west of Junction City, and it was a rare transient in Ellis, Rooks, and Rawlins counties in the 1930s. It is now reported over a larger area of the west, especially during migration. Its current breeding range nearly meets that of the Black-headed Grosbeak in the northern half of the state, and the amount of hybridization is expected to increase. Most of the hybrids reported during midsummer are from areas where Black-headed Grosbeaks predominate. However, hybrids may occur anywhere during the nonbreeding season. In recent years, increasing numbers of migrating grosbeaks have appeared at feeding stations in residential areas.

Banding: 384 banded; no encounters.

References: Busby and Zimmerman, 2001; Imler, 1937; Janzen, 2007; Thompson and Ely, 1992; Tiemeier, 1942.

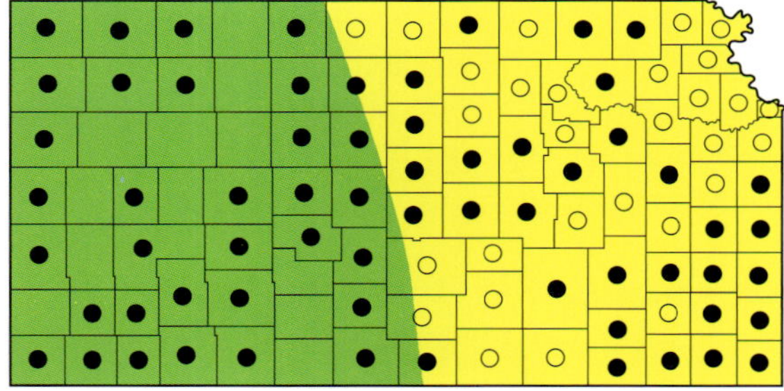

Black-headed Grosbeak

Pheucticus melanocephalus (BHGR)

Status: Uncommon transient and summer resident in the west; casual eastward; occasional in winter.

Habitat: Riparian woods, windbreaks, parks, and residential yards.

Migration: The median first arrival for Ellis County is 2–3 May; late observations are 25 May–10 June. Outside breeding areas, presumed transients are recorded 21 April–4 June with most during May. In fall the first transients (some perhaps hatched nearby) arrive in early August through mid-September with stragglers to 11 October. Occasional birds appear at feeders during early winter, including 17 December (Chase Co.) and 16–22 January 1974 (Lyon Co.).

Breeding: Unexpectedly, KBBAT confirmed nesting in only four blocks, three in the northwestern tier of counties and one in Finney County. R. Johnston reported 16 records of breeding between 11 May and 10 July with a modal date of egg-laying of 5 June. Nest-building has been reported 16–20 May, eggs 21 May–11 June (median 7 June), young in nest 11–30 June and 15 August, and recently fledged young 10 July–10 August.

Comments: During presettlement and early settlement years it was common at Fort Hays (Ellis Co.), "fairly common" in Decatur County, and "rare" in Finney County during summer. Rising noted that it was common in the northwest and probably only a transient in the southwest. Its current range extends somewhat farther east barely meeting that of the Rose-breasted Grosbeak. Although actual nesting is rarely documented, most recent summer records are near this boundary. Most summer records in the west are of territorial males in deciduous riparian growth along the Smoky Hill River drainage and northward. Smaller numbers occur in parks and residential areas of towns.

Banding: 197 banded; one encounter: in-state, at banding site. Oldest 5 years.

References: Allen, 1872; Busby and Zimmerman, 2001; Cable et al., 1996; Goss, 1891; Jansen, 2007; Johnston, 1964a; Thompson and Ely, 1992.

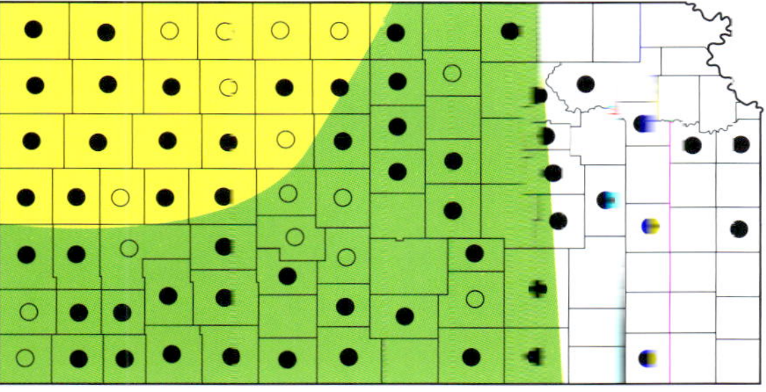

Blue Grosbeak

Passerina caerulea (BLGR)

Status: Common transient and summer resident in the west; uncommon in the east.

Habitat: Riparian woodlands, trees and brushy areas in grassland, windbreaks, and parks.

Migration: Extreme dates for spring transients are 12 April and 8 June with most migration during May. The median early arrival date for Ellis County is 8 May. An obvious migration was noted in Meade County on 21 May. Extreme dates for fall departure are 9 September–13 October with most migration during September. The median departure date for Ellis County is 3 October. A most unusual sighting is of a male found on the Wichita CBC by C. Miller, observed by others, and photographed by M. Heaney on 20 December 2008.

Breeding: KBBAT reported the highest frequency of confirmed nestings within the forest mosaic of the Osage Plains and Red Hills. Lowest frequencies were in the Glaciated Region and (unexpectedly) the Smoky Hills. Perhaps the brushy areas with scattered trees in gullies and ravines in prairie and around abandoned farmsteads were too scattered to be fully sampled. Nest-building has been reported 23 May–14 June, eggs 2 June–10 July, young in nest 9 June–7 August, and recently fledged young 20 June–13 August.

Comments: The record from the Wichita 2008 CBC is one of the latest for the central United States. The latest date reported for Missouri is 4 December 1952; for Nebraska, 4 January 1948. It is less dependent on tree cover than the other two grosbeaks and is therefore more widespread through western Kansas. It is less likely to appear in towns and residential yards even as a transient.

Banding: 189 banded; two encounters: both instate. Oldest 2 years, 3 months.

References: Busby and Zimmerman, 2001; Cable et al., 1996; Janzen, 2007; Robbins and Easterla, 1992; Sharpe et al., 2001; Thompson and Ely, 1992; Young et al., 2009.

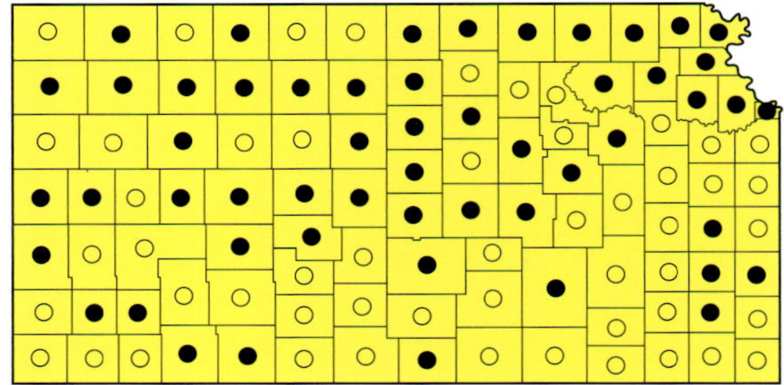

Lazuli Bunting

Passerina amoena (LAZB)

Status: Uncommon transient in the west, less common in the east; breeds at least occasionally in the far west.

Habitat: Riparian areas, thickets and brushy areas in grassland, hedgerows, and residential yards.

Migration: Extreme spring migration dates are 17 March (Cherokee Co.), 24 April, and 16 June with most during the first half of May. The median first arrival for Ellis County is 11–12 May; the median latest departure is 23 May. There are several reports of males during midsummer in eastern Kansas. Extreme fall migration dates are 10 August–20 September with stragglers through 2 October. The number of sightings at feeders during migration has increased considerably since 2000.

Breeding: There are currently only two recorded nestings from Kansas, both in Morton County. The first is from 18 July 1958; the second is from KBBAT. The first nest was in a cottonwood–tamarisk–sweet clover association along the Cimarron River. The female flushed from the nest and was joined by her mate. Other males were singing along the river, but only one nest was found.

Comments: H. Menke considered it a "common summer resident" but without any mention of physical evidence. A male apparently spent the summer of 1995 in southern Cowley County, and a hybrid was seen in the same area on 15 June 1996. In 1993 one was seen regularly in Geary County from Memorial Day through July. A mixed pair was reported from Geary County on 20 May 1973. Lazuli Buntings and Indigo Buntings hybridize where their ranges meet, and presumably this occurs in Kansas as well. Hybrid individuals are regularly seen during migration.

Banding: 53 banded; no encounters.

References: Busby and Zimmerman, 2001; Cable et al., 1996; Janzen, 2007; Thompson, 1958; Thompson and Ely, 1992.

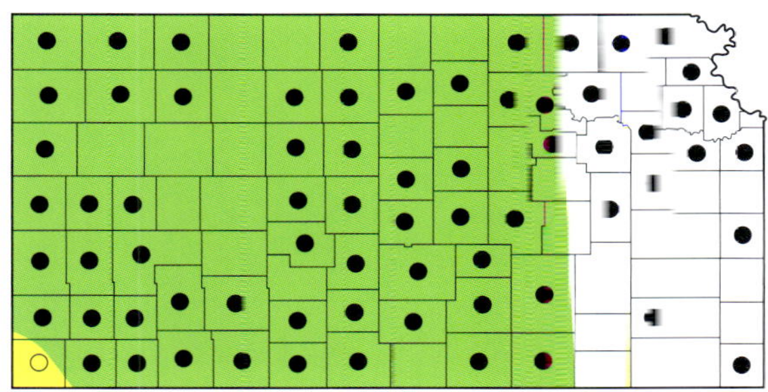

Indigo Bunting

Passerina cyanea (INBU)

Status: Common transient statewide; common summer resident statewide though less common in the southwest.

Habitat: Woodland edge, riparian areas, forest edge, brushy areas in grassland, windbreaks, roadsides, and, during migration, parks and residential yards.

Migration: The median first arrival for the east is 1 May; for central and western Kansas, 6 May. Stragglers occur into early June. The median first arrival for Ellis County is 8 May. Fall migration is poorly documented, but the median late date for Ellis County is 10 October. Statewide, flocking begins in late August with most migration from mid-September to mid-October with stragglers to 31 October and, exceptionally, 18 November. One CBC record on 27 December 1992, Arkansas City (Cowley Co.).

Breeding: R. Johnston reported 24 records of breeding between 11 May and 20 August with 15 June as the modal date for egg-laying. Nest-building has been reported 14 May–12 June, eggs 15 May–18 August (median 12 June), young in nest 13 June–29 July, and recently fledged young 18 July–7 September. It is unknown whether late dates are a second clutch attempt after a failed first clutch.

Comments: KBBAT found highest frequencies in the east through the Flint Hills to a line from Pratt to Jewell counties with only scattered records of probable breeding westward. As with other "cardulines" this species seems to be underreported in the west. During the breeding season its nests are restricted to brushy vegetation and low trees along streams, in gullies with brush, around farm ponds with trees, and less often in ornamental plantings. During migration it is more widespread and often occurs in residential areas as well.

Banding: 1,553 banded; four encounters: three in-state. One banded in Kansas on 5 June 2002 was killed by a cat in Iowa on 25 July 2005. Oldest 3 years, 1 month.

References: Busby and Zimmerman, 2001; Cable et al., 1996; Janzen, 2007; Johnston, 1964a; Thompson, 1993; Thompson and Ely, 1992.

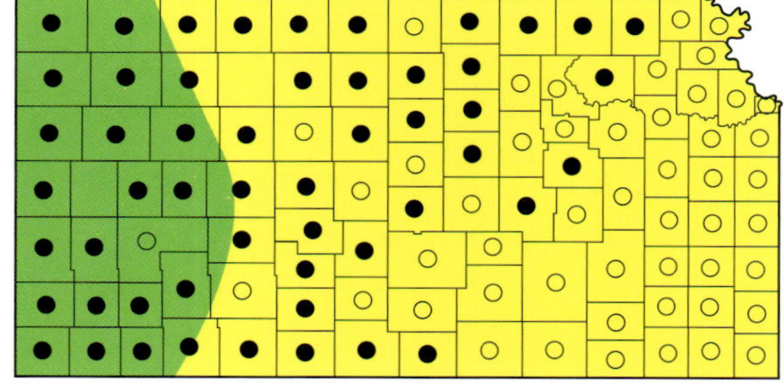

Painted Bunting

Passerina ciris (PABU)

Status: Uncommon transient and summer resident in the southeast, becoming less common northward and westward in the south to the Red Hills.

Habitat: Brushy areas in grassland, scrub oak hillsides, cedar glades, parks, and residential yards.

Migration: Extreme dates for presumed spring transients are 19 April and 24 May. The fall migration is poorly documented. Migration probably begins in late August with the peak in September. There are few records after 20 September with only stragglers through 2 October. Median departure for presumed transients is 26 September.

Breeding: KBBAT confirmed breeding in only seven plots, most in the Cross Timbers or the Red Hills. However, it is a local and low-density breeder north, at least to the Kansas River, and occurs regularly at numerous localities in most years. Few data are available, but nest-building was reported 27 May, eggs 6 June–7 July, young in nest 22–23 July, and recently fledged young 18 July–2 September.

Comments: Early 19th-century ornithologists reported it from southwestern Kansas, and C. Bunker specifically called it a common summer resident in the southeast. H. Tordoff specifically extended the range, including breeding, into the northeast. R. Mengel reviewed its status, noting that it had been in the area since at least 1954 and provided specific breeding data. By examining specimens in suspected breeding condition he concluded that the actual range was much wider than suspected. Despite its dramatic coloration and a distinctive song usually delivered from an exposed perch, the species is underreported in summer. At the edge of its range, this is due in part to its occurrence as small, isolated populations. However, recent records indicate that these "pockets" of occurrence are stable for many years, for example, in the Stockdale area (Riley Co.) and near Junction City (Geary Co.). Females with brood patches and pairs with territorial males during summer suggest that its range is still too narrowly defined or that the species is still expanding its range northward. Nesting in Saline County in 1918–1919 suggests the former; its increase in the Topeka area since 1947 and near Lawrence since 1954 suggests the latter. In recent years, it has been reported with increasing frequency at residential feeders

Banding: 43 banded; no encounters.

References: Bunker, 1913; Busby and Zimmerman, 2001; Cable et al., 1996; Janzen, 2007; Mengel, 1970a; Messerly, 1972; Thompson and Ely, 1992; Tordoff, 1956.

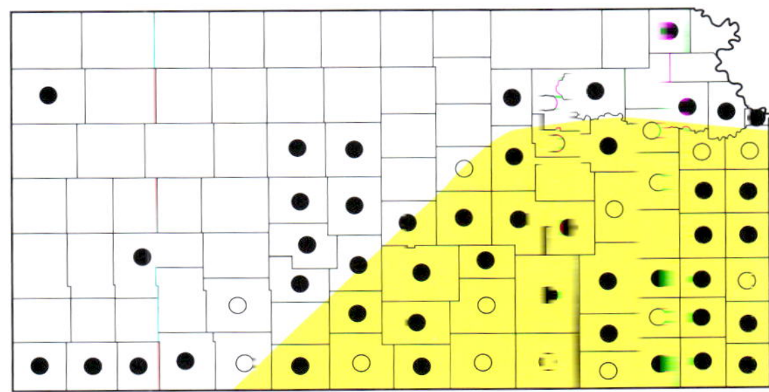

Dickcissel

Spiza americana (DICK)

Status: Common transient and summer resident in eastern and central Kansas, becoming uncommon and local westward.

Habitat: Tallgrass prairie, alfalfa fields, meadows, overgrown or fallow fields, and roadsides.

Migration: The earliest reported arrivals are 5 and 6 April, but the median arrival date statewide is 5 May. "Woods" (unpubl. manuscript, 1976) reported nocturnal migration 3 May–6 June over Topeka. High spring counts include 600 on 11 May (Sedgwick Co.). Postbreeding flocking begins by 19 August and continues through early September after which Dickcissels have either departed or become very inconspicuous. E. Young and M. Thompson observed about 5,000 entering into SCW at dusk to roost on 1 September 1994. Stragglers have been observed through 6 November. Nocturnal migration has been reported between 8 August and 17 October. Dickcissels are frequently involved in tower kills, usually during September. Individuals have remained into the CBC period on at least four occasions (Douglas, Lyon, and Sedgwick [two] cos.). One with a flock of Harris Sparrows on 4 February 1966 (Kingman Co.) may have been wintering.

Breeding: J. Zimmerman reported nesting on Konza Prairie from 24 May to 19 August (116 nests). Statewide eggs have been reported 13 April–20 July, nestlings 9 June–20 July, and recently fledged young 11 June–4 September. Males are polygynous and in high-quality habitat have two or three, sometimes up to six, mates, resulting in greater reproductive nesting success. Cowbird parasitism is common, often with multiple cowbird eggs per nest.

Comments: It occurs statewide with the lowest frequencies in the High Plains. During the 19th century, it was "abundant on Big Timber Creek (Rush Co.) and some were seen along the Saline [River]," apparently areas of better habitat than the shortgrass plains near Fort Hays. The species is believed to have increased in numbers in the west during the 20th century due to an increase in irrigation, CRP lands, and weedy fields. Locally, numbers may vary greatly from year to year especially in the west. The dust bowl era (1933–1939) severely affected western populations, and during 1933 and 1934 Dickcissels were extremely rare or absent from Ellis and Rooks counties.

Banding: 1,496 banded; two encounters: both in-state.

References: Busby and Zimmerman, 2001; Cable et al., 1996; Ely, 1971; Imler, 1937; Janzen, 2007; Thompson and Ely, 1992; Tordoff and Mengel, 1956; Young, 1993; Young and Thompson, 1995; Zimmerman, 1989.

Bobolink

Dolichonyx oryzivorus (BOBO)

© David Seibel

Status: Irregular transient and summer resident (local breeder) in eastern and central Kansas; casual westward.

Habitat: Wet meadows, alfalfa, hayfields, and tallgrass prairie.

Migration: Extreme spring migration dates are 2 April and 11 June with most birds seen during May. In Ellis County, where bobolinks do not nest, the median spring date is 11 May. High numbers include flocks of 150+ in Douglas and Franklin counties on 5 May, 100+ in Woodson County on 7 May, and an astounding 2,000–3,000 in several alfalfa fields in Sumner County on 12 May 2006. In fall, most migration is east of Kansas with the few birds reported between 15 August (Gray Co.) and 7 November (Douglas Co.), with a median of 9 October.

Breeding: Most of the few confirmed nestings are from Barton, Stafford, and Cloud counties. Females are inconspicuous, and nests are exceedingly difficult to locate. The few data are of eggs 18 June–16 July, young in nest 19–29 June, and recently fledged young 30 June–14 July. The best-known colony (Stafford Co.) was active from at least 16 June through 25 July 1956 and contained about 40 males. One active nest was found on 18 June, but no young were ever seen. Colonies were reported in the general area during at least six subsequent seasons (1972–1983). A colony of 17 males nested at CBWA in 1971, with additional nestings through at least 1983. A smaller colony at Jamestown (Cloud Co.) was active 25 June–1 July 1940, and young were being fed on 25 June. Nesting continues irregularly at or near the CBWA and QNWR localities and at a few sites in northeastern Kansas (Nemaha Co.). The most recent nesting was of two females (no males seen) at the Konza Prairie in Riley County during July 2007. The nests were at the top of adjacent hills in tallgrass prairie, much drier habitat than is normal for Kansas colonies. Both nests were depredated, but a female was heard in the area on 1 August.

Comments: Most migrating birds pass through rapidly, but males may sing and display very actively while here. Most of the reports of very early or very late birds are from outside known breeding areas. Small groups of actively displaying males are often reported from areas where nesting has not been known to occur. Three such males (two singing persistently) were in a lush wet meadow in Wallace County on 29 June 1979. Whether such flocks attempt to nest is unknown.

References: Blundell and Von Korff, 2018; Busby and Zimmerman, 2001; Schwilling, 197[illegible]a; Thompson and Ely, 1992; Tordoff, 1957.

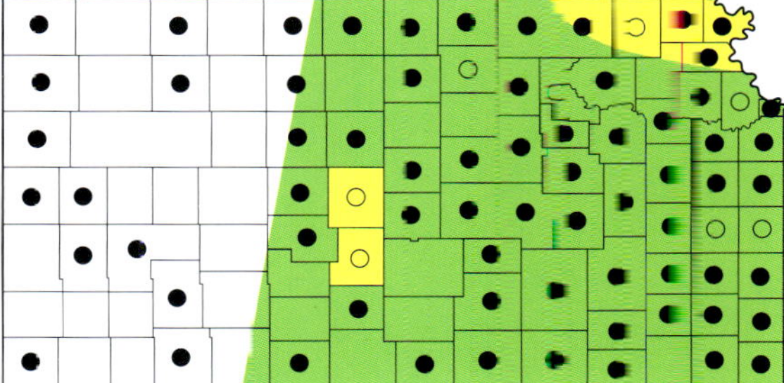

Red-winged Blackbird

Agelaius phoeniceus (RWBL)

© David Seibel

Status: Common transient and summer resident statewide; uncommon to locally abundant in winter.

Habitat: Breeds in marshes, wet areas in alfalfa and grain fields, rank growth near ponds, gullies, and along roadsides; at other times almost anywhere, especially grain fields and feedlots. Roosts in cattail marshes, stands of cedars, and riparian areas.

Migration: The spring migration starts in late February and continues through May. Locally, breeding males arrive on territories by mid-March to mid-April and are soon joined by females. Flocking begins by late July, and large flocks of transients begin appearing by September and into October (tens of thousands) and early November (hundreds of thousands). Local roosts (most at large marshes or in the southeast) may contain up to 3–6 million birds during winter. Birds from such roosts spread out over many square miles of feeding territory during the day. Winter roosts are still active through late February, some years into early April.

Breeding: KBBAT confirmed breeding on 72 percent of all blocks, making it one of the most widespread species in the state. It was recorded in the highest number of blocks in the High Plains. Originally a breeder in marshes, it now occupies low, wet spots with weedy rank vegetation in upland areas including alfalfa and wheat fields, roadside ditches, and farm ponds. Nest-building has been reported 25 April–6 June, eggs 29 March–21 July, young 8 May–21 July, and recently fledged young 9 June–30 July (and 28 September). From May to June 1989, M. Thompson and E. Young found 17 of 21 nests parasitized by Brown-headed Cowbirds.

Comments: Mention Red-winged Blackbird and most people think immediately of a spring male calling from a marsh with his red, yellow-bordered "epaulets" raised in display. Less familiar are the flocks of dull brownish birds that roam the countryside most of the year. Flocks congregate in grain fields and around feedlots and in winter gather in huge roosts for the night, traveling many miles and forming seemingly endless streams of birds as they approach the roost. Anyone fortunate enough to be in the midst of such a roost will long remember the noise, activity, and odor of the occasion.

See page 504 for banding information.

References: Besser and Steffen, 1988; Busby and Zimmerman, 2001; Cable et al., 1996; Cink and Boyd, 2005; Janzen, 2007; Thompson and Ely, 1992; Young, 1993; Young and Thompson, 1995.

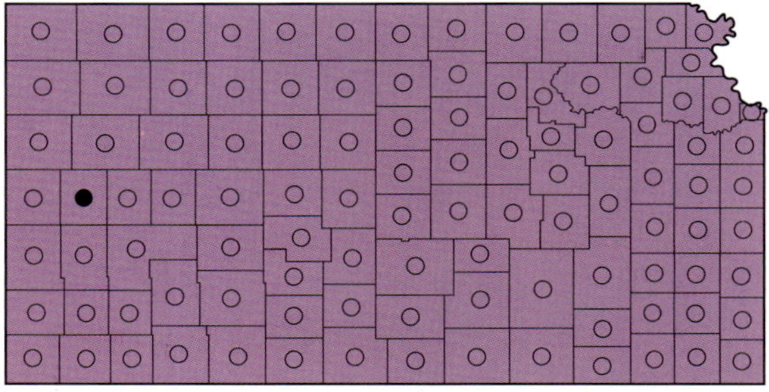

Eastern Meadowlark

Sturnella magna (EAME)

Status: Common transient and summer resident south of a line from Washington County to Clark County; becoming less common west and largely absent from the southwest; uncommon statewide in winter.

Habitat: Tallgrass and mixed-grass prairie, meadows, hayfields, pastures, cultivated areas, and fallow fields.

© Thane Rogers

Migration: There is general agreement that at least some breeding populations move southward in winter and are replaced by more northerly birds. Complicating the already difficult problem of identifying nonsinging birds is the flocking and local dispersal of birds in late fall and winter. "Woods" (unpubl. manuscript, 1976) noted in Shawnee County that the spring movement began in early February with summer flocks forming by early August. The few data suggest a spring movement from late February through mid-April and a fall movement from late September into November. In the west, most records (singing individuals) are mid-March through late May. The few fall reports from the west (unverified) are late September to early October. Clearly the distribution and movements of the two meadowlarks in Kansas deserve serious study.

Breeding: This is the species of the humid tallgrass prairie, breeding westward through the Red Hills (local) and in the north locally westward in areas of wet grassland. For example, at CBWA Western Meadowlarks occupy the drier upland rim whereas Easterns nest in the wetter bowl of the bottoms proper. A similar pattern is noticed at SCW. Elsewhere, small groups also nest in the taller vegetation below large dams and in subirrigated fields. Nest-building has been reported 20 June, eggs 22 April–6 August, young 18 June–22 July, and recently fledged young 21 May.

Comments: S. Rohwer visited various sites along the major river systems during summer 1968 and 1969. He concluded that the Eastern Meadowlark had extended westward along the Smoky Hill River to Ellis County since the 1930s. Expansion was more recent and probably ongoing along the Arkansas River to Gray Co. in 1970. The western limit on the Cimarron River was in Clark County. KBBAT and its map suggest that the westward movement is continuing.

Banding: 637 banded; one encounter: in-state.

References: Busby and Zimmerman, 2001; Cable et al., 1996; Janzen, 2007; Rohwer, 1972; Thompson and Ely, 1992; Young, 1993.

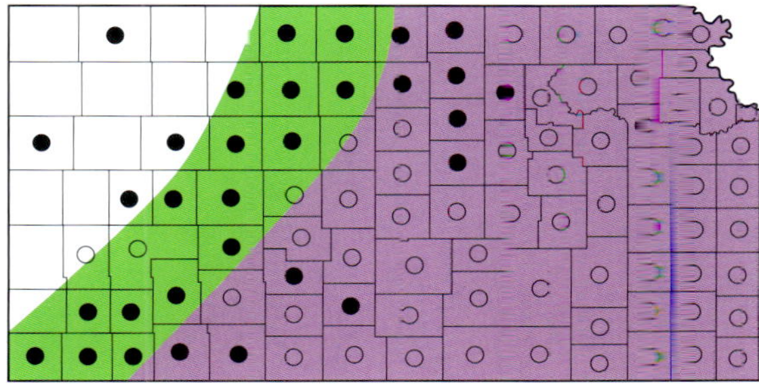

Western Meadowlark

Sturnella neglecta (WEME)

© David Seibel

Status: Common transient and summer resident north of a line from Barber County to Doniphan County; becoming less common east of the Flint Hills and largely absent in the southeast; uncommon statewide in winter.

Habitat: Drier habitats than the Eastern Meadowlark, primarily midgrass and shortgrass prairie but also alfalfa and grain fields, roadsides, and open areas.

Migration: As with the Eastern Meadowlark, it occurs in all months, with breeding birds forming flocks in late summer. It is presumed that summer populations move southward and/or eastward to be replaced by more northerly ones. In most areas numbers are highest in March and April and again in October and November, indicating a migration. In Greeley County, it was considered "abundant" from 25 September to 18 November. In the east, most spring records are 23 February–14 May (Johnson Co.). In the west, there is a marked increase in singing activity as birds move into breeding areas from mid-March to early and mid-April. A definitive study is clearly needed.

Breeding: KBBAT found it occurred in the highest number of blocks in the High Plains. Eastward, it overlaps the breeding range of the Eastern Meadowlark, with the Western occupying the shorter grass of hilltops and disturbed areas. Although usually separated ecologically, both species often occur together in the same field in central Kansas. Nest-building has been reported 6 April–10 June, eggs 14 April–12 July, young 26 April–20 July, and fledged young 1 June–19 July.

Comments: During winter, birds often move into farmsteads during inclement weather, feeding with livestock and even roosting in buildings. Song is the best means of distinguishing the two meadowlarks, and individuals often sing during fall and occasionally even in winter on warm, sunny days. The careful observer should note that the seasonal changes in appearance of each meadowlark species (through molt and feather wear) are more extreme than the differences between the two species. Hybridization has been reported from northwestern Missouri and probably occurs in Kansas, but the resulting offspring are said to be sterile. D. Seibel and others once observed a single bird in Leavenworth County alternately singing typical songs of both Eastern and Western Meadowlarks!

See page 504 for banding information.

References: Busby and Zimmerman, 2001; Cable et al., 1996; Janzen et al., 2007; Thompson and Ely, 1992; Young, 1993.

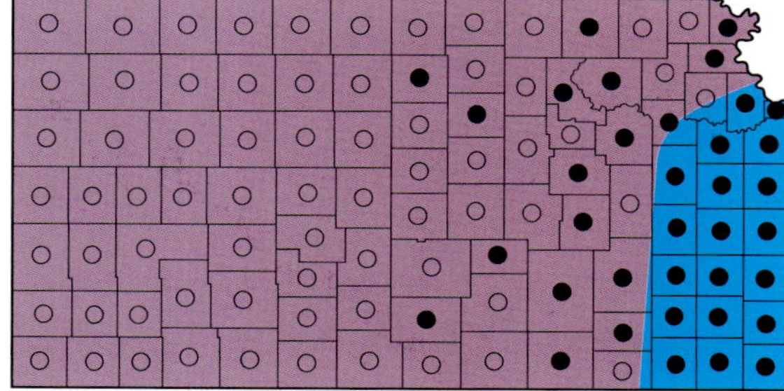

Yellow-headed Blackbird

Xanthocephalus xanthocephalus (YHBL)

Status: Common transient and local summer resident in the west; less common eastward.

Habitat: Breeds in cattail marshes; at other seasons, feedlots, farmsteads, and cultivated areas.

Migration: Extreme dates of presumed transients are 11 March (Sumner Co.) to 5 June (in the east) with most migration from mid-April through early May. Median arrival dates include 11 April (Barton Co.). Spring flocks are usually small, but 300–400 were reported from Washington County on about 30 April. Early flocks are predominately males, including 500 on 10 April (Barton Co.), and with flocks of 300 females on 2 May (Mitchell Co.). The fall migration is poorly defined. Postbreeding flocking begins by July. Peak migration is apparently late August to late September with stragglers into the CBC period. A surprising 82 individuals were killed at a television tower in Goodland (Sherman Co.) on 12–16 September 1975. About 300 were roosting at CBWA on 1 January 1972, but only one remained on 8 February.

© David Seibel

Breeding: Males start setting up territories soon after arriving at a nesting site with nest-building by mid-May and postbreeding flocking by July. Statewide, eggs have been reported 14 May–5 July, young in nest 7 June–9 July, and recently fledged young 13 June–30 July. Cattails standing in water are a requirement for successful nesting, so the largest and most consistent colonies are at CBWA and QNWR. However, small groups frequently attempt nesting in small marshes when conditions are favorable. Among these are documented nestings from Mitchell, Kearny, Finney, and Sedgwick counties and unsuccessful attempts in Harvey, Ellis, and Russell counties.

Comments: Yellow-heads arrive at the nesting marshes later than the more numerous Red-winged Blackbirds; they typically occupy areas where cattails are standing in water and displace the Red-winged Blackbirds outward to less favored areas. However, all colonies are subject to extreme weather conditions, and on occasion, hailstorms decimate the colonies. During early winter birds may appear at residential feeding stations. Whether any birds successfully overwinter is unknown.

See page 504 for banding information.

References: Barkley et al., 1977; Busby and Zimmerman, 2001; Cable et al., 1996; Janzen, 2007; Thompson and Ely, 1992; Young, 199[illegible]

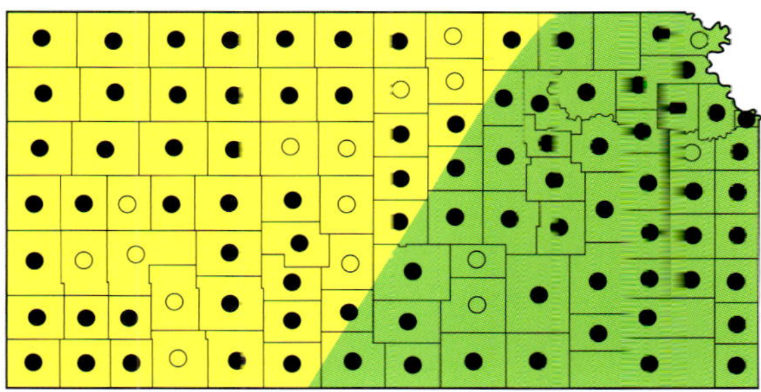

Rusty Blackbird

Euphagus carolinus (RUBL)

© David Weible

Status: Uncommon transient and local winter resident, chiefly in the east.

Habitat: Flooded woods, riparian areas, lake margins, cultivated fields, and feedlots.

Migration: The spring migration begins in mid-February, peaks in March, and is over by early April with stragglers to 17 April and 1 May (once, Shawnee Co.). High counts include 350 on 25 March (Linn Co.). August dates are unacceptable; September dates need verification. The earliest fall dates are 6 and 15 October (east) and 24 and 25 October (west). High counts include "large flock" on 13 October (Jefferson Co.) and 200 on 11 November (Pottawatomie Co.). Wintering birds may be widespread, often consisting of small flocks in wooded areas near water, through the CBC period to at least mid-February. Wintering numbers are higher in some years, especially in the southeast where they may become part of mixed winter roosts. During 1998 and 1999, state CBC totals for the Rusty Blackbird were 50,682 and 23,099, respectively, due to huge numbers at a winter roost in Arkansas City. Subsequent totals have averaged 840 individuals (357–1,445), largely due to the loss of this roost.

Comments: Once common during migration and during the winter, it has become irregular with reduced numbers. Analysis of sightings is difficult because of frequent confusion with Brewer's Blackbird.

Banding: 28 reported banded; no valid encounters. Seven encounters all to Kansas and reported from one bander at the same locality are rejected as an error in identification. The same situation was reported in Nebraska by R. Sharpe and others.

References: Cable et al., 1996; Janzen, 2007; Sharpe et al., 2001; Thompson and Ely, 1992; Thompson and Young, 1999, 2000.

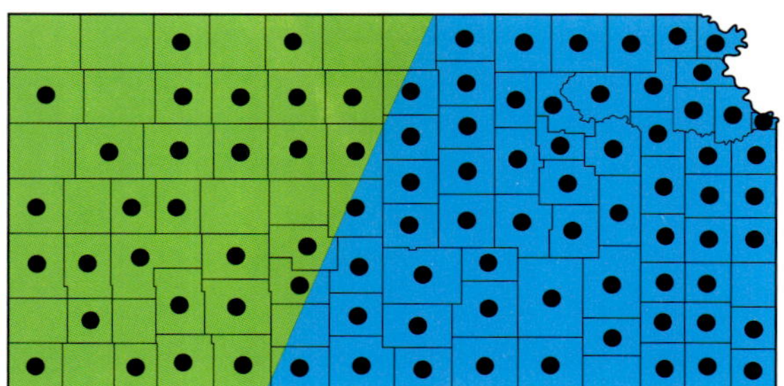

Brewer's Blackbird

Euphagus cyanocephalus (BRBL)

© Michael Heaney

Status: Uncommon transient and irregular winter resident.

Habitat: Pastures, cultivated fields, prairies, and feedlots.

Migration: Extreme dates for spring migration are 8 March (west) and 28 April (east) with most migration during April. Bent gave 10 April (23 years, Pottawatomie Co.) for median arrival. Most flocks reported in spring are under 500 individuals. E. Young (pers. comm.) noted a major migration in the southern Flint Hills on 11–12 April with more than 40,000 individuals in Butler, Cowley, Greenwood, and Elk counties. A report of 200 individuals on the late date of 3–6 June (Mitchell Co.) was recognized as unusual and was carefully double-checked and confirmed. Extreme dates for fall migration are 5 October and 30 November. September records are suspect. Median fall arrival in Ellis County is 19 October. In fall, most sightings are of small flocks (<100) but with numbers increasing locally during the CBC period and into the winter.

Comments: Snow considered it "quite common" in eastern Kansas, but there are relatively few specimens and verified reports. Suggestions that it was a summer resident or a "probable" breeder in the northwest are unfounded. However, future nesting is expected, because it currently nests regularly in southeastern Colorado not far from the Kansas border. Currently, most midsummer records are unverified. Confusion with Rusty Blackbirds and with other blackbirds continues, and counts from feedlots and winter roosts need careful confirmation. For example, a report of 70,000–100,000 on 5 November (Barton and Stafford cos.) may be (in part) an error in identification. However, an estimated 20,000 were killed at a feedlot in the area. During most years it greatly outnumbers the Rusty Blackbird on most counts. Removal of roost sites, the weather, and differences in coverage by counters combine to produce dramatic variation in numbers of most blackbirds. One roost in Arkansas City (Cowley Co.), for example, was responsible for most of the state high of 18,645 in 1999, but numbers dropped dramatically following destruction of the roost. In various years, flocks of several thousand have been reported from such diverse localities as Kanopolis Reservoir (Ellsworth Co.), the Red Hills area, Meade County, and near Newton (Harvey Co.).

See page 504 for banding information.

References: Bent, 1958; Cable et al., 1996; Janzen, 2007; Johnston, 1965; Sharpe et al., 2001; Snow, 1903; Thompson and Ely, 1992; Thompson and Young, 1999; Young, 1993.

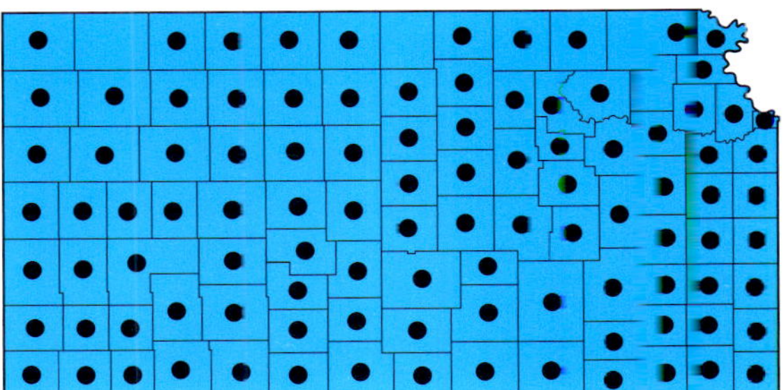

Common Grackle

Quiscalus quiscula (COGR)

© David Weible

Status: Common transient and summer resident statewide; winter resident in the east, local westward.

Habitat: Breeds in woodland edge, riparian areas, open areas, farmsteads with scattered trees, cemeteries, parks, and residential yards; at other seasons also cultivated fields and feedlots.

Migration: Migration is difficult to define because of overlap of wintering birds and the arrival or departure of summer residents. It was still one of the three predominate species in a mixed-species winter roost in Arkansas City (Cowley Co.) on 13 March. Migration is probably from late February to mid-April. Summer residents arrive in March and are nesting by early April, but nonincubating birds in some colonies continue to use nocturnal roosts some distance away for at least a few more weeks. Statewide it is earlier, about 18 March. In Ellis County the local breeding colonies are deserted soon after the young fledge (by early July), and roosting flocks are established, usually in Hays. Numbers typically peak by the end of September, and most depart soon after. These roosts are reestablished or others form during October and November. These are presumably transient birds. The mean fall departure date from Hays is 12 November. As with other blackbirds, the numbers that overwinter vary greatly among areas and years. The highest numbers of wintering birds are near feedlots and in the southeast. In recent years (1998–2008), total numbers on CBCs have varied from 100,000+ during five winters before 2002–2003 to a few thousand since 2005–2008.

Breeding: Statewide, nest-building has been reported 6 April–10 June, eggs 13 April–22 June, young 17 May–6 July, and recently fledged young 22 May–20 July. It may nest as single pairs but more often in small colonies, often in conifers or in stands of Osage orange.

Comments: KBBAT found that it was fairly uniformly distributed statewide and missing only from closed-canopy forest and open grassland. Much of the nesting in Kansas is in close association with humans, and the sweeping of large flocks though residential areas and cropland is a familiar sight during migration and winter. At such times the flocks must consume enormous amounts of insects, mast, or grain.

See page 504 for banding information.

References: Busby and Zimmerman, 2001; Cable et al., 1996; Janzen, 2007; Thompson and Ely, 1992; Young and Thompson, 1995.

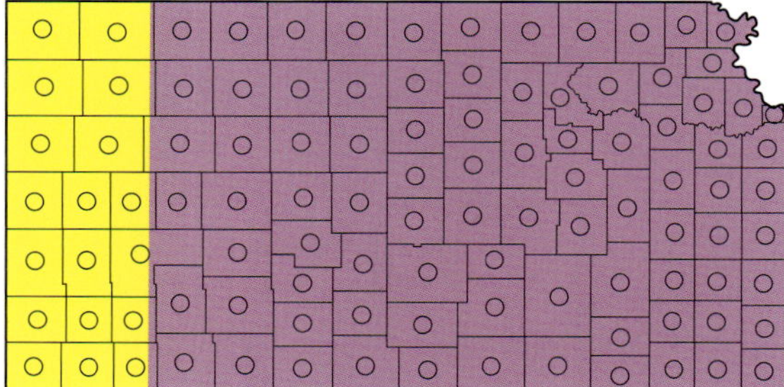

Great-tailed Grackle

Quiscalus mexicanus (GTGR)

Status: Immigrant. Currently uncommon transient nearly statewide and common but local resident in the south, southwest, and east.

Habitat: Breeding is in marshes and open areas with groups of trees including at industrial sites and in roadside parks; at other seasons in towns and cities, fields, and feedlots.

Migration: Median arrival is probably 17 March. Flocks outside breeding colonies during mid-March and April are probably transients. Postbreeding flocking begins by late July, and through mid-September large flocks are present in favored feeding areas (500, Sedgwick Co.). It becomes widespread by early October through mid-November including large flocks of presumed transients. Overwintering began with a few individuals at CBWA in 1969, and by 1974 significant numbers were present there and in Sedgwick County. Since 2000, hundreds to thousands have overwintered in the southwest (Finney and Seward cos.), south-central region (Barton, Stafford, Sedgwick, and Cowley cos.), and in the northeast (Johnson, Douglas, and Leavenworth cos.). By far the highest CBC total to date was in 2002 with 24,382 individuals, of which an estimated 20,000 were on the Olathe count. High winter counts outside roosts include 7,500 near Basehor (Leavenworth Co.) on 5 January.

Breeding: Typical nesting is in small colonies in groves of thickly branched trees or in cattail marshes. Nest-building has been reported 15 May–22 June, eggs 1 May–25 June (median 21 June), young in nest 31 May–18 July, and recently fledged young 26 May–27 June.

Comments: The first sighting (unpublished) was 6 August 1963 from Harvey County by D. Platt followed by a sighting from Sedan (Chautauqua Co.) in early April 1964 by J. Humphrey. The first report of breeding was during 1969, with small colonies found by M. Schwilling near Great Bend (Barton Co.) and by K. Downing in Wichita (Sedgwick Co., two specimens, ESU). By fall of 1971, birds were reported in Sumner, Ford, Ellis, and Russell counties and again bred in or near the three previous colonies. By 1980, confirmed nesting (or an attempt) had expanded outward to include 11 more counties, including Morton, Ford, Mitchell, and Cowley counties. It has now been reported from all counties, with confirmed breeding in more than half of them, mostly south and east of the Flint Hills. It is a very sociable and noisy species, especially during the breeding season. A few may visit feeders.

© Rob Graham

Banding: 27 banded; no encounters.

References: Busby and Zimmerman, 2001; Cable et al., 1996; Cink and Boyd, 2002; Janzen, 2007; Schwilling, 1971b; Thompson and Ely, 1992.

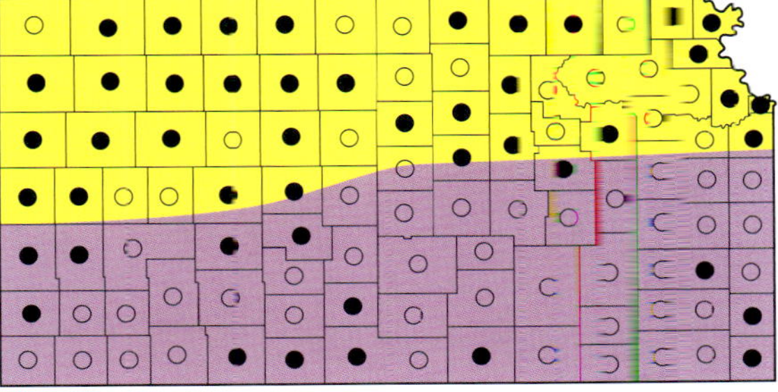

Black-and-white Warbler
Mniotilta varia (BAWW)
178 banded; one encounter. One banded in Hays (Ellis Co.) on 27 September 1973 was shot in Sonora, Mexico, on 25 December 1974, presumably on its wintering grounds.

Worm-eating Warbler
Helmitheros vermivorum (WEWA)
Eight banded; no encounters. M. Thompson netted and banded three in Cowley County in April and May 1974. One was captured each day for 3 successive days in the same net, each being caught within 2 feet of the same spot in the net. The species was not seen in the county again for 35 years, when a lone bird responded to a song recording played by M. Thompson in Winfield (Cowley Co.) on 7 May 2009.

Ovenbird
Seiurus aurocapilla (OVEN)
429 banded; one encounter. One banded in Minnesota on 23 August 1986 was found dead in northeastern Kansas on 23 May 1987, presumably while returning to its breeding grounds.

Common Yellowthroat
Geothlypis trichas (COYE)
1,864 banded; no encounters. Oldest 5 years, 11 months (T. Flowers).

Spotted Towhee
Pipilo maculatus (SPTO)
666 banded; two encounters: both in-state. Oldest 5 years, 1 month.

Eastern Towhee
Pipilo erythrophthalmus (EATO)
264 banded; two encounters: both in-state. Oldest 5 years, 1 month.

American Tree Sparrow
Spizella arborea (ATSP)
14,952 banded; 37 encounters: 27 in-state; 5 from Kansas to: AB, NE, ND, OK, SK; 5 to Kansas from: MB, MN, ND, NE, SD.

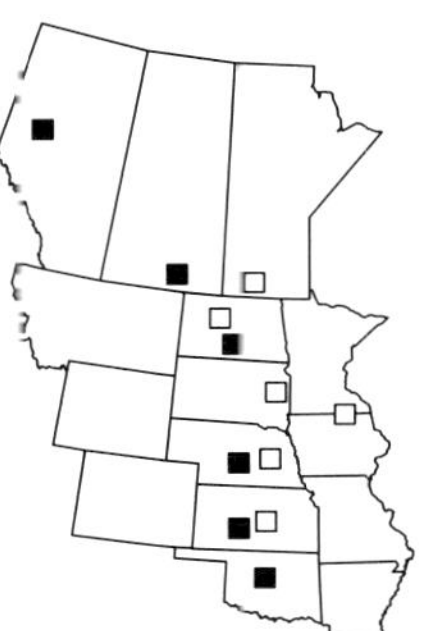

Vesper Sparrow
Pooecetes gramineus (VESP)
69 banded; one encounter. One banded 3 October 1966 in Ellis County was shot in Manitoba on 10 June 1967, presumably on its breeding grounds.

Harris's Sparrow
Zonotrichia querula (HASP)
13,602 banded; 116 encounters: 94 in-state; 6 from Kansas to: NE (2), TX (2), OK, SK; 16 encountered in Kansas from: SD (6), ND (5), NE (3), NW, SK. Oldest 10 years, 10 months. Banded Harris's Sparrows consistently return to the same wintering site where banded and presumably return to the same breeding site. Of the two oldest birds encountered in Kansas one returned to the same site 8 years later. The second, at least 1 year old when banded and possibly older, returned to very near the banding site 10 years, 10 months later, having made the journey from at least northern Saskatchewan or northern Manitoba to central Kansas for the 12th time. That is a lot of miles for a small passerine!

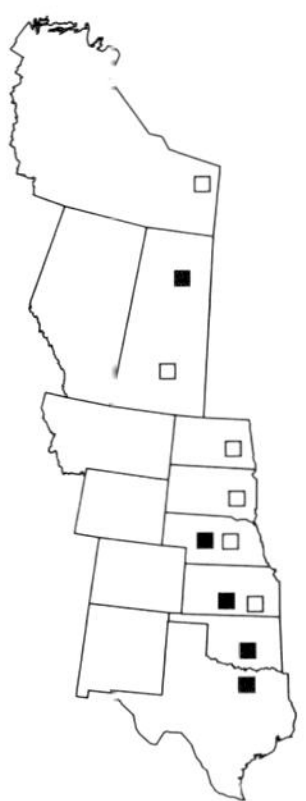

Dark-eyed Junco

Junco hyemalis (DEJU)

17,004 banded; 140 encounters: 123 in-state; 12 from Kansas to: MN (2), ND (2), TX (2), AR, CO, IA, MT, SK, WI; five encountered in Kansas from: SD (3), MB, NE. Oldest 3 years, 2 months. The breakdown by race is: Slate-colored, 14,755; Oregon, 2,168; White-winged, 3; Gray-headed, 2; unidentified, 76. As expected, the three recoveries of Pink-sided were from the Rockies.

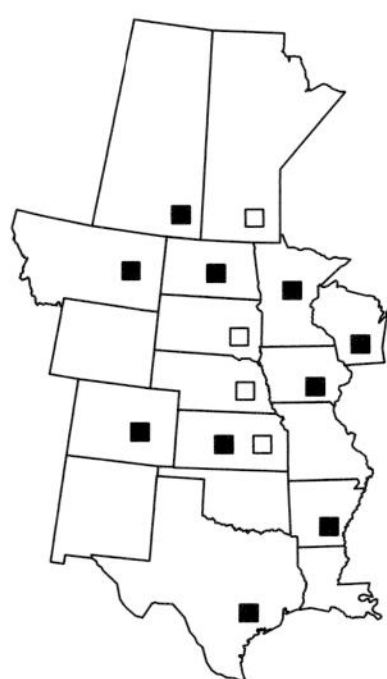

Red-winged Blackbird

Agelaius phoeniceus (RWBL)

10,548 banded; 148 encounters: 83 in-state; 41 from Kansas to: TX (20), NE (5), OK (5), SK (4), AB, MB, MN, MT, ND, NM, SD; 24 encountered in Kansas from: ND (8), SD (6), OK (3), AB (2), MN (2), MO (2), NE. Oldest 7 years, 3 months. Besser and Steffen examined data for the 120 recoveries from birds banded in Kansas through 1988. One hundred eleven of these (92.5%) were banded by F. Robl, a pioneer duck bander near CBWA, most during 1937–1940. Forty-seven were recovered by the public outside of Kansas and provide information on the breeding grounds and wintering area of red-wings banded in central Kansas. The breeding area was essentially southeastern Alberta, southern Saskatchewan, eastern Montana, and north-central North Dakota; the wintering area was along and near the Red River of northern Oklahoma, west through the Texas Panhandle, and in extreme eastern New Mexico. The map of current banding results extends that pattern only slightly.

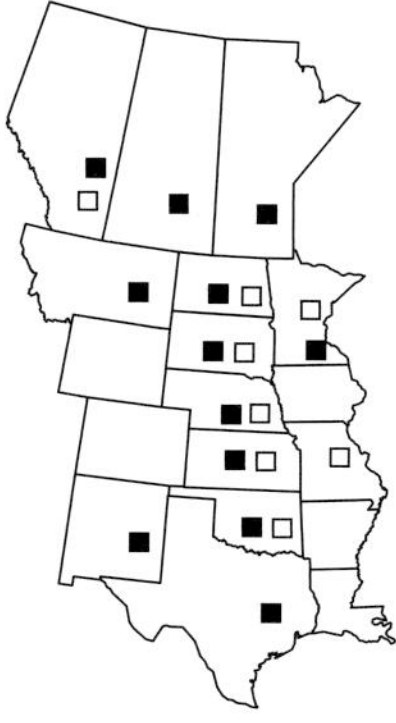

Western Meadowlark

Sturnella neglecta (WEME)

221 banded; two encounters: one in-state. One banded in Kansas on 16 June 1969 was electrocuted in Texas on 24 November 1969.

Yellow-headed Blackbird

Xanthocephalus xanthocephalus (YHBL)

4,635 banded; 48 encounters: 17 in-state; 22 from Kansas to: Mexico (9), SD (3), TX (3), MN (2), ND (2), NE, WI, unknown; 9 encountered in Kansas from: SD (6), ND (2), WY. Oldest 8 years, 10 months.

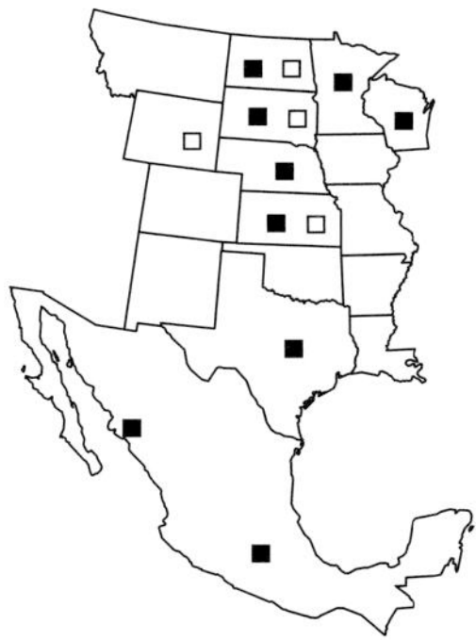

Brewer's Blackbird

Euphagus cyanocephalus (BRBL)

74 banded; no encounters. One banded in Texas on 5 February 1925 and found dead in Kansas on 27 June 1925 is likely (from the late date) an error in identification.

Common Grackle

Quiscalus quiscula (COGR)

10,623 banded; 527 encounters: 179 in-state, 84 from Kansas to: TX (31), LA (16), AR (8), OK (8), NE (7), SD (4), MS (2), MT (2), CO, IA, MO, ND, OH, SK; 264 encountered in Kansas from: AR (144), TX (75), OK (16), SD (7), NE (5), LA (4), MO (3), CO (2), MN (2), ND (2), MS, ON, TN, WI. Oldest 4 years, 10 months.

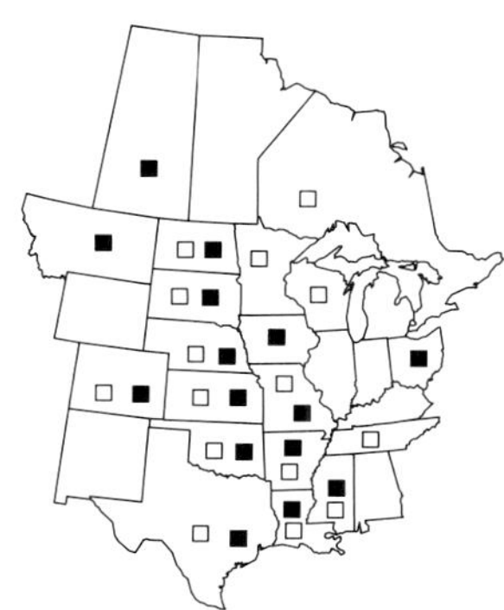

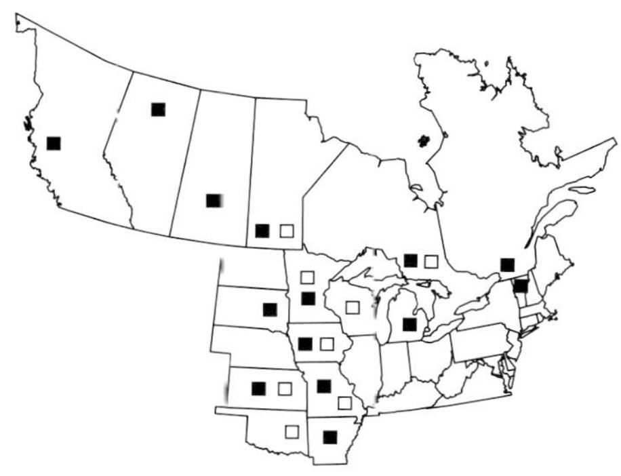

Brown-headed Cowbird

Molothrus ater (BHCO)

13,839 banded; 87 encounters: 21 in-state; 37 from Kansas to: Mexico (17), TX (8), OK (5), MN (3), IA, ND, SD, SK; 29 encountered in Kansas from: TX (21), OK (3), AR, IN, LA, MI, PA. Oldest 3 years.

Baltimore Oriole

Icterus galbula (BAOR)

2,744 banded (includes 60 hybrids); nine encounters: all in-state.

Purple Finch

Carpodacus purpureus (PUFI)

8,804 banded; 74 encounters: 44 in-state, 30 from Kansas to: MN (11), MO (3), ON (3), AR (2), IA (2), SK (2), AB, BC, MI, MB, QC, SD, VT; 14 encountered in Kansas from: MN (7), MB (2), IA, MO, OK, ON, WI. Oldest 7 years, 10 months.

House Finch

Carpodacus mexicanus (HOFI)

12,084 banded; 55 encounters: 40 in-state; 9 from Kansas to NE (3), IA (2), MO (2), MN, ND; 6 encountered in Kansas from: IA (2), MN, NE, SD, TX. Oldest 9 years, 4 months (Ely).

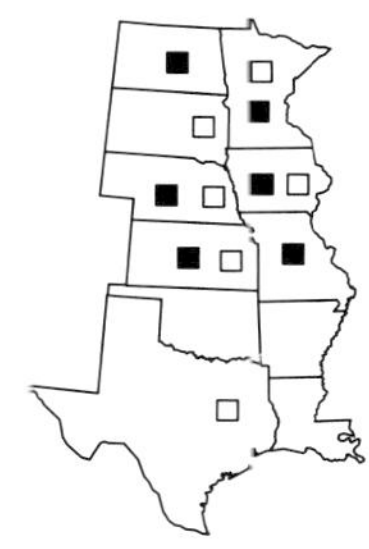

Pine Siskin

Spinus pinus (PISI)

47,065 banded; 181 encounters: 110 in-state; 55 from Kansas to: SD (8), MN (6), NE (4), WY (4), CO (3), NY (3), TX (3), WI (3), ID (2), MO (2), OR (2), AB, CA, IL, IN, MA, MB, ME, MI, MT, OH, OK, QC, SC, SK, UT 16 encountered in Kansas from: SD (4), MN (2), WI (2), AL, MI, MO, NY, ON, QC, TX, UT. Oldest 6 years.

American Goldfinch

Spinus tristis (AMGO)

31,660 banded; 66 encounters: 18 in-state, 32 from Kansas to: NE (8), SD (4), SK (4), OK (3), MO (2), TX (2), WI (2), WY (2), AR, IA, IL, ND, TN; 16 encountered in Kansas from: NE (5), MO (3), MN (2), WI (2), IA, MI, ND, SD. Oldest 5 years, 1 month.

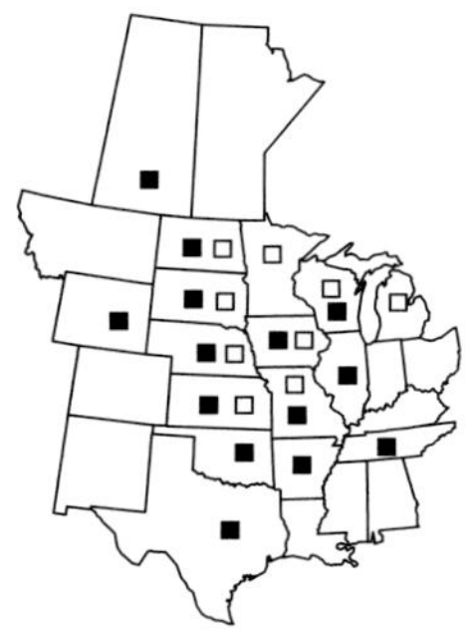

References

Alderfer, J., ed. 2006. Complete Birds of North America. National Geographic Society, Washington, DC. 664 pp.

Alisauskas, R. T., S. M. Slattery, D. K. Kellett, D. Stern, and K. D. Warner. 1998. Spatial and temporal dynamics of Ross's and Snow Goose colonies in Queen Maud Gulf Bird Sanctuary, 1966–1998. Progress Report on Numbers of Geese and Colonies, September 1998. Canadian Wildlife Service, Saskatoon, Saskatchewan.

Allen, J. A. 1872. Notes of an ornithological reconnaissance in portions of Kansas, Colorado, Wyoming, and Utah. Pt. 2. Bull. Mus. Comp. Zool. 3(6):113–183.

American Ornithologists' Union. 1998. Check-list of North American Birds, 7th ed. American Ornithologists' Union, Washington, DC. 829 pp.

———. 2000. Forty-second supplement to the American Ornithologists' Union *Check-list of North American Birds*. Auk 117(3):847–858.

———. 2002. Forty-third supplement to the American Ornithologists' Union *Check-list of North American Birds*. Auk 119(3):897–906.

———. 2003. Forty-fourth supplement to the American Ornithologists' Union *Check-list of North American Birds*. Auk 120(3):923–931.

———. 2004. Forty-fifth supplement to the American Ornithologists' Union *Check-list of North American Birds*. Auk 121(3):985–995.

———. 2006. Forty-seventh supplement to the American Ornithologists' Union *Check-list of North American Birds*. Auk 123(3):926–936.

———. 2007. Forty-eighth supplement to the American Ornithologists' Union *Check-list of North American Birds*. Auk 124(3):1109–1115.

———. 2008. Forty-ninth supplement to the American Ornithologists' Union *Check-list of North American Birds*. Auk 125(3):758–768.

———. 2009. Fiftieth supplement to the American Ornithologists' Union *Check-list of North American Birds*. Auk 126(3):705–714.

Anderson, T. R. 1982. Song Sparrow nesting in Kansas. Kansas Orni. Soc. Bull. 33(2):23–24.

———. 2001. Extralimital nesting of the White-winged Dove, *Zenaida asiatica*. Kansas Orni. Soc. Bull. 52(4):47–48.

Anthony, L. W., and C. A. Ely. 1976. Breeding biology of Barn Swallows in west-central Kansas. Kansas Orni. Soc. Bull. 27(4):37–41.

Applegate, R. D., B. E. Flock, and D. R. Applegate. 2004. Types of perches used by fall migrant and wintering Red-tailed Hawks (*Buteo jamaicensis*) in Kansas. Kansas Orni. Soc. Bull. 55(2):1–4 [sic], 21–24.

Applegate, R. D., and G. J. Horak. 1999. Status and management of the Greater Prairie-Chicken in Kansas. Pp. 113–122 *in* The Greater Prairie-Chicken: A National Look (W. D. Svedarsky, R. H. Hier, and N. J. Silvy, eds.). Miscellaneous Publication 99-1999. Minnesota Agricultural Experiment Station, University of Minnesota, Saint Paul.

Arteburn, J. W. 2003. Oklahoma Bird Records Committee 2003. Bull. Oklahoma Orni. Soc. 37:25–29.

Austin, J. E., C. M. Custer, and A. D. Afton. 1998. Lesser Scaup (*Aythya affinis*). The Birds of North America Online (A. Poole, ed.). Cornell Lab of Ornithology, Ithaca, NY.

Austin, J. E., and M. R. Miller. 1995. Northern Pintail (*Anas acuta*). The Birds of North America Online (A. Poole, ed.). Cornell Lab of Ornithology, Ithaca, NY.

Austin, O. L. 1953. The migration of the Common Tern (*Sterna hirundo*) in the Western Hemisphere. Bird-Banding 24:39–55.

Balda, R. 2002. Pinyon Jay (*Gymnorhinus cyanocephalus*). The Birds of North America Online (A. Pool, ed.). Cornell Lab of Ornithology, Ithaca, NY.

Ball, L. G., K. Zyskowski, and G. Escalona-Segura. 1995. Recent bird mortality at a Topeka television tower. Kansas Orni. Soc. Bull. 46(4):33–36.

Baltosser, W. H., and S. M. Russell. 2000. Black-chinned Hummingbird (*Archilochus alexandri*). The Birds of North America Online (A. Poole, ed.). Cornell Lab of Ornithology, Ithaca, NY.

Baltosser, W. H., and P. E. Scott. 1996. Costa's Hummingbird (*Calypte costae*). The Birds of North America Online (A. Poole, ed.). Cornell Lab of Ornithology, Ithaca, NY.

Banks, R. C., and M. R. Browning. 1999. Questions about Thayer's Gull. Ontario Birds 17:124–130.

Bannor, B. K., and E. Kiviat. 2002. Common Moorhen (*Gallinula chloropus*). The Birds of North America Online (A. Poole, ed.). Cornell Lab of Ornithology, Ithaca, NY.

Barber, D. R., P. M. Barber, and P. G. Jablonski. 2000. Painted Redstart (*Myioborus pictus*). The Birds of North America Online (A. Poole, ed.). Cornell Lab of Ornithology, Ithaca, NY.

Barkley, R., C. A. Elk [sic = Ely], and J. Palmquist. 1977. Recent TV tower kills at Goodland, Kansas. Kansas Orni. Soc. Bull. 28(1):10–12.

Barlow, J. C., S. N. Leckie, and C. T. Baril. 1999. Gray Vireo (*Vireo vicinior*). The Birds of North America Online (A. Poole, ed.). Cornell Lab of Ornithology, Ithaca, NY.

Barlow, J. C., and J. D. Rising. 1965. The summer status of wood pewees in southwestern Kansas. Kansas Orni. Soc. Bull. 16(2):14–16.

Barr, J. F., C. Eberl, and J. W. McIntyre. 2000. Red-throated Loon (*Gavia stellata*). The Birds of North America Online (A. Poole, ed.). Cornell Lab of Ornithology, Ithaca, NY.

Barrows, W. H. 1889. The English Sparrow (*Passer domesticus*) in North America, especially in its relation to agriculture. U.S. Dept. Agric., Div. Econ. Orni. Mamm. Bull. No. 1. 405 pp.

Baumgartner, F. M., and A. M. Baumgartner. 1992. Oklahoma Bird Life. University of Oklahoma Press, Norman. 443 pp.

Bechard, M. J., and J. K. Schmutz. 1995. Ferruginous Hawk (*Buteo regalis*). The Birds of North America Online (A. Poole, ed.). Cornell Lab of Ornithology, Ithaca, NY.

Bechard, M. J., and T. R. Swem. 2002. Rough-legged Hawk (*Buteo lagopus*). The Birds of North America Online (A. Poole, ed.). Cornell Lab of Ornithology, Ithaca, NY.

Bedell, P. A. 1996. Evidence of dual breeding ranges for the Sedge Wren in the central Great Plains. Wilson Bull. 108(1):115–122.

Bednarz, J. C. 1995. Harris's Hawk (*Parabuteo unicinctus*). The Birds of North America Online (A. Poole, ed.). Cornell Lab of Ornithology, Ithaca, NY.

Bednarz, J. C., and R. J. Raitt. 2002. Chihuahuan Raven (*Corvus cryptoleucus*). The Birds of North America Online (A. Poole, ed.). Cornell Lab of Ornithology, Ithaca, NY.

Bent, A. 1929. Life Histories of North American Shore Birds, Part 2. U.S. Natl. Mus. Bull. 146, Pt. 2. 429 pp.

———. 1932. Life Histories of North American Gallinaceous Birds. U.S. Natl. Mus. Bull. 162. 490 pp.

———. 1946. Life Histories of North American Jays, Crows and Titmice. U.S. Natl. Mus. Bull. 191. 495 pp.

———. 1953. Life Histories of North American Wood Warblers. U.S. Natl. Mus. Bull. 203. 734 pp.

———. 1958. Life Histories of North American Blackbirds, Orioles, Tanagers, and Their Allies. U.S. Natl. Mus. Bull. 211. 549 pp.

———. 1968. Life Histories of North American Cardinals, Grosbeaks, Buntings, Towhees, Finches, Sparrows, and Allies. U.S. Natl. Mus. Bull. 237, Pts. 1–3. 1,889 pp.

Besser, J. F., and D. K. Steffen. 1988. Breeding and wintering areas of Red-winged Blackbirds banded in Barton County, Kansas. Kansas Orni. Soc. Bull. 39(4):33–36.

Betts, A. J. 1958. An autumnal roost of robins. Kansas Orni. Soc. Bull. 9(1):10–11.

Bibles, B. D., R. L. Glinski, and R. R. Johnson. 2002. Gray Hawk (*Asturina nitida*). The Birds of North America Online (A. Poole, ed.). Cornell Lab of Ornithology, Ithaca, NY.

Bildstein, K. L., and K. Meyer. 2000. Sharp-shinned Hawk (*Accipiter striatus*). The Birds of North America Online (A. Poole, ed.). Cornell Lab of Ornithology, Ithaca, NY.

Blachly, C. P. 1879–1880. Ornithology of Riley County, Kansas. Trans. Kansas Acad. Sci. 7:102–110.

Blanco, D., R. Banchs, P. Canevari, and M. Osterheld. 1993. Critical sites for the Eskimo Curlew (*Numenius borealis*) and other Nearctic grassland shorebirds in Argentina and Uruguay. Unpublished report prepared by Wetlands for the Americas, Buenos Aires, Argentina, and U.S. Fish and Wildlife Service (agreement 1448-0007-92-7778). 86 pp.

Blundell, M. A., and B. Von Korff. 2008. Bobolinks (*Dolichonyx oryzivorus*) nesting at Konza Prairie Biological Station, Riley, Kansas. Kansas Orni. Soc. Bull. 59(2):21–23.

Boarman, W. I., and B. Heinrich. 1999. Common Raven (*Corvus corax*). The Birds of North America Online (A. Poole, ed). Cornell Lab of Ornithology, Ithaca, NY.

Bond, M. W. 1965. Did a Barbados hunter shoot the last Eskimo Curlew? Audubon 67:314–316.

Booms, T. L., T. J. Cade, and N. J. Clum. 2008. Gyrfalcon (*Falco rusticolus*). The Birds of North America Online (A. Poole, ed.). Cornell Lab of Ornithology, Ithaca, NY.

Bordage, D., and J. P. Savard. 1995. Black Scoter (*Melanitta nigra*). The Birds of North America Online (A. Poole, ed.). Cornell Lab of Ornithology, Ithaca, NY.

Bowen, D. E. 1976. Coloniality, reproductive success, and habitat interactions in Upland Sandpipers, *Bartramia longicauda*. Ph.D. dissertation, Kansas State University, Manhattan. 127 pp.

Boyd, R. L. 1972. Breeding biology of the Snowy Plover at Cheyenne Bottoms Waterfowl Management Area, Barton County, Kansas. M.S. thesis, Emporia State University, Emporia, KS. 86 pp.

———. 1985. First nesting record of the Ash-throated Flycatcher in Kansas and an additional nesting record for the Black-billed Magpie. Kansas Orni. Soc. Bull. 36(4):34.

———. 1986. First nesting record of the Cerulean Warbler in Kansas. Kansas Orni. Soc. Bull. 37(3):37–38.

———. 1991. First nesting record for the Piping Plover in Oklahoma. Wilson Bull. 103:305–307.

Brennan, L. A. 1999. Northern Bobwhite (*Colinus virginianus*). The Birds of North America Online (A. Poole, ed.). Cornell Lab of Ornithology, Ithaca, NY.

Brisbin, I. L., Jr., and T. B. Mowbray. 2002. American Coot (*Fulica americana*). The Birds of North America Online (A. Poole, ed.). Cornell Lab of Ornithology, Ithaca, NY.

Brookhout, T. A. 1995. Yellow Rail (*Coturnicops noveboracensis*). The Birds of North America Online (A. Poole, ed.). Cornell Lab of Ornithology, Ithaca, NY.

Brown, P. W., and L. H. Fredrickson. 1997. White-winged Scoter (*Melanitta fusca*). The Birds of North America Online (A. Poole, ed.). Cornell Lab of Ornithology, Ithaca, NY.

Brua, R. 2002. Ruddy Duck (*Oxyura jamaicensis*). The Birds of North America Online (A. Poole, ed.). Cornell Lab of Ornithology, Ithaca, NY.

Brumwell, M. J. 1951. An ecological survey of the Fort Leavenworth Military Reservation. American Midl. Nat. 45(1):187–231.

Brush, T., and J. W. Fitzpatrick. 2002. Great Kiskadee (*Pitangus sulphuratus*). The Birds of North America Online (A. Poole, ed.). Cornell Lab of Ornithology, Ithaca, NY.

Buckley, N. J. 1999. Black Vulture (*Coragyps atratus*). The Birds of North America Online (A. Poole, ed.). Cornell Lab of Ornithology, Ithaca, NY.

Buehler, D. A. 2000. Bald Eagle (*Haliaeetus leucocephalus*).

The Birds of North America Online (A. Poole, ed.). Cornell Lab of Ornithology, Ithaca, NY.

Bunker, C. 1913. The birds of Kansas. Kansas Univ. Sci. Bull. 7(5):137–158.

———. 1919. Harris's Hawk (*Parabuteo unicinctus harrisi*) in Kansas. Auk 36:283.

Burger, J. 1996. Laughing Gull (*Larus atricilla*). The Birds of North America Online (A. Poole, ed.). Cornell Lab of Ornithology, Ithaca, NY.

Burger, J., and M. Gochfeld. 2002. Bonaparte's Gull (*Larus philadelphia*). The Birds of North America Online (A. Poole, ed.). Cornell Lab of Ornithology, Ithaca, NY.

———. 2009. Franklin's Gull (*Larus pipixcan*). The Birds of North America Online (A. Poole, ed.). Cornell Lab of Ornithology, Ithaca, NY.

Busby, W. H., D. W. Mulhern, P. G. Kramos, and D. A. Rintoul. 1997. Nesting Piping Plover and Least Tern on the Kansas River. Prairie Nat. 29(4):257–262.

Busby, W. H., S. T. Patti, and M. Rader. 1999. Summer record of the Rufous-crowned Sparrow in Kansas. Kansas Orni. Soc. Bull. 50(2):27–28.

Busby, W. H., and J. L. Zimmerman. 2001. Kansas Breeding Bird Atlas. University Press of Kansas, Lawrence. xii + 466 pp.

Butler, R. W. 1992. Great Blue Heron (*Ardea herodias*). The Birds of North America Online (A. Poole, ed.). Cornell Lab of Ornithology, Ithaca, NY.

Cable, T. T. 1987. Pacific Loon captured at Milford Lake. Kansas Orni. Soc. Bull. 38(3):26–27.

Cable, T. T., and J. S. Bond. 1991. Food habits of Harlan's Hawk and Long-eared Owls in Kansas. Kansas Orni. Soc. Bull. 42(2):25–27.

Cable, T. T., and D. A. Rintoul. 1985. Thayer's Gull in Riley County: first documented occurrence in Kansas. Kansas Orni. Soc. Bull. 36(2):21–22.

Cable, T. T., S. Seltman, and K. J. Cook. 1996. Birds of Cimarron National Grassland. Gen. Tech. Rep. RM-GTR-281. U.S. Department of Agriculture, Forest Service, Rocky Mountain Forest and Range Experiment Station, Fort Collins, CO. 108 pp.

Calder, W. A., and L. L. Calder. 1992. Broad-tailed Hummingbird (*Selasphorus platycercus*). The Birds of North America Online (A. Poole, ed.). Cornell Lab of Ornithology, Ithaca, NY.

Cannon, T. A., and C. D. Hall. 1977. Black Skimmer at Wilson Reservoir. Kansas Orni. Soc. Bull. 28(3): 27–28.

Carnes, G. 2004. Purple Gallinule: *Porpyrula martinica*. Pp. 130–131 *in* Oklahoma Breeding Bird Atlas (D. L. Reinking, ed.). University of Oklahoma Press, Norman.

Carson, L. B. 1954. New records for fall migrants in eastern Kansas. Kansas Orni. Soc. Bull. 5(4):27–29.

Cavitt, J. F., A. T. Pearse, and D. A. Rintoul. 1998. Hybridization of Mountain Bluebird and Eastern Bluebird in northeastern Kansas. Kansas Orni. Soc. Bull. 49(2):21–25.

Chandler, R. M. 1987. The first record of a Prairie Falcon from the Pleistocene of Kansas. Kansas Orni. Soc. Bull. 38(3):27.

Cink, C. L. 1987. Distribution and abundance of the Whip-poor-will and Chuck-will's-widow in Kansas. Nongame Wildlife Project, submitted to Kansas Fish and Game Commission, August 1987. 15 pp.

———. 2002. Whip-poor-will (*Caprimulgus vociferus*) The Birds of North America Online (A. Poole, ed.). Cornell Lab of Ornithology, Ithaca, NY.

———. 2006. Recoveries of Eastern Phoebes banded as nestlings in northeastern Kansas. Kansas Orni. Soc. Bull. 57(1):12.

Cink, C. L., and R. L. Boyd. 1982. Ovenbird nesting in Douglas County, Kansas. Kansas Orni. Soc. Bull. 33(1):17–19.

———. 2002. The winter bird count for 2001. Kansas Orni. Soc. Bull. 53(1):1–20.

———. 2003. The winter bird count for 2002. Kansas Orni. Soc. Bull. 54(1):1–20.

———. 2004. The winter bird count for 2003. Kansas Orni. Soc. Bull. 55(1):1–20.

———. 2005. The winter bird count for 2004. Kansas Orni. Soc. Bull. 56(1):1–11, 13–20.

———. 2006. The winter bird count for 2005. Kansas Orni. Soc. Bull. 57(1):1–11, 13–20.

———. 2007. The winter bird count for 2006. Kansas Orni. Soc. Bull. 58(1):1–10, 13–20.

Cink, C. L., and C. T. Collins. 2002. Chimney Swift (*Chaetura pelagica*). The Birds of North America Online (A. Poole, ed.). Cornell Lab of Ornithology, Ithaca, NY

Clubine, S. 2002. Editorial. Native Warm-season Grass Newsletter 21(3). Missouri Department of Conservation, Clinton.

Collins, C. P., and T. D. Reynolds. 2005. Ferruginous Hawk (*Buteo regalis*): a technical conservation assessment. 2 September [Online]. U.S. Department of Agriculture Forest Service, Rocky Mountain Region. Available: http://www.fs.fed.us/r2/projects/scp/assessments/ferruginoushawk.pdf.

Collins, J. T. 1985. Natural Kansas. University Press of Kansas, Lawrence. xii + 226 pp.

Collins, J. T., S. L. Collins, J. Horak, D. Mulhern, W. Busby, C. C. Freeman, and G. Wallace. 1995. An Illustrated Guide to Endangered and Threatened Species in Kansas. University Press of Kansas, Lawrence. 160 pp.

Colvin, W. J. 1936. Nesting of the Louisiana Waterthrush in Kansas. Auk 53(4):451.

Colwell, M. A., and J. R. Jehl, Jr. 1994. Wilson's Phalarope (*Phalaropus tricolor*). The Birds of North America Online (A. Poole, ed.). Cornell Lab of Ornithology, Ithaca, NY.

Connelly, J., M. Gratson, and K. Reese. 1998. Sharp-tailed Grouse (*Tympanuchus phasianellus*). The Birds of North America Online (A. Poole, ed). Cornell Laboratory of Ornithology, Ithaca, NY.

Conway, C. J. 1995. Virginia Rail (*Rallus limicola*). The Birds of North America Online (A. Poole, ed.). Cornell Lab of Ornithology, Ithaca, NY.

Conway, C. J., W. R. Eddleman, and S. H. Anderson. 1994. Nesting success and survival of Virginia Rails and Soras. Wilson Bull. 106:466–473.

Cooke, W. W. 1888. Report on bird migration in the Mississippi Valley in the years 1884 and 1885. U.S. Dept. Agri., Div. Econ. Orni. Bull. No. 2. 313 pp.

Corbat, C. A., and P. W. Bergstrom. 2000. Wilson's Plover (*Charadrius wilsonia*). The Birds of North America Online (A. Poole, ed.). Cornell Lab of Ornithology, Ithaca, NY.

Corder, M. 2006. First Kansas nesting record of the Vermilion Flycatcher. Kansas Orni. Soc. Bull. 57(3):25–26.

Coulter, M. C., J. A. Rodgers, J. C. Ogden, and F. C. Depkin. 1999. Wood Stork (*Mycteria americana*). The Birds of North America Online (A. Poole, ed.). Cornell Lab of Ornithology, Ithaca, NY.

Cullen, S. A., J. R. Jehl, Jr., and G. L. Nuechterlein. 1999. Eared Grebe (*Podiceps nigricollis*). The Birds of North America Online (A. Poole, ed.). Cornell Lab of Ornithology, Ithaca, NY.

Curry, R. L., A. T. Peterson, and T. A. Langen. 2002. Western Scrub-Jay (*Aphelocoma californica*). The Birds of North America Online (A. Poole, ed.). Cornell Lab of Ornithology, Ithaca, NY.

Curtis, O. E., R. N. Rosenfield, and J. Bielefeldt. 2006. Cooper's Hawk (*Accipiter cooperii*). The Birds of North America Online (A. Poole, ed.). Cornell Lab of Ornithology, Ithaca, NY.

Cuthbert, F. J., and L. R. Wires. 1999. Caspian Tern (*Sterna caspia*). The Birds of North America Online (A. Poole, ed.). Cornell Lab of Ornithology, Ithaca, NY.

Dabbert, C. B., G. Pleasant, and S. D. Schemnitz. 2009. Scaled Quail (*Callipepla squamata*). The Birds of North America Online (A. Poole, ed.). Cornell Lab of Ornithology, Ithaca, NY.

Davis, W. E., Jr. 1993. Black-crowned Night-Heron (*Nycticorax nycticorax*). The Birds of North America Online (A. Poole, ed.). Cornell Lab of Ornithology, Ithaca, NY.

Davis, W. E., Jr., and J. Kricher. 2000. Glossy Ibis (*Plegadis falcinellus*). The Birds of North America Online (A. Poole, ed.). Cornell Lab of Ornithology, Ithaca, NY.

Davis, W. E., Jr., and J. A. Kushlan. 1994. Green Heron (*Butorides virescens*). The Birds of North America Online (A. Poole, ed.). Cornell Lab of Ornithology, Ithaca, NY.

Davis, W. E., Jr., and S. M. Russell. 1990. Birds in Southeastern Arizona, 3rd ed. Tucson Audubon Society, Tucson, AZ.

Day, R. H., I. J. Stenhouse, and H. G. Gilchrist. 2001. Sabine's Gull (*Xema sabini*). The Birds of North America Online (A. Poole, ed.). Cornell Lab of Ornithology, Ithaca, NY.

Diamond, A. W., and E. A. Schreiber. 2002. Magnificent Frigatebird (*Fregata magnificens*). The Birds of North America Online (A. Poole, ed.). Cornell Lab of Ornithology, Ithaca, NY.

Dickerman, R. W. 1989. Identification of Red-tailed Hawks wintering in Kansas. Kansas Orni. Soc. Bull. 40(4):33–34.

Drilling, N., R. Titman, and F. McKinney. 2002. Mallard (*Anas platyrhyncos*). The Birds of North America Online (A. Poole, ed.). Cornell Lab of Ornithology, Ithaca, NY.

Droege, M. 2004. Broad-winged Hawk (*Buteo platypterus*). Pp. 98–99 *in* Oklahoma Breeding Bird Atlas (D. L. Reinking, ed.). University of Oklahoma Press, Norman.

Dubowy, P. J. 1996. Northern Shoveler (*Anas clypeata*). The Birds of North America Online (A. Poole, ed.). Cornell Lab of Ornithology, Ithaca, NY.

Dugger, B. D., and K. M. Dugger. 2002. Long-billed Curlew (*Numenius americanus*). The Birds of North America Online (A. Poole, ed.). Cornell Lab of Ornithology, Ithaca, NY.

Dugger, B. D., K. M. Dugger, and L. H. Fredrickson. 2009. Hooded Merganser (*Lophodytes cucullatus*). The Birds of North America Online (A. Poole, ed.). Cornell Lab of Ornithology, Ithaca, NY.

Dumas, J. V. 2000. Roseate Spoonbill (*Platalea ajaja*). The Birds of North America Online (A. Poole, ed.). Cornell Lab of Ornithology, Ithaca, NY.

DuMont, P. A. 1940. Relation of Franklin's Gull colonies to agriculture on the Great Plains. Trans. N. American Wildl. Conf. 5:183–189.

Dunk, J. R. 1995. White-tailed Kite (*Elanus leucurus*). The Birds of North America Online (A. Poole, ed.). Cornell Lab of Ornithology, Ithaca, NY.

Dykstra, C. R., J. L. Hays, and S. T. Crocoll. 2008. Red-shouldered Hawk (*Buteo lineatus*). The Birds of North America Online (A. Poole, ed.). Cornell Lab of Ornithology, Ithaca, NY.

Eadie, J. M., M. L. Mallory, and H. G. Lumsden. 1995. Common Goldeneye (*Bucephala clangula*). The Birds of North America Online (A. Poole, ed.). Cornell Lab of Ornithology, Ithaca, NY.

Eadie, J. M., J.-P. L. Savard, and M. L. Mallory. 2000. Barrow's Goldeneye (*Bucephala islandica*). The Birds of North America Online (A. Poole, ed.). Cornell Lab of Ornithology, Ithaca, NY.

Eaton, S. W. 1992. Wild Turkey (*Meleagris gallopavo*). The Birds of North America Online (A. Poole, ed.). Cornell Lab of Ornithology, Ithaca, NY.

Eddleman, W. R., R. E. Flores, and M. Legare. 1994. Black Rail (*Laterallus jamaicensis*). The Birds of North America Online (A. Poole, ed.). Cornell Lab of Ornithology, Ithaca, NY.

Elder, B. L. 1986. Rapid range expansion of the House Finch in Kansas. M.S. thesis, Fort Hays State University, Hays, KS. 17 pp. + figures.

Elliott-Smith, E., and S. M. Haig. 2004. Piping Plover (*Charadrius melodus*). The Birds of North America Online (A. Poole, ed.). Cornell Lab of Ornithology, Ithaca, NY.

Elphick, C. S., and J. Klima. 2002. Hudsonian Godwit (*Limosa haemastica*). The Birds of North America Online (A. Poole, ed.). Cornell Lab of Ornithology, Ithaca, NY.

Elphick, C. S., and T. L. Tibbitts. 1998. Greater Yellowlegs (*Tringa melanoleuca*). The Birds of North America Online (A. Poole, ed.). Cornell Lab of Ornithology, Ithaca, NY.

Ely, C. A. 1961. Cassin's Finch and Pine Grosbeak in west-central Kansas. Condor 63(5):418–419.

———. 1969. Common Bushtit—an addition to the Kansas avifauna. Kansas Orni. Soc. Bull. 20(4):26.
———. 1971. A history and distributional list of Ellis County, Kansas, birds. Ft. Hays Studies, New Series, Sci. Series No. 9. 115 pp.
———. 1977. Mid-winter bird count for 1976. Kansas Orni. Soc. Bull. 28(1):1–9.
———. 1985. Birds. Pp. 173–193 *in* Natural Kansas (J. T. Collins, ed.). University Press of Kansas, Lawrence.
Ely, C. A., and L. W. Anthony. 1968. Scott's Oriole—an addition to the Kansas avifauna. Kansas Orni. Soc. Bull. 19(3):19.
Ely, C. R., and A. X. Dzubin. 1994. Greater White-fronted Goose (*Anser albifrons*). The Birds of North America Online (A. Poole, ed.). Cornell Lab of Ornithology, Ithaca, NY.
England, A. S., M. J. Bechard, and C. S. Houston. 1997. Swainson's Hawk (*Buteo swainsonii*). The Birds of America Online (A. Poole, ed.). Cornell Lab of Ornithology, Ithaca, NY.
Evers, D. C., J. D. Paruk, J. W. McIntyre and J. F. Barr. 2010. Common Loon (*Gavia immer*). The Birds of North America Online (A. Poole, ed.). Cornell Lab of Ornithology, Ithaca, NY.
Ewins, P. J., and D. V. Weseloh. 1999. Little Gull (*Larus minutus*). The Birds of North America Online (A. Poole, ed.). Cornell Lab of Ornithology, Ithaca, NY.
Fellows, S. D., and R. J. Gress. 1999. Breeding Mountain Plovers in Kansas. Kansas Orni. Soc. Bull 50(4):29–35.
Fellows, S. D., and S. L. Jones. 2009. Status Assessment and Conservation Action Plan for the Long-billed Curlew (*Numenius americanus*). Bio. Tech. Publ. FWS/BTP-R6012-2009. U.S. Department of the Interior, Fish and Wildlife Service, Washington, DC.
Fitch, H. S., and P. von Achen. 1973. Yellow-billed Cuckoo nesting at the University of Kansas Natural History Reservation. Kansas Orni. Soc. Bull. 24(2):12–15.
Fleharty, E. D. 1995. Wild Animals and Settlers on the Great Plains. University of Oklahoma Press, Norman. 316 pp.
Flowers, T. L. 1992. Golden Eagles nesting in Meade County, Kansas. Kansas Orni. Soc. Bull. 43(4):33–37.
———. 1995a. A History and Distributional List of Meade County, Kansas Birds. Privately published by the author, Meade, KS. 148 pp.
———. 1995b. Two new records for Meade County. Kansas Orni. Soc. Bull. 46(4):39–40.
———. 1998. Rookery in Meade County, Kansas. Kansas Orni. Soc. Bull. 49(3):33–38.
Frederick, P., and D. Siegel-Causey. 2000. Anhinga (*Anhinga anhinga*). The Birds of North America Online, (A. Poole, ed.). Cornell Lab of Ornithology, Ithaca, NY.
Fredrickson, R. W. 1951. Alterations in the list of Kansas birds since Long (1940). Kansas Orni. Soc. Bull. 2(2):10.
Frey, C. M., and B. D. Monser. 2009. Recent and historical sightings of the Magnificent Frigatebird preceded by hurricanes in the Gulf of Mexico with notes in Kansas. Kansas Orni. Soc. Bull. 60(3):25–28.
Galbreath, E. C. 1955. An avifauna from the Pleistocene of central Kansas. Wilson Bull. 67:62–63.
Gammonley, J. H. 1996. Cinnamon Teal (*Anas cyanoptera*). The Birds of North America Online (A. Poole, ed.). Cornell Lab of Ornithology, Ithaca, NY.
Gauthier, G. 1993. Bufflehead (*Bucephala albeola*). The Birds of North America Online (A. Poole, ed.). Cornell Lab of Ornithology, Ithaca, NY.
Gehlbach, F. R. 1995. Eastern Screech-Owl (*Megascops asio*). The Birds of North America Online (A. Poole, ed.). Cornell Lab of Ornithology, Ithaca, NY.
Gibbs, J. P., F. A. Reid, S. M. Melvin, A. F. Poole, and P. Lowther. 2009. Least Bittern (*Ixobrychus exilis*). The Birds of North America Online (A. Poole, ed.). Cornell Lab of Ornithology, Ithaca, NY.
Gilchrist, H. G. 2001. Glaucous Gull (*Larus hyperboreus*). The Birds of North America Online (A. Poole, ed.). Cornell Lab of Ornithology, Ithaca, NY.
Gill, R. E., Jr., P. Canevari, and E. H. Iversen. 1998. Eskimo Curlew (*Numenius borealis*). The Birds of North America Online (A. Poole, ed.). Cornell Lab of Ornithology, Ithaca, NY.
Gillihan, S. W., D. Rubenstein, and D. Hanni. 2004. Ferruginous hawk (*Buteo regalis*) conservation assessment for Great Plains national grasslands. Unpublished report. U.S. Department of Agriculture Forest Service Chadron, NE.
Giudice, J. H., and J. T. Ratti. 2001. Ring-necked Pheasant (*Phasianus colchicus*). The Birds of North America Online (A. Poole, ed.). Cornell Lab of Ornithology, Ithaca, NY.
Godfrey, W. E. 1979. The Birds of Canada. National Museum of Canada, Ottawa, Ontario. 428 pp.
Goering, D. K. 1964. The Upland Plover in the Flint Hills of Kansas. M.S. thesis, Kansas State Teachers College, Emporia. 28 pp.
Goldstein, M. I., B. Woodbridge, M. A. Zaccaginini, S. B. Canavelli, and A. Lanusse. 1996. An assessment of mortality of Swainson's Hawks on wintering grounds in Argentina. J. Raptor Res. 30:106–107.
Gollop, J. B. 1988. The Eskimo Curlew. Pp. 583–595 *in* Audubon Wildlife Report 1988/1989 (W. J. Chandler, ed.). Academic Press, Inc., New York.
Gollop, J. B., T. W. Barry, and E. H. Iversen. 1986. Eskimo Curlew: a vanishing species? Saskatchewan Nat. Hist. Soc. Spec. Publ. 17. 160 pp.
Good, T. P. 1998. Great Black-backed Gull (*Larus marinus*). The Birds of North America Online (A. Poole, ed.). Cornell Lab of Ornithology, Ithaca, NY.
Goodrich, A. L. 1946. Birds in Kansas. June 1945 Report of the Kansas State Board of Agriculture, Topeka. 340 pp.
Goodrich, L. J., S. C. Crocoll, and S. E. Senner. 1996. Broad-winged Hawk (*Buteo platypterus*). The Birds of North America Online (A. Poole, ed.). Cornell Lab of Ornithology, Ithaca, NY.
Goss, N. S. 1883. A Catalogue of the Birds of Kansas. Kansas Publication House, Topeka. 37 pp.
———. 1886. A Revised Catalogue of the Birds of Kansas. Kansas Publication House, Topeka. 76 pp.

———. 1891. History of the Birds of Kansas. Geo. W. Crane and Co., Topeka, KS. 692 pp.

Goudie, R. I., G. J. Robertson, and A. Reed. 2000. Common Eider (*Somateria mollissima*). The Birds of North America Online (A. Poole, ed.). Cornell Lab of Ornithology, Ithaca, NY.

Graber, R., and J. Graber. 1950. New birds for the state of Kansas. Wilson Bull. 62(4):206–209.

———. 1951. Notes on the birds of southwestern Kansas. Trans. Kansas Acad. Sci. 54(2):145–174.

Gratto-Trevor, C. 1992. Semipalmated Sandpiper (*Calidris pusilla*). The Birds of North America Online (A. Poole, ed.). Cornell Lab of Ornithology, Ithaca, NY.

———. 2000. Marbled Godwit (*Limosa fedoa*). The Birds of North America Online (A. Poole, ed.). Cornell Lab of Ornithology, Ithaca, NY.

Greene, E., W. Davison, and V. R. Muehter. 1998. Steller's Jay (*Cyanocitta stelleri*). The Birds of North America Online (A. Poole, ed.). Cornell Lab of Ornithology, Ithaca, NY.

Gress, R. J. 1982. Red-breasted Nuthatch nesting in Sedgwick County. Kansas Orni. Soc. Bull. 33(4): 37–39.

———. 1984. Great Egrets nesting in Sedgwick County. Kansas Orni. Soc. Bull. 35(2):21–22.

Grzybowski, J. A. 1995. Black-capped Vireo (*Vireo atricapilla*). The Birds of North America Online (A. Poole, ed.). Cornell Lab of Ornithology, Ithaca, NY.

Grzybowski, J. A., and V. W. Fazio III. 2004. First observations of Cliff Swallows in Oklahoma. Bull. Oklahoma Orni. Soc. 37:9–14.

Hardy, J. W. 1957. Sight record of a Golden-crowned Sparrow in Kansas. Kansas Orni. Soc. Bull. 8(2):11.

Harrington, B. A. 2001. Red Knot (*Calidris canutus*). The Birds of North America Online (A. Poole, ed.). Cornell Lab of Ornithology, Ithaca, NY.

Harris, H. 1919. Birds of the Kansas City region. Trans. Acad. Sci. St. Louis 23(8):213–371.

Hatch, J. J. 2002. Arctic Tern (*Sterna paradisaea*). The Birds of North America Online (A. Poole, ed.). Cornell Lab of Ornithology, Ithaca, NY.

Hatch, J. J., and D. V. Weseloh. 1999. Double-crested Cormorant (*Phalacrocorax auritus*). The Birds of North America Online (A. Poole, ed.). Cornell Lab of Ornithology, Ithaca, NY.

Hatch, S. A., G. J. Robertson, and P. H. Baird. 2009. Black-legged Kittiwake (*Rissa tridactyla*). The Birds of North America Online (A. Poole, ed.). Cornell Lab of Ornithology, Ithaca, NY.

Haymes, G. T., and H. Blokpoel. 1978. Seasonal distribution and site tenacity of the Great Lakes Common Tern. Bird-Banding 49:142–151.

Hayward, J. L., and N. A. Verbeek. 2008. Glaucous-winged Gull (*Larus glaucescens*). The Birds of North America Online (A. Poole, ed.). Cornell Lab of Ornithology, Ithaca, NY.

Heath, J. A., P. Frederick, J. A. Kushlan, and K. L. Bildstein. 2009. White Ibis (*Eudocimus albus*). The Birds of North America Online (A. Poole, ed.). Cornell Lab of Ornithology, Ithaca, NY.

Heath, S. R., E. H. Dunn, and D. J. Agro. 2009. Black Tern (*Chlidonias niger*). The Birds of North America Online (A. Poole, ed.). Cornell Lab of Ornithology, Ithaca, NY.

Hedges, H. 1953. The Prairie Warbler in eastern Kansas. Kansas Orni. Soc. Bull. 4(4):30–31.

Hejl, S. J., K. R. Newlon, M. E. McFadzen, J. S. Young, and C. K. Ghalambor. 2002. Brown Creeper (*Certhia americana*). The Birds of North America Online (A. Poole, ed.). Cornell Lab of Ornithology, Ithaca, NY.

Helmers, D. L. 1991. Habitat use by migrant shorebirds and invertebrate availability in a managed wetland complex. M.S. thesis, University of Missouri, Columbia. 135 pp.

Hepp, G. R., and F. C. Bellrose. 1995. Wood Duck (*Aix sponsa*). The Birds of North America Online (A. Poole, ed.). Cornell Lab of Ornithology, Ithaca, NY.

Herbert, L. 1980. Overwintering of White-necked Raven in southwestern Kansas. Bull. Oklahoma Orni. Soc. 13:31.

Hertzel, P., W. R. Silcock, and S. J. Dinsmore. 2006. Identification of Cackling and Canada Geese in Iowa. [Online]. Available: http://www.iowabirds.org/ID/geese.asp.

Hibbard, C. W. 1964. Occurrences of the Ground Dove and Band-tailed Pigeon in Kansas. Kansas Orni. Soc. Bull. 15(3):19.

Hicks, T. L. 2009. Fish Crow (*Corvus ossifragus*) range expansion in Kansas. Kansas Orni. Soc. Bull. 60(4):29–36.

Highfill, K. M. 1990. A study of single adult Bald Eagle rearing young in Kansas. Kansas Orni. Soc. Bull. 41(2):21–24.

———. 1997. Great Horned Owls (*Bubo virginianus*) successful nesting in flower pot in northeast Kansas. Kansas Orni. Soc. Bull. 48(2):23–24.

Hill, R. A. 1976. Host–parasite relationships of the Brown-headed Cowbird in a prairie habitat of west-central Kansas. Wilson Bull. 88(4):555–565.

Hobson, K. A., and M. B. Robbins. 2009. Origins of late-breeding nomadic Sedge Wrens in North America: limitations and potential of hydrogen-isotope analyses of soft tissue. Condor 111(1):188–192.

Hohman, W. L., and R. T. Eberhardt. 1998. Ring-necked Duck (*Aythya collaris*). The Birds of North America Online (A. Poole, ed.). Cornell Lab of Ornithology, Ithaca, NY.

Hohman, W. L., and S. A. Lee. 2001. Fulvous Whistling-Duck (*Dendrocygna bicolor*). The Birds of North America Online (A. Poole, ed.). Cornell Lab of Ornithology, Ithaca, NY.

Holmes, R. T., and F. A. Pitelka. 1998. Pectoral Sandpiper (*Calidris melanotos*). The Birds of North America Online (A. Poole, ed.). Cornell Lab of Ornithology, Ithaca, NY.

Horak, G. J. 1985. Kansas Greater Prairie-Chickens. Kansas Fish and Game Commission, Wildlife Bull. No. 3. Emporia. 65 pp.

Horak, G. J., and R. D. Applegate. 1998. Greater Prairie-Chicken Management. Kansas School Nat. 45:1–15.

Houston, C. S., and D. E. Bowen, Jr. 2001. Upland Sandpiper (*Bartramia longicauda*). The Birds of North America Online (A. Poole, ed.). Cornell Lab of Ornithology, Ithaca, NY.

Hubbard, J. P., Carla Dove, and C. M. Milensky. 2001. T. C. Henry's Harlan's Hawk and other 1850's Kansas birds. Kansas Orni. Soc. Bull. 52(4):42–47.

Hunt, P. D., and D. J. Flaspohler. 1998. Yellow-rumped Warbler (*Dendroica coronata*). The Birds of North America Online (A. Poole, ed.). Cornell Lab of Ornithology, Ithaca, NY.

Imler, R. H. 1937. An annotated list of the birds of Rooks County, Kansas, and vicinity. Trans. Kansas Acad. Sci. 39:295–312.

Institute for Bird Populations. 2010. English and scientific alpha codes for North American birds through the 50th AOU Supplement (2009). [Online]. Available: http://www.birdpop.org/alphacodes.htm.

Jackson, B. J., and J. A. Jackson. 2000. Killdeer (*Charadrius vociferus*). The Birds of North America Online (A. Poole, ed.). Cornell Lab of Ornithology, Ithaca, NY.

Jackson, J. A., and H. R. Ouellet. 2002. Downy Woodpecker (*Picoides pubescens*). The Birds of North America Online (A. Poole, ed.). Cornell Lab of Ornithology, Ithaca, NY.

Jackson, J. A., and J. D. Rising. 1968. Mid-winter bird count for 1967. Kansas Orni. Soc. Bull. 19(1):3.

James, J. D., and J. E. Thompson. 2001. Black-bellied Whistling Duck (*Dendrocygna autumnalis*). The Birds of North America Online (A. Poole, ed.). Cornell Lab of Ornithology, Ithaca, NY.

Janzen, P. 1998. Winter round-up: 1 December, 1997 through 28 February, 1998. Kansas Orni. Soc. Horned Lark 25(2):8–12.

———. 2001. Fall season round-up: August 1, 2000 through November 30, 2000. Kansas Orni. Soc. Horned Lark 28(1):6–15.

———. 2002a. Revisions to the status of the Rufous-crowned Sparrow in Kansas. Kansas Orni. Soc. Bull. 53(3):29–33.

———. 2002b. New breeding bird records from the Red Hills region of Kansas. Kansas Orni. Soc. Bull. 53(4):37–39.

———. 2007. The Birds of Sedgwick County. Kansas Orni. Soc., Monograph 1. 118 pp.

Jehl, J., and J. R. Jehl, Jr. 1998. Stilt Sandpiper (*Calidris himantopus*). The Birds of North America Online (A. Poole, ed.). Cornell Lab of Ornithology, Ithaca, NY.

Jehl, J. R., Jr., J. Klima, and R. E. Harris. 2001. Short-billed Dowitcher (*Limnodromus griseus*). The Birds of North America Online (A. Poole, ed.). Cornell Lab of Ornithology, Ithaca, NY.

Jenkins, M. A. 2004. Golden Eagle (*Aquila chrysaetos*). Pp. 106–107 *in* Oklahoma Breeding Bird Atlas (D. L. Reinking, ed.). University of Oklahoma Press, Norman.

Jenkinson, M. A. 1968. Early records of the Chuck-will's-widow at Manhattan, Kansas. Kansas Orni. Soc. Bull. 19(3):17–18.

———. 1984. Correction of a purported nesting of the Chestnut-sided Warbler from Kansas. Kansas Orni. Soc. Bull. 35(2):22.

———. 1991. Fork-tailed Flycatcher in Barton County. Kansas Orni. Soc. Bull. 42(3):29–30.

Johnsgard, P. A. 1973. Grouse and Quails of North America. University of Nebraska Press, Lincoln. 553 pp.

———. 1979. Birds of the Great Plains. University of Nebraska Press, Lincoln. 539 pp.

———. 1990. Hawks, Eagles, and Falcons. Smithsonian Institute Press, Washington, DC. 403 pp.

Johnson, J. 2010. Migratory movement of Short-eared Owls. Unpublished data. [Online]. Available: http://www.seaturtle.org/tracking/index.shtml?project_id=419.

Johnson, K. 1995. Green-winged Teal (*Anas crecca*). The Birds of North America Online (A. Poole, ed.). Cornell Lab of Ornithology, Ithaca, NY.

Johnson, L. B. 2008. Extralimital Ladder-backed Woodpecker of apparent extended longevity in Riley County, Kansas. Kansas Orni. Soc. Bull. 59(4):33–36.

Johnson, O. W., and P. G. Connors. 1996. American Golden-Plover (*Pluvialis dominica*). The Birds of North America Online (A. Poole, ed.). Cornell Lab of Ornithology, Ithaca, NY.

Johnston, R. F. 1958. Breeding of the Brown Thrasher in Kansas. Kansas. Orni. Soc. Bull. 9(3):17–18.

———. 1960. Directory to the Bird-Life of Kansas. Univ. Kansas, Mus. Nat. Hist. Misc. Publ. 23:1–69.

———. 1963. Distributional records of some Kansas birds. Kansas Orni. Soc. Bull. 14(4):27.

———. 1964a. The breeding birds of Kansas. Univ. Kansas Mus. Nat. Hist. 12:575–655.

———. 1964b. Traill Flycatchers breeding in Kansas. Kansas Orni. Soc. Bull. 15(1):7.

———. 1965. A directory to the birds of Kansas. Univ. Kansas, Mus. Nat. Hist. Misc. Publ. 41:1–67.

———. 1992. Rock Pigeon (*Columba livia*). The Birds of North America Online (A. Poole, ed.). Cornell Lab of Ornithology, Ithaca, NY.

Johnston, R. F., and S. G. Johnson. 1985. The breeding season of feral pigeons in Kansas. Kansas Orni. Soc. Bull. 36(4):32–33.

Kansas Ornithological Society. 2010. Kansas Ornithological Society birds of Kansas checklist, 11th ed. [Online]. Available: http://ksbirds.org/.

Kaufman, K. 1990. A Field Guide to Advanced Birding. Houghton Mifflin Co., Boston, MA. 299 pp.

Kennedy, E. D., and D. W. White. 1997. Bewick's Wren (*Thryomanes bewickii*). The Birds of North America Online (A. Poole, ed.). Cornell Lab of Ornithology, Ithaca, NY.

Keppie, D. M., and R. M. Whiting, Jr. 1994. American Woodcock (*Scolopax minor*). The Birds of North America Online (A. Poole, ed.). Cornell Lab of Ornithology, Ithaca, NY.

Kessel, B., D. A. Rocque, and J. S. Barclay. 2002. Greater Scaup (*Aythya marila*). The Birds of North America Online (A. Poole, ed.). Cornell Lab of Ornithology, Ithaca, NY.

Kirk, D., and M. Mossman. 1998. Turkey Vulture (*Cathartes aura*). The Birds of North America Online (A. Poole, ed.). Cornell Lab of Ornithology, Ithaca, NY.

Klima, J., and J. R. Jehl, Jr. 1998. Stilt Sandpiper (*Calidris himantopus*). The Birds of North America Online (A. Poole, ed.). Cornell Lab of Ornithology, Ithaca, NY.

Kluza, D. A., K. S. Bostwick, and E. A. Young. 2001. Late fall bird mortality at a Topeka television tower. Kansas Orni. Soc. Bull. 52(2):21–24.

Knopf, F., and R. Evans. 2004. American White Pelican (*Pelicanus erythrorhyncos*). The Birds of North America Online (A. Poole, ed.). Cornell Lab of Ornithology, Ithaca, NY.

Knopf, F. L., and M. B. Wunder. 2006. Mountain Plover (*Charadrius montanus*). The Birds of North America Online (A. Poole, ed.). Cornell Lab of Ornithology, Ithaca, NY.

Kochert, M. N., K. Steenhof, C. L. McIntyre, and E. H. Craig. 2002. Golden Eagle (*Aquila chrysaetos*). The Birds of North America Online (A. Poole, ed.). Cornell Lab of Ornithology, Ithaca, NY.

Koenig, W., and M. D. Reynolds. 2009. Yellow-billed Magpie (*Pica nuttalli*). The Birds of North America Online (A. Poole, ed.). Cornell Lab of Ornithology, Ithaca, NY.

Kraft, M. J. 1990. Kansas resident Canada Goose management plan. Kansas Department of Wildlife and Parks. 20 pp. Adopted October 8, 1990.

Kuchler, A. W. 1974. A new vegetation map of Kansas. Ecology 55:586–604.

Kuenning, R. R. 1998. Scaled Quail (*Callipepla squamata*). Pp. 150–151 *in* The Colorado Breeding Bird Atlas (H. Kingery, ed.). Colorado Bird Atlas Partnership and Colorado Division of Wildlife, Denver.

Lanctot, R. B., J. Aldabe, J. Bosi de Almeida, D. Blanco, J. P. Isacch, J. Jorgensen, S. Norland, P. Rocca, and K. M. Strum. 2009. Conservation Plan for the Buff-breasted Sandpiper (*Tryngites subruficollis*). Version 1.0. U.S. Fish and Wildlife Service, Anchorage, AK, and Manomet Center for Conservation Sciences, Manomet, MA. 114 pp.

Lanctot, R. B., and C. D. Laredo. 1994. Buff-breasted Sandpiper (*Tryngites subruficollis*). The Birds of North America Online (A. Poole, ed.). Cornell Lab of Ornithology, Ithaca, NY.

Land, M. E. 2010. Report of the Kansas Bird Records Committee. Kansas Orni. Soc. Bull. 61(2):21–24.

Langley, W. 2000. Changes in wintering crow populations in Kansas. Kansas Orni. Soc. Bull. 51(2):21–22.

Lantz, D. E. 1901. A list of the birds seen in Dickinson County, Kansas, from August 1898, to August, 1900. Trans. Kansas Acad. Sci. 17:116–121.

Larrabee, A. P. 1937. Nesting of the Pine Siskin in South Dakota and Kansas. Wilson Bull. 49(2):116.

LaShelle, D. 1988. Spotted Redshank in Jefferson County, Kansas. Kansas Orni. Soc. Bull. 39(4):38–39.

———. 1990. Gray Hawk in northeastern Kansas. Kansas Orni. Soc. Bull. 41(4):29–30.

Latta, S. C., and M. E. Baltz. 1997. Lesser Nighthawk (*Chordeiles acutipennis*). The Birds of North America Online (A. Poole, ed.). Cornell Lab of Ornithology, Ithaca, NY.

Leonard, D. L., Jr. 2001. American Three-toed Woodpecker (*Picoides dorsalis*). The Birds of North America Online (A. Poole, ed.). Cornell Lab of Ornithology, Ithaca, NY.

Leschack, C. R., S. K. McKnight, and G. R. Hepp. 1997. Gadwall (*Anas strepera*). The Birds of North America Online (A. Poole, ed.). Cornell Lab of Ornithology, Ithaca, NY.

Leukering, T. 2000. Re: NC Pacific-slope Flycatcher (discussion on ID-Frontiers listserv, posted 27 January 2000). [Online]. Available: http://www.virtualbirder.com/bmail/idfrontiers/200001/w4/index.html#28.

Lewis, E. R. 1980. First winter record of the Lesser Goldfinch in Kansas. Kansas Orni. Soc. Bull. 31(2):21.

Lewis, J. C. 1995. Whooping Crane (*Grus americana*). The Birds of North America Online (A. Poole, ed.). Cornell Lab of Ornithology, Ithaca, NY.

Limpert, R. J., and S. L. Earnst. 1994. Tundra Swan (*Cygnus columbianus*). The Birds of North America Online (A. Poole, ed.). Cornell Lab of Ornithology, Ithaca, NY.

Linsdale, J. M. 1927. Notes on summer birds of southwestern Kansas. Auk 44:47–58.

———. 1928. Birds of a limited area in eastern Kansas. Univ. Kansas Sci. Bull. 18:517–626.

———. 1933. The nesting season of birds in Doniphan County, Kansas. Condor 35:155–160.

Lohoefener, R. R. 1977. Comparative nesting ecology of solitary and colonially nesting Barn Swallows in west-central Kansas. M.S. thesis, Fort Hays State University, Hays, KS. 55 pp.

Lohoefener, R., L. Lohmeier, and C. A. Ely. 1983. Riparian habitats and nesting bird associations in north-central Kansas. Kansas Fish and Game Contract No. 71. 109 pp.

Loncore, J. R., D. G. Mcauley, G. R. Hepp, and J. M. Rhymer. 2000. American Black Duck (*Anas rubripes*). The Birds of North America Online (A. Poole, ed.). Cornell Lab of Ornithology, Ithaca, NY.

Long, W. S. 1934. The Birds of Kansas. Unpublished manuscript. University of Kansas, Lawrence. 292 pp.

———. 1940. Check-list of Kansas birds. Trans. Kansas Acad. Sci. 43:433–456.

Lowther, P. E. 1977. Chestnut-sided Warbler nesting record from Kansas. Kansas Orni. Soc. Bull. 28(3):32.

———. 1979. The nesting biology of House Sparrows in Kansas. Kansas Orni. Soc. Bull. 30(3):23–28.

Lowther, P. E., H. D. Douglas III, and C. L. Gratto-Trevor. 2001. Willet (*Tringa semipalmata*). The Birds of North America Online (A. Poole, ed.). Cornell Lab of Ornithology, Ithaca, NY.

Lowther, P. E., D. E. Kroodsma, and G. H. Farley. 2000.

Rock Wren (*Salpinctes obsoletus*). The Birds of North America Online (A. Poole, ed.). Cornell Lab of Ornithology, Ithaca, NY.

Lowther, P. E., and R. T. Paul. 2002. Reddish Egret (*Egretta rufescens*). The Birds of North America Online (A. Poole, ed.). Cornell Lab of Ornithology, Ithaca, NY.

Lowther, P., A. F. Poole, J. P. Gibbs, S. Melvin, and F. A. Reid. 2009. American Bittern (*Botaurus lentiginosus*). The Birds of North America Online (A. Poole, ed.). Cornell Lab of Ornithology, Ithaca, NY.

MacCarone, A. D., and P. Janzen. 2005. Winter diet of Long-eared Owls (*Otus asio*) at an urban roost in Wichita, Kansas. Trans. Kansas Acad. Science 108(3–4):116–120.

MacWhirter, B., P. Austin-Smith, Jr., and D. Kroodsma. 2002. Sanderling (*Calidris alba*). The Birds of North America Online (A. Poole, ed.). Cornell Lab of Ornithology, Ithaca, NY.

MacWhirter, R. B., and K. L. Bildstein. 1996. Northern Harrier (*Circus cyaneus*). The Birds of North America Online (A. Poole, ed.). Cornell Lab of Ornithology, Ithaca, NY.

Marks, J. S., D. L. Evans, and D. W. Holt. 1994. Long-eared Owl (*Asio otus*). The Birds of North America Online (A. Poole, ed.). Cornell Lab of Ornithology, Ithaca, NY.

Marti, C. D., A. F. Poole, and L. R. Bevier. 2005. Barn Owl (*Tyto alba*). The Birds of North America Online (A. Poole, ed.). Cornell Lab of Ornithology, Ithaca, NY.

Matiasek, J. J. 1998. Nest-site selection and breeding behavior of the migratory Rock Wren (*Salpinctes obsoletus*) in western Kansas. M.S. thesis, Fort Hays State University, Hays, KS.

McCallum, D. A. 1994. Flammulated Owl (*Otus flammeolus*). The Birds of North America Online (A. Poole, ed.). Cornell Lab of Ornithology, Ithaca, NY.

McCormack, J. E., and J. L. Brown. 2008. Mexican Jay (*Aphelocoma ultramarina*). The Birds of North America Online (A. Poole, ed.). Cornell Lab of Ornithology, Ithaca, NY.

McCrimmon, D. A., Jr., J. Ogden, and G. T. Bancroft. 2001. Great Egret (*Ardea alba*). The Birds of North America Online (A. Poole, ed.). Cornell Lab of Ornithology, Ithaca, NY.

McGowan, K. J. 2001. Fish Crow (*Corvus ossifragus*). The Birds of North America Online (A. Poole, ed.). Cornell Lab of Ornithology, Ithaca, NY.

McKinley, D. J. 1964. History of the Carolina Parakeet in its southwestern range. Wilson Bull. 76:68–93.

McNicholl, M. K., P. E. Lowther, and J. A. Hall. 2001. Forster's Tern (*Sterna forsteri*). The Birds of North America Online (A. Poole, ed.). Cornell Lab of Ornithology, Ithaca, NY.

Melvin, S. M., and J. P. Gibbs. 1996. Sora (*Porzana carolina*). The Birds of North America Online (A. Poole, ed.). Cornell Lab of Ornithology, Ithaca, NY.

Mengel, R. M. 1970a. A second definite nesting record of the Painted Bunting, and notes on the species in Kansas. Kansas Orni. Soc. Bull. 21(1):7–8.

———. 1970b. Black Skimmer in Douglas County, Kansas. Kansas Orni. Soc. Bull. 21(2):15.

Menke, H. W. 1894. List of birds of Finney County, Kansas. Kansas Univ. Quart. 3(2):129–135.

Messerly, E. H. 1972. Forgotten records of the Painted Bunting in Kansas. Kansas Orni. Soc. Bull. 23(4):20.

Meyer, K. D. 1995. Swallow-tailed Kite (*Elanoides forficatus*). The Birds of North America Online (A. Poole ed.). Cornell Lab of Ornithology, Ithaca, NY.

Miller, J. L. 1975. Little Gull at John Redmond Reservoir, Coffey County, Kansas. Kansas Orni. Soc. Bull. 26(2):9–10.

Mitchell, C. D. 1994. Trumpeter Swan (*Cygnus buccinator*) The Birds of North America Online (A. Poole, ed.). Cornell Lab of Ornithology, Ithaca, NY.

Moldenhauer, R. R., and D. J. Regelski. 1996. Northern Parula (*Parula americana*). The Birds of North America Online (A. Poole, ed.). Cornell Lab of Ornithology, Ithaca, NY.

Molina, K. C., J. F. Parnell, and R. M. Erwin. 2009. Gull-billed Tern (*Sterna nilotica*). The Birds of North America Online (A. Poole, ed.). Cornell Lab of Ornithology, Ithaca, NY.

Moore, L. 2001. Kansas summer season roundup: June 1 2001 through July 31, 2001. Horned Lark 28(4):6–10.

———. 2003. Kansas fall season roundup: August 1, 2002 through November 3, 2002. Horned Lark 30(1):7–17.

———. 2004. Kansas fall season roundup: August 1, 2003 through November 30, 2003. Horned Lark 31(1):6–12.

Moorman, T. E., and P. N. Gray. 1994. Mottled Duck (*Anas fulvigula*). The Birds of North America Online (A. Poole, ed.). Cornell Lab of Ornithology, Ithaca, NY.

Morrison, R. I. G., A. Bourget, R. Butler, H. L. Dickson, and C. Gratto-Trevor. 1994. A preliminary assessment of the status of shorebird populations in Canada. Progress Notes 208. Canadian Wildlife Service, Ottawa, Ontario.

Morrison, R. I. G., R. E. Gill, B. A. Harrington, S. Skagen, G. W. Page, C. L. Gratto-Tever, and S. M. Haig. 2000. Population estimates of Nearctic shorebirds. J. Waterbird Soc. 23(3):337–352.

Moskoff, W. 1995. Solitary Sandpiper (*Tringa solitaria*). The Birds of North America Online (A. Poole, ed.). Cornell Lab of Ornithology, Ithaca, NY.

Moskoff, W., and L. R. Bevier. 2002. Mew Gull (*Larus canus*). The Birds of North America Online (A. Poole, ed.). Cornell Lab of Ornithology, Ithaca, NY.

Moskoff, W., and R. Montgomerie. 2002. Baird's Sandpiper (*Calidris bairdii*). The Birds of North America Online (A. Poole, ed.). Cornell Lab of Ornithology, Ithaca, NY.

Mowbray, T. B. 1999. American Wigeon (*Anas americana*). The Birds of North America Online (A. Poole, ed.). Cornell Lab of Ornithology, Ithaca, NY.

———. 2002. Canvasback (*Aythya valisineria*). The Birds of North America Online (A. Poole, ed.). Cornell Lab of Ornithology, Ithaca, NY.

Mowbray, T. B., F. Cooke, and B. Ganter. 2000. Snow

Goose (*Chen caerulescens*). The Birds of North America Online (A. Poole, ed). Cornell Lab of Ornithology, Ithaca, NY.

Mowbray, T. B., C. R. Ely, J. S. Sedinger, and R. E. Trost. 2002. Canada Goose (*Branta canadensis*). The Birds of North America Online (A. Poole, ed.). Cornell Lab of Ornithology, Ithaca, NY.

Mueller, H. 1999. Wilson's Snipe (*Gallinago delicata*). The Birds of North America Online (A. Poole, ed.). Cornell Lab of Ornithology, Ithaca, NY.

Mulhern, D. W., and M. A. Watkins. 2008. An attempt to relocate pre-fledged Least Tern chicks on the Kansas River. Kansas Orni. Soc. Bull. 59(2):23–26.

Muller, M. J., and R. W. Storer. 1999. Pied-billed Grebe (*Podilymbus podiceps*). The Birds of North America Online (A. Poole, ed.). Cornell Lab of Ornithology, Ithaca, NY.

National Audubon Society. 2007. 2002–2007. The Christmas bird count historical results. [Online]. Available: http://www.audubon.org/bird/cbc.

Nebel, S., and J. M. Cooper. 2008. Least Sandpiper (*Calidris minutilla*). The Birds of North America Online (A. Poole, ed.). Cornell Lab of Ornithology, Ithaca, NY.

Nelson, D. L. 1998. Chihuahuan Raven. Pp. 328–329 *in* The Colorado Breeding Bird Atlas (H. Kingery, ed.). Colorado Bird Atlas Partnership and Colorado Division of Wildlife, Denver.

Nettleship, D. N. 2000. Ruddy Turnstone (*Arenaria interpres*). The Birds of North America Online (A. Poole, ed.). Cornell Lab of Ornithology, Ithaca, NY.

Nisbet, I. C. 2002. Common Tern (*Sterna hirundo*). The Birds of North America Online (A. Poole, ed.). Cornell Lab of Ornithology, Ithaca, NY.

Nol, E., and M. S. Blanken. 1999. Semipalmated Plover (*Charadrius semipalmatus*). The Birds of North America Online (A. Poole, ed.). Cornell Lab of Ornithology, Ithaca, NY.

Norment, C. J., and S. A. Shackleton. 1993. Harris's Sparrow (*Zonotrichia querula*). The Birds of North America Online (A. Poole, ed.). Cornell Lab of Ornithology, Ithaca, NY.

North, M. R. 1994. Yellow-billed Loon (*Gavia adamsii*). The Birds of North America Online (A. Poole, ed.). Cornell Lab of Ornithology, Ithaca, NY.

North American Breeding Bird Survey. 2010. North American Breeding Bird Survey Website. Available: http://www.pwrc.usgs.gov/bbs.

O'Brien, M., R. Crossley, and K. Karlson. 2006. The Shorebird Guide. Houghton Mifflin Co., New York. 477 pp.

Oring, L. W., E. M. Gray, and M. Reed. 1997. Spotted Sandpiper (*Actitis macularius*). The Birds of North America Online (A. Poole, ed.). Cornell Lab of Ornithology, Ithaca, NY.

Otte, C. 2004. 2003 Report of the Kansas Bird Records Committee. Kansas Orni. Soc. Bull. 55(3):25–28.

———. 2005. 2004 Report of the Kansas Bird Records Committee. Kansas Orni. Soc. Bull. 56(2):21–23.

———. 2006. 2005 Report of the Kansas Bird Records Committee. Kansas Orni. Soc. Bull. 57(2):13–15 [sic = 21–23].

———. 2007. 2006 Report of the Kansas Bird Records Committee. Kansas Orni. Soc. Bull. 58(2):21–23.

———. 2008. 2007 Report of the Kansas Bird Records Committee. Kansas Orni. Soc. Bull. 59(2):26–28.

———. 2009. 2008 Report of the Kansas Bird Records Committee. Kansas Orni. Soc. Bull. 60(2):21–24.

Page, G. W., L. E. Stenzel, G. W. Page, J. S. Warriner, J. C. Warriner, and P. W. Paton. 1995. Snowy Plover (*Charadrius alexandrinus*). The Birds of North America Online (A. Poole, ed.). Cornell Lab of Ornithology, Ithaca, NY.

Parker, J., E. Bennett, and R. Chipman. 1983. Second record of the Magnificent Frigatebird for Kansas. Kansas Orni. Soc. Bull. 34(1):18–19.

Parker, J. W. 1999. Mississippi Kite (*Ictinia mississippiensis*). The Birds of North America Online (A. Poole, ed.). Cornell Lab of Ornithology, Ithaca, NY.

Parkes, K. C. 1951. The genetics of the Golden-winged × Blue-winged Warbler complex. Wilson Bull. 63:5–15.

Parmelee, D. F. 1961. Evening Grosbeaks at Emporia, Kansas. Kansas Orni. Soc. Bull. 12(2):11.

———. 1992. White-rumped Sandpiper (*Calidris fuscicollis*). The Birds of North America Online (A. Poole, ed.). Cornell Lab of Ornithology, Ithaca, NY.

Parmelee, D. F., M. D. Schwilling, and H. A. Stephens. 1969a. Charadriiform birds of Cheyenne Bottoms, part I. Kansas Orni. Soc. Bull. 20(2):9–13.

———. 1969b. Charadriiform birds of Cheyenne Bottoms, part II. Kansas Orni. Soc. Bull. 20(3):17–24.

———. 1970. Gruiform birds of Cheyenne Bottoms. Kansas Orni. Soc. Bull. 21(4):25–27.

Parmelee, D. F., and H. A. Stephens. 1963. A second breeding colony of the Double-crested Cormorant in Kansas. Kansas Orni. Soc. Bull. 14(4):21–22.

———. 1964. Status of the Harris's Hawk in Kansas. Condor 66(5):443–445.

Parsons, K. C., and T. L. Master. 2000. Snowy Egret (*Egretta thula*). The Birds of North America Online (A. Poole, ed.). Cornell Lab of Ornithology, Ithaca, NY.

Patti, S. T. 1972. Brown Towhee—a species new to Kansas. Kansas Orni. Soc. Bull. 23(3):14.

———. 2004. Chihuahuan Raven (*Corvus cryptoleucus*). Pp. 278–279 *in* Oklahoma Breeding Bird Atlas (D. L. Reinking, ed.). University of Oklahoma Press, Norman.

Patti, S. T., and T. G. Shane. 2001. Cave Swallow in Kansas—a species new to the state. Kansas Orni. Soc. Bull. 52(4):39–42.

Paulson, D. R. 1995. Black-bellied Plover (*Pluvialis squatarola*). The Birds of North America Online (A. Poole, ed.). Cornell Lab of Ornithology, Ithaca, NY.

Pearson, S. F. 1997. Hermit Warbler (*Dendroica occidentalis*). The Birds of North America Online (A. Poole, ed.). Cornell Lab of Ornithology, Ithaca, NY.

Peterson, R. T. 1980. A Field Guide to the Birds, 4th ed. Houghton Mifflin Co., Boston, MA. 384 pp.

Petit, L. J. 1999. Prothonotary Warbler (*Protonotaria citrea*). The Birds of North America Online (A. Poole, ed.). Cornell Lab of Ornithology, Ithaca, NY.

Pierotti, R. J., and T. P. Good. 1994. Herring Gull (*Larus argentatus*). The Birds of North America Online (A. Poole, ed.). Cornell Lab of Ornithology, Ithaca, NY.

Piper, W. C. 1997. Bird sightings in Thomas County, Kansas. Kansas Orni. Soc. Bull. 48(3):28.

Pittman, G. L. 1992. 1991 Report of the Kansas Bird Records Committee. Kansas Orni. Soc. Bull. 43(2):18–19.

———. 1993. 1992 Report of the Kansas Birds Records Committee. Kansas Orni. Soc. Bull. 44(2):21–23.

———. 1994. 1993 Report of the Kansas Bird Records Committee. Kansas Orni. Soc. Bull. 45(4):36.

———. 1995. 1994 Report of the Kansas Bird Records Committee. Kansas Orni. Soc. Bull. 46(3):28–29.

———. 1996. 1995 Report of the Kansas Bird Records Committee. Kansas Orni. Soc. Bull. 47(3):34–35.

———. 1997. 1996 Report of the Kansas Bird Records Committee. Kansas Orni. Soc. Bull. 48(4):34–36.

———. 1998. 1997 Report of the Kansas Bird Records Committee. Kansas Orni. Soc. Bull. 49(2):26–29.

Platt, D. R. 2002. Fifty years of early winter bird counts in Harvey County, Kansas. Kansas Orni. Soc. Bull. 54(2):21–36.

Podrebarac, D. K., and E. J. Finck. 1991. Winter distribution of the House Finch in Kansas. Kansas Orni. Soc. Bull. 42(4):33–36.

Poole, A. F., L. R. Bevier, C. A. Marantz, and B. Meanly. 2005. King Rail (*Rallus elegans*). The Birds of North America Online (A. Poole, ed.). Cornell Lab of Ornithology, Ithaca, NY.

Poole, A. F., R. O. Bierregaard, and M. S. Martell. 2002. Osprey (*Pandion haliaetus*). The Birds of North America Online (A. Poole, ed.). Cornell Lab of Ornithology, Ithaca, NY.

Porter, J. M. 1951. Sight records of bird migration in north-central Kansas. Kansas Orni. Soc. Bull. 2(3):21–26.

Ports, M. A. 1978. A survey of the avifauna of Morton County, Kansas. Unpublished report to the Kansas Fish and Game Commission. 88 pp.

Post, W., and D. B. McNair. 1995. Evaluation of an historical egg set of the Passenger Pigeon in Kansas. Kansas Orni. Soc. Bull. 46(2):23–24.

Powers, D. R. 1996. Magnificent Hummingbird (*Eugenes fulgens*). The Birds of North America Online (A. Poole, ed.). Cornell Lab of Ornithology, Ithaca, NY.

Powers, D. R., and S. M. Wethington. 1999. Broad-billed Hummingbird (*Cynanthus latirostris*). The Birds of North America Online (A. Poole, ed.). Cornell Lab of Ornithology, Ithaca, NY.

Preston, C. R., and R. D. Beane. 2009. Red-tailed Hawk (*Buteo jamaicensis*). The Birds of North America Online (A. Poole, ed.). Cornell Lab of Ornithology, Ithaca, NY.

Ptacek, J., and M. Schwilling. 1983. Mountain Plover reintroduction in Kansas. Kansas Orni. Soc. Bull. 34(2):21–22.

Rakestraw, J. 1995. Large frog predation by a Greater Yellowlegs. Kansas Orni. Soc. Bull. 46(4):40.

Reed, A., D. H. Ward, D. V. Derksen, and J. S. Sedinger. 1998. Brant (*Branta bernicla*). The Birds of North America Online (A. Poole, ed.). Cornell Lab of Ornithology, Ithaca, NY.

Rice, N. H., K. Zyskowski, and W. H. Busby. 2001. Charadriiform bird surveys in north central Kansas. Kansas Orni. Soc. Bull. 52(3):29–36.

Rice, O. O. 1961. Pine Grosbeaks in Topeka. Kansas Orni. Soc. Bull. 12(1):2–3.

———. 1965. Lark Bunting nesting colony, Shawnee County, 1964. Kansas Orni. Soc. Bull. 16(1):1–2.

———. 1980. Tree Swallow nesting colony at the Marais des Cygnes Wildlife Management Area. Kansas Orni. Soc. Bull. 31(3):23–24.

Rich, L., and B. Rich. 1994. First verified record of the Phainopepla from Kansas. Kansas Orni. Soc. Bull. 45(3):23.

Rintoul, D. A. 1999. 1998 Report of the Kansas Bird Records Committee. Kansas Orni. Soc. Bull. 50(2):22–27.

———. 2000. 1999 Report of the Kansas Bird Records Committee. Kansas Orni. Soc. Bull. 51(2):22–24.

———. 2001. 2000 Report of the Kansas Bird Records Committee. Kansas Orni. Soc. Bull. 52(2):24–28.

———. 2002. 2001 Report of the Kansas Bird Records Committee. Kansas Orni. Soc. Bull. 53(2):24–28.

———. 2003. 2002 Report of the Kansas Bird Records Committee. Kansas Orni. Soc. Bull. 54(3):39–42.

Rintoul, D., and T. T. Cable. 1990. Breeding record for the Black-shouldered Kite in Kansas. Kansas Orni. Soc. Bull. 41(3):26–28.

Rising, J. D. 1974. The status and faunal affinities of the summer birds of western Kansas. Univ. Kansas Sci. Bull. 50(8):347–388.

———. 1983. The Great Plains hybrid zones. Current Ornithol. 1:131–157.

Rising, J. D., and D. L. Kilgore, Jr. 1964. Notes on birds from southwestern Kansas. Kansas Orni. Soc. Bull. 15(4):23–25.

Robb, L. A., and M. A. Schroeder. 2005. Greater Prairie-Chicken (*Tympanuchus cupido*): a technical conservation assessment. 15 April [Online]. U.S. Department of Agriculture Forest Service, Rocky Mountain Region. Available: http://www.fs.fed.us/r2/projects/scp/assessments/greaterprairiechicken.pdf.

Robbins, M. B. 2007. Buff-Breasted Sandpiper (*Tryngites subruficollis*) fall migration at sod farms in Kansas. Kansas Orni. Soc. Bull. 58(3):25–28.

Robbins, M. B. and D. A. Easterla. 1981. Range expansion of the Bronzed Cowbird with the first Missouri record. Condor 83:270–272.

———. 1992. Birds of Missouri. Their Distribution and Abundance. University of Missouri Press, Columbia. 399 pp.

Robbins, M. B. B. R. Barber, and E. A. Young. 2000. Major bird mortality at a Topeka television tower. Kansas Orni. Soc. Bull. 51(3):29–30.

Robbins, M. B., S. Patti, A. Nyari, C. Hobbs, and M. C. Thompson. 2006. Common Raven nesting attempt in Morton County, Kansas. Kansas Orni. Soc. Bull. 57(3):27–28.

Robbins, M. B., A. T. Peterson, and M. A. Ortega-Huerta. 2002. Major negative impacts of early intensive cattle stocking on tallgrass prairie: the case of the Greater Prairie-Chicken (*Tympanuchus cupido*). North American Birds 56(2):239–244.

Robbins, M. B., D. E. Seibel, and C. Cicero. 2005. Probable Yellow-bellied (*Sphyrapicus varius*) × Red-breasted Sapsucker (*S. ruber*) hybrid from eastern Kansas, with comments on the field identification of adult sapsuckers. North American Birds 59:360–363.

Robel, R. J. 1966. Booming territory size and mating success of the Greater Prairie-Chicken (*Tympanuchus cupido pinnatus*). Anim. Behav. 14:328–331.

Robel, R. J., J. N. Briggs, J. J. Cebula, N. J. Silvy, C. E. Viers, and P. G. Watt. 1970. Greater Prairie-Chicken ranges, movements, and habitat usage in Kansas. J. Wildl. Manage. 34:286–306.

Robertson, G. J., and R. I. Goudie. 1999. Harlequin Duck (*Histrionicus histrionicus*). The Birds of North America Online (A. Poole, ed.). Cornell Lab of Ornithology, Ithaca, NY.

Robertson, G. J., and J.-P. L. Savard. 2002. Long-tailed Duck (*Clangula hyemalis*). The Birds of North America Online (A. Poole, ed.). Cornell Lab of Ornithology, Ithaca, NY.

Robins, J. D., and G. L. Worthen. 1973. The Christmas bird count in Kansas, 1949–1971. Kansas Orni. Soc. Bull. 24(3):17–30.

Robinson, J. A., L. W. Oring, J. P. Skorupa, and R. Boettcher. 1997. American Avocet (*Recurvirostra americana*). The Birds of North America Online (A. Poole, ed.). Cornell Lab of Ornithology, Ithaca, NY.

Robinson, J. A., J. M. Reed, J. P. Skorupa, and L. W. Oring. 1999. Black-necked Stilt (*Himantopus mexicanus*). The Birds of North America Online (A. Poole, ed.). Cornell Lab of Ornithology, Ithaca, NY.

Rodgers, J. A., Jr., and H. T. Smith. 1995. Little Blue Heron (*Egretta caerulea*). The Birds of North America Online (A. Poole, ed.). Cornell Lab of Ornithology, Ithaca, NY.

Rohwer, F. C., W. P. Johnson, and E. R. Loos. 2002. Blue-winged Teal (*Anas discors*). The Birds of North America Online (A. Poole, ed.). Cornell Lab of Ornithology, Ithaca, NY.

Rohwer, S. A. 1972. Distribution of meadowlarks in the central and southern Great Plains and the desert grasslands of eastern New Mexico and west Texas. Trans. Kansas Acad. Sci. 75(1):1–19.

Rolfs, M. E., C. A. Ely, J. K. Wilson, and R. A. Hill. 1974. Pine Siskin nesting in west-central Kansas. Kansas Orni. Soc. Bull. 25(4):26–28.

Romagosa, C. M., and T. McEneaney. 1999. Eurasian Collared-Dove in North America and the Caribbean. North American Birds 53:348–353.

Rosenberg, K. V., S. E. Barker, and R. W. Rohrbaugh. 2000. An Atlas of Cerulean Warbler Populations. Final Report to USFWS: 1997–2000 Breeding Season. December. Cornell Lab of Ornithology, Ithaca, NY. 56 pp.

Roth, S. D., Jr., and J. M. Marzluff. 1989. Nest placement and productivity of Ferruginous Hawks in western Kansas. Trans. Kansas Acad. Sci. 92:132–148.

Rubega, M. A., D. Schamel, and D. M. Tracy. 2000. Red-necked Phalarope (*Phalaropus lobatus*). The Birds of North America Online (A. Poole, ed.). Cornell Lab of Ornithology, Ithaca, NY.

Rusch, D. H., S. DeStefano, M. C. Reynolds, and D. Lauten. 2000. Ruffed Grouse (*Bonasa umbellus*). The Birds of North America Online (A. Poole, ed.). Cornell Laboratory of Ornithology, Ithaca, NY.

Russell, R. W. 2002. Pacific Loon (*Gavia pacifica*). The Birds of North America Online (A. Poole, ed.). Cornell Lab of Ornithology, Ithaca, NY.

Ryder, J. P., and R. T. Alisauskas. 1995. Ross's Goose (*Chen rossii*). The Birds of North America Online (A. Poole, ed.). Cornell Lab of Ornithology, Ithaca, NY.

Ryder, J. R. 1993. Ring-billed Gull (*Larus delawarensis*). The Birds of North America Online (A. Poole, ed.). Cornell Lab of Ornithology, Ithaca, NY.

Ryder, R. A., and D. E. Manry. 1994. White-faced Ibis (*Plegadis chihi*). The Birds of North America Online (A. Poole, ed.). Cornell Lab of Ornithology, Ithaca, NY.

Sauer, J. R., J. E. Hines, and J. Fallon. 2008. The North American Breeding Bird Survey, results and analysis 1966–2007. Version 5.15.2008. [Online]. U.S. Geological Survey Patuxent Wildlife Research Center, Laurel, MD. Available: http://www.pwrc.usgs.gov/.

Savard, J.-P. L., D. Bordage, and A. Reed. 1998. Surf Scoter (*Melanitta perspicillata*). The Birds of North America Online (A. Poole, ed.). Cornell Lab of Ornithology, Ithaca, NY.

Schneider, R. J. 1996. Rufous Hummingbird. *In* The Kansas City Star. 13 and 14 November.

Schorger, A. W. 1955. The Passenger Pigeon: Its Natural History and Extinction. University of Wisconsin Press, Madison. 424 pp.

Schukman, J. M. 1993. Breeding ecology and distributional limits of phoebes in western Kansas. Kansas Orni. Soc. Bull. 44(3):25–29.

———. 1996. Temporal and spatial relationships of three canopy-dwelling warblers in a Missouri River bottomland forest. Kansas Orni. Soc. Bull. 47(4):37–40.

Schulenberg, J. 1977. Parasitic Jaeger in Coffey County. Kansas Orni. Soc. Bull. 28(3):28–29.

Schulenberg, J. H., G. L. Horak, M. D. Schwilling, and E. J. Fink. 1994. Nesting of Henslow's Sparrow in Osage County, Kansas. Kansas Orni. Soc. Bull. 45(3):25–28.

Schwilling, M. D. 1951. Mountain Chickadee. American Birds 33:293.

———. 1954. Black-throated Sparrow in Kansas. Wilson Bull. 66(2):151.

———. 1956. Bird notes and nesting records from the Marais des Cygnes Waterfowl Refuge and surrounding area. Kansas Orni. Soc. Bull. 7(4):21–22.

———. 1969. A Band-tailed Pigeon specimen from Kansas. Kansas Orni. Soc. Bull. 20(4):26.

———. 1971a. Bobolinks nest again in Kansas. Kansas Orni. Soc. Bull. 22(3):14–15.

———. 1971b. Rapid increase and dispersal of Boat-tailed Grackles in Kansas. Kansas Orni. Soc. Bull. 22(3):15–16.

———. 1972. Violet-green Swallow at the Cheyenne Bottoms Waterfowl Management Area. Kansas Orni. Soc. Bull. 23(4):18.

———. 1980. A review of Curve-billed Thrasher records for Kansas. Kansas Orni. Soc. Bull. 31(3):24–25.

Schwilling, M. D., D. Mulhern, and G. Horak. 1989. The Bald Eagle nesting in Kansas. Kansas Orni. Soc. Bull. 40(4):35–36.

Schwilling, M. D., and S. Roth. 1987. Violet-green Swallow nesting in Wallace County, Kansas. Kansas Orni. Soc. Bull. 38(4):35.

Schwilling, M. D., E. Schulenberg, and J. Schulenberg. 1981. Southeast Kansas nesting notes. Kansas Orni. Soc. Bull. 32(1):18–19.

Seibel, D. E. 1978. A Directory to the Birds of Cowley and Sumner Counties, Kansas, and the Chaplin Nature Center. Wichita Audubon Society Miscellaneous Publication No. 1, Wichita, KS. 74 pp.

Self, H. 1978. Environment and Man in Kansas. Regents Press of Kansas, Lawrence. 288 pp.

Senner, S. E., and M. A. Howe. 1984. Conservation of Nearctic shorebirds. Pp. 379–421 *in* Behavior of Marine Animals. Vol. 5 (J. Burger and B. L. Olla, eds.). Plenum Press, New York.

Senner, S. E., and E. F. Martinez. 1982. A review of Western Sandpiper migration in interior North America. Southwest. Nat. 27:149–159.

Shackford, J. S., D. M. Leslie, Jr., and W. D. Harden. 1999. Range-wide use of cultivated fields by Mountain Plovers during the breeding season. J. Field Orni. 70(1):114–120.

Shane, T. G. 1966. Chuck-will's-widow breeding in Geary County, Kansas. Kansas Orni. Soc. Bull. 17(2):12–14.

———. 2005. A significant midcontinental stopover site for the Long-billed Curlew. Kansas Orni. Soc. Bull. 56(4):33–37.

Shane, T. G., and R. LaShelle. 1974. Red-breasted Nuthatch apparently breeding in Kansas. Kansas Orni. Soc. Bull. 25(3):22–23.

Shane, T. G., and S. S. Seltman. 1995. The historical development of wintering Lark Bunting populations north of the thirty seventh parallel in Colorado and Kansas. Kansas Orni. Soc. Bull. 46(4):36–39.

Shane, T. G., and S. J. Shane. 1995. A late fall flock of Mountain Plovers in Kearny County, Kansas. Kansas Orni. Soc. Bull. 46(2):22–23.

———. 2000. The Cedar Waxwing: a western Kansas breeding species. Kansas Orni. Soc. Bull. 51(4):33–35.

———. 2008. Observations of wintering juncos in a Garden City, Kansas backyard. Horned Lark 35(2):11–12.

Shane, T. G., S. J. Shane, M. B. Osterbuhr, and R. G. Osterbuhr. 2001. Late summer Roseate Spoonbills in western Kansas. Kansas Orni. Soc. Bull. 52(4):37–39.

Sharpe, R. S., W. R. Silcock, and J. G. Jorgensen. 2001. Birds of Nebraska. Their Distribution and Temporal Occurrence. University of Nebraska Press, Lincoln. 520 pp.

Shields, M. 2002. Brown Pelican (*Pelecanus occidentalis*). The Birds of North America Online (A. Poole, ed.). Cornell Lab of Ornithology, Ithaca, NY.

Shirling, A. E. 1920. Birds of Swope Park in the Heart of America, Kansas City, Missouri. McIndoo Publishing Co., Kansas City, MO. 117 pp.

Sibley, D. A. 2000. National Audubon Society: The Sibley Guide to Birds. Knopf, New York. 544 pp.

———. 2004. Distinguishing Cackling and Canada Goose. [Online]. Available: http://www.sibleyguides.com/2007/07/identification-of-cackling-and-canada-goose.

Skeel, M. A., and E. P. Mallory. 1996. Whimbrel (*Numenius phaeopus*). The Birds of North America Online (A. Poole, ed.). Cornell Lab of Ornithology, Ithaca, NY.

Smallwood, J. A., and D. M. Bird. 2002. American Kestrel (*Falco sparverius*). The Birds of North America Online (A. Poole, ed.). Cornell Lab of Ornithology, Ithaca, NY.

Smith, P. W. 1987. The Eurasian Collared-Dove arrives in the Americas. American Birds 41:1370–1379.

Snell, R. R. 2002. Iceland Gull (*Larus glaucoides*). The Birds of North America Online (A. Poole, ed.). Cornell Lab of Ornithology, Ithaca, NY.

Snow, F. H. 1872. A catalogue of the birds of Kansas. Kansas Educ. J. 8:376–383.

———. 1878. Additions to the catalogue of Kansas birds. Trans. Kansas Acad. Sci. 6:38.

———. 1903. A catalogue of the birds of Kansas. Trans. Kansas Acad. Sci. 18:154–176.

Snyder, L. 1919. Harris's Hawk in Kansas. Auk 36:567.

Spahn, R., and D. Tetlow. 2006. Observations of the Cave Swallow invasion of November 2005. Kingbird 56(3):216–225.

Squires, J. R., and R. T. Reynolds. 1997. Northern Goshawk (*Accipiter gentilis*). The Birds of North America Online (A. Poole, ed.). Cornell Lab of Ornithology, Ithaca, NY.

Stedman, S. 2000. Horned Grebe (*Podiceps auritus*). The Birds of North America Online (A. Poole, ed.). Cornell Lab of Ornithology, Ithaca, NY.

Steenhof, K., M. R. Fuller, M. N. Kochert, and K. K. Bates. 2005. Long-range movements and breeding dispersal of Prairie Falcons from southwest Idaho. Condor 107:481–496.

Steeves, J. B., and S. Holohan. 1995. Calidrid spring migration on the east and west Canadian prairie. Wader Study Group Bull. 77:38–43.

Storer, R. W., and G. L. Nuechterlein. 1992a. Clark's Grebe (*Aechmophorus clarkii*). The Birds of North America Online (A. Poole, ed.). Cornell Lab of Ornithology, Ithaca, NY.

———. 1992b. Western Grebe (*Aechmophorus*

occidentalis). The Birds of North America Online (A. Poole, ed.). Cornell Lab of Ornithology, Ithaca, NY.

Stout, B., and G. Nuechterlein. 1999. Red-necked Grebe (*Podiceps grisegena*). The Birds of North America Online (A. Poole, ed.). Cornell Lab of Ornithology, Ithaca, NY.

Sullivan, J. 1995. *Buteo lagopus. In* Fire Effect Information System. [Online]. U.S. Department of Agriculture, Forest Service, Rocky Mountain Research Station, Fire Sciences Laboratory (producer). Available: http://www.fs.fed.us/database/feis/.

Sutton, G. M. 1967. Oklahoma Birds: Their Ecology and Distribution, with Comments on the Avifauna of the Southern Great Plains. University of Oklahoma Press, Norman. 674 pp.

Suydam, R. 2000. King Eider (*Somateria spectabilis*). The Birds of North America Online (A. Poole, ed.). Cornell Lab of Ornithology, Ithaca, NY.

Svedarsky, W. D., J. E. Toepfer, R. L. Westemeier, and R. J. Robel. 2003. Effects of management practices on grassland birds: Greater Prairie-Chicken. Northern Prairie Wildlife Research Center, Jamestown, ND. [Online]. Available: http://www.npwrc.usgs.gov/resource/literatr/grasbird/gpch/gpch.htm (Version 28MAY2004).

Svedarsky, W. D., R. L. Westemeier, R. J. Robel, S. Gough, and J. E. Toepfer. 2000. Status and management of the Greater Prairie-Chicken *Tympanuchus cupido pinnatus* in North America. Wildl. Biol. 6:277–284.

Swan, T., and M. C. Thompson. 1997. Records of the Yellow Rail in Kansas. Kansas Orni. Soc. Bull. 48(3):25–27.

Swanson, D. L., J. L. Ingold, and G. E. Wallace. 2008. Ruby-crowned Kinglet (*Regulus calendula*). The Birds of North America Online (A. Poole, ed.). Cornell Lab of Ornithology, Ithaca, NY.

Swenk, M. H. 1926. The Eskimo Curlew in Nebraska. Wilson Bull. 38:117–118.

Tacha, R. W. 1975. A survey of rail populations in Kansas with emphasis on Cheyenne Bottoms. M.S. thesis, Fort Hays Kansas State College, Hays. 54 pp.

Tacha, T. C., D. C. Martin, and C. T. Patterson. 1981. Common Crane (*Grus grus*) sighted in west Texas. Southwest. Nat. 25(4):569.

Tacha, T. C., S. A. Nesbitt, and P. A. Vohs. 1992. Sandhill Crane (*Grus canadensis*). The Birds of North America Online (A. Poole, ed.). Cornell Lab of Ornithology, Ithaca, NY.

Taggart, T. W., J. T. Collins, and C. Schmidt. 2010. Kansas herpetofaunal atlas: on-line reference. Electronic Database. Sternberg Museum of Natural History, Fort Hays State University, Hays, KS. Available: http://webcat.fhsu.edu/ksfauna/herps.

Tarvin, K. A., and G. E. Woolfenden. 1999. Blue Jay (*Cyanocitta cristata*). The Birds of North America Online (A. Poole, ed.). Cornell Lab of Ornithology, Ithaca, NY.

Telfair, R., and M. Morrison. 2005. Neotropic Cormorant (*Phalacrocorax brasilianus*). The Birds of North America Online (A. Poole, ed.). Cornell Lab of Ornithology, Ithaca, NY.

Telfair, R. C., II. 2006. Cattle Egret (*Bubulcus ibis*). The Birds of North America Online (A. Poole, ed.). Cornell Lab of Ornithology, Ithaca, NY.

Terres, John K. 1948. Bird of tragedy. Audubon Mag. 50(2):90–95.

———. 1980. The Audubon Society Encyclopedia of North American Birds. Alfred A. Knopf, New York. 1,109 pp.

Thompson, B. C., J. A. Jackson, J. Burger, L. A. Hill, E. M. Kirsch, and J. L. Atwood. 1997. Least Tern (*Sterna antillarum*). The Birds of North America Online (A. Poole, ed.). Cornell Lab of Ornithology, Ithaca, NY.

Thompson, M. 1958. Additional nesting records for the state of Kansas. Kansas Orni. Soc. Bull. 9(3):18–19.

———. 1971. Some winter records of warblers in Kansas and Oklahoma. Kansas Orni. Soc. Bull. 22(2):11–12.

———. 1993. The winter bird count for 1992. Kansas Orni. Soc. Bull. 44(1):1–16.

———. 1997. The winter bird count for 1996. Kansas Orni. Soc. Bull. 48(1):1–20.

Thompson, M. C., W. Champeny, and J. Newton. 1983. Records of the Garganey in Kansas. Kansas Orni. Soc. Bull. 34(4):29–30.

Thompson, M. C., and H. Chaplin. 1971. Lesser Goldfinch in Kansas. Kansas Orni. Soc. Bull. 22(1):7–8.

Thompson, M. C., and C. Ely. 1989. Birds in Kansas. Vol. 1. Univ. Kansas Mus. Nat. Hist. Publ. Ed. Ser. No. 11. 404 pp.

———. 1992. Birds in Kansas. Vol. 2. Univ. Kansas Mus. Nat. Hist. Publ. Ed. Ser. No. 12. 422 pp.

Thompson, M. C., and C. S. Holmes. 1963. Occurrence of the Pygmy Nuthatch in Kansas. Kansas Orni. Soc. Bull. 14(3):18.

Thompson, M. C., M. Schwilling, and J. A. White. 1980. New distributional records for the state of Kansas. Kansas Orni. Soc. Bull. 31(3):26–27.

Thompson, M. C., and E. A. Young. 1991. Waterbirds of Slate Creek Wetlands. Report submitted to Kansas Department of Wildlife and Parks for grant #180. 25 pp.

———. 1995. The winter bird count for 1994. Kansas Orni. Soc. Bull. 46(1):1–20.

———. 1996. The winter bird count for 1995. Kansas Orni. Soc. Bull. 47(1):1–20.

———. 1998. The winter bird count for 1998 [sic = 1997]. Kansas Orni. Soc. Bull. 49(1):1–20.

———. 1999. The winter bird count for 1998. Kansas Orni. Soc. Bull. 50(1):1–20.

———. 2000. The winter bird count for 1999. Kansas Orni. Soc. Bull. 51(1):1–20.

———. 2001. The winter bird count for 2000. Kansas Orni. Soc. Bull. 52(1):1–20.

Thoreau, H. D. 1910. Notes on New England Birds. Houghton Mifflin Co., Boston, MA. 452 pp.

Tibbitts, T. L., and W. Moskoff. 1999. Lesser Yellowlegs (*Tringa flavipes*). The Birds of North America Online (A. Poole, ed.). Cornell Lab of Ornithology, Ithaca, NY.

Tiemeier, O. W. 1938. Summer birds of Rawlins County, Kansas. Trans. Kansas Acad. Sci. 40:397–399.

Titman, R. D. 1999. Red-breasted Merganser (*Mergus serrator*). The Birds of North America Online (A. Poole, ed.). Cornell Lab of Ornithology, Ithaca, NY.

Tomback, D. F. 1998. Clark's Nutcracker (*Nucifraga columbiana*). The Birds of North America Online (A. Poole, ed.). Cornell Lab of Ornithology, Ithaca, NY.

Tordoff, H. B. 1956. Check-list of the birds of Kansas. Univ. Kansas Publ. Mus. Nat. Hist. 8:307–359.

———. 1957. Nesting of the Bobolink in Kansas. Kansas Orni. Soc. Bull. 8(3):13–14.

Tordoff, H. B., and J. R. Alcorn. 1957. Northeastward extension into Kansas of winter range of Sage Sparrow. Kansas Orni. Soc. Bull. 8(3):14.

Tordoff, H. B., and R. M. Mengel. 1956. Studies of birds killed in nocturnal migration. Univ. Kansas Publ. Mus. Nat. Hist. 10(1):1–44.

Tracy, D. M., D. Schamel, and J. Dale. 2002. Red Phalarope (*Phalaropus fulicarius*). The Birds of North America Online (A. Poole, ed.). Cornell Lab of Ornithology, Ithaca, NY.

Trautman, M. B. 1964. Probable breeding of the Clay-colored Sparrow in Morton County, Kansas. Kansas Orni. Soc. Bull. 15(4):26–27.

Trost, C. H. 1999. Black-billed Magpie (*Pica hudsonia*). The Birds of North America Online (A. Poole, ed.). Cornell Lab of Ornithology, Ithaca, NY.

U.S. Department of the Interior, Fish and Wildlife Service, and U.S. Department of Commerce, U.S. Census Bureau. 2002. 2001 National Survey of Fishing, Hunting, and Wildlife–Associated Recreation. U.S. Department of the Interior, Fish and Wildlife Service, and U.S. Department of Commerce, U.S. Census Bureau, Washington, DC.

U.S. Fish and Wildlife Service. 1999. Endangered and threatened wildlife and plants: proposed threatened status for the Mountain Plover. Federal Register 64(30):7587–7601.

———. 2003. Birding in the United States: a demographic and economic analysis. Addendum to the 2001 National Survey of Fishing, Hunting, and Wildlife–Associated Recreation. Report 2001-1. U.S. Fish and Wildlife Service, Washington, DC.

———. 2008. Species assessment and listing priority assignment form: Lesser Prairie-Chicken. [Online]. Available: http://ecos.fws.gov/docs/candforms_pdf/r2/B0AZ_V01.pdf.

Vannoy, D. 1991. First Anna's Hummingbird in Kansas. Kansas Orni. Soc. Bull. 42(1):22–23.

Verbeek, N. A., and C. Caffrey. 2002. American Crow (*Corvus brachyrhynchos*). The Birds of North America Online (A. Poole, ed.). Cornell Lab of Ornithology, Ithaca, NY.

Versaw, A. E. 2004. Scaled Quail (*Callipepla squamata*). Pp. 120–121 *in* Oklahoma Breeding Bird Atlas (D. L. Reinking, ed.). University of Oklahoma Press, Norman.

Villasenor G., L. E. 1988. Nesting of the House Finch (*Carpodacus mexicanus*) in Hays, Kansas. M.S. thesis. Fort Hays State University, Hays, KS. 23 pp. + 3 figs. and 11 tables.

Waldon, B. 1995. Possible sighting of Eskimo Curlews (*Numenius borealis*). Blue Jay 54:123–124.

Walters, E. L., E. H. Miller, and P. E. Lowther. 2002. Red-breasted Sapsucker (*Sphyrapicus ruber*). The Birds of North America Online (A. Poole, ed.). Cornell Lab of Ornithology, Ithaca, NY.

Warkentin, I. G., N. S. Sodhi, R. H. M. Espie, A. F. Poole, L. W. Oliphant, and P. C. James. 2005. Merlin (*Falco columbarius*). The Birds of North America Online (A. Poole, ed.). Cornell Lab of Ornithology, Ithaca, NY.

Warnock, N. D., and R. E. Gill. 1996. Dunlin (*Calidris alpina*). The Birds of North America Online (A. Poole, ed.). Cornell Lab of Ornithology, Ithaca, NY.

Watkins, M. A., and D. W. Mulhern. 1997. Bald Eagle nesting activity in Kansas—1996. Kansas Orni. Soc. Bull. 48(2):21–23.

———. 1998. Bald Eagle nesting activity in Kansas—1997. Kansas Orni. Soc. Bull. 49(2):29–32.

———. 1999. Ten years of successful Bald Eagle nesting in Kansas. Kansas Orni. Soc. Bull. 50(3):29–33.

Watkins, M. A., D. W. Mulhern, and E. Willis. 1996. Bald Eagle nesting activity in Kansas—1995. Kansas Orni. Soc. Bull. 47(3):29–33.

Watkins, M. A., E. Willis, and D. W. Mulhern. 1994. A history of successful Bald Eagle nesting in Kansas. Kansas Orni. Soc. Bull. 45(4):29–35.

Watts, B. D. 1995. Yellow-crowned Night-Heron (*Nyctanassa violacea*). The Birds of North America Online (A. Poole, ed.). Cornell Lab of Ornithology, Ithaca, NY.

West, R. L., and G. K. Hess. 2002. Purple Gallinule (*Porphyria martinica*). The Birds of North America Online (A. Poole, ed.). Cornell Lab of Ornithology, Ithaca, NY.

White, C. M. 1994. Population trends and current status of selected western raptors. Pp. 161–172 *in* A Century of Avifaunal Change in Western North America (J. R. Jehl, Jr., and N. K. Johnson, eds.). Studies in Avian Biology No. 15.

White, C. M., N. J. Clum, T. J. Cade, and W. G. Hunt. 2002. Peregrine Falcon (*Falco peregrinus*). The Birds of North America Online (A. Poole, ed.). Cornell Lab of Ornithology, Ithaca, NY.

Wiebe, K. L., and W. S. Moore. 2008. Northern Flicker (*Colaptes auratus*). The Birds of North America Online (A. Poole, ed.). Cornell Lab of Ornithology, Ithaca, NY.

Wiens, G. 1993. White-throated Swift (*Aeronautes saxatalis*) from Cowley County, Kansas. Kansas Orni. Soc. Bull. 44(3):30–31.

Wiggins, D. 2005a. Western Scrub-Jay (*Aphelocoma californica*). Pp. 268–269 *in* Oklahoma Breeding Bird Atlas (D. L. Reinking, ed.). University of Oklahoma Press, Norman.

———. 2005b. Pinyon Jay (*Gymnorhinus cyanocephalus*). Pp. 270–271 *in* Oklahoma Breeding Bird Atlas (D. L. Reinking, ed.). University of Oklahoma Press, Norman.

Wiley, R. H., and D. S. Lee. 1998. Long-tailed Jaeger (*Stercorarius longicaudus*). The Birds of North America Online (A. Poole, ed.). Cornell Lab of Ornithology, Ithaca, NY.

———. 1999. Parasitic Jaeger (*Stercorarius parasiticus*). The Birds of North America Online (A. Poole, ed.). Cornell Lab of Ornithology, Ithaca, NY.

———. 2000. Pomarine Jaeger (*Stercorarius pomarinus*). The Birds of North America Online (A. Poole, ed.). Cornell Lab of Ornithology, Ithaca, NY.

Williamson, S. 1974. The summer of the Cassin's Sparrow. Kansas Orni. Soc. Newsletter 2(6):1–2.

Williamson, S. L. 2001. A Field Guide to Hummingbirds of North America. Houghton Mifflin Co., New York. 263 pp.

Wilson, J. K. 1976. Nesting success of the Lark Bunting near the periphery of its breeding range. Kansas Orni. Soc. Bull. 27(2):13–22.

Wilson, W. H. 1994. Western Sandpiper (*Calidris mauri*). The Birds of North America Online (A. Poole, ed.). Cornell Lab of Ornithology, Ithaca, NY.

Winkler, D. W. 1996. California Gull (*Larus californicus*). The Birds of North America Online (A. Poole, ed.). Cornell Lab of Ornithology, Ithaca, NY.

Withgott, J. H., and K. G. Smith. 1998. Brown-headed Nuthatch (*Sitta pusilla*). The Birds of North America Online (A. Poole, ed.). Cornell Lab of Ornithology, Ithaca, NY.

Wolf, B. O. 1997. Black Phoebe (*Sayornis nigricans*). The Birds of North America Online (A. Poole, ed.). Cornell Lab of Ornithology, Ithaca, NY.

Wolfe, D. H., and M. Wolfe. 1994. King Rail impaled on barbed wire fence. Kansas Orni. Soc. Bull. 45(4):35.

Wolfe, L. R. 1961. The breeding birds of Decatur County, Kansas: 1908–1915. Kansas Orni. Soc. Bull. 12(4):27–30.

Woodin, M. C., and T. C. Michot. 2002. Redhead (*Aythya americana*). The Birds of North America Online (A. Poole, ed.). Cornell Lab of Ornithology, Ithaca, NY.

"Woods" ("the man who walks in the woods" = R. Sutherland). 1972. A note on the early history of the House Sparrow in Kansas. Kansas Orni. Soc. Bull. 23(2):11.

Young, E. A. 1993. A survey of the vertebrates of Slate Creek Salt Marsh, Sumner County, Kansas, with an emphasis on waterbirds. M.S. thesis, Fort Hays State University, Hays, KS. 187 pp.

———. 1995. Green-winged Teal nest in south-central Kansas. Kansas Orni. Soc. Bull. 46(3):29–30.

———. 2007. Note on the spring migration of the Buff-breasted Sandpiper in the Flint Hills of south-central Kansas. Kansas Orni. Soc. Bull. 58(4):32.

———. 2009. Bald Eagle nest surveys along the Arkansas River Basin: Mulvane (Kansas) to Kaw Reservoir (Oklahoma), 2009. Final report for Kaw Nation.

Young, E. A., M. N. Harding, M. Rader, and L. Wilgers. 2005. Notes on food habits of wintering Long-eared Owls in north-central Kansas. Kansas Orni. Soc. Bull. 56(3):25–29.

Young, E., J. Gabriele, and E. Agpalo. 2010. The winter bird count for 2009–2010. Kansas Orni. Soc. Bull. 61(1):1–20.

Young, E. A., and M. B. Pate. 1995. Winter distribution of the Great Blue Heron in Kansas. Kansas Orni. Soc. Bull. 46(3):25–28.

Young, E. A., and M. C. Thompson. 1995. Notes on some large concentrations of migrating birds in south-central Kansas. Kansas Orni. Soc. Bull. 46(3):30–32.

———. 2008. The winter bird count for 2007. Kansas Orni. Soc. Bull. 59(1):1–20.

Young, E., M. C. Thompson, and E. Agpalo. 2009. The winter bird count for 2008. Kansas Orni. Soc. Bull. 60(1):1–20.

Young, J. R., C. E. Braun, S. J. Oyler-McCance, J. W. Hupp, and T. W. Quinn. 2000. A new species of sage-grouse (Phasianidae: *Centrocercus*) from southwestern Colorado. Wilson Bull. 112(4):445–453.

Zimmerman, J. L. 1978. Ten year summary of the Kansas breeding bird survey: an overview. Kansas Orni. Soc. Bull. 29(4):26–30.

———. 1979. Mid-winter bird count for 1978. Kansas Orni. Soc. Bull. 30(1):1–16.

———. 1987. Non-passerine breeding birds of Konza Prairie. Kansas Orni. Soc. Bull. 38(4):29–33.

———. 1989. Passerine breeding birds of Konza Prairie. Kansas Orni. Soc. Bull. 40(2):23–28.

———. 1993. The Birds of Konza: The Avian Ecology of the Tallgrass Prairie. University Press of Kansas, Lawrence. 198 pp.

Zimmerman, J. L., and S. Patti. 1988. A Guide to Bird Finding in Kansas and Western Missouri. University Press of Kansas, Lawrence. 230 pp.

Zuvanich, J. R. 1963. Forster Terns breeding in Kansas. Kansas Orni. Soc. Bull. 14(1):1–3.

Index